Praise for *The Battle of Arnhem*

"Beevor conveys a clear sense of what was happening in each fight and the knock-on consequences for the others. What's more, the compressed time scale and limited strategic scope of Market Garden ideally suit the author's testimony-rich approach. . . . Mr. Beevor is a highly accomplished architect of what the American literary scholar Samuel Hynes calls 'battlefield gothic': the nightmarish horrors and absurdities of combat which themselves become a badge of authenticity for war stories. . . . No one could be better placed to explore these topics."

—*The Wall Street Journal*

"[*The Battle of Arnhem*] is destined to be a World War II military history classic. . . . Excellent maps make the action easy to follow, and the author's clear, quick prose makes for fascinating, informative reading. . . . Beevor's superb latest offering, in keeping with his established record of excellence, is a must-read for the general military history enthusiast and the WWII history expert."

—*Publishers Weekly* (starred review)

"*The Battle of Arnhem* brings a wealth of new detail to a major World War II disaster. . . . Beevor brings to the familiar story a vast amount of research in German, British, American, Polish, and Dutch archives. As usual, his narrative bristles with specifics, including countless observations gleaned from eyewitnesses to every stage of Market Garden. Devoted readers of military history will enjoy the wealth of details."

—*The Christian Science Monitor*

"In this new volume, Sir Antony Beevor takes a fresh look at this battle first popularized by Cornelius Ryan's landmark *A Bridge Too Far*. . . . Sir Antony describes the unfolding of the battle in marvelous detail with numerous recollections from both Allied and German participants. One aspect of the battle he covers much better than older narratives is the heavy fighting beyond the Arnhem bridge, the usual focus of Market Garden histories."

—*New York Journal of Books*

"In the meticulous narrative style he first employed in *Stalingrad*, [Beevor] recreates the operation from the dropping of the first troops on September seventeenth to the evacuation of the remnants of the British 1st Airborne

Division eight days later. . . . The outline of the story of 'Arnhem' may be familiar, but Sir Antony's unearthing of neglected sources from all the countries involved—British, American, Polish, Dutch, and German—brings to life every aspect of the battle."

—*The Economist*

"Beevor tells a story that is more human and complex than what he calls 'the great myth of heroic failure,' a tale of vanity, hubris, occasional incompetence, human frailty, and remarkable grit. . . . In Beevor's hands, Arnhem becomes a study of national character."

—*The Times* (London)

"Beevor describes the battle and its aftermath with his customary deep understanding of the human factor—both of the soldiers who risked everything and of the plight of the Dutch civilians."

—General Sir Mike Jackson, *The Spectator* (London)

PENGUIN BOOKS

THE BATTLE OF ARNHEM

Antony Beevor is the bestselling author of ten books, including *D-Day*, which received the Royal United Services Institute's Duke of Westminster Medal for Military Literature; *The Battle for Spain*, the La Vanguardia prize-winner for nonfiction; *Paris After the Liberation 1944–1949*; *Stalingrad*, winner of the Samuel Johnson Prize, the Wolfson History Prize, and the Hawthornden Prize for Literature; *The Fall of Berlin* 1945, which received the first Longman-History Today Trustees Award; and *Ardennes 1944*, which was shortlisted for the Prix Médicis. His books have appeared in thirty-three languages and have sold more than eight million copies. He is the recipient of the 2014 Pritzker Military Museum & Library Literature Award for Lifetime Achievement in Military Writing and was knighted in 2017.

THE BATTLE OF ARNHEM

THE DEADLIEST AIRBORNE OPERATION OF WORLD WAR II

Antony Beevor

PENGUIN BOOKS

PENGUIN BOOKS
An imprint of Penguin Random House LLC
penguinrandomhouse.com

First published in Great Britain as *Arnhem: The Battle for the Bridges, 1944* by Viking,
an imprint of Penguin Random House UK, 2018

First published in the United States of America by Viking,
an imprint of Penguin Random House LLC, 2018
Published in Penguin Books 2019

Map illustrations by Jeff Edwards

Illustration of Arnhem Bridge on page 128 by Michael White from John Waddy,
A Tour of the Arnhem Battlefields, Barnsley 2011

ISBN 9780143128830 (paperback)

THE LIBRARY OF CONGRESS HAS CATALOGED THE HARDCOVER EDITION AS FOLLOWS:
Names: Beevor, Antony, 1946– author.
Title: The Battle of Arnhem : the deadliest airborne operation of WWII, 1944 / Antony Beevor.
Description: New York : Viking, [2018] | Includes bibliographical references and index. |
Identifiers: LCCN 2018031831 (print) | LCCN 2018032733 (ebook) |
ISBN 9780698409408 (ebook) | ISBN 9780525429821 (hardcover)
Subjects: LCSH: Arnhem, Battle of, Arnhem, Netherlands, 1944.
Classification: LCC D763.N42 (ebook) | LCC D763.N42 B424 2018 (print) |
DDC 940.54/219218—dc23
LC record available at https://lccn.loc.gov/2018031831

Printed in the United States of America
1 3 5 7 9 10 8 6 4 2

Set in Ehrhardt MT

For Artemis

Contents

List of Illustrations

Illustration acknowledgements

The majority of the photographs come from the Imperial War Museum and private collections via Robert Voskuil and Bob Gerritsen. Other photographs are from: 2, Aviodrome in Lelystad; 3, 26, Beeldbank WO2 – NIOD; 7, Ehrhard Schmidt; 11, 23, 25, 45, 51, Getty Images; 15, Air Historical Branch, Ministry of Defence; 17, S. L. A. Marshall Collection via USAMHI; 18, 24, Karel Margry Collection; 22, 36, Cornelius Ryan Collection of World War II Papers, Mahn Center for Archives and Special Collections, Ohio University Libraries; 27, Karl-Heinz Kaebel; 38, The Polish Institute and Sikorski Museum in London; 47, SS-PK Raske; 49, Sem Presser via Maria Austria Instituut. Every reasonable effort has been made to trace copyright but the publisher welcomes any information that clarifies the copyright ownership of any unattributed material displayed and will endeavour to include corrections in reprints.

List of Maps

Key to Military Symbols

ALLIED	GERMAN
Army Group headquarters	Army Group headquarters
Army	Panzer Corps
Armoured/Infantry Corps	Infanterie-Division
Armoured Division	Fallschirmjäger-Division
Infantry Division	Fallschirmjäger-Regiment
Infantry Brigade	Panzer-Division
Infantry Regiment	Panzer-Brigade
Airborne Division	Pioneer Battalion
Parachute Regiment	Flak Brigade
Parachute Battalion	Artillery Regiment

Glossary

Compo	British army slang for its 'composite' rations in tins.
Coup de main parties	Assault troops to be landed by glider very close to an objective to seize it by surprise, like those who seized Pegasus Bridge in Normandy.
Divers	*Onderduikers*, literally under-divers, were those who had gone into hiding from the Nazis, including Jews, those evading forced labour, and members of the underground on the run.
DZ	Drop zone.
Fallschirmjäger	German paratrooper belonging to the Luftwaffe. By 1944 there were few Fallschirmjäger left who had taken part in parachute operations, such as the invasion of Holland and Belgium in May 1940, and the invasion of Crete in May 1941. Most were Luftwaffe ground crew transferred into so-called Fallschirmjäger regiments and divisions in 1944.
Firing on fixed lines	Machine guns can be set up by day with particular settings to allow them to be fired later in darkness on fixed lines at a certain height in a particular direction to cover likely enemy routes of approach.
Forward air controllers	Specially trained air force or army NCOs and officers in radio vehicles who could direct air strikes by radio.
Jedburgh teams	The British SOE (Special Operations Executive), in co-operation with the American OSS

(Office of Strategic Services), trained small multi-national groups to parachute in to join local Resistance groups in 1944 to create mayhem behind German lines in the liberation of western Europe. During Operation Market Garden, a Jedburgh team was allocated to each airborne division, each with a Dutch officer, to liaise with local Resistance groups and organize their activities in support of the Allied forces.

Kampfgruppe
Battle group.

KP (or LKP)
The Landelijke Knokploegen (Fighting Group) was the main Dutch organization which engaged in sabotage. Between 500 and 1,000 strong.

Landser
The German name for an ordinary front-line soldier.

LO
The Landelijke Organisatie voor Hulp aan Onderduikers, the Central Government Organizations for Help to People in Hiding. This helped *onderduikers*, or 'divers' (*qv*), to survive by providing false or stolen ration books, and arrange their exfiltration from the Netherlands. Jews, shot-down Allied airmen and Resistance members on the run from the Germans were helped along escape lines running through Belgium and France to Spain.

LZ
Landing zone.

MI9
The British organization to help prisoners of war or those trapped behind enemy lines to escape.

Micks
Guards nickname for members of the Irish Guards.

Moffen
Derogatory Dutch name for Germans, more or less the equivalent of 'Krauts'.

Nebelwerfer
German six-barrelled rocket-firing mortar which made a screaming, braying noise. This led to British soldiers calling it the 'moaning minnie' or the 'screaming meenie'. Americans called it the 'screaming meemie'.

NSB
Nationaal-Socialistische Beweging (National Socialist Movement).

Oberst i.G.
Oberst im Generalstab, or colonel of the general staff.

OD	The Orde Dienst (Order Service) had the mission of preparing for the return of the Dutch government from London as the country was liberated. Its organization was based on officers and civil servants of the original administration from 1940. Its duty was to gather intelligence and maintain order during the interregnum. Its intelligence arm was the GDN (Geheim Dienst Nederland). For example in Eindhoven, the GDN based itself in the local museum to camouflage the coming and going of informants.
Orders group	British army term for a meeting summoned by a commander to deliver operational orders and other instructions.
PAN	Partisanen Actie Nederland: this was another Resistance group separate from the KP and from March 1944 was particularly strong in Eindhoven and the surrounding area. It could call some 600 young men into action when necessary.
PIAT	The Projector Infantry Anti-Tank was the British counterpart to the American bazooka. It was spring-loaded and fired its bomb just over a hundred metres.
Polder	The low-lying areas and fields reclaimed in the Netherlands which usually lay below sea-level and were protected by dykes.
Reichsarbeitsdienst (RAD)	The Reich Labour Service.
Royal Tiger	The seventy-two-ton Mark VI Tiger II tank was called a Königstiger, but this has usually been wrongly translated as King Tiger, when in fact it refers to the Royal, or Bengal, Tiger.
RVV	The Raad van Verzet (Council of Resistance) helped *onderduikers* and carried out acts of sabotage. During Operation Market Garden, the government-in-exile in London gave the RVV the important role of organizing the railway strike which so enraged the Germans.
SD	Sicherheitsdienst, the SS intelligence agency. During the war it was part of the Reich Main Security Office along with the Gestapo (secret police) and other such agencies.
Stick	An aircraft load of paratroopers, usually about eighteen men.
Stonk	British Army slang for a mortar bombardment.

Table of Military Ranks

American	British	German army	Waffen-SS
Private	Private/Trooper	Schütze/Kanonier/Jäger	Schütze
Private First Class		Oberschütze	Oberschütze
	Lance-Corporal	Gefreiter	Sturmmann
Corporal	Corporal	Obergefreiter	Rottenführer
Sergeant	Sergeant	Feldwebel/Wachtmeister	Oberscharführer
Staff Sergeant	Staff/Colour Sergeant	Oberfeldwebel	Hauptscharführer
Technical Sergeant	Regtl Quartermaster Sgt		
Master Sergeant	Coy/Sqn Sergeant Major	Stabsfeldwebel	Sturmscharführer
	Regimental Sergeant Major		
2nd Lieutenant	2nd Lieutenant	Leutnant	Untersturmführer
Lieutenant	Lieutenant	Oberleutnant	Obersturmführer
Captain	Captain	Hauptmann/Rittmeister	Hauptsturmführer
Major	Major	Major	Sturmbannführer
Lieutenant Colonel	Lieutenant Colonel	Oberstleutnant	Obersturmbannführer
Colonel	Colonel	Oberst	Standartenführer
Brigadier General	Brigadier *	Generalmajor	Oberführer
			Brigadeführer
Major General	Major General **	Generalleutnant	Gruppenführer

Lieutenant General	Lieutenant General	***	General der Infanterie/	Obergruppenführer/
			Artillerie/Panzertruppen	General der Waffen-SS
General	General	****	Generaloberst	Oberstgruppenführer
General of the Army	Field Marshal	*****	Generalfeldmarschall	

This can only be an approximate guide to equivalent ranks since each army has its own variations. Some ranks have been omitted in the interests of simplicity. In the British and Canadian and US armies the following ranks command the following sub-units (below a battalion), units (battalion or regiment) and formations (brigade, division or corps).

Rank	British and Canadian Army	US Army	Approx. number of men at full strength
Corporal	Section	Squad	8
2nd/Lieutenant	Platoon	Platoon	30
Captain/Major	Company	Company	120
Lieutenant Colonel	Battalion or Armoured Regiment	Battalion	700
Colonel		Regiment	2,400
Brigadier	Brigade	Combat command	2,400
Major General	Division	Division	10,000
Lieutenant General	Corps	Corps	30,000–40,000
General	Army	Army	70,000–150,000
Field Marshal/ General of the Army	Army Group	Army Group	200,000–350,000

A complete Order of Battle is available online at www.antonybeevor.com

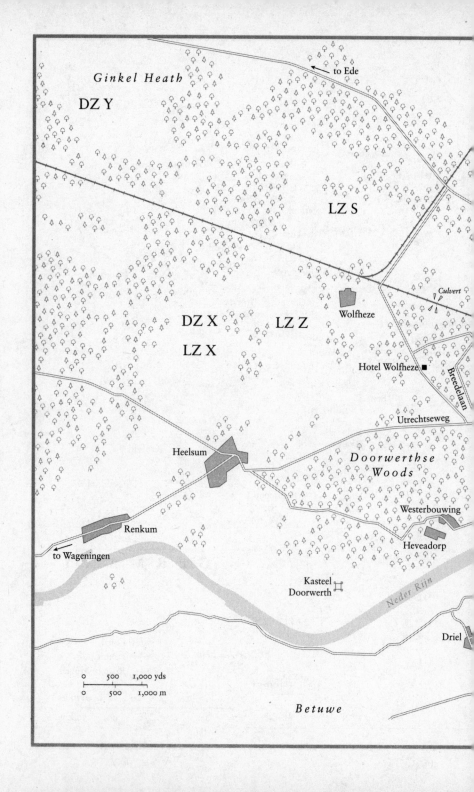

Ginkel Heath

DZ Y

to Ede

LZ S

DZ X

LZ Z

LZ X

Culvert

Wolfheze

Hotel Wolfheze ■

Breedelaan

Utrechtseweg

Heelsum

*Doorwerthse
Woods*

Westerbouwing

Renkum

Heveadorp

to Wageningen

Kasteel
Doorwerth

Neder Rijn

Driel

| 0 | 500 | 1,000 yds |
| 0 | 500 | 1,000 m |

Betuwe

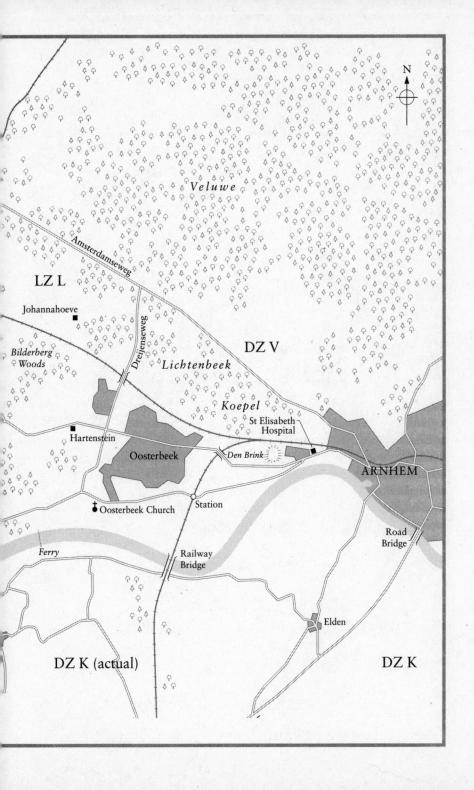

1

The Chase is On!

Sunday 27 August 1944 was a day of perfect summer weather in Normandy. The soporific sounds of a cricket match could be heard from a field at Saint-Symphorien-les-Bruyères, south-west of Evreux. In the adjoining pear orchard, Sherman tanks of the Sherwood Rangers Yeomanry had just been refitted and repaired after the battle of the Falaise Gap, the culmination of the battle for Normandy. Bats, balls, pads and stumps had been smuggled ashore on one of their supply trucks. 'Never let it be said that we invaded the Continent unprepared,' wrote one of the players.

The regiment was supposedly on twenty-four hours' notice to move, but just after lunch the order came to move out in an hour. Its tanks were on the road in seventy minutes, heading for the River Seine, which the first British formation, the 43rd Wessex Division, had crossed at Vernon the day before. British troops were rather jealous that General George Patton's US Third Army had beaten them to a Seine crossing by six days.

On 29 August the Allied armies, now nearly a million strong, lunged forward from their bridgeheads east of the Seine, heading for Belgium and the German border. The battle for Normandy had finally been won, and the German army was in chaotic retreat. 'Along the main supply routes', an American officer wrote in his diary, 'you see the evidence of our air effort against the enemy. Trucks have been bombed and strafed, rusted and twisted in wild profusion along the roads, occasionally a truck load of gas cans with the cans bulging out like a swollen dead cow, black and charred, or a train with mounds of bulging cans, twisted steel frames from the destroyed box cars.'

For British cavalry regiments, the chase was on. Lieutenant General Brian Horrocks, the commander of XXX Corps, mounted in the turret of a command tank, could not resist joining in. 'This was the type of warfare I thoroughly enjoyed,' he wrote later. 'Who wouldn't?' With more than 600

tanks – Shermans, Churchills and Cromwells – the Guards Armoured Division, the 11th Armoured Division and the 8th Armoured Brigade charged
forward on a frontage of eighty kilometres, 'scything passages through the
enemy rear areas', he added, 'like a combine-harvester going through a field
of corn'.

The country between the Seine and the Somme was 'open and rolling
with wide fields, no hedges and good roads'. The dangerous Norman *bocage*
of tightly enclosed pasture and sunken roads lay far behind them. The
Sherwood Rangers adopted their old desert formation from the North African campaign, with a squadron of Shermans spread out in front, regimental
headquarters just behind it and the other two sabre squadrons on the flanks.
'To travel at top speed across hard, open country on a lovely morning,' a
cavalry troop leader wrote, 'knowing that the Germans were on the run, was
exhilarating to say the least, and everyone was in the best possible spirits. It
was almost like taking part in a cross-country steeplechase.'

Church bells pealed at their approach. Almost every house was festooned
in the French national colours of red, white and blue. Villagers, overjoyed
to be spared the destruction of Normandy, waited to greet them with bottles
of wine and fruit. Unshaven members of the Resistance, wearing armbands,
tried to mount the leading vehicles to show the way. A staff officer with the
Guards Armoured Division in a Staghound armoured car noticed 'their odd
assortment of weapons which they brandished with more exuberance than
safety'.

From time to time a tank would run out of fuel. The vehicle then had to
sit immobilized by the side of the road until one of the regiment's three-
tonners caught up and pulled alongside. Jerrycans would then be swung
across to the crew members standing on the engine deck. There were the
occasional short, sharp firefights when a German group, overtaken by the
advance, refused to surrender. Clearing out such pockets of resistance was
called 'de-lousing'.

On the afternoon of 30 August, Horrocks felt the advance was still not
fast enough. He ordered Major General 'Pip' Roberts to send his 11th
Armoured Division through the night to take Amiens and its bridges over
the River Somme by dawn. Although the tank drivers were falling asleep
from exhaustion they made it to the bridges, and three-ton trucks brought
in a brigade of infantry at first light to secure the town. Horrocks was close
behind to congratulate Roberts on the success. After reporting on the operation, Roberts then said to his corps commander, 'I have a surprise for you,
General.' A German officer in black panzer uniform was brought round. He
was unshaven and his face was scarred from a wound received in the First

World War which had removed most of his nose. Roberts, Horrocks noted, 'was exactly like a proud farmer leading forward his champion bull'. His trophy was General der Panzertruppe Heinrich Eberbach, the commander of the Seventh Army, who had been surprised in his bed.

The next day, 1 September, was the fifth anniversary of the German invasion of Poland which had started the war in Europe. By a curious coincidence, both Allied army group commanders of the Normandy campaign happened to be sitting for portraits at their respective headquarters. Basking in the glow of victory after General George C. Patton's triumphant charge to the Seine, General Omar N. Bradley near Chartres was being painted by Cathleen Mann, who was married to the Marquess of Queensberry. They could at least enjoy cool drinks on that beautiful day. The supreme commander, General Dwight D. Eisenhower, had just sent Bradley a refrigerator, with the message: 'Goddamit, I'm tired of drinking warm whiskey every time I come to your headquarters.'

Field Marshal Sir Bernard Montgomery, wearing his trademark outfit of grey polo-neck sweater, corduroy trousers and black, double-badged beret, was sitting for the Scottish portraitist James Gunn. His tactical headquarters and caravan were in the park of the Château de Dangu, halfway between Rouen and Paris. Despite the messages of congratulation that morning on his promotion to field marshal, Montgomery was in such a bad mood that he refused to meet his host, the duc de Dangu, and members of the local Resistance. All Montgomery's hopes of a joint offensive under his leadership into northern Germany had been dashed, because Eisenhower was replacing him as commander-in-chief land forces. Bradley was no longer his subordinate, but his equal. In Montgomery's view, Eisenhower was throwing away the victory by a refusal to concentrate his forces.

Senior American officers, on the other hand, were far angrier at Montgomery's promotion. It made him a five-star general, while Eisenhower, his superior, still had only four stars. Patton, whose Third Army troops were already close to Verdun in eastern France, wrote to his wife that day, 'The Field Marshal thing made us sick, that is Bradley and me.' Even a number of senior British officers thought that Winston Churchill's sop to Monty and the British press to camouflage the implied demotion was a grave mistake. Admiral Sir Bertram Ramsay, the Allied naval commander-in-chief, wrote in his diary: 'Monty made a Field Marshal. Astounding thing to do and I regret it more than I can say. I gather that the PM did it on his own. Damn stupid and I warrant most offensive to Eisenhower and the Americans.'

The next day, Saturday 2 September, Patton, Eisenhower and Lieutenant

General Courtney H. Hodges, the commander of the First US Army, met at Bradley's 12th Army Group headquarters, where Lady Queensberry had put away her paintbrushes. According to Bradley's aide, Hodges was 'neat and trim as usual in his battle dress', while Patton was 'gaudy with brass buttons and the big car'. They were there to discuss strategy and the great supply problem. The unexpectedly rapid advance meant that they were out-running the capacity of even the huge American military transport fleet. Patton begged Bradley that morning: 'Give me 400,000 gallons of gasoline and I'll put you in Germany in two days.'

Bradley had every sympathy. So keen was he that all available aircraft continue to supply Patton's Third Army that he had opposed the plans for airborne drops ahead to speed the Allied advance. Patton, who longed 'to go through the Siegfried Line like shit through a goose', was already bribing the transport pilots with cases of looted champagne, but that was still in-sufficient. Eisenhower refused to budge. He was also being badgered by Montgomery, who demanded the bulk of supplies to enable him to mount the main attack in the north.

Allied diplomacy required the supreme commander to balance the rival demands of the two army groups as far as was humanly possible. This led to Eisenhower adopting a 'broad-front strategy', which satisfied neither com-mander.* Eisenhower's chief of staff, Lieutenant General Walter Bedell Smith, commented after the war on the problems with Montgomery and Bradley. 'It is amazing', he said, 'how good commanders get ruined when they develop a public they have to act up to. They become prima donnas.' Even the seemingly modest Bradley 'developed a public, and we had some trouble with him'.

Eisenhower's failure to resolve the competing strategies of Montgomery and Bradley was then made worse by an accident. After leaving 12th Army Group headquarters near Chartres that afternoon, he was flown back to his own command post at Granville on the Atlantic coast of Normandy. It was a grave mistake to have chosen a spot so far behind the rapidly developing battlefronts. In fact, as Bradley pointed out, he would have been better placed for communications if he had stayed in London. Towards the end of the flight back to Granville, his light aircraft developed engine trouble and

---

* Eisenhower's broad-front strategy was greeted with relief by the German high com-mand, the OKW. 'According to German conceptions,' wrote a staff officer, 'it remained a mystery why the enemy had failed to mass all his troops at one point and force a breakthrough . . . Instead, the enemy did the German command the favour of distrib-uting his forces in a fan-type manner over the entire front.'

the pilot had to land on a beach. Eisenhower, who had already damaged one knee, now wrecked the other one when helping to turn the aircraft round on the sand. He was confined to bed, with the leg in plaster, just before Bradley and Montgomery were due to meet. He stayed immobilized for a whole week, which proved to be a crucial one.

That same evening of 2 September, Horrocks arrived at the headquarters of the Guards Armoured Division in Douai. He felt frustrated by the need to hold back his troops that day to allow an airborne drop on Tournai. It had then been cancelled at the last moment due to bad weather and because the American XIX Corps had already reached the drop zones. So with a certain theatrical flourish, Horrocks announced to the assembled Guards officers that their objective for the next day was Brussels, some 110 kilometres further on. There was a gasp of delighted astonishment. Horrocks also ordered Roberts's 11th Armoured Division to charge straight for the great port of Antwerp in Operation Sabot.

With the Welsh Guards preceded by the armoured cars of the 2nd Household Cavalry Regiment on the right and the Grenadier Guards group on the left, 'the spirit of competition was irresistible and nothing could stop us that day,' an officer recorded. The betting on who would reach Brussels first was intense. '*Les jeux sont faits – rien ne va plus!*' was apparently the roulette croupier's cry at 06.00 hours, as both contingents set off. The Irish Guards group in reserve followed a few hours later. 'It was our longest drive, 82 miles in 13 hours,' their 2nd (Armoured) Battalion noted in the war diary. But for some units the headlong advance did not turn out to be so sporting. The Grenadiers lost more than twenty men in a vicious engagement with a group of SS.

The unexpected appearance of the Guards Armoured Division in the Belgian capital that evening triggered an even greater jubilation than had been seen during the liberation of Paris. 'The chief trouble was the mobbing of the crowds,' the Household Cavalry noted as they were constantly brought to a halt by exultant Belgians, packed along the road a dozen deep, singing 'Tipperary' and making V for Victory signs. 'Another universal habit of the liberated is to write messages of welcome all over the vehicles as they slowly nose their way through the crowd,' wrote the same officer. 'If you stop they swarm over the vehicle, cover it with fruit and flowers and offer wine.' The Household Cavalry and the Welsh Guards 'won the race by a short head', although 'it was a hazardous task, because every time one stopped to ask the way one was hauled from the car and soundly kissed by both sexes.'

German troops still held the aerodrome outside the capital and 'fired five rounds of high explosive' into the park in front of the Royal Palace, where Major General Allan Adair was establishing his command post under canvas. British troops were greatly helped by the Armée Blanche of the Belgian Resistance which 'proved of enormous value for rounding up the many stray Germans who were trying to escape'. Civilians, when not kissing their liberators, hissed and booed and kicked any German prisoners they saw.

Many British soldiers were struck by the contrast with Normandy, where the welcome had often been half-hearted, amid the terrible destruction wreaked on their towns and villages. 'The people dressed better,' an officer wrote, 'clothes seemed more plentiful, everyone looked clean and healthy, whereas France gave one the impression that everyone was shoddy and tired.' But appearances of comparative prosperity could be misleading. The German occupiers had seized food supplies, coal and other resources for themselves, and more than half a million Belgians had been shipped off for forced labour in German factories. Belgium, however, at least benefited from the rapidity of the Allied advance. This saved it from the destruction of battle, last-minute looting and the usual scorched-earth tactics of the Wehrmacht. But to the south-east reckless attacks by the Belgian Resistance on retreating groups of German soldiers led to vicious and indiscriminate reprisals by SS units in particular.

The Germans were shaken by the rapidity of the Allied advance that day. An NCO described it in his diary as 'An event that surpasses all expectations and calculations, and even puts our "Blitzkrieg" in the summer of 1940 in the shade'. Oberstleutnant Fullriede noted 'the conversation of officers in the barracks. The western front has had it: the enemy is already in Belgium and on the German border. Roumania, Bulgaria, Slovakia and Finland are asking for peace. It's just like in 1918.' Others blamed their first ally most of all. 'The Italians are the most guilty,' Unteroffizier Oskar Siegl wrote home. And some compared Italy's 'betrayal' of Germany to that of Austria in the First World War. In some cases, this produced reactions of bewildered self-pity. 'We Germans have only enemies in the world, and one has to ask why we are so hated everywhere? There is no nation which wants to know us.'

Allied generals also drew parallels with the end of the First World War. The optimism was such that Bradley's 12th Army Group headquarters had already ordered up 25 tons of maps 'for operations in Germany'. And Bradley's aide Major Chester B. Hansen remarked that 'everyone was getting as excited as a sophomore class on the eve before a dance.' At 12th Army

Group headquarters 'everything we talk about now is qualified by the phrase "if the war lasts that long".'

They had completely misunderstood the consequences of Oberst Claus Graf Schenk von Stauffenberg's attempted bomb attack against Hitler on 20 July. Allied commanders assumed that this event had signalled the start of the German army's disintegration. In fact its failure, and the repression which followed, meant the very opposite. The Nazi Party and the SS now had total control, and the general staff and all army formations would be forced to fight to the Führer's last breath.

On the morning of 3 September, while Allied spearheads advanced on Antwerp, Brussels and Maastricht, Generals Bradley and Hodges flew to the headquarters of Lieutenant General Miles Dempsey's Second British Army. The purpose was to discuss 'future operations towards the Ruhr' with Montgomery. Apart from Eisenhower, laid up with his bad leg in Granville, another absentee from the conference was Lieutenant General Henry Crerar, the commander of the First Canadian Army, who had insisted on staying in Dieppe to take a memorial parade for all of his countrymen killed in the disastrous raid of August 1942. He would have pointed out the difficulties of seizing the Channel ports and dealing with the German Fifteenth Army, which had retreated from the Pas de Calais to a pocket west of Antwerp on the Scheldt estuary. The port of Antwerp was also vital to any idea of advancing across the Rhine into Germany, yet both Montgomery and Bradley were fixated with their own diverging intentions: the British heading north, and the Americans heading east.

No proper minutes of this conference were taken, and afterwards Bradley became convinced that Montgomery had deliberately misled him. Bradley said that the airborne drop planned for the next day on the bridges over the River Meuse (or Maas in Dutch) around Liège should be cancelled. Montgomery apparently agreed. 'We both consider', the field marshal said afterwards, 'that all available aircraft should go on transport work so that we can maintain momentum of advance.' Yet later that very afternoon, at 16.00 hours, Montgomery ordered his chief of staff to ask the First Allied Airborne Army back in England to start working on another plan, a far more ambitious one. His new idea was to seize the bridges 'between Wesel and Arnhem' to launch his 21st Army Group across the Rhine north of the Ruhr. Montgomery evidently calculated that if he could be the first to establish a bridgehead over the Rhine, Eisenhower would have to give him the bulk of the supplies, and support him with American formations.

It was a great pity that Eisenhower had not been at the meeting. When

Bradley found out that Montgomery had reneged on what had been agreed without telling him, he was furious. Montgomery refused to acknowledge what almost all other senior British officers had understood. Britain was now very much the junior partner in the alliance because the Americans were providing the bulk of the troops, much of the hardware and most of the oil. The idea that Britain remained a first-rate power was a fantasy which Churchill desperately tried to promote, even though he knew in his heart that it was not the case. In fact one could argue that September 1944 was the origin of that disastrous cliché which lingers on even today about the country punching above its weight.

2

'Mad Tuesday'

On Monday 4 September, the second day of celebration in Brussels, Queen Wilhelmina of the Netherlands broadcast a message from London: 'Compatriots – You know our liberation is coming. I wanted you to know that I have nominated Prins Bernhard as commander of the Dutch forces under the supreme commander General Eisenhower. Prins Bernhard will be the commander of the armed resistance. Until soon. Wilhelmina.'

The German retreat through the Netherlands towards the Reich had begun on 1 September, and reached its peak four days later on what became known as *Dolle Dinsdag* – or 'Mad Tuesday'. Rumours spread that Montgomery's armies were already at the border, and a mistaken report by the Dutch Service of the BBC radio on the evening of 4 September even claimed that the Allies had reached Breda and Roermond. In Amsterdam people went out the next morning, expecting to see Allied tanks on their way in.

Most retreats are sorry sights, but the bedraggled, dejected mass of Wehrmacht stragglers from France and Belgium caused an unusual degree of jubilation, disdain and harsh laughter in the Dutch people after the humiliations of the arrogant occupation. 'Never have we enjoyed anything as much as watching the disorderly retreat of this once great army,' a woman in Eindhoven wrote. Some in improvised units, such as Kriegsmarine sailors formed into Schiffs-Stamm-Abteilungen, had trudged most of the way from the Atlantic coast. Others had seized any vehicle they could find along the way, cars such as old Citroëns with running boards and wood-burning trucks with smoke-stacks.

The spectacle, which fascinated and thrilled the Dutch, seemed to confirm the impression of total defeat. They took chairs out on to the side of the street to watch. The formerly invincible and mechanized Wehrmacht, which had crushed their country so easily in the summer of 1940, had now been reduced to stealing every imaginable form of conveyance, especially bicycles.

There had been 4 million bicycles in the Netherlands at the beginning of the war, half as many as the total population. The Wehrmacht had commandeered 50,000 at the beginning of July 1942, and now thousands more were headed for Germany, most of them loaded with soldiers' equipment and booty as they pushed them along the roads. With no rubber for tyres, pedalling them on wooden wheels was heavy work. But their loss hit hard. The Dutch underground movement needed them for their couriers, and ordinary families relied on bicycles for seeking out food from farms in the countryside.

Most of the motorcars looted in France and Belgium also lacked tyres. Driven on the rims of their wheels, they made a noise which caused everyone to wince. The majority were occupied by German officers, and as an onlooker in Eindhoven noted, 'Many vehicles had young women sitting in them – the sort that usually fraternised with Germans.' These French, Belgian and Dutch women, who were presumably guilty of *collaboration horizontale*, clearly wanted to avoid a predictable fate at home. In Arnhem too, the neurologist Louis van Erp saw a number of German officers with 'women on their laps, partly German, partly French women'. And the officers were flourishing bottles of brandy. In some towns the day was called 'Cognac Tuesday'. German soldiers tried to sell some of the bottles and other items they had stolen. Only a few Dutch took advantage of the bargains offered, which included sewing machines, cameras, watches, textiles and birds in cages unlikely to survive the journey.

Some motorcars belonged to Dutch Nazi sympathizers in the NSB – the Nationaal-Socialistische Beweging. They knew that the southern Netherlands province of Brabant would prove too dangerous for them without German protection. Others fleeing vengeance included collaborators from France and arch-Catholic, pro-Nazi Rexists from Belgium. The loyal Dutch called members of the NSB the 'wrong' Netherlanders, or the 'black *Kameraden*', and saw them as somehow worse than the Germans. 'The attitude of the Dutch population towards the NSB remains totally opposed,' a German officer in Utrecht reported. 'Better ten Germans than one NSBer is the general view, and considering the rejection of everything German, that really means something.'

Other vehicles included the odd omnibus and Red Cross ambulances packed with soldiers and their weapons, contrary to all the rules of war. There were German soldiers on horse-drawn farm-carts, loaded with chickens, ducks and geese in wooden cages; and trucks with stolen sheep and pigs. Somebody spotted two oxen stumbling about in a bus, and a nun saw a cow in an ambulance. Such sights produced a bitter smile at the shameless theft of food from occupied countries. There was the odd fire-engine and even a hearse with ostrich plumes covered in dust. Wehrmacht vehicles had branches from pine trees tied to the front in an attempt to sweep away the tacks and nails scattered on roads by members of the underground.

The exhausted footsoldiers, the 'Moffen' as the Dutch called their German occupiers contemptuously, looked dishevelled, bearded and black with dirt.* Their appearance and that of their officers sitting back in cars caused a sensation once the dismal cavalcade crossed the Reich frontier. There were wild rumours and numerous black jokes. A Gefreiter heard from his family: 'Yesterday evening people were saying that in Kaiserslautern the Führer himself was inspecting the cars.' Civilians also resented the privileges of officers, and their treatment of the ordinary soldier, the *Landser*. 'The "Gentlemen" travelled in their fully loaded automobiles, leaving the *Landser* in the lurch.'

A marked difference in attitude had developed in Germany towards the eastern-front soldier and his counterpart, the *Westfrontkämpfer*. There was a general suspicion that the German army in the west had been softened by its four years of easy occupation in France and the Low Countries. 'The feeling of the civilian population towards the soldier on the western front is not altogether good,' a woman wrote to her husband, 'and I too am convinced that if the soldier of the eastern front had been in the west, then the break-through would not have happened.'

A gunner wrote home rather confirming the impression of collapse in the West: 'I cannot convey what the scene is like. This isn't a retreat, but a flight.' Yet he went on to admit that it was a well-provisioned departure. 'The cars were laden with Schnapps, cigarettes, and hundreds of tins of fats and meat.' The German occupation authorities also engaged in last-minute plundering. Having already seized church bells to melt down, they hurriedly shipped raw materials, especially coal and iron ore, to the Reich, and held on to the engines and wagons. Such acts were justified on the grounds

---

* The Dutch word 'Moffen' for Germans was the equivalent of 'Kraut' or 'Boche' in English or French. It dated from the early seventeenth century when the areas of northern Germany just east of the Netherlands were referred to as the Muffe. The much richer and more sophisticated Dutch looked down on their inhabitants as unsophisticated and crude. The term was revived during the German occupation.

that they should not leave 'an economic advantage' to the Allies. A certain amount of scorched-earth actions were also carried out. In Eindhoven, a series of enormous explosions could be heard as the Germans destroyed installations on the airfield and blew up munition dumps. A huge pall of smoke blotted out the sun.

Transporting all these resources to the Reich was not easy. The Dutch underground carried out acts of sabotage during the first part of September. Yet a German officer observed that 'the fact that railway traffic is almost at a standstill is not a question of fuel, but can be put down much more to the effects of English fighter pilots, who have shot to death the majority of locomotives.' To the dismay and even anger of the Dutch government-in-exile in London, RAF fighter pilots could not resist the thrill of blasting railway engines with cannon fire, because it produced such a spectacular explosion of steam.

The only satisfaction for civilians was to see how NSB members and their families were made frantic by these delays in their desperation to escape to Germany. In a town south-west of Arnhem, their plight produced intense *Schadenfreude*. 'It was a wonderful sight,' a local called Paul van Wely wrote. 'The station waiting room looked like a junk store with tramps. Crying faces and hanging heads.' Around 30,000 NSB members and their families went to Germany where they were ignored in the disintegration of the last months of the war. As one historian put it, 'Organised Fascism in the Netherlands virtually collapsed on 5 September.'

During what appeared to be an interregnum, and with the Dutch police more or less in hiding after their equivocal role during the occupation, underground groups kidnapped members of the NSB and even a few German officials. Some were freed soon afterwards by the German police. On that 'Mad Tuesday', the Reichskommissar, Dr Arthur Seyss-Inquart, declared a state of emergency.* 'Resistance against the occupying forces will be broken with arms, in accordance with the orders given to German troops.' He went on to threaten death sentences for the slightest opposition.

Many German officers were angry that the Dutch were preparing to welcome their Anglo-Saxon liberators with flowers and flags. This was a typical Nazi confusion of cause and effect. Having treacherously invaded and occupied a neutral country, they still expected the population to remain loyal to

* Seyss-Inquart's full title of 'Reichskommissar für die besetzten niederländischen Gebiete' ('Reichskommissar for the occupied Netherlandish areas') reflected the earlier Nazi plan of incorporating the Netherlands into the Reich.

them. 'The Dutch are not just cowardly, but lazy and slow,' wrote Ober-leutnant Helmut Hänsel with bitterness.

Many ordinary soldiers did not, however, agree. Those who were sick of the war used to remark ironically: 'My longing for a heroic death has been fully satisfied.' Reich Germans residing or working in Holland, even the sixty-year-olds, were appalled to be mobilized during this crisis. 'They wear civilian clothing under their uniforms hoping to escape,' a sympathetic Dutchman observed, 'but are never left alone.'

'A very wet and stormy day,' Admiral Ramsay noted in his diary. 'British in Brussels and Antwerp. Latter port not badly damaged but of course it is useless until the estuary and approaches are cleared of the enemy.' Ramsay's concern did not register with his colleagues in khaki. They were still glowing with the success of their great advance.

The 11th Armoured Division's progress into Antwerp 'was extremely difficult owing to the great joy and enthusiasm shown by the enormous crowds'. The Germans had been so taken by surprise that only a few of them put up a determined fight. Most important of all, the Resistance had managed to secure the port installations and prevent any last-minute destruction by the Germans. Its members had also proved 'of great assistance in dealing with snipers and prisoners'. The prisoners were locked up in empty cages in Antwerp zoo, one for German officers, NCOs and soldiers. Others held traitors and collaborators, and another held their wives and children, as well as young women accused of having slept with Germans. The animals had starved to death or been eaten during the occupation.

To protect the narrow Allied corridor to Antwerp, forces were pushed out sideways to defend it. The Sherwood Rangers reached Renaix south of Ghent after a 400-kilometre advance from their abandoned game of cricket eight days before. With their Sherman tanks they surrounded a German regiment, some 1,200 men strong. The German commander, 'a stout, dapper little man with a bull neck', insisted during protracted negotiations that his honour as an officer required at least an impression of fighting on. Time was wasted, but the Sherwood Rangers knew that this was better than even a one-sided battle which would take longer.

The German commander finally agreed that he and his men would march out that evening bearing arms, and would surrender on condition that no German soldier was handed over to the Resistance. The Oberst insisted on addressing his men for about fifteen minutes, assuring them that they had made an honourable surrender. He then nodded to his Stabsfeldwebel who shouted an order, and almost as one they smashed the butts of their rifles on the road. 'Then each man raised his right hand and shouted "*Sieg Heil!*" three times,' which seemed rather paradoxical at the moment of giving in. Members of the Resistance, deprived of their revenge, watched angrily as their former occupiers were marched off to a holding camp.

Horrocks's two armoured divisions, having achieved their dramatic dash forward, halted where they were in Antwerp and Brussels to service their vehicles and rest. Horrocks, on his way to Brussels, was shot at by a German tank overtaken in the advance. Armoured cars of the 2nd Household Cavalry were sent back to patrol the road, while their corps commander set up his headquarters in the park of the Palace of Laeken. It was another day of celebration in the city, with a triumphal procession through the town. The Guards Armoured Division was followed by a brigade of Belgian troops brought forward to share in the event. A Guards officer called it 'a most remarkable sight with literally the whole of Brussels lining the streets and cheering. Meanwhile batches of prisoners were being marched about by the members of the Belgian resistance's Armée Blanche who, from time to time fired their rifles in the air.'

Shortly afterwards the Grenadier Guards group, one battalion of infantry and one of tanks, moved due east from Brussels to take Louvain (or Leuven in Flemish). For many in the regiment it brought back memories of an action there during the retreat towards Dunkirk just over four years before. Field Marshal Montgomery also returned to old haunts. He set up his headquarters at the Château d'Everberg fifteen kilometres east of Brussels on the road to Louvain. Montgomery knew the place well. This eighteenth-century building, restyled later, had been the 3rd Division's headquarters just over four years before in the late spring of 1940. The chatelaine, the Princesse de Merode, was not overjoyed to see her visitors as she apparently remembered how Montgomery's staff officers had depleted the wine cellar on the previous occasion. She could not help feeling that her home was being treated 'just like a hotel'. Only that morning Luftwaffe fighter pilots from J G 51 – the famed Jagdgeschwader Mölders – had pulled out hurriedly, and three hours later the British arrived to take possession.

By the end of the first week in September, the fuel shortage had really started to affect both Montgomery's 21st Army Group and Bradley's 12th Army Group. Bradley's aide Hansen wrote on 6 September that even corps commanders 'were forced to go borrowing cans of gas to keep their cars fueled'. With none of the Channel ports yet open, supplies had to be brought all the way from western Normandy in a constant shuttle, known as the 'Red Ball Express', with thousands of trucks driven by African-American

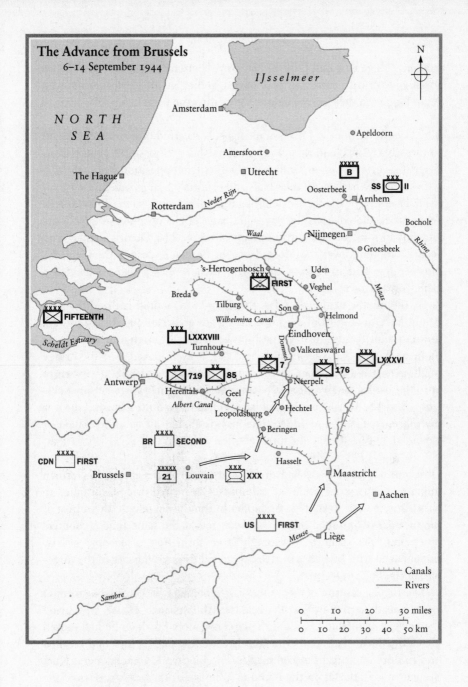

The Advance from Brussels
6–14 September 1944

N

NORTH SEA

IJsselmeer

Amsterdam

Apeldoorn

Amersfoort

The Hague

Utrecht

B

Oosterbeek

SS II

Arnhem

Bocholt

Rotterdam

Neder Rijn

Waal

Nijmegen

Groesbeek

Rhine

's-Hertogenbosch

Uden

FIRST

Breda

Tilburg

Veghel

Maas

Son

Wilhelmina Canal

Helmond

LXXXVIII

Turnhout

Dommel

Eindhoven

Valkenswaard

LXXXVI

7

176

Antwerp

719

85

Neerpelt

Scheldt Estuary

FIFTEENTH

Herentals

Geel

Albert Canal

Hechtel

Leopoldsburg

Beringen

BR SECOND

Hasselt

Maastricht

CDN FIRST

Brussels

21

Louvain

XXX

Aachen

US FIRST

Meuse

Liège

Sambre

Canals
Rivers

0   10   20   30 miles

0   10 20 30 40 50 km

soldiers. 'Huge Red Ball Express convoys', Hansen added, 'are speeding up the highways with tons and tons of gas, rolling at fifty miles an hour all night long with their bright lights illuminating the road.'

The Guards Armoured Division in Brussels received orders to advance on to the Albert Canal and then on to Leopoldsburg, close to the Dutch frontier, before carrying on to Eindhoven. Only 'slight opposition was expected', with resistance harder 'on the canals and bridges'. A large warehouse full of drink reserved for the Wehrmacht had been discovered, so the Irish Guards sent a truck and collected twenty-eight cases of champagne as well as wine and liqueurs to fuel their triumphant advance. The Guards managed to secure a foothold over the Albert Canal at Beringen, despite the Germans blowing the bridge. During the night, their sapper squadron erected a Bailey bridge to replace it.

By the middle of the next day, the Guards Armoured realized that 'we would have to stop thinking in terms of flowers, fruit and kisses and get down to some steady stuff.' Opposition had suddenly strengthened. 'At one moment during that very complicated day, it even looked as if the bridge might go when a desperate force of one officer and forty SS troops crept onto the barges nearby after knocking out no less than forty supply vehicles.' 'Both the Welsh and the Coldstream had taken quite a knock,' the war diary keeper noted, and added: 'SS troops should all be either killed or wounded, but preferably the former.'

Observant Dutch civilians had already started to notice a change in German military activity, even while the columns of dispirited troops continued to pass through their town. One bystander in Eindhoven noted: 'the retreat of the Germans continued on the Monday, but at the same time a counter-movement was seen to develop: a large formation of troops, heavily camouflaged with branches of trees, marched through the city in the direction of the Belgian frontier.'

The British capture of Antwerp on 4 September had created a storm at Führer headquarters in East Prussia, the Wolfsschanze. Hitler, on hearing the news, wiped from his mind the circumstances in which he had sacked Generalfeldmarschall Gerd von Rundstedt at the end of June and recalled him to duty once again as commander-in-chief west. Generaloberst Kurt Student was in Berlin on the island of Wannsee at the headquarters of the Luftwaffe's Fallschirmjäger or paratroop arm when a call came through from the Wolfsschanze. Student, the architect of the Fallschirmjäger force, had commanded the airborne operations in the Netherlands in 1940 and in

Crete the following year. The order from Hitler was 'to build a new defence line along the Albert Canal and to hold it indefinitely'. Student's formation was given the inflated designation of First Fallschirm Army. According to one of his more cynical officers, Hitler chose Student because 'the Führer "the Greatest Commander of all time" said to himself: "Who shall defend Holland? Only he who conquered Holland can do that." So Student came to Holland.'

Student was to take every paratroop unit he could lay his hands on, starting with Oberstleutnant Friedrich Freiherr von der Heydte's 6th Fallschirmjäger-Regiment. He also brought in new formations, those in training establishments and even Luftwaffe ground crew turned into infantry battalions. Heydte, a veteran of the airborne invasion of Crete in 1941, was scathing about the way untrained Luftwaffe personnel were being designated as Fallschirmjäger. 'Those new paratroop *"Divisionen"* are second-rate Flak field divisions,' he told fellow officers. 'It's just pure vanity on Göring's part . . . The point seems to be that he thinks: "If peace breaks out I don't see why Himmler should be the only one to have a private army."'

The VI Luftwaffe Battalion (for special missions) was in fact a penal battalion brought back from Italy. It consisted of Luftwaffe airmen and ground crew convicted of crimes and officers sacked for incompetence. Their weaponry was pitiful and they were still wearing tropical uniforms. Even Heydte's famous regiment was a shadow of its former self after its battles against the American 101st Airborne in Normandy. 'The fighting strength of the regiment was weak,' he reported. 'The men were not yet welded together, the young replacements made up 75% of the strength, and they were barely trained. Hundreds of members of the regiment had never had a weapon in their hand and fired the first shots of their lives in their first engagement!'

Three of the new regiments were formed into the 7th Fallschirmjäger-Division. Student told his chief of staff, Generalleutnant Erdmann, to command it. Student was also given the 719th Infanterie-Division of coastal defence, and the 176th Infanterie-Division composed mostly of battalions with convalescents and the chronically sick. To command them, he had the headquarters of the LXXXVIII Corps under General der Infanterie Hans-Wolfgang Reinhard, 'a calm and experienced troop leader'. Although he received a brigade of assault guns, including some heavy Jagdpanther tank destroyers, his 'small and barely mobile' army had only twenty-five tanks along a front which stretched for nearly 200 kilometres all the way from the North Sea to Maastricht.

Student's Parachute Army was to come under the command of Army Group B. Having no artillery, Student ordered in flak units from Luftflotte

Reich because their 88mm anti-aircraft guns were also devastatingly effective against tanks. 'And then', he wrote with only slight exaggeration, 'one could admire once again the astonishing precision of German organisation and of the general staff. All these troops, which were strewn all over Germany, from Güstrow in Mecklenburg to Bitsch in Lorraine, were sent as "*Blitz*" transports to the Albert Canal. Here they arrived on 6 and 7 September, 48 to 72 hours after being alerted. The most remarkable aspect was that when the troops arrived at the stations, arms and equipment lay ready for five newly formed Fallschirmjäger regiments, having been brought in from other parts of Germany.'

There had been also some spontaneous reactions against the headlong retreat. On 4 September Generalleutnant Kurt Chill, with the remnants of his 85th Infanterie-Division, had halted at Turnhout on hearing that the British had entered Antwerp and Brussels. He turned his men around to redeploy along the Albert Canal. Chill's division had been reduced to less than a single regiment in Normandy. It had retreated via Brussels, having picked up a battalion of barely armed replacements on the way. Purely by chance, General Reinhard had come across the 85th Division's signals officer and was thrilled to hear that Chill had begun rounding up stragglers and seizing any artillery units still withdrawing. He was using them to man a defence line along the Albert Canal between Hasselt and Herentals.

The 85th Division thus became one of the key building blocks of Student's Parachute Army. In many places, officers and the hated Feldgendarmerie – known as 'chain-dogs' or *Kettenhunde* because of the metal gorget worn on a chain round their necks – had seized stragglers at gunpoint and forced them into scratch units. In a retreat a Kampfkommandant was designated, and as one officer explained: 'He is an officer who has the right to stop any officer up to and including the rank of Oberst, at any time, and to force him to go into action immediately, even at pistol point if necessary.'

On Tuesday 5 September, Student flew to see Model at Verviers near Liège. He argued that their only hope of obtaining enough troops to hold the line was General Gustav-Adolf von Zangen's Fifteenth Army. Thanks to the British decision to halt at Antwerp and not secure the Scheldt estuary, Student did indeed start to receive reinforcements from the Fifteenth Army. Its men and guns were shipped in barges across the Scheldt estuary at night to avoid Allied air attack. This failure to trap such a large force was to have a major influence later in the month when these German troops were able to attack the western flank of the American paratroopers trying to defend the route north towards Arnhem.

Student went on to see General Reinhard of LXXXVIII Corps. On the way he passed shire horses pulling the wagons of the 719th Division. This provided a bleak reminder that Germany was now fighting a poor man's war. On the next day, 6 September, when Generalleutnant Chill finally had a chance to report to Student, the two men heard that British tanks had crossed the canal at Beringen. Student ordered Chill to supervise a counterattack with Heydte's 6th Fallschirmjäger-Regiment and the battalion of the 2nd Fallschirmjäger. They were supported by an army Panzerjäger battalion of tank destroyers. Just north of Beringen at Beverlo, there was hard fighting in the village, with the Guards Armoured Division losing a number of tanks to Panzerfaust rocket-propelled grenades.

Allied commanders underestimated the energy of Generalfeldmarschall Walther Model, whom Hitler had brought in to take over Army Group B during the final crisis in Normandy. Model, a short, stocky man with a monocle, was totally unlike the sort of aristocratic staff officer whom Hitler loathed. From a modest background and with a popular touch, Model was unswervingly loyal to Hitler, who in turn had trusted him implicitly as his 'fireman' to resolve a crisis on the eastern front.

Model provoked mixed reactions among his own officers. While one regimental commander in an SS Panzergrenadier division said that 'Model is the grave-digger of the Western Front,' another from the same division clearly admired him. 'He is a first-rate artist of improvisation. He is an exceptionally cold-blooded dog, extraordinarily popular with the men because he has a certain amount of feeling for them and doesn't push himself forward in any theatrical sort of way, but is thoroughly hated by his own headquarters staff because he demands as much from them as from himself . . . Model is conceited and exuberant, always has new ideas, and at least three solutions to any awkward situation and is the complete autocrat. He won't stand any contradiction.' Another senior officer agreed that Model never let his subordinates get a word in edgeways, and was 'a little Hitler'.

The retreat of the stragglers from France horrified General der Flieger Friedrich Christiansen, the Wehrmacht commander-in-chief for the Netherlands. He felt that their dishevelled appearance demoralized his own troops. At bridges over the main rivers, especially the Waal, men were halted and re-formed into scratch groups called Alarmeinheiten.

Christiansen, one of the three men who wielded power in the Nazi-controlled Netherlands, had been a seaplane ace in the First World War. He was not known for his intelligence, only for his passionate admiration for the Führer and his total subservience to Reichsmarschall Hermann Göring. His second-in-command was Generalleutnant Heinz-Hellmuth von Wühlisch, a gaunt old Prussian warhorse, who had gathered a staff of like-minded officers. Christiansen, however, had a deeply suspicious streak. He tried to recruit spies in the wake of the bomb plot against Hitler, because he regarded Wühlisch as a real or potential traitor. 'He was guilty,' Christiansen insisted after the war. 'He committed suicide,' he added, as if that proved his point.

In theory, the leadership of the Nazi administration in the country lay with an Austrian, Reichskommissar Dr Arthur Seyss-Inquart. Seyss-Inquart, a bespectacled lawyer, had in March 1938 been the organizer of Hitler's *Anschluss*, turning their mother country into the Ostmark province of Großdeutschland. Seyss-Inquart became its governor and promptly ordered the confiscation of Jewish property. After the invasion of Poland, he became deputy to Hans Frank, the notorious Nazi in charge of the Generalgouvernement in Poland. Then, following the invasion and occupation of the neutral Netherlands in May 1940, this convinced anti-semite instigated the persecution of all Jews in the country. Tragically, Dutch officials had failed to destroy the administrative records before the Wehrmacht seized public buildings. The religious affiliation of each person marked in the official rolls identified the vast majority of the 140,000 Dutch and foreign Jews. Now in September 1944, Seyss-Inquart, greatly overestimating the strength of the Dutch underground movement, feared a general uprising, so he planned to make Rotterdam, Amsterdam and The Hague into centres of defence.

The third, and in some ways the most powerful, member of the Nazi triumvirate in the Netherlands was another Austrian, SS-Obergruppenführer Hanns Albin Rauter, the Höhere SS- und Polizeiführer. When the main German round-up of Jews took place in June 1942, there were strikes and protests, but apart from demonstrating great bravery they only increased the repression. Approximately 110,000 Jews out of 140,000 were deported from the Netherlands, and only 6,000 of these survived the war. The other 30,000 were in most cases hidden or smuggled out of the country by ordinary Dutch people. More than 1,500 of Arnhem's 1,700 Jews were deported to concentration camps in Germany and murdered. A number, however, were hidden and saved by the underground, especially by Johannes Penseel and his family.

A fugitive from the Germans, whether Jewish or Gentile, who disappeared was known as an *onderduiker*, or 'diver'. Some areas were better than others in hiding Jews. For example, as many as half of Eindhoven's 500 Jews were concealed as divers and saved. Since armed resistance was almost impossible in a country lacking mountains and large forests, the Dutch underground concentrated on helping those in danger with fake identities and ration books, as well as collecting intelligence for the Allies and passing shot-down pilots along escape lines through Belgium and France to Spain.

Rauter was merciless. He proudly reported on 2 March 1944, 'The Jewish problem in the Netherlands properly speaking can be considered solved. Within the next ten days the last full Jews will be taken away from Westerbork camp to the East.' He also ordered many reprisals for acts of resistance, which were later termed 'systematic terrorism against the Netherlands people'. Prominent Dutchmen were seized as hostages and executed. After a train had been blown up by the Dutch underground, the Germans seized as a hostage Count Otto van Limburg Stirum, the uncle of Audrey Hepburn, who was then living just outside Arnhem. He was executed with four others on 15 August 1942. Mostly the German authorities picked doctors and teachers as hostages. By 1944, their expectation of an Allied invasion made them nervous and cruel, with constant reprisals for sabotage or the killing of German personnel.

Mad Tuesday had its own tragic consequences. In the general panic, the SS decided to evacuate the remaining 3,500 prisoners in the concentration camp at Vught (known to the Germans as Konzentrationslager Herzogenbusch). Few Jews were left in the Netherlands by this stage, so most of the prisoners were Gentiles – Dutch, but also French and Belgian. Some 2,800 men were sent to Sachsenhausen and more than 650 women to Ravensbrück.*

The occupation of the Netherlands was probably the most brutal of all those in western Europe. German Nazis had hoped that the Dutch would join their cause as fellow Aryans. Rauter even insisted on referring to the Dutch SS as the 'Germanic SS'. So the German authorities were first astonished, then enraged by the determined opposition from the great majority of the population. All students were ordered to declare their support for the Nazi regime. Any who refused were arrested on 6 February 1943 in mass round-ups. Those who escaped had to disappear and become divers too. Almost 400,000 citizens of the Netherlands were conscripted and sent to the Reich for *Arbeitseinsatz*, which effectively meant slave labour.

The country's food supplies were systematically looted. Those living near the coast were forcibly removed, and large areas of farmland were

---

* It has been suggested that, of all nationalities, the Dutch suffered the lowest survival rate in concentration camps because their bodies had been used to a diet of high fat content from dairy products. The sudden change to 'an almost total lack of fat in the camp food' proved devastating.

deliberately flooded by breaking dykes. This part of Hitler's plan to defend 'Fortress Europe' made further inroads into a food supply already greatly reduced by German depredations. Malnutrition began to have its effect, especially on children. Diphtheria and even typhus spread.

In certain secret places the brutality was far worse. Generalleutnant Walter Dornberger, the Inspector of Long-Range Rocket Troops, was later recorded secretly in a British prisoner-of-war camp speaking of the activities of his colleague SS-Standartenführer Behr. 'In the Netherlands he made Dutchmen build the sites for the V2,' Dornberger told fellow officers, 'then he had them herded together and killed by machinegun fire. He opened brothels for his soldiers with twenty Dutch girls. When they'd been there for two weeks they were shot and new ones brought along, so that they couldn't divulge anything they might discover from the soldiers.'

Unfortunately, the Dutch suffered from their allies as well as from their enemy occupiers. The most unforgivable security lapses in the whole war by the Special Operations Executive in London led to the serial betrayal of Dutch agents parachuted in to help the underground. The *Englandspiel* operation mounted by the Abwehr, German counter-intelligence, hoodwinked the British SOE officers in charge and constituted a huge blow to Anglo-Dutch relations. And on 22 February 1944, a terrible mistake was made. When part of an American bomber force, heading for the Messerschmitt factory at Gotha, was recalled, the formation decided to drop their bombs instead on a German town. Not realizing that they had just crossed the border of the Netherlands, the American bomber crews destroyed a large part of the old town in Nijmegen and killed 800 people that day. Sadly, the battles ahead to liberate southern Holland were to lead to even greater suffering, but the Dutch, so desperate to be free, proved not just remarkably brave, but also remarkably forgiving.

3

The First Allied Airborne Army

While the British and the Americans were charging forward from the River Seine towards the German border, the British 1st Airborne Division back in Britain seethed with frustration as one operation after another was cancelled. 'Saturday, 2 September,' Major J. E. Blackwood of the 11th Parachute Battalion wrote in his diary. 'Briefed to drop SE of Courtrai to stem the Hun retreat across the River Escaut. Cancelled because of storm. Damn the storm! Sunday, 3 September, Briefed to drop near Maastricht. Operation cancelled because Yankee armour advancing too fast. Damn the Yanks!'

Members of the 1st Airborne Division were the most exasperated because they had been left out of the D-Day operation. Kept in reserve for a follow-up or for an operation of opportunity, they been stood to and stood down so many times that they were starting to become cynical. On a couple of occasions, the operation had not been cancelled until after they had been loaded into their aircraft and gliders on the runway.

The first plan hatched by Montgomery in the second week of June was to drop the division around Évrecy to create a breakthrough to seize Caen. For a number of reasons Air Chief Marshal Sir Trafford Leigh-Mallory opposed the idea with determination. He was almost certainly right to do so, but as he had wrongly predicted total disaster for the airborne drops on D-Day, Montgomery felt confirmed in his opinion that the airman was just a 'gutless bugger'.

In August, with Patton's breakout from Normandy, one airborne operation after another was dreamed up and the transport aircraft were consigned to fuel deliveries to help his advance. Lieutenant General Lewis H. Brereton, the air force commander of the newly created First Allied Airborne Army, complained to the supreme commander: 'I must emphasize that continued cargo carrying will render the Troop Carrier Command unfit for a successful airborne campaign.' He had a point. It was Eisenhower who had insisted, when appointing Brereton, that his chief priority was to improve the navigation training of IX Troop Carrier Command so that paratroops were no longer dropped in the wrong places, as had happened in the invasion of Sicily in 1943 and then again in Normandy.

The next idea was to seize crossings across the River Seine, but General Patton was already there. On 17 August, planning started on a drop in the Pas de Calais east of Boulogne. But then Brereton and Montgomery's chief of staff, Major General Francis de Guingand (known as 'Freddie'), agreed that the effort should be switched to the enemy's main line of retreat. Operation Linnet, planned for 3 September, would aim for Tournai over the Belgian border and for a bridgehead over the River Escaut. Linnet was cancelled on 2 September, with the possibility of switching to a Linnet II to seize bridgeheads over the River Meuse with three airborne divisions ahead of the American First Army. That too was cancelled at the meeting between Montgomery and Bradley the next day.

The First Allied Airborne Army had only been called into being on 2 August 1944 by General Eisenhower. Despite Eisenhower's devotion to balanced Allied relations, General Lewis Brereton's staff consisted mainly of American air force officers. At their headquarters, Sunninghill Park near Ascot, they enjoyed Saturday-night dances at their own club and watched movies such as *Kansas City Kitty* and *Louisiana Hayride*.

The only senior British officer with the First Allied Airborne Army was Brereton's deputy, Lieutenant General Frederick Browning. The whole set-up, with a USAAF general and staff commanding two major army formations – the American XVIII Airborne Corps and the British I Airborne Corps – was bound to complicate priorities and roles. Matters were not helped by a strong mutual dislike between Brereton and 'Boy' Browning. The only characteristic the two men had in common was vanity. Brereton, a small, difficult man, was such a compulsive womanizer that his activities provoked a severe rebuke from General George C. Marshall, the American chief of staff and a man of the strictest moral rectitude.

Browning, a hawk-faced Grenadier Guards officer with the air of a matinée idol, was married to the writer Daphne du Maurier. (She had chosen maroon for the paratrooper's beret as it was 'one of the General's racing colours'.) Although undoubtedly brave, Browning was highly strung. He could not help tugging at his moustache when nervous. His barely concealed ambition, combined with an immaculate uniform and a peremptory manner, did not endear him to other senior officers, especially the American paratroop commanders. They regarded 'the suave and polished Boy Browning' as a patronizing and manipulative empire-builder.

Unfortunately, when the tensions came to a head, Browning picked the wrong fight with Brereton, threatening to resign. On 3 September, he wrote to oppose Operation Linnet II which was intended to help Bradley's advance: 'Sir, I have the honour to forward my protest, in writing . . .', he began in the formal way. He went on to list his reasons for concluding that dropping three airborne divisions, one British and two American, to seize crossings over the River Meuse between Maastricht and Liège would fail. The whole enterprise was to be launched in less than thirty-six hours. The First Allied Airborne Army had no maps of the area to brief troops, no information on enemy dispositions and flak defences, and Allied fighter cover would not include the whole area of operations.

Browning was undoubtedly right, but Linnet II was cancelled by Bradley and Montgomery during their meeting that same day on very different grounds: the greater need for fuel deliveries. As a result Browning's protest served only to rile Brereton, who seemed much keener to help Bradley's forces than the British. And whatever the circumstances, a threat to resign cannot be repeated with any effect soon afterwards. Browning, who was desperate to command an airborne corps in action before the war came to an end, knew only too well that next time it would be seized upon. His American counterpart, Major General Matthew Bunker Ridgway, the commander of XVIII Airborne Corps, longed to take over and was better qualified. Ridgway had led the 82nd Airborne Division into Sicily, into Italy and into Normandy in June, so he had seen far more airborne combat. Browning had not been in action since the First World War.

Immediately after Montgomery's meeting with Bradley on 3 September (where he had disingenuously agreed not to use airborne forces), he promptly signalled his chief of staff Freddie de Guingand at 16.00 hours: 'Require airborne operation of one British division and Poles on evening 6 September or morning 7 September to secure bridges over Rhine between Wesel and Arnhem.' This was to be called Operation Comet.

De Guingand contacted Brereton's headquarters and at 22.30 hours Brigadier General Floyd L. Parks, Brereton's chief of staff, telephoned General Browning to pass on the order. 'You will immediately prepare detailed plans for an airborne operation along the River Rhine between Arnhem and Wesel.' Browning did not object this time. As well as his own determination to lead an airborne attack, the morale of the 1st Airborne Division badly needed an end to the dispiriting series of last-minute cancellations.

Browning was far from alone in his desire to use airborne forces in a dramatic and decisive way. Both Brigadier General James M. Gavin, the commander of the 82nd Airborne, and Major General Maxwell D. Taylor, who commanded the 101st, were keen to prove that airborne troops were critical to winning the war. Churchill also wanted the operation to boost British prestige just as it was flagging. And Montgomery saw it as a chance 'to seize control of Allied strategy'.

Both the Americans and the British had invested major resources to create the First Allied Airborne Army with six and a half divisions.* Although a small army in conventional terms, it was by far the largest and best-equipped airborne force ever assembled. General Marshall, chairman of the joint chiefs of staff in Washington, and General 'Hap' Arnold, head of the US Army Air Force, were impatient to use it in a major strategic operation. The American press was carried away by the idea that airborne operations represented the future of warfare. *Time* magazine even believed that 'peace could be maintained in the postwar world with the establishment of an airborne international army.' This was a fantasy which ignored basic limitations, such as the comparatively short range of fully loaded troop-carrying aircraft. It was a mistake often shared by generals who should have known better.

On 4 September, Browning and de Guingand flew to France, and at 19.00 hours a conference began at Dempsey's Second Army headquarters. 'We discussed plans for the capture of Nijmegen and Arnhem,' Dempsey noted. 'I will start with XXX Corps from Antwerp on the morning of 7 September 44 and Airborne Corps will drop two or three airborne brigades on the morning of 7 September to get the bridges.'

Back in England, British and Polish airborne officers did not share their superiors' enthusiasm for Operation Comet. The plan for a parachute brigade to drop nearly 110 kilometres behind German lines to seize the bridge over the Neder Rijn, or Lower Rhine, at Arnhem, and for Major General Stanisław Sosabowski's Polish Independent Brigade and an airlanding brigade to take Nijmegen, the great bridge and the high ground to the south-east of the city, prompted ironical remarks about 'the British and the Poles capturing Holland all by themselves'. Sosabowski, who had been a

---

* The First Allied Airborne Army consisted of the American XVIII Airborne Corps, with the 82nd and 101st Airborne Divisions, and the 17th Airborne Division still in training; and the British I Airborne Corps, with the 1st and 6th Airborne Divisions, the Polish 1st Independent Parachute Brigade attached and the 52nd (Lowland) Division as an airlanding formation to be flown in later to a captured airfield.

professor at the Polish war college, interrupted Major General Roy Urquhart in the briefing. 'But the Germans, General . . . The Germans!' He also referred sarcastically to these 'planning geniuses' who had come up with such an idea. Brigadier John 'Shan' Hackett also became restless at the naive assumptions that all would go well on the day. Lieutenant Colonel John Frost, who would command the troops at Arnhem bridge, was completely frank with his officers. 'Believe me, it will be some bloodbath,' he told them.

Encouraged by the heady optimism prevailing in headquarters on the continent, the First Allied Airborne Army also grossly underestimated the determination of the enemy. 'Large forces of airborne troops,' their intelligence chief wrote, 'having the audacity to drop in daylight, may well scare the enemy into a state of complete disorganization.' Despite Eisenhower's instruction that the First Allied Airborne Army was to support Montgomery's forces, Brereton also favoured using it to help Bradley. On 5 September, two days after agreeing to Comet, Brereton even approved the preparation of 'a plan to lift the US Airborne corps and drop [it] back of the Siegfried Line in the vicinity of Cologne'. This would have led to a terrible disaster if it had gone ahead, because the Germans would have concentrated all available forces to defend the city and the Rhine crossings there.

Eisenhower had insisted that something must be done to secure the Scheldt estuary to open the port of Antwerp and trap the German Fifteenth Army. Montgomery's headquarters reacted to this only on 8 September, demanding an airborne assault on the island of Walcheren, despite the fact that planning for Comet was under way. This time Browning and Brereton were united in their opposition. Browning 'believed that the Air Forces could achieve almost as much by attacking the shipping by which troops are being evacuated from south of the Scheldt estuary', but this would have been hard since the Germans were moving them only at night. Brereton turned the project down because the 'small size of [the] island indicates excessive losses due to drowning of troops dropped in the water'. The terrain was no good for gliders, and Walcheren had strong flak defences.

The almost casual way in which both First Allied Airborne Army and Montgomery's headquarters came up with one airborne plan after another, and in this case two at the same time, almost beggars belief. Brigadier Edgar 'Bill' Williams, Montgomery's chief intelligence officer, admitted later that 'we didn't work in the serious way we did for D-Day. We were in Brussels where we had parties and a gay time. Everyone worked, but the psychology was wrong.' In addition, Montgomery saw only Browning when discussing airborne operations. He did not want to consult the RAF, even though the War Office and Air Ministry had agreed after the airborne chaos in Sicily that the air force side must lead the planning process. And Browning probably did not want to admit to the field marshal that the real decisions would be taken by USAAF officers at Brereton's headquarters. In any case, the lack of liaison between ground and air was pitiful, if not scandalous. It was bad even on the air side. Leigh-Mallory had to write to Brereton to point out that he had failed to invite to planning meetings the RAF commanders of 38 and 46 Groups whose transport aircraft would be an integral part of Operation Comet.

On 9 September Sosabowski, accompanied by Major General Urquhart, the commander of the 1st Airborne Division, met Browning at Cottesmore airfield in the Midlands to discuss Comet. 'Sir,' Sosabowski said to Browning without any preamble, 'I am very sorry, but this mission cannot possibly succeed.'

'Why?' Browning demanded. Sosabowski replied that it would be suicide with such small forces. Browning then attempted flattery. 'But my dear Sosabowski, the Red Devils and the gallant Poles can do anything.' Sosabowski, although distinctly unimpressed by such a facile compliment, restricted himself to the observation: 'Human abilities do have limits after all.' He then told Urquhart that he would have to have all his orders in writing as he refused to be held responsible for such a disaster. Browning, even though he had obliquely acknowledged that the forces might be insufficient, took deep offence at Sosabowski's attitude.

In Belgium General Dempsey had just reached similar conclusions to those of Sosabowski. The day before he had summoned General Horrocks of XXX Corps to Brussels aerodrome for a quick conference. As he expected, Horrocks confirmed that their bridgehead over the Albert Canal was 'being strongly opposed by the enemy'. Dempsey expressed his concerns to Montgomery the next day, then flew to see Horrocks again in the afternoon. 'It is clear', Dempsey wrote in his diary, 'that the enemy is bringing up all the reinforcements he can lay his hands on for the defence of the Albert Canal, and that he appreciates the importance of the area Arnhem–Nijmegen. It looks as though he is going to do all he can to hold it. This being the case, any question of a rapid advance to the northeast seems unlikely. Owing to our maintenance situation, we will not be in a position to fight a real battle for perhaps ten days or a fortnight. Are we right to direct Second Army to Arnhem, or would it be better to hold a left flank along the Albert canal and strike due east towards Cologne in conjunction with First Army?' But this was the last thing that Montgomery wanted. He wanted to go north and force the Americans to support him.

Early the next morning, Sunday 10 September, Dempsey went to Montgomery's headquarters and managed to persuade him that 'in view of increasing [German] strength on the Second Army front in the Arnhem–Nijmegen area the employment of one airborne division in this area will not be sufficient. I got from C-in-C his agreement to the use of three airborne divisions.'

Montgomery liked the idea of cancelling Operation Comet and replacing it with a larger one which brought the American 82nd and 101st Airborne Divisions under his command. But to Dempsey's dismay Montgomery also brandished a signal at him which had arrived from London the day before. Two V-2 rockets had exploded in England having apparently been fired from the area of Rotterdam and Amsterdam. The government asked urgently for an estimate of how long it would take his army group to seal off the area. For Montgomery, who wanted to go north via Arnhem, and not east via Wesel as Dempsey and others on his staff preferred, this was just the confirmation he needed to justify his decision.

There was only one cloud on the field marshal's horizon, but for him it was a dark one. Eisenhower, he discovered, was allowing Bradley and Patton to advance into the Saar, south-east of Luxembourg. The supreme commander was not according full priority to his Northern Group of Armies, as he thought had been promised. Matters were not improved by communications failures at Eisenhower's tactical headquarters back at Granville, 650 kilometres to the west. At that moment, Montgomery was having typed a long letter to Field Marshal Sir Alan Brooke, the chief of the imperial general staff, complaining that Eisenhower was totally out of touch, that there was no 'grip' on operations, and it included the lines: 'Eisenhower himself does not really know anything about the business of fighting the Germans: he has not got the right sort of chaps on his staff for the job, and no one there understands the matter.'

Dempsey summoned Browning to his tactical headquarters, where in the next two hours they put together an outline plan. The new operation, which would be called Market Garden, consisted of two parts. Market was the airborne operation, in which the American 101st and 82nd Airborne Divisions would seize river and canal crossings from Eindhoven to Nijmegen, with the big bridges over the Rivers Maas and Waal, the largest in Europe; while, further on, the British 1st Airborne Division and the Polish brigade would drop near Arnhem to capture the great road bridge over the Neder Rijn. Browning was pleased with his phrase, describing Market as an 'airborne carpet', as if it simply had to be unrolled in front of the ground troops.

Operation Garden would consist principally of Horrocks's XXX Corps led by tanks, charging north up a single road, with polderland flood plain on either side broken only by woods and plantations. They would keep going all the way over the bridges secured by the paratroopers. After crossing the bridge at Arnhem, they would occupy the Luftwaffe air base of Deelen. The 52nd (Airlanding) Division would be flown in, and from there XXX Corps would carry on all the way to the shore of the IJsselmeer, a total distance of more than 150 kilometres from the start-line. The objective for the British Second Army was to cut off the German Fifteenth Army and the whole of the western Netherlands, outflank the Siegfried Line, be across the Rhine and in a position to encircle the Ruhr from the north, or even charge on towards Berlin.

Montgomery, meanwhile, headed for Brussels aerodrome to see Eisenhower, who had flown in with his deputy, Air Chief Marshal Sir Arthur Tedder. This meeting had been arranged some days before, and discussion of the airborne operation was not on the agenda. Eisenhower, still suffering badly from his knee, could not descend from the aircraft, so proceedings took place on board. Montgomery, incensed by the frustration he had been expressing in his letter to Brooke, was in a fractious mood. He refused point blank to allow Eisenhower's chief supply officer, Lieutenant General Sir Humfrey Gale, to be present, but insisted that his own chief administrative officer, Major General Miles Graham, should remain.

Montgomery pulled from his pocket a sheaf of telegrams. 'Did you send me these?' he demanded, waving them.

'Yes, of course,' Eisenhower replied. 'Why?'

'Well, they're nothing but balls, sheer balls, rubbish.' After letting him run on for a short time, Eisenhower leaned forward, put his hand on Montgomery's knee and said: 'Monty, you can't speak to me like that. I'm your boss.'

Halted in his harangue, Montgomery could only mumble an apology. But he still insisted that Patton must be stopped, that his own army group should be given two American corps from Hodges's First Army and that it should receive 'absolute priority' in supplies, 'if necessary to the exclusion of all other operations'. Eisenhower rejected that interpretation of the word 'priority' and emphasized that the objective was the Ruhr, not Berlin. He was prepared to give Montgomery priority, but he was not going to halt Patton. Eisenhower reminded him that he already had the support of the First Allied Airborne Army. This led to a very brief discussion of the latest airborne plan.

Eisenhower followed standard US Army practice. Having agreed an overall strategy, he did not believe in interfering further. Montgomery was able to use this later to imply that at this meeting Eisenhower had given his blessing to the new Market Garden plan. They discussed only the timing and the problem of supplies, which Montgomery dramatized in order to obtain more. Eisenhower should perhaps have raised the question of aircraft range. He had received a warning from Brereton that the Allied airborne divisions and troop carrier formations should move to the continent, otherwise an operation across the Rhine would be too far. He was, however, 'alarmed at the administrative picture as painted by Monty', and agreed to see if supplies to Dempsey's Second Army could be increased. Graham, who should have known the situation, believed that the 500 tons a day they were receiving was more than enough for Market Garden, but not enough for the deep penetration into the North German plain which Montgomery wanted. Both Eisenhower and Tedder considered it 'fantastic to talk of marching to Berlin with an army which is still drawing the bulk of its supplies over beaches north of Bayeux'. The port of Antwerp had to be opened first.

Dempsey, meanwhile, had worked fast. By the time Montgomery returned from Brussels aerodrome to his tactical headquarters, Dempsey had 'fixed with [Browning] the outline of the operation', his diary entry stated. 'He can be ready to carry this out on 16 September at the earliest.' Horrocks was his next visitor that afternoon. 'Saw Commander XXX Corps at my headquarters and gave him the plan for the operation to be carried out by Airborne Corps and XXX Corps with the co-operation of VIII Corps on the right and XII Corps on the left.'

Montgomery had wanted to present the First Allied Airborne Army with a fait accompli, approved by the supreme commander, and this he achieved. He had also decided on Arnhem and not Wesel, a crossing which he would almost certainly have had to share with the American First Army.

There have been suggestions that Browning too preferred Wesel, but Browning had strenuously supported Comet, which included Arnhem. Now, he was to command three and a half airborne divisions to do the same job, not just one and a half, so he was unlikely to oppose the field marshal on the subject. And the suggestion that on 10 September Browning had said to Montgomery that Arnhem might be going 'a bridge too far' is highly improbable, since they do not appear to have met that day. There is no mention in Dempsey's diary of Browning at the early-morning meeting with Montgomery, and he had reached Dempsey's headquarters only at midday when Montgomery was with Eisenhower.

Browning's excitement was quite palpable at the prospect of the airborne corps seeing action at last. He sent the single codeword 'New' from Demp-sey's headquarters back to the First Allied Airborne Army at Sunninghill Park. This signified that a planning conference was to be called that evening when he returned.

General Brereton, on the other hand, must have felt deeply affronted that Montgomery had made no attempt to consult him in advance. His resent-ment would have been perfectly justified. Eisenhower's original directive had insisted that planning should be shared.* Montgomery had deliberately ignored this. He wrote to Field Marshal Brooke: 'Airborne Army HQ had refused my demand for airborne troops to help capture Walcheren . . . and they are now going to be ordered by Ike to do what I ask.'

Twenty-seven senior officers gathered in the Sunninghill Park confer-ence room at 18.00 hours to hear Lieutenant General Browning's account of decisions taken that day in Belgium. Brereton was there, so were his chief of staff Brigadier General Parks, Major General Paul L. Williams of IX Troop Carrier Command, Brigadier General James Gavin of the 82nd Air-borne Division and Brigadier General Anthony C. McAuliffe of the 101st. Astonishingly, neither Major General Urquhart of the 1st Airborne nor Major General Sosabowski had been invited. The only British officer present from outside Brereton's staff was Air Vice Marshal Hollinghurst of 38 Group. It is more than likely that Browning did not want Urquhart pres-ent so that he controlled his planning entirely.

Browning presented what he and Dempsey had worked out, using an air-lift timetable based on Operation Linnet. Disingenuously, he implied that it had Eisenhower's blessing, when the supreme commander had not seen it. Brereton and his staff privately dismissed it as just 'a tentative skeleton plan'. Browning finished by declaring that the operation would take place between 14 and 16 September, just over three days away. It was a danger-ously short time.

Brereton raised the first key decision: was it to be a night or a day oper-ation? German night fighters 'would be more effective than their day fighters, but flak would be much more accurate by day than by night'. Brere-ton decided on a daylight operation 'in the belief that a proper employment of the supporting air forces available could knock out flak positions in advance and beat them down during the airborne operations themselves'.

---

* 'The commander in chief Northern Group of Armies, in conjunction with the Com-manding General First Allied Airborne Army, will plan and direct the employment of the entire Airborne force which is made available to the Northern Group of Armies to expedite the accomplishment of its assigned missions.'

His headquarters claimed that 'this was a bold decision since the flak was known to have increased by 35% in the Market area, the troop carrier aircraft were unarmoured, were not equipped with leak-proof tanks, and flew at speeds between 120 and 140 miles an hour.' But Brigadier General Gavin's chief intelligence officer, who was present, felt they had exaggerated. Brereton's 'estimate of flak differed widely from that given me at Second US Bombardment Division just four hours previous. This bombardment division was flying missions daily over the Nijmegen area.'

Brereton then asked Major General Williams to speak. The troop carrier commander's words must have come as a bombshell to Browning. Most of the key assumptions on which he and Dempsey had worked that day were now thrown in the air. 'General Williams stated that the lift would have to be modified, due to the distance involved, which precluded the use of double tow lift . . . single tow only could be employed.' This meant that with each plane towing one American glider, instead of two, as Browning had calculated with Dempsey, only half the number of gliders could be taken on each lift. And since the mid-September days were shorter and the mornings mistier, Williams ruled out two lifts in a day.

These changes meant that it would take up to three days to deliver the airborne divisions, and that depended on perfect flying weather. Operation Market, the airborne side of Market Garden, would thus not be landing any more assault troops on the crucial first day than Operation Comet, because half the force would have to be left behind to guard landing and drop zones for the subsequent lifts. And the Germans, having identified Allied intentions, would be able to concentrate troops and anti-aircraft batteries against these areas on subsequent days. Williams's obdurate attitude might be seen to contain an element of revenge after the deliberate refusal to consult the air force side in advance, but the fault lay far more with Montgomery and his determination to impose an ill-considered plan.

Next morning, 11 September, Major General Urquhart attended Browning's briefing. The headquarters of British 1 Airborne Corps was just north-west of London in the large and elaborate Palladian building of Moor Park, with its great portico of Corinthian columns. Browning drew three large circles on the talc-covered map to show the objectives of the three divisions. As he finished drawing the third one, he fixed Urquhart with a deliberately unsettling stare, saying 'Arnhem Bridge – and hold it.'

Later, a more detailed examination of the terrain revealed that the high ground north of the Neder Rijn meant that their defence plan would have to include the whole city of Arnhem, with a population of nearly 100,000,

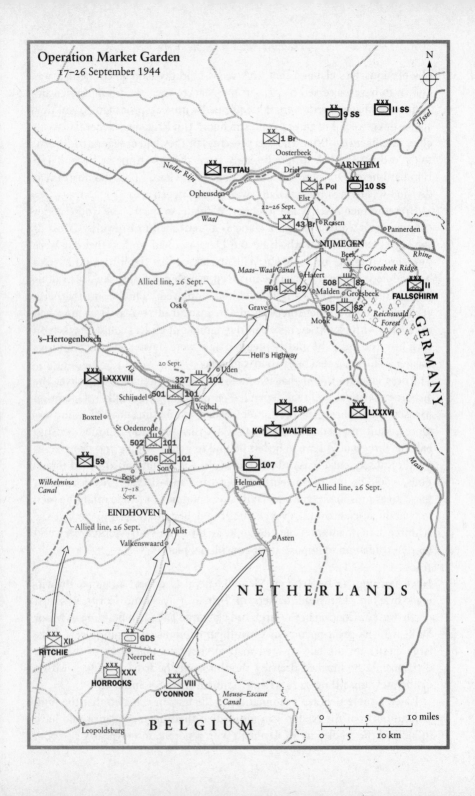

as well as the drop zones outside. That signified a perimeter many times the size of a usual division frontage. Urquhart could not help wondering whether his 1st Airborne had been given the furthest and most dangerous objective as a compliment to its effectiveness or because Allied diplomacy could not survive a disaster to an American formation under British command. He strongly suspected the latter, and he was right.*

A follow-up meeting took place at IX Troop Carrier Command's headquarters at Eastcote, also on the north-western edge of London. American air force officers more or less dictated the choice of drop and landing zones. Their main priority was to avoid German flak batteries on the way in and on the way out. For simplicity in the short time available, the air transport chiefs were working from the plans elaborated for earlier operations. Yet Major General Williams rejected the glider-borne *coup de main* parties to seize the main bridges by surprise attack, which had been a key element in the previous plan. Air Vice Marshal Hollinghurst of the RAF's 38 Group said that he was perfectly happy to go ahead with them. Williams overruled him on the grounds that 'normal sized coup de main parties would not have been strong enough to seize and hold the major bridges.' But according to Hollinghurst in a memo, the decision to mount the whole operation 'in broad daylight' was 'because the [American] Eighth Air Force cannot operate their fighters at early dawn or dusk' and this was why the *coup de main* parties were cancelled. The Americans had stricter rules on visibility than the RAF. But it was also true that a company landed before dawn, like the Pegasus Bridge operation in Normandy, would have attracted all available German forces to the bridge well before the arrival of the main force, and Browning refused to consider a daylight *coup de main*.

Major General Maxwell Taylor, the commander of the 101st Airborne which was responsible for the first sixty kilometres of the road, refused drop zones 'in seven separate areas' close to the seven bridges he had to seize. He feared too great a dispersal of his division. They were reduced to two, and later after a meeting with Dempsey, his responsibility for defending the route north was reduced to twenty-five kilometres.

Gavin was also unhappy with the dispersion of his dropping zones. Williams flatly refused to change them. The 101st at least was to have the

* Eisenhower's chief of staff, Lieutenant General Walter Bedell Smith, when asked after the war whether SHAEF dictated that the division at Arnhem should be the British one, replied: 'No we did not dictate it but I am damned glad it was. The political fallout in the United States would have been disastrous if an American airborne division had been chewed to pieces in a British plan.'

greatest number of aircraft because it was closest to the base of the operation. The 82nd Airborne had the next largest allocation and the British 1st Airborne the fewest, partly because General Browning appropriated thirty-eight gliders for his own corps headquarters. (German officers when analysing the operation afterwards came to the opposite conclusion. They believed that the furthest division should have been the strongest.)

German flak concentrations dominated the planning of the air routes and the drop zones. Troop Carrier Command wanted to stay well away from the key objectives of Arnhem and Nijmegen bridges because of their anti-aircraft defences. At Arnhem, they were also threatened by the Luftwaffe airfield of Deelen just to the north of the town. As a result the British division was to be dropped well to the west, with an approach march of between ten and thirteen kilometres to the road bridge through a major town. Surprise, the most vital element in airborne operations, was therefore lost before they even took off.

'One of the greatest difficulties in mounting this operation rested on the inflexible planning of Troop Carrier Command,' Gavin's chief intelligence officer, Colonel Norton, recorded. 'The ground plan became practically secondary to the air plan.' Major General Urquhart of 1st Airborne simply did not have the experience to negotiate forcefully with Troop Carrier Command. He accepted the landing and drop zones he had been given. 'The airmen had the final say,' Urquhart wrote later, 'and we knew it.' But those airmen were firmly convinced that there were no alternative sites.

Many historians, with an 'if only' approach to the British defeat, have focused so much on different aspects of Operation Market Garden which went wrong that they have tended to overlook the central element. It was quite simply a very bad plan right from the start and right from the top. Every other problem stemmed from that. Montgomery had not shown any interest in the practical problems surrounding airborne operations. He had not taken any time to study the often chaotic experiences of North Africa, Sicily and the drop on the Cotentin peninsula in Normandy. Montgomery's intelligence chief, Brigadier Bill Williams, also pointed to the way that 'Arnhem depended on a study of the ground [which] Monty had not made when he decided on it.' In fact he obstinately refused to listen to the Dutch commander-in-chief Prince Bernhard, who had warned him about the impossibility of deploying armoured vehicles off the single raised road on to the low-lying polderland flood plain.

Williams also acknowledged that at 21st Army Group 'enemy appreciation was very weak. We knew very little about the situation.' Yet towering over everything else, and never openly admitted, was the fact that the whole operation depended on everything going right, when it was an unwritten rule of warfare that no plan survives contact with the enemy. This was doubly true of airborne operations. The probability of the Germans blowing the huge road bridge at Nijmegen over the River Waal was barely discussed. Had they done so, XXX Corps could not possibly have reached the 1st Airborne at Arnhem in time. The German failure to destroy it was an astonishing and totally uncharacteristic mistake on their part, and one which Allied planners should never have counted on.

Also on 11 September, Admiral Ramsay flew to Granville, to where Eisenhower had returned after the meeting with Montgomery at Brussels aerodrome. 'Went on to see Ike and found him in pyjamas with his knee bad again,' Ramsay wrote in his diary. 'Stayed to tea and he let himself go on subject of Monty, command, his difficulties, future strategy etc. He is clearly worried, and the cause is undoubtedly Monty who is behaving badly. Ike does not trust his loyalty and probably with good reason. He has never let himself go to me like this before.'

Over the next few days Ramsay kept trying to have a meeting with Montgomery about the Scheldt estuary to open the great port of Antwerp. The field marshal would not see him. As far as he was concerned, Antwerp had been settled as an objective for the First Canadian Army. But his obsessively tidy mind had insisted on a geographical progression. The Canadians should continue advancing up the coast to capture and open the much smaller and more damaged Channel ports first. In any case Montgomery clearly believed that if he could get across the Rhine, then Antwerp could be dealt with later.

At the same time, Montgomery was trying to extract everything he could. On 11 September, the day after their meeting in the aircraft at Brussels aerodrome, he sent a signal to Eisenhower: 'Your decision that the northern thrust towards the Ruhr is *not* to have priority over other operations will have certain repercussions which you should know . . . Revised Operation Comet can NOT repeat NOT take place before 23 September at the earliest . . . The delay will give the enemy time to organize better defensive arrangements.' He claimed that he now found that he lacked sufficient supplies. Eisenhower, horrified that the Allies might fail both to achieve a bridgehead across the Rhine and to secure Antwerp, sent his chief of staff, General Walter Bedell Smith, to sort things out.

The next day, Bedell Smith flew to the field marshal's tactical headquarters. He promised an extra 500 tons of supplies a day, even if that meant depriving three American divisions of their transport, and assured Montgomery that the US First Army would receive priority too so that his right flank would be protected. This would mean holding back Patton in the Saar. Montgomery felt he had won 'a great victory'. He boasted to Field Marshal Brooke that his signal to Eisenhower had 'produced electric results. Ike has given way and he sent Bedell to see me today. The Saar thrust is to be stopped.'

Montgomery, having obtained what he wanted, despatched another signal to Eisenhower: 'Thank you for sending Bedell to see me. As a result of the guarantee of 1,000 tons a day and of fact that Hodges will now get all the maintenance he needs I have investigated my own problem again. I have now fixed D Day for Operation MARKET for Sunday 17 September.' Bradley, meanwhile, was furious that he had never been consulted, and as soon as he heard he told Eisenhower he 'objected strenuously' to the plan. Patton was sickened. 'Monty does what he pleases,' he wrote in his diary, 'and Ike says "yes, sir".' In fact Montgomery received nothing like what he had been promised, and he used this later in an attempt to divert blame for the failure of Operation Market Garden. General Eisenhower, until the very end of his life, could not get over the way Montgomery was never able to admit that he had been responsible for anything going wrong.

4

Doubts Dismissed

Early on 10 September, when Dempsey had persuaded Montgomery to cancel Operation Comet, a message with the news reached the British 1st Airborne Division. According to an officer in Frost's 2nd Battalion, 'the whole brigade went to Nottingham and Lincoln to get tight, as only the 1st Para Brigade knows how.' But on returning with massive hangovers, they heard that they were going after all, but on a new and bigger mission.

Lieutenant Colonel Charles Mackenzie, Urquhart's chief of staff, was a small man with a neatly trimmed moustache, an amused look in his eyes and a dry sense of humour. He and some fellow officers, when they heard of the cancellation, decided to enjoy that day boating on the Thames. When they arrived back in the afternoon, they found General Urquhart excited. 'Come on,' he told them. 'We're on with the next one and we've got some work to do.' They started to pore over the maps, trying to work out what might have changed. They did not have a clear idea, of course, until after the two briefing sessions the next day. Mackenzie thought the new operation with more than three divisions seemed at least more realistic than some of the previous plans.

American paratroopers, who had seen their fill of action in Normandy, did not suffer from the same sort of cynicism which had started to build up in the British 1st Airborne. Their own version was part of the devil-may-care self-image which they cultivated. Frank Brumbaugh in the 82nd Airborne had returned to Nottingham from Normandy with a 'barracks bag of German helmets' to sell as souvenirs. But he found his customers wanted the beaten-up ones with bullet holes in, not the shiny new ones, so he began firing at his stock with a looted Walther P-38, and the price went up from one pound to five pounds. 'We also took every chance we got to comfort the English wives and girls whose husbands and boyfriends were off in the Far

East . . . With the blackout, one had to shuffle one's feet walking through the parks so as not to step on the many loving couples entwined on the ground, while looking for a place for [ourselves] and our own temporary girlfriends.'

Losses had been so heavy in Normandy that in some battalions new replacements accounted for up to 60 per cent of their strength. The 508th Parachute Infantry Regiment had returned with only 918 men out of 2,055. Training was intensified to get the new arrivals prepared for combat, but the jokes kept coming. American paratroopers claimed that, unlike the British 1st Airborne, they were not disappointed when operations were cancelled. 'Combat is a place where a guy could get hurt!' and 'Let Patton win the war!' became the cry after missions were cancelled at the last moment because the Third Army's rapid advance had overrun the target area.

Most of the 101st Airborne felt relief when an operation was cancelled, unlike their commander. Major General Maxwell Taylor was thought to be too much of an 'eager beaver'. He kept telling his men 'that he would not rest until he had a good mission for us'. They preferred to boast of a different sort of combat, 'that a military police unit would be given a presidential citation if they were on duty when the 101st were in town on leave'. It was fortunate that the 82nd Airborne was quartered in the east Midlands while the 101st was in the south of England, as the two enjoyed coming to blows. The 82nd would provoke the 101st by pointing at their shoulder badge and cry in mock terror, 'Screaming Eagles – Help! Help!'

Not all members of the two American airborne divisions were obsessed with women, drink, gambling and fighting. The poet Louis Simpson in the 327th Glider Infantry with the 101st reflected on the character of their host nation. 'The English are a very great race, and take things in their stride without the dramatization Americans love. Any girl will show you a picture of her family and mention as tho' it were funny, that they were blitzed and that brother John was killed in Africa last year. Sometimes this apparent coldness makes me shiver. I prefer our over-emphasis on the value of life.'

Polish paratroopers could not have been more different. They were not like the British who just wanted to make the best of a bad war by joking and referring to any battle as 'a party'. Nor were they like the Americans who wanted to finish it quickly so that they could go home. The Poles were exiles, fighting for the very survival of their national identity. An American officer who saw them in training described them as 'killers under the silk'. Polish patriotism was nothing like the rather embarrassed British equivalent: theirs was a burning, spiritual flame.

At that moment their countrymen and -women were suffering terribly in the Warsaw Uprising against impossible odds. 'As Poles we knew we had to die for a lost cause,' said Corporal Wojewódka, 'but as soldiers we wanted to fight hoping that it would shorten the war. Some of us hoped that the Russians would be stopped before taking Poland and very naively we were praying for miracles.' The British could not really understand what the war meant to Poland. 'My Scottish girlfriend is crying,' wrote one paratrooper. 'She knows we have to part. Maybe forever. She cannot understand that a soldier must carry on the battle for Poland's sake.'

Their commander, Major General Stanisław Sosabowski, was a difficult and demanding man. He was not loved by his men, but they respected, feared and also trusted him, because he would do anything that he asked of them. They referred to him as '*Stary*' – the 'old one' in Polish. This violently patriotic and tough fifty-two-year-old had deep-set eyes and a weather-beaten face. He was fiercely obstinate and far from deferential when it came to dealing with senior officers when he thought they were wrong.

Sosabowski and his men had one idea which dominated everything. Their brigade motto was 'The Shortest Way', and their mission was to spearhead the liberation of their homeland. As early as October 1940, the Polish commander-in-chief, General Władysław Sikorski, issued his 'Order Regarding Preparations to a National Rising in Poland'. It was, like many of the papers which followed, a remarkable document, far-sighted about the likely course of the war, and yet also hopelessly optimistic that Polish forces in Britain could come to grips with the enemy on home territory. They even considered the future possibility of flying in armoured divisions.

Sikorski was undeterred by British officialdom. He had insisted that when the 1st Polish Independent Parachute Brigade was set up under Sosabowski, it would not be deployed under Allied command, but held back to assist an uprising in Poland. The British accepted this stipulation, although no doubt with some head-shaking and mutters about 'the crazy Poles'. But on 17 May 1943 Browning approached Sosabowski with a view to changing the agreement as plans began to be considered for the invasion of France. According to Sosabowski, four months later Browning told him that 'unless you become part of the British airborne forces, I will take away your equipment and training opportunities.'

The following year, when planning for D-Day was well advanced, the War Office considered any rising or operation in Poland as nothing more than a diversion to the main effort in Normandy. Montgomery 'refused to accept any restrictions upon the use of the brigade'. Sosabowski's command was to be deployed as part of the British 1 Airborne Corps.

The tragedy for Poland was the unexpectedly rapid advance of the Red Army in Operation Bagration, which brought it almost to the gates of Warsaw by the end of July 1944. Polish plans had never intended the great uprising to take place until 'the defeat of Germany becomes inevitable'. But desperate to forestall a Soviet occupation of the Polish capital, the Home Army, or Armia Krajowa, started the Warsaw Uprising on 1 August.

Just over two weeks later, as Warsaw burned in the vicious battle, the Polish commander-in-chief wrote half-apologetically to Sosabowski. 'I made every effort, about which you will hear at the right time, for at least part of the Brigade to be used where your hearts and dreams have driven you for the past years. Unfortunately, obstacles proved more powerful than my will or yours. But we shall bite the bullet and carry on along our straight and honest road. Keep a cheerful spirit and show the world the grand Polish soldierly flair which challenges fate and breaks through all obstacles . . . Beat the Germans and fight well, thus helping Warsaw at least indirectly. We for our part will not cease in efforts to organise sufficient help for her in weapons and ammunition.' But resupply by air was almost as difficult for the insurgents in Warsaw as it would prove to be for paratroopers at Arnhem.

Despite a recent training accident, in which thirty-six of their comrades had been killed when two Dakota C-47s collided, Sosabowski's men had lost none of their determination. They still tried to comfort themselves with the idea that if they were not dropping on Warsaw, they would at least be close 'to walking into Germany through the kitchen'. But as the uprising approached its terrible climax they were 'boiling' with rage not to be dropped there. That was where they should be, and that was what they had trained for. The fact that the C-47 simply lacked the capacity to deliver a full load of paratroopers over Poland and return to British bases did not diminish the intensity of their emotions.

On 12 September at Moor Park, Sosabowski had another meeting with Urquhart, who told him that the Polish Brigade Group had been allocated only 114 aircraft and 45 Horsa gliders. Sosabowski was not pleased. It meant that he would have to leave behind his artillery, while his anti-tank detachment could take just their guns and Jeeps and a crew of only two men each. They were to be landed with the 1st Airborne Division north of the Neder Rijn, while the bulk of the Polish brigade was to land on the south side.

Flaws in the plan became even more evident day by day. On 14 September at 16.00 hours, Sosabowski met Urquhart at Wittering airfield near Stamford in Lincolnshire. He pointed out that his brigade would be able to cross the Neder Rijn at Arnhem only if the British had already secured the bridges. In his minute of the meeting, the Polish commander wrote in his stilted way: 'Sosabowski permitted himself the liberty of pointing out that the bridgehead to be held by the 1st Airborne Division's 1st Brigade is more than ten miles away. And before the Polish brigade arrives, it might not even have reached the area and might be surrounded in an even smaller area. In that case the Polish brigade would have to wait for them before they can take up positions.'

He also pointed out that 'the bridgehead to be held by 1st Airborne Division and 1st Polish Parachute Brigade Group extends for over ten miles in difficult terrain, and there is always the possibility that until the Polish Brigade Group arrives on D+2 its defensive positions might be seized and held by the enemy, as 1st Airborne Division might be unable to establish and hold such a large perimeter. In this case the Polish Brigade Group will have to attack in order to reach the allotted positions to the east of Arnhem.' Urquhart apparently agreed that such a situation might occur, but he did not 'expect any strong enemy opposition'.

Sosabowski emphasized that 'in order to enable the Brigade Group to cross the River Neder Rijn, the 1st Airborne Division should hold the bridge or should possess some other means of crossing the river.' Apparently Urquhart assured him that 1st Airborne Division would be able to do that, and protect the drop zone of the Polish Brigade Group. Events would prove Sosabowski's concerns to be abundantly justified.

The British brigade commanders were not nearly so critical of the plan, mainly because the 1st Airborne simply could not face another cancellation. They just wanted to get on with it. And, in the view of Brigadier Philip Hicks, who commanded the 1st Airlanding Brigade, Market Garden at least seemed to stand a better chance of success than several of the previous plans. 'Some of them were absolutely insane,' he said. Another factor could not be ignored. Officers and men alike knew that if they were not dropped in an operation, then either they would be forced to serve as an ordinary infantry division in the field, or the whole formation would be split up as replacements for other units.

Brigadier General Jim Gavin of the 82nd Airborne was appalled that Urquhart should have accepted drop and landing zones so far from his main objective. Yet Gavin himself had been told by Browning that his first priority was to secure the Groesbeek heights south-east of Nijmegen. They overlooked the Reichswald, a great forest just across the German border, which was thought to conceal tanks. Browning's argument was that if the Germans occupied the Groesbeek heights, then their artillery could stop XXX Corps reaching Nijmegen. Its great road bridge thus slipped down to become a lower priority, partly because the First Allied Airborne Army refused to land *coup de main* glider parties. General Brereton meanwhile complained to General Arnold in Washington that the ground-force planners 'persist in presenting a multitude of objectives'. That, of course, was hardly surprising when Montgomery's plan involved crossing no fewer than three major and countless lesser water obstacles. Nobody, Brereton included, dared to say that it was a thoroughly bad plan based purely on the assumption that the German army was collapsing.

Even though the British were over the Albert Canal at Beringen on 6 September, General Student was comforted by the idea that they would find the terrain ahead far from easy. 'The general consensus of opinion', he wrote later, 'was that the enemy would now enter the maze of the Dutch canal system, a terrain most favourable for defence and in which the enemy would be unable to use his masses of tanks to the same extent.'

On 7 September, while the battle continued at Beringen and Hechtel, Dempsey ordered the 50th (Northumbrian) Division to cross the Albert Canal south of Geel. This sector was defended by the Kampfgruppe Dreyer, led by Generalleutnant Chill's most energetic regimental commander. The 6th Green Howards managed to establish a bridgehead. Oberstleutnant Georg Dreyer, no doubt furious that his men had been surprised, counter-attacked again and again. The 50th Division commander, seeing that this was developing into a serious battle, called for support from another brigade near Brussels. The following morning, 9 September, the tanks of the Sherwood Rangers Yeomanry rattled over a prefabricated Bailey bridge erected by Royal Engineers the night before. They were to support the 6th Durham Light Infantry and together they captured the town of Geel on 10 September. As a troop leader in the Sherwood Rangers wrote later, 'I ought to have known enough about the German Army from my time in Normandy to realise that wounded and cornered tigers have to be treated with the greatest caution and respect. This lesson I was soon to learn in Geel.' General Reinhard lost little time. He ordered in a company of the Heavy Panzerjäger Battalion 559, and a battalion of Heydte's 6th Fallschirmjäger-Regiment to help Dreyer's Kampfgruppe retake the place.

After the first day of fighting, C Squadron of the Sherwood Rangers in Geel were well satisfied with their capture of the town, and the pleasure it seemed to give many of its inhabitants. But towards the end of the day the tank crews began to feel apprehensive. They noticed that the locals were hurriedly taking down their Belgian and Allied flags. The squadron was very short of ammunition, and the Durhams were already short of men after all their casualties in Normandy. The Germans still left in positions around the town were shouting defiance as night fell. Over the radio, reports came in of German tanks or Panzerjäger self-propelled guns in the area. Fortunately, a courageous sergeant from headquarters squadron drove a truck stacked with ammunition through the German positions to get to them.

German infantry made probing attacks. A troop leader was shot through the head as he peered out of the turret of his Sherman, then the tank itself was hit and burst into flames, burning the rest of the crew to death. Stuart Hills, another troop leader, spotted a Panzerjäger just in time. His gunner knocked it out just as it was aiming at their Sherman. Another tank in the troop, a Firefly with the immensely powerful 17-pounder gun, managed to ambush a heavy Jagdpanther at a range of ten metres as it came round a corner. The blast from the explosion could be felt at some distance.

By dawn, the Sherwood Rangers were concerned that the Durhams, exhausted by all their battles, were starting to abandon positions. It soon became clear that they had no infantry left in front to protect them from being stalked by German *Landsers* with Panzerfaust rocket-propelled grenades. By late morning the squadron was down to six tanks, and by the time the order to withdraw came, eleven of the Sherwood Rangers tanks had been destroyed and two badly damaged. It was a bloodier engagement than any they had experienced in Normandy. They were not facing a defeated army.

5

The Day of the Hatchet

Although the British Second Army was starting to receive a bloody nose as it approached the Dutch frontier from the south, German occupation forces in the Netherlands were distinctly nervous, and Dutch collaborators in the NSB were again fleeing the country.

On 8 September, Paymaster Heinrich Klüglein in Utrecht described another wave of chaotic withdrawal. 'When news arrived of the offensive with British tanks towards the southern Netherlands border,' he wrote, 'an almost completely unplanned retreat of military and civil establishments led to some random looting [of transport]. Trains and vehicles, occupied by those fleeing, caused jams and were shot up by [Allied] ground-attack aircraft and set alight: in short a very regrettable image which unfortunately showed a lack of leadership and discipline.' His own department had summoned all their female staff from Rotterdam and Amsterdam to Utrecht, and trains were waiting ready if needed to take people to Germany or the northern Netherlands. 'The Dutch have behaved themselves in a comparatively calm fashion,' he went on.

Top Nazi officials in the Netherlands were clearly a good deal more anxious than Paymaster Klüglein. They greatly overestimated the strength of the Dutch underground, whose members in some places had started blowing trees down across the road. They feared a *Bijltjesdag*, or 'day of the hatchet', when the underground would rise up and kill them. Seyss-Inquart feared being torn limb from limb by the populace, yet he knew that to escape back to Germany risked a tribunal and hanging on Hitler's orders. His plan was to make Amsterdam, The Hague and Rotterdam the kernel of the German defence, and withdraw there with what forces remained. SS-Obergruppenführer Rauter was furiously opposed to such a defensive response. Despite their shared Austrian background, the two men did not get on. Seyss-Inquart once remarked in a striking understatement that the Höhere SS- und Polizeiführer, proud of his mass murder of Dutch Jews, was simply 'a big child with a child's cruelty'.

To calm Seyss-Inquart, General von Wühlisch announced that he would issue a proclamation threatening that in any case of sabotage the Germans would set fire to houses in the neighbourhood and seize their inhabitants as hostages. Seyss-Inquart was impressed by such ruthlessness, but Rauter, who disliked and distrusted Wühlisch as well, decided to issue his own order the next day which would go much further. Thus the leadership of both the Wehrmacht and the SS in Holland were vying with each other to see who could display the most violence to deter the Dutch underground.

The next day, Rauter issued his secret order, '*Bekämpfung von Terroristen und Saboteuren*', to the Gestapo and SD (Sicherheitsdienst), stating that any 'illegal assemblies must be blown up mercilessly' and the houses 'smoked out using English explosives and handgrenades'.* Three days later, Rauter received an order by teleprinter from Reichsführer-SS Heinrich Himmler, saying 'Model is in your area. Contact him immediately.' Rauter discovered that Army Group B's headquarters had been withdrawn to Oosterbeek. He went to the Hotel Tafelberg where he had a discussion with Model and his chief of staff, Generalleutnant Hans Krebs.

Rauter later claimed that at this meeting he had predicted the Allied airborne operation to capture the bridges over the Maas, Waal and Neder Rijn, but Model and Krebs had dismissed his idea. They argued that the bridge at Arnhem was far too distant from the troops who would have to come to relieve the parachute formation entrusted with its capture. 'That the English will come to Arnhem is not possible,' Model apparently said. He considered the whole plan far too reckless for a commander as cautious as Montgomery. In any case, airborne divisions were too valuable to be thrown away. 'England only has two, as has America.' The Allies would therefore hold on to them until they really were in a position to cross the Rhine.

Christiansen and his headquarters, known as WBN for Wehrmacht-befehlshaber der Niederlande, did expect airborne landings, but only if combined with an amphibious invasion on the Dutch coast. The Luftwaffe 3rd Fighter Division, based at Deelen just north of Arnhem, was more prescient. It had recorded in its war diary a few days before that a 'parachute landing in our area is expected'.†

---

* The explosive was from supplies dropped by SOE with the unfortunate Dutch agents captured on arrival as a result of British incompetence.

† A myth arose just after the war that the plan for Market Garden had been betrayed to the Germans by a traitor in the Dutch underground called Christiaan Antonius

Himmler had told Rauter that he was responsible for the demolition of the key bridges should the Allies invade south-east Holland, so on this visit to Oosterbeek Rauter raised the question with Model. Model insisted that the decision on blowing the bridges was entirely his to make. He said later that his intention had always been to keep the Nijmegen bridge intact so that he could counter-attack any spearhead and cut it off. He had even ordered that the explosive charges already laid should be removed in case they were set off by artillery fire.

SS-Obergruppenführer Rauter, satisfied with his savage record in the Netherlands, was now longing to assume an active military role. The airborne landings a week later would give him the opportunity to command what he called Kampfgruppe Rauter. This would consist of the SS guard or Wachbataillon *Nordwest* from Amersfoort concentration camp, a regiment of Ordnungspolizei and the so-called 34th SS Grenadier-Division *Landstorm Nederland*, in fact just a couple of battalions of Dutch volunteers who had already been mauled on the Albert Canal by the Princess Irene Brigade of the Royal Netherlands Army. Bradley's troops, on the other hand, reported a very tough battle with Dutch SS just to the south-east. 'XIX Corps on the 14th was fighting a brigade of Dutch SS troops who continued to fight stubbornly,' Bradley's aide wrote. 'They were mercenaries with little to look forward to and had to be killed almost mercilessly. [We] compared their fighting to that of the Japs in their refusal to surrender.'

Rauter was proud of his Dutch 'Germanic SS', yet many in its ranks were not even members of the NSB. Most were simply weak-willed or opportunistic youngsters who wanted to avoid being sent to Germany as forced labourers. They were promised that all they had to do on joining the SS was to guard Jews and political prisoners in the concentration camp at

---

Lindemans, known as 'King Kong' because of his size. Lindemans, born in Rotterdam, worked in his father's garage. During the war he helped an escape line of the Dutch underground. In March 1944, he was recruited by Major Hermann Giskes, the Abwehr counter-intelligence chief in the Netherlands. The suggestion that the whole plan had been betrayed was never convincing because all German sources admit that they were taken completely unawares. Sentenced to death by a Dutch court, Lindemans committed suicide in prison in 1946.

According to the end-of-war report by Hugh Trevor-Roper, the historian and wartime intelligence officer, SS-Brigadeführer Walter Schellenberg, the head of the SD foreign intelligence department, received information in mid-September 1944 predicting an Allied airborne landing in Holland to seize a Rhine bridge, but he took no action in response.

Amersfoort. They would not be in danger and their families would benefit with extra rations of food and fuel. Since there were insufficient volunteers even then, numbers were made up through recruitment in prisons and corrective schools. These 'volunteers' were forced to sign a contract in German, which most of them could not read.

Their officers and senior NCOs were German and the battalion commander, Sturmbannführer Paul Helle, was an Austrian from the Tyrol. Helle was a shamelessly corrupt opportunist. 'Although he had wife and children in Germany,' wrote the Dutch historian of the battle, Colonel Theodor Boeree, 'he had a very intimate lady friend. She was rather brown as her cradle had been in Java, and the whole battalion grinned when Helle held his usual lecture about the superiority of the Nordic race, with their fair hair and blue eyes.' Helle's subordinates loathed him because he fawned on his superiors and treated his juniors with arrogance. Neither Helle nor his men expected that they would ever have to do more than bully the prisoners in their charge, certainly not fight British paratroopers.

A very different force north of the Neder Rijn was the II SS Panzer Corps. Commanded by SS-Obergruppenführer Wilhelm Bittrich, it consisted of the 9th SS Panzer-Division *Hohenstaufen* and the 10th SS Panzer-Division *Frundsberg*. Constant air attacks and fatigue, as well as the loss of almost all its tanks in the retreat from Normandy, had reduced what he called its 'feeling of combat superiority'. Even its manpower was down to less than 20 per cent of full strength.

On 3 September, the 10th SS Panzer-Division *Frundsberg* had been ordered to Maastricht, where it was told to re-equip itself by requisitioning motor-vehicles and ammunition from the supplies of retreating Luftwaffe elements. The 9th SS Panzer-Division *Hohenstaufen* and corps headquarters staff were directed to Hasselt in Belgium, thirty-five kilometres to the west. The very next day, Bittrich received orders to withdraw his two divisions north of the Neder Rijn to the area of Apeldoorn and Arnhem to refit but to remain combat ready. He took his staff, as well as some corps units, to Doetinchem with its fine, moated castle thirty kilometres east of Arnhem.

Bittrich was just about the only Waffen-SS general respected and liked by his counterparts in the army. Tall and erect, he was intelligent, cultivated and thoughtful, and had a good sense of humour. He had originally wanted to be a musician and conductor, having studied at the conservatoire in Leipzig. Although officially a Nazi, he had nothing but contempt for senior Party members and Hitler's entourage. In a conversation with Generalfeldmarschall Erwin Rommel on 16 July in Normandy, he was so critical of Führer headquarters and its refusal to acknowledge the developing disaster in the west that he indicated his agreement to Rommel's plan to enter secret negotiations with the Allies. Bittrich's fierce objection to the hanging of Generaloberst Erich Hoepner, who had been implicated in the 20 July plot against Hitler, was reported back to Berlin by one of his officers. He was ordered to surrender his command, but as the situation in Normandy became catastrophic he could not be spared. Generalfeldmarschall Model then thwarted further attempts to discipline him during the retreat to the Netherlands.

Bittrich's priority was to restore the fighting strength of his two divisions. Apart from eight antiquated Renault tanks brought back by the 9th SS *Hohenstaufen*, there were just three serviceable Mark V Panther tanks left in the *Frundsberg* 10th Panzer Division, with another two in workshops. In addition, the two divisions had a combined total of twenty assault guns, self-propelled artillery and heavy mortars. In those desperate days, Bittrich had to weaken his command still further. He was told to send the Kampfgruppe Segler of 9th SS *Hohenstaufen* and the Kampfgruppe Henke to strengthen the very mixed force under Oberst Walther facing the newly won British bridgehead across the Maas–Scheldt Canal almost on the Dutch border. On the other hand, the reconnaissance battalion of the *Hohenstaufen* and three panzergrenadier battalions remained formidable fighting units.

There has been much debate about the strength of the II SS Panzer Corps when Market Garden was being planned. Its presence in the Arnhem area had been known to Allied intelligence through the Dutch underground and from Ultra signals intercepts even while Comet was being prepared. But partly because of a belief that it had been virtually destroyed in the retreat from France, and partly in a misguided attempt to avoid dismaying the troops, little mention of its presence was made in briefings.

When Bedell Smith went to see Montgomery on 12 September to promise him the extra supplies demanded, he took the chief intelligence officer at SHAEF, Major General Kenneth Strong. 'The operation was conceived at 21st Army Group,' Bedell Smith said after the war. 'We were always a bit dubious about it. Strong thought there might be parts of three panzer divisions in and around where the 1st Airborne was to drop.' Bedell Smith also thought that the British force being sent to Arnhem 'was too weak'.

Montgomery's headquarters, on the other hand, had passed on their view to the First Allied Airborne Army that 'the only reinforcements known to be arriving in Holland are the demoralized and disorganized remnants of the Fifteenth Army now escaping from Belgium by way of the Dutch islands.' Montgomery refused even to allow Strong into his presence, with the retort 'I have my own intelligence,' and he 'waved [Bedell Smith's] objections airily aside'.

The rivalry and mutual dislike between intelligence chiefs was sometimes even greater than that between their respective commanders. Brigadier Bill Williams, Montgomery's brilliant but also erratic intelligence chief, was vitriolic about Eisenhower's Major General Strong. 'He worried about everything,' Williams told Forrest Pogue, the American official historian, after the war, and called Strong the 'headless horror' and the 'faceless wonder'. He even considered him a 'coward', saying that he 'wouldn't go near the front'.

Leaving aside the clash of personalities, they were all wrong in their different ways. The *Hohenstaufen* and the *Frundsberg* were indeed in the area, and were not the entirely spent force which Montgomery and Williams imagined. But with only three serviceable Panther tanks and fewer than 6,000 men between them, they could hardly be counted as proper SS panzer divisions. 'In point of fact', one of their commanders said, 'they had scarcely the strength of regiments.'

What all those involved in the argument on the Allied side failed to grasp was the extraordinary ability of the German military machine to react with speed and determination. And the two panzer divisions, even in their weakened state, were able to form a nucleus on to which other, less experienced units could be grafted.

Browning's intelligence officer, Major Brian Urquhart, on the other hand, became increasingly nervous at his chief's complacency. He was so convinced that there were German tanks in the Arnhem area that he requested a photo-reconnaissance mission. The shots revealed Mark III and Mark IV tanks used for driver training which belonged to the training and replacement battalion of the *Hermann Göring* Division. They were not part of the II SS Panzer Corps, as Urquhart thought. The vast majority of the tanks which Allied troops faced in Market Garden were not present at the start of the operation, but were brought in from Germany with astonishing speed on *Blitztransport* trains.

Whatever the strengths or weaknesses of the II SS Panzer Corps, the survival of the British 1st Airborne Division entirely depended on the speed with which Horrocks's XXX Corps could advance up a single road all the way to Arnhem for 103 kilometres. The original distance had been reduced because the Guards Armoured Division now occupied a bridgehead over the Maas–Scheldt Canal at Neerpelt.

Lieutenant Cresswell's troop of the 2nd Household Cavalry Regiment had managed to outflank the Germans in front of the canal, as the division reported, 'with their uncanny knack of finding a way round'. They concealed their armoured and scout cars in a wood well to the rear of German lines. Cresswell and Corporal of Horse Cutler stole bicycles for their reconnaissance and finally climbed up on to a factory roof, from where they could survey the German positions from behind. They reported that the bridge at the De Groote barrier was intact, but although it was strongly held they could identify the positions on the map.

'We reached the area of the bridge as light was falling,' the war diary of the 3rd Battalion Irish Guards recorded on 10 September, 'and the commanding officer [Lieutenant Colonel J. O. E. Vandeleur], after a rapid recce, decided to try and rush it. No. 2 Company and one squadron of tanks were detailed for the job. The tanks put down a hail of fire on the area of the bridge itself and succeeded in knocking out several 88 mm guns. Lieutenant Stanley-Clarke's platoon, preceded by a troop of tanks, then charged the bridge and succeeded in reaching the other side. The remainder of No. 2 and No. 3 Companies were quickly pushed across to join them and the position was rapidly consolidated. The R[oyal] E[ngineers] officer with the Battalion succeeded in disconnecting all the charges which were in position to blow the bridge.' This remarkable *coup de main* was achieved at the cost of only one man killed and five wounded.

The Irish Guards, intensely proud of their exploit, called their prize 'Joe's Bridge' after Lieutenant Colonel J. O. E. Vandeleur. 'Our success had saved the whole of Second Army days in its advance,' the war diary of their companion armoured battalion boasted. Next day at 09.00 hours, the Germans counter-attacked with self-propelled assault guns and infantry. One of the assault guns got within a hundred metres of battalion headquarters, but the Germans were thrown back with heavy losses. The Irish Guards infantry battalion suffered fourteen casualties, including a captain killed while stalking an assault gun with a PIAT anti-tank launcher.

The divisional commander Major General Allan Adair asked the Household Cavalry to scout out the road leading north to Eindhoven. He wanted to know whether the bridge over the River Dommel near Valkenswaard was strong enough to take tanks. With the nascent Kampfgruppe Walther reinforcing the sector rapidly, it was a formidable mission. Lieutenant Rupert Buchanan-Jardine, a German-speaker, took just two scout cars. In the morning, before the mist gave way to sun, they charged through German lines, passing virtually unchallenged. They drove almost to Valkenswaard, some ten kilometres behind German lines. Buchanan-Jardine asked locals about the bridge, and having had a good look himself, he returned to the vehicles. They closed their hatches, and charged back through the German positions, deafened by the machine-gun and rifle fire peppering their armour. They were exceedingly fortunate that the Germans along the road had had no time to swing round anti-tank weapons. Their little sortie caused a great commotion well behind German lines. The police in Eindhoven, using loudspeakers, ordered all civilians to clear the streets immediately.

At first light on 13 September, the Germans launched a small counter-attack on the Neerpelt bridgehead. The Guards, automatically on dawn stand-to, were not taken by surprise. Their supporting artillery, having registered the likely forming-up points, reacted immediately, and the attack was over almost before it began. In Eindhoven, a woman diarist recorded that morning: 'We hear artillery fire. The latest news is that the Allies have come closer by 15 kilometres . . . They must be in Valkenswaard. Will Eindhoven be the first liberated city in Holland? Will the liberation come without too much bloodshed? We pray to God that our country will be saved too much agony.' That same day, Oberstleutnant Fullriede of the *Hermann Göring* Division passed down the road up which XXX Corps would advance less than a week later. He considered the major bridges at Nijmegen and Grave to be 'guarded by totally insufficient forces'. And in his view they had not been properly prepared for demolition. 'That is a crime,' he added in his diary.

The Guards Armoured Division settled into 'several days' respite' as its battalions prepared for Operation Garden and received replacement tanks to bring them up to strength. The Irish Guards described the XXX Corps order on the subject as 'Top up, tidy up, tails up – and no move for several days.' For officers, 'tails up' seems to have meant slipping away to Brussels to visit newly acquired girlfriends and enjoy the restaurant Le Filet de Sole, where payment was refused. Guardsmen were not so fortunate. Their NCOs kept them hard at work on the vehicles.

Liaison between the First Allied Airborne Army and the British commanders in Belgium who had thought up the plan did not improve. Brereton and his staff only discovered several days after planning had started that 'XXX Corps' advance was going to be thirty feet wide and seventy miles deep.' Nobody had worked out exactly when the airborne corps' main reinforcement, the British 52nd (Airlanding) Division, was to land. There was a general assumption that it might be flown into the Luftwaffe airfield of Deelen once that was taken.

On 12 September, the First Allied Airborne Army held a conference to discuss air support, principally the bombing targets of German barracks and flak defences. This was followed by a larger meeting three days later, with representatives from the US Eighth Air Force, the US Ninth Air Force, Bomber Command, Air Defence of Great Britain which would provide the RAF fighter escorts, Coastal Command and the Allied navies. Nobody came from Second Army, XXX Corps or even the RAF's 2nd Tactical Air Force on the continent. Only the American 101st Airborne made an effort to liaise with XXX Corps. Brigadier General Anthony McAuliffe, the deputy commander, flew to Brussels on 12 September with Lieutenant Colonel C. D. Renfro, who was to be its liaison officer with Horrocks's staff. They went to Dempsey's headquarters and then to see Horrocks south of Hechtel, where Renfro stayed on, politely ignored.

Also on Tuesday 12 September, Major General Urquhart called an orders group to brief his brigade and some unit commanders. Robert Urquhart, known as Roy, was a large, heavy man with a thick black moustache. A brave infantry brigadier in Italy, he had been astonished when told that he was to command the 1st Airborne Division. 'I had no idea at all how these chaps functioned,' he confessed. He had never parachuted in his life, knew nothing of airborne operations and suffered from terrible airsickness. Yet he could hardly refuse such a promotion.

At the beginning of January 1944, Urquhart had reported to Browning, still dressed in the tartan trews of his old regiment, the Highland Light Infantry. Browning observed briskly: 'You had better go and get yourself properly dressed.' Urquhart suggested that, considering his inexperience, he had better do some practice parachute jumps. Browning glanced at his bulk, and replied: 'I shouldn't worry about learning to parachute. Your job is to prepare this division for the invasion of Europe. Not only are you too big for parachuting, you are also getting on.' Urquhart was forty-two. Browning explained that he had done two jumps, and had injured himself both times. That is why he had decided to train instead as a glider pilot.

Well aware that he would be seen as an outsider, even a curiosity, by the airborne fraternity, Urquhart knew that officers and soldiers alike would be sizing him up. Nobody disliked him, and most came to admire him for his courage, good humour and fairness. But perhaps the biggest disadvantage of his conventional military background was the simplistic assumption that 'an airborne division was a force of highly trained infantry, with the usual gunner and sapper support, and once it had descended from the sky it resorted to normal ground fighting.' This was not exactly the case. As soon as an airborne division landed, it had to exploit the element of surprise immediately to make up for the fact that it lacked the transport and the bulk of the artillery and heavy weapons of its conventional counterpart.

Urquhart had three brigadiers under him. The oldest, Pip Hicks, commanded the 1st Airlanding Brigade with three glider-borne infantry battalions. Hicks, a reserved and unexciting commander, had nearly drowned in a glider which had crash-landed in the sea during the invasion of Sicily. Gerald Lathbury, the tall and elegant leader of the 1st Parachute Brigade, was rather different. According to Urquhart, he spoke in a languid drawl, but had a very good brain. Lathbury had the 1st, 2nd and 3rd Battalions of the Parachute Regiment, many of whose officers and men had endured trial by fire in Tunisia and Sicily. The youngest and most intelligent brigadier of all was Shan Hackett, a small, yet supremely confident cavalryman from the 8th King's Royal Irish Hussars. Hackett, who did not suffer fools gladly, commanded the 4th Parachute Brigade. His three battalions, however, could not quite match the experience and professionalism of Lathbury's men.

Urquhart had wanted part of the first lift to be dropped on the polderland south of the Neder Rijn, but the RAF refused point-blank because of the German flak positions close to the Arnhem bridge. The aircraft bringing the 1st Airborne would constitute the northern and left-hand stream coming out from England, so after dropping their paratroopers or releasing their gliders, they had to turn left to avoid clashing with those dropping the 82nd Airborne at Nijmegen. If they went as far as Arnhem south of the river, then they would be turning over the flak positions and circling back right by the Luftwaffe airfield at Deelen. With all the restrictions imposed by IX Troop Carrier Command, Urquhart had little choice but to go for dropping and landing zones short of the Arnhem–Deelen area. Sosabowski's Polish Parachute Brigade was due to be dropped on the southern side of the Arnhem road bridge, but only on the third day. By which time, IX Troop Carrier Command assumed, the bridge and all the flak positions would be secured.

Anyone with any experience of airborne operations could see that the British landing and dropping zones, up to thirteen kilometres to the west of Arnhem, were too far away to achieve surprise. Major General Richard Gale, who had commanded the 6th Airborne Division on D-Day, warned Browning that the lack of *coup de main* parties was likely to be disastrous and that he would have resigned rather than accept the plan. Browning refused to agree and asked Gale not to mention it to anyone else as it might damage morale. Urquhart, all too conscious of this fundamental handicap, planned to use the reconnaissance squadron, mounted in Jeeps armed with machine guns, to race on ahead. It was perhaps not a good augury that Freddie Gough, the 'cheerful, red-faced, silver-haired major' who commanded the reconnaissance squadron, turned up late for the orders group, and was thoroughly reprimanded.

There was little Urquhart could do about the other basic flaw in the forth-coming operation. While Lathbury's 1st Parachute Brigade was to march off towards the bridge, Hicks's 1st Airlanding Brigade would have to remain behind to guard the drop and landing zones ready for Hackett's 4th Brigade to land on the second day. This meant that Urquhart would have just a single brigade to secure his chief objective. Right from the start, his division would be split in two with a wide gap in between. To make matters worse, one of his signals officers became concerned that the standard 22 Set radio might not work over that distance, with the town of Arnhem and the woods in between.

6

Final Touches

In the Netherlands, tensions between occupiers and occupied had suddenly increased. On Sunday 10 September in Nijmegen, all males between the ages of seventeen and fifty-five were ordered to report for digging defences. A warning was proclaimed that those who failed to turn up would have their houses destroyed by fire, their possessions seized and their wives and children arrested. The German-appointed burgemeester, a hated member of the NSB, summoned schoolteachers to a meeting to order them to police their students. The teachers stayed away. Next day a woman recorded in her diary, 'The houses of teachers not attending are being plundered by the Germans as a reprisal, and passers-by are forced to help.' According to the Germans, the furniture was being confiscated and given instead to families in the Reich who had been bombed out. The teachers had to disappear into hiding as divers.

On 13 September, the able-bodied young men of Nijmegen still refused to turn up with spades ready to dig defences. The next day, when Radio Oranje announced that Maastricht had been liberated, heavily armed members of the SS appeared on the streets. Few male civilians dared venture out for fear of being seized. A German proclamation announced that any form of sabotage would also be dealt with by executions and the burning of houses. Student's First Fallschirm Army reported 'nine terrorists shot' and another five arrested for espionage.

On 15 September, SS-Obergruppenführer Rauter sent a message to the headquarters of Model's Army Group B in Oosterbeek to express his fear of an imminent uprising and to suggest that every Dutch policeman should be disarmed in case he were 'a camouflaged terrorist'. That day at Molenbeke on the edge of Arnhem a group of boys tried to set fire to a munitions dump. Three people, one of them a headmaster, were executed as a reprisal. Many older boys at this time were cutting telephone lines and slashing the tyres of Wehrmacht vehicles. As one of them said later, 'We did not know what danger was.' Dr van der Beek, the neurologist at the clinic of Wolfheze to the west of Arnhem, recorded a warning that another three people would be executed if a member of the NSB who had been kidnapped two days before was not handed over. An anonymous telephone call revealed that he was alive and he was found unhurt.

The small village of Wolfheze, which contained both an institute for the blind and an asylum for the mentally handicapped, lay in the woods by a small railway station. This made it an ideal place for the Germans to hide troops and munitions. On 11 September forty 105mm howitzers had been delivered brand new from the factory, and 600 artillerymen, a mixture of youngsters and older men, arrived by rail to camp under the trees. Their commander, Hauptmann Bredemann, claimed to have had a hard task restoring order because some of the buildings were used to house female Luftwaffe signals personnel known as *Blitzmädel*. 'The lunatic asylum had long since been occupied by a great number of German sluts,' Bredemann recounted. 'They worked at the aerodrome of Deelen, partly as "*Blitzmädel*", which was a new name for whores, because of the exceedingly short pleasure they gave the soldiers – sometimes waiting in queues – in that moment of intimate team-work.'

On Friday 15 September, the ammunition for the guns arrived and a large dump was established near by in the woods. A dozen of the guns, drawn by requisitioned horses, were taken to Doesburg, north-east of Arnhem, as part of the plan to defend the line of the River IJssel. Purely by chance, Wolfheze was targeted in an air strike two days later, at Urquhart's request because it was right next to the 1st Airborne's drop zone and assembly area. Apparently the US Army Air Force demanded an assurance that there were German troops in and around the Institute, rather than just inmates. Colonel Mackenzie, Urquhart's chief of staff, gave it, even though he could not be sure. The consequences would be tragic, but mainly because of a direct hit on the concealed ammunition dump.

The Landelijke Knokploegen Resistance network (LKP or KP) in the area of Arnhem was extremely well organized under the leadership of Piet Kruijff. Kruijff, an engineer with rayon manufacturers AKU, ran a tight ship with good security. He set up different groups, with each leader picking their own members secretly. Weapons and explosives had been parachuted to them by SOE in August in the Veluwe, the high ground north of Arnhem. Kruijff's main associates included Albert Horstman, a colleague from work; Lieutenant Commander Charles Douw van der Krap, a naval officer who received the highest Dutch decoration for bravery, the Willemsorde;

Harry Montfroy who looked after the explosives, and Johannes Penseel who was in charge of communications. The group had carried out various acts of sabotage, such as blowing up a train in Elst.

On 15 September, Kruijff's group blasted part of a key viaduct. Although the damage was not as great as they had hoped, the Germans issued a proclamation the next day saying that unless the perpetrators gave themselves up, they would start shooting twelve hostages at midday on Sunday 17 September. Doctors, teachers and other prominent citizens immediately went into hiding to avoid the inevitable round-up. Several of Kruijff's colleagues argued that they should give themselves up rather than let innocent people die. Kruijff was firm. They were at war. Nobody was to surrender themselves. Fortunately, intense Allied air attacks on the Sunday morning solved the dilemma. The Germans had more urgent matters to consider.

Kruijff's network in Arnhem and others, especially in Nijmegen, had recognized the importance of telecommunications. They either recruited telephone operators or infiltrated some of their own people. Nicholas de Bode, an engineer with the Dutch telephone organization PTT, helped set up a secret system whereby the underground, using special numbers with twenty-nine digits, could link up the north and south of the country with automatic dialling. The Germans were none the wiser, even though they had installed their own nationals in every exchange to keep an eye on suspicious activity and handle Wehrmacht calls. They also did not know that the PGEM electricity company in the region had its own private telephone network between Arnhem and Nijmegen, which the underground used. Unfortunately, the British army did not really trust any Resistance group, purely as a result of a few bad experiences elsewhere. Major General Urquhart, who had received unreliable information from Italian partisans, tended to think that all such sources simply offered 'patriotic little fairytales'. And Field Marshal Montgomery made it clear to Prince Bernhard that he 'did not think the resistance people would be of much use'. Some intelligence briefings before Market Garden even suggested that the Dutch population close to the border, particularly round Nijmegen, might well turn out to be pro-German.

On 14 September, one of Piet Kruijff's colleagues, Wouter van de Kraats, noticed an unusual amount of German military traffic in Oosterbeek, five kilometres west of Arnhem. This quiet and peaceful village consisted mainly of large villas and houses set back in well-tended gardens. The mixture of architectural styles included immaculately thatched roofs, almost a Dutch equivalent of Arts and Crafts, and birthday-cake stucco villas with pink-tiled roofs. Oosterbeek, spread out along the north bank of the Neder

Rijn, on rising ground, with trees and beautiful views over the river and the polderland of the Betuwe beyond, had for many years appealed to senior officials and prosperous merchants from the Dutch East Indies as an ideal place to retire.

Without warning, large signs were erected in Oosterbeek saying '*Deutsche Wehrmacht – Eintritt Verboten!*' ('German Wehrmacht – Entry Forbidden!'). Anti-aircraft guns and even an anti-tank gun guarded one road in particular, the Pietersbergseweg. Wouter van de Kraats saw that the activity focused on the Hotel Tafelberg. Pretending that he lived near by, he persuaded the first sentry to let him pass. A second, more officious guard further on levelled his rifle and ordered him to leave the area immediately. Wouter van de Kraats was happy to comply. He had seen all that he needed. The chequered metal pennant outside the hotel signified an army group headquarters, and that could mean only one person.

The restlessly energetic Model did not waste any time after a rapid glance over his new headquarters. He immediately set off to see the most important formation commander in the area, SS-Obergruppenführer Bittrich, who had established his own command post in the moated castle of Slangenburg at Doetinchem, twenty-five kilometres east of Arnhem.

Model reached Kasteel Slangenburg well before dusk on 14 September. Unaccompanied this time by his chief of staff Generalleutnant Krebs, he strode in wearing his grey leather greatcoat, and with his monocle firmly screwed in place. Bittrich towered over his short army group commander. 'He came up only to my ear,' he said later. Bittrich had summoned his two divisional commanders, Brigadeführer Heinz Harmel of the 10th SS Panzer-Division *Frundsberg* and Standartenführer Walter Harzer of the 9th SS *Hohenstaufen*.

Model never sat down. He spent the whole time firing questions. 'What do you have left? How quickly can you get back on your feet?'

Bittrich replied that his front-line combat strength was little more than 1,500 men in each division, although the total manpower was double that. They went on to discuss rearming. A decision had been made back in the Reich by Waffen-SS headquarters that one of the two divisions was to be returned for complete re-equipment. The other should stay where it was in the Netherlands and regroup there. Bittrich, favouring his old division the 9th SS *Hohenstaufen*, had selected it to return to Germany. Model then ordered its officers to hand over their armoured vehicles and heavy weapons to the sister division before they left, as well as a number of men. Harmel cannot have been pleased. He felt that, since his division was the weaker of the two, it should be the one sent back to re-form.

'Any other questions, gentlemen?' Model asked, barely looking around at them. 'Anything else? No? Goodbye then.'

Although Model had protected Bittrich in Normandy and during the retreat, there were some things which the commander of II SS Panzer Corps did not want his superior to know. Bittrich's 'campaign books' may have been Goethe's *Faust* and Plato's *Republic*, but his favourite diversion was less elevated. He had 'a little dancer' in Berlin. Standartenführer Harzer, who had been his chief of staff, had always covered up for him when Model demanded to know where he was. Bittrich had now made Harzer take over command of the 9th SS Panzer-Division, while its commander SS-Brigadeführer Stadler remained in hospital recovering from wounds received in Normandy.

Harmel, who commanded the 10th SS *Frundsberg*, was slightly jealous of the preference Bittrich showed for Harzer, especially after all he, Harmel, had been doing to reanimate his own division. During the chaotic retreat, the *Frundsberg* had come across an abandoned German train loaded with field guns.

Harmel had ordered his men to seize them and take them with them. And as soon as they reached the Netherlands, he had started an intense training programme, also with emphasis on physical fitness. He had even established a *Frundsberg* slogan '*Keiner über Achtzehn*', which meant that every soldier had to be as agile as a boy under eighteen.

As soon as Model had departed, Bittrich observed that since reinforcements and replacement vehicles were allocated by the Waffen-SS Führungshauptamt (headquarters) near Berlin, everything would be achieved more rapidly if one of them went in person. He decided to send Harmel, who was more senior in rank, as that would count for something. Harmel should go in two days' time, on 16 September. They would not mention anything to Model.

After Harmel had left to return to his division, Harzer told Bittrich that as a precaution he was planning to hold on to all of the *Hohenstaufen* reconnaissance battalion's vehicles until the very last moment by removing their tracks and dismounting the guns. This would qualify them as unserviceable. 'I haven't heard a thing,' Bittrich replied quietly.

Generalfeldmarschall Model held his first conference at the Tafelberg the next evening, with SS-Obergruppenführer Rauter and Generalleutnant von Wühlisch. The whole hotel had been searched in the greatest detail to make sure that no microphones or explosives had been hidden, and yet Russian Hiwis, former prisoners of war forcefully recruited as menial labour, were peeling potatoes in the kitchen. They were no doubt carefully watched by members of Model's defence detachment of 250 Feldgendarmerie.

The happiest people at the Tafelberg appeared to be Model's staff officers. They felt that they could at last settle down for a bit in one place. Leutnant Gustav Jedelhauser wrote in his diary that Oosterbeek looked 'like a paradise – everything was so clean and pretty'. There was also the chance, after the last few weeks of constant movement, of having their laundry done. They were told it would be ready on 19 September, in four days' time. Officers on the staff also decided to organize a party that evening to cele-brate the promotions from Normandy which had eventually been confirmed. Unlike some members of his staff, Model had not started to relax in the deceptive calm of Oosterbeek.

'Each day we await the enemy's major offensive,' Oberstleutnant Full-riede wrote in his diary on 15 September. Model's immediate superior, Generalfeldmarschall von Rundstedt, whom Hitler had brought back as commander-in-chief west, sent a warning that day to Generaloberst Jodl at Führer headquarters. 'The situation facing Army Group B has further worsened in the last week. It is fighting on a front around 400 kilometres long with a battle strength of some twelve divisions and at the moment 84 serviceable tanks, assault guns and light tank destroyers against a fully mobile enemy with at least twenty divisions and approximately 1,700 ser-viceable tanks.' He then went on to ask whether it would be possible to transfer individual panzer divisions or at least more assault gun brigades from the eastern front to the west.

Both Model and Rundstedt had their eye on the counter-attack to be launched that day against the Neerpelt bridgehead across the Maas–Scheldt Canal. The Kampfgruppe Walther, with its command post at Valkenswaard, just to the north, came under General Student's First Fallschirm Army. Yet Walther lacked staff officers, signals personnel and even supply personnel. The German command was 'as bad as can be imagined', Oberstleutnant von der Heydte of the 6th Fallschirmjäger-Regiment remarked. Heydte thought it ridiculous that the main road up which the enemy was clearly going to charge should be the boundary between his regiment and the two battalions of panzergrenadiers from the 10th SS *Frundsberg*. He warned Walther's senior operations officer that nobody was directly responsible for the defence of the road, but it did little good.

Once again the German attack, which had no artillery support, was rap-idly broken up by the accuracy of British gunnery. In that flat countryside, Heydte believed in blasting church towers with anti-tank guns to deal with forward observation officers. As soon as Heydte arrived at his command post, the British batteries put down a rapid barrage on the house. Leutnant Volz described the scene as the shells landed: 'With an elegant leap [Heydte] disappeared through the ground floor window. I – with splinters flying around, covered in plaster and dust – got further under the table. The insanely jangling telephone slowly got on my nerves. I could not reach the receiver, which in this storm of buzzing splinters would have meant suicide. During a short fire pause, Major Schacht on the staff of First Parachute [Fallschirm] Army explained he was not used to being made to wait on the telephone, without at least some information on the immediate situation – as military protocol demanded.'

Heydte was furious. His regiment's losses were 'considerable'. And an angry Fullriede wrote in his diary that evening: 'Some of the barely trained recruits, once their officers are out of action, lose their heads and run into the tank fire. The only good thing is that their relatives in Germany have no idea of the pointless, irresponsible way that their boys are being sacrificed here.' Student's headquarters ordered more attacks, but Oberst Walther did not want to lose more men to no purpose. He simply launched token feints.

German soldiers in the west were often terrorized by Allied airpower, which dwarfed anything they had seen in the east. 'The fireworks at the front', remarked a soldier in a rear-area security battalion, 'are not as dangerous as the low-level strafing attacks.'

In England, the final touches were being put to the air plan which in two days' time would unleash the first lift of 1,500 transport aircraft and 500 gliders, to say nothing of the hundreds of bombers, fighter-bombers and fighters, whose mission was to destroy airfields, barracks and flak positions in advance. In the early hours of 17 September, 200 Lancasters from Bomber Command and 23 Mosquitoes would attack the German airfields at Leeuwarden, Steenwijk-Havelte, Hopsten and Salzbergen, dropping 890 tons of bombs. Soon after dawn another eighty-five Lancasters and fifteen Mosquitoes, escorted by fifty-three Spitfires, would attack the coastal-defence flak batteries of Walcheren with 535 tons of bombs. (As a comparison, the heaviest Luftwaffe raid on London during the Battle of Britain dropped only 350 tons.) Flying Fortresses of the US Eighth Air Force would bomb Eindhoven airfield, while the main force, escorted by 161 P-51 Mustangs, would attack 117 flak positions along the troop carrier routes and around the dropping and landing zones.

While Brereton's First Allied Airborne Army exuded confidence in its plans, a number of officers in the airborne divisions became increasingly uneasy as various details emerged. The Americans had allocated only one pilot per glider, which meant that if he were killed or wounded, one of the soldiers would have to take over, having never flown a glider before. Gliders bringing in senior officers were, however, allowed two pilots. Although horrified by the plan of the British 1st Airborne at Arnhem, Brigadier General Jim Gavin of the 82nd Airborne never challenged General Browning's argument that 'The Groesbeek high ground was of far greater importance to the success of this and subsequent operations than the Nijmegen bridges.' Browning had emphasized to Gavin that German counter-attacks would come from the Reichswald, just over the border to the south-east of Nijmegen. If the Germans managed to secure the high ground, then they could shell some of the bridges and the road, up which XXX Corps and its supplies would be advancing. Yet Gavin still felt it was strange not to go straight for the main objective, the great Nijmegen road bridge, which was presumably prepared for demolition. In any case, Gavin had not forgotten how in Sicily his 505th Parachute Infantry Regiment had found itself up against the *Hermann Göring* Panzer-Division. This time he intended to bring in his own glider-borne artillery as soon as possible.

Major General Urquhart also had good reasons to be apprehensive. His command caravan was parked under a large elm facing the fairway of the golf course at Moor Park, so on Friday 15 September he took a little time off to play a few holes. He looked up to see his chief of staff waiting to speak to him. Colonel Mackenzie looked grave. They had just heard that the number of gliders had been reduced. Urquhart thought hard, and then said that whatever they had to cut, it must not be the anti-tank guns, especially the 17-pounders.

Urquhart was in a difficult position. Officers at all levels were reluctant to criticize a plan passed down to them since it might suggest they were faint-hearted. He clearly did not think that Operation Market was going to be plain sailing, otherwise he would not have laid such emphasis on keeping their anti-tank guns. At the same time he had to conceal his fears from all those under his command. There is no hint in any of Urquhart's reports, or in his book written after the war, that he opposed the plan he was ordered to carry out. But then he was not a man to seek controversy and he certainly would not have wanted to contradict the subsequent version of events that the battle of Arnhem had been a heroic, worthwhile gamble. Yet according to General Browning's aide, Captain Eddie Newbury, on 15 September Urquhart appeared in Browning's office on the second floor at Moor Park and strode over to his desk. 'Sir,' he said, 'you've ordered me to plan this operation and I have done it, and now I wish to inform you that I think it is a suicide operation.' He apparently then turned and walked out of Browning's office.

7

Eve of Battle
Saturday 16 September

Leopoldsburg was a rather dismal garrison town south-west of the Neerpelt bridgehead. On the morning of Saturday 16 September its streets became crowded with Jeeps, bringing unit and formation commanders of XXX Corps to the cinema opposite the railway station where Lieutenant General Brian Horrocks was going to brief them. Redcapped military police with white gauntlets tried to direct the traffic, but many senior officers ignored their instructions and simply parked where they liked.

The lobby of the cinema buzzed as more than a hundred colonels, brigadiers and major generals in a variety of coloured berets and khaki forage caps chatted away, catching up with friends. After showing their identity cards to more military policemen, they filed into the cinema and took their places. At 11.15 hours, Horrocks made his entrance. Keeping to the Eighth Army's insouciant attitude to uniform since the desert war, he wore a polo-neck jersey under a battledress blouse and a camouflage-pattern airborne smock. A popular commander of great charm, Horrocks was greeted with cheers on all sides as he made his way down the central aisle to the stage, where a huge map of the south-western Netherlands awaited him.

The excited hubbub finally quietened as Horrocks turned to face them. 'This next operation', he declared, 'will give you enough to bore your grandchildren for the rest of your lives.' The release of tension produced a roar of laughter. He then proceeded in the standard format to outline the current situation, enemy strength and own troops, before coming on to the object of Operation Garden. He described the 'airborne carpet' stretching ahead of XXX Corps from Eindhoven to Arnhem. The Guards Armoured Division, supported by fourteen regiments of artillery and squadrons of rocket-firing Typhoons, would break the German line to their north. Then they would follow the single road, what Horrocks called the 'Club Route', but which the Americans would soon dub 'Hell's Highway', over 103 kilometres to Arnhem.

There were seven major water obstacles to cross, but the 43rd Division, right behind the Guards, would be equipped with boats and bridging equipment in case of German demolitions. There would be 20,000 vehicles on the road, and the strictest traffic controls would be enforced. The low polderland on either side of the banked-up road meant that only infantry could deploy out to the flanks because it was too soggy for heavy armoured vehicles. After Arnhem, their ultimate objective was the IJsselmeer (also known as the Zuyder Zee), to cut off the remnants of the German Fifteenth Army to the west, and then attack the Ruhr and its industries to the east. As the ambitious scope of the operation became clear, reactions differed between those who were inspired by its daring and those who feared the consequences of such rashness, advancing on a one-tank front.

Horrocks spoke for an hour, hardly ever referring to his notes. Colonel Renfro, the 101st Airborne liaison officer with XXX Corps, was 'impressed with his enthusiasm and his confidence in the operation'. But he remained deeply sceptical of the idea that 'the Guards Armoured Division would be in Eindhoven in two to three hours' and in Arnhem in sixty.

Several Dutch officers present from the Princess Irene Brigade did not think much of Horrocks's joke that the operation should be called Goldrush because the Netherlands was such a rich country. More to the point, they felt that the British were taking far too much for granted. 'First we'll take this bridge, then that one, hop this river and so on.' The terrain and its difficulties were well known to them, as this very route constituted one of the key questions in their staff college exams. Any candidate who planned to advance from Nijmegen straight up the main road to Arnhem was failed on the spot, and this was exactly what the British were planning to do. Unfortunately, the British planners had failed to consult them. Their brigade major, who was also present, reminded the brigade commander Colonel de Ruyter van Steveninck, of the Napoleonic maxim: never fight unless you are at least 75 per cent certain of success: the other 25 per cent you can leave to chance. Horrocks's plan, they agreed, appeared to reverse the proportions.

Horrocks, with his prematurely white hair and beguiling smile, made some people think he looked more like a bishop than a general. He never revealed how much pain he was in a lot of the time. This did not come from the severe stomach wound he had received in the First World War, but from a German fighter's strafing run in Italy the year before. One bullet went through his leg while another punctured his lungs and hit his spine on exit. He was extraordinarily lucky not to have died or been paralysed. Surgery followed surgery and the general medical opinion was that he would never return to active service. But Montgomery, who had a very soft spot for 'Jorrocks', as he called him, had summoned him back in August to take over command of XXX Corps. This was premature. Horrocks still suffered from severe bouts of sickness which, with high temperature and intense pain, could last for up to a week. His most recent collapse had taken place just as his divisions were about to cross the Seine. Montgomery, who had guessed what was happening, turned up unannounced at his command post and reassured him that he would not send him home. He moved Horrocks's caravan to his own tactical headquarters, where he would bring in the army's top medical specialists to care for him.

It is impossible to assess how much Horrocks's judgement might have been affected by these attacks that autumn. All one can say is that in December, during the great German offensive in the Ardennes, he came up with such a mad idea – he wanted to let the Germans cross the Meuse and then defeat them on the field of Waterloo – that even Montgomery insisted on sending him back to England on sick leave. In any case, Horrocks's plan for Operation Garden was the obvious one, given the orders he had received from Montgomery and Dempsey. He has, however, been criticized for choosing the Guards Armoured Division to lead the charge north, rather than Roberts's 11th Armoured Division. Horrocks said later that he chose them 'for the breakout because I was sure they could do it, "no matter what the cost". They had the better infantry, with officers prepared to give their lives without qualm or question.'

The Guards Armoured Division had been set up in England in June 1941 to make up for the shortage of tank formations in the event of a German invasion. When Hitler attacked the Soviet Union later that month a German cross-Channel assault became an even more unlikely event, but the transformation went ahead anyway because the Foot Guards had so many spare battalions. The Guards, benefiting from their close relationship with the royal family, had long wielded enormous influence and to a large degree were a law unto themselves. Even their recruiting system remained independent, and as a result the so-called 'Brigade of Guards' was able to expand to a total of twenty-six battalions. But it struck many people as strange that an organization which deliberately selected tall men for their parade-ground presence should then force them into the restricted space of a tank. Perhaps a rather more pertinent paradox, however, was their excessive respect for the chain of command, which led to a suppression of initiative, that vital element in fast-moving armoured warfare.

Professor Sir Michael Howard, a Coldstreamer himself, always felt that setting up the Guards Armoured Division had been 'a big mistake'. Guards regiments, he argued, were 'very good on defence, but never very good at offensive operations'. They were 'taught to die', but never taught to kill. 'We lacked the killer instinct.' In his view, only the Irish Guards had it. So Horrocks, or Major General Allan Adair, the divisional commander, at least picked the right regiment to lead the attack.

Lieutenant Colonel Vandeleur, who commanded the 3rd (Motorized) Battalion of the Irish Guards, was a tall, solid, red-faced figure of good fighting stock. His ancestors had fought at many battles, including Waterloo, yet his reaction on hearing from Horrocks that the Irish Guards were to lead the attack north was 'Oh, Christ!' That evening Brigadier Norman Gwatkin briefed the officers of the Irish Guards group at his 5th Brigade command post. 'Orders were issued for a breakout from the bridgehead on the following day and an advance north to the Zuyder Zee [IJsselmeer].' Vandeleur cannot have been surprised to hear 'a half-moan' go up when his officers heard that they were to be the spearhead once again. They felt they had deserved a break after seizing Joe's Bridge. 'We have 48 hours to reach the 1st Airborne at Arnhem,' Gwatkin announced. Several shook their heads in disbelief. They knew how much tougher German resistance had become in the last ten days. And the IJsselmeer was more than 145 kilometres away.

Back in England, briefings that day prompted a variety of reactions, ranging from overconfidence to outright scepticism. Most paratroopers were told that Market Garden would bring the war to a speedy end. Some officers even said that they should be home by Christmas if all went well. Browning suggested at his final briefing at Moor Park that the strike north would cut off so many German troops that the shock would bring about a surrender within a matter of weeks.

Almost everyone was relieved to hear that the operation was going to take place in daylight. Normandy veterans could not forget the chaos of the night drop there, with sticks of paratroopers scattered all over the Cotentin peninsula. A platoon commander in the 82nd Airborne described their briefing with officers from Troop Carrier Command. Once Colonel Frank Krebs of the air force had finished speaking, Lieutenant Colonel Louis G. Mendez, a battalion commander in the 508th Parachute Infantry Regiment, stood up and looked around slowly. After a heavy silence he addressed the pilots: 'Gentlemen, my officers know this map by heart, and we are ready to go. When I brought my battalion to the briefing prior to Normandy I had the finest combat-ready force of its size that will ever be known. Gentlemen, by the time I had gathered them together in Normandy, half of them were gone.' Apparently, tears were rolling down his cheeks by this point. 'I charge you all – put us down in Holland or put us down in Hell, but put us ALL down in one place or I will hound you to your graves.' He then turned and walked out.

A few paratroopers were slightly dismayed by the codename, Operation Market Garden, 'which made it sound like we were going to be picking apples or tiptoeing through the tulips. We thought it should have been called something a little more rugged sounding.' Veterans of Normandy tended to dismiss the encouraging intelligence reports on enemy strength as 'the usual old-men-too-weak-to-pull-the-trigger and ulcer-battalion stories'. But they also preferred to believe that the planners would not send them into a disaster. 'We were damned sure General Brereton wasn't going to let his brand new Allied Airborne Army get the hell kicked out of it,' a captain in the 82nd Airborne recorded.

Several American airborne briefings revealed reservations about their British ally. Colonel Reuben H. Tucker of the 504th announced to his officers: 'I'm supposed to tell you – and I'll quote – "we will have the world's greatest concentration of armor with us on this operation."' Then, to great laughter, he muttered: 'One Bren-gun carrier might turn up.' The 504th Parachute Infantry Regiment under Colonel Tucker had dropped in Sicily, then was held back in Italy to fight in the Apennines as infantry and even took part in the Anzio landings. As a result of the hardships it had undergone, the regiment was spared the D-Day operation with the 82nd Airborne. For some reason, this seems to have contributed to some bad blood between Tucker and Jim Gavin, the 82nd Airborne's divisional commander, but it did not last.

For the Poles, the point of the war was to close with the enemy and kill Germans, and now the moment had come. 'Everyone is serious, aware that we are going,' wrote a Polish paratrooper. 'To a keen eye, the men's faces speak of longing for vengeance and even fear – a wholly natural feeling, for we are not going to exercise, but to face the enemy eye to eye. In spite of everything, there is a spirit of joy.'

When he wrote 'in spite of everything', he referred of course to the Warsaw Uprising where they all longed to be, fighting alongside the Home Army. As they were shown maps and aerial pictures of their objective in the Netherlands, Stanley Nosecki visualized with his eyes closed 'the Poniatowski bridge, the Column of Zygmunt, the King's Castle and the Tomb of the Unknown Soldier'. He wondered, 'Are they still fighting in Warsaw on those famous streets of Nowy Swiat and Tamka? Is the Holy Cross Church still there, where I used to serve as an altar-boy every other Sunday?'

British briefings usually took place around sand models. Sergeant Robert Jones of Frost's 2nd Battalion had worked for hours from air-reconnaissance photographs to create a seven-metre-square reproduction of the road bridge at Arnhem and its approaches. This was on the floor of the library at Stoke Rochford Hall, a Victorian country house near Grantham in the east Midlands.

Some thought that the briefing sounded uncomfortably like the one less than two weeks earlier for Operation Comet, although this time there were the two American airborne divisions to beef it up. They assumed that Market Garden would also be cancelled at the last moment, and once again they would be stood down as soon as they were loaded and ready to take off. The more experienced paratroopers in the 1st Parachute Brigade, who had seen service in North Africa and Sicily, were unconvinced by assurances that German resistance would be light, but they said nothing. One officer in the 1st Battalion claimed that he and several others objected strongly to the dropping zone so far from the bridge, 'and volunteered *en masse* to jump on, or a bit to the south of, the objective. This request and the reason for it was passed on to higher command and refused because the vicinity of Deelen airfield to the north and the wetness of the polders to the south might cause unacceptable casualties. As it proved the "safe" DZ cost us infinitely more casualties.'

Whatever the concerns officers still held about the plan, they knew they had to get on with it and set a good example. In the British army, that usually meant falling back on the old jokes. In the airborne, when drawing parachutes, it also meant the storeman saying, 'Bring it back if it doesn't work and we'll exchange it.'

In the Netherlands the Dutch tried to stick with their weekend routine, but fear and expectation dominated everything. Martijn Louis Deinum, the director of the great De Vereeniging concert hall in Nijmegen, wrote in his diary that the whole city felt very tense. 'Something was going to happen.' In Oosterbeek next to Arnhem, the young Hendrika van der Vlist smuggled some breakfast out to her brother, who was in hiding. Their father owned the Hotel Schoonoord, which had been taken over by the Germans. They left a terrible mess and picked all the flowers they could find to decorate their rooms. German soldiers still tried to believe that they would win the war. One of them said to her, 'You just wait until the new weapons arrive.'

SS-Obergruppenführer Rauter issued orders that morning forbidding the civil population to 'halt on or near bridges, any sort of bridge approach, and underpasses at any German command post or establishment'. Yet

Generalfeldmarschall von Rundstedt's headquarters at that moment was far more preoccupied with the American First Army's advance on the city of Aachen. He was ordering in the 12th Infanterie-Division and the 116th Panzer-Division, as well as the 107th Panzer-Brigade and the 280th Assault Gun Brigade from Denmark.

It was a momentous day in the Wolfsschanze in East Prussia. Hitler, who had recently risen from his sickbed after an attack of jaundice, astonished the assembled generals after the morning situation conference. He cut Generaloberst Jodl short, to announce his determination to launch a major counter-attack from the Ardennes with Antwerp as its objective. He had dreamed this up in his drug-fuelled fantasy during the illness. Their surprise was even greater when he talked of an offensive with more than thirty divisions at a time when they did not have enough to defend Aachen. Jodl tried to bring in an air of reality when he pointed to Allied air superiority and the fact that they expected parachute landings any day in Denmark, Holland or even northern Germany. Hitler's attention was brought back to the imminent threat to Aachen, but he had no intention of abandoning his new idea.

That evening a Führer Order was transmitted. 'The battle in the west has spread in wide sectors to the German homeland – German towns and villages are becoming battle zones. These facts must make our war leadership fanatical and, with every man able to carry a gun, the fight must be escalated with the hardest of hearts – every Bunker, each housing block in a German town, each German village must become a fortress so that the enemy is either bled to death or its garrison is buried within it in man to man combat.'

A scorched-earth policy had already been declared for the Netherlands and the besieged Channel ports. The chief of staff of the Fifteenth Army reported that 'in Ostend harbour 18 ships have been sunk.' Discussions were conducted about destroying the ports of Rotterdam and Amsterdam. General von Zangen meanwhile continued to bring back troops and field guns at night across the Scheldt estuary.

SS-Brigadeführer Harmel of the *Frundsberg* left that afternoon by car for Berlin, to discuss the re-equipment of Bittrich's panzer corps. But because of the state of the roads, with many cratered by bombing, he did not reach Berlin until the middle of the following morning. For Harmel, the timing could not have been worse.

Unlike Harmel in Berlin, SS-Sturmbannführer Sepp Krafft was going to be right on the spot when the landings took place west of Arnhem the next day. Krafft, who was thirty-seven years old, had been an officer of the security police on the eastern front and had transferred to the Waffen-SS only the year before. A tall man with dark-blue eyes, he was very ambitious even though he commanded nothing more than the 16th SS Panzergrenadier Training and Reserve Battalion. He may not have seen himself as a man of destiny before the airborne landings, but there can be little doubt that he did soon afterwards. He was also slightly paranoid, claiming later that Obergruppenführer Bittrich 'regarded me as a police spy for Himmler'. After the battle of Arnhem was over, Krafft seems to have believed that Bittrich should have recommended him for the Knight's Cross of the Iron Cross and was angry not to have received it. Bittrich, with a certain hauteur, insisted: 'I simply cannot remember the man at all.'

Krafft's battalion of three companies was spread between Arnhem and the area of Oosterbeek. The thousand recruits he had been promised for training had not yet arrived. He had been there for only a few days when a major on the staff arrived to say that he must leave because Generalfeldmarschall Model's headquarters was moving to Oosterbeek. As a result Krafft positioned part of his force out in the woods, just to the north-east of the town. One detachment, close to Wolfheze, was almost on the edge of the landing and drop zones chosen for the 1st Airborne Division.

On the evening of 16 September, Krafft was on his way into Arnhem when he encountered General Walter Grabmann, a veteran of the Condor Legion (the Luftwaffe force in the Spanish Civil War supporting General Franco). Grabmann now commanded the Luftwaffe 3rd Fighter Division at Deelen. He invited Krafft to dinner to see his new command bunker. During dinner Grabmann remarked that he felt on edge. The weather remained clear and yet Allied air activity had virtually ceased. 'The English cannot afford to let one single day go by; now more than ever before.' In his view this suggested that they might be preparing something big, perhaps even an airborne operation. He had been to Model's headquarters and expressed his fears to the chief of staff Generalleutnant Hans Krebs. But Krebs had laughed at the suggestion and said that he would make himself look ridiculous if he repeated such things. Krafft decided to post a lookout in the tower of the grandiose villa he occupied, the Waldfriede.

That Saturday night, Krafft's men were celebrating their luck at being quartered in such pleasant surroundings. 'Life there was as if in the lap of peace,' observed SS-Sturmmann Bangard. Each man had received a bottle of Danziger Goldwasser liqueur, someone played an accordion, they sang favourite songs, and many of them did not go to bed until three in the morning.

The same evening in England, paratroopers in the 82nd Airborne listened to a band playing. 'Some troopers were dancing on their own and others clapped their hands in time to the music,' Dwayne T. Burns recorded. 'Some were playing ball while others lay on their cots, dead to the world and oblivious to worry or to noise. It was going to be a day jump and we knew this had to be better than the night drop into Normandy.' The hard core of compulsive gamblers played on. Others sharpened their jump knives, made jokes about the Krauts suffering from lead poisoning or discussed their weapons, a passionate and deeply personal subject. Some paratroopers even had a pet name for their rifle or Thompson sub-machine gun. In many cases, they adapted their Tommy guns by removing the butt or made other illegal modifications. Quite a few, however, hated the weapon with a passion. 'We were disenchanted with that gun,' said Staff Sergeant Neal Boyle. 'When mine jammed on me I wouldn't carry one again.'

Lieutenant Ed Wierzbowski, a platoon commander in the 101st Airborne, had a troubling conversation that night. His sergeant approached him between the pyramidal tents in the marshalling area, where they had been locked down. 'Lieutenant, I've got a feeling I'm not coming back from this one,' Staff Sergeant John J. White said to him. Wierzbowski tried to snap him out of it with a joke, but to no avail. The sergeant was calm while his eyes revealed that he remained totally convinced of his fate. 'He then parted with a smile and said "See you in the morning, Lieutenant."' Wierzbowski found it very hard to sleep. The look in White's eyes stayed with him.

8

Airborne Invasion
Sunday Morning 17 September

Soon after first light on what was to be a very busy day, a total of eighty-four Mosquito fighter-bombers, as well as Boston and Mitchell medium bombers of the 2nd Tactical Air Force, took off to attack German barracks at Nijmegen, Cleve, Arnhem and Ede. This followed the raids on Luftwaffe airfields during the night by Bomber Command and the US Eighth Air Force. At the same time another 872 B-17 Flying Fortresses, loaded with fragmentation bombs, were heading out in groups to smash identified flak and troop positions in the Netherlands. They were escorted by 147 P-51 Mustangs, flying flank and top cover. The escorts had little to do. 'Luftwaffe reaction was hesitant,' was the verdict that day. Only fifteen Focke-Wulf 190s were seen and seven were shot down for the loss of one US fighter.

While the Allied aircraft were on the way to their targets, American and British paratroopers queued for breakfast. The Americans had hotcakes and syrup, fried chicken with all the trimmings and apple pie. British paratroopers in John Frost's 2nd Battalion piled their mess tins with smoked haddock, 'quite a lot of which ended up on the floor of the aircraft', a sergeant remarked.

Frost himself had eggs and bacon. He was in a good mood. Having been dismayed by Operation Comet, he thought that this time the arrangements at least seemed much better. Frost, who had led the highly successful Bruneval Raid in February 1942, seizing a German radar set in northern France, had also known disasters in Tunisia and Sicily. He did not expect the coming battle to be easy, but he still ordered his batman Wicks to pack his dinner jacket, golf clubs and shotgun ready to come over with the staff car later. He then checked his own equipment, including a forty-eight-hour ration pack, his Colt .45 automatic and the hunting horn with which he rallied the battalion. Frost, a religious man of firm convictions, was admired by his men.

'There's old Johnny Frost,' they would say, 'a Bible in one hand and a .45 in the other.'

By the time the three divisions deployed to their respective airfields, eight for the British and seventeen for the Americans, the sun was starting to burn through the morning mist to make a beautiful early-autumn day. Altogether a total of 1,544 transport aircraft and 478 gliders stood ready for the first lift of more than 20,000 troops. The runways provided an impressive sight, with each tug aircraft and glider lined up perfectly for take-off. The troop carrier command C-47 Dakotas were also carefully aligned ready to become airborne at twenty-second intervals.

General Boy Browning was at Swindon airfield in excellent spirits. He was finally taking an airborne corps to war. His glider, which was to be flown by Colonel George Chatterton, who commanded the Glider Pilot Regiment, would carry the general's entourage including his batman, cook and doctor, as well as his tent, Jeep and luggage. According to his biographer, Browning had also packed three teddy bears. The fact that he had appropriated no fewer than thirty-eight gliders for his corps headquarters in the first lift, especially when the 1st Airborne's allocation had been cut back, struck a number of people as an act of pure vanity. The three divisions would be operating independently of each other, so there would be very little a corps headquarters could usefully do, above all on the vital first day.

At the airfield, Urquhart suddenly realized that he had not clarified which of the brigade commanders should take over if he became *hors de combat*. So he drew his chief of staff aside and said, 'Look, Charles, if anything happens to me, the succession is to be Lathbury, Hicks, Hackett in that order.' 'All right, sir,' Mackenzie replied, not imagining that it would ever come to that. They would both regret later that Urquhart had not made it clear in advance to the brigadiers concerned.

As the 1st Airborne lined up for tea and sandwiches before boarding, some paratroopers seemed to display an ostentatious optimism. A sergeant had brought a deflated football ready for a game once they had captured the bridge. Another soldier, when asked why he had a dartboard with him, replied that a game of darts always helped 'to pass away dull evenings'. And a captain with the 1st Parachute Brigade headquarters insisted on taking a bottle of sherry to celebrate the taking of the bridge. Those going by glider competed in the ribald messages they chalked up on the fuselage of camouflage canvas. General Urquhart noted an 'Up with the Frauleins' skirts' scrawled on a Horsa. Gallows humour abounded. 'The chaps are just the same,' a glider pilot recorded in his diary. 'One fellow is taking bets as to how many of us will get the chop; I wonder if he will come back to collect his debts, or maybe pay out.'

American optimism appeared to consist mostly of fantasies about yet another foreign country. A young lieutenant remembered wondering 'what all those blonde girls really looked like, with wooden shoes on their feet and windmills in their eyes'. A number of paratroopers had heard that the Netherlands was the country of diamonds, and they dreamed of returning home with enough loot to set themselves up in style.

On the other hand, the possibility of imminent death revived religious thoughts. Catholics especially took the opportunity of spiritual consolation. The American airborne divisions included a rich ethnic mix from Catholic cultures, including men of Spanish, German, Polish, Irish and Italian descent. As there was no time for individual confession, Father Sampson of the 101st Airborne gave a general absolution to the group of bare-headed men kneeling at the edge of the airfield. 'The gold and white vestments of the Catholic priest looked incongruous against the olive drab around,' wrote an onlooker.

Far from feeling optimistic, a few young paratroopers were in a state of mortal dread. The day before, two had gone absent without leave after the briefing. Then, just before the 101st climbed on to trucks to be taken to the airfield, another had shot himself through the foot with his M-1 rifle. Next to the runway, yet another one had slipped behind a C-47 where he did the same. 'Some men went AWOL and quite a few parachutes accidentally on purpose came out of their packets in the aircraft,' Brigadier General McAuliffe acknowledged later. A parachute spilled in that way meant that a man could not jump, but if it was deliberate, then he faced a court martial for cowardice. Many were afraid of losing their nerve in the aircraft at the last moment and refusing to jump.

Paratroopers were so heavily loaded that they could hardly move, and needed to be pushed or pulled up the steps into the aircraft. They had helmets covered with camouflage netting and strapped under the chin, webbing equipment, musette bags with personal items such as shaving kit and cigarettes, three days of K-rations, extra ammunition in beige cloth bandoliers, hand grenades and a Gammon grenade of plastic explosive for use against tanks, their own M-1 rifle or Thompson sub-machine gun, as well as mortar rounds, machine-gun belts or an anti-tank mine for general use, and of course every man carried his parachute behind. Bazooka men, mortar men, machine-gunners and signallers shouldered all or part of their own weapon or radio. On average each man carried the equivalent of his own weight. Since few of them could reach their cigarettes, a sergeant moved down the aisle of the aircraft handing them out and lighting them.

Before boarding his plane, Brigadier General Jim Gavin was talking to his attached Dutch officer, Captain Arie Bestebreurtje, who revealed that he had never jumped from the door of a C-47. He had only dropped through a hole in the floor from British aircraft, so Gavin gave him a lesson on the spot. 'Just step out, like stepping out of a bus,' he said. Bestebreurtje, who at six foot three was taller than Gavin, wore a commando green beret and British battledress with a shoulder patch showing an orange lion and 'NED-ERLANDS' written underneath. He was a member of a Jedburgh team, one of which was attached to each airborne division and another to corps head-quarters. These teams, formed by the British Special Operations Executive in co-operation with the American Office of Strategic Services, trained small multi-national groups to parachute in to join up with the local Resist-ance and create mayhem behind German lines. Their main task in the Netherlands was to liaise with the underground and organize their activities in support of the Allied forces.

The first aircraft to take off carried each division's pathfinders. They would land on their drop and landing zones, fight off any Germans, set up Eureka homing beacons to guide in the waves of troop carriers and set off coloured smoke grenades on their approach. Twelve RAF Stirlings from Fairford in Gloucestershire took the 21st Independent Parachute Company to mark the 1st Airborne's drop and landing zones. At least twenty of its members were German and Austrian Jews who had transferred from the Pioneer Corps. In case of capture, their dog-tags and identity papers carried Scottish or English names, usually with 'Church of England' marked under religion so that they could not be identified as Jews. They would fight fero-ciously, taunting the enemy in his own language.

Next to leave were the tug planes and their 320 gliders carrying the 1st Airlanding Brigade, divisional headquarters and the field ambulances. As well as troops, supplies and ammunition, the Horsa gliders carried Jeeps, trailers, motorcycles and 6-pounder anti-tank guns, while the larger Hamil-cars took Bren-gun carriers and the 17-pounders. The tug plane advanced slowly until the tow rope tightened and then finally the glider began to move down the runway. The glider pilot would shout back over his shoulder, 'Hook your safety belts, the towline is fastened . . . they're taking up the slack . . . hold on!' Then with a lurch, a second lieutenant recounted, 'the tail comes up, the nose goes down, the plywood creaks, and we are barrelling down the runway. Long before the tow plane leaves the ground the speed sends the flimsy glider skywards.'

Finally, it was the turn of the C-47 troop carriers. With a deafening roar their engines suddenly speeded up, the propeller blast flattening the grass beside the runway, then the heavily laden aircraft accelerated away. Inside the strutted metal cave of the fuselage the paratroopers sat wedged in their aluminium bucket seats, facing each other across the narrow aisle, mostly avoiding eye contact until they reached cruising height.

In Belgium General Horrocks asked Colonel Renfro, the liaison officer of the 101st Airborne, to brief him again on the airborne plan. 'How many days' rations will they jump with?' he asked. 'How long can they hold out?' These questions slightly surprised Renfro after Horrocks had declared at the briefing that the Guards Armoured Division would be in Eindhoven in a few hours. Horrocks and his chief of staff Brigadier Harold Pyman then asked Renfro what he thought of their plan. 'It's all right,' he replied without any warmth. Horrocks, aware of his hesitation, laughed. Renfro could not tell whether this was a nervous laugh or bluff.

While they were speaking, the corps and divisional artillery near the canal carried on with their preparations to support the Guards Armoured attack. One heavy, three medium and ten field artillery regiments were ready in their gun lines to provide a rolling barrage which would advance at 200 yards a minute. They had been ordered to avoid cratering the road ahead at all costs. Fortunately the road was quite straight. The massive convoy of vehicles which would follow the Guards Armoured Division was being sorted out in the rear by movement officers and military police.

The bombers and fighter-bombers attacked flak positions in Nijmegen and Arnhem just before 10.30. Electricity for the whole area was cut off almost immediately because the PGEM generating plant on the banks of the Waal had been hit. The wise began filling baths and pails immediately in case the pumps would not come back on. Those who had binoculars or old telescopes climbed on to roofs and tried to watch the action. They had to be quick. Mosquito fighter-bombers screamed in at low level over Arnhem to attack the main barracks, the Willemskazerne, but they also hit the Restaurant Royale opposite. An antiquarian bookseller near by saw 'Germans stumbling from the blasted rubble of the Willems barracks with blood pouring from their noses and ears from the concussion.' By mistake, Allied bombers hit an old people's home, the St Catharina Gasthuis, next to a German warehouse, which the Wehrmacht had in fact abandoned. A number of residents were buried under the rubble. Strafing fighters came in low. Sister Christine van Dijk saw German soldiers ducking round tree trunks to avoid their machine-gun fire.

The Dutch used to joke that the safest place to go in an air raid was the railway station as the RAF never managed to hit it, but in parts of Arnhem there was little cause for laughter. A large number of houses round the barracks caught fire, and nothing could be done to help. 'Fire engines [are] unable to work as Germans are shooting at them,' an anonymous diarist recorded in this first example of revenge against the Dutch for supporting the Allied attack, even though some 200 civilians were killed in the raid. The RAF's key targets were the anti-aircraft batteries around the Arnhem road bridge, yet Model's headquarters instinctively assumed that the 'air raids on flak positions near Arnhem were believed to be made in an effort to destroy the bridge'.

Ton Gieling, a young keeper at the Arnhem zoo, was on his way home on that Sunday morning when the Allied bombing raid started. German soldiers were lying dead and wounded in front of a café in the Bloemstraat. Then, to his surprise, 'a badly burnt rabbit dashed across the road in front of me and disappeared.' Further on, he found a gravely wounded man being helped on to a stretcher. Gieling, who was strong, grabbed one end and they hurried the injured man to the St Elisabeth Hospital only to find that he had died on the way. Gieling, like many others, stayed at the hospital to help as a Red Cross volunteer. West of Arnhem, the town of Ede which contained just 180 German soldiers was smashed by air attack.

Wolfheze was also heavily hit at 11.40, having been targeted at General Urquhart's request. Unfortunately one of the bombs scored a direct hit on the artillery ammunition dump under the trees, and the massive explosion caused great damage and killed a number of people. After the Wolfheze Institute for the Blind had been hit, the matron organized a well-disciplined evacuation to a shelter prepared in the woods. But many of the 1,100 mentally infirm patients at the next-door institute were traumatized by the bombing. The nurses began laying out white sheets on the ground in the shape of a huge cross in case more aircraft came to attack. Dr Marius van de Beek and other doctors began operating on some eighty wounded, and the eighty-one dead were buried on the following Friday.

On this Sunday morning, both Catholic and Dutch Reformed churches were not as full as usual, as the congregations were made up almost exclusively of women and children. The men had 'dived' to avoid being taken hostage or shot in reprisal for the attack on the viaduct. Explosions made windows rattle and the sudden cut in the electricity supply brought church organs to a groaning halt as the lights went out. In some churches, the priest blessed the congregation and everyone filed out quickly. The Dutch Reformed congregation in Oosterbeek guessed that the attacks signified imminent liberation. Spontaneously, they burst into the national anthem, '*Het Wilhelmus*', which dated back to the sixteenth-century revolt against the Spanish occupation of the Netherlands.

In the Betuwe, the low-lying land between Arnhem and Nijmegen, people hurried to climb the dykes for a better view of the columns of smoke rising from both towns. In the city of Nijmegen itself, people were understandably anxious after the disastrous American bombing of 22 February mentioned earlier, but soon relaxed when they saw that the main targets for the Typhoons and Mosquitoes were the flak batteries by the bridges on the north side and German positions on the Hazenkampseweg to the southwest. As soon as the hissing whoosh of the rockets had died away and the aircraft disappeared into the distance, people poured out into the streets. There was an air of expectancy after all the premature rumours of the Allied advance.

Generaloberst Student and his First Fallschirm Army headquarters were south of Vught not far from the notorious concentration camp. Student was struggling under a mountain of paperwork in a villa taken over by his staff. 'Annoying red tape followed us even here on to the battlefield,' he complained. 'I had opened wide the windows of my room. In the late forenoon, enemy air activity suddenly became very lively. Columns of fighter planes and formations of small bombers flew over constantly. In the distance one could hear bombs dropping, aircraft machine-guns, and anti-aircraft fire.' He did not regard it as particularly significant at the time.

In Arnhem railway station, panzergrenadiers from the 9th Panzer-Division *Hohenstaufen* continued loading weapons and equipment on to trains to return to Germany where the formation was to be rebuilt. A certain amount had already been handed over to the 10th SS Panzer-Division *Frundsberg*, and although part of the *Hohenstaufen* had departed over the last two days, there was still quite a force left in the area. It included tank crews from the 9th SS Panzer-Regiment which had no tanks, two battalions of panzergrenadiers, an artillery battalion, the 9th SS Panzer Reconnaissance Battalion next to Deelen airfield, an engineer company, the divisional escort company and a couple of half-tracks with quadruple 20mm flak guns.

At 10.30, just as the bombing attacks started, Standartenführer Harzer, accompanied by two of his officers from the *Hohenstaufen*, drove to the reconnaissance battalion's base at Hoenderloo on the northern edge of Deelen aerodrome. The battalion of around 500 men commanded by SS-Sturmbannführer Viktor Gräbner was drawn up in an open square on parade, flanked by several eight-wheeler armoured cars and half-tracks. Harzer addressed them, and then presented Gräbner with the Knight's Cross of the Iron Cross for his bravery and leadership in Normandy. When the ceremony was over, Harzer accompanied Gräbner and his officers to lunch.

Harzer was well aware that Gräbner, reluctant to transfer his vehicles to the 10th SS Panzer-Division *Frundsberg*, had had his men remove many of their guns, tracks and wheels so that he could declare them 'not ready for use'. With the nearest enemy forces at least ninety kilometres to the south, there appeared to be no reason why their armoured fighting vehicles needed to be ready to move at short notice.

The Irish Guards Group moved across Joe's Bridge and took up position in the bridgehead a thousand metres south of the frontier. They could just see the border post through their binoculars. Many had that strange feeling of imminent danger in the pit of the stomach. Joe Vandeleur, who had been a keen horseman before he severely damaged a leg, thought that 'it felt like the start of a race. We were lining up at the start line and the finish was the Zuyder Zee ninety miles away.' He had been partially reassured by the promise of the rolling barrage and rocket-firing Typhoons swooping down to attack enemy gun positions ahead. He had a forward air controller from the RAF in the next vehicle and a direct radio link to the artillery.

Vandeleur wore his usual parachute smock, the Micks' emerald-green cravat around his throat and a pair of corduroys. Horrocks, who was hardly in a position to criticize, liked to tease him on his unguardsmanlike turnout. Mounted in a scout car, Vandeleur took up position behind the second squadron of tanks. His infantry were riding on the Sherman tanks of the 2nd (Armoured) Battalion of the Irish Guards commanded by Lieutenant Colonel Giles Vandeleur. The two cousins were closer than brothers.

As the C-47 troop carriers circled, waiting for their formations to assemble, a number of men began to suffer from airsickness. A lieutenant in the 82nd was entranced when he looked down from the open door and saw a convent below, with a group of nuns in the courtyard staring up at them in amazement. Others gazed at the 'tiny checker box fields' of the English countryside.

The glider, because it was so light, always tended to fly higher than the tow plane, which gave their occupants a chance to see the sky full of other aircraft. But their flimsy construction made them dangerous. To the horror of the crew in one Stirling, the wings broke off the Horsa glider they were towing, and the fuselage crashed to the ground, killing everyone inside. In a very different case, a soldier in one of the 101st Airborne's Waco gliders over East Anglia was suddenly overtaken by panic. He 'jumped up and released the control that connected the glider to the tow ship. The glider went down in England.' He faced a general court martial and a long prison sentence. A British glider pilot, on glancing over his shoulder, saw to his disbelief that a group of the King's Own Scottish Borderers were brewing up a mess tin full of tea on the plywood floor. He shouted back, furious at such recklessness, but they just asked if he wanted a cup too. Another example of obtuseness was demonstrated by a newly arrived second lieutenant in the 82nd Airborne. He wore a white silk scarf, which he evidently considered rather dashing. He was advised to take it off since anything white made an easy aiming mark, but he did not and received a serious head wound soon after landing.

The coastline slipped by a thousand feet below. They were now over the North Sea, what American pilots called 'Blitz Creek'. After all the earlier aborted operations, someone joked, 'They're leaving the cancellation a bit late this time.' Looking down at the shadows of the aircraft on the sea, pilots spotted a couple of Horsa gliders and a C-47 which had crash-landed on the water. Men were standing on the wings, waiting for the RAF air-sea rescue tender, which was racing towards them. One glider 'stayed afloat for two and a half hours and had to be sunk by naval fire'. The record established a few days later was a glider remaining afloat for seventeen hours. From time to time they spotted the odd warship, but the most impressive spectacle was the vast air armada, escorted by squadrons of Thunderbolts, Mustangs, Spitfires and Typhoons. 'Wow!' said a paratrooper from Ohio. 'What Cleveland wouldn't give for this air show.'

During the crossing, a Parachute Regiment private observed of his companions, 'some [were] cocky and confident, some quiet and thoughtful, and some scared and on edge. Strangely enough the latter were mostly the veterans of the savage North African fighting. They knew what lay ahead.' Another paratrooper remarked, 'We tried to fake a smile at each other occasionally, but not much was said.' On some planes, paratroopers – usually the replacements – tried to get an airborne song going. A universal favourite, sung to the tune of 'John Brown's Body', was 'Gory, Gory what a hell of a way to die . . . They picked him off the tarmac like a pot of strawberry jam.' American paratroopers also sang to a similar tune, 'I ain't gonna jump no more, no more.'

Some slept, or at least pretended to by shutting their eyes. Lieutenant Colonel Patrick Cassidy, who was in the same aircraft as Major General Maxwell Taylor of the 101st, recorded that their divisional commander 'slept most of the distance. He awakened once to eat a K-Ration, then dozed off again.' Not surprisingly, there was no singing in his aircraft. 'Most of the men also slept and there was little conversation.'

Pilots were nervous. The Netherlands was known as 'flak alley', because of the massive enemy anti-aircraft defences guarding the shortest route for Allied bombers heading to Germany. Glider pilots with so little control over their flimsy craft felt especially vulnerable when tracer bullets curved lazily up at them. The idea of shrapnel coming up from below made many sit on their flak jackets to give added protection to their private parts. A few pilots even brought a sandbag to sit on, not that it would have done much good. They were not allowed parachutes simply because their passengers did not have them.

The imminence of danger tended to prompt premonitions of death and superstition. A number read different passages in the Bible to find an indication of their likely fate. Pfc Belcher, a bazookaman in the 82nd, seemed convinced that he was going to die. He asked his team-mate, Patrick O'Hagan, to make sure his girlfriend got his ring and Bible. 'He was shot in the air as he descended,' O'Hagan recorded. On the other hand, most of those who had predicted their own death and survived tended to forget about it afterwards. Yet there was a certain logic among the veterans of North Africa, Sicily and Italy, who had started to believe that their ration of luck was running low. One staff sergeant described himself as 'a fugitive from the law of averages'.

As they reached the Dutch coast, they also reached the line of anchored barges with flak batteries mounted on them. 'We could see the tracers', wrote Chaplain Kuehl, with the 504th Parachute Infantry Regiment, 'and knew that between each visible bullet there were many more rounds. We saw troopers jumping out of one of our wing planes and were shocked to look down and see only water below. Then we noticed the plane was on fire.' One paratrooper described the apparently curving machine-gun fire as looking like 'golf balls of red tracer'.

Much of the land in from the coast had been deliberately flooded by the Germans breaching the dykes. Those who had dropped in June on the base of the Cotentin peninsula in Normandy were painfully reminded of comrades drowned there in similar circumstances. The sight of inundated villages, with just the roofs of houses, a church spire or the odd tree appearing out of this desolation, was most depressing. Only after they were over dry land did paratroopers discard their Mae Wests.

Captain Bestebreurtje, the Dutch officer attached to 82nd Airborne headquarters, was deeply moved as he looked at the familiar, flat terrain of the enemy-occupied country which he had not seen for four years. 'It was a feeling of warmth for the land,' he explained later. 'I saw the fields and farmhouses and I could even see a windmill turning. I remember distinctly thinking to myself: "Here is my poor old [Netherlands] and we have come to liberate you."'

Taking a more southerly route, the 101st Airborne passed over Belgium. As an aircraft carrying a stick of the 502nd Parachute Infantry Regiment flew low over Ghent, exultant civilians in the street started giving the V for Victory salute. A cynic remarked to an excited private, 'Look, they're giving you two to one we don't come back.' A BBC correspondent in a scout plane over Belgium sighted the air armada. 'The sky was black with transport aircraft flying in perfect formation,' he recorded. 'They were completely surrounded by Typhoons, Spitfires, Mustangs, Thunderbolts and Lightning fighters. It was an aerial layer cake . . . As my pilot shouted to me, "No room up here for Jerry!"'

Some in that armada had never seen flak before. The C-47 with Major General Maxwell Taylor on board also carried a USAAF colonel who had come along as an observer. 'What's that stuff?' he asked, pointing at the black puffs of smoke. 'Colonel,' the co-pilot replied, 'you can rest assured it ain't fluff.' Paratroopers hated flak, because they felt helpless – 'there is no way to fight back.' Paratroopers wounded by flak in a plane and unable to jump were pushed to the rear and taken back to England for treatment. Some officers had their sticks stand up and hook up as soon as the flak started so that they were ready to jump if the plane caught fire.

Those in gliders felt even more vulnerable. As a group from the 326th Airborne Engineer Battalion crossed the coast, flak shrapnel came through the floor, wounding the glider pilot in one leg, his chest and an arm. There was no co-pilot, so an airborne engineer called Melton E. Stevens climbed into the empty seat and the pilot was just able to give him some 'instructions for flying and landing the glider before he passed out'. They carried on all the way to their LZ and somehow survived the landing, even though 'dirt was piled against the nose of the glider up above the windshield.' Stevens and his companions were then able to load the wounded pilot on to their hand-drawn ammunition cart and carry him off to find a medic.

British airborne sappers, strapped in a glider, spent most of the flight nervously eyeing the Jeep right in front of them, which was loaded with explosive. Even a near-miss from a flak shell could set off the whole lot. The only consolation was that death would be instantaneous. There was no alternative to 'sweating out the flak'. Their only hope were their escorts. As soon as a German flak position opened fire, Spitfires, rocket-firing Typhoons and Thunderbolt P-47s would roll and dive steeply with all guns blazing. The men in one glider suddenly saw a P-51 Mustang come alongside them. The pilot waggled his wings in greeting, then dived on the offending flak position, knocked it out, then came up again to waggle his wings once more, before charging off again.

The redoubtable Colonel Robert Sink, who commanded the 506th Parachute Infantry Regiment, was standing by the door of his C-47 watching the flak strike other aircraft in their formation. Suddenly, his own plane lurched and he saw that part of the wing had been blown off. 'Well, there goes the wing,' he said to the rest of the stick. Evidently the pilot performed miracles because he got them to the drop zone just north-west of the bridge at Son, their first objective. In several cases, the transport carrier pilots displayed self-sacrificial courage when their plane was on fire, by holding her steady to give all the paratroopers on board a chance to jump.

Lieutenant Colonel Cassidy watched flames start to consume a neighbouring plane. The pilot courageously kept it on the level to allow the paratroopers to jump, while knowing that he and his crew would crash to their deaths. Distracted by this drama, he failed to see that the green light had come. 'Cassidy,' General Maxwell Taylor said calmly, 'the green light is on.' 'Yes sir,' he said. And with his eyes still on the burning plane, he jumped, followed by his divisional commander. Bizarrely, General Taylor, later chairman of the joint chiefs of staff under President Kennedy, was then followed by his bodyguard, Stevan Dedijer, a Princeton graduate of Yugoslav origin, who claims to have shouted 'Long live Stalin!' as he threw himself out.

Inevitably, there were one or two paratroopers who panicked. According to Lieutenant Colonel Hank Hannah, the operations officer of the 101st, a paratrooper on his plane 'suddenly chickened out and, pulling the rip cord of his reserve chute, said: "See, I can't jump now."' Hannah bawled him out and told him he'd have to jump anyway. Then the plane was hit and the nervous paratrooper was glad to bale out using his emergency parachute. Another paratrooper, purely by accident, caught his ripcord on some projection and his chute opened. In furious embarrassment he had to return with the aircraft to England.

As they approached their designated drop zones, officers searched around trying to find landmarks to orientate themselves. Captain Bestebreurtje, with a pang of excitement, sighted the wooded ridge from Nijmegen to Groesbeek, where Gavin and his headquarters were to jump. After Colonel Mendez's famous outburst about being dropped in Holland or in hell, some officers teased their pilot about how far they had been dropped from their DZs in Normandy. Lieutenant Colonel Warren R. Williams in the 504th had to eat his words. Their pilot put them down within 200 metres of the school which had been selected back in England as the regimental command post.

The broadcaster Edward R. Murrow, on one of the troop carrier planes, recorded for radio what he saw as it happened: 'By now [we're] getting towards the dropping area and I [sit] looking down the length of the fuselage. The crew chief is on his knees back in the very rear speaking into his inter-com, talking with the pilots . . . We [see] the first flak. I think it's coming from that little village just beside the canal. More tracer coming up now, just cutting across in front of our nose. They're just queued up on the door now, waiting to jump . . . you can probably hear the snap as they check the lashing on the static line – do you hear them shout 3–4–5–6–7–8–9–10–11– 12–13–14–15–16–17–18 – there they go – every man out.' Fortunately for Murrow's listeners all went according to plan, but two paratroopers from the 506th died in a terrible way. Their own aircraft had disgorged the whole stick of paratroopers correctly, but 'then a falling plane whose occupants had already baled out struck against them and the prop cut them to pieces.'

A jump-master in the 501st stood in the door of his plane and waved back to the Dutch jumping up and down in excitement a few hundred feet below. Some paratroopers were almost surprised to find that the countryside beneath them was exactly what they had expected, dykes, windmills and lush green grass. The senior officer present usually jumped first, with the next most senior acting as 'push-master', bringing up the rear and shoving out anyone who hesitated. Captain Ferguson in the 82nd stood ready in the open doorway, waiting for the green light, with 'the plane throttling down, the wind screeching and tingling against my face, as I looked down and out'. The plane lurched with the blast from each shell burst, so it was a relief when the green light finally came on. In their eagerness to get out, the stick of paratroopers waddled forward in a line as rapidly as they could without slipping on the vomit and urine slopping around on the floor. The pilot also had to remember to pull the lever to release the parapacks with heavy loads fastened under the plane's belly. One load of anti-tank mines dropped like a stone when its parachute failed to open, and caused a huge explosion.

'Get ready, we're cutting loose!' a Waco glider pilot shouted back as he dropped the nylon tow rope. The glider then banked round and round to reduce speed, but it would still hit the ground at sixty miles an hour with dirt flying up all around as it ploughed across the landing field. 'Let's go!' came the cry when they finally came to a halt, and everyone piled out of the side. Landing in a ploughed field was fine for the paratroopers as the freshly turned earth was soft, but it could be disastrous for gliders which did not land along the line of the furrows. They often ended up on their nose.

'The medics', wrote a doctor from the 101st, 'had a busy time trying to extricate the broken and bloody bodies from the chewed up wreckage.' The worst accident happened when two gliders of the 506th Parachute Infantry Regiment collided in mid-air, killing several of those on board and leaving the landing zone a mad crash-site of smashed plywood. As it was happening, 'a Jeep came flying out making everyone scatter,' a trooper remembered. 'Among the hundreds of gliders in the awkwardest positions,' wrote an officer in the 82nd, 'one was jammed into a windmill with its tail jutting into the air at an angle of about 65 degrees.'

The British 1st Airborne which had followed the northern route came in over the orchards and polderland of the Betuwe, between the River Waal and the Neder Rijn. Tension mounted as they came close to the drop zone. 'The transparent insincerity of their smiles', wrote Colonel Frost, 'and the furious last minute pulling at their cigarettes reminded me that the flight and the prospect of jumping far behind the enemy's lines was no small test for anyone's nervous system.'

Starting from the back, the stick lined up along the aisle with each man placing his left hand on the shoulder of the man in front. The C-47 bringing Captain Eric Mackay and men of the 1st Para Squadron Royal Engineers was hit on the approach, when a shell, almost certainly a 20mm, took out the red and green lights over the door. As a result, Mackay had to watch from the open door for when the paratroopers in the other aircraft jumped and simply follow suit.

A glider's chance of survival was slim if hit by anything larger than a machine gun. Not far from the landing zone, the crew of a Stirling tug plane felt a sudden jolt. Flak had taken off the tail of the Horsa they were towing, then a wing sheared off and the tow rope broke. They heard later from the pilot of a neighbouring aircraft that he had seen bodies falling out as the glider disintegrated.

One glider pilot recorded their approach over the Neder Rijn. 'We were almost at the release point now and the scene below looked exactly as it had appeared on the photographs at briefing the previous day. To starboard I could see the main reason for our trip – the bridge across the Rhine.' There was chaos ahead as scores of gliders tried to land at the same time on the heathland north-west of Wolfheze. There was no air traffic control, so the co-pilot, if they had one, kept looking in all directions watching for other gliders while the pilot focused on landing. The other problem was cows. Sergeant Roy Hatch became desperate when a cow kept running ahead madly rather than escaping to the side. Even once the glider came to a rest, the men were still not safe. There was always the chance of another glider, out of control, crashing into it. Since it was safer in the open, and doors often jammed, soldiers slashed or smashed their way out of the side of the fuselage.

General Horrocks climbed an iron ladder and took up position on the factory roof near Joe's Bridge. Once the formations of troop carriers and gliders with the 101st Airborne had passed over their heads, he passed the order to his signaller that H-Hour would be 14.35 hours. The 350 guns of the Royal Artillery behind opened fire at exactly 14.00 hours, and under cover of the bombardment the Irish Guards battle group moved into their final positions on the start-line. The clock ticked away until H-Hour, while the gunners continued to pound the forward German positions. Then, with the order 'Driver advance!', the lead tank commanded by Lieutenant Keith Heathcote set off.

For the first few minutes everything seemed to go well, but as they passed the border post into the Netherlands one tank after another was hit. Soon nine were blazing. Vandeleur called in the RAF. 'It was the first time I had ever seen Typhoons in action,' he recorded later, 'and, Jesus, I was amazed at the guts of those pilots. They came in one at a time, head to tail, and flew right through our own barrage. I saw one disintegrate right above me. The noise was unimaginable. Guns firing, the screams of planes overhead and the shouts and curses of the men. I had to scream into the microphone to be heard.' In the middle of all this mayhem, divisional headquarters radioed to ask how the battle was going. 'My second-in-command Denis Fitzgerald just held up the microphone and said "Listen."' In the cacophony of explosions and shouting all around, one officer found the noise of wireless 'mush' in his earphones rather comforting.

Just behind Vandeleur's scout car came two RAF vehicles with the forward air controllers, Squadron Leader Max Sutherland and Flight Lieutenant Donald Love. Love saw cows, maddened with fear, galloping in circles in the fields on either side as the battle raged. At the border post, 'one of those little striped boxes', he also spotted 'a severed head, with a headless German body lying several yards away'. Love found to his dismay that some of the Typhoon pilots did not have the right gridded map, so when Squadron Leader Sutherland gave them their targets, they could do little. Instead, they had to use the tanks burning up front as 'a landmark to show the positions of forward troops'.

The Typhoons were coming in so close that Sutherland wanted to use yellow smoke grenades to mark their own troops, but that was dangerous as German gunners would immediately use them as an aiming mark. Vandeleur thought the Typhoons were attacking his Irish Guards by mistake with cannon fire, then he admitted his mistake. What tank crews had thought to be rounds striking their turrets turned out to be the cannon shell cases ejected from Typhoons flying low overhead.

Lieutenant John Quinan, who had abandoned his blazing Sherman, was standing by a man who was shot through the heart by a sniper. 'As he fell, he very clearly said "Oh, God!",' Quinan reminisced later. 'I have often thought it a nice theological speculation whether he spoke before, or after, death.'

As soon as the Shermans of the second company had been set ablaze, Major Edward Tyler took his tanks down off the road on to the polder, which was fortunately dry, and swung round to the right. Lance Sergeant Cowan, famous for his eagle eye, spotted a camouflaged self-propelled assault gun and knocked it out with his Firefly's 17-pounder. The crew commander surrendered to him, so Cowan told them to jump up on the back of his tank. He then continued his advance, only to find that his prisoner tapped him on the shoulder and pointed out another assault gun which he had not spotted. This too was destroyed. 'And this extraordinary combination of ex-enemy self-propelled gun commander and Irish Guards sergeant went on to deal with a third.' The German spoke reasonable English and was delighted with the Firefly's straight shooting. His explanation for this bizarre behaviour was that he was a professional soldier, and he could not bear to see anyone adopting the wrong tactics, as he thought Cowan had.

Accompanying infantry from the 3rd Battalion brought back prisoners. The guardsmen were very rough with snipers, whom they forced to trot down the road at the double, while prodding them with bayonets. One prisoner, perhaps out of panic, tried to break away and run. 'Frankly, he was dead the second the thought entered his mind. Everyone seemed to take a shot at him. He only got about fifteen to twenty yards before he was shot to pieces.'

As the German prisoners came back with their hands on their heads past the line of vehicles, 'I caught a movement out of the corner of my eye,' Vandeleur recorded. 'One of the bastards had taken a grenade he had concealed and lobbed it into one of our gun carriers . . . I saw one of our sergeants lying in the road with his leg blown off.' The German, who was gunned down in an instant, belonged to the Fallschirmjäger-Regiment von Hoffmann in Kampfgruppe Walther. Because of the dirty fighting methods of Hoffmann's men, the Irish Guards took it for granted that they were to kill as many as possible.

The wild reconnaissance ride of Lieutenant Buchanan-Jardine a few days before had revealed that the Germans had forced locals to dig an anti-tank ditch outside Valkenswaard. As a result, Vandeleur had ordered a bulldozer-tank to take position close to the head of the column. This was fortunate since it was badly needed to clear the road of the nine shot-up tanks before those coming up behind could continue. After the nasty shock of the ambush destroying so many of their tanks, Vandeleur was concerned at what else lay ahead.

9

The German Reaction
Sunday 17 September

On that Sunday morning of early-autumn sunshine, members of Krafft's 16th SS Training and Replacement Battalion who were not on duty rose late after their drinking the night before. 'In the distance,' SS-Sturmmann Bangard noted, 'we heard the streetcar rumbling from Oosterbeek to Arnhem.' Krafft himself was engaged in paperwork in his command post by the railway halt Oosterbeek Hoog. When the Mosquitoes flew in to attack Arnhem and the B-17s bombed Wolfheze, he was perplexed. They were hardly major military targets. A little later, when fighter-bombers attacked the anti-aircraft batteries in the area, he ordered his own 20mm flak crews into action. 'What a wonderful sound, like the beat of a drum,' Krafft enthused as soon as he heard them in action. 'It warms our hearts.'

Near Vught, Generaloberst Student had carried on with his own paperwork. 'I was suddenly startled at my desk', he wrote, 'by a rushing sound which became louder and louder. I stepped out on to the balcony. Everywhere I looked I saw aircraft – troop transporters and gliders – which flew past in loose formation and very low.'

Student, the old paratrooper warhorse, found himself thinking back nostalgically to his own airborne assaults, both the Netherlands in 1940 and Crete in 1941. 'I was deeply impressed by this mighty spectacle so suddenly presented to me. At that moment, I didn't think of the danger to our position, but I thought instead, filled with reflection and longing, of our own earlier operations.' When his new chief of staff, Oberst i.G. Reinhard, rushed out to join him on the balcony Student said: 'If only I had had such mighty means at my disposal!' The two men then climbed up to the flat roof of the house. Down below, drivers and clerks from the headquarters had appeared with their rifles and were shooting at the aircraft flying so low overhead.

Generalfeldmarschall Model had stood for a short time outside the Hotel Tafelberg watching the B-17 Flying Fortresses overhead. He assumed that they were heading for Germany. Later, during lunch, Oberst i.G. Hans Georg von Tempelhoff was summoned to the telephone and told to look out of the window. Tempelhoff saw paratroopers and gliders. He alerted Model and Krebs who joined him. Both men wore monocles, which apparently fell out as their eyebrows shot up in astonishment. Krebs said: 'This will be the decisive battle of the war.'

'Don't be so dramatic,' Model reproved him. 'It's obvious enough. Tempelhoff, get to work!' As operations officer, Tempelhoff dashed back to the telephone to ring all formations in the area, the II SS Panzer Corps first of all. After contacting as many as possible, he rang Generalfeldmarschall von Rundstedt's headquarters. Tempelhoff was rather taken aback by their unperturbed reaction – which he described as 'almost callously normal'.

Accounts vary of the departure from the Hotel Tafelberg. Some say it was panic-stricken. According to Obergruppenführer Bittrich who was not there, '[Model] ran to his bedroom, he crammed his belongings in his suitcase. He hastened downstairs, crossed the street and the suitcase burst open, all his toilet articles lay scattered all over the street. Helped by his men, he gathered them up a second time and off he went.' Another said that Krebs forgot his cap and pistol belt and the entire set of operations maps, which showed German dispositions along the whole front from the Netherlands to Switzerland. Other, more convincing versions imply that, although hurried, they set off in an orderly manner.

There were, of course, inconveniences. A staff officer who remembered that he had left his cigars in his room at the Tafelberg was furious that some enemy officer would enjoy them instead. More, like Leutnant Jedelhauser, regretted the loss of their laundry, having departed with no more than the uniform they were wearing. All agree on one thing, however. Model and his staff were convinced that the airborne landings were part of a plan to capture the head of Army Group B. They assumed that their presence in Oosterbeek must have been betrayed by the Dutch.

Model's convoy of vehicles drove fast towards Arnhem. They stopped briefly at the headquarters of Generalmajor Kussin, the town commandant. Model told him to find out exactly what was happening. The convoy, with its Feldgendarmerie escort in motorcycle combinations, carried on first to

Model's rear headquarters at Terborg, and then to Bittrich's headquarters in the castle of Slangenburg at Doetinchem, only a few kilometres away.

In Oosterbeek, following the rapid departure of Army Group B headquarters, wild scenes took place at the Schoonoord Hotel just up the road. German officers ran around madly, throwing their luggage into cars and trucks, while German women auxiliaries, known as 'grey mice' because of their uniforms, were hurrying back to their billet on the Utrechtseweg to retrieve their things and escape.

'A panic flight of the rear services located at Arnhem started,' a Dr Gerhardt recorded. 'Passenger cars with officers, paymasters and female military helpers, packed high with suitcases and other baggage, trucks with men, cyclists, soldiers marching in groups or alone, all were striving to leave the endangered city as quickly as possible.' Dutch civilians, standing outside their doors and by their garden gates, were eager to find out what was happening. Since the electricity had failed, the wireless was no help.

Panic appears to have overcome the headquarters of the Luftwaffe's 3rd Fighter Division at Deelen. Expecting to be captured by paratroopers, their chief operations officer ordered the destruction of their war diary for the last six months. They sent a signal: 'Command post attacked by fighter-bombers.' It was impossible to leave their bunkers, they claimed, with landings to the 'west, south-west, south and north-west of the divisional command post'. They received orders from the I Fighter Corps to blow up their bunker and retreat to Duisburg in the northern Ruhr. In contrast, a hastily assembled force of their ground crew was marched south to block any British paratroopers advancing down the Amsterdamseweg.

For Krafft's battalion, things had seemed to have calmed down again by midday. 'It was Sunday and we therefore got a good meal,' Bangard recorded. 'We received a wonderful chop per person and had a large plateful of pudding for dessert.' At 13.40 hours, according to Bangard, 'we heard the cry "Paratroopers!"' At first they thought it must be a mistake. Krafft himself heard 'the spine-chilling cry' of 'Gliders!' Over the tops of the trees to the west, he could make out tug aircraft releasing gliders. 'I felt sick to my stomach,' Krafft subsequently recounted with Germanic frankness in such matters. 'I unbuckled my belt and went behind the bushes.' Clearly feeling better as a result, he 'pulled up his pants', went back into his command post and issued the order 'Battalion, prepare to march!'

Krafft's men, while they listened to his instructions, loaded extra ammunition and grenades into pouches and pockets. 'In a feverish hurry the last things were packed,' Bangard said, 'steel helmet on, weapon in hand and *raus*!' Krafft had now worked out that the enemy operation must have the Arnhem road bridge as its principal objective. It was too big for a raid on Model's headquarters and the bridge was the only strategic target in the area. 'It was up to me to stop them,' he wrote in his report. He decided to establish a defensive line extending across the two main roads into Arnhem from the west and the railway line, 'but I didn't have enough men to extend to the Rhine.' Krafft's battalion comprised 13 officers, 73 NCOs and 349 men, a total of only 435. As far as he knew there were few other military organizations near by, except 'Army Group B, whose assistance we can probably not depend upon'. It would indeed have been unusual to see officers, with the broad burgundy stripes of the general staff on their breeches, wearing helmets and carrying machine pistols into battle. 'My soldiers were young and raw, but I had good NCOs and officers,' Krafft recorded, 'although one Leutnant deserted and was later court-martialled.' Less convincingly, since there were no reports of armed Dutch civilians at this stage, he also boasted, 'We did have trouble with Dutch terrorists . . . They were suitably dealt with!'

Krafft claims that he sent a motorcycle and sidecar with a runner to the heavy-machine-gun group and No. 2 Company near the Hotel Wolfheze with the order: 'Attack immediately. Send accurate intelligence of enemy's positions.' But British reports do not reflect the impression of an immediate counter-attack. Krafft also claims to have ordered his mortar battery into action. It was equipped with the Raketenwerfer multiple rocket launcher, which made a terrifying noise, and therefore would give the impression of far greater firepower than the battalion really possessed. In fact the fighting did not really start until at least an hour or more later, when the first British forces moving towards Arnhem ran into the initial blocking line which he set up west of the Bilderberg woods.

Krafft, in his bombastic way, later claimed to have reasoned that although it was often argued that a small force should not attack a far greater one, 'In this present fight for existence by the German people, there are occasions every day when only a virile offensive spirit can lead to success.' His men certainly fought effectively, but in defence, not in attack as he pretended.

Just after 15.00 hours, Generalmajor Kussin, the town commandant for Arnhem, appeared at the Hotel Wolfheze to say that he had called General der Flieger Christiansen, the Wehrmacht commander-in-chief Netherlands. Reinforcements should arrive by dusk. Krafft warned Kussin not to return by the Utrechtseweg. But Kussin, who was accompanied by two officers and a driver, was convinced that they would be all right. Within minutes they were all dead, having driven straight into a point platoon of British paratroopers.

*

At 13.40 hours, towards the end of lunch with the *Hohenstaufen* reconnaissance battalion, Standartenführer Harzer received an urgent call from his command post. The Luftwaffe communications network had just informed Obergruppenführer Bittrich of the first parachute drops and glider landings. His message to Harzer read: 'Paratroopers have landed near Arnhem. Immediate Alarm. Orders will follow.' Harzer could only yell to Gräbner and tell him to get his men to work. He needed to know how long it would take them to put their half-tracks back together again and remount their guns. There was no point cursing about bad luck. Without Gräbner's little trick of making them temporarily unserviceable, they would not have managed to hold on to the vehicles at all. After conferring with his head mechanic, Gräbner promised that they would be ready to move in three hours.

Harzer tried rapidly to work out what troops he had available. Some had already left for Siegen in Germany, and would have to be called back. The *Hohenstaufen* 'panzer regiment did not have a single tank in an operational state', so the crews would act as infantry. His greatest regret was to have been forced to send two panzergrenadier battalions to the Kampfgruppe Walther south of Eindhoven and hand the excellent Euling Battalion over to their sister division, the *Frundsberg*. Much would therefore depend on the other divisional elements: pioneers, artillery and flak detachments.

In Brummen, north-east of Arnhem on the road to Zutphen, SS-Hauptsturmführer Hans Möller of the *Hohenstaufen* pioneer battalion was outside enjoying the beautiful day with his adjutant, Untersturmführer Grupp. A collection of tiny white spots far away in the sky suddenly caught his attention. 'Cirrocumulus?' he suggested to his companion, then contradicted himself. 'No, flak bursts! No, there are too many for that.' He noticed that Dutch civilians near by had stopped to look too. 'Good grief, Grupp, those are parachutes!' They ran to sound the alarm.

Unlike the British army, German officers did not wait for orders from above, so it was not just the Krafft Battalion which mobilized on its own initiative. Both Möller's under-strength pioneer battalion and the *Hohenstaufen* artillery regiment, which was several kilometres closer at Dieren, moved as fast as they could towards the enemy. Möller sent off his reconnaissance platoon under Oberscharführer Winnerl immediately. The rest followed over the next two hours. The old Prussian army dictum of 'march towards the sound of gunfire' was followed by other units too. By dusk, the commander of the artillery regiment, SS-Obersturmbannführer Spindler, would be leading a combined force of odd *Hohenstaufen* units designated the Kampfgruppe Spindler.

Soon, any rear unit capable of firing a weapon was being mobilized in the

Netherlands and in Wehrkreis VI, the neighbouring military district in the
Reich. They included police battalions and even Reichsarbeitsdienst teenagers on labour service in their brown uniforms, which made the Dutch
think they were simply Hitler Youth. A corporal noted in his diary when
they received the call: 'We learn that paratroop forces have landed in the
area of Arnhem and Nijmegen. We have been ordered out. Weapons, ammunition and iron rations are being issued. Exact details are not known.'

Herbert Stelzenmüller, a Kriegsmarine cadet, was out on a Sunday stroll
in the ancient city of Cleve, just over the German border, when sirens
sounded. Members of the Feldgendarmerie drove through the streets ordering all service personnel back to barracks. The cadets were issued with Dutch
or Belgian rifles captured in 1940, and driven to Nijmegen. Stelzenmüller
and his companions saw a Reichsarbeitsdienst officer with two Dutch
teenagers, who had been captured wearing orange armbands. 'The RAD
commander took out his pistol and shot the two unarmed Dutch boys in cold
blood. Both fell dead in the roadway.'

SS-Brigadeführer Harmel of the *Frundsberg* had not reached Berlin until
the middle of that Sunday morning. Only then did he discover that the
Waffen-SS Führungshauptamt had just moved out to Bad Saarow, east of
the capital, to avoid the bombing. He reached Bad Saarow at midday. He
had to wait before his meeting started with SS-Obergruppenführer Hans
Jüttner who, with his white hair, smooth pale skin and rimless glasses, looked
more like a prosperous dentist than the head of the Waffen-SS. It was clear
that the move and the desperate circumstances of the retreat from France
had left the headquarters in a state of some confusion.

During the meeting, an aide brought in a teleprinter message and laid it
in front of Jüttner. He read it out to Harmel. It was from Bittrich. 'Harmel:
return immediately. Airborne landings in Arnhem area.' With the briefest
of goodbyes, Harmel raced for his car and told his driver to go like the devil.
It would be a nine-hour journey at least, largely because of the bombing of
the Ruhr and the need to proceed with screened headlights once night fell.
Harmel was desperate to be back with his men. He knew that they 'could
rely only on rapid action'.

SS-Obergruppenführer Hans Rauter was in The Hague when he received
news of the airborne landing. His first telephone call was to Sturmbannführer
Helle of the Dutch SS-Wachbataillon *Nordwest* at Amersfoort concentration
camp. Helle, however, was ensconced with his Javanese mistress. He had given
his adjutant, Obersturmführer Naumann, the strictest orders that he was not

to be disturbed. Following his instructions, Naumann had done nothing when the town major rang to say that large numbers of paratroopers had dropped to the east. But when the telephone rang once more, and he found Obergruppenführer Rauter himself on the line, Naumann 'leaped to his feet'. The battalion was to be ready to march immediately, Rauter told him. Sturmbannführer Helle was to report at once to General von Tettau. This time Naumann did disturb his commanding officer.

Generalleutnant Hans von Tettau's headquarters were at Grebbeberg near Wageningen to the west of Arnhem. Christiansen had billeted most of the dejected and weaponless troops who had escaped from Normandy along the north bank of the Neder Rijn. He had not wanted them to lower the morale of his own troops in the Netherlands, so he kept them apart. Tettau's command had been responsible for rounding up these stragglers crossing the Neder Rijn, bringing them back to discipline and incorporating them into scratch units. But Tettau, with his tired, gaunt face, was hardly an inspiring leader, and like a number of senior officers he assumed at first that the British had landed at Deelen airfield. 'Our commanders are simply pitiful,' Oberst Fullriede ranted in his diary. 'Tettau and his staff give the impression of an old gentlemen's club.'

Rauter then called Generalleutnant von Wühlisch, the deputy to General Christiansen. He told him about the orders he had given to Helle's battalion at Amersfoort. Rauter claimed that Wühlisch, afraid that the 'day of the hatchet' had finally arrived, then said, 'Yes, but can you weaken your position in such a way?'

'Right now our front line is Arnhem,' Rauter retorted. 'I want every available soldier fit to fight there. If there is a revolt behind the front, then we'll fight it with orderlies, clerks and telephone operators. My reserves are on the march already.' Considering that Helle was probably not yet dressed by then, the idea of his 'reserves' being 'on the march' was optimistic.

'Good luck then,' Wühlisch replied coldly and hung up.

According to his own account, Rauter also telephoned Reichsführer-SS Heinrich Himmler in Berlin to warn him of the invasion. 'What are you going to do?' Himmler asked.

'I'm going to Arnhem at once! I have already thrown in my entire reserves. I hope that the Resistance will leave me alone at this critical moment!'

'I wish you strength, Rauter,' Himmler replied. Rauter left immediately afterwards and was not ambushed by 'terrorists'. 'I had soldier's luck,' he claimed.

10

The British Landings
Sunday 17 September

The first members of the British 1st Airborne to land were the pathfinders of the 21st Independent Parachute Company. They jumped right on time from the twelve Stirling bombers at 12.40 hours. An unfortunate corporal dropped his Sten gun, a notoriously unsafe weapon, as he landed and it went off, killing him. A platoon each secured Landing Zones S and Z, and Drop Zone X. They then set up the Eureka homing devices. A German motor-cyclist rode up to ask if they had seen any Tommies. It was 'a rather fatal mistake', as one of the pathfinders observed.

At 13.00 hours the first of 300 gliders began to land, having had their tow cast off about a kilometre and a half before. The airlanding brigade came in just north of the railway line on Landing Zone S. Medical teams were soon treating the casualties from crashed gliders. Sixteen of the brigade's gliders had failed to appear, half of them with men from the 7th Battalion King's Own Scottish Borderers. A piper began playing 'Blue Bonnets over the Border' to signal that they should form up in their companies. A rapid roll call indicated that, even with the missing gliders, the KOSB still mustered 40 officers and 700 men. Their task was to defend the drop and landing zones, together with part of the 2nd Battalion the South Staffordshire Regiment and the 1st Battalion the Border Regiment.

Over the next forty minutes, divisional troops in Horsas and some of the large Hamilcars came in on Landing Zone Z. They carried the 75mm pack howitzers of the Light Regiment as well as anti-tank guns, Jeeps, Bren-gun carriers, the airborne squadron of the Royal Engineers, the field ambulances and the reconnaissance squadron. One Hamilcar 'made a bad landing', the senior medical officer reported. 'It appeared to have come down very fast in a potato field, collected a lot of earth under its bows which acted as a stop and turned it arse over tip. One pilot was killed and the other injured and pinned down by the load inside.'

Among the gliders which failed to arrive, one bringing a Bren-gun carrier had apparently been shot down by a detachment belonging to 'a battalion of Moors' from the SS Regiment *Götz Berens von Rautenfeld.** Ordered to defend an intersection on the Breda–Tilburg road, they had managed to bring the glider down with small-arms fire. Their commander, a Leutnant Martin, recorded in his diary that on the glider was written in chalk, 'Is this journey absolutely necessary?' This fragment of British humour, sending up the government slogan to reduce domestic travel, seems to have left the young officer totally mystified.

A postman called Jan Donderwinkel, wearing his uniform and carrying a first-aid kit, turned up on Landing Zone S to help. He was astonished to see soldiers pulling the tail off a glider, and a Jeep being driven out. He found a soldier lying on the ground whose feet had been crushed in the glider landing. 'Are you a postman?' the soldier asked. 'Yes,' replied Donderwinkel. 'Well then, have you a letter for me?'

'No,' he said, 'but do you have a cigarette for me?' The injured soldier laughed and handed him a packet of Player's. Donderwinkel carried the soldier to the Wolfheze asylum close by where the 131st (Parachute) Field Ambulance had already established a casualty clearing station. Patients from the asylum wandering in the woods were still in shock from the explosion when the ammunition dump had been hit. It was very hard to persuade them to return.

An idea arose that Major Freddie Gough's reconnaissance squadron had lost a large number of its thirty-two armed Jeeps in the crossing, when in fact only four failed to arrive. But another six Jeeps were trapped in crash-landed gliders, because they could be driven out only when the tail section had been removed. 'Our glider had a rough landing,' a young reconnaissance officer recounted, 'and finished with her tail in the air. It took us four and a half hours to unload.'

The reconnaissance squadron was supposed to be the force that would carry out the lightning dash to the bridge. The delay was made worse by Gough's insistence on parachuting, because he hated gliders. Most of his men felt the same and chose to parachute too. As a result they did not arrive

* The presence in the Netherlands of Muslims from the 13th SS Division *Handschar*, which was then still fighting partisans in Yugoslavia, is surprising but not impossible, as they may have been attached to the XII SS Armeekorps.

with their Jeeps, which had twin Vickers K machine guns mounted. Gough
was angry that they had not been given the same task as in the planning for
Operation Comet, where his squadron was to have been dropped near Elst,
south of the Neder Rijn between Arnhem and Nijmegen. In the end the
first troop of the reconnaissance squadron did not set off until just after
15.40 hours, two hours after all gliders had landed.

At 13.50 hours, formations of 145 C-47 Dakotas appeared and began to
drop some 2,700 men, mostly from the 1st Parachute Brigade, commanded
by Brigadier Gerald Lathbury. Lieutenant Patrick Barnett, who commanded the defence platoon for brigade headquarters, jumped first from his
aircraft, and he could not understand on landing what had happened to the
rest of the stick. Only later did he find that his batman had lost his nerve at
the last moment and just sat down, preventing everyone else from jumping.
The pilot had been forced to come round again.

Local farmers and their wives had by then appeared and they helped cut
rigging lines, if only to carry off the valuable silk canopies to be refashioned
as dresses and underwear. Within little more than ten minutes, all paratroopers had landed, with remarkably few broken bones. Corporal Terry
Brace, a medic, was combing his hair just after landing. His sergeant major,
on seeing this, shouted at him: 'Brace, there is no point in worrying about
your hair if you are going to lose your bloody head.'

Once on the ground, members of the 2nd Parachute Battalion were summoned to the familiar braying of Lieutenant Colonel John Frost's hunting
horn. Frost did not waste time. His battalion group set off at 15.00 hours
south towards Heelsum. They then swung east through the Doorwerthse
woods along his route codenamed 'Lion' which was the closest to the river.
Their main objective was the great steel road bridge over the Rhine, 600
metres long with its ramps on both sides.

Proving that speed counted for everything that day, the fastest group to
move off had been the military police detachment of eleven men. They
marched straight into Arnhem, encountering no opposition, and headed
for their objective, which was police headquarters. They remained there in
splendid isolation until the building was stormed by SS troops nearly forty-
eight hours later.

The 3rd Battalion, meanwhile, which was also ordered to head for Arnhem, took the central route along the Utrechtseweg, codenamed 'Tiger'.
Deciding that all was going well, Lathbury ordered the 1st Battalion, his
reserve, to take the northern route into Arnhem, the Amsterdamseweg,
codenamed 'Leopard'. He then heard the misleading report about the

reconnaissance squadron, so he sent a message to Frost to push on as fast as he could. At this stage, radio communications seemed to work quite well, but soon the woods and buildings made messages break up. The 22 Set was simply not powerful enough, as signals officers had warned. The Germans were also operating a powerful jamming station on the divisional net. Regrettably, clear instructions on switching frequencies had not been distributed in advance. Finally, at 17.30 hours a despatch rider was sent off by motorcycle to 1st Parachute Brigade with a message bearing the new frequency. He returned a few hours later having failed to find them.

Communications were little better for a large American air support party led by Lieutenant Paul B. Johnson from the 101st Airborne. They had flown in by glider with the British. They made a smooth landing and within five minutes they had unloaded their Jeeps and driven to the assembly point. One of their other gliders, however, had dug its nose into the soft field and the men in it were 'a bit shaken up'. As soon as Johnson's team reached the temporary divisional command post on the edge of the landing zone, they tuned their wireless set but found it would not transmit. The other team had the same problem. 'During the afternoon we made contact with a station several times who would not answer our authenticator but instead asked for his signal strength and us to send him a series of V's.' This led them to believe that it was a German Y-service set intent on mischief. The signallers kept trying all night, but without any luck.

At 15.30, just as the 1st Battalion moved out, so did the Jeeps of the 1st Parachute Squadron Royal Engineers. To raise morale, somebody had wired in a radio which was playing 'Tiger Rag' as they set off. When the Jeeps towing the howitzers of the Light Regiment moved out, Lance Bombardier Jones instinctively drove on the left side of the road. His battery sergeant major cursed him for giving away the fact that they were British.

It seemed all too easy. Paratroopers were amazed at how well this daytime drop had gone in comparison to the chaotic night-landings in Sicily and the 6th Airborne's drop on Normandy. 'Casualties had been lighter than antici- pated as there was virtually no enemy opposition during the flight or on landing,' Colonel Graeme Warrack, the deputy director of medical services, noted. Their first impression was of individual German soldiers surrender- ing. A few were even encountered in the woods, including one with a Dutch girlfriend, who appeared far more embarrassed than her *Landser* lover who surrendered willingly.

Everything then changed rather quickly. The first real clashes with Krafft's men happened when Lieutenant Bucknell's troop of the reconnais- sance squadron crossed the railway line at Wolfheze and set off towards

Arnhem along a track beside the high railway embankment. In a defile less than a kilometre down this track, the Jeeps came under heavy fire from Krafft's No. 2 Company in well-sited positions. Bucknell and six others were dead, with four more wounded and taken prisoner. Gough, who was following, had heard the firing ahead. He knew his Jeeps were involved, because he could distinguish the sound of their Vickers K machine guns. He turned back to warn the 1st Parachute Battalion under Lieutenant Colonel David Dobie that the way was blocked. Dobie decided to go further north to follow the Amsterdamseweg into Arnhem.

It was about this time that General Urquhart, impatient at the lack of information on the advance, went to the command post of Hicks's 1st Airlanding Brigade at the Wolfheze level-crossing to find out what he knew. Hicks's main concern at that time was the absence of the commanding officer of the Border Regiment, whose glider had not turned up. He was however amused when a very young German Luftwaffe female auxiliary was brought to him, as their first prisoner. The poor girl was absolutely terrified and refused both a cup of tea and some chocolate, no doubt afraid that they contained some fearful substance.

This is when Urquhart heard the inaccurate report about the reconnaissance squadron Jeeps failing to arrive. He sent a message to Gough, who was in fact very close by, telling him to report in as soon as possible. He wanted to change the reconnaissance squadron's role from being a *coup de main* force at the bridge to one of reconnoitring the three main routes in front of the battalions. Gough set off for the divisional command post back at the edge of the landing zone, but in the meantime Urquhart had gone off to find Lathbury and the headquarters of the 1st Parachute Brigade. So Gough began a wild-goose chase, while Urquhart made the great mistake, compounded of course by the collapse in wireless communications, of losing touch with his own headquarters. Almost everything was now starting to go wrong.

The 1st Battalion, advancing north through the woods to the Amsterdamseweg, ran straight into the scratch Luftwaffe unit from Deelen and suffered a number of casualties. This Luftwaffe Alarmeinheit was soon reinforced by some of the first armoured cars from Gräbner's *Hohenstaufen* reconnaissance battalion, effectively blocking the northern, 'Leopard' route. Around dusk, Dobie heard a message over the radio, one of the very few times it worked that day, saying that Frost's 2nd Battalion was getting through to the bridge. So Dobie decided to abandon his task of sealing off north Arnhem. He turned his battalion around, and headed south again to help Frost.

The 3rd Battalion, whose lead platoon had gunned down Generalmajor Kussin, followed the Utrechtseweg, the centre route. Short of Oosterbeek, they were attacked by a German self-propelled assault gun charging at them down the road. It managed to destroy a Jeep and a 6-pounder anti-tank gun. Eventually it pulled back under heavy small-arms fire. Lieutenant Colonel John Fitch, concerned that the road ahead might be blocked, sent off C Company under Major Peter Lewis to try another route. Lewis took his men up to the railway line, and they followed the track all the way into Arnhem, fighting successful little skirmishes. They would manage to reach the road bridge before midnight, an impressive achievement.

It was probably one of their little skirmishes with part of Krafft's battalion which convinced the SS-Sturmbannführer that he was in danger of being cut off. He decided to abandon any further attempt to maintain his positions, and pulled his men back to the north-east as darkness fell. They encountered part of the Kampfgruppe Spindler, which was starting to set up its own *Sperrlinie*, or blocking line. Spindler, who had no idea of Krafft's existence until then, was told by Bittrich to include the battalion as part of his own force.

Major General Urquhart, by now deeply concerned at the slowness of the advance, was still in search of Brigadier Lathbury. He found Lathbury's brigade major, Tony Hibbert. 'The General drove up,' Hibbert recorded, 'and I could see that he was angry. He said that we were moving "too bloody slowly".' Urquhart drove off again to find Lathbury. Hibbert warned Frost of Urquhart's concerns.

The rest of Fitch's 3rd Battalion, on reaching Oosterbeek with its redbrick roads, began to experience embarrassing scenes of joy and generosity. 'The people were shouting and pointing in the streets,' wrote Jan Voskuil, 'laughing and clapping. Small boys jumped up and down.' Because the paratroop helmet was round and unlike the usual British soup-plate shape, Jan Eijkelhoff asked if they were American. 'Not bloody likely,' came the offended reply. 'We're British.'

Pretty Dutch girls kissed the soldiers sweaty from the heat and the march. 'Everywhere the Churchill V-sign was used as a currency of friendship and greeting.' Cheering civilians, women and old men, offered fruit and drinks, including gin. Officers shouted orders that nobody was to drink alcohol or stop. Younger men emerged from hiding and begged to be allowed to accompany them and fight too. Some Dutch nevertheless felt that the British advance was over-cautious, even hesitant. 'The British soldiers arrive,' a woman wrote. 'We wave at them with white handkerchiefs and orange ribbons to encourage them to come on and that it is safe.' But then they heard the sound of German motorbikes approaching. 'Like a film in slow motion, the British take their guns which had been slung over their shoulders.' The Dutch slipped back into their houses, and the more nervous went down into their cellars.

Freddie Gough, meanwhile, had driven back to the divisional command post to find Urquhart. Charles Mackenzie, the chief of staff, had told him that the general was with Lathbury, so he finally found the 1st Parachute Brigade headquarters in Oosterbeek, but Tony Hibbert had no idea where Urquhart and Lathbury were. Hibbert shrugged. 'They're together some place, but they've both gone off.' In fact matters were far worse. Just as Urquhart recognized that he was dangerously out of touch, he found that a German mortar shell had exploded by his Jeep in his absence, and his signaller was badly wounded. Private Sims, a mortarman himself with the 2nd Battalion, had a healthy respect for the accuracy of his German counterparts. 'Hold a mess-tin out half a mile away and the bastards will put the third bomb in it.'

On the southern route, Frost's 2nd Battalion was led by A Company commanded by the eccentric and fearless Major Digby Tatham-Warter. They were all fit because Frost had trained his paratroopers to a basic of thirty miles a day with 60 pounds of equipment on their backs. Once they had passed the rectory and church in Oosterbeek, watched by Kate ter Horst and her five young children, C Company under Major Victor Dover struck off to the right to capture the railway bridge. They advanced rapidly across the polder where a number of cows lay dead. Dover told Lieutenant Peter Barry to take his platoon on to the bridge, with some sappers to deal with any charges. They were quite close to the bridge when they saw a German soldier run on to it from the southern side. 'He got to the middle and I saw him kneel down and start doing something. I put one section down and told them to open fire. The range I gave the Bren gunner was 500 yards. With another section, I ordered a rush on the bridge to get across.' They were already on the bridge with water beneath them when the central span blew up in their faces.

The rest of Frost's battalion carried on towards Arnhem, followed by part of Lathbury's brigade headquarters, Captain Mackay and his sappers, 16th (Parachute) Field Ambulance and part of the Jedburgh Team Claude, in the form of the Dutch Captain Jacobus Groenewoud and the American Lieutenant Harvey Todd. Their task was to advance with the leading elements of the 1st Parachute Brigade into Arnhem. There, they were to contact the ex-burgemeester and ex-chief of police and get them to administer

Arnhem until the military government officers arrived with XXX Corps. As soon as they had landed, Groenewoud had gone straight into Oosterbeek to get help and transport to clear supplies off the landing zone. He had returned with three wagons and a German Opel Blitz truck. He had shot down the two German soldiers standing by the truck. 'They might have surrendered,' he told Todd, 'but no time for PoWs here.'

One of Tatham-Warter's platoon commanders thought that their advance had been almost 'like a triumphal procession' until they were surprised by a German 'arc', an eight-wheeler armoured car, firing its machine gun and 20mm cannon. The closer Frost's force came to Arnhem, the greater the resistance became. Tatham-Warter led his men over one garden fence or wall after another to outflank German machine-gun positions. It was not Frost's hunting horn which could be heard now, but Tatham-Warter's bugler sounding the charge. Tatham-Warter, who did not trust radios in battle to communicate orders, had trained his men with the old light infantry bugle calls.

The toughest opposition came soon after they had gone under the railway line from Nijmegen. Up to their left stood a wooded bluff called Den Brink. This commanding feature had been occupied by an advance group of Kampfgruppe Spindler. Frost ordered B Company under Major Douglas Crawley to clear them out, while A Company pushed on, but it all took time and cost several casualties, including a sergeant badly shot through both legs. Corporal Terry Brace, the medic, placed a lighted cigarette between his lips to calm him down. The sergeant had lost a great deal of blood. He grasped both of Brace's wrists. 'Am I going to be all right?' he asked.

'Sure you are,' said Brace.

'Please try to do something for me,' he pleaded. 'I've got two children at home. Please.'

'Don't worry,' Brace reassured him. 'You'll be fine.' But he knew that the sergeant would be dead very soon.

A terrible moment occurred when a little Dutch girl, thrilled to see British soldiers, ran out into the street crying '*Chocolade!*' Two paratroopers yelled at her to go back, but she was cut down in the cross-fire. Somebody dashed out and collected her body and carried it across the road. The Dutch, in spite of the heavy firing, pulled the wounded into their houses to care for them.

When they reached the Y-junction just short of the St Elisabeth Hospital, the main column forked right down towards the bridge. The doctors and orderlies of 16 (Para) Field Ambulance went straight to the hospital entrance, where 'casualties were almost waiting on the doorstep'. Inside, they found that the Dutch doctors had rightly placed the British wounded on one side of the hospital and the Germans on the other.

The officers and men of the field ambulance, carrying most of their equipment on their backs, received the warmest possible welcome. When the first news of the airborne landing had arrived, 'dozens of nurses and doctors poured out into the street and they formed a circle, joined hands and whirled around, delirious with joy.' The forty German Catholic nuns, who were also working there, became very nervous at the unexpected turn of events. All the Dutch medical personnel gathered round a piano to sing the '*Wilhelmus*', many with tears running down their cheeks. Then they sang 'God Save the King'.

'While they were singing, a British soldier appeared with his rifle in the back of a German officer. It turned out that the German was a surgeon and he stood to attention until the anthem drew to a close.' The German doctor was pressed into service in the hospital. The staff now included Dutch, British and German doctors, German nuns, Dutch nurses, British orderlies, Dutch volunteers from the underground and Red Cross assistants.

Sister van Dijk said proudly to the captured German doctor, 'Now we are free.' He shook his head. 'Don't say that. It is just the beginning.' One of the wounded German prisoners asked her if she knew where he would be going. 'Probably to England,' she replied confidently. 'Thank God!' he said. The St Elisabeth Hospital neurologist asked one of the British officers what he thought would happen. 'Well, we'll have two days of terrible fighting, and then Monty will arrive.' That night some thirty Austrian Luftwaffe personnel who had been forced to act as infantry came to the hospital, making a great deal of noise about their wounds, which were superficial. They were all armed, so the hospital staff had to take their weapons and lock them in a secure room. These Austrians were happy to give up their weapons since, as they made very clear, they did not want to fight for the Germans.

Generalfeldmarschall Model and his staff reached Bittrich's command post by 15.00 hours. 'I'm looking for a new headquarters,' he announced. 'They almost got me.' Bittrich probably had to conceal a smile at his superior's vanity in believing himself to have been the prime target. Bittrich had at first assumed that the Allied plan was to cut off General von Zangen's Fifteenth Army. Now the point of the operation was quite clear. Generaloberst Student became very excited that evening when a patrol returned with detailed Allied orders found on a crashed Waco glider near Vught, but as soon as the German command linked the assault on the bridges to the attack of XXX Corps, Allied intentions became self-evident. The real importance of these papers, however, was to reveal details of subsequent lifts which enabled the Germans to concentrate their anti-aircraft guns against the landing zones.

Bittrich had already issued his orders to the II SS Panzer Corps. 'The Division will reconnoitre in the direction of Arnhem and Nijmegen,' he instructed Standartenführer Harzer of the 9th *Hohenstaufen*. 'Quick action is imperative! The taking and securing of Arnhem Bridge is of decisive importance.' Since Bittrich was planning to give the 10th *Frundsberg* the responsibility for securing Nijmegen, it was a mistake to mention the city to Harzer, because he allowed his reconnaissance battalion under Viktor Gräbner to go charging off too far from the key objective.

Model was much clearer in his ideas. He wanted Harzer's *Hohenstaufen* to stop the British from taking Arnhem, while Harmel's *Frundsberg* was to cross the Neder Rijn and ensure that the British Second Army could not get through to the paratroopers. The polderland of the Betuwe, with the single main road via Elst, would be the perfect place to stop them. Model ruled out any suggestion of blowing up the road bridges at Arnhem and Nijmegen. They had to be held to allow a full counter-attack. Bittrich agreed that the Arnhem bridge should be kept, but he was dismayed that the Waal bridge at Nijmegen could not be touched.

Although Model's Army Group B had lost contact with Rundstedt's headquarters, it could still transmit via Luftwaffe West. A stream of orders and instructions poured forth, including the codeword 'Gneisenau', which prompted the immediate mobilization of all designated Kampfgruppen. Corps Feldt with the 406th Landesschützen-Division was ordered to attack the 82nd Airborne south-east of Nijmegen from Cleve and Goch. The II Fallschirm Corps, commanded by General der Fallschirmtruppen Eugen Meindl in Cologne, was ordered to Cleve, 'taking every man who could just carry a gun'. Their mission was to drive back the 82nd Airborne and join up with the troops defending Nijmegen, even though neither Meindl nor Model at that stage had any idea who they were.

The Generalfeldmarschall demanded from Rundstedt's headquarters the 'fastest possible provision of reinforcements with heavy mobile anti-tank weapons. Lack of close-range anti-tank weapons [Panzerfausts] and fuel is delaying all counter-measures.' Model also demanded the diversion of the 107th Panzer-Brigade and the assault gun brigade heading to Aachen from Denmark. In addition, he wanted a heavy panzer battalion of Mark VI Royal Tiger tanks, 88mm flak batteries and just about every unit available to be sent to prevent an Allied breakthrough.

Model was ferocious in his criticism of the Luftwaffe. 'The almost complete lack of counter-attack from air and ground was of decisive significance. It is absolutely essential that we have fighters in the sky day and night.' Apparently, he yelled his complaints down the telephone at Generalleutnant Bulovius of the 2nd Fighter Corps. Bulovius tried to claim that his pilots had shot down ninety Mustangs, a futile and preposterous lie.

Things did not bode well for General der Flieger Werner Kreipe, the Luftwaffe chief of staff at Führer headquarters in East Prussia. During the afternoon the first reports came in of 'landings and parachute jumps over Holland', he recorded in his diary. The Wolfsschanze was engulfed by a frenzy of telephone calls and 'instructions for counter-measures'. In the panic, the Oberkommando der Wehrmacht (OKW) even informed Rundstedt's headquarters that an American airborne division had 'landed in Warsaw'.

Kreipe noted 'quite an excitement' as he was summoned to a meeting with the Führer and Jodl. Hitler was furious that the Luftwaffe had not attacked the air armada. He said the Luftwaffe was 'inefficient, cowardly, and has failed to support him'. Kreipe had become used to such outbursts. He asked the Führer to give examples. 'I decline any further conversations with you,' Hitler retorted. 'I want to see the Reichsmarschall [Göring] tomorrow. I hope that you will at least be able to arrange that.'

Hitler was powerfully affected when informed of Model's narrow escape from British airborne troops. He decided that the defences of the Wolfsschanze should be massively increased to prevent the Red Army from launching a similar coup against him. His greatest terror was to be captured by the Soviets and taken to Moscow as a trophy prisoner. 'Here I sit with my whole supreme command. Here sits the Reichsmarschall; the OKW; the Reichsführer-SS; the Reich Foreign Minister. Well then, this is the most valuable catch, that is obvious. I would not hesitate to risk two parachute divisions here, if with one blow I could get my hands on the whole German command.'

11

The American Landings
Sunday 17 September

General Reinhard, the commander of LXXXVIII Corps, was returning at lunchtime to his headquarters at Moergestel, just east of Tilburg, when he sighted the air armada. He had already been forced to abandon his staff car on five occasions to throw himself in the ditch as strafing fighters came in low. 'In order not to offer too large a target to the enemy "*Jabos*" [fighter-bombers], I continued the journey in the sidecar of one of the motorcycles in my escort.'

When he finally reached his headquarters in the Villa Zonnewende, his staff told him of the parachute landings at Son, but they had also received a false report of another landing at Udenhout, just north of Tilburg. Reinhard assembled about a thousand men in scratch units, and sent one force to Son, the other to Udenhout and two companies from the 245th Infanterie-Division to Best. His only reserve was 'a police battalion at Tilburg whose entire personnel consisted of old men'.

In Eindhoven, the Knokploegen, the military wing of the underground, seized the telephone exchange. They found that the Germans had not damaged the system on their departure, and they could even ring Amsterdam and The Hague. 'Peter Zuid', the *nom de guerre* of Johannes Borghouts, called his wife in Oosterbeek. He broke down in tears on hearing her voice, having not spoken to her during all his time in hiding.

In Nijmegen, the heavy roar of aircraft engines and a mass of black silhouettes approaching from the south-west caused great excitement. People shouted, 'The Tommies are coming!' and some started to climb on to the roofs of houses to get a better view. They were to be disappointed when no paratroops appeared within their view. One of them suddenly spotted on the roof of a neighbouring house a helmeted German machine-gunner. He had an MG-42, which the Allies called a 'Spandau', and belts of ammunition wrapped diagonally around his torso 'like a Mexican bandit'.

Many of the German troops started to leave Nijmegen, most to counter-attack the paratroopers, a few to flee over the border to Germany. The troops remaining were nervous as they set up machine-gun posts and began to barricade streets with barbed-wire chevaux-de-frise barriers. If they saw civilians out on the street, they shouted, 'Go away, or you'll be shot!' Reinforcements also began to appear. A group of arrogant young Fallschirmjäger arrived by truck to defend Hunner Park and the great traffic circle of Keizer Lodewijkplein leading to the main bridge. One of them claimed to civilians that 'the Fallschirmjäger pushed back the Americans immediately'.

Shopkeepers rapidly boarded up their windows, not that that would do much good once the fighting started. At the same time, leaders of the local underground began to issue orders from the Bonte Os restaurant in Molenstraat. They divided the town into four, for the OD or Order Service to maintain security, even though they possessed only seven rifles between them. The Knokploegen combat groups were much better armed.

Further down the Molenstraat, trunks were being hurriedly loaded into a grey military truck outside Gestapo headquarters. Those people watching from behind curtains were convinced that they were filled with loot. One Gestapo man stopped by the OD was found to have his pockets filled with watches and jewellery. Collaborating officials and any remaining NSB members slipped away that afternoon, usually saying that they needed to fetch something from home. Yet several German policemen made no attempt to leave, and neither did the hated Inspector Verstappen, an arch-collaborationist, who surrendered a little later at the Groenestraat police station.

Out in the countryside people hurried to the drop and landing zones, offering to help. Everyone wanted to shake hands with a liberator. And after enduring the near-sawdust of Consi cigarettes during the occupation, the prospect of being offered a Lucky Strike seemed an unimaginable treat to dedicated Dutch smokers. The taste of their first American cigarette provided the most intense experience for many people, and they boasted about it to friends who had not yet undergone this rite of passage.

For the majority of American paratroopers, the operation was most unlike the wild scattering they had experienced in Normandy; in fact they descended in such a tight pattern that they were almost coming down on top of each other. One or two even became snagged in each other's rigging or were hit by weapon containers. Father Sampson, a Catholic padre with the 101st Airborne, nearly made the chute of a man descending below him collapse. He called his post-war memoir *Look Out Below!*

When there was firing from the ground, almost every paratrooper in the sky felt that the Germans were targeting him and nobody else. Lieutenant James Coyle descended, shooting at distant Germans with a .45 automatic pistol. He never expected to hit any of them, but it alleviated the sense of helplessness. After hitting the ground, they struggled out of their parachute harnesses. One man enmeshed in his lines looked up in terror to see a civilian standing over him with a large knife, but he had come over to help. One Dutchman, who had proudly put on his army tunic and helmet from 1940 to bicycle out to greet the paratroopers, 'came very close to being shot because of the strange uniform he was wearing'. He proved to be extremely useful, however, as he spoke both English and German.

Lieutenant Colonel Cassidy landed on a barbed-wire fence, and took some five minutes to free himself. In a couple of cases, Gammon grenades – the individual paratrooper's anti-tank weapon – exploded when leg bags came adrift and plummeted to the ground. The first task was to locate and open up the bundles which had been dropped from under the plane. A sergeant in the 101st was moved to find that a Dutch woman, whose husband had been killed only two days before by Allied planes attacking flak positions, still helped them retrieve parachute bundles from the fields near Son. Paratroopers were touched by the help offered by locals.

'The Dutch', a corporal reported in contrast to the scenes near Wolfheze, 'even gathered our chutes and placed them by the road for salvage, rather than scurrying off with them as the French so often did.' American officers, on the other hand, were once again dismayed by the wasteful habits of many of their soldiers. 'When a man landed with one piece of heavy equipment', a member of the 506th Parachute Infantry Regiment observed, 'and did not find anyone immediately who had the corresponding pieces, he tended to throw his away.' The 2nd Battalion found that night that it had only two mortars which were complete.

With greater haste than the British to the north, the American paratroopers set off towards their first objective, a column on each side of the road. Dutch onlookers watched in amazement as they chewed gum on the march. They were also intrigued by the practical informality of their uniforms. Supply officers tried to find civilian vehicles to transport ammunition and rations from the drop zone, but many Dutch farmers, having guessed immediately what was needed, turned up to help with large carts drawn by a couple of horses. They refused the mimeographed forms which would have enabled them to claim payment later. Several paratroopers even used cows as ammunition carriers, much to the amusement of their comrades.

A few gliders crash-landed in enemy territory. The Dutch used hollowed-out haystacks to hide those on board, and then provided bicycles and guides to get them back to their own forces. One glider came under heavy fire from German soldiers just before it landed two kilometres south-east of Boxtel. Dutch civilians ran up to help, and started to carry away a gunner called James Seabolt who had broken his leg in the crash. They and the Americans came under fire again. A few moments later, 'a beautiful Dutch girl arrived with a wheel-barrow.' Seabolt was placed in it and they trundled him off. He was in such pain that his comrades had to leave him in a barn in the care of the girl. They gave him a morphine shot and handed him a pistol, which seemed an unsafe combination, but they and Seabolt were all returned to American lines over the next week thanks to their helpers.

The 101st Airborne Division dropped north of Eindhoven in four different places round Veghel and Son. American paratroopers of its 501st Parachute Infantry Regiment heading for Veghel asked for directions to what they called the 'double A bridge'. Dr Leo Schrijvers was rather perplexed until he realized they meant the bridge over the River Aa. The 502nd, dropping further south, had to split its forces, with one battalion going for St Oeden-rode on the River Dommel, and Best to the south-west, while the first objective of Colonel Sink's 506th Parachute Infantry Regiment was the bridge at Son over the Wilhelmina Canal.

Generaloberst Student claimed to have taken personal charge of the bat-tle against the 101st. 'Better than anyone else I knew that airborne troops are at their weakest during the first few hours and thus rapid and decisive action on our part was called for.' He had no reserves to hand, but there were several thousand replacements for Fallschirmjäger units at 's-Hertogenbosch (also known as Den Bosch). One hastily assembled march battalion was sent against St Oedenrode and another against Veghel. He ordered Generalleutnant Walter Poppe's 59th Infanterie-Division, the first of the Fifteenth Army formations, to head for Boxtel at once. Its advance units, however, were to make for Son, where the bridge was held by part of the training battalion of the *Hermann Göring* Division, which had rapidly learned its battlecraft in the fighting at Beverloo a few days before.

As the 506th was dropping north-west of Son, the paratroopers were alarmed to see five, some say eight, enemy tanks. These tanks were from Oberstleutnant Fullriede's training and replacement battalion of the *Hermann Göring* Division, which Major Urquhart's photo-reconnaissance sortie had picked up. Fortunately for the paratroopers, 'the fighter-bombers attacked, destroying two and driving the rest away.' The 506th landed on a soft ploughed field, and Sink's first impression was that his regiment was 'in good shape'. As the first groups reached the wood where they were to

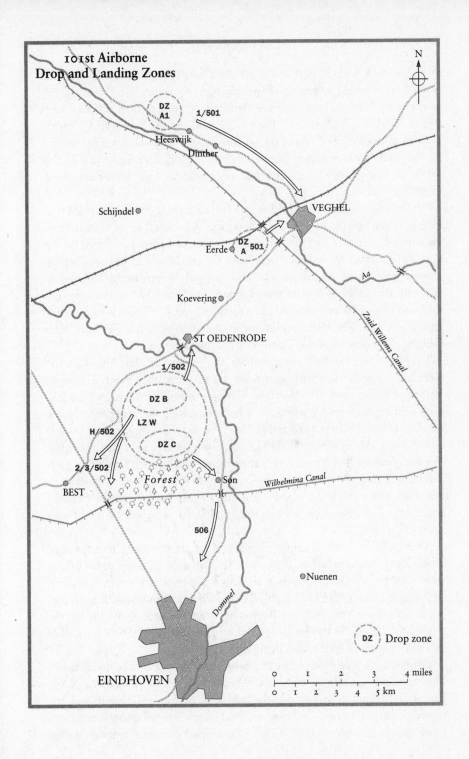

101st Airborne
Drop and Landing Zones

N

DZ
A1

1/501

Heeswijk

Dinther

Schijndel

VEGHEL

DZ
A   501

Eerde

Aa

Koevering

ST OEDENRODE

Zuid Willems Canal

1/502

DZ B

LZ W

H/502

DZ C

2/3/502

Forest

Son

Wilhelmina Canal

BEST

506

Nuenen

Dommel

DZ   Drop zone

0   1   2   3   4 miles

0   1   2   3   4   5 km

EINDHOVEN

assemble, Sink sent off part of the 1st Battalion towards the bridge at Son. It would have been too much to hope to achieve total surprise. 'Within sight of the first objective,' a lieutenant reported, 'three German officers were encountered in a Volkswagen. They were immediately "neutralized" with Tommy guns. We killed two of the officers and severely wounded the other.' As the 101st's commander, Major General Taylor, advanced towards the firing, his bodyguard claimed that his only comment was: 'You're supposed to go ahead of me.'

An unsuspecting German soldier on a bicycle rode right into the point platoon as it reached the edge of Son. Shouting '*Kamerad!*' as he tried to raise his arms in surrender, he fell off. A moment later, an 88mm positioned on the town's main street opened fire. Luckily for the 1st Battalion, the round struck a house, causing no casualties. The lead company immediately deployed to deal with the gun. Lacking infantry support, the 88mm had no flank protection, so a bazooka team managed to creep round and Pfc Thomas G. Lindsey knocked it out. The surviving gunners turned to run, but Sergeant Rice brought them down with his Thompson sub-machine gun.

Everything so far had gone well for the Americans, but although the German troops in Son had been taken by surprise, they reacted quickly, especially those from the *Hermann Göring* training battalion, which had been split up to defend key bridges. They dismantled the firing mechanism for the explosive charges and reinstalled it in the cellar of Konings Garage on the south side of the canal. As D Company advanced towards the bridge, German soldiers in a house across the canal opened up with machine guns and rifles. Other 88mm guns by the canal began firing at the rest of the battalion attacking from the woods. The tree bursts caused fearful wounds; altogether a dozen paratroopers were killed or crippled by the flying splinters.

The Germans ceased firing, allowing other paratroopers to approach. The silence was oppressive. Then there was a huge explosion as the bridge went up in their faces. Debris rained down everywhere on the soldiers, 'stunned by the surprise of the blast'. Major Dick Winters, of Easy Company 506th Parachute Infantry Regiment, threw himself to the side of the road as the chunks of concrete rained down. He thought, 'God damn, what an awful way to die in the war, being hit by a rock.'

Colonel Sink was dejected by the failure to seize the bridge undamaged. His regiment was supposed to be in Eindhoven ready to welcome XXX Corps. But he noted that at least the central pillar was intact, so it could be repaired. Major James L. LaPrade and two others jumped into the canal and swam across. (Winters claimed that they ripped off some wooden garage doors and threw them in the canal in an attempt to cross without getting their feet wet.) Others found boats and soon part of the battalion was across. In less than two hours airborne engineers had improvised a footbridge. The men from the 326th Airborne Engineer Battalion, who had carted off their glider pilot to be treated by the medics, arrived to build 'a float of barrels and timbers large enough to handle light traffic across the canal by a hand drawn cable'.

The engineers and paratroopers enjoyed every possible assistance from the town's population, as Lieutenant Colonel Hannah recorded. 'We received ovations, cheers, offers of food, smiles and an acceptance so wholehearted and unrestrained – so unlike our reception in Normandy – that it nearly brought tears to my eyes. The whole village turned out, and the young Dutch officer who jumped with me was overwhelmed with welcomes – it was undoubtedly the greatest day in his life.' Dr Schrijvers of the St Joseph Hospital helped deal with jaw and ankle fractures from the jump. He was fascinated to encounter penicillin for the first time, liberally supplied to the American medical services.

The 502nd Parachute Infantry Regiment, which dropped just north of Sink's regiment, faced the dreaded task of splitting its strength. The 1st Battalion set off north towards St Oedenrode. 'The march was terribly hot and the men were suffering greatly from too much clothing.' They came to an old bridge unmarked on their maps. Just beyond lay a church, and Germans concealed in the graveyard began firing mortars at them. The 1st Battalion's mortar platoon fired back with their 60mm mortars, but the Germans were too well protected among the tombstones. Eventually the firefight was won when some paratroopers sprinted across the bridge and forced the Germans to pull out. There was little resistance along the rest of the way. A number of Germans rose very cautiously from the ditches with their hands held high in surrender as the lead platoon approached. By dusk St Oedenrode was secured, and the battalion sent a patrol north-east up the road to link up with the 501st Regiment in Veghel.

A far more dangerous task awaited Company H, sent in the opposite direction to secure Best and the bridge beyond. General Taylor had recognized the risk of losing the bridge at Son, so he had decided to secure the crossing south-east of Best as a back-up. According to the intelligence available, the mission did not appear to require more than a company and a platoon of engineers. This small force, under Captain Robert Jones, set out from the drop zone following the edge of the forest between Son and Best. His overloaded men also suffered in the heat. Several of the replacements quietly dumped some of the machine-gun ammunition along the way.

The scouts ahead lost their bearings in the woods, so the company emerged out of the trees too close to the village of Best, rather than 500 metres further south from where they could charge the bridge. The company immediately came under small-arms fire. Lieutenant Wierzbowski's platoon deployed to outflank the German positions, but then came under accurate rifle fire from some other buildings. Wierzbowski recounted how Staff Sergeant White, his platoon sergeant who had predicted his own death the night before, 'stepped out from the cover of a corner of one of the buildings, as he was sighting his rifle toward a second storey window. The sniper hiding there beat him to it and caught him right between the eyes. As he was falling, my thoughts went back to his predictions of the night before.' White was their very first casualty.

Soon afterwards, H Company's position became even more precarious. 'Coming down the road was a motorized German column of twelve trucks with German infantry' and three half-tracks with 20mm light flak guns, the German equivalent of what the Americans called their 'meat-choppers'. The convoy was led by a lone German motorcycle escort. Captain Jones, seeing the opportunity for a good ambush, yelled the command to hold all fire. He hoped to riddle the column as it passed in front of them, but 'some of the headquarters men, not hearing the command, opened fire at the motorcyclist, his body seemed to halt in mid-air as the motor-cycle continued on'. The trucks braked hard and the troops inside jumped down to deploy into a skirmish line.

The failed ambush had drawn into the battle for Best the reinforcements that General Reinhard was sending to Son. Jones's company now faced nearly a thousand men, with six 88mm guns and the three half-tracks with 20mm flak. Hiding behind a hedgerow, Wierzbowski and his platoon attempted to outflank the new force, but Captain Jones called him back. The Americans were losing too many men mainly from tree bursts fired by the 88s, and Jones had just received an order from Lieutenant Colonel Robert Cole, their battalion commander, to reach the bridge whatever the cost. The company withdrew into the woods, from where they could make their way to the canal.

Wierzbowski's own command, which was given the task of taking the bridge, had been reduced to eighteen men in his platoon and twenty-six engineers. They made their way cautiously through the forest and plantations of young pine trees, crossing the firebreaks in small groups at a run. Rain began to fall, and dusk came early with the black clouds. Proceeding mainly at a crawl, with two scouts ahead, they reached the dyke of the canal bank unseen. Dreading a flare that might reveal them at any moment, they halted short of the bridge, which they could just see in silhouette against the night sky. Wierzbowski and one of the scouts slithered forward on their bellies for a closer look, but while they hid almost under the feet of the sentries, the paratroopers left behind became restless and started muttering. The German guards heard them and began throwing grenades, then a machine gun opened up.

Several of the paratroopers panicked in their exposed position on the canal side of the dyke, and ran away. Wierzbowski had to race back to lead the remainder back behind the dyke, where he ordered them to dig in on the reverse slope. By then he was down to a combined total of eighteen men. He tried to call Captain Jones on the radio to warn him of their position, but found a piece of shrapnel had wrecked the set. The search patrols which Captain Jones sent out failed to find them, even though firing continued intermittently into the night. Wierzbowski did not know whether to long for dawn or dread it.

The small town of Veghel was taken by Colonel Howard Johnson's 501st Parachute Infantry Regiment. The 1st Battalion commanded by a young Texan, Lieutenant Colonel Harry Kinnard, came from the north-west. The rest of the regiment arrived from their drop zone to the south, securing the bridge over the River Aa on the way. Kinnard, on hearing that the NSB mayor had fled (some sources insist that he was lynched), picked a prominent citizen, Cornelis de Visser, and said, 'You're mayor.' The local Catholic priest, a leading figure in the local underground, arrived to offer men as scouts or guards for prisoners. Yet Kinnard was worried that if the Dutch demonstrated their patriotism too openly and the Germans then retook the town, there would be terrible reprisals.

Soon after his arrival, Colonel Johnson was standing on the bridge, 'looking extremely martial, with leafy twigs in the camouflage net on his helmet', according to Cornelis de Visser. A car containing two German soldiers approached, and came to a sudden halt when the driver saw they were Americans. Johnson shouted '*Hände hoch! Raus!*' ('Hands up! Get out!'). The two men tried to escape down the slope of the raised road, but a Polish-American paratrooper shot them both with his service pistol. Johnson set up his command post in the house of Dr Kerssemakers in the centre of Veghel, and gave it the codename of Klondyke. The town was rapidly bedecked with orange bunting and the Dutch flag in horizontal stripes of red white and blue, and all the locals celebrated.

Padre Sampson, who had nearly collapsed the chute of a paratrooper below him as he jumped with Kinnard's battalion, landed in the wide moat

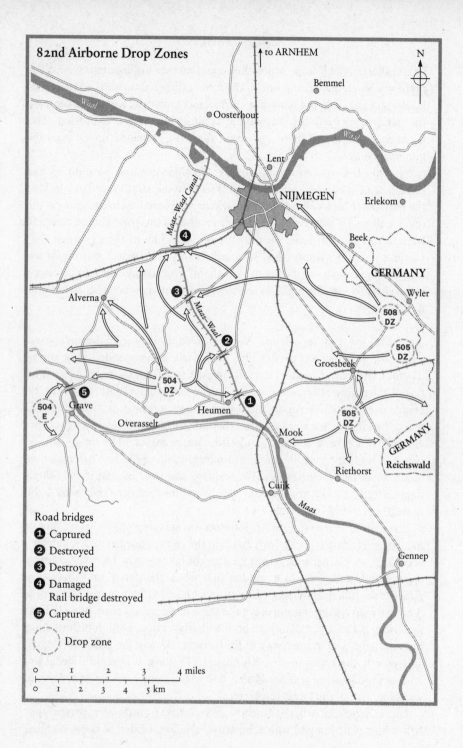

82nd Airborne Drop Zones

to ARNHEM

N

Waal

Bemmel

Oosterhout

Waal

Lent

NIJMEGEN

Erlekom

Maas-Waal Canal

4

Beek

GERMANY

Wyler

3

Alverna

Maas-Waal

**508
DZ**

2

**505
DZ**

Groesbeek

**504
DZ**

**505
DZ**

5

**504
E**

Grave

1

Heumen

Overasselt

Mook

GERMANY

Riethorst

Reichswald

Cuijk

Maas

Gennep

Road bridges

1 Captured

2 Destroyed

3 Destroyed

4 Damaged
Rail bridge destroyed

5 Captured

Drop zone

0   1   2   3   4 miles

0   1   2   3   4   5 km

of Kasteel Heeswijk. With the battalion doctor, Sampson decided to set up their aid station in this eleventh-century fortress. The padre then discovered that it had been made into a museum, with 'torture racks, implements for mutilation, scourges, iron masks', he wrote. 'Not the ideal place to inspire patients with confidence in an army doctor.' Once the casualties from the drop had been moved there, Sampson went off after Kinnard to see about moving them all into Veghel, but by the time he returned German troops had seized the castle and the aid post. All their injured were now prisoners.

The C-47 Dakotas bringing the 82nd Airborne encountered 'quite a bit of flak' on approaching the drop zone near Groesbeek. Five of the aircraft were hit. 'One was burning from the tip of one wing to the tip of the other. Men were baling out of the burning ship.' An air force officer recounted their experience. 'All of the 18 paratroopers jumped. Our radio operator baled out at 500 feet, and he got to the ground with a strained back. Our crew chief also baled out but he was killed by small arms fire or flak on the way down. The first pilot, 1st Lieutenant Robert S. Stoddard, stayed in the plane, and he was burned to death as it hit the ground. I baled out at 200 feet. I fractured my ankle. The Dutch dragged me and some of the wounded into their houses. Later they helped us get to a field hospital.'

Arie Bestebreurtje, the Dutch liaison officer with the 82nd Airborne, may have been thrilled to recognize the contours ahead round Groesbeek, but the pilot failed to gain height to compensate for the rising ground. As a result Brigadier General Jim Gavin 'had a helluva landing' from only about 400 feet. 'It seemed I hardly got out of the plane before I landed. I really bumped my ass like it had never been hit before.' In fact he cracked his spine in two places. 'I'm so excited, the Germans were in the woods nearby shooting at us. So I got my pistol out and laid it on the ground to grab it quick if I needed it while I was trying to get out of my harness, and I had my rifle.'

Gavin was famous among his men for always carrying his M-1 rifle like an ordinary trooper. Born in Brooklyn, he had joined the US Army as an orphan. His intelligence and military qualities were so evident that he was selected for West Point and rose rapidly to become the youngest general of his generation. His film-star good looks, intelligence and charm attracted Marlene Dietrich and Martha Gellhorn, and he had affairs with both of them.

Although in great pain, Gavin set off with an engineer officer and Bestebreurtje up a sunken track which led to a plantation of pine trees. A machine gun suddenly opened fire on them, but either the engineer officer or Bestebreurtje (depending on different sources) managed to hit the gunner in the forehead with a single shot. This small group of officers was soon joined by Gavin's divisional artillery commander. He had broken an ankle in the drop, so one of his men had to ferry him around in a wheelbarrow. This enabled him to report in person to Gavin: 'All guns ready to fire, on call.' Gavin had insisted on having this battalion of parachute artillery in the first wave, because he had never forgotten facing the Tiger tanks of the Panzer-Division *Hermann Göring* with just a bazooka.

Whatever the rules of warfare, American paratroopers did not take kindly to Germans who had just been trying to kill them. 'We got out of our 'chutes and headed for where we had seen the 20mm gun battery,' one of them recounted. 'Four Germans stood by their guns, hands held high, shouting "Kamerad!" Kamerad hell! They were cut to ribbons by tommy guns and rifle slugs.' This took place near the Hotel Berg en Dal, close to Beek and right on the border with Germany. Paratroopers from the 508th Parachute Infantry Regiment discovered a couple of German officers in bedrooms who had changed into civilian clothes.

Later that afternoon Bestebreurtje found one of the local Resistance leaders near the Hotel Berg en Dal, which was just three kilometres from the centre of Nijmegen, then set up his headquarters in the Hotel Sionshof on the Groesbeek road. From there he began telephoning into the city to discover German strength and positions. Gavin refused to set up his command post in the Hotel Berg en Dal. He preferred a tented camp in the woods a few hundred metres away.

General Browning had also selected the sector for his command post, and set up camp in the woods close to Gavin. After his glider had landed, Browning proudly produced a Pegasus pennant in silk to fly from the aerial on his Jeep. (The winged-horse symbol had been another suggestion from his wife Daphne du Maurier.) Soldiers in his headquarters then had to prepare the general's sleeping arrangements. This meant digging a deep, grave-like hole in the ground to take his camp-bed, with a tent erected over the top.

One company in the 508th had two planeloads of paratroopers who, instead of baling out over the Groesbeek heights, were dropped eight kilometres too far east and landed in Germany. 'We joke and laugh as we move out,' recorded Dwayne T. Burns. 'It's hard to believe that we are in German territory, miles from our own front lines. I keep waiting for something to happen.' Lieutenant Combs, who had been wounded by flak before jumping, managed 'with the aid of a Ukrainian deserter from the German army' to bring his twenty-two men back to rejoin their battalion. According to the official report, they killed some twenty Germans on the way and brought in forty-nine prisoners.

Close to the southern end of the Groesbeek landing zone was a company of convalescents from Ersatz-Bataillon 39. They had been sent from Cleve to round up stragglers retreating from France and Belgium. They were led by a young lieutenant who had never seen combat, so Hauptfeldwebel Jakob Moll, a veteran of the French campaign and the eastern front, assured the youth that he would take over command if they had to fight. The company was on patrol in the woods when the 82nd Airborne began to land. Reaching the edge of the trees they peered out and were amazed by the sight. 'The field was covered with gliders, and paratroopers were dashing about, getting equipment together and unloading cargo gliders.' The Germans were awed by the organization and the quantity of material, and they saw Dutch civilians arriving to help. The young lieutenant wanted to attack immediately, but Moll persuaded him that it would be suicide using ill-armed men. The company had some old machine guns, but no tripods. To fire them, they would have to rest the barrel on somebody's shoulder, which was a deafening experience for the man concerned. At Breedeweg, a hamlet just south of Groesbeek, the local priest recorded that German officers jumped into cars and drove off, while one young soldier was so 'frightened out of his wits' by the airborne landings that he shot himself.

In Groesbeek captured Germans, their hands held high, were marched to the school. Others were made to face the wall of the local shoe factory. The town's inhabitants cheered the Americans who were running along the road. 'They hardly noticed us,' a young woman recorded in her diary. 'Our liberators look strange and lugubrious with their blackened faces from camouflage cream, where the white of the eyes stood out. Their clothing looked more like an overall than a uniform, with pockets in the most unusual places.' As soon as they started to dig foxholes, 'smiling kids' turned up begging to be allowed to take over the small picks and shovels.

Members of the Dutch underground had immediately appeared on the streets to help. They were 'solidly built men in their blue overalls, which look like a primitive uniform, and they all carry guns', the same diarist noted. They rounded up members of the NSB, exciting the admiration of their fellow citizens. 'The people who have been terrorizing the village for the last couple of years are now lying on the verge of the road in a sad little troupe, with many passers-by making nasty remarks and insults, in which they can express their bottled-up hate and fear.' These prisoners would be held in the camp with a munitions dump in the Wolfsberg Forest, just to the west of Groesbeek.

A local recounted that one German soldier was not locked up with the others. 'One of the Americans had hurt his ankle on landing and had taken a German prisoner in full uniform who pulled him around the country lanes on a child's cart. He reclined like Madame Récamier, smoking a cigarette with a smirk on his face.' Further to the south in Mook, the villagers raised the Dutch flag over the school and danced around singing 'Cowboy Joe', the only American song they knew.

While the 508th and the 505th Parachute Infantry Regiments secured the Groesbeek heights facing the Reichswald, the 504th had the tricky task of capturing the large bridge over the River Maas at Grave and five bridges over the Maas–Waal Canal. Only the southernmost bridge of the five at Heumen was taken completely intact. Three were blown by the Germans and a fourth badly damaged.

The C-47s approached the drop zone for the Grave bridge at 600 feet. As a 20mm anti-aircraft gun began firing, Sergeant Johnson shook his fist and shouted: 'You dirty Krauts. You wait a minute and we'll be down there to get you.' Colonel Reuben Tucker, the redoubtable commander of the 504th, considered their drop a 'parade-ground jump'. Out of 1,936 men in his regiment, one of his soldiers was killed when his parachute failed to open, and forty-four men suffered injuries. One of them, Tucker's regimental adjutant, smashed through a tiled roof.

While two companies of the 2nd Battalion of the 504th jumped on the north side of the Maas near Grave, Easy Company dropped to the south. Part of the company had jumped too soon, but the platoon which was closest did not wait. It assembled on the road 'in very brief order'. As the men approached the huge bridge, wading along drainage ditches, they came under small-arms fire. Then, a machine gun opened up from a camouflaged flak tower. Two German trucks arrived and they engaged them too. Fortunately, the soldiers they contained did not have much stomach for the fight, and they soon slipped away. This allowed the platoon to storm a building some fifty metres from the bridge and then to knock out the crew of a light flak gun mounted on a pillbox. The 20mm gun itself was undamaged, and they turned it to take on the corresponding pillbox at the northern end. The bridge was theirs.

The rest of the battalion which had dropped on the north side of the Maas made contact. They began to prepare a night attack on the town of Grave. 'Just about this time, up the road from the south there came a tank. It pulled up within about 25 yards of our land mines and stopped. We had three bazooka teams covering the tank, but before they could open fire, somebody hollered: "Don't fire! Don't fire! It's British armor." (We had been told to expect the British within six to twenty-four hours). By the time this unknown person was through shouting "British armor", the [German] tank had opened up with a 75mm gun. After firing about six rounds into and around our positions, the tank pulled out. One officer was killed and about fifteen men wounded.' Their only consolation was that a German scout car and two motorcycles with sidecars blew themselves up on the mines they had laid.

As dusk began to fall, the tension in Nijmegen was unbearable. 'People were nervous and so were the Germans,' wrote Martijn Louis Deinum, the director of the great concert hall, in his diary. Firing could be heard in the distance. The Allies had landed somewhere outside, but nobody in the city really knew what was going on. The Germans, afraid of losing control, sent troops 'goose-stepping through the streets, guns at the ready'. Another diarist wrote that the sound of hobnailed jackboots marching rapidly in step was 'the most unpleasant sound imaginable at the moment'. The mixture of fear, anticipation and excitement meant that few would sleep that night.

A crowd stormed the warehouse of the Turmac plant, because that was where the Wehrmacht had stored all its looted alcohol. Doors were smashed in, and people emerged triumphant with crates or armfuls of bottles. Some people were appalled at the risks other civilians took, plundering a goods train in the station, while the Germans still had heavily armed troops near by. 'Men, women and children are lugging parcels, crates and barrels and it would seem that they do not even bother to inspect exactly what they have laid their hands on. I see a small girl carrying a pile of wooden shoes, a young woman with an armful of broom handles. And all of them are wildly excited, swearing at each other for good measure.'

Bestebreurtje was frustrated by Gavin's insistence on securing the Groesbeek heights before making a serious attempt to seize the bridge. 'We are not interested in the bridge at this moment,' the divisional commander told him, because he still expected 'a helluva [German] reaction from the Reichswald'. Gavin reluctantly allowed Bestebreurtje to go into the city to reconnoitre. He had, however, ordered Colonel Roy E. Lindquist of the 508th to send a battalion into Nijmegen on the off-chance of taking the bridge once the area north of Groesbeek had been secured. Gavin later admitted that he did not rate Lindquist nearly as highly as his other two regimental commanders because he lacked a 'killer instinct' and did not 'go for the jugular'. Gavin told Lindquist not to send his battalion through the town. They should skirt it to the east and approach the bridge from the flat land of the riverbank.

Yet Lindquist and the commander of his 1st Battalion, Lieutenant Colonel Shields Warren, ignored this instruction. Following the advice of a local member of the underground, the 1st Battalion advanced straight into Nijmegen up the main road from Groesbeek. Word of their presence spread instantly. Crowds assembled to cheer them, to shake hands, to admire their brown paratrooper boots, which were so quiet with their rubber soles. These soldiers were so relaxed, so unlike the Germans with their shouting and stamping. Assuming that the moment of liberation had come, with German troops withdrawn to the north of the town to defend the bridge, two youths climbed the façade of the infantry barracks to chip away at the great stone Nazi eagle until it came crashing down, and the crowd surged forward to smash up the larger fragments.

Firing broke out at around 22.00 hours, the director of the concert hall noted. 'We heard the first death-cry of a human being. Ghastly.' There were cries of 'Medic!' as paratroopers were hit, but the Dutch were quick to pull the wounded into their houses and care for them there. Chaotic fighting in the darkness followed, sometimes close combat with trench knives. Although one company pushed forward far enough to have a view of the bridge, the battalion as a whole never managed to advance further than the large traffic circle, the Keizer Karelplein, which German reinforcements had started to defend. Bestebreurtje and his fellow member of the Jedburgh Clarence team George Verhaeghe were shot at in their Jeep. Verhaeghe was badly wounded in the thigh, and Bestebreurtje less seriously in the hand and arm.

A great opportunity had been missed. The Nijmegen road bridge at the start of that evening had been defended by just nineteen SS troopers from the *Frundsberg*, a dozen from the *Hermann Göring* training battalion and a handful of reluctant Landsturm militia. Explosives were in place – 950 kilograms on the southern side, and the same on the northern end, but not wired up for demolition. Warren's battalion had clashed with German reinforcements which had literally just arrived.

For paratroopers dropped just a few hours before in a foreign country far behind enemy lines, that first night was disorientating. 'Just east of Groesbeek,' a lieutenant with the 505th recorded, 'we were around a hundred yards from a railroad track. As some of us sat talking, a railroad train manned by the enemy approached from our rear and passed through our position. We were taken so completely by surprise we just watched the train go by.' Brigadier General Gavin, trying to sleep under a tree, was instantly awake when he heard it, and demanded to know why it had not been stopped.

That night on 'tree row', the front line on the Groesbeek heights facing the Reichswald, a nervous sentry in the dark shot an inquisitive cow. On the landing grounds, some battalion personnel quite shamelessly stole supplies from the gliders belonging to other units. Out to the east of Nijmegen and also west of Utrecht, RAF Bomber Command dropped parachute puppets to confuse the enemy. General Eisenhower made a broadcast to the people of the Netherlands urging them not to rise en masse, but to use any covert action to dismantle the enemy's transport.

In northern Belgium at XXX Corps headquarters near Hechtel, Lieutenant Colonel Renfro, the 101st Airborne liaison officer, was uneasy. The battering which the Sherman tanks of the Irish Guards had received that afternoon meant that 'the quick "ride into the blue" which had been expected did not materialize'. His confidence was not helped by the pretence of Horrocks's chief of staff, Brigadier Pyman, that everything was going well.

Colonel Joe Vandeleur had halted the Irish Guards in Valkenswaard on the orders of Brigadier Norman Gwatkin, the commander of the 5th Guards Brigade, who joined him there. While they enjoyed a glass of champagne together from their captured supplies, Gwatkin told him 'to take [his] time getting to Eindhoven, that there was no hurry because the Son bridge had been blown, and [they] would have to wait for the bridging to be brought up'. This decision was clearly approved by Horrocks, who wrote later: 'In my opinion it was the act of an experienced commander to halt, rest his troops etc., while the bridge was being repaired.' But this makes no sense. Son was north of Eindhoven, and work could not start until the engineers accompanying the Guards Armoured Division arrived to construct a Bailey bridge. If Horrocks seriously imagined that the 101st Airborne's engineers were capable of constructing a bridge to take tanks, then he should have checked with Colonel Renfro. That Gwatkin, presumably with Horrocks's approval, could have told Vandeleur to take his time beggars belief.

12

Night and Day Arnhem
17–18 September

A Dutch diarist, whose house overlooked the approaches to the great Arnhem road bridge, guessed that the British must be close when a flare went up. A German sentry could be heard calling out in panic: '*Ich bin ganz allein!*' – 'I am all alone!'

The leading platoon of Frost's 2nd Battalion reached the Arnhem road bridge at about 20.00 hours, soon after night had fallen. Major Digby Tatham-Warter kept his men of A Company hidden under it, allowing German traffic to continue. He sent two platoons out to the sides to prepare some of the nearby houses for defence. Sergeants and corporals knocked respectfully on doors, explained what they had to do and recommended that the family sought shelter elsewhere to avoid the coming battle. Not surprisingly, most were very upset. Their spotless houses were rapidly transformed for fighting. Baths and basins were filled to ensure a supply of water, because the electricity was bound to go off again. Curtains, blinds and anything flammable were ripped down, furniture moved to make firing positions and windows smashed out to reduce casualties from flying glass. The battalion padre, Father Bernard Egan, who was helping these paratroopers, confessed to deriving 'somewhat of an unholy glee from pitching a chair through a window, knowing full well there were no police around to reprimand me'.

As darkness fell, Lieutenant Colonel Frost remembered the German army saying that 'Night is the friend of no man,' yet it certainly seemed to be helping his paratroopers. He caught up with the rest of A Company lying quietly on the embankment of the bridge, while Germans still passed back and forth. Frost probably arrived about an hour after most of Gräbner's reconnaissance battalion of the 9th SS *Hohenstaufen* stormed south over it towards Nijmegen on Bittrich's order. Yet Standartenführer Harzer, the *Hohenstaufen* divisional commander, had overlooked the second part of

Bittrich's instructions – to secure the bridge itself. Only a handful of men from the original guard detachment remained on the bridge.

Frost had been disappointed to find that the pontoon bridge they had passed a kilometre back had been dismantled. After the loss of the railway bridge in the explosion, it was now impossible to send men across to seize the south end of the road bridge except in boats, but groups sent off in search of them had no luck. Tatham-Warter had been waiting until they could rush both ends at the same time, but they could delay no longer. Lieutenant John Grayburn's platoon was chosen for the task. Grayburn, who won the Victoria Cross for this action, seems to have been determined to display conspicuous gallantry. He led his men up the steps on to the roadway. Sticking close to the massive steel girders on each side, his platoon charged against the fire of an armoured car and 20mm twin flak guns. Grayburn was hit in the shoulder and other men were wounded, so they had to withdraw.

During this first attempt to secure the bridge, more and more houses overlooking the ramp and the approaches were occupied. (See plan.) The Jeeps and the 6-pounder anti-tank guns were at first parked in a space concealed by houses west of the bridge. The headquarters and defence platoon of the 1st Parachute Brigade (minus Brigadier Lathbury who was still with General Urquhart and the 3rd Battalion on the far side of Oosterbeek) took over buildings on the west side of the ramp next to Frost's headquarters.

Major Freddie Gough of the reconnaissance squadron arrived with his headquarters in three Jeeps and reported to Frost just as a second attempt was made to seize the bridge. To deal with a pillbox on the side of the bridge, another platoon and an airborne engineer with a flamethrower got into position. But the operator's number two tapped him on the shoulder just as he was about to fire, and he jerked back in surprise. As a result the spurt of flame went over the top of the pillbox and hit a pair of wooden shacks just behind. They must have contained ammunition, fuel and dynamite because an almighty explosion and fireball followed. It looked as if they had set the whole bridge on fire, which produced some sarcastic comments about capturing the bridge and not destroying it. There was one advantage. Three trucks full of German troops approached over the bridge, and as their drivers tried to manoeuvre past the fires, Frost's paratroopers began shooting. Soon all three vehicles were blazing, as well as several of the unfortunate soldiers, who were cut down.

Remembering how the Germans had blown up the railway bridge in front of their noses, Frost was still concerned that the great road bridge could also be brought down, but a Royal Engineer officer assured him that the heat

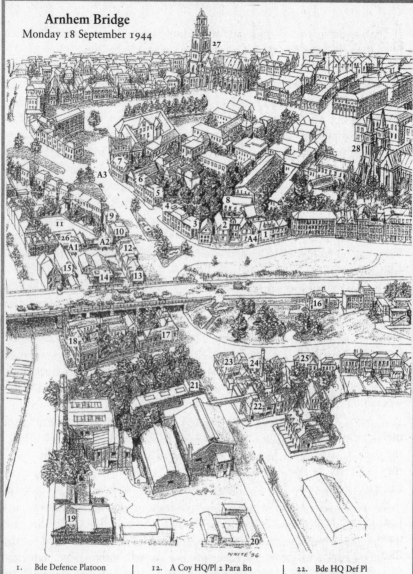

Arnhem Bridge
Monday 18 September 1944

1. Bde Defence Platoon
2. HQ 1 Para Bde
3. HQ 2 Para Bn
4. Mor Pl 2 Para Bn
5 & 6. HQ/Sp Coy 2 Para Bn
7. HQ 1 Atk Bty RA
8. RASC Pl
9 & 10. B Coy 2 Para Bn
11. Pl A Coy 2 Para Bn

12. A Coy HQ/Pl 2 Para Bn
13. Pl A Coy 2 Para Bn
14. 9 Fd Coy RE (18th only)
15. Pl A Coy/MMG 2 Para Bn
16. C Coy HQ/9 Pl 3 Para Bn
    A Tp 1 Para Sqn RE
17. Pl A Coy 2 Para Bn
18. A/B Coy 2 Para Bn
19, 20 & 21. 8 Pl C Coy 3 Para Bn

22. Bde HQ Def Pl
23. Sigs/RASC/Ord
24 & 25. Sigs/RE
26. 6 pdr Atk gun/Jeep park
27. St Eusebius Church
    (Grote Kerk)
28. St Walburgis

A1–A4. 6 pdr Atk guns

from the fires would have destroyed the wires leading to any explosive charges. Even so, Frost spent a restless night. The big attack would come in the morning, and despite the urgent efforts of the signallers, they were not yet in touch with divisional headquarters or the other battalions. The reasons for the 1st Airborne Division's disastrous communications have still not yet been fully explained, and perhaps never will be. They include a problem of terrain, with woods and buildings, insufficiently powerful sets, run-down batteries and, in the case of some sets, the wrong crystals being issued.

Assessing the perimeter they needed to hold around the northern end of the road bridge, Frost wished he still had C Company under Major Dover, but his signaller could not make radio contact to recall them. After the railway bridge had been blown up, C Company had set off for its secondary objective, the German headquarters in Nieuwe Plein. As it passed the St Elisabeth Hospital, Dover's company surprised thirty German soldiers climbing down from two buses. They killed most of them in a one-sided firefight and captured five. But as they proceeded they started to come up against soldiers and vehicles of what soon became the Kampfgruppe Brinkmann, based on the reconnaissance battalion of the SS *Frundsberg*. Even though C Company managed to knock out an armoured car with a PIAT anti-tank launcher, they were forced to pull back. They were eventually surrounded, yet managed to hold out for another sixteen hours until their ammunition was exhausted.

As if to balance the loss of Frost's C Company, an unexpected reinforcement arrived in the form of Major Lewis's C Company of the 3rd Battalion, the one which had made its way into Arnhem along the railway track. As they crept down towards the road bridge through the centre of the city, they had a chaotic and murderous encounter in the dark streets.

A unit of Reichsarbeitsdienst teenagers from a heavy flak detachment had been waiting in Arnhem station to return to Germany. Late that afternoon on learning of the airborne landings, their commander, Hauptmann Rudolph Mayer, had gone to the town commandant's office to find out what they should do. He returned to announce that they would be armed and that they would be coming under SS command. The boys were marched to a nearby barracks where they were issued with old carbines. The bolts did not work properly and the only way to open the chamber was to knock them against something hard. 'Their morale was not high, but it really hit the bottom when they saw these old guns,' one of their officers recorded. That evening they had still received no orders and no food. In fact they had not eaten for nearly forty-eight hours, because of the delay at the station.

As dusk fell, SS-Obersturmführer Harder appeared and announced that they were now part of Kampfgruppe Brinkmann from the 10th SS Panzer-Division *Frundsberg*. They would attack from the town centre towards the Rhine. In the pitch dark, they became aware of other soldiers who they assumed were also part of the same Kampfgruppe. Suddenly a British para-trooper yelled: 'Germans!' Everyone began firing in panic. The wild scene was illuminated for odd moments by flashes or explosions. At close quarters, British Sten guns killed more efficiently than the antiquated bolt-action rifles issued to the RAD teenagers. Almost half of Mayer's boys were killed and the rest must have been traumatized, yet Lewis's company also lost a platoon commander and a sergeant, and a third of his men were captured by SS panzergrenadiers.

The remnants of this 3rd Battalion company joined the engineer troop led by Captain Mackay in two buildings of the Van Limburg Stirum School on the east side of the bridge ramp. Not long afterwards, panzergrenadiers, either from the Kampfgruppe Brinkmann or the SS Battalion Euling, crept up and tossed grenades through the windows of the house furthest from the bridge.

'We fought hand to hand in the rooms,' Mackay wrote. 'One of them brought a Spandau [MG-42] and poked it right through the window spray-ing the room. I was standing there with my .45 and just pushed it in his mouth and pulled the trigger. It blew his head off, or all that was not held on by his chin strap. I grabbed the Spandau and turned it on the Germans out-side.' In other parts of the building there was fighting with fists, boots, rifle butts and bayonets before the Germans were dislodged. Mackay recognized that the smaller of the two buildings on the north side was far too vulner-able, with bushes in which German attackers could hide, so he decided to abandon the house. They pulled out their wounded, whom they had to haul over a two-metre wall with Mackay straddling it as each man was handed up to him.

Altogether Frost's force was probably more than 700 strong with all of the attached arms and services, ranging from the Royal Engineers to the Royal Army Ordnance Corps. In brigade headquarters, the signallers installed themselves in the roof, having removed a few tiles for their antennae. They spent the night trying to make contact with divisional headquarters and the other two battalions, sending messages that the 2nd Battalion was at the bridge and urgently needed reinforcements.

Major Dennis Munford of the Light Regiment Royal Artillery knew that without a working radio set he could not direct fire support from their pack howitzers taking position around Oosterbeek church. He and another officer therefore decided to drive back that night through German lines in Jeeps to Wolfheze. They retuned their No. 22 Sets there, collected more batteries, reported on the situation at the bridge and drove back once more through German lines. Only Munford's Jeep got through. The other officer received a serious stomach wound and was captured. At dawn, Munford would range in the 75mm howitzers on the enemy's likely avenues of approach both from the south end and around the northern perimeter. One of the inhabitants in a house very close to the church and the gun line recounted how a British gunner knocked politely at their door, urging them not to be frightened when the guns began firing. 'When you hear a boom and a whistle it is ours,' he explained. 'When you hear a whistle and bang it is one of theirs.'

Lieutenant Colonel Dobie with his 1st Battalion, having abandoned the attempt to follow the northern route into Arnhem, was determined to get to the bridge to support Frost after his radio operator had picked up one of the messages. They made their way south during that first night, until Dobie decided to take the Utrechtseweg in the middle as a shorter route. But when his lead company reached the railway embankment east of Oosterbeek they came up against Möller's 9th SS Pioneer Battalion. Möller himself wrote melodramatically, 'With the coming of the dawn, the dance began . . . It was a battle man against man – the "Red Devils" against the "Men in Black", elite against elite.' The 1st Battalion could not get through. Still missing one company after the clash with the Luftwaffe Alarmeinheit and now weakened by further casualties, the battalion zigzagged down to follow the southern road close to the river. Dobie's men were tired, having had very little rest.

Lieutenant Colonel Fitch's 3rd Battalion, which had halted for much of the night near the Hotel Hartenstein on the western side of Oosterbeek, set off again at 04.30 hours. Fitch also chose the southern route. Both Brigadier Lathbury and Major General Urquhart carried on forward with the lead company: an unwise surfeit of senior officers so close to the front. The battalion had to pass through a wooded area where German riflemen had climbed trees. These harassing attacks delayed the rear half of the two-kilometre-long column. An inhabitant of Oosterbeek was thrilled to see a British soldier kill a sniper, 'just like shooting a crow'.

Further delays occurred as they advanced cautiously at dawn through Oosterbeek. Locals would throw open their windows and call 'Good morning!' across the street. 'Good morning to you,' came the unenthusiastic reply to their presence being revealed. Soon families were pouring out into the street, some wearing a coat thrown over their pyjamas or night-dress, to offer tomatoes, pears and apples from their gardens and cups of coffee or tea.

These distractions, after the shooting, delayed the rear of the battalion, and they lost touch with the vanguard, which by then had passed under the railway bridge a kilometre east of Oosterbeek church. To confuse matters even more, Dobie's 1st Battalion also joined the southern road, mixing in with the rear part of the 3rd Battalion, which did not follow the route taken by the leading company with Lathbury and Urquhart. This vanguard had wasted precious time waiting for the other companies to catch up. On continuing the advance, they came up against the southern end of Spindler's second *Sperrlinie* around the St Elisabeth Hospital, some two kilometres short of the road bridge. By now Spindler's blocking force was being strengthened with self-propelled assault guns (often misleadingly described as tanks in British accounts). The 1st Battalion, meanwhile, soon found itself under fire from the high ground of Den Brink. The planners back in England had failed to see the danger on the map. The two roads from the west reached western Arnhem on the side of a hill between the railway line and the river. This provided an ideal choke point to slow or halt the British advance.

The Germans of course suffered from confusion too. Presumably as the result of a radio message from Gräbner's reconnaissance force charging south the previous evening, Model's Army Group B had reported at 20.00 hours 'Arnhem–Nijmegen road free of enemy. Arnhem Nijmegen bridges in German hands.' But not long afterwards two German women telephonists in the Arnhem exchange warned Bittrich that British paratroopers had secured the northern end of the road bridge, and they proceeded to pass information throughout the night. Bittrich awarded them both the Iron Cross after the battle. He went to Harzer's command post in the early morning in an angry mood, because Gräbner had ignored his 'order that the bridge be taken and firmly held'.*

Model also appeared at Harzer's command post set up in Generalmajor Kussin's headquarters in north Arnhem. There was low cloud that day, he observed, which should at least frustrate the Allied air forces. He told Harzer that the Heavy Panzer Battalion 503 with Mark VI Royal Tigers was

---

* The headquarters of the Wehrmacht commander-in-chief Netherlands was still so obsessed about an uprising of the Dutch underground that it stated in a signal on the morning of 18 September, 'Arnhem road bridge occupied by terrorists'.

being brought across Germany by *Blitztransport* from Königsbrück near Dresden. This meant that the Reichsbahn had to clear every line and every train, short of the Führer's personal *Sonderzug*, out of the way. Another fourteen Tiger Mark VI tanks from Heavy Panzer Battalion 506 at Paderborn were already on their way. Their crews had been wakened at 00.30 hours in their barracks at Sennelager, and by 08.00 hours every tank had been loaded on to railway flat-cars. Model also announced that he would have the water supplies cut off to Oosterbeek, as that was where the bulk of the British would be forced to withdraw. Although Model still refused Bittrich's requests to blow the bridge at Nijmegen, he sent a curt order by teleprinter later in the morning: 'Destruction of Rotterdam and Amsterdam harbours to proceed'. This was one of the first stages of German retaliation for the rail strike to help the Allies.

All through the night, Model's staff had been ordering in reinforcements towards Arnhem, using the town of Bocholt as railhead. The 280th Assault Gun Brigade, en route from Denmark to Aachen, was diverted to Arnhem. Other units included three battalions of around 600 men each; nine Alarmeinheiten of scratch units totalling 1,400 men; two panzerjäger companies of tank destroyers from Herford; six motorized Luftwaffe companies totalling 1,500 men; and a Flakkampfgruppe made up of ten batteries, with a total of thirty-six 88m guns and thirty-nine 20mm guns. They were 'temporarily motorized' which meant that civilian tractors and trucks were used to tow them. The 20mm light flak guns were sent forward to the landing zones to take on any more airborne lifts or drops.

As these units reached the Arnhem area, Bittrich distributed them between the two divisions. To Harzer he allocated a police battalion from Apeldoorn, a veteran reserve battalion from Hoogeveen and a flak brigade due to arrive a little later. These additions would bring Harzer's *Hohenstaufen* up to nearly 5,000 men. Harmel's *Frundsberg* would receive the company of Tiger Mark VI tanks from Paderborn, although because of breakdowns only three would arrive; an SS-Werferabteilung (a heavy mortar battalion); an engineer battalion with flamethrowers brought in from Glogau, and a panzergrenadier training and replacement battalion, arriving from Emmerich.

This last unit did not sound very promising. Many of its men had suffered amputations, while its commander Major Hans-Peter Knaust led his battalion on crutches. But Knaust, who had lost a leg in the battle for Moscow when with the 6th Panzer-Division, was a formidable leader. Without bothering to consult the local authorities, he ordered his men to seize the fuel reserves at the town of Bocholt to fill their tanks. Going ahead of his men in the only half-track his Kampfgruppe had been allowed, he reported to Bittrich's headquarters at 02.00 that morning. Bittrich's SS aide announced Knaust rather disparagingly as 'someone from the army'. Bittrich, who in any case enjoyed good relations with the regular army, was certainly pleased to see him. He needed every unit possible, and Knaust, with his four panzergrenadier companies, would also receive a platoon of assault guns and a company of seven Mark III and eight Mark IV tanks from a driver-training school in Bielefeld.

Model's plan was not just to block the rest of the 1st Airborne Division from reaching the Arnhem road bridge, it was to crush it between two forces. He had sent instructions during the night by teleprinter to General Christiansen, the Wehrmacht commander-in-chief Netherlands. His forces under General von Tettau were to attack the 'air-landed enemy from the west and north-west' and link up with II SS Panzer Corps on the northern side. Tettau had done little on 17 September, apart from telling Sturmbannführer Helle to take his SS Wachbataillon from Amersfoort concentration camp to Ede. Helle, no doubt regretting the abrupt farewell to his mistress, somehow imagined that the British were advancing west towards him, when they were pushing east to Arnhem. His guard battalion, which had been promised it would never have to fight, was starting to dwindle even before a shot was fired. A third of them deserted on the way, or soon after their first taste of combat.

A far more reliable unit was the SS Unteroffizier Schule commanded by Obersturmbannführer Hans Lippert. While Lippert waited at Grebbeberg for his own men to arrive, he was given a naval contingent – Schiffs-Stamm-Abteilung 10 – whose commander warned him that his men had no infantry training, and a so-called Fliegerhorst-Bataillon of Luftwaffe ground crew, whose military experience had been 'limited to rolling fuel drums'. Lippert's growing but very mixed force was designated the 'Westgruppe', supposedly the counterpart to the far more powerful 'Ostgruppe' based on the *Hohenstaufen* Division. Bittrich rashly predicted that 'with a counter-attack from both east and west, the enemy forces would be destroyed on 19 September.'

Aware that only a small proportion of the airborne division had reached the bridge, Bittrich ordered Harzer's *Hohenstaufen* to concentrate all available forces on building two blocking lines to ensure that no more British troops got through. Möller's pioneer battalion of the *Hohenstaufen* had already taken up position on the eastern edge of Oosterbeek along the railway line which ran south to Nijmegen. His was the force which had repulsed Dobie's 1st Battalion in the night. 'Around us frightened people in houses looked at us with hostile expressions,' he wrote. 'We dug in amid this jungle of gardens and villas like imitation chateaux, of hedges and fences and outhouses.' They were soon reinforced with the divisional flak detachment. Beyond them Möller had positioned another company, commanded by Obersturmbannführer Voss, in and around a large house on the corner of the Utrechtseweg partly concealed by thick rhododendron bushes.

So while Harzer's *Hohenstaufen* faced west to block the rest of the 1st Airborne, the bulk of Harmel's *Frundsberg* Division was ordered to destroy resistance at the bridge as soon as possible so that reinforcements could be sent south to ensure the defence of Nijmegen. The only alternative route was round to the east and then to ferry troops and vehicles across the Neder Rijn at Pannerden, two kilometres north of the River Waal.

The 1st Battalion of the 21st SS Panzergrenadier-Regiment was ordered to secure key buildings just to the north of the bridge. One company had a single half-track, which panzergrenadiers usually called a 'rolling coffin'. A British 6-pounder armour-piercing round went through one side and out the other, leaving little damage except for two round holes. Amazed at their luck, they pulled back rapidly. 'We all acted like heroes for each other's benefit,' a panzergrenadier called Horst Weber admitted, 'when actually inside we were quivering with fear.'

Their company was ordered to occupy the imposing courthouse – the Paleis van Justitie. Convinced that British paratroopers had occupied it, they wheeled up their anti-tank gun and simply blasted a side wall at pointblank range until they had a breach large enough to enter. A soldier from the panzer regiment in the company, who was known simply as 'Panzermann' because he still wore his black uniform, was the first through the hole. It was a large building with marble columns in the hall and many cellars, but no British. They set up their machine guns to cover the Walburgstraat and the market place.

Another member of his battalion 'saw some Dutch civilians during the fighting. They came out on the street to bandage the wounded. We used to try and avoid shooting them, although this was not always possible.'

At the northern end of the road bridge, Frost's force stood-to before dawn on that Monday morning. With spare magazines to hand and grenades ready primed, they waited to see what daylight would bring. 'A cold mist rising off the Rhine almost obscured the bridge,' wrote a member of the mortar platoon. His lieutenant decided to set up his observation post on the top of the warehouse facing the bridge where the battalion's Vickers machine guns were installed. 'Their ugly snouts were a little back from the windows in the shadows, but they still had a very fine field of fire.' While awaiting the inevitable German counter-attack, the machine-gun crews busied themselves on needless little tasks in the tense atmosphere. But when the mortar platoon commander checked the line they had just laid down to the field telephone in one of the mortar pits, he found that the handset they had brought with them did not work. He flung it against the wall with fearful swearing. They had to try another method, with a paratrooper taking down the range he estimated from the map, and then shouting it down from the back of the building to the mortar pits dug in on the grass islands either side of the main road.

Several German trucks, whose drivers seemed unaware of recent developments around the bridge, were shot to pieces with rapid fire from Bren guns, rifles and Stens. The soldiers on board who were not killed were taken prisoner. Several of them came from a V-2 rocket group, but naturally did not admit that to their captors. The PIAT teams and the crews of 6-pounder anti-tank guns held back. They knew better than to waste ammunition on soft-skinned vehicles. The American OSS officer Lieutenant Harvey Todd with the Jedburgh team was installed in the attic of brigade headquarters, as he recounted in his after-battle report. 'I had a good o[bservation] p[ost] and sniper position in the rafters of a building near a small window in the roof overlooking the road and the bridge. I killed three Germans here as they tried to cross the road.' 'One badly wounded German', noted a mortarman, 'pulled himself with his hands to within a couple of yards of safety and then was despatched by one of our own snipers who had been following his progress with detached interest.'

At 09.00, just out of sight on the southern part of the bridge a column of some twenty vehicles was forming up from Sturmbannführer Gräbner's reconnaissance battalion of the *Hohenstaufen*. Gräbner had briefly halted on the bridge just out of view. Round his neck, he wore the *Ritterkreuz*, which he had received the day before. Gräbner was known to despise half-measures. Evidently convinced that a sudden attack at full speed would do the trick, he raised his arm. All the drivers began revving their engines. Gräbner gave the signal, and all the vehicles accelerated forward. Puma armoured cars, the latest version of the eight-wheeler, led the way followed by open half-tracks, and finally Opel Blitz trucks with only sandbags as protection for the soldiers on board.

A signaller up in an attic shouted 'Armoured cars coming across the bridge!' Frost experienced an irrational surge of hope that this might be the vanguard of XXX Corps arriving ahead of time, but he was swiftly disabused. He and his men watched in fascination as the column had to slow down to weave its way through the burned-out trucks on the northern ramp. The paratroopers expected the leading vehicles to blow up on the necklace of anti-tank mines they had laid across the bridge, but the first four Pumas, firing their 50mm guns and machine guns, accelerated away past them into the town.

Determined to make up for their slow start, Frost's paratroopers finally reacted with every rifle, Bren and Sten gun available. The mortar platoon and the Vickers machine guns also opened up with devastating effect. The anti-tank gunners from the Light Regiment found their range, and the next seven vehicles were hit and set ablaze. Gräbner's men, having never experienced a battle in such a confined space, tried to escape, but vehicles crashed into each other. A half-track backed into the one behind and they became locked. The open half-tracks proved to be death-traps. Their ambushers were able to fire down and lob grenades into both the driver and panzer-grenadier compartments. One tried to escape down the side bank of the ramp and smashed into the school building. Another crashed through a barrier and fell to the riverside road which ran under the bridge.

Some of those trapped on the bridge jumped from the parapet into the Neder Rijn. Gräbner himself is said to have been killed when he climbed out of his captured Humber armoured car to try to sort out the chaos. The smell of roasted flesh permeated the air for hours afterwards, mixed with the stench of the oily-black smoke from the blazing vehicles. Gräbner's body was never identified among all the other carbonized corpses.

Lieutenant Todd up in the roof shouted down targets to the 6-pounder anti-tank crew below. 'Several German infantrymen tried to cross the bridge, but from my OP I couldn't miss,' he reported. 'Killed six as they tried to cross the roadblock along the bannister of the bridge. Then someone spotted me. A sniper's bullet came thru the window and glanced off my helmet, but glass and splinters from the window were in my eyes and face.' Todd was taken down to the aid station in the cellar. The paratrooper who took over his position in the roof was wearing his maroon beret instead of a helmet. A German sniper saw it and killed him.

Mackay's sappers in the school building had no anti-tank weapons, so they could do no more than fire their personal weapons and throw grenades down into the backs of half-tracks. At one point mortar shells began to fall on the school, but Mackay quickly realized that they were being fired at by one of their own teams. 'Cease fire, you stupid bastards!' he yelled. 'We're over here.' Major Lewis in the same building recorded that they could hear a badly wounded German soldier, who must have crawled from one of the burning half-tracks, calling for his mother. They could not see him, but the calls went on for most of the day and half the night until he fell silent. It was 'a ghostly feeling', Lewis recalled.

Once the furious firing had died down, a defiant 'Whoa Mahomet!' rang out. This was the 1st Parachute Brigade's war cry from North Africa. 'Soon it was reverberating all around that bridge,' Mackay recorded. It would follow almost every engagement from then on because it was also a good way of establishing which buildings the defenders still held. When the cheering ended, all that could be heard was a siren howling away. 'Will we be getting overtime for this, Sir?' called a platoon joker. 'The whistle's just gone.'

After only a short pause, the Germans launched another attack from the opposite direction, with infantry, several half-tracks and intense mortar fire. The PIAT teams and anti-tank gun crews accounted for another four armoured vehicles, but the desperate calls for stretcher-bearers indicated a heavy toll of British casualties too. When there were not enough stretchers, the wounded were carried on doors ripped from their hinges to the cellar under brigade headquarters. It began to fill rapidly. The two doctors, Captains Logan and Wright, and their orderlies were overwhelmed with work, but there was no hope of evacuating any wounded to 16 (Para) Field Ambulance in the St Elisabeth Hospital. The dead were stacked in a yard behind brigade headquarters.

Colonel Frost wondered how on earth they were going to feed their increasing bag of prisoners. One of them held in the cellars of the government building was identified as a Hauptsturmführer in the 9th Panzer-Division *Hohenstaufen*. Frost went down to ask him what SS panzer divisions were doing in Arnhem. 'I thought you were supposed to be finished after the Falaise Gap,' Frost said. The SS officer replied that they might have received a good beating there, but they had been refitting round Apeldoorn. 'We are the first instalment,' he told Frost confidently, 'and you can expect more.'

Although firing died away from time to time, any movement between houses could be dangerous, with German riflemen constantly waiting for targets. British paratroopers noted that German marksmanship was very bad in the initial engagements, perhaps because they were so tense.

The mortar platoon commander at the top of the building with the Vickers machine guns was able to work out the ranges easily from a map. He soon had his 3-inch mortars below in the weapon pits dropping their bombs on the German vehicles gathered at the south end of the bridge. Through his binoculars, he could watch several direct hits with fierce satisfaction at such a successful 'stonk'. But by the afternoon Knaust's Kampfgruppe, including the panzer company from Bielefeld, had assembled just to the east of the bridge ramp in a dairy on the Westervoortsedijk. Using that street and the one parallel running along the line, they attacked houses held by Digby Tatham-Warter's A Company. Although they seized two buildings and penetrated under the bridge, Knaust was clearly shaken on losing three out of his four company commanders in the savage battle.

What with the fighting at the bridge, several British groups besieged close to the centre and a major battle developing west of the St Elisabeth Hospital, the city of Arnhem had become even more of a battleground than many of its inhabitants realized. Those in the northern part of Arnhem had no idea of what was happening in the centre and towards the bridge. They assumed that the fighting that they could hear was south of the Neder Rijn. Those who went off to try to buy bread returned rapidly 'looking as white as death because of the shooting in the streets'. Many buildings including the two barracks, the Willemskazerne and the Saksen-Weimar-kazerne, as well as the big Wehrmacht depot, were still on fire.

Much of the town centre was also blazing. What sounded like heavy rain 'turned out to be the crackle of flames', one man wrote. The Germans, convinced that enemy spotters or snipers were in the huge tower of St Eusebius, known as the Grote Kerk, kept shooting at it. The company of the 21st Panzergrenadiers even began firing at the tower with their 75mm anti-tank gun. 'The noise it made in these narrow streets was deafening. The reverberations seemed to go on endlessly.' Several people saw 'the hands of the large clock on the church spin round crazily – as if time were racing by'.

From Den Brink round to the grim façade of the St Elisabeth Hospital and beyond, the Germans had the advantage of the high ground. The 1st and 3rd Parachute Battalions struggled in vain to depose them. To make matters worse, as they tried to attack north around the Y junction they were exposed to the fire of German flak batteries positioned on the south bank of the Neder Rijn. And ahead of them, a German Mark IV panzer, an assault gun or an armoured car would emerge to shell them, then pull back quickly as soon as they saw a 6-pounder anti-tank gun deployed.

A platoon commander in the 1st Battalion was at first encouraged by their progress. 'Advancing on high ground,' he jotted in his diary. 'Ordered to capture the hill in front with houses and a wool factory with high chimneys. Got to houses. Had a good shoot from a house still occupied by screaming Dutch. What a row! Little girl about ten years of age from another house hit, shot in thigh. My medics attended to her, but we had to hold the mother off as she went berserk. Huns running.' But then the attack flagged and the reinforced Germans came back. 'Hit by a sniper and then by a machine-gun.' Platoon commanders were suffering a terrible attrition rate. 'Under fire from across the river,' wrote another. 'Cut off. German grenade in the arm and in the eye. It was just like being stabbed with a red-hot needle. I was very frightened because I thought I was blind.'

There were many grisly sights. 'Smoke and fire darkened the streets. Broken glass and broken vehicles, and debris littered the road.' A paratrooper with the 1st Battalion described 'the smouldering body of a lieutenant' ahead of them. A tracer bullet had ignited the phosphorus bomb in one of his pouches and he had burned to death. A distraught father was seen pushing a handcart with the body of a child. 'A dead civilian in blue overalls lay in the gutter, the water [from a burst main] lapping gently around his body.' There were also bizarre moments in the middle of this battle. A Dutchman stepped out of his house and asked two British soldiers in English if they would like a cup of tea. A little further back along the route they had come, the bodies of British paratroopers lay 'everywhere, many of them behind trees or poles', Albert Horstman of the Arnhem underground recorded. He then saw 'a man, about middle-aged, who wore a hat. This man went to every dead soldier, lifted his hat, and stood in silence for a few seconds. There was something terribly Chaplinesque about the scene,' Horstman concluded.

The confused fighting meant that there were many stragglers from both the 1st and 3rd Para Battalions. Regimental Sergeant Major John C. Lord, an imposing moustachioed Grenadier recruited by Boy Browning (and known as 'Lord Jesus Christ' by the paratroopers), was trying to get a grip on the situation round the St Elisabeth Hospital when struck by a German bullet. 'It felt exactly like I had been hit in the arm by a hammer,' he recorded. The impact spun him round and he landed flat on his back. 'My arm was paralysed and bleeding badly, but strangely enough it did not hurt.' Lord was carried into the hospital, where he soon acquired a deep admiration for the professionalism and good humour of the nurses. None of them had opted to leave even while the battle raged round the hospital, and the building was hit by heavy flak shells from across the river.

One of the German nuns was spoon-feeding a ninety-year-old man when his head was literally severed by a shell, which must have passed within millimetres of the nun. Frozen in horrified disbelief, 'she sat there staring with the plate still in her hand.' Because of the heavy firing, Dutch doctors began transferring their civilian patients to the Diaconessenhuis, a clinic outside the battleground. To identify themselves they wore sheets and helmets painted white with a red cross. Sister van Dijk thought they looked like crusaders.

*

Soon after midday, a still optimistic Bittrich estimated that Frost's force at the bridge was only 'around 120 strong'. The British may have suffered a lot of casualties that morning, but the *Frundsberg* was not going to destroy them as quickly as he had hoped.

At the road bridge, Tony Hibbert, the brigade major, suggested that in Lathbury's absence Lieutenant Colonel Frost should become acting brigade commander, while his second-in-command should take over the battalion. They hoped that this would be a very temporary measure. One of Frost's radio operators picked up the net of XXX Corps. The signal sounded so strong that they assumed they could not be very far off. Frost and his officers imagined that the arrival of the Guards Armoured Division was only a matter of hours away.

13

Arnhem – The Second Lift
Monday 18 September

Divisional headquarters had spent the night by the landing ground beyond Wolfheze with little idea of what was happening. At dawn there was still no sign of General Urquhart nor any report about where he might be, so his chief of staff Colonel Mackenzie and his fellow officers decided to move towards Arnhem. They assumed that Urquhart had spent the night with the 1st Parachute Brigade headquarters. Mackenzie was not too concerned, but the lack of radio contact and information troubled him.

Mackenzie and the chief artillery officer, Lieutenant Colonel Robert Loder-Symonds, went in search of Brigadier Hicks, whom they found just after 06.00 hours in a house on the Utrechtseweg. They persuaded him to take over command of the division until Urquhart or Lathbury reappeared. Hicks also agreed to their recommendation that he should push another battalion through to reinforce Frost's 2nd Battalion at the bridge. They suggested sending the 2nd Battalion the South Staffordshire Regiment forward, even though it lacked two companies. The rest could follow on as soon as they landed by glider. A further reinforcement in the push to break through to the bridge could be the 11th Parachute Battalion from Hackett's 4th Parachute Brigade, which was due to drop at 10.00 hours. The 11th Battalion was chosen because its dropping zone was the closest to Arnhem. Well aware of Brigadier Hackett's 'volatile' temperament, Mackenzie knew that he would not take this well, nor the news that Hicks, to whom Hackett was senior, had taken command of the division.

Hicks himself did not welcome his temporary promotion. It was a bad moment because the officer in line to replace him at the head of 1st Airlanding Brigade had 'fallen to pieces – simply lost his nerve'. Another colonel had to be found from divisional headquarters. Hicks found the situation at divisional headquarters 'somewhat confusing' with missing commanders, bad communications and a lack of clarity about the situation. The only certainty was that the German reaction had been 'quick and fierce'. 'It was one of the worst few hours I have ever spent in my life,' Hicks admitted later.

The Staffords did not set off until 09.30 hours. There seems to have been no great sense of urgency because they followed the standard routine of fifty minutes' marching to ten minutes' rest. They lost several men from strafing Messerschmitts on their way through Oosterbeek, and later when they reached the railway embankment defended by Möller's pioneer battalion they suffered rather more casualties. Then, just like their predecessors, they had to switch to the lower road close to the Neder Rijn, and they also came under heavy German fire from Den Brink. They were not to make contact with the 1st and 3rd Parachute Battalions near the St Elisabeth Hospital until nearly 19.00 hours that evening.

Moving that morning with divisional headquarters towards Oosterbeek was the USAAF officer Lieutenant Bruce E. Davis of the 306th Fighter Control Squadron. His role was to task Allied aircraft in support of ground troops. 'About 10.30 we spotted some sixty planes flying quite high,' he reported later. 'Thinking they were Typhoons we tried to contact them by VHF to have them make a Reccy for us. We were a bit humiliated, or rather prostrated, when instead they suddenly dove and came in strafing, turning out to be Me 109s.'

The other two battalions still defending the landing and drop zones for the arrival of the second lift, the King's Own Scottish Borderers and the Border Regiment, were already under attack by dawn. Since they were spread over a large area and surrounded by woods, they found it almost impossible to defend the zones effectively.

A company of the Border Regiment at Renkum had to withdraw into a brickworks when surrounded by the Schiffs-Stamm-Abteilung 10. The commander, Fregattenkapitän Ferdinand Kaiser, complained that his men were armed with old Mauser rifles and a French Hotchkiss machine gun from the First World War. Their Kampfgruppe leader, Obersturmbannführer Lippert, came to see him during this engagement when a mortar shell exploded close to them. 'I flew into a bush hit in the thigh by a piece of shrapnel. An SS man who received a whole "splinter salad" in the face, screamed loudly that he couldn't see anything. Everyone else was unscathed.' Kaiser was evacuated to the German military hospital in Apeldoorn, where surgeons were operating for twenty-hour hours at a stretch. 'It was atrocious,' he recounted.

The Border company, heavily outnumbered, had to escape later having lost six Jeeps and both its anti-tank guns. To their north round Ginkel

Heath, a company of the Scottish Borderers was attacked at dawn by a company of Helle's SS Wachbataillon *Nordwest*. An isolated platoon, out of radio contact, was cut off and forced to surrender. As a result these Dutch SS were in position to fire directly at Hackett's 4th Parachute Brigade when it dropped later in the day. Another company of the Borderers fared better, knocking out a half-track with the first round from one of their 6-pounder anti-tank guns.

By mid-morning, even battalion headquarters staff were taking part in bayonet charges to push back German marauders. Adriaan Beekmeijer, a Dutch commando officer attached to their intelligence section, found himself in heavy fighting. One of Beekmeijer's tasks was to interrogate enemy captives. He 'was ashamed to discover that there were many Dutchmen'. He identified them as Helle's SS Wachbataillon from Amersfoort. One of the prisoners was a Hauptsturmführer Fernau, who had been a servant of the former Kaiser at Doorn.

Around 11.00 hours, both battalions survived strafing attacks from Jagdgeschwader 11 fighters, but tracer rounds started dangerous fires on the heathland where the paratroopers and gliders were to land. The Luftwaffe's belated entry into battle that morning had been accelerated by Hitler's fury at its unimpressive performance the day before.* Some 300 Messerschmitt Me 109s and Focke-Wulf 190s were allocated. Most of them, however, were held back, with pilots sitting strapped in their cockpits, waiting for a radio signal from the besieged garrison in Dunkirk to warn them of another airborne armada approaching.

The weather was clear but because there was no radio contact with Browning's headquarters, Brigadier Hicks had no idea that bad visibility in England had delayed their departure. (General Brereton had warned Eisenhower that 'weather in the United Kingdom is often different from weather on the Continent,' which was another reason why the airborne bases should have been moved to France.) 'The hours literally dragged by,' Hicks recorded. The wait was made even more intolerable by the lack of clear information on the situation at the bridge and the fighting round the St Elisabeth Hospital, but a clear account would have been hard to come by in

---

* The Luftwaffe chief of staff described another Hitlerian rant that morning. 'The Führer becomes violent with rage about the failure of the Luftwaffe, wants to know immediately how many and what fighter forces are committed for the defence of Holland. My telephone call to Luftwaffe Reich revealed that only minor forces were committed. The Führer used my report as an excuse for the severest reprimands: the entire Luftwaffe which is incompetent and cowardly, had deserted him.'

the confusion of the fighting. The hospital was taken by the Germans, who marched off most of 16th (Parachute) Field Ambulance as prisoners, leaving only the surgical teams in place. The British reoccupied it in the evening, but failed to hold it for long.

While the vanguard of the 3rd Parachute Battalion waited close to the St Elisabeth Hospital for its other companies to catch up, the flak guns across the river as well as mortar and small-arms fire from the high ground above forced them to take shelter. When pinned down in houses on the north side of the Utrechtseweg the only response to the self-propelled assault guns trundling down the road was to hurl a Gammon grenade from a window. Both Brigadier Lathbury and General Urquhart were also unable to move. They were in a house in the Alexanderstraat, which ran parallel to the Utrechtseweg right up to the side of the St Elisabeth Hospital.

Only at 15.00 hours did the rest of the battalion catch up, bringing a Bren-gun carrier full of much-needed ammunition. Major Peter Waddy was killed as he insisted on helping to unload it. The officer casualty rate was alarming and contributed greatly to the confusion later. Colonel Fitch, still determined to reach the bridge, decided that the only chance was to attack to the north and move along the railway line, but the intensity of German firepower forced back any attempt.

With reckless bravery, Lathbury and Urquhart appeared in the open hoping to find a way forward. A burst of machine-gun fire caught Lathbury in the thigh. Urquhart and two other officers dragged him to a small house where a courageous local couple took them in. A German appeared in the doorway a moment later. Urquhart managed to draw his service pistol rapidly and fired two rounds into him. They carried Lathbury down into the cellar of the house, then Urquhart and the two other officers slipped out of the back entrance. Their escape did not take them away from the Germans, in fact it had trapped them. The commander of the 1st Airborne Division, burning with impatience and frustration, would have to spend the second night of the battle hiding in an attic.

Even though 16 (Para) Field Ambulance was still operating in the St Elisabeth Hospital, the fighting all around made it almost impossible to evacuate any more wounded there. A solution had to be found further back in Oosterbeek. Hendrika van der Vlist, whose father owned the Hotel Schoonoord, described how a British doctor arrived in a Jeep. He asked straight out, 'Can you turn this hotel into a hospital within an hour?' She explained that it was in a terrible mess from the Germans using it as a billet. He told her to recruit people off the street if necessary. When they heard, neighbours hurried to help clean the place. An hour later patients began to be brought in on stretchers. Straw and mattresses were put down in the small salon, and rows of beds erected in the large salon.

The Hotel Schoonoord was 'a long low building of two storeys. Facing the Arnhem road, on either side of the main entrance were large glass-fronted rooms normally in use as dining room and bar-lounge.' The 181st (Airlanding) Field Ambulance from Hicks's brigade took over both the Schoonoord and the Hotel Tafelberg, which Model had abandoned the day before. The Tafelberg became the surgical annexe, with portable operating tables set up in offices. The Schoonoord was only 300 metres from divisional headquarters in the Hotel Hartenstein, but its prominent position beside the Utrechtseweg would render it very vulnerable later. Other young Dutch women helped in any way they could, even though some of the patients were so disfigured by their wounds that it was hard to look at them. They lit cigarettes for them, which was usually their first request, while the second was to take down a letter for their families as best they could in English. The letter-writers could not help crying when it became clear that the most gravely hit were dictating their farewell. Among the first casualties brought in were those from an improvised aid centre in a warehouse down by the river, which had been hit by a strike from a Nebelwerfer battery of multi-barrelled mortars on the southern bank.

While Urquhart remained absent from his division, SS-Brigadeführer Harmel had returned that morning from Berlin to the *Frundsberg* forward command post at Velp on the eastern edge of Arnhem. 'Thank God you're back!' was how he claims his acting chief of staff greeted him. Bittrich had been giving orders to the *Frundsberg* in Harmel's absence. Harmel rang Bittrich, then went to see Standartenführer Harzer at the *Hohenstaufen* command post in north Arnhem. Pulling rank over the more junior Harzer, who was briefing him on the situation, Harmel suddenly said, 'I'm ordered to go down to Nijmegen with my division. Do you have the bridge open yet? Get rid of these Tommies, Harzer.'

'Me?' Harzer claims to have replied. 'I'm seeing to it that the paratroopers don't get into Arnhem. I don't have time to take care of the bridge at the same time.' Harzer was clearly taken aback to find that Harmel still did not have a clear idea of their respective responsibilities and had to explain the situation clearly again.

Harmel was particularly angry at Gräbner's wild-goose chase with the *Hohenstaufen* reconnaissance battalion towards Nijmegen, because after it had been 'totally shot to pieces' on the bridge, Bittrich then told his division to hand over its reconnaissance battalion to the 9th *Hohenstaufen*. He found Gräbner's conduct 'utterly inexplicable' and now 'the burning half-tracks are distributed the whole length of the bridge and are blocking the width of the carriageway.' He went off in an armoured vehicle to have a look at the fighting for the north end of the bridge. 'I could see a dead soldier lying there whom we had not been able to remove because he was in the English line of fire. There were a lot of snipers. I decided that the only way to take care of them was by using heavy guns on the houses. There was artillery there and I ordered them to fire, starting right under the gables and shooting metre by metre until the house collapsed.'

German artillery at that moment in central Arnhem consisted of a single 150mm gun. Its crew started against the buildings on the west side of the wide Eusebiusbinnensingel, which led to the bridge. 'It was the best and the most effective artillery fire I have ever seen,' the young panzergrenadier Horst Weber recorded. 'They shot metre by metre starting from the top. Buildings would finally collapse like dolls' houses.' Frost started thinking of ways to mount a sudden raid to knock the gun out when a lucky shot from either a howitzer or a mortar killed the crew and rendered the gun unserviceable.

Another threat was the arrival of German 40mm flak guns south of the river. They proceeded to destroy the roofs of the building from where the Vickers machine guns controlled the bridge. It was not long before the building itself caught fire, and the machine-gun platoon had to escape to find new positions. Yet the 75mm howitzers of the Light Regiment were still being directed on to their targets by Major Munford, acting as a forward observation officer. He had been careful when ranging in to keep their fire on the approaches and away from the bridge itself, which they needed intact for XXX Corps.

After a long wait out by the landing and drop zones, aero engines could finally be heard just before 14.00 hours. A cry of relief went up, 'They're here!' The 127 C-47 Dakotas carrying Hackett's 4th Parachute Brigade were heading for Ginkel Heath, which the King's Own Scottish Borderers were struggling to defend. Another 261 gliders, having dropped their tow ropes, headed for the landing zones. They were bringing the rest of divisional headquarters and its personnel, together with vehicles, the rest of the Light Regiment Royal Artillery, part of the Polish anti-tank squadron and the remainder of the airlanding brigade, including the last companies of the South Staffords. They were followed by another thirty-one RAF Stirlings to drop supplies.

The greatly increased Luftwaffe presence kept the RAF's 259 Spitfires, Tempests, Mustangs and Mosquitoes busy, even though there were fewer flak batteries to knock out on the second day. The Eighth Air Force clashed with ninety Messerschmitt 109s, losing eighteen aircraft, while the RAF lost six. Airborne casualties in the crossing had been comparatively light, but the drop and the landing operation received 'a much warmer reception than we did on the preceding day', Lieutenant Davis noted. His American team was still trying to contact Allied aircraft on VHF, but without any success.

Having worked out where the follow-up drop zones would be, the Germans had redeployed all available flak guns. The paratroopers preparing to jump felt a sickening lurch every time a flak shell exploded near by. Captain Frank King in the 11th Parachute Battalion recounted how, as they approached in their C-47, he noticed that the American crew chief had fallen asleep, 'slumped back with his chin on his chest'. He moved over to shake him and found the man was dead. There was a hole in the fuselage behind him. King stood in the doorway and noticed that the other aircraft in their formation were gaining altitude while theirs was not. Then he saw that one of the engines was on fire. He turned and shouted to Company Sergeant Major Gatland at the other end of the stick. 'We're on fire! Check with the pilot.' As Gatland opened the door to the cockpit, a blast of flame came through, and he slammed it shut. King ordered the stick to jump immediately and led the way. They were in a shallow dive only some 200 feet up, which meant that their chutes hardly had time to open. Most of them suffered severe jarring as they hit the ground at speed. One man's chute did not open at all.

Major Blackwood, also with the 11th Battalion, kept a detailed diary. 'At 13.55 the pilot gave me the red light and I ordered action stations. I had a good but not comforting view from my position at the door. Flak was now dangerously close. We passed over a wood at some 1,500 feet and the whole edge of that wood erupted into flame. Holes appeared in the port wing but with no material effect. Two of our battalion planes were hit about now and went down in flames. Even though they flew into a barrage of fire, the pilots were flying magnificently in formation. I got my green light at 14.10 hrs. I gave my stick a final "Hi-de-hi!" and heard their yelp as I jumped.' But the jerk of the chute opening tore loose his weapon bundle and he lost his Sten gun, magazines, two 24-hour ration packs and toilet kit.* 'I watched it crash

---

* Each 24-hour ration pack contained meat cubes, concentrated oatmeal, boiled sweets, plain chocolate, cigarettes, benzedrine tablets and a powder of tea-leaves, sugar and dried milk ready-mixed for the addition of hot water.

to earth.' He then noticed that his parachute 'contained a modicum of bullet holes'. They were under fire from a German machine gun at the edge of the wood and mortar shells were falling. 'Men were coming down dead in the harness and others were hit before they could extricate themselves.' Blackwood sent his men into action as soon as they were on their feet to attack the Dutch SS. 'Young Morris gleefully brought in a sniper about twice his size,' he noted.

German fire also caused casualties on Landing Zone X, two kilometres west of Wolfheze. Several gliders were set ablaze, confirming their nickname of 'matchboxes'. The glider pilot padre, the Rev. G. A. Pare, seized a Red Cross flag and ran out into the open accompanied by stretcher-bearers. 'Five of the gliders were just ashes, bodies could be seen on the grass. The first man was dead. Another groaned in thankfulness. I moved to the next body. I waved my hand and the Jeep came out of the wood with the other bearers. The casualties had all been shot in the back as they tried to get to shelter. None of the gliders had been unloaded. The last man I came to was beside a dead body. I found to my astonishment that he was not wounded, but prostrate with grief at the death of his pal, and was unwilling to leave him. I spoke rather sharply to him and a bearer assisted him off.'

On the heath with its sandy tracks, Staff Sergeant Les Frater saw a burned-out Jeep, and next to it what looked like a charred sack of flour. He prodded it with his foot and then recoiled in horror when he saw it was a human torso. One glider had tipped on to its nose and the vehicle inside crushed the pilot and co-pilot, who were still alive but completely trapped. They could be given shots of morphine, but later it was said that since nothing could be done to release them, there was no alternative. 'Someone shot one or both of them to put them out of their misery.' Apparently, a major in the South Staffords was also found lying with his legs shredded in a glider crash and he too begged to be shot.

There were similar gruesome episodes on the drop zone. A platoon commander in the 156th Battalion had been hit by 20mm tracer bullets, and by the time his soldiers reached him, smoke was coming from his chest wounds. He was in such terrible pain that he begged them to shoot him, 'so we handed him his cocked pistol', one of them recounted, 'and he shot himself.' Thanks to that morning's fires on the heathland and German mortar fire, ammunition canisters were exploding just after they landed. At the battalion rendezvous point, Major John Waddy was told by his company sergeant major that one of his platoon commanders, Lieutenant John Davidson, had not arrived. It appeared that Davidson, who broke his leg very badly when landing on a patch of the heather which was ablaze, had shot himself before

the fire ignited the phosphorus grenades he was carrying. A number of paratroopers whose chutes had caught in the tops of trees on the far side of the
heath became helpless targets for Helle's Dutch SS.

The five Polish anti-tank gun crews who landed by glider were determined to get into action as soon as possible. They had not even been
distracted at the airfield near Salisbury when young WAAFs had smiled at
them when handing out rations. 'They are young and pretty,' a Polish paratrooper wrote in his diary. 'We are young too, but [our] only thoughts are
[focused on] the fact that we have had no report on the first contingent
landing.'

Pathfinders from the 21st Independent Parachute Company remained at
the landing grounds to help the new arrivals, and to kill Germans. A British
member of the company was struck by 'the hatred of one of our German
Jews as he emptied a whole Sten magazine into a German'. There were
reasons for harshness round Ginkel Heath. Sergeant Stanley Sullivan
'found three young boys between the ages of 12 and 14 all dead lying spread-
eagled on the ground wearing orange armbands', probably victims of the
SS guard battalion from Amersfoort in their own civil war.

A Dutch officer attached to Hackett's headquarters was angry to see British soldiers giving cigarettes to some Dutch SS – 'traitors all' – whom they
were guarding. A Polish liaison officer was equally irritated. When one
of the prisoners complained loudly about something, he strode over and
threatened him into instant silence.

The pathfinder commander, the middle-aged but extremely tough Major
Bob Wilson, described how his men heard Germans shouting from the
adjoining wood, calling on them to surrender. 'They shouted back that they
were too frightened and would they come and get them. Sixty Germans
came out and they were mowed down by two Brens firing from a distance of
about 150 yards. They died screaming.' A German loudspeaker van moved
up and started playing music. A voice announced that a panzer division was
advancing towards them, that their commanding general had been captured
and that they would be treated well if they surrendered. Somebody managed to silence it with a PIAT bomb.

There were lighter moments. Major John Waddy recounted how they
captured a soldier in German uniform just after landing. 'We were interrogating him in painful, schoolboy German, and after five minutes he asked in
perfect English "Do you speak English?" He was a Pole.'

Colonel Mackenzie, Urquhart's chief of staff, found Hackett on the landing
zone and told him straight out that Hicks had taken over. 'Look here,

Charles,' Hackett replied. 'I am senior to Hicks and should therefore assume command of the division.'

'I quite understand, sir,' Mackenzie replied. 'But the General did give me the order of succession and furthermore Brigadier Hicks has been here 24 hours and is much more familiar with the situation.' Urquhart's failure before leaving England to inform the brigadiers of his designated successor now proved an unnecessary distraction. He had given priority to Hicks because he had more experience handling infantry battalions on the ground than Hackett, the dashing young cavalryman.

Hackett was also unhappy that he had not been consulted in advance about the transfer of the 11th Battalion, but seemed to accept the arrangement. Mackenzie then went to the Hotel Hartenstein, and went upstairs to get some rest. Half an hour later he was told that he had better comes downstairs because 'the two brigadiers, Hicks and Hackett, were having a flaming row'. Mackenzie, prepared to support Hicks entirely, found that the storm was over. Hackett had vented his irritation, and accepted the new status quo.

The 11th Parachute Battalion did not set off quite as smartly as it might have done towards Arnhem along the Amsterdamseweg. Stuart Mawson the battalion doctor was called to tend to Major Richard Lonsdale, the second-in-command and a formidable warrior. But Lonsdale, who had been badly wounded in the hand while still in the aircraft, was more interested in looking at the map. Mawson warned him that he might lose the use of his hand if it were not treated properly, but Lonsdale told him to 'Stop flapping around like a wet hen' and showed no interest. 'To try to persuade him to regard his wound from a medical point of view', Mawson wrote, 'was as useless as passing a bottle of milk round the sergeants' mess.'

According to Major Blackwood, the 11th Battalion did not move off towards Arnhem until dusk, 'picking up *en route* our transport and anti-tank guns which had landed very successfully by glider. We had little opposition in this phase, bar snipers, and could appreciate the *Esquire* nude by Vargas, which some cheerful idiot had pinned to a tree with a couple of bayonets.' Other sources indicate an earlier departure at around 17.00 hours, but that was still nearly three hours after landing.

The rest of Hackett's brigade, the 156th and the 10th Battalions, were no quicker departing, partly due to the chaos of the landing ground on Renkum Heath where it was proving very difficult to extricate Jeeps from smashed gliders. Casualties needed to be treated and the field ambulance escorted eastwards. Mawson noted that his patients 'seemed more surprised about their wounds than hurt'. Hackett pointed out that he had lost 200

men, either in the air or on landing, which represented a tenth of his brigade strength, before the battle had even started. Yet Urquhart's absence
and the row between the two brigadiers was presumably also a factor in the
delay. The 10th Battalion soon followed the 156th along the railway tracks
towards Arnhem. The plan was to force their way forward between the railway line and the Amsterdamseweg to the north, seizing the high ground at
Koepel.

Things were no better ahead. The 1st and 3rd Parachute Battalions had suffered significant losses and were tied down just west of the St Elisabeth
Hospital. Those who had not been there, including the two brigadiers back
at the Hotel Hartenstein in Oosterbeek, had no idea what a choke point the
area offered for the Germans to trap troops trying to fight their way into
Arnhem.

On the far side of the Arnhem road bridge, German troops began searching houses in this southern extension of the town. They were clearly on
edge and this made them dangerous. 'Most of the German infantry were no
older than seventeen or eighteen, smoking heavily with great bravado,' one
of the inhabitants stated. 'Some looked nervously around. An older soldier
came walking up with about five of these "children", pale and upset. They
followed him like dogs. You could really see that these boys were totally
dependent on this older man. Five German soldiers and a Feldwebel came
into the garden of a neighbour and ordered me and four other men up
against a wall. They told us we would be shot as they had been fired on from
the direction of our houses. A neighbour of mine, who was rather German-
orientated, started talking to the Feldwebel. He raised two fingers and
claimed under oath that nobody had been shooting from our block. The
soldiers left and we were deeply relieved.'

Around the British perimeter at the north end of the bridge, the morale
of the young panzergrenadiers was high, even if they were still frightened
underneath. 'We were raring to fight,' Horst Weber recorded. The panzergrenadiers were helmeted, heavily armed with their MP-40 sub-machine
guns and grenades, and wearing their Waffen-SS camouflage smocks (similar to the British airborne ones, but 'more leopardy-looking', as an English
sergeant put it). They had been encouraged by the dejected expressions of
the locals as they marched in. 'A short while before the Dutch had greeted
the British like victors,' Weber said proudly. 'Now they scurried away as we
approached.' But in retrospect he had to confess: 'We were only little boys
playing at being soldiers. We were idiots. But we were absolutely convinced
that we would win.'

In the late afternoon, the 10th SS Reconnaissance Battalion, a far weaker force than Gräbner's, arrived to join the battle at the bridge. 'The fighting in this part of the city increased in severity every hour,' SS-Brigadeführer Harmel wrote. 'The enemy appeared to be excellently trained in street and house to house fighting and defended his rapidly established pockets of resistance with great determination.'

Nightfall brought only a temporary relief to the British defenders. Colonel Frost went round visiting the different houses. He told the men that they could expect XXX Corps to arrive the next day. Some considered it 'our most enjoyable battle', as they recounted to each other how many Germans they had killed that day. But there was little opportunity for rest. The Germans managed to set fire to the school on the east side of the ramp that night. Mackay's sappers and Lewis's men fought it with fire extinguishers, and even had to beat at the flames with their parachute smocks. It took them until the early hours to bring the blaze under control. For the rest of the night, the flickering light from other fires made sentries jumpy.

14

The American Divisions and XXX Corps Monday 18 September

Frost's assurance to his men that XXX Corps would be with them by Tuesday was sadly far off the mark. The Irish Guards group, convinced by Brigadier Gwatkin's mistaken notion that they need not hurry until the bridge at Son was rebuilt, moved out of Valkenswaard at what Joe Vandeleur himself described as a 'leisurely pace'.

The Germans, on the other hand, were still rushing in reinforcements. Generaloberst Kurt Student claimed credit for concentrating against the 101st Airborne on the Eindhoven sector. The first major formation to be brought in, Generalleutnant Walter Poppe's 59th Infanterie-Division, arrived by rail at Boxtel. This was just ten kilometres north-west of Best, where Lieutenant Wierzbowski's platoon was so dangerously isolated on the bank of the Wilhelmina Canal. The 59th was very far from a full-strength division. The advance guard had five battalions of fewer than 200 men each. Their horse-drawn artillery was following on behind by night marches to avoid Allied aircraft. The division's rearguard was still being brought across the Scheldt, and most of their ammunition had been left behind in the Breskens pocket south of the Scheldt estuary. The whole division had no more than a hundred rounds of 105mm ammunition. Montgomery's failure to secure the north side of the estuary had allowed the Germans to extricate almost all of the Fifteenth Army, for use against the left flank of Operation Market Garden.

During the night Captain Jones, the commander of Company H, had sent out several patrols to contact Wierzbowski but each one came up against heavy resistance. Lieutenant Colonel Cole, the commanding officer of the 3rd Battalion, was convinced that Wierzbowski's platoon and the engineers had all been wiped out. 'They've been annihilated without a doubt,' he told his executive officer.

The coming of dawn allowed Wierzbowski a glimpse of their surroundings.

They were very close to the concrete road bridge, and they could just see the railroad bridge some 300 metres beyond. Close to the road bridge was a German barracks, surrounded by trenches and gun pits. The moment any of Wierzbowski's men raised his head, a fusillade followed immediately. They spotted some Germans trying to steal up on them from some trees. Wierzbowski told his men to hold their fire until the last moment, and then they caused carnage.

At about 10.00 hours, a German officer arrived in a car. He issued some orders, then left. Soon afterwards, there was a massive explosion. The Germans had now blown the bridge at Best. The American paratroopers had to duck down in their foxholes as chunks of concrete rained down. With the radio out of action, Wierzbowski could not warn either Captain Jones or battalion headquarters. By then many of his men were wounded, and though they could be patched up by their medic, there was no prospect of evacuating them. To make matters worse, they were then strafed by their own P-47 Thunderbolts, whose pilots ignored the orange smoke grenade they set off to identify themselves. Yet in the course of the day Wierzbowski and his men managed to inflict far more casualties on the Germans than they had suffered themselves. His bazooka team even managed to knock out one of the 88mm guns along the canal.

In the afternoon, they heard vehicle engines and assumed they were German reinforcements. Instead, they were thrilled to see on the other side of the canal a British armoured car and a scout car from the Household Cavalry Regiment. This half-troop scared off the nearest Germans with machine-gun fire. Shouting across the canal, Wierzbowski asked them to contact the 101st Airborne by radio to warn them that the bridge had been destroyed, but the armoured car radio operator could not raise them. Instead, the corporal of horse in charge reported back to his own squadron, asking the message to be relayed to the Americans.

Unable to evacuate Wierzbowski's wounded, the Household Cavalry gave them all their medical supplies and spare ammunition, and these were ferried across in a dilapidated rowboat. Later, another platoon from Captain Jones's company appeared, and its commander Lieutenant Nick Mottola agreed to dig in on the left flank of Wierzbowski's position. The British reconnaissance troop, assuming that the embattled platoon was now safe, moved on. But Wierzbowski's experience of encircled combat was far from over. Fortunately, three of his men 'made a prowl', during which they captured a German officer and two medics. They were put to work looking after the wounded, but there was still no plasma for those who had lost a lot of blood.

*

The commander of the 502nd Parachute Infantry Regiment, Colonel John Michaelis, faced a major problem that day on his western flank round Best, which went well beyond the suspected destruction of Wierzbowski's platoon. Wierzbowski's battalion commander, Lieutenant Colonel Robert Cole, had won the Medal of Honor in the fighting for Carentan in Normandy against the 17th SS Panzergrenadier-Division and Oberstleutnant von der Heydte's 6th Fallschirmjäger-Regiment. Famous for his temper as well as his kindness and bravery, Cole was known as the 'cussing colonel of Carentan'.

Cole's battalion was tied down in the Sonsche Forest between Son and Best, so Michaelis sent the 2nd Battalion under Lieutenant Colonel Steve Chappuis to help extricate it. 'The Germans at this point had caught us in some open ground', one of Chappuis's company commanders wrote, 'and pulled a brilliant strategic move, practically pinning the two battalions down. The 2nd Battalion was in regimental reserve and we pulled out to attempt to out-flank the Germans.'

But Chappuis soon found that advancing across such open and flat countryside was hard going without tank or artillery support. The Dutch had been haymaking and 'the fields ahead were covered by these small piles of uncollected hay. That was the only cover,' his report stated. They attacked by dashing from heap to heap, which offered minimal protection. Tracer bullets set the hay on fire and many men were hit. 'The platoon leaders urged them on. Those who kept going usually managed to survive. Those who held back were killed.' Chappuis eventually had to call it off, at least for the time being, because they were losing too many men.

'In a day and a half fifty percent of our battalion were casualties,' the battalion doctor recorded with a certain exaggeration. The true figure was closer to half that. 'I had to put wounded men in zigzag trenches, and give them plasma. The fighting was very nasty.' He claimed that the Germans shot down a medic trying to carry a wounded man, and when they tried to evacuate patients by Jeep with four litters, they fired at that too, even though 'the Red Cross was plainly marked on that Jeep.'

Cole's force in the woods meanwhile was under heavy artillery fire, and Germans were starting to infiltrate their positions, despite the risk of being hit by their own guns. Cole needed air support, but 'a shell had just hit his radio operator in the head and blown his brains out. Cole went to the radio and wiped the blood and brains from it. It was still working.' A strike of P-47 Thunderbolts was called in. Cole decided to check the recognition panels put out at the edge of the wood to identify their own position. He stepped out from the trees, put a hand up to shield his eyes as he searched the sky and a single shot rang out from a house some 200 metres away. The bullet, hitting him in the temple, went right through his head. A German was seen soon afterwards, running from a corner of the house. He was gunned down and Cole's men convinced themselves that they had at least got his killer. His men placed his body in a foxhole and covered it with an equipment chute.

Chappuis's men had been forced to dig in where they were. 'We were in a slit trench in an open field and I was on the machine-gun when the Germans started attacking across the field. One fellow lost all his nerve and started to bang his head on the side of the trench and cry like a baby.' The casualties mounted again. The battalion doctor established his aid station in a depression in the ground. 'When we had a patient needing plasma we put him in the lowest part of the depression, because you could stand up there [holding the plasma bag] without being in the line of machine-gun bullets that whipped through the trees from north and west.' After such a battering all the two battalions could hope to do was hold on until the next morning and pray for relief.

The detached 1st Battalion of the 502nd at St Oedenrode suspected that German forces were gathering to their west round Schijndel, ready to attack. So Lieutenant Colonel Cassidy was furious that morning when seven Jeeps charged through St Oedenrode, moving 'like bats out of hell'. They were heading for Schijndel, and had not bothered to stop to enquire about the situation.

The Germans were even closer than Cassidy imagined. The column of Jeeps ran straight into an ambush just a couple of kilometres along the road. Only the last Jeep of this party of war tourists managed to turn round in time and escape. It contained Colonel Cartwright of the First Allied Airborne Army, who ran back to tell Cassidy to send men immediately. They had to save the occupants of the other Jeeps, who had thrown themselves into ditches beside the road and were tied down by machine-gun fire. Cassidy was outraged that their 'pure bull-headedness' meant that he would have to sacrifice some of his men to get them out. 'Why in hell did you go up that road?' he demanded. Cartwright replied that a guide had thought it was safe.

Fortunately one of Cassidy's platoons, commanded by Lieutenant Mewborn, had sighted the Jeeps, two of which were blazing. They eventually managed to fight off the Germans in the ambush, and even drove two of the Jeeps back. General Taylor, on a tour of inspection from Son with his Communist bodyguard from Princeton, had meanwhile reached St Oedenrode.

When he heard what had happened, he told Cassidy, 'Don't send another man out on such a mission. Your assignment is to hold the town.'

Completely unaware of the desperate battle the 502nd was fighting round Best, Colonel Sink had left only a platoon and an engineer detail in Son, as the 506th marched fast due south to Eindhoven. Most of his regiment had crossed by the improvised footbridge, and several Jeeps had been brought across by the raft made with oil drums. The 3rd Battalion in the lead came up against artillery, mortar and rifle fire at Woensel on the northern edge of Eindhoven. Captain John W. Kiley was killed by a sniper in a church tower. 'A bazooka rocket then hit the tower and silenced the sniper.'

A Dutch policeman who insisted on accompanying the 3rd Battalion saw that people were cowering in the houses along the Woenselsestraat. To the dismay of the paratroopers, he began shouting: 'These men are not Germans, but Americans – Liberators!' The last thing the advancing paratroopers wanted was people hurrying out of their houses to welcome them and shake their hands and kiss them, especially when they were involved in sporadic clashes with retreating Germans. The streets cleared only when a German 88mm gun in the Kloosterdreef began firing.

At 12.15 hours, a troop of the Household Cavalry Regiment, which had circumvented Aalst and Eindhoven, met up with Colonel Sink in Woensel. To pass back the news that they had met up with the Screaming Eagles, the patrol commander reported by radio, using his own regiment's nickname in the Guards Armoured Division: 'Stable boys have contacted feathered friends.'* Part of this troop then carried on along the southern bank of the Wilhelmina Canal towards Best and they were the ones who helped Wierz-bowski's platoon. Soon afterwards, thanks to the Dutch telephone service through German lines, an American major at Son provided all the bridge's dimensions for the Royal Engineers.

Colonel Sink then ordered his second battalion round to the east towards the city centre to seize the bridges, but diverted one company to deal with the 88mm gun which was causing trouble. There turned out to be two. The company of paratroopers were guided by a local man who knew exactly where the guns were positioned. Just as the Americans were about to attack the first gun from two sides, Sergeant Taylor saw a woman gesturing to him urgently from a first-floor window. She signalled that three Germans were

---

* British officers believed that their veiled speech, mostly using nicknames, cricketing metaphors and schoolboy slang, was impenetrable to German listening stations. All too often this was not the case.

coming. Taylor, deeply relieved that they had not charged out at that moment, pulled back until they had gone past, and then took them prisoner from behind. A squad with rifle grenades led by Lieutenant Hall stalked the battery. They had no clear line of sight, but one of the rifle grenades struck home. Then a 6omm mortar, brought up without its baseplate, and just held steady between a paratrooper's legs, knocked out the second gun.

Even before the wounded gun crews had been captured in a house just behind the battery, people were dancing in the Woenselse market place. One inhabitant described how 'the crowd goes crazy and "the boys" who are tired and sweaty can hardly get through. They have to shake everyone's hand.' One of Sink's officers wrote: 'Dutch civilians crowded round the troops, offering them apples, bottles of jam and an occasional nip of gin. The reception was terrific. The air seemed to reek with hatred for the Germans.'

There were more 'running fire-fights' as American paratroopers continued to clear the town, which made celebrating civilians dive for cover. Members of the PAN (Partisanen Actie Nederland) rapidly emerged, ready to help. People were amazed by their sudden appearance. 'Everywhere you look you see men in blue overalls with armbands saying "PAN". They carry a gun over their shoulders and charge around on motorcycles and in cars with flags.' Any remaining German soldiers and NSB men were flushed out of houses and made to lie face down in the street. Soldiers from the Dutch army forced to surrender in 1940 reappeared in their old uniforms, ready to guard prisoners. 'After four years, four months and six days, we are liberated,' an inhabitant wrote thankfully. The fact that they had woken that morning to find there was no gas or electricity seemed petty in comparison.

Colonel Sink had been deeply concerned that they might not have the city cleared in time for the Guards Armoured Division. Then at 13.00 hours, just before General Taylor arrived, he heard from Lieutenant Colonel Robert L. Strayer of the 2nd Battalion that they had secured all four bridges over the Dommel and checked them for demolition charges. Taylor climbed a church steeple to get a better view of the city. He spoke to Colonel Strayer by radio. 'Where did you say you are?' the divisional commander asked. Back came the triumphant reply, 'I'm sitting on all the bridges, General.' Strayer's men had also captured the police station.

'The flags are out everywhere,' a diarist recorded. 'A jubilant crowd, with Orange scarves, paper hats etc. are dancing in the road.' Young men tore down the Wehrmacht signposts and levered off street-names which had been changed by the occupiers. It was not long before a huge portrait of Princess Juliana hung outside the Hotel Royal, and photographs of the Dutch royal family appeared in windows.

There were still odd nervous moments. Two paratroopers, who were enjoying the attention of several girls while they kept a sharp lookout on the Augustijnerdreef, jerked into action on sighting a black-uniformed figure approaching on a bicycle. Dr J. P. Boyans, who was present, saw them raise their sub-machine guns and cried, 'Don't shoot! Don't shoot! That's a Dutch policeman.' The paratroopers looked surprised for a moment. 'Okay,' one of them said. 'I thought it was an SS.' Boyans asked him what would have happened if he had not warned him. 'Oh, nothing much. Just a little hole between the eyes.' He grinned. 'I'm a very good shot.'

After the long occupation, revenge was in the air. Major Dick Winters suddenly heard booing. He turned and saw a prostitute approaching them in a very suggestive way. 'And the people grabbed her,' he recounted, 'and the last we saw her, she was, I guess, heading for a haircut.' Inhabitants of the city were amused to hear that earlier in the day the NSB burgemeester had become terrified that he might be lynched. 'He and his wife went to ask for shelter at the Marechaussee-kazerne [gendarmerie barracks]; [but] on the way his bicycle was seized by a fleeing German soldier.'

'At 3 o'clock,' another diarist recorded, 'with screaming and shouting from the crowds, a whole group of NSB are collected and locked up in the school near the Jewish cemetery.' More and more young men begged officers of the 101st to give them the weapons and uniforms of the dead and wounded so that they could continue the fight. The Americans were much less bureaucratic than the British in this way, and even though it was strictly against regulations, a number of civilians joined their ranks. A few even served with them right up to the end of the war.

At 15.30 on that eventful afternoon, the second lift came in on the landing zone north-east of Son. The poet Louis Simpson, serving in the 327th Glider Infantry Regiment, described their arrival. 'When we are over the landing area, the glider pilot pulls the lever that releases the cable. For the first time, the kite has a character of its own. It soars like a bird. Then it travels on the air currents in silence. All that we hear is the creaking of struts. Then it slams down tilting on one wing. Your life is in the hands of the pilots.' There was a palpable sense of relief as the glider bumped along the field then ground to a stop.

'The land is flat and everywhere gliders are strewn, pointing in every direction,' he wrote. Companies marched off hurriedly in open formation. 'On the horizon, a windmill, like a Dutch painting. Somewhere guns are rumbling. The sun is warm; under your woollen shirt you begin to sweat. At dusk we entered a village. At the entrance a German tank had been blown apart. On it and under it were the blackened forms of the crew; they appeared vulcanized, melted; through the crust of black gleamed streaks of ruby-red flesh.'

Simpson was intrigued by the mentality of the German soldier. 'I skirted a pit shaped like a grave. At the end of the pit stood a cross from which hung an American helmet with a bullet hole through it. On the cross was written in Gothic lettering, "Welcome 101st Airborne Division". Krauts are strange. Imagine, in the press of battle thinking up a trick like that and putting it into execution!'

Out of the 450 gliders which had taken off, towed by C-47 Dakotas, 428 reached the 101st landing zone. They did not just deliver the 327th Glider Infantry, but also two parachute field artillery battalions, an engineer battalion, and even a surgical team bringing in an X-ray machine. The 327th reported that 'in some places German soldiers could be seen lined up in columns firing at the gliders. Generally their aim was poor as they did not give enough lead, but a number of light streaks began to filter thru the rear of Colonel Harper's craft.' Colonel Joseph H. Harper, their regimental commander, did not intend to take enemy fire sitting down, so he and his Jeep driver fired back with their personal weapons from the glider.

Brigadier General Anthony McAuliffe, Taylor's deputy commander and the chief artilleryman of the 101st Airborne, came in with the 377th Parachute Field Artillery Battalion. He also had a young Walter Cronkite of United Press in his glider. 'Our helmets came flying off on impact,' Cronkite wrote later with a touch of journalistic licence, 'and were worse than the incoming shells. I grabbed a helmet, the trusty musette bag with the [typewriter] inside, and began crawling toward the canal which was the rendezvous point. When I looked back I had half a dozen guys crawling after me. Seems I was wearing the lieutenant's helmet, with that neat stripe down the back.'

Soon after all the gliders were on the ground, B-24 Liberators flew over the landing zone dropping supplies. The 327th Glider Infantry regretted letting their guard down that night. 'Seventy-five percent of all supplies lashed in gliders were removed by other troops and Dutch civilians,' they reported. From then on they had armed sentries in Jeeps patrolling to prevent further thefts.

The 101st Airborne realized that they had been very fortunate. The German garrison defending Eindhoven had consisted of little more than a hundred men. Brigadier General Jim Gavin, on the other hand, knew that the Germans would reinforce Nijmegen as rapidly as they could. They had also been concentrating their troops in the centre and north of the city.

Following the landings on Sunday and the initial probes of Lieutenant Colonel Warren's battalion into the city from the south, the Germans had blown up their ammunition dumps in a series of massive explosions in the early hours, waking the city's population.

According to Harmel of the 10th SS *Frundsberg*, who was now responsible for the defence of Nijmegen, the garrison at the time of the airborne landings consisted of 'Germany's worst soldiers' and had been less than 750 strong. Apart from the arrogant 1st Fallschirmjäger Training Regiment under Oberst Friedrich Henke which arrived soon afterwards, the city had been defended with 'railway security guards, a few local militia, members of a police band, a few scattered SS men, and other units'. Many of them were armed with rifles from the First World War and even, Harmel claimed, from the Franco-Prussian War of 1870. They had been issued five-round clips which they simply stuffed in their pockets as they had no ammunition pouches. Their only anti-tank weapons were the surviving flak guns from the road bridge.

To prevent the British XXX Corps from joining up with the 1st Airborne at Arnhem, Obergruppenführer Bittrich wanted to blow both the railway bridge and the great road bridge at Nijmegen. But for that task to be accomplished, they had to be properly defended first. He had therefore issued his orders to Harmel just after midnight during the first hour of 18 September. '10th SS Panzer-Division will go south-eastwards from Arnhem to cross the Lower Rhine by ferry and hold a bridgehead on the south bank of the Waal. The bridges are to be prepared for demolition.'

The obvious way to prevent the Allied link-up was to blow the bridge at Nijmegen, but Generalfeldmarschall Model again overruled Bittrich later that morning. 'We still need the bridges,' he insisted. 'We need them to counter-attack.' Bittrich was unconvinced, certain that they lacked sufficient forces for an effective counter-attack. Frustrated and annoyed, he doubted that Model had a special plan, but at least he, Bittrich, was in the clear now that he had formally made the request.

A company of Harmel's 10th SS Pioneer Battalion had left on requisitioned bicycles in the early hours for Pannerden, on the Neder Rijn just north of where it split from the Waal. One advantage of bicycle transport was the ability to dismount rapidly and throw yourself in a ditch in the event of enemy fighters. These troops were followed by advanced elements of what was to be the Kampfgruppe Reinhold. Reinhold, the commander of the *Frundsberg* panzer regiment, brought his dismounted tank crews, the Euling panzergrenadier battalion, only 200 strong, and a battery of guns. SS-Hauptsturmführer Karl-Heinz Euling who commanded the 2nd Battalion of the 21st SS Panzergrenadier-Regiment was, according to Harmel, 'a fantastic fellow and a good soldier'.

Despite the delays of ferrying panzergrenadiers across the Neder Rijn in rubber dinghies tied together, Euling's battalion reached the road bridge by midday. Reinhold wasted no time in taking command of the defence of the city and preparing his forces to repel any Allied attack 'with great vigour'. Ferrying field guns and half-tracks, however, was to prove intensely frustrating. Because of Allied airpower, they could only cross at night and they could not use lights, so the commanders, walking backwards, had to signal to their drivers, waving a white handkerchief in the dark to pull left or right as they manoeuvred them on to the ferry.

As soon as Reinhold arrived, he ordered that all forces should be concentrated in the north of the city round the approaches to the two bridges. The ancient fortress of the Valkhof, which dated back to Charlemagne, would become the core of their defence. He also brought into the defended perimeter the youths of the Reichsarbeitsdienst. Reinhold had a special task for them as he intended to defend Nijmegen bridge by fire.

General Browning had emphasized to Gavin that the main threat would come from tanks in the Reichswald. Although this turned out not to be true, almost every unit imaginable in north-west Germany was being mobilized to counter-attack the 82nd Airborne on its eastern flank. An optimistically named Corps Feldt, under General der Kavallerie Kurt Feldt, based north of Krefeld had already been gathering. It included the 406th Division under Generalleutnant Gerd Scherbening, which Feldt described as entirely a 'makeshift formation'. It included a non-commissioned officer training school and replacement units, as well as 'ear' and 'stomach' battalions – convalescents who could hardly hear and gastric cases who needed special diets.

This was just a temporary solution. Model and Student intended to bring in the rather more professional II Fallschirmjäger Corps under General der Fallschirmtruppen Eugen Meindl as soon as it could be assembled. General Feldt admitted, 'I had no confidence in this attack since it was almost an impossible task for the 406th Division to attack picked troops with its motley collection.' Apart from Army Group B's insistence on an immediate advance, Feldt thought the only justification for it was to forestall an American advance to the east and try to give an impression of strength.

Units of the 406th Division panicked south-east of Mook. 'It was with the greatest difficulty that General Scherbening and I succeeded in halting our troops in the jump-off positions. On this occasion I just managed to avoid being taken prisoner myself in the area of Papen Hill.' At midday Feldt heard that the advance detachments of the 3rd and 5th Fallschirm-jäger divisions had reached Emmerich. He immediately went there but was taken aback to find that 'they consisted of a weak battalion of each division, mostly organized from service troops who had survived the Battle of Nor-mandy. They had practically no heavy weapons.' Feldt, on returning to his command post, found Model and General Meindl already there. Feldt expressed his astonishment at the condition of the two Fallschirmjäger divisions. He said they must amalgamate the two into a Kampfgruppe under Major Karl-Heinz Becker.

Having slept under the tree where he heard the train, Brigadier General Gavin was barely able to move at first with his cracked spine. Ignoring the pain, he still picked up his M-1 rifle and trudged off to check on positions. One of the key tasks that day was to clear the landing zones as 454 gliders for the 82nd Airborne were due to land that afternoon. But first he met up with Captain Bestebreurtje at the Hotel Sionshof. Bestebreurtje had assem-bled nearly 600 members of the Resistance wearing orange armbands.

Gavin warned them that the Germans would kill them if they captured them. 'We don't care,' they replied. 'Give us the weapons from your dead and wounded, and we'll fight with you.' Gavin agreed and told them that their main mission was to make sure that the Germans did not blow the bridge.

According to Martijn Louis Deinum, the director of the De Vereeniging concert hall, a small group of American paratroopers from the failed attempt to reach the bridge had stayed on all night to fight the Germans on their own. 'Three grim-looking and filthy young parachutists came in with their machine guns and started shooting from the windows. We went to the cellar. No elec-tricity.' Deinum wondered whether they were drunk. One of them said to him, 'The Germans are such rotten shots.' What Deinum did not grasp was that Lieutenant Colonel Warren's battalion, which had failed to get to the bridge, was still fighting in Nijmegen against the Kampfgruppe Henke. In other parts of the town, American paratroopers were invited into houses to wash and brush their teeth and shave. 'Some brush their teeth three times a day,' mevrouw Wisman was surprised to find. 'They don't like being com-pared to the Tommies [British],' she added. 'They think of them as a little bit slow, and they the Americans are the ones who have to go in first.'

After his meeting at the Sionshof, Gavin went to the command post of the 508th Parachute Infantry Regiment to discover exactly what had hap-pened to Warren's battalion. Early reports of his success in taking the bridge turned out to be false. Gavin was furious that Warren had not followed the riverbank as ordered, and instead had gone straight into the city, thinking 'that this would be all right'. Warren's battalion was still tied down in the centre of Nijmegen, just when the 508th outside the city was coming under pressure from the east.

Around the middle of the morning, Gavin received reports that the Germans were moving close to the glider landing zone. This was part of Corps Feldt's attempt at a counter-offensive. There was an attack on Groesbeek spotted by American observers in the church spire. Father Hoek the parish priest insisted on going from house to house checking on his flock, despite the firing and occasional shelling. Paratroopers became used to this, and he recounted that when things became dangerous, a head would appear out of a foxhole and shout 'Father, cover!' And he would throw himself flat.

During the first night, when manning the 'tree line' overlooking the Reichswald, the 508th Parachute Infantry Regiment was very conscious of being right on the frontier of Germany. Men were ordered not to challenge anyone to their front, but just shoot them, 'as everyone would be enemy'. Inevitably, there was the odd tragic mistake, including a platoon commander shot by his own men. A lieutenant in the regiment also admitted that their men 'were not very careful about the way they cleaned out a town. As an example, they would locate a German in a house. They would go up to the door and say "*Kommen Sie hier!*" As soon as someone stirred inside the house, they would spray the interior with their Tommy guns.'

The Dutch, however, seemed able to forgive their liberators almost anything. 'The people came out of their homes', Dwayne Burns with the 508th at Beek recorded, 'to find deep holes dug into their front yards and the heads of troopers sticking up from them. They were very friendly and glad to see us, offering us both food and drinks, but mostly, they wanted to talk and give us what information they could.' One of Burns's squad had been killed during the night. 'We buried him on the corner of the vacant lot across from the road block. A trooper whose father was a minister read some verses from his Bible and said a prayer. Then, we, his buddies, covered him and smoothed over the dirt, placing his helmet and one dog tag on the grave as a marker. The Dutch people in the area came later and put flowers from their gardens on the grave.'

In Mook, some ten kilometres to the south, a paratrooper moving under fire from house to house was startled when a door suddenly opened. 'I pulled my .45 and was about to fire,' he wrote. 'Standing in the doorway was an elderly Dutch woman, holding in her hand a cup containing coffee with a piece of cake between two slices of bread.' The paratrooper, a little shaken, thanked her for her hospitality, but begged her to stay inside for her own safety.

The German attacks that morning against roadblocks and villages were as ill-coordinated as General Feldt described, but some still presented a real threat to the landing zones. Captain Anthony Stefanich's C Company of the 505th south-east of Groesbeek had been fired at by some Germans concealed in haystacks. Stefanich, a devout Catholic and 'a legend in the regiment', was worshipped by his men. He gave the order and the company advanced in extended line to chase the Germans off the field just as the gliders were coming in to land. 'The C Company troopers were firing', wrote one of his officers, 'and the Germans were running away from us. It looked like a line of hunters in a rabbit drive. All of a sudden one lone German soldier, running down a small gulley about 75–100 yards in front of us stopped, turned round and fired one shot in the direction of Captain Stefanich and me. The bullet struck "Stef" near the heart and he fell at my feet.' Another account says that Stefanich was trying to rescue a glider pilot under fire when he was hit, but the outcome was the same. Two of his lieutenants remained with him as he was dying, and Stefanich urged them repeatedly to 'see that C Company does a good job'. His soldiers cried unashamedly for the leader they had lost, and they covered his body with a parachute for a shroud.

Altogether 385 gliders landed safely out of the 454 which had taken off. Nineteen of them overflew into German territory to the anguish of those watching from the ground. Some gliders ploughed across a beet field, hurling the beets high into the air. Many crashed, but their passengers or contents survived. Gavin was greatly relieved to hear that the newly arrived battalion of artillery had lost only six out of thirty-six pack howitzers. The glider pilots had managed to do the best expected of them. But unlike the British Glider Pilot Regiment, which had trained its men to fight alongside the airborne soldiers once they landed, their American counterparts belonged to the USAAF and had no infantry skills. In fact they expected to be protected as soon as they had landed their men and cargoes. According to one USAAF officer, as soon as XXX Corps reached the 101st Airborne, their glider pilots began to hitchhike back via Brussels. 'A few of the most enterprising had worn their Class A uniform under their flying overalls, and hitched rides to Paris instead of returning to England. One apparently even made it to the Riviera.' Gavin found the situation intolerable. He preferred the British system of glider pilots fighting on as infantry, but inter-service demarcation disputes were just as bad on both sides of the Atlantic.

Gavin had little option but to accede to the orders of his immediate superior, Lieutenant General Browning. But he was keen to put the exact circumstances on record in the operations log. 'At 15.30, 18 September, General Gavin had a conference with General Browning at which General Browning asked for the plans for the ensuing 24 hours. General Gavin stated [that] his plan for the night of 18–19 September was to seize the bridge north of Nijmegen using one battalion of 504 and in conjunction with 508 envelope the bridgehead from the east and west. General Browning approved the plan in general, but on giving it more thought, in view of the situation in the XXX Corps, he felt that the retention of the high ground South of Nijmegen was of greater importance, and directed that the primary mission should be to hold the high ground and retain its position west of the Maas–Waal Canal. Therefore, General Gavin assembled the regimental commanders and issued an order for the defence of the position.'

With their command posts so close together, Browning could not resist looking over Gavin's shoulder. Yet it is rather strange, as Gavin's record shows, that Browning should still have put so much emphasis on defending the flank, and so little on securing the Nijmegen bridge which was absolutely essential if his own 1st Airborne Division was to be saved from destruction.

Browning had clearly become frustrated. He spent much of the time driving fast all over the place in his Jeep, the Pegasus pennant fluttering proudly from a wireless aerial. He still expected any passenger to be able to map-read while being thrown around, as the vehicle lurched and bounced over the rutted tracks. 'He drove at a furious rate of speed and was completely unmindful of danger,' his aide recounted. 'He did it as a matter of course – he was the commander and it was the right thing to do.' This self-dramatizing behaviour revealed his exasperation that the battle was being fought individually by the airborne divisions until Horrocks arrived to take over. Browning still could not admit that both he and his heavily manned corps headquarters were utterly redundant.

Horrocks's XXX Corps, led by the Irish Guards group, was more than twenty-four hours behind schedule, largely due to the halt at Valkenswaard for 'a quiet night' and a late start on the advice of Brigadier Gwatkin. They did not set off until 10.00 hours, although the two battalion war diaries gave different reasons for the delay. The 3rd Battalion claimed they were waiting to be replaced by an infantry battalion from the 50th Division, while the 2nd (Armoured) Battalion said that they were 'delayed until 10.00 hours by a report of one Jagd Panther and two self-propelled guns at Aalst'.

An armoured car troop from the Household Cavalry Regiment led the way up the Club Route towards Aalst, just six kilometres south of Eindhoven.

Colonel Joe Vandeleur gave the accompanying RAF air controller, Flight Lieutenant Love, the target ahead for the Typhoon squadrons to attack. After the heavy losses of the day before – nine Sherman tanks, twenty-three dead and thirty-seven wounded – the Irish Guards were reluctant to charge straight up an open road again.

While they waited for the Typhoons, Vandeleur halted the column for lunch. He and his cousin Giles found a villa by the road with its own swimming pool. They had a swim and revived themselves with more champagne afterwards when a young woman war correspondent joined them. Finally, two hours after the initial request, Love heard that the strike had been cancelled due to poor flying conditions. Vandeleur was livid. 'What's the matter?' he demanded sarcastically. 'Is the RAF afraid of the sunshine?' The only assistance they received that day was a tactical reconnaissance mission which confirmed that the bridge at Son really had been destroyed.

A senior member of the great Philips electrical company at Eindhoven crossed through the lines with a map showing the position of all the German guns. This was a great help, but a series of delays still dogged the advance. There was another hold-up later when four 88mm guns supported by infantry were found to be defending a line north of Aalst. While No. 2 Squadron engaged the German gun crews to keep them occupied, No. 1 Squadron and a company of infantry tried to outflank their positions, but wide ditches defeated cross-country movement. Artillery was brought up and opened fire. At 17.00 hours, Major General Adair and Brigadier Gwatkin arrived to see what was causing the delay, and soon afterwards the Household Cavalry troop reported that the Germans had departed. The column was on the move again up the Aalsterweg by 17.30, and half an hour later the armoured cars were racing through Eindhoven. Their crews drove with hatches closed down, thinking the town was still held by the Germans. As a result, they missed out on the riotous welcome.

At about 19.30, people in Eindhoven heard shouting in the streets. 'The English are coming on the Aalster road!' Abandoning dinners on the table, they bustled out of their houses, and soon there were just 'the cries of joy, laughter and the jumping up and down from young and old'.

Guardsmen in tanks and other vehicles made V for Victory signs back to the crowds, as the column was brought almost to a halt by cheering civilians. Miraculously nobody was crushed under the tank tracks, as people of all ages chalked slogans and messages of thanks on the hulls of Shermans as they passed. According to one woman in Eindhoven, British soldiers observed that 'whatever the Dutch and Belgians were in want of, they were certainly not in want of chalk.' One Irish Guards officer, astonished by the

1. Admiral Sir Bertram Ramsay (*right*) with Field Marshal Montgomery, who ignored his urgent requests to secure the Scheldt estuary to open the port of Antwerp.

2. (*Following two pages.*) The vital bridge at Arnhem over the Neder Rijn, or Lower Rhine, photographed just before the war.

3. A pre-war group of Dutch Nazis from the NSB, or Nationaal-Socialistische Beweging.

4. Teenage Waffen-SS recruits.

5. 'Boy' Browning (*right*) with the Polish paratroop commander Major General Sosabowski, an outspoken critic of his plans.

6. Viktor Gräbner on 17 September receiving the Knight's Cross, which he lived to wear for less than a day.

7. Sepp Krafft, the commander of the SS troops who slowed the advance to Arnhem.

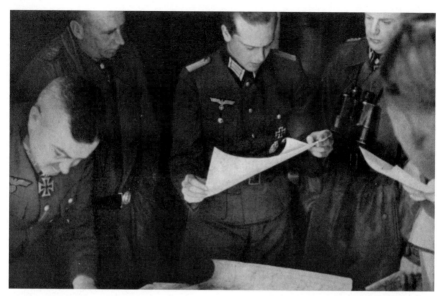

8. The German command plans its response. (*L to r*) Model, Bittrich, a staff officer and Harmel (10th SS Panzer-Division).

9. Walter Harzer (9th SS Panzer-Division *Hohenstaufen*).

10. Horrocks, Montgomery and Prince Bernhard.

11. Major General Maxwell Taylor, 101st Airborne.

12. Brigadier General Jim Gavin, 82nd Airborne.

13. The 21st Independent Parachute Company of pathfinders before boarding their Stirlings. Some twenty of its members were German Jews intent on revenge.

14. Gliders of the 1st Airborne towed over the Neder Rijn with the flood plain of the Betuwe beyond.

15. (*Previous page.*) The air armada over the Netherlands.

16. Glider landing zone north-west of Arnhem, 17 September.

17. Brigadier General Anthony McAuliffe (*left*, later of Bastogne fame) with officers of the 101st Airborne.

18. 101st Airborne parachute drop north-west of Son, 17 September.

19. British paratroopers having tea with locals.

20. A Sherman Firefly pushes past Irish Guards tanks destroyed in the first few minutes of Operation Garden.

21. Another XXX Corps vehicle ambushed south of Valkenswaard.

22. The liberation carnival of shaving the heads of Dutch women who had slept with Germans had 'none of the sickening and almost animal glee that French crowds showed on similar occasions'.

23. Proud members of the Dutch underground with weapons taken from the Germans including an MG-34.

24. Crowds in Eindhoven on 19 September, cheering a very delayed Guards Armoured Division.

25. (*Following page*.) British soldiers were amazed by the Dutch chalking messages of thanks and greeting all over their tanks.

patriotic displays of the national colour in every direction, observed that 'all those orange flags made it very like Ulster.' He also suspected that the American paratroopers had already 'managed to kiss all the girls who wanted to be kissed'.

While the Irish Guards pushed their tanks through the crowds, Joe and Giles Vandeleur slipped away in a scout car through the city and on to the canal at Son. They found a rowing boat and crossed to the other bank where they encountered some paratroopers from the 101st Airborne. 'They were drinking coffee and smoking cigarettes. You would never have thought there was a war on, they were so completely relaxed,' Joe Vandeleur noted, perhaps forgetting his own swim earlier in the day. 'We said hello and they shuffled to their feet and gave us a few half-hearted salutes.'

Neither the citizens of Eindhoven, cheering themselves hoarse, nor the 101st Airborne had any idea that the 107th Panzer-Brigade was close by. Commanded by Major Berndt-Joachim Freiherr von Maltzahn, its Mark V Panther tanks had reached Venlo on railway flat-cars early that morning. By the time the Vandeleurs reached the canal by Son, the brigade had halted at the Soeterbeek Bridge over the River Dommel on the north-east edge of Eindhoven. As the Germans had no reconnaissance aircraft, Maltzahn had little idea of where the Allied forces were. According to local legend, Maltzahn was told by a quick-thinking gardener called Willem Hikspoors that the bridge ahead was not strong enough to take his tanks. Maltzahn apparently decided not to take the risk and turned his column round.

Gavin had been exasperated the previous evening when that German train had escaped Nijmegen, puffing its way right through the lines of his division. It was, however, a trick which could not be pulled twice. 'A train approached heading for Germany,' a paratrooper recounted. 'Several bazooka rounds in the engine halted the train. It had a number of passenger cars containing all sorts of artworks.' According to Lieutenant Jack P. Carroll of the 505th, 'there were quite a few people on the train, all loaded down with loot, which they intended to take back to Germany. The loot consisted of cigars, hosiery and clothing which had been taken from the Dutch. One of the cars was loaded with woollen socks, another was filled with new handkerchiefs. We killed five soldiers on the train and captured forty.' One paratrooper was greatly impressed by 'a group of people in fine looking uniforms – black trimmed with red, highly polished boots and belts'. He asked one of the Americans guarding them if they belonged to the German general staff. The guard laughed and replied, 'No, this is the train crew.'

*

A dozen kilometres to the north in Nijmegen there was nothing to laugh about. The arrival of the Kampfgruppe Reinhold marked the start of a pitiless battle waged largely against the citizens of Nijmegen. To strike fear into the people, SS patrols cleared civilians from the streets. On Smidstraat, one detachment halted in front of a house where they heard children crying. One of them shouted a command for them to be quiet, but the noise continued. He pulled out a grenade, but fortunately his companion persuaded him not to throw it into the cellar.

While the Kampfgruppe Reinhold prepared to defend the Valkhof, the Belvedere, the Keizer Lodewijkplein and Hunner Park on the southern approach to the great road bridge, German artillery deployed ready in the Keizer Karelplein, the huge traffic circle in the centre of the city. As dusk fell, Reinhold sent parties of marauding troops and the RAD youth as fireraisers into the town. They banged on doors and shouted, 'Anybody still here? You must leave the house at once, it's going to be set on fire.' They burst into the Carmelite monastery on Doddendaal, claiming that they had been fired upon from it. 'While the Prior was trying to convince them that their allegations were all wrong,' Father Wilhelmus Peterse recorded, 'soldiers were already busy throwing wood kindling drenched in gasoline into the rooms.'

According to some accounts, the Germans were attempting to bolster their courage with looted gin. There was a good deal of general plundering. Two German soldiers in the Molenstraat smashed in the plate-glass window of a shop with their rifle butts, then climbed in to snatch what they could. The KP underground group also took advantage of the confusion. 'In the St Annastraat, an abandoned German truck is raided by the resistance,' a diarist recorded. 'They take a large number of rifles, ammunition and grenades, load them on a hand-cart and trundle them back rapidly to their headquarters.'

Members of an air-raid precaution group had been round warning householders in the north of the city to open their windows to save them being shattered if the great bridge over the Waal was blown up. But once the fires started consuming whole houses, the chief sound was of glass panes exploding in the heat.

'The fires are taking on fantastic dimensions,' noted Albertus Uijen. Whole blocks were ablaze, as the battle went on with German and American machine guns firing. 'Flames leap up to great heights . . . Walls cave in, rafters crash down and in between are the cries of fleeing people and the sharp crack of rifles and machine-gun fire . . . It is a stampede. Nobody remains in the danger zone. A few have salvaged the barest necessities such as clothing and blankets and in fear haul these along to a safer place. Mothers hold their crying tots close to them. Desperate fathers carry the bigger children as well as hastily packed suitcases. The anxieties they have been through can clearly be read on their faces.'

Only the very impressive civil defence organizations and the Red Cross just managed to prevent total panic. The evacuation of the Protestant hospital went smoothly and just in time, using cars and handcarts to transfer the patients elsewhere. As soon as the fire brigade put out one blaze, the Germans would start it again. They apparently shot a fireman who went to their headquarters to plead with them, and in an effort to block the Nijmegen fire brigade completely, they ordered them to drive over the border to Cleve. The firemen drove off in the right direction, but once out of sight, they turned round and concealed their vehicles in a factory. 'It looks as if the whole of Nijmegen will be reduced to ashes,' a shocked Albertus Uijen concluded in his diary that night.

15

Arnhem
Tuesday 19 September

After the confused fighting on the Monday, with the 3rd and 1st Battalions trying to break through to the bridge, their last hope was another push that evening. In the end it did not take place until the early hours of Tuesday. At a candle-lit council of war in a ruined house, Lieutenant Colonel Dobie of the 1st Parachute Battalion took the lead in the absence of any formation commander. They were close to the Rhine Pavilion, a waterside building below the St Elisabeth Hospital. A mistaken report that the Germans had recaptured the north end of the bridge prompted divisional headquarters to tell them to cancel the attack, but then it was on again.

Dobie was joined by Lieutenant Colonel Derek McCardie of the South Staffords and Lieutenant Colonel George Lea of the 11th Parachute Battalion. There was no contact with Fitch of the 3rd Parachute Battalion, even though he could not have been far away. Dobie was still utterly determined to support Frost at the bridge, despite the fact they would again suffer from machine-gun fire from the left, assault guns ahead and flak guns firing across the river into their right flank. The idea was to attack in the dark and fight through to the bridge before first light.

The Germans had pulled back their blocking line. This allowed the British to reoccupy the St Elisabeth Hospital and Major General Urquhart to escape from his attic hideout. But Standartenführer Harzer's decision to withdraw to a new line on the far side of some open ground, some 500 metres east of the Rhine Pavilion and 200 metres beyond Arnhem's Municipal Museum, was to create a better killing field.

Soon after 03.00, Dobie's battalion advanced rapidly along the riverfront, only to encounter Fitch's 3rd Battalion withdrawing, after their own bruising battle to get through. Fitch had little more than fifty men standing out of the whole battalion. Dobie refused to believe they could not break

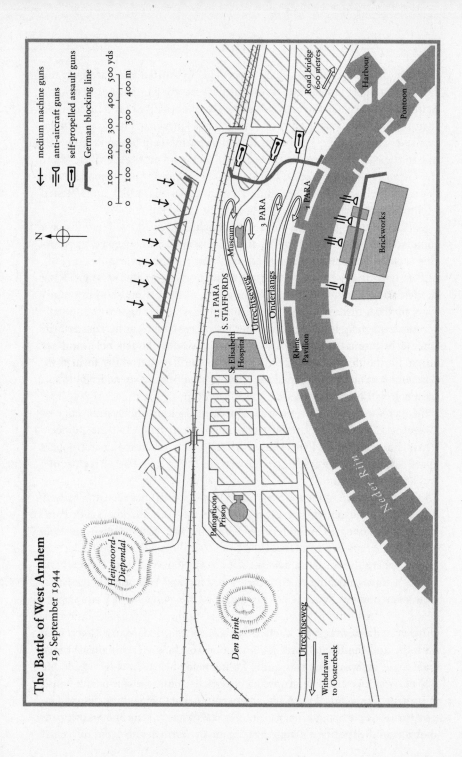

The Battle of West Arnhem
19 September 1944

medium machine guns
anti-aircraft guns
self-propelled assault guns
German blocking line

N

0   100   200   300   400   500 yds
0   100   200   300   400 m

Road bridge
600 metres

Harbour

Pontoon

Brickworks

1 PARA

3 PARA

Onderlangs

Museum

Utrechtseweg

Rhine Pavilion

11 PARA
S. STAFFORDS

St Elisabeth Hospital

Neder Rijn

Panopticon Prison

Den Brink

Heijenoord-Diependal

Utrechseweg

Withdrawal to Oosterbeek

through, and marched on. Fitch turned his exhausted men around, and agreed to support Dobie's attack. On the Utrechtseweg up the hill, the South Staffords, followed by the 11th Parachute Battalion, skirted the Museum and then ran into the assault guns of Harzer's blocking line. They too suffered fusillades and machine-gun bursts from the embankment beyond the railway line to their left, and heavier-calibre flak firing from across the river, where the Germans had occupied a brickworks. The 88mm shells exploded with devastating effect, while the rounds from the dual 20mm flak guns blasted off limbs with such force that the shock alone could kill.

A Parachute Regiment lieutenant identifiable only as 'David' wrote down some impressions while in hiding after the battle. 'I was obsessed by recurring scenes of the nightmare passed – of Mervyn with his arm hanging off, of Pete lying in his grotesque attitude, quite unrecognizable, of Angus lying in the dark clinging to the grass in his agony, of the private shouting vainly for a medical orderly – there were none left – of the man running gaily across an opening, the quick crack and his surprised look as he clutched the back of his neck, of his jumps so convulsive as more bullets hit him. How stupid all this war game is, I only hope the sacrifice that was ours in those days will have achieved something – yet even at this moment I feel that it hasn't. It will remain a gesture.'

Möller's 9th SS Pioneers, well concealed back on the eastern edge of Oosterbeek, ambushed British troops coming on behind. 'The pioneers fired,' he recounted. 'Panzerfausts literally blew groups of paratroopers apart, and flamethrowers sprayed fire at the enemy . . . The Utrechtseweg was a channel of death.'

The rest of Kampfgruppe Spindler to the north, between the railway line and the Amsterdamseweg, was fighting the 10th and the 156th Parachute Battalions. They were also harassing the King's Own Scottish Borderers, preparing to defend Landing Zone L, north of the Bilderberg woods, where the third lift was due later in the day. And with General von Tettau's forces pushing in from the west, the 1st Airborne Division was nearly surrounded.

Further to the east on the Utrechtseweg near the hospital, Major Robert Cain with the 2nd South Staffords saw a man beckon him over. He then handed Cain a rifle and pack. He was caring for a wounded British soldier inside and did not want to suffer the consequences of having a weapon in the house. 'Germans,' he said apologetically, and to emphasize the point, he put two fingers to his temple to represent a pistol. Soon afterwards, Cain and his company took up another position to fight back against a German sally from the centre of Arnhem. Cain grabbed the Bren gun and fired off a whole magazine. Realizing that he was standing on a pile of flat stones, he looked down and saw that they were gravestones with Hebrew inscriptions. They were standing in a Jewish graveyard which had been presumably been smashed by the Germans or Dutch Nazis.

With German reinforcements arriving with heavy weapons, the British did not stand a chance against intense fire from three sides. After the near-destruction of Fitch's 3rd Battalion, Dobie's 1st Battalion was broken in semi-suicidal attacks against German positions. Hardly a man was left unwounded. The only escape was to seek shelter in nearby houses, but the panzergrenadiers, supported by assault guns, had them trapped, and took most of them prisoner little more than an hour later.

A couple of hundred metres to the north, the South Staffords were running low on anti-tank PIAT rounds. The Museum, which the British called the Monastery, had been their aid post. It now had to be evacuated, but the doctor there, 'Basher' Brownscombe, remained with those who could not be moved. He was murdered several days later in hospital by a Danish member of the SS, who was later tried and hanged for the crime. A defensive position in the dell behind the Museum was also abandoned due to concentrated mortar fire.

Major Blackwood, arriving with the 11th Battalion, saw signs of the previous day's fighting: 'Wires and cables down, an occasional barricade of burned out vehicles, some dead Germans cluttering the streets. We moved under fire to a position on the hill near the big hospital and dug in there while a battalion put in an attack on the lower level. The noise was terrific. Somewhere behind the hospital was a large calibre gun popping off, but an attempt to find out more about it only brought a shower of Spandau bullets about my ears. So for the most part we lay on the *qui vive* looking at the horribly stiff bodies of an officer and men of the 1st Brigade which blocked the gateway on our flank.'

At around 09.00, German Mark IV tanks appeared, as well as assault guns. They were held off at first by the last few PIATs, as a member of the South Staffords recorded, 'but at about 11.00 all PIAT ammunition was exhausted and tanks over-ran the position, inflicting heavy casualties and splitting the Battalion into pockets.' They had no anti-tank guns forward because the convex curve of the hill shielded enemy armoured vehicles until they were almost on top of them. As the Staffords pulled back near the St Elisabeth Hospital, the same private saw a British soldier jump from a first-floor window of a house on to the back of a tank in an attempt to drop a grenade into the turret, but he was shot down before he had a chance.

Behind the South Staffords, the 11th Parachute Battalion tried to advance on the railway line and embankment up to the left, but the attack never got off the ground. Between the Utrechtseweg and the river, survivors from the 1st and 3rd Parachute Battalions pulled back to the Rhine Pavilion. Colonel Fitch was not among them. He had been killed by a mortar bomb. With hardly any medics or stretcher-bearers left, the wounded were told to try to make their way as best they could to the St Elisabeth Hospital, even though it was now back under German control.

At 10.30, Colonel Warrack, the deputy head of medical services, managed to contact the 16th (Parachute) Field Ambulance in the St Elisabeth Hospital. He was using the telephone of a civilian in Oosterbeek, whose son was in the Dutch SS. Warrack heard that, although the Germans had taken away the head of 16 Field Ambulance and many of the orderlies, two surgical teams were still operating. They had nearly a hundred casualties, many of them serious cases. Warrack could hear the sound of battle in the background, with machine guns and an assault gun firing constantly, as he conversed with the field ambulance's dental officer. Later in the morning Brigadier Lathbury was brought into the St Elisabeth Hospital from his hiding place, with the bad wound in his thigh. He had removed all badges of rank and pretended to be Corporal Lathbury.

Bizarrely in the circumstances of such a British disaster, a German SS panzergrenadier with only a flesh wound was crying in the hospital. One of the remaining British doctors told him to shut up because he was not dying. A Dutch nurse explained that the man was crying not from pain, but because the Führer had decreed that the Allies must never cross the Rhine, and they had done so.

Even the 11th Parachute Battalion behind the South Staffords found itself forced to retreat, as Major Blackwood recounted: '13.00 hrs, message to say that our attack on the Arnhem bridge had been beaten back and that German tanks had outflanked and surrounded us . . . B Company took up positions in houses overlooking a main crossroads. Our orders were brief – wait for the tanks, give them everything we had in the way of grenades, shoot up as many infantry as we could before we died. With Scott I entered one of the corner houses, said "Good morning" to the worried looking tenant, and went upstairs to the room with the most commanding view. It was a remarkably fine room to die in. A plaster cast of a Madonna in the corner, two crucifixes, three ornately framed texts, and a picture of the Pope. We removed all glass and china to a remote corner, laid out our grenades, ammunition and weapons on the bed, and had a drink of water. Scott, who is an RC, made furtive use of some of the religious adornments and I put in a wee word or two of my own.'

Just outside the hospital, Major Cain was taking shelter in a long air-raid trench on the east side of the St Elisabeth Hospital. He told his men to stay down as they could hear a German assault gun approaching. It was little more than fifty metres away. Peering over the rim of the trench, Cain could see the commander standing, with head and shoulders exposed. He wore black gloves and held some binoculars. Cain, who had nothing more than his service revolver, was horrified to hear a burst of fire from along the trench. One of his men had tried and failed to kill the commander, who dropped inside and closed the hatch with a clang, and then the assault gun turned towards them. Three of Cain's men panicked. They scrambled from the trench and were cut down by machine-gun fire. Cain pulled himself out of the trench as the assault gun manoeuvred, and then rolled down the reverse slope behind, which led to a steep drop into the courtyard of the hospital. Just beyond the hospital, he came across men from the 11th Battalion. He wanted to get his revenge on the assault gun, but they had no PIAT ammunition left.

Instead, Cain was told to round up as many men as he could and seize the high ground at Den Brink. The plan was for Cain's force on Den Brink to act as a pivot, for the 11th Parachute Battalion to attack another hill to the north of the railway line called Heijenoord-Diependal. Cain and his men passed the round panopticon prison with its shallow dome and then rushed Den Brink from the side. To Cain's relief, there was little resistance when they put in their attack and took the feature, but a tangle of tree roots made digging trenches difficult. He urged his men to hurry. He knew how fast the Germans would range in with their mortars, and they did, with tree bursts. In a short time, two-thirds of his force had suffered shrapnel wounds. Soon after 14.00, Cain felt there was no alternative but to pull back. Not only was the attempt to get through to Frost's force at the bridge defeated, but four battalions had been savaged in the attempt. With most officers killed or wounded, a chaotic retreat was under way. Men appeared out of the smoke of battle, running back in ones and twos 'like animals escaping from a forest fire'.

Once released from hiding early in the morning, General Urquhart and his two companions found a Jeep and drove to the Hartenstein. 'As I came down the steps,' wrote the padre of the Glider Pilot Regiment, 'who should be ascending but the General. Several saw him but nobody said a word. We were completely taken aback. His return was the signal for a great resurgence of confidence.'

Confidence was needed badly, as Urquhart's chief of staff Charles Mackenzie had just found. On a check of the divisional area, he was disturbed to find a machine-gun nest and a Bren-gun carrier abandoned. He then came across a group of about twenty soldiers in a panic, with some of them shouting 'The Germans are coming! The Germans are coming!' He and Loder-Symonds calmed them down and Mackenzie drove the carrier back to the Hartenstein. He found Urquhart, standing on the steps, about to explode, no doubt because on his return he had found that nothing was going to plan. 'We assumed, sir, that you were gone for good,' Charles Mackenzie said to him.

Around the Hartenstein, armed members of the LKP underground group were forcing the NSB collaborators they had rounded up to dig trenches. Other Dutch volunteers were collecting corpses to move them to burial places. The glider pilot padre, meanwhile, set off in a Jeep with two young SS trooper prisoners, still in their tiger camouflage smocks, sitting on the front. They were going to bury General Kussin and his companions.

Early that morning staff officers at the Hartenstein suddenly discovered that 'a BBC set, brought in to send news releases back to London, had communication with its base set so we received permission to send our messages over it. Arrangements were made by BBC in London to get personnel from SHAEF to receive the messages and relay them to British Airborne headquarters at Moor Park.' For the next two days, 'this was the only reliable radio contact we had in the Division to the outside world.'

Just north of Oosterbeek, while the other four battalions tried and failed to get through to the bridge, Hackett's 4th Parachute Brigade had been fighting its own battle. During the night the 156th Parachute Battalion, commanded by Lieutenant Colonel Sir Richard Des Voeux, had continued its advance between the railway line and the Amsterdamseweg towards Arnhem. Hackett's plan was to seize the high ground at Koepel beyond a north–south road through the woods called the Dreijenseweg, which ran down to Oosterbeek, but this was the blocking line of the Kampfgruppe Spindler. It was a strongly held position with steeply rising wooded ground on the eastern side of the road where Spindler's force of panzergrenadiers and gunners was dug in, supported by eight-wheeler armoured cars, halftracks and assault guns. At around midnight, the 156th Battalion had run into outposts west of the road. Colonel Des Voeux decided to back off and wait until first light to get a better idea of what they were up against.

Expecting a dawn attack, the Germans pulled in their outposts. First one company of the 156th attacked and, as soon as it had crossed the road, suffered devastating losses from the concentration of German firepower. It was virtually wiped out. Another company was sent in supposedly to turn the

German flank, but it was a continuous line. They too could not spot the well-camouflaged trenches and gun pits in the woods.

Major John Waddy sighted a German half-track with 20mm double flak guns, and began to stalk it. High in one of the trees, however, was a sniper who shot him in the groin before he could fire the PIAT. One of Waddy's sergeants, a huge Rhodesian, picked him up in his arms like a child, saying to him, 'Come on, Sir. This is no place for us,' and carried him back to the battalion aid post. Waddy's travails were not over. As a patient in the Hotel Tafelberg he was wounded twice more, first by German mortar fire and, towards the end of the battle, by shell fragments from British artillery firing from south of the river.

In the course of the morning, the 156th Battalion lost almost half its strength. Brigadier Hackett had to pull it back. To the north, the 10th Parachute Battalion commanded by Lieutenant Colonel Ken Smyth advanced past the discouraging sight of casualties brought back on a procession of Jeeps. Smyth's lead company encountered a similar volume of fire to the 156th and went to ground. Reluctant to destroy another company, Smyth asked Hackett's permission to try to outflank the end of the blocking line by sending a company round north of the Amsterdamseweg. Soon the 10th Battalion was pinned down by the much stronger and better-munitioned Kampfgruppe Spindler.

Hackett's brigade needed to hold that line, even if no further advance was possible, because less than a kilometre to the west of the Dreijenseweg lay Landing Zone L where part of the third lift was due to arrive that afternoon. Already the King's Own Scottish Borderers were having a hard time trying to defend its perimeter. Meanwhile, General von Tettau's forces were advancing on Wolfheze to their rear, while the very high railway embankment along their southern flank risked trapping them in a desperately vulnerable position. Both Urquhart and Hackett now suddenly recognized the danger the 4th Parachute Brigade was in.

When the order to fall back reached the 156th Battalion, Major Geoffrey Powell was furious. They were given just fifteen minutes' warning, and to withdraw quite openly in daylight invited disaster. 'It was ludicrous, insane. We were ordered to just break off and fall back. The move was chaotic.' Under constant attack by the Germans, the battalion was split and then fragmented.

Captain Lionel Queripel had taken over command of the 10th Battalion company north of the Amsterdamseweg. With his slightly whimsical expression, Queripel did not seem to be a man likely to win the Victoria Cross for a whole series of actions. His men referred to him as Captain Q, and thought

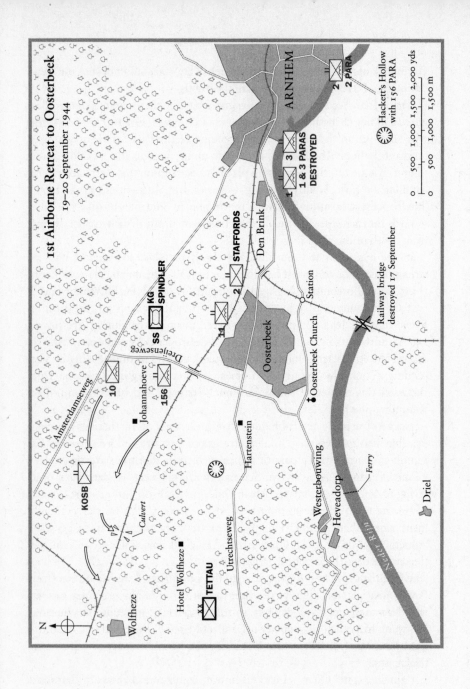

1st Airborne Retreat to Oosterbeek
19–20 September 1944

ARNHEM

2 PARA

1 & 3 PARAS
DESTROYED

Hackett's Hollow
with 156 PARA

0   500   1,000   1,500   2,000 yds

0   500   1,000   1,500 m

Railway bridge
destroyed 17 September

STAFFORDS

Den Brink

SS KG
SPINDLER

Station

Oosterbeek

† Oosterbeek Church

Dreijenseweg

10

Johannahoeve

156

Amsterdamseweg

Hartenstein

Westerbouwing

Heveadorp

Ferry

KOSB

Culvert

Utrechtseweg

Nede Rijn

Hotel Wolfheze

TETTAU

Wolfheze

Driel

N

he looked more like 'a country parson than a soldier'. Yet bravery can never be judged by appearances. Although himself wounded in the face, he first carried a crippled sergeant out of danger. He then stormed a German position, which had two machine guns and a captured British 6-pounder anti-tank gun, killing the crews. He was hit again. Then, as Germans threw stick grenades, he picked them up and threw them back. 'Finally, as the German counter-attack increased greatly in strength, he ordered his men to pull back while he held off the Germans with hand grenades and a Sten gun.' Queripel's self-sacrifice could end only in death.

Sergeant Fitzpatrick, the man he had carried out of danger, was tended to by their medical officer, Captain G. F. Drayson, kneeling beside him. A mortar bomb came down. It exploded and almost decapitated the doctor who fell across Fitzpatrick's body, pinning the weakened man to the ground. Sergeant Fitzpatrick began to sob, appalled that Drayson should have died trying to help him.

The broken battalion reached the landing zone as the gliders carrying the Polish anti-tank squadron began to approach. Back at the Hotel Hartenstein, the American fighter control team led by Lieutenant Davis were trying to contact Allied fighters to protect the incoming lift. Davis managed no more than one brief exchange with a Spitfire pilot, who then could not hear anything because of the flak explosions all around him. 'All through the operation the Luftwaffe was active, but it was a very peculiar activity,' Davis reported after the battle. 'The FW 190s and Me 109s were over every day except two, and their tactics were always the same. They would sweep back and forth about 4,000 feet, drop to 2,000 and then peel off as if to strafe us. But I doubt whether they fired over 500 rounds in all the passes they made at us. It looked as if they were afraid to use their ammunition and then be unarmed in case our fighters would come, and were merely trying to bolster German morale.'

On the ground, the withdrawal of the 10th and 156th Battalions enabled the Germans to start attacking the landing zone from the woods. The King's Own Scottish Borderers found themselves under heavy fire. 'See my first live Jerry and put a bullet through him,' one of them recorded. 'He went down on his knees, so I rolled out of Tony Morgan's way, and he put a burst into him. More Jerries coming out of the woods under cover of M.G.34 and Schmeisser fire, which we return. I got another cert.'

At about four the cry went up 'Third lift here!', the chaplain of the Glider Pilot Regiment recorded. 'All we could do was gaze in stupefaction at our friends going to inevitable death. We watched in agony the terrible drama. It was heroic in the extreme. We saw more than one machine blazing yet continuing on its course. It now became borne in on us that we faced terrible opposition.'

While the departure of the Polish Parachute Brigade had been cancelled from airfields in the Midlands because of bad visibility, the second glider group bringing the rest of the anti-tank squadron managed to lift off in thirty-five gliders from the airfields of Salisbury Plain well to the south. But only twenty-six arrived together with British gliders on Landing Zone L. 'The landing took place in the midst of the fiercest battle and sustained enormous losses,' a Polish account stated. 'Gliders were literally shot to pieces in the air, during landing and on the ground.' Many were injured on landing. 'The British could not help as they had their own problems.'

The Germans were even firing with Nebelwerfer multi-barrelled mortars on to the landing ground. The confusion was such that Polish soldiers opened fire on 10th Battalion paratroopers retreating across the landing zone, thinking they were Germans. They killed several of them including Lieutenant Paddy Radcliffe, the commander of the machine-gun platoon. 'Absolute hell,' wrote Major Francis Lindley of the 10th Battalion. 'Germans had the open ground surrounded with flak guns and machine-gun. Gliders landing all round us. C-47 flew over with flames shooting out of it. Stirling crashed near the road. Poles just started firing at everything.' Finally the Poles realized from the yellow triangles being waved at them that they were firing at the British. Lieutenant Colonel Smyth of the 10th Battalion apparently had 'tears in his eyes' when looking at the sad remnants of his command.

'Later in the afternoon the resupply ships, Stirlings and Dakotas, came over and ran into terrific ack-ack barrages,' one report stated. 'Too many of them get hit and go down flaming and too much of the supply drop goes to the Germans . . . It had been expected that we would control the area where the supplies were dropped. Evidently no message had got through changing the DZ. We tried while the planes were overhead to contact them with VHF on the three frequencies but got no reply. Yellow ground panels and smoke pots were set out but only a few of the planes were able to see them because of the tall trees and the low altitude of the planes.'

Another posthumous Victoria Cross was awarded for bravery that afternoon. Flight Lieutenant David Lord had brought his C-47 Dakota down below cloud cover just north of Nijmegen. A German flak battery opened fire and set his starboard engine ablaze. Lord asked how much longer to the drop zone. 'Three minutes' flying time,' came the reply. The plane began to list as the fire spread. Over the intercom Lord told his crew: 'They need the stuff. We'll go in and bale out afterwards. Get your chutes on.' He told his navigator to go back and help the four Royal Army Service Corps soldiers who would be pushing out the baskets. The mechanism was broken, so they had to manhandle each container of ammunition out of the door. They managed only six out of eight, so Lord insisted on going round again to drop the last two. As soon as they were gone, Lord shouted 'Bale out! Bale out!' Lord kept the aircraft steady long enough for them to jump, but it was not long enough for him and he was killed.

Flying Officer Henry King, his navigator, had no idea after parachuting whether Lord had died or had managed to crash-land the plane. 'Lord was a strange fellow,' he observed later. 'He had studied for the ministry, but left a seminary to join the RAF in 1936. He was rather a grimly determined chap.' King encountered some members of the 10th Battalion. They offered him a cup of tea and some chocolate. 'That's all we've got,' one of them said.

'What do you mean, that's all you've got?' King replied. 'We just dropped supplies to you.'

'Sure you dropped our tins of sardines, but the Huns got them. We got nothing.'

Many if not most of the containers drifted towards German positions, to the frustration of the paratroopers. 'Now we too smoked English cigarettes and ate English chocolate,' SS-Hauptsturmführer Möller exulted.

Möller's divisional commander, Standartenführer Harzer of the *Hohenstaufen*, described how Model visited his command post daily. He arrived with a small escort, and demanded a short, sharp situation report as soon as he stepped in the door. Whenever there was a problem, the commander on the spot had to offer three different solutions. Once that was over, Harzer was allowed to request more men, vehicles, weapons, ammunition and supplies. Model would then make his decision, and telephone his chief of staff General Krebs, 'and a few hours later, transport columns and troops were re-directed towards Arnhem'. Since the *Hohenstaufen* lacked transport, the Wehrmacht trucks would deliver the shells straight to the gun lines. When flamethrowers were requested for street-fighting, Model had them flown to the division from an ordnance department in central Germany. The German army was based on a ruthless prioritization which the British army manifestly failed to match.

Once Model had finished with Harzer, he then went forward to visit the command post of each Kampfgruppe, where he would question officers and soldiers alike on the progress of the attack and on morale. As Möller indicated, morale was high not just because of their certainty of winning this battle after the defeat in Normandy, but because of the cornucopia of Allied parachute containers raining down on them. Having captured the orders which revealed the signals and identification panels for guiding the Allied supply drops, further generous supplies could be expected. The panels were quickly manufactured and distributed the next day.

In addition, the British in their retreat were losing control of their drop zones and lacked radio contact to warn the RAF. Allied aircraft would soon be at even greater risk. Harzer's strength was about to be increased by the arrival of a flak brigade commanded by Oberstleutnant Hubert von Swoboda of the Luftwaffe, an Austrian. This consisted of five flak battalions from the Ruhr, with a mixture of 20mm, 47mm, 88mm and even 105mm anti-aircraft guns. Most of the guns had to be towed by farm tractors or even wood-burning trucks, but the II SS Panzer Corps was still able to assemble nearly 200 anti-aircraft guns west of Arnhem, positioned to support the ground troops as well as engage Allied aircraft. And yet, according to Major Knaust, Bittrich was still anxious about the outcome of the battle. When he visited Knaust at his command post just east of the ramp that day, he said: 'Knaust, can we hold out here another 24 hours? We've got to gain time to allow the divisions from Germany to arrive.' Both Knaust's and Heinrich Brinkmann's Kampfgruppen had suffered heavy casualties in the house-to-house fighting north of the bridge. Knaust's well-worn tanks either broke down or were knocked out rapidly by the British 6-pounder anti-tank guns. 'It would seem a miracle how they manhandled heavy guns up on to the upper floors,' Harzer commented later. 'The heavy infantry weapons fire from basements or withdrawn from windows so they cannot be spotted.'

In Arnhem during the previous night, the Germans had forcibly evacuated any remaining Dutch civilians from houses near the northern end of the road bridge. One of the last sounds that Coenraad Hulleman remembered before leaving his home was the unearthly racket of an upright piano upstairs being riddled with bullets.

As expected, the German attack came at dawn. The defenders at the bridge had already heard all the firing to the west where the other battalions around St Elisabeth Hospital were trying to fight through to them. Harmel's *Frundsberg* seemed to be concentrating its efforts on finishing off the school on the east side of the ramp, using Knaust's Kampfgruppe and his few remaining panzers. 'On Tuesday morning', Lieutenant Donald Hindley recalled, 'the tanks came back and they started shelling this house very heavily.' Three of the airborne sappers managed to stalk one of the tanks and knock it out. 'The crew got out and crept along the wall of the house till they came to rest beneath the window where I was sitting. I dropped a grenade on them and that was that. I held it for two seconds before I let it drop.'

Sapper John Bretherton was shot through the forehead. 'Bretherton, for a split-second, looked surprised. Then he dropped to the ground without a cry.' Another sapper suddenly gripped Sergeant Norman Swift's arm and asked him if he was all right. Swift could not understand since he felt fine. He followed the soldier's gaze and saw a large pool of what looked like blood by his feet, and then realized it was rusty water which had seeped from one of the bullet-ridden radiators. Another sapper, who was badly shell-shocked, walked out of the building. He was calling out, 'We're all going to die.' Everyone yelled at him to come back, 'but he was too far gone to understand and walked straight into the line of German fire.'

In a house opposite the school the panzergrenadier Rottenführer Alfred Ringsdorf was exasperated by the way the school's defenders 'were shooting through the windows in the stairwell so that we could not use the stairs'. The only way of dealing with its defenders, he argued, was to fire a Panzerfaust to explode just below the windowsill. That would kill any rifleman waiting to pop up for another shot. Along with the rest of Obersturmführer Vogel's company, he had no cigarettes, and they were desperate to capture some prisoners in order to take theirs.

Captain Mackay had issued the stimulant Benzedrine to his men, which caused double vision in some and occasionally provoked hallucinations, of which the most common was that XXX Corps had arrived on the other side of the bridge. Some men became obsessed with this vision. Others, without the influence of Benzedrine, were eagerly awaiting the drop of the Polish Parachute Brigade on the polderland near the southern end of the bridge. Frost, knowing that the Poles would face a desperate battle there, had assembled a 'suicide squad' led by Freddie Gough to fight across the bridge to join them. He was not to know that Sosabowski himself was fuming, because he had been told at the last moment that only his anti-tank squadron was going in on that day.

With German snipers focusing on the windows of the school, the sappers and paratroopers from the 3rd Battalion had to be silent as well as invisible. 'We bound up our feet with strips of rags,' Mackay wrote, 'to make our movements through the house silent. The stone floors were covered with glass, plaster and were slippery with blood, especially the stairs.' German marksmanship had improved. 'We were now getting a considerable number of sniper bullets entering our houses,' another paratrooper wrote in a diary, 'and needless to say suffering considerable casualties, although it seemed to us that we had inflicted at least double the amount on the enemy. We were still unable to contact the Divisional Commander, although the wireless team had received the Second Army quite clearly, but unfortunately they were not receiving us.'

The American OSS lieutenant Harvey Todd recorded with satisfaction three more kills during the Germans' dawn attack. He left his perch in the roof of brigade headquarters a little later. Around midday the enemy launched another counter-attack, a much more serious one. Todd recorded five more kills from his position in the roof, but then had to get out rapidly when a German machine-gunner zeroed in on him. A Bren-gunner in the building was killed so Todd took over his weapon. He spotted a 20mm flak gun being used against another house, and managed to shoot the crew.

'Great joy all round' broke out when a Focke-Wulf 190 roared in from the south over the bridge to drop a bomb, which proved a dud as it bounced up the main concourse of the Eusebiusbinnensingel towards the town centre. Sappers in the school fired Bren guns at the plane. The pilot banked to escape their bursts, but his port wing caught the church steeple to the west and the plane crashed with a massive explosion. This produced another roar of 'Whoa Mahomet!' from all the buildings around the bridge.

The defiance belied the fact that Frost's force was suffering badly. 'We now had over 50 casualties in our building alone,' Lieutenant Todd reported. The battalion doctor Captain Jimmy Logan and his orderlies won universal praise for accomplishing what they did without running water, and when they were almost out of clean bandages, morphine and the other medical necessities of war. Patients had to use empty wine bottles and fruit jars to urinate in. The Rev. Father Bernard Egan had worked well with Logan ever since the battalion's battles in North Africa. Logan knew by then which of his patients were Catholic, and he would warn Father Egan as soon as one of them needed the last rites. One man just before dying of his wounds said, 'And to think I was worried that my chute wouldn't open.'

Captain Jacobus Groenewoud, the Dutch leader of the Jedburgh team, tried to ring the St Elisabeth Hospital but the line was dead. Groenewoud and Todd decided to run to a doctor's house near by to ring the hospital from there. When about halfway, and just as they were steeling themselves for the next dash across a street, Captain Groenewoud was killed by a sniper. 'The bullet went in his forehead and out the back of his head,' Todd wrote. Todd ducked into a doorway, and found a man who spoke a little English. They managed to sneak to the next-door house where there was a telephone which worked. He called the hospital, but the doctor he spoke to explained it would be impossible to send an ambulance. They had tried already, but the Germans warned that any ambulance sent out would be fired on. The doctor also explained that as the Germans controlled the hospital approaches, where a considerable battle was going on, they wanted the British wounded moved so there was more space for their own casualties. When Todd managed to return to brigade headquarters, the news was equally bad there. In one of the few radio transmissions to work, they had learned that XXX Corps had still not captured the bridge at Nijmegen, but were about to make an attempt that evening.

Later that morning, the Germans bombarded the school with Panzerfausts. Thinking that they had silenced the defenders, they surrounded the school. Mackay told his men to prepare two grenades each, and on his command they dropped them from the upper windows. They grabbed their weapons and finished off any who had not been blasted by the grenades. 'It was all over in a matter of minutes leaving a carpet of field-grey around the house.' Mackay was recognized by his men as being one of those rare beings who were virtually fearless.

Another was Major Digby Tatham-Warter. He inspired everyone, almost playing the fool, by walking up and down in the open twirling an umbrella he had found in one of the houses, and putting on a bowler hat like Charlie Chaplin. When Freddie Gough pointed this out to Colonel Frost, he simply said, 'Oh yes, Digby's quite a leader.' Lieutenant Patrick Barnett, who commanded the brigade defence platoon, saw Tatham-Warter walking along the street in a heavy mortar barrage with his umbrella up. Barnett stared at him in astonishment and asked him where he was going. 'I thought I'd go and see some of the chaps over there.' Barnett laughed and pointed at the umbrella as German mortars kept firing. 'That won't do you much good.' Tatham-Warter looked at him, eyes wide open in mock surprise. 'Oh? My goodness, but what if it rains?'

Some soldiers became fired up with bloodlust. Private Watson was sent to replace a Scot, predictably known as 'Jock'. 'He told me to get the bloody hell out. He said he had ten notches on his [rifle] butt already and he planned to get ten more of the bastards before they got him. He looked like the kind of crazy bastard who'd do it.' Watson went back a couple of hours later. 'Jock was sprawled on the floor. He'd taken a bullet right through the mouth.' Freddie Gough remembered that one of their best snipers was Corporal Bolton, one of the few black soldiers in the division. Bolton, a 'tall, languid' man, took great satisfaction in his work, 'crawling all over the place, sniping', and would 'grin widely' after each victory.

Brigadeführer Harmel ordered his men to cease fire while he sent a captured British soldier to Colonel Frost, to suggest they meet to discuss surrender. The panzergrenadiers seized the opportunity to eat or sleep.

'After a pause', wrote Horst Weber, 'the English paratroopers suddenly let out a terrific yell: "Whoa Mahomet!" We all sprang up, wondering what was happening. We were frightened at first by this terrible yell . . . Then the shooting began again.'

Frost was determined to fight on, yet because they were so short of ammunition he felt compelled to issue an order to shoot only when repelling German attacks. During the next onslaught a voice was heard to shout at the enemy, 'Stand still you sods, these bullets cost money!'

Now pushed back well to the west of the bridge, the remnants of the four battalions which had tried to break through were in full retreat, harried by their German pursuers. 'At every house we passed was a man or a woman with a pail of water and several cups. We needed those drinks,' wrote Major Blackwood in the 11th Parachute Battalion. 'The people flocked round us, smiling, laughing, offering us fruit and drink. But when we told them the Boche was coming, their laughter turned to tears. As we dug our slit-trenches in the gardens, the melancholy procession of blanket carrying refugees began to move past.'

Blackwood's men cannot have occupied those trenches for long, because the retreat gathered pace and became even more chaotic. Most platoons and companies had lost their officers in the fighting. 'A sergeant whose boots were squelching blood from his wounds', recorded a soldier from the South Staffords, 'gave us the order to try to get out of it, and make our way back to the first organised unit we came to . . . Everyone still alive seemed to be wounded somewhere or deeply shocked.'

The other retreat westwards, that of the 4th Parachute Brigade, was to escape being caught against the steep railway embankment. There were only two ways to get through, the level crossing at Wolfheze and a culvert under the railway through which a Jeep could just be driven, providing the windscreen was folded flat and the driver lay almost sideways. The 6- and 17-pounder anti-tank guns were too large. Using all their remaining strength, some anti-tank crews tried to manhandle their guns up the vertiginous slope of the embankment. The Germans, seizing the opportunity, sent machine-gun groups up on to the embankment to fire along the railway tracks.

When self-propelled assault guns appeared, even the bravest paratroopers were shaken, knowing how ill-armed they were. A chief clerk of the 4th Parachute Brigade recounted how a major shouted, 'You white-livered bastards. Come and get them!' He did not last long, brought down by German fire as he charged forwards. A pathfinder sergeant near Wolfheze saw 'hundreds of airborne running in panic. They were pouring back, some of them without arms . . . We went along the railway line and I remember seeing a Pole up on top of the embankment trying to fire a six-pounder anti-tank gun. He was shouting in Polish. We saw that the breech block of the gun had been removed. We tried to make him understand the gun wouldn't fire, but it was no use. We left him. He was out of his mind and I felt terribly sorry for him.'

The King's Own Scottish Borderers also took part in the disastrous withdrawal from the landing zone and the adjoining farm of Johanna Hoeve. Colonel Payton-Reid, its commanding officer, described how his battalion, 'which at four o'clock in the afternoon was a full-strength unit, with its weapons, transport and organisation complete, whose high morale had been further boosted by a successful action against attacking enemy, and which was prepared to meet anything coming [at] it, was reduced within the hour to a third of its strength, with much of its transport and many of its heavy weapons lost, one company completely missing and two more reduced to half-strength'. Payton-Reid led the remainder all the way round and back to north Oosterbeek to a small hotel called the Dreijeroord, which the regiment would always know as 'the White House'. Payton-Reid knocked on its door at 21.00, to be greeted as a liberator, but he felt a hypocrite. He knew he was 'bringing them only danger and destruction. By the next night the building was reduced to a shell.'

Caring for the wounded in such a retreat became doubly difficult. With the advance of General von Tettau's forces from the west, Colonel Warrack had to organize the rapid evacuation of patients from the dressing station at Wolfheze. Most were moved to the Hotel Schoonoord. Warrack visited it at 11.00 and found that 'casualties were coming in fast'. In fact the total had passed 300, and they had taken over nearby buildings to house the overflow. Hendrika van der Vlist, the daughter of the owner, had put on her girl-guide uniform because it was made of tough material. Along with other young women volunteers, they started by washing the faces of the wounded and their hands to reduce the danger of infection.

They also had to act as interpreters. Both British and German wounded were brought in, and at first it was too complicated to keep them apart. Even though the Germans were prisoners, their attitude had not changed. One of them summoned her: 'Nurse, cold towel! I have a headache.' She observed that 'The Herrenvolk has become so used to commanding that they do not know how to behave differently.' On the other hand, a German who had never wanted to be in the army soon made friends with the British soldiers either side of him. They started teaching each other words and phrases in their own language.

She then found a Dutch boy in German uniform who had been shot through the jaw. He was a traitor, but she could not help feeling pity. Later in the week, she discovered that he was 'mentally defective'. She was surprised to find how quickly she adapted to dealing with horrible wounds. 'A week ago I would have been frightened at the sight of such a horribly injured face. Now I am used to it. It is nothing but wounds that I see here. And the heavy sickly smell of blood hanging all over the place.'

Urquhart went to the Schoonoord to visit the wounded that afternoon. Soon afterwards the rest of the 131st (Parachute) Field Ambulance arrived from Wolfheze, having just got out in time as Helle's SS Wachbataillon approached. To help feed such a crowd, farmers brought in livestock killed in the fighting and locals arrived with produce from their gardens and orchards, especially tomatoes, apples and pears. The wounded were not very hungry but they badly needed water, the hospital's greatest problem. The bathtubs in the hotel had fortunately all been filled on Sunday as a precaution just after the airborne landings. Volunteers now started to drain the central heating system and radiators to replace what was being used from the baths.

Other civilians turned up at the Schoonoord, particularly divers who had emerged from hiding, including former political prisoners and several Jews. They had come because they thought they must be safe there. The general impression that the Allies had as good as won the war was already proving very dangerous for many in occupied Europe.

With German losses mounting at the bridge that day, Brigadeführer Harmel welcomed the arrival of the 280th Assault Gun Brigade from Denmark, which had been diverted to Arnhem instead of Aachen. One of their men later recounted that they lost 80 per cent of their vehicles in the fighting in and around Arnhem, which he described as far more savage than anything he had witnessed in Russia. British paratroopers would hold their fire and let the assault guns pass, then shoot them from behind because the armour was so much thinner there. The close-quarter fighting wrecked the nerves of the crews, he added. They were terrified of being burned alive by phosphorus grenades.

Above all Harmel eagerly awaited the arrival of Kompanie Hummel from the 506th Heavy Panzer Battalion, with its Tiger tanks. They had been unloaded early that morning in Bocholt, close to the Dutch border, after their *Blitztransport* across Germany. But only two of the Tiger tanks survived the eighty-kilometre road-march. The rest were rendered useless along the way, mostly from broken tracks and sprockets. The two serviceable tanks went into action that evening, guarded by panzergrenadiers from the SS *Frundsberg*. Their armour-piercing rounds went right through a house, leaving a hole each side. 'They looked incredibly menacing and sinister in the half-light,' Colonel Frost recounted, 'like some prehistoric monster as their great guns swung from side to side breathing flame.' When the ammunition was switched to high explosive, their 88mm guns began to smash the houses around the heads of the defenders. At times it was hard to breathe, so thick was the dust of pulverized masonry. The building which housed battalion headquarters was hit, and Digby Tatham-Warter and Father Egan were both wounded.

In the school, Major Lewis ordered his men into the cellars, since the Tigers could not depress their guns far enough to shoot so low. Once they withdrew, the defenders reoccupied the first floor. A brave anti-tank gunner took on one of the Tigers single-handed. He ran out, loaded his gun and fired, then ran back behind the house. Fortunately he was under cover when the tank destroyed the gun, yet one of the two Tigers was knocked out that very evening. A round from a different 6-pounder hit the turret, badly wounding the commander and another member of the crew, while a second round jammed the main armament. The second Tiger then developed mechanical problems and also had to be withdrawn for major repairs at Doetinchem. 'Thus ended the first day's engagement in a fiasco,' wrote a member of the Kompanie Hummel.

Harmel ordered heavy howitzers and more assault guns to be brought in to take over the task of blasting British strongpoints at close range. To the British defenders, this suggested that the Germans were not in a hurry, which meant that XXX Corps had still not crossed the bridge at Nijmegen. In fact Harmel was under great pressure. Generalfeldmarschall Model wanted the 1st Airborne destroyed and the Arnhem bridge opened quickly so that they could speed reinforcements to Nijmegen, having heard that XXX Corps had reached the edge of the city. That evening Model put the so-called Division von Tettau, which had just occupied Wolfheze, under the command of II SS Panzer Corps 'for the complete destruction of the enemy west of Arnhem'. The Germans could not help exaggerating their already considerable successes that day. Bittrich claimed 1,700 prisoners taken, four British tanks and three armoured cars knocked out. It seems that Bren-gun carriers now counted as tanks.

The bombardment of the houses round the bridge was far worse than what the 2nd Battalion had endured in Sicily. 'It seemed impossible for the mortaring to get any heavier but it did,' wrote Private James Sims, 'bomb after bomb rained down, the separate explosions now merging into one

continuous rolling detonation, the ground shook and quivered as the deto-
nations overlapped.' He was curled up at the bottom of a trench out on the
Eusebiusbinnensingel. 'Alone there in that trench it was like laying in a
freshly dug grave waiting to be buried alive.' It was not just the shrapnel
which killed. In brigade headquarters, Lieutenant Buchanan, the intelligence officer, dropped dead from bomb blast without a scratch on him.

At one stage in the fighting that day, Lieutenant Barnett of the defence
platoon saw two German medics dash out to tend to British wounded in the
street, until they were shot by a German MG-34 and fell across the bodies
of those they were trying to help. 'They had been shot down by their own
people.' The artillery forward observation officer was badly wounded, so
Lieutenant Todd took over, having served in the cannon company of his
American division. To speed things up, Harmel sent in the newly arrived
pioneers with flamethrowers to set fire to the houses. 'As night came, rows
and rows of houses stood in flames,' Harmel recorded. 'But still the British
did not give up.' As a house was set on fire, they 'mouseholed' through from
one to another. There was no water to extinguish the blaze.

Some of the fires had been started to make sure that the streets were
constantly lit, as one panzergrenadier explained. 'Then if they tried to run
across they made good targets.' But now Harmel's own panzergrenadiers
were also suffering from the fires. 'The houses were burning and it was terribly hot,' Alfred Ringsdorf recorded. 'I got cinders in my eyes more than
once and the smoke made them smart. It also made you cough. Ashes and
soot from the rubble made things even worse. It was hell.' He had still not
entirely recovered from a close shave earlier in the day. 'I took a prisoner,
quite a heavy, strong man. I had him stand up and raise his hands so that I
could search him. I bent down in my search and at that very moment he
uttered an "Oh," and crumpled up dead. It was an English bullet meant for
me which had killed him. For a second I was paralysed. Then, I broke out
in a cold sweat and, driven by habit, dived for cover.'

Ringsdorf hated close combat, because 'it was one man against another,
face to face, and also you never knew when the enemy would pop up.' He
avoided the danger of moving around at night and stumbling into the enemy.
The one thing he longed to do was to take off his helmet because it was so
heavy and his neck was so stiff. 'The English were very good sharpshooters.
Most of the German soldiers, dead and wounded, were hit in the head.' He
thought that the only reason he survived the battle was because he was leading. 'The enemy rarely shoots at the first man, but wait to see if there are
more soldiers coming. They let the first couple of men go by, then attack
those coming up next.'

As well as the fires deliberately started, much of the city centre was ablaze, including the towers of the two churches, the St Eusebius and the St Walburgis. Their bells made strange noises when struck by bullets. Because of the conflagration, the prison director in Arnhem opened the cells of all but the most dangerous prisoners. The liberated inmates emerged with white faces and heads shaved, in their prison clothes. The blaze continued to spread. 'You can read the newspaper by the light of the fires,' an anonymous diarist wrote laconically. Civilians started to flee the burning city whenever there was a lull in the shelling. The old and the ill had to be transported on handcarts or even in wheelbarrows.

The British at the bridge had no illusions about the danger. The crackle of burning buildings and the occasional crump as floors and façades collapsed gave an apocalyptic impression. Frost and Gough climbed to the attic to watch. If the wind changed direction then they would be trapped in a conflagration which might turn into a firestorm.

16

Nijmegen and Eindhoven
Tuesday 19 September

After all the delays to XXX Corps, the 14th Field Squadron Royal Engineers worked through the night at Son. They excelled themselves by assembling a Bailey bridge over the Wilhelmina Canal in less than eight hours, and by 06.15 on Tuesday the armoured cars of the Household Cavalry were rattling across it. Making up for lost time, they were over the River Aa and through Veghel half an hour later. The Grenadier Group had taken over the lead from the Irish Guards and they drove steadily all morning on towards the bridge over the River Maas at Grave. 'No sign of enemy, save prisoners,' the Irish Guards noted in their war diary.

As the huge snake of XXX Corps followed, a squadron of Cromwell tanks from the 15th/19th Hussars was diverted to support the embattled 502nd Parachute Infantry Regiment at Best. In the two battalions dug in on the edge of the Sonsche forest, nobody yet knew that Wierzbowski's platoon was still resisting at dawn by the blown bridge little more than a kilometre further on. Wierzbowski hoped that the message about their plight, sent via the Household Cavalry armoured car, would lead to their deliverance.

The remnants of Wierzbowski's little force were now on their own because Mottola's platoon, dug in on their left, had disintegrated and disappeared during the night. Wierzbowski and his men were so exhausted that they could hardly stay awake, but they knew they could not abandon their wounded comrades.

Dawn revealed a heavy mist over the canal. Suddenly figures loomed out of the haze on all sides. Wierzbowski shouted a warning, but the Germans had thrown their potato-masher grenades first. Some men were quick enough to throw them back out of their trenches before they exploded, but one blew up in a paratrooper's face, blinding him completely. Another fell in the trench next to Wierzbowski and just behind Pfc Mann who was 'propped against the back of the trench, and who had both arms wrapped in slings from his previous wounds'. Mann yelled 'Grenade!' and Wierzbowski saw him 'deliberately slide his back on the grenade, covering it'. The grenade went off, muffled by his sacrifice. Wierzbowski caught him by the shoulders. Mann looked up at him and said, 'Lieutenant, my back's gone.' Without another sound, he closed his eyes. Wierzbowski and two others in the trench were only slightly wounded as a result. Mann was awarded a posthumous Medal of Honor.

Soon Wierzbowski's platoon had fired their last rounds. They had no option but to surrender. Two German medics, whom they had captured earlier, jumped up to beg their comrades not to kill anyone. Wierzbowski and half a dozen survivors were taken back to a German field hospital. Some time later, the Germans became very agitated when a thunderous vibration began. The tanks of the Guards Armoured Division were approaching. Wierzbowski, working through one of his men who spoke German, persuaded the major in charge to lay down their weapons, which the Americans promptly seized. Their return next day to the 502nd caused astonishment, for everyone had assumed they were dead.

The rapid advance of the Guards Armoured Division against negligible opposition caused a good deal of false optimism. 'It was an express drive right across Holland,' Frank Gillard reported for the BBC, 'linking up all the way with parachutists and airborne forces who prepared the ground and made the advance possible by seizing the bridges and road junctions. In five hours, five hours only – an advance of almost thirty miles had been made . . . It's an incredible achievement.'

On hearing that the Guards Armoured Division had reached the Grave bridge, Browning told Colonel Chatterton to drive down with him to meet them and Brigadier General Gavin at Overasselt. Browning, although outwardly calm, was deeply concerned at the lack of contact with the 1st Airborne at Arnhem. The congratulations he had received in a signal from Montgomery were turning bitter, but he could not admit it. A strange rumour had also emerged back in Britain. Browning's wife, the novelist Daphne du Maurier, was rung at three in the morning by a journalist 'asking if it were true that my husband had been taken prisoner'.

Browning failed to recognize the Grenadier officer who greeted him, because his face was caked with the dust and dirt thrown up by the armoured vehicles. 'General "Boy" Browning,' he wrote, 'accompanied by an escort of very tough looking glider pilots, was as ever immaculately dressed, a contrast to our filthy appearance.' Gavin exulted at the sight of the tanks. 'I was really living,' he said later. The 82nd Airborne's isolation was over and with the tanks of the Guards Armoured Division he was now confident that they could both seize the Nijmegen bridge and fight off any attack from the Reichswald.

Gavin and Browning met Major General Allan Adair, the commander of the Guards Armoured Division, who was taken aback to hear that the Americans had not already captured the bridge. He had assumed that it had been the 82nd Airborne's first priority and that his tanks would simply 'sweep through' the city and on to Arnhem. Gavin, who had been keeping his best battalion in reserve, now proposed that it should ride the Sherman tanks of the Grenadier Guards and charge the bridge along with their infantry battalion. In return he asked for a battalion of the Coldstream to replace it on the Groesbeek sector. All the British officers agreed, unaware of the *Frundsberg* reinforcements which had reached northern Nijmegen. In fact it was 'suggested that the town was not strongly held and that a display of force in the shape of tanks would probably cause the enemy to withdraw'.

The Grenadier Guards group, with Captain the Duke of Rutland commanding the lead motor company and Major Alec Gregory Hood the armoured squadron, had meanwhile been diverted east via Groesbeek. A party of Royal Engineers, after checking bridges, had decided that only the span at Heuman was sufficiently robust to bear tanks.

The Grenadiers had been told to meet Captain Bestebreurtje at the Convent of Marienboom five kilometres south of Nijmegen. They parked their tanks outside, but then came under air attack. Lieutenant Colonel Rodney Moore, whose aircraft-recognition skills were notoriously bad, became convinced that the plane attacking them was an Allied fighter. He started throwing yellow smoke grenades to identify themselves. This rather blinded his own adjutant, Captain Tony Heywood, who was frantically firing the Sherman's turret-mounted machine gun at the strafing Messerschmitt.

Once the aircraft had departed, Bestebreurtje led the officers over to the Hotel Sionshof. Word had spread of the meeting, and almost every member of the different underground groups converged on the place, causing chaos. Major Henry Stanley of the Grenadiers described the scene. 'It was a lovely sunny day and the café had already attracted the attention of the crowds. Groups of excited civilians were pushing their way in and talking to anyone prepared to listen. The underground supporters were being marshalled together in one room by the Dutch liaison officer all talking at once. Dutch guards, obviously impressed by the importance of the occasion, were ineffectively trying to prevent anyone coming in or out. Outside, a battery of American 75s were firing away as hard as they could, and as our tanks began to arrive still more excited and delighted spectators joined the crowds. Meanwhile inside the café the owners were doing a record business. In the midst of all this we were trying to evolve a plan to capture two bridges over one of the largest rivers in Europe.'

Gavin and his most trusted battalion commander, Lieutenant Colonel Benjamin H. Vandervoort, also arrived and the plan was rapidly agreed. Members of the Dutch underground insisted that the plunger to blow the main bridge was in the post office building held by the Germans. Gavin promised an extra platoon of his paratroopers to help take the place. He went out and grabbed the first platoon he came across. Bestebreurtje had meanwhile selected four members of the underground to act as guides for the three combat teams and the post office group.*

Gavin left to meet General Horrocks, accompanied by Adair, in a school-house near Malden. Gavin told Horrocks that he wanted boats to launch an attack on the northern end of the bridge in case they did not manage to seize it that evening. Horrocks agreed and Adair said that he could bring up about twenty-eight assault boats that night. Thus contrary to the belief of many at the time, the plan to launch an opposed crossing of the Waal was entirely Gavin's.

The Grenadiers mounted their tanks and began the advance into Nijmegen. Part of Vandervoort's 2nd Battalion of the 505th Parachute Infantry rode on the engine decks, and the rest ran from tree to tree on the flanks up the broad avenue of the Groesbeekseweg. According to an American source, as the Grenadiers advanced towards the huge traffic circle of the Keizer Karelplein, the column came to a halt. The sharp crack of 88s firing could be heard, and tracer was flying overhead down the street. Captain Robert Franco, the surgeon of the 2nd Battalion, decided to leave his Jeep and walk ahead with an aid man to see what was happening. 'Captain Franco, look!' his aid man suddenly called out, pointing. 'The source of wonder-ment was a pair of tankers in their black berets, sitting in the middle of the

---

* One volunteer whose services were rejected was called Jan van Hoof, a lanky boy scout. Bestebreurtje refused to use him as 'he was very young and seemed very ner-vous'. Yet after the war a legend emerged in Nijmegen, promoted by a Jesuit priest, that Jan van Hoof had cut all the wires to the explosive charges on the bridge and thus saved it. This story is hard to credit. Jan van Hoof was killed very soon afterwards in the fight-ing, and would not have had a chance to get near to the bridge which was by then heavily guarded. And if he had cut the wires beforehand, why did he not tell Bestebreurtje, which was surely his duty in the circumstances? Once again the bridge's survival came back to Model's categorical order that it was not to be blown.

street, making tea over the usual square oil can half-filled with sand and drenched with gasoline. I looked at my watch. It was 4 p.m.' Even allowing for soldiers' tales, there are too many similar accounts to dismiss them. Major Dick Winters of the 101st Airborne recounted that 'the British custom of wanting – insisting – on stopping to "brew up a cup of tea" left us speechless.' He concluded that the British, with the exception of their airborne units, were 'not aggressive'.

The Grenadier Group consisted of the 1st Motor Battalion and the 2nd (Armoured) Battalion, now reinforced by Vandervoort's battalion. A battery of the 153rd Field Regiment and Q Battery of the 21st Anti-Tank Regiment also supported it. While the British and American guns hammered away at the north end of the great road bridge, the two main attacking columns advanced into the city. One headed for the railway bridge and the other for the road bridge, but they came up against heavy resistance at the Keizer Karelplein. German 88mm guns, well dug in, were shielded by blazing buildings. Fire-raising groups increased the destruction begun the day before, and German artillery north of the River Waal was also firing into the city.

The only group to enjoy any success at this attempt was the smallest one. Captain George Thorne, commanding a troop of Shermans, a platoon of Grenadiers and a platoon of paratroopers, headed for the post office 'where it was rumoured a horrible little man was sitting with a plunger, waiting to blow the bridge by remote control'. As they entered the southern part of Nijmegen, people emerged from their houses to wave and welcome them. According to Major Stanley, 'the guide who was with them showed a remarkable capacity for receiving the admiration of the crowd until the first shot was fired, whereupon he subsided to the bottom of the tank and refused to stir an inch. Finally he was hoisted up by the scruff of the neck and forcibly asked the whereabouts of the Post Office. He gazed around and then pointed to the building alongside which the tank had pulled up. The Post Office was stormed and taken, but no horrible little man was found.' The Grenadiers were rightly sceptical of the whole story, since the logical place for any detonating device would be on the north bank of the River Waal, not in the town. But although the Germans inside the post office surrendered immediately, eight Guardsmen were killed by a shell, fired from across the river, which exploded in the front of the building.

Some SS soldiers, including an Obersturmführer, were captured, totally drunk, in business premises on Van Welderenstraat. They were taken back to the post office to join the other prisoners. The Obersturmführer, finding that Gerardus Groothuijsse was a member of the underground and now with the Guardsmen, told him that when the Germans recaptured the city he and all his fellow terrorists would be shot. A Grenadier hauled the Obersturmführer off, shot him and took his watch which he proudly offered back to Groothuijsse as a 'nice souvenir'.

From the post office, Thorne's force advanced towards the Keizer Lodewijkplein, a smaller traffic circle close to the south end of the road bridge. But with the open area of Hunner Park in front they came into plain view of the 88mm guns and had to beat a rapid retreat, suffering more casualties. The German defence system ahead was formidable. To the west of the bridge on the edge of the escarpment stood the Valkhof, the Carolingian citadel, and the Belvedere, a sixteenth-century watchtower high above the Waal. And the Kampfgruppe Reinhold, including the Euling Battalion of SS panzergrenadiers, reinforced by a mixed group under Major Bodo Ahlborn, had wasted no time since their arrival in digging foxholes and slit trenches. The bridge approach was also blocked by wrecked vehicles.

'The town was on fire,' one of Vandervoort's officers reported, 'and the flames silhouetted the British tanks so they were good targets for the German 88s. The tanks had to pull out. I was trapped there by the bridge. I had two platoons reinforced with 15 British Tommies. The Germans attempted to flank us. We gathered up our wounded, six American and British soldiers, and we carried them through a burning apartment building, and to the back yard.' They found it had a three-metre wall, so it was hard work passing the wounded over the top. German soldiers had also been spotted digging defences on the north bank of the Waal, so some of Vandervoort's paratroopers went up on to the rooftops opposite and picked them off as they dug.

Even if the sally to the bridges failed, the arrival of the Grenadiers' tanks in Nijmegen seems to have saved a number of people. A party of German soldiers was chasing a policeman working with the underground, who had tried to steal a German truck full of ammunition. He fled through the air-raid precaution headquarters and out of a back door. The Germans charged in and levelled their rifles at everyone working there. All the staff, nearly forty strong, had to stand with their hands above their heads as the German officer ranted that fresh German troops were arriving from all sides. 'The town is surrounded!' he shouted. He claimed that he and his men had been shot at it from this building. 'We're burning the whole town to the ground.' At that moment, one of the men with his hands up asked if he could stub out his cigarette as it was about to burn his fingers. This provoked an explosion of nervous laughter from the others, which did not improve the Germans' mood. The officer said that he would hand them all over to the Gestapo, but then the rolling thunder of approaching tanks made the Germans flee for their lives. 'It is only when one faces death', observed one of the men there, 'that one realises the great value of life.'

This sentiment was reflected in much of the population. People showed a remarkable resignation when forced to abandon their houses and possessions to the flames. They were simply thankful that they and their family were at least still alive as they fled through showers of sparks from the burning buildings. Of course, a number broke down under the strain and horror of what they had seen. After the fires set by German soldiers and the teenagers of the Reichsarbeitsdienst the evening before, most families had prepared 'flight cases' with essentials and valuables ready for a rapid departure.

A diarist described their whole street burning, the blaze started by the Germans, the occupants having to escape over garden walls. 'Some Germans throw hand-grenades behind them,' he wrote, but 'one soldier helps to lift children and suitcases over the walls.' One group of Germans even apologized to the inhabitants of the house they were about to set ablaze. 'We are very sorry but we have to set light to it.' In another of the houses, a drunken German soldier continued to play the piano. Just south of their Valkhof defences the SS were having a wild party, throwing beer bottles. A couple of them apparently danced with wooden mannequins seized from smashed shop windows. Fleeing inhabitants gave them a wide berth, fearing what they might do in their madness.

A woman described how German youths from the RAD and the SS, some of them very drunk, went shouting and screaming through the streets: 'they shot left and right, and doused houses in petrol . . . They torched our whole city.' Another wrote, 'We hear that a middle aged couple have been driven back into the flames by those bastards! Their name was Frederiks and they were people whose son had been executed the year before during the strikes in 1943. He had been caught distributing leaflets.'

The fighting amid the blazing buildings became savage that night. A lieutenant in Vandervoort's battalion described it as 'a fierce hand-to-hand battle in which trench knives were the only weapons used'. He added that 'the ceaseless hunt for snipers made psycho cases out of us.' The director of the concert hall described the fighting around the Keizer Karelplein, where the Germans had started so many fires. 'The racket of guns, mortars and machine guns was terrible.'

Most of the buildings around the Keizer Karelplein were ablaze, including the university building, the courthouse and the houses near the St Josephkerk. Smoke made the air almost unbreathable. 'As evening falls over the town, the air is coloured red from the countless fires.' Many similar

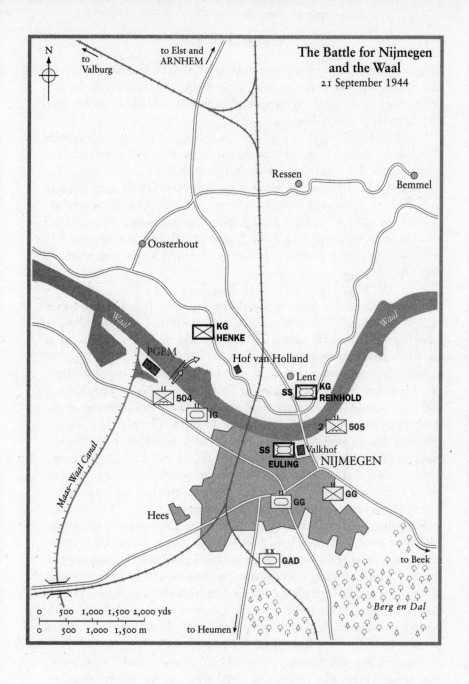

N
to Valburg

to Elst and
ARNHEM

**The Battle for Nijmegen
and the Waal**
21 September 1944

Ressen

Bemmel

Oosterhout

Waal

Waal

**KG
HENKE**

PGEM

Hof van Holland

Lent

SS **KG
REINHOLD**

504

IG

2 505

SS Valkhof
EULING NIJMEGEN

Maas-Waal Canal

Hees

GG

GG

XX GAD

to Beek

Berg en Dal

o 500 1,000 1,500 2,000 yds

o 500 1,000 1,500 m

to Heumen

images of Nijmegen burning were recorded. 'The centre of the town looks like hell. A red glow hangs against the black sky. The crackling of the fires can be heard from afar.' An increasing number of the population began to flee the town in fearful despair.

SS-Brigadeführer Harmel of the *Frundsberg* refused to acknowledge after the war that the fires had been started deliberately by his own men, and tried to argue that it was simply an unfortunate consequence of battle. 'After the violent street fighting, the whole of the north part of Nijmegen was seen to be on fire.' At 21.30 that evening Harmel's superior Obergruppenführer Bittrich signalled to Model's headquarters, 'Commanding general II SS Panzer Corps emphasizes that the Nijmegen garrison is very weak.' To conceal comparative weakness with extreme violence was a standard SS response.

Allied commanders at Nijmegen soon saw that their frontal attack on the bridges would fail. Different methods were needed. They would have to clear the town, sector by sector, and Gavin's idea of an assault crossing of the River Waal became essential.

Gavin had suddenly appeared at the command post of the 504th Parachute Infantry Regiment. According to Captain Louis A. Hauptfleisch, Colonel Reuben Tucker's regimental adjutant, Gavin had been very apologetic about the plan for a river assault in broad daylight. Hauptfleisch assumed that the order had come from General Browning, when the idea was entirely Gavin's. Tucker was stoical. 'OK, we will do the best we can,' was his response. He told Hauptfleisch to summon the three battalion commanders for an orders group to be held on his return from the conference at Gavin's headquarters in the forest near Berg en Dal.

Browning, accompanied by Colonel George Chatterton of the Glider Pilot Regiment, was there along with senior officers from XXX Corps. Chatterton described a Guards brigadier (probably Gwatkin), wearing corduroys and suede desert boots, sitting on a shooting stick. Reuben Tucker wore a helmet, had a hefty pistol strapped under his left armpit, and a trench knife on his belt. Tucker was chewing a cigar 'and occasionally he would remove it long enough to spit. Every time he did, I could see looks of faint surprise flicker over the faces of the Guards officers.'

The plan was that once the town had been secured, Tucker's 3rd Battalion, under cover of a smokescreen and with supporting fire from the Shermans of the 2nd (Armoured) Battalion of the Irish Guards, would paddle across the Waal well to the west of the road and rail bridges. They would then swing right along the bank of the river and, as soon as they reached the north end of the road bridge, the tanks of the Grenadiers would charge across. It sounded quite straightforward.

The 3rd Battalion of the 504th Parachute Infantry Regiment was commanded by Major Julian Cook. He briefed his officers that night on the 1st Airborne's situation, and the need to cross the Waal to capture the Nijmegen bridge. His officers were rather shaken to hear that things were not going well in Arnhem. A shot went off during the briefing. Private Gittman, who had been cleaning Captain T. Moffat Burriss's pistol for him, had fired it accidentally, forgetting there was a round in the chamber. The bullet went through his hand. As soon as his comrades heard of their mission the next day, they teased Gittman with the suggestion that he had done it deliberately to avoid the mission. Gittman, furious at any suggestion of a self-inflicted wound, was determined to join them the next day, even heavily bandaged.

Brigadier General Gavin's surge of confidence, prompted by the arrival of the Guards Armoured Division, would not last long. That night a German counter-attack on the 508th sector by the hill in the Den Heuvel woods was beaten back with help from the armoured battalion of the Coldstream Guards. But the next morning the tanks had to move south rapidly, as a far more dangerous situation developed near Mook, putting the vital bridge at Heumel under threat. German attacks in preparation, up and down the XXX Corps lifeline, would threaten the whole operation. Horrocks's cosy term the 'Club Route' was rapidly forgotten. The American name of 'Hell's Highway' was far more descriptive.

St Oedenrode, which the Guards Armoured Division had passed through that morning, was also under attack. Fortunately for Colonel Cassidy and the 1st Battalion of the 502nd Parachute Infantry Regiment, one of the Irish Guards Shermans had suffered mechanical problems in the small town and remained behind for repairs to the engine. When Company C reported that Germans were approaching the town, Captain James J. Hatch ran over to the tank, commanded by Sergeant Paddy McCrory, to ask if he could help. 'Hell, yes!' came the reply. Capable of no more than five miles an hour, the tank clanked up another road to strengthen the defence. McCrory advanced with his head out of the turret, despite the hail of bullets. Then, spotting a track off to the left, he followed it. After about 200 metres he suddenly saw a battery of three German light flak 20mm guns ahead which were firing at Company C. They were concentrating so much on their work that they did not see the tank until McCrory's gunner opened fire, putting them out of action. McCrory pushed on across to the Schijndel road. An American paratrooper helping out in the tank spotted a camouflaged gun ahead. He yelled at McCrory, and the turret traversed on to the target. A few moments later the gunner also hit a German truck which, to judge by the explosion, turned out to be full of ammunition. Some thirty German dead were counted and fifty-three prisoners taken.

When Colonel Cassidy thanked Paddy McCrory for his contribution afterwards, saying that his tank had changed the whole course of the engagement, the Irish Guards sergeant replied simply, 'When in doubt, lash out.' Cassidy decided to make it his motto too. His men would have little rest. Another advance on St Oedenrode took place that afternoon, as Model's headquarters reported: '16.00, counter-attack by 59th Infanterie-Division slowly winning ground on western edges Oedenrode.'

British tanks made a vital contribution to a much larger battle further south at Best. Here the other two battalions of the 502nd were launching a counter-attack by the Sonsche forest, supported by two battalions of the 327th Glider Infantry Regiment. One report also mentions the presence of nearly a hundred armed members of the Dutch underground group PAN.

The squadron of the 15th/19th Hussars in Cromwell tanks was greeted enthusiastically by the paratroopers. Their squadron leader asked the Americans to stand back as they lined up on the edge of the forest. The Cromwells opened fire together and maintained a rapid rate of reloading. 'The tanks turned the tide of battle,' Lieutenant John L. Cronin reported. 'The Germans saw the tanks and they started to wave handkerchiefs and white paper. Some of the bitter-end chaps shot the Germans who were offering to surrender.' German officers appear to have ordered machine-gunners to shoot them down.

'Our men wanted to kill off the Germans,' Cronin continued, 'but the battalion [commanding officer] said we must take prisoner every German who wanted to surrender. Then we saw them standing there, cowering before our weapons. They looked like broken men. Even the kids looked broken. They were asked why they had not surrendered sooner. "Officers wouldn't let us," was the answer.'

Lieutenant Colonel Chappuis agreed that 'the tanks were the decisive factor.' Reports vary, some claiming 2,600 prisoners and 600 bodies counted. Captain LeGrand K. Johnson called it 'one of the worst massacres that I have ever seen. The firing was so heavy that most of the Germans were surrendering and quite a few of them did not have a chance and just had to stand there and take it.' Another officer simply said, 'The operation was hardly more than a mop-up. Within two hours the 2nd Battalion captured seven hundred prisoners.' Chappuis had to radio for more military police as they had so many prisoners. The 3rd Battalion's executive officer 'got together a group of cooks, messengers and oddments and took over the guard detail until the MPs arrived'.

By 14.15 the 502nd, still supported by the Cromwell tanks, had captured Best and routed the remnants of the garrison there which had already been savaged by Lieutenant Wierzbowski and his men. Towards the end of the afternoon the squadron of the 15th/19th Hussars had to leave in a hurry, trundling due east towards Son. They had just received a message saying that the headquarters of the 101st was under attack, from part of Major von Maltzahn's 107th Panzer-Brigade.

Hauptmann Wedemeyer had found a crossing over the Dommel, a massive culvert which separated the river from the Wilhelmina Canal. With a group of Mark V Panther tanks, Wedemeyer surprised Major General Taylor in his command post at Son where he had no more than a platoon to defend the new Bailey bridge. Shells started to explode in the small town and a British truck on the bridge was set on fire. Taylor sent some men off to stalk the Panthers with bazookas, while he drove straight to the nearby landing ground. He rounded up some men and a 57mm anti-tank gun from the 327th Glider Infantry, and brought them back in a hurry. A hit from a bazooka and another from the anti-tank gun convinced Wedemeyer that the bridge was more heavily defended than they had thought, and he withdrew his force just before the squadron of the 15th/19th Hussars arrived.

General Taylor, now fully aware of how vulnerable Hell's Highway really was, brought back a battalion of the 506th from Eindhoven to ensure the safety of the Bailey bridge. The attack of the 107th Panzer-Brigade from the east was supposed to have been co-ordinated with the attack of the 59th Division from the west, so the Allies had been lucky that this had not worked. But it underlined the fact that the Germans could strike at will almost anywhere along the route and cut it. General Sir Miles Dempsey's other two corps in the Second Army, VIII and XII Corps, which should have been flanking the XXX Corps advance, had been delayed, XII Corps by heavy resistance and VIII Corps, on the right, by the fuel crisis.

Eindhoven had enjoyed another day of celebration, singing and dancing in the streets. Girls dressed themselves in orange, 'with big orange bows in their hair', and horizontal red, white and blue flags could be seen everywhere. 'A dummy in the uniform of a Dutch Nazi was hung from a lamppost and streets returned to their original names.'

'We are free, thank God!' another diarist wrote. 'In the morning all the flags were out. The city is full of troops, mostly Americans. A never ending line of vehicles (the English Second Army) is coming from the south and going north. The PAN or Netherlands Partisans (hundreds of armed men) are guarding public buildings and collecting NSBers, whom they keep under guard. Women and girls who have fraternized with the Germans are being shorn of their hair. In Strijp this work is being done by an NSB hairdresser in a convent in the Bezemstraat.'

Dr Boyans saw a group on the edge of the town surrounding two attractive women. They were about to have their heads shorn. The shearer was clicking his scissors when two American paratroopers from the 101st Airborne with Thompson sub-machine guns broke the circle. They aimed their weapons at the self-appointed hairdressers. 'Stop that nonsense!' they ordered. Then, each one took a woman by the arm and led them off through the throng and into town. The frustrated avengers could do little but mutter. An elderly man, standing next to Dr Boyans, remarked quietly: 'They're no fools, these Americans. They're looking for women with experience of life, and if you ask me, they've picked the right ones.'

Both General Brereton, the commander of the First Allied Airborne Army, and Major General Matthew Ridgway, the commander of XVIII Airborne Corps, arrived that evening in Eindhoven. Brereton was staying at Dempsey's headquarters, because he knew Browning would not welcome his presence. And Ridgway was naturally still sore that his two American airborne divisions had been put under Browning instead of himself. In any case, the two generals could not have picked a worse moment to visit Eindhoven. Ridgway later claimed that he was bombed 'every time he goes anywhere with Brereton'.

First of all, word spread of the 107th Panzer-Brigade rampaging to the north of the town. 'We will never forget that evening and night of terror,' a woman diarist wrote. 'About 7 o'clock we heard the rumour that the Germans would re-enter Eindhoven and that there would be a great battle with tanks. We all had to quickly get back into our houses. Just when we had done so we were warned to take all our flags back inside – the flags that we had raised so full of pride and hope that morning. We were told the Germans would shoot at those houses showing [them].'

But the real danger came from the skies. Earlier in the day two squadrons of the Household Cavalry Regiment had begun escorting more than 800 vehicles north from Leopoldsburg, heading for Nijmegen. Night had just fallen as the head of this interminable column passed through Eindhoven. Parachute flares were dropped, lighting up the whole city in a deathly glare. This signalled the start of an extended raid by Luftwaffe bombers. Eighteen ammunition trucks and petrol bowsers of the Royal Army Service Corps went up in flames, causing 'huge explosions'. As the fires reached the small-arms ammunition and shells it sounded as if a major battle had started. Captain John Profumo, the second-in-command of A Squadron (and many years later Britain's secretary of state for war), organized civilian working parties with great speed to clear the debris and allow the column to continue. If it remained blocked in Eindhoven, then the bombers would keep coming back. The fire brigade could do little as bombs had also smashed the water mains, although British and American troops did what they could to fight the fires and rescue people.

'A dreadful night,' an inhabitant wrote. 'A bombing of half an hour. Storm winds howl through the basements and cellars where people shelter. A latecomer is hurled inside by the blast. After the bombardment there remains a huge roar as if from cannon fire, but later we heard it was the noise from the burning trucks loaded with munitions.' The woman diarist was deeply shaken too. 'We all knew what fear was that night. People were killed in their cellars and we who did not have a cellar were standing in our kitchen and prayed without stop and prayed again. We were even given absolution as we had a priest visiting us at that time and that made us calmer. It was as if it would never end. Roof-tiles came down, all sorts of things came down, and always everything was accompanied by the ceaseless howling of shells overhead.' Altogether 227 civilians were killed and another 800 wounded. With Arnhem and Nijmegen ablaze, and the centre of Eindhoven blasted by explosions, the joy of liberation had been cut short with brutality.

17

Nijmegen – Crossing the Waal
Wednesday 20 September

After the failure to get to the Nijmegen road bridge the evening before, the two very dissimilar divisional commanders, the lanky Jim Gavin and the Guards major general Allan Adair with his First World War moustache, were in complete agreement. Their only hope now was to clear the northern part of the city block by block. Each infantry company, whether Vandervoort's paratroopers or Grenadiers, was to be supported by a troop of tanks.

Major Stanley waited with his company of Grenadiers for dawn in the Juliana Park, with much of the city ablaze around them. 'It was a pretty tense business,' he wrote, 'just waiting, houses on fire and the fire coming our way, driving before it various bands of homeless natives. It was heart-breaking to see their helplessness.' The huge numbers rendered homeless congregated in the St Canisius Hospital, which was experienced in dealing with disasters after the mistaken bombing of Nijmegen by American aircraft seven months before. The staff were having to feed up to 4,000 people a day.

The task facing the combat teams involved in each phase was made doubly dangerous with German assault guns moving around and suddenly opening fire. Adair therefore ordered that each street, once it had been cleared, should be blocked by an M-10 Achilles from Q Battery 21st Anti-Tank Regiment. This tank destroyer's powerful 17-pounder gun could even knock out a Tiger tank. But, with most of the houses on fire, clearing block by block was going to be hard when faced with determined SS panzergrenadiers. The fire-raising continued during the gradual German withdrawal towards the Valkhof. Pioneers with flamethrowers smashed a window in each house, then blasted a stream of blazing fuel inside.

'From the first five minutes the fighting did not conform in the slightest to my original plan,' Stanley confessed. They were suffering heavy casualties out in the street so they needed to go through the houses and over garden walls, although the fires were spreading rapidly. Stanley saw a German throw a stick grenade which exploded at the feet of a fellow officer and Sergeant Partridge. 'There was a hell of a bang, but the amazing thing was the only damage sustained was to Sergeant Partridge, who took the full blast right in his face, and was then only dazed for a few minutes, after which he got really angry and fairly set about the Hun.' A very large house still lay ahead, and 'we had not enough men to clear it,' Stanley continued. 'As we were having a bit of impertinence from them, we decided to cover the exits with Brens and to cook them. Phosphorus grenades and a borrowed incendiary from the Americans did the trick.' The house caught fire and later began to explode. The *Frundsberg* had used it as their ammunition dump. Prisoners interrogated later claimed that there had still been many SS troopers trapped inside.

Eventually, Stanley was able to report that his area had been cleared. 'Charlie Rutland was then unleashed. Having seen No 2 Company on their way, I went back to see the Commander who had set up his HQ in the Post Office.' He had a quick sleep there after the long night. 'But one's peace of mind', Stanley noted, with the slightly flippant hauteur of the Foot Guards, 'was constantly and rudely jolted by a large and exceedingly rude enemy gun, either 150mm or 210mm, which intermittently plastered the whole area and made an awful mess of anything it hit.'

The third phase turned out to be the most bitter. With the thick smoke, tank commanders had to stick their heads out of the turret hatch if they were to see anything at all. German snipers and machine-gunners in the tops of buildings managed to kill or seriously wound four tank commanders in Major James Bowes-Lyon's squadron. Major Gregory Hood's squadron, working in from the east with Vandervoort's paratroopers, experienced a savage battle with the SS panzergrenadiers defending the Keizer Lodewijk-plein traffic circle by the Hunner Park.

Out to the west, Colonel Reuben Tucker's paratroopers and Lieutenant Colonel Giles Vandeleur's Shermans cleared the area behind the huge PGEM power station on the southern bank of the Waal. The two men had met at the XXX Corps command post early in the morning, and had left together in a scout car. The power station was close to where Major Julian Cook's battalion was to launch its boats. Unfortunately the trucks bringing the boats were slowed at Son, where the 107th Panzer-Brigade was attacking again. A German shell reduced the number of serviceable boats from thirty-two to twenty-six.

A most unenviable task later that day awaited the King's Company of the Grenadiers. Their objective was the Carolingian fortress, the Valkhof. The

King's Company first of all seized the police station, which had a commanding position. The attached machine-gun platoon found that it provided 'a wonderful shoot'. The King's Company went on to seize the port, and from there they could pour flanking fire on to the Valkhof. 'All we knew was that it was going to take everything we had got to make headway towards that bloody bridge.' While his division fought with Gavin's paratroopers to clear the approaches to the southern end of the bridge, Major General Allan Adair expected the Germans to blow the whole structure at any moment. 'I sat there gritting my teeth, dreading the sound of an explosion.'

One troop of Grenadier tanks had been 'left out of battle'. The troop leader, Sergeant Peter Robinson, a tough and experienced regular soldier, knew that in the army there was no such thing as a free rest during a battle, and he wondered what their task would be. Just after midday, he received the order from his squadron commander, Major John Trotter, to go forward with him in a scout car to reconnoitre the road bridge. Trotter briefed him to have his troop of Shermans ready to charge it as soon as he received the signal. 'You've got to get across at all costs.' Trotter then tried to make reassuring comments about contacting Robinson's wife 'if anything happens to you'.

At the end of the morning, once the north-western section had been cleared, Major Cook, his company commanders and Captain Henry Keep, the battalion operations officer, drove in Jeeps to the power plant on the banks of the Waal, close to where they were to make the assault crossing. They climbed to the ninth floor, where they had a clear view right across the river to the German positions on the far side. They were joined by their regimental commander Colonel Tucker and Giles Vandeleur, but also by Browning, Horrocks and Gavin.

Through their binoculars the officers studied the far bank of the River Waal, which was some 300 metres wide at that point. 'We saw green, grassy flatlands that ran for about 900 yards,' wrote Henry Keep, 'then rose to form a dyke with a two-lane road on it. This was the route we would follow to the railroad and highway bridges . . . We could see enemy machine-gun positions along the dyke and also on the flat terrain. We observed mortar and artillery units behind the dyke and 20mm guns on the railroad bridge . . . I felt rather funny inside. I think everyone else did too although no one said a word – we just looked.' While they were studying the lie of the land, Allied supply aircraft flying north to Arnhem were greeted by 'a veritable wall of small arms and flak' from the positions across the river. Horrocks told Gavin how impressed he was that his paratroopers were able to sleep before such an ordeal. 'Fortunately, none of them had seen what we had,' Henry Keep observed.

The original idea was for the assault companies to get into their boats in the Maas–Waal Canal, just to the west of the PGEM building, as they would be out of sight. But 'the current was too swift where the canal entered the river,' so they had to launch the boats from the bank just upriver from the power station.

Vandeleur, whose tanks were to provide fire support for the crossing, had also brought Major Edward Tyler to discuss details with Colonel Tucker. The plan to cross the river 'put the fear of God in me', Tyler said. He asked Tucker if his paratroopers were trained in assault crossings. Tucker replied that it would be a case of 'on-the-job training'. He added, 'Just stop the Krauts shooting at us and we'll do the rest.' Tyler was concerned about his tanks hitting the paratroopers, but Tucker told him to keep firing. If they were too close then his men would fire flares or wave banners.

Tyler was concerned that his sixteen tanks silhouetted on a skyline would be vulnerable, so he spaced them out as much as he could with twenty metres between them. There was a tall wire fence in front which the Shermans would push flat by advancing slowly. Tyler was dismayed to find that at ground level it was impossible to identify the well-camouflaged German gun positions, which had been quite easy to spot from the top of the power station. Tucker's 2nd Battalion, with every machine gun they could lay their hands on, also took up position to increase the volume of fire. Well to their rear, the Leicestershire Yeomanry with their Sexton self-propelled 25-pounder guns would be providing the smoke screen.

The delay to the trucks bringing the boats did not help Cook's battalion to relax. 'As the hour of three o'clock approached,' Lieutenant Virgil F. Carmichael observed, 'the men became more nervous and tense. I clearly remember one man taking out a Camel cigarette, lighting it with a valued Zippo lighter and throwing the pack away and throwing the Zippo away, saying that he would have no need of them no more. As it turned out, he did not.' Major Cook tried to lighten the atmosphere by joking that 'he was going to imitate George Washington in the well-known picture crossing the Delaware. He was going to stand erect in the boat and with clenched right fist pushed forward overhead, he was going to shout: "Onward men, onward!"' Purely because another officer had been expected to take command of the battalion, Cook had not been well received when he arrived, but that was about to change dramatically with the bravery and leadership he would show that day.

Behind the embankment and the tanks, Cook's officers split their platoons, allocating thirteen men to each assault boat. When the trucks eventually arrived just before 15.00, the paratroopers were appalled to find that the twenty-six boats were just canvas on a flat-bottomed wooden frame. Two companies, H and I, were to form the first wave. G Company would follow as soon as the three men of the 307th Airborne Engineers, who were to crew each boat, managed to bring them back. As many recognized, the engineers had the most terrifying job of all.

The Leicestershire Yeomanry opened fire with smoke shells at exactly 15.00. When the order was given at 15.15, the paratroopers and engineers 'shouldered the boats like coffins, with their outside hand carrying weapons', and ran over the top of the dyke, then down the slope. They slipped and slid in the mud, struggling to get their boats straight in the water as they clambered aboard.

As soon as the assault boats were in the water, the Irish Guards in the Shermans opened up with their thirty-two Browning machine guns, and so did Tucker's 2nd Battalion with theirs. The 376th Parachute Field Artillery Battalion took on targets further to the rear. At first the smokescreen provided by the Leicestershire Yeomanry worked quite well, but soon large gaps started to appear. Tucker asked Giles Vandeleur if his tanks could help. Each Sherman had only a dozen smoke shells, so they did not last long. The Irish Guards also found that their Browning machine guns had got so hot from firing that they 'ran away', which meant that even when the trigger was released they carried on firing until the belt was finished.

Lieutenant Carmichael, who was in the first boat with Major Cook, a devout Catholic, heard him 'saying his Rosary and as he struck the water with his paddle, you could hear him say: "Hail Mary, full of grace", on through the Rosary, repeating it over and over again as he paddled as hard as he could toward the other bank'. There was no question of standing in the prow like Washington. Everyone paddled as hard as they could, some even using their rifle butts or hands. Henry Keep, who had been an oarsman at Princeton, was counting 'one-two-three-four', but their efforts were all over the place. Keep had 'a rather incongruous vision of our coxswain at Princeton on Lake Carnegie pounding rhythmically on the sides of the flimsy shell and of our rowing in unison pulling to the time of his beats'. Then, the Germans began firing in earnest, with small-arms and machine-gun fire from the positions in front, and machine-gun and 20mm fire from the small nineteenth-century Hof van Holland fortress slightly to their right, and even from the railway bridge a whole kilometre beyond that.

At first the fire was erratic, but then the Germans started to get the range and it increased greatly in intensity. 'There was smoke on the water,'

Lieutenant John Gorman of the Irish Guards noted. 'You could see the splashes as the bullets hit [and] the Americans sitting in the boats suddenly slump over.' Some compared the effect of bullets on the water's surface to a hailstorm. 'It was a horrible, horrible sight,' Giles Vandeleur recorded. 'Boats were literally being blown out of the water. I could see huge geysers of water shooting up as the shells hit the water, and the small arms fire coming from the northern bank made the river look like some sort of seething cauldron.' If one of the engineers steering a boat was hit, then it circled aimlessly until someone else took over.

'In everyone's ears', wrote Henry Keep, 'was the constant roar of bursting artillery shells, the dull wham of a 20mm, or the disconcerting ping of rifle bullets.' There was also the unmistakable thwack whenever a bullet struck a body. One boat had so many holes in it that men were bailing water with their helmets. The arm muscles of those paddling screamed with the strain. Lieutenant Hyman D. Shapiro, the assistant medical officer, recognized that in such a battle all he could do was bring extra dressings and morphine. 'Doctors were little more than glorified aid-men,' he said. 'I looked up at the man sitting beside me and saw his head disappear,' presumably the result of a direct hit from a 20mm shell. Like the Protestant chaplain who sat just behind him, Shapiro's main purpose was to provide moral support. The chaplain, Captain Delbert Kuehl – 'a rough tough Alaska sourdough who saw the light . . . really saw it' in Shapiro's words – was exhausted from paddling. Shapiro did not notice him hand his paddle to someone else, so on seeing that Kuehl's hands were empty, he handed him his.

Every man on that crossing had a sensation of utter vulnerability. 'I felt as naked as the day I was born,' Henry Keep wrote. 'We were soaked, gasping for breath, dead tired, and constantly expecting to feel that searing sensation as the bullet tears through you. I wanted to vomit; many did. Somehow or other we were three-quarters of the way across. Everyone was yelling to keep it up, but there was little strength left in anyone . . . But at last we reached the other side. We climbed over the wounded and dead in the bottom of the boat. And up to our knees in water waded to shore, where behind a small embankment we flopped down gasping for breath, safe for the moment from the incessant firing.'

Out of the twenty-six boats that made the initial crossing, only eleven returned to collect the second wave. Some had sunk, others drifted with the strong current, with their cargo of dead and men so badly wounded that they could do nothing. Dutch civilians further downstream, having seen what was happening, waded out to pull the casualties into shore.

Lieutenant Gorman of the Irish Guards watched the first wave reach the bank. 'I was horrified by the smallness of their numbers. I didn't see how they could possibly get a foothold with so few men.' Along with Browning, Horrocks and Tucker, Giles Vandeleur had a grandstand view from the top of the power station. 'My God! What a courageous sight it was! They just moved across that field steadily. I never saw a single man lie down until he was hit.' Yet from across the river the effect of distance made it look as if the paratroopers were just strolling about. Once the first wave was on the far bank, Major Tyler ordered his sixteen tanks to lift their machine-gun fire and to start hammering the Hof van Holland with their 75mm guns. They began with armour-piercing, then switched to high explosive. That prompted the crews of the two twin 20mm guns on the fort to switch their fire to the Shermans, and they killed one of Tyler's tank commanders.

At one point Tyler saw a grey horse towing an anti-tank gun on its own towards the railway bridge. The crew must have been killed. He gave the order to fire at it. And one of the tank gunners, a former groom who loved horses, managed to hit the weapon with a solid armour-piercing round, destroying it utterly without harming the grey. The range was almost a kilometre. The horse walked on 'as unconcerned as if he had been out making the morning milk deliveries'.

The tanks started to run short of ammunition and a haze from the fighting made it extremely hard to distinguish American soldiers from German. But by then there was no doubt who was winning. 'All along the shore line now our troops were appearing deployed as skirmishers,' Keep's account continued. 'They were running into murderous fire from the embankment 800 yards away, but they continued to move forward across the plain in a long single line many hundreds of yards wide. They cursed and yelled at each other as they advanced, non-coms and officers giving directions, the men firing from the hip their BARs [Browning Automatic Rifles], machine-guns and rifles. Steadily they moved forward. All this time the 2nd Battalion and the tanks on the other side of the river were giving us marvellous support.

'Many times I have seen troops who are driven to a fever pitch – troops who, for a brief interval of combat, are lifted out of themselves – fanatics rendered crazy by rage and the lust for killing – men who forget temporarily the meaning of fear. It is then that the great military feats of history occur which are commemorated so gloriously in our text books. It is an awe-inspiring sight, but not a pretty one.' Staff Sergeant Clark Fuller described his own experience of this sudden metamorphosis from fear to fearlessness. 'When we finally got to the opposite shore, I experienced a feeling I never felt before. All the fear of the past fifteen or twenty minutes seemed to leave me, to be replaced by a surge of reckless abandon that threw caution to the winds. I felt as though I could lick the whole German army.' The courage and aggression of the American paratroopers prompted one Guards officer to observe: 'I think these paratroopers must be fed on dynamite or raw meat.'

Any notion of belonging to a particular platoon or company had disappeared in the confusion. Officers collected whatever men were near them and charged off in small groups to attack the isolated strongpoints on the way to the bridge. Most of the German troops defending this sector of the Waal came from a replacement battalion which had arrived from Herford the day before. SS-Untersturmführer Gernot Traupel, Reinhold's adjutant, had been shaken to see them when they arrived. 'The soldiers were very young, about seventeen years of age, and they looked to me like children even though I was only twenty-one years old.' When paratroopers killed them in their foxholes they hauled the bodies out and, using them as sandbags, fired from behind them until they had caught their breath again. Colonel Tucker, catching up with his men, pulled one of the boys out of his foxhole by the scruff of his neck. They were all quivering in fear. He told them in German that they were prisoners of war and would not be shot. As soon as Tucker loosened his grip the boy jumped back into his hole to cower there.

As Cook's men moved east along the embankment towards the railway bridge, they first had to deal with the Hof van Holland fort surrounded by its stagnant moat. According to Lieutenant Carmichael, one man managed 'through some vigorous action [by swimming the moat and climbing the wall] to get on top of Fort van Holland and while there our men would toss live hand grenades up to him, and he would pull the pin and drop them into the portholes from his protected position on top of the fort.' At the same time, a small group of men charged over the wooden bridge and into the tunnel which led to the open courtyard within. Those inside surrendered quickly. Bill Downs of CBS reported that seventy-five German bodies were dumped in the algae-covered moat.

Pushing on towards the railway bridge, Lieutenant Richard G. La Riviere, always known as 'Rivers', reported that they ran into a bunch of German soldiers who wanted to surrender. He estimated that there were thirty or forty of them, 'ordinary run of the mill soldiers', but as there were only fifteen to twenty paratroopers, they shot the Germans on the spot. In the chaos of the fight, paratroopers found money scattered along the road after a German paymaster had abandoned his case in flight. They grabbed just a few banknotes as souvenirs, not imagining that they were valid currency.

By this time it was almost dusk. Anyone who looked back across the river would have seen the dreadful sight of Nijmegen on fire, with the flames reflected on the water. As Captain Carl W. Kappel's group came to the railway bridge, they saw Germans jumping in panic from the side, nearly a hundred feet above the water. Some were so scared that they leaped even though they were still over the riverbank. According to some accounts, they had tried to surrender and been told to give themselves up to the paratroopers on the south side. 'There was confusion,' a captain reported, 'and at that point several Germans threw grenades on our men who opened fire with rifles and machineguns.' Once firing started, there was no stopping it. Some of the paratroopers tried to shoot the Germans jumping from the bridge in mid-air, but Kappel ordered them to stop as they were running short of ammunition. They swung German machine guns, mounted to cover the bridge, and opened fire with them instead.

Trapped by men from the 2nd Battalion on the southern side, the Germans suffered a fearful massacre. 'I did see old German men grab our M1s and beg for mercy,' Corporal Jack Bommer recounted. 'They were shot point blank. Such is war.' He remembered an officer saying before they climbed into the boats, 'No prisoners, just shoot them. There's no time.' Captain Kappel spoke to the company commander from the 1st Battalion which had followed them. This officer boasted that they had taken many more prisoners than Cook's battalion. 'You captured yours,' Kappel retorted. 'We shot ours.'

Without counting those who jumped, 267 bodies were retrieved from the railway bridge alone, but one report states that 175 prisoners were taken there. There were apparently also cases of paratroopers removing gold wedding rings from dead Germans, which usually required cutting off the finger. A number of their comrades strongly disapproved, but it did little good in the savage atmosphere of victory. Word spread in the German army about the massacre. Oberst Fullriede wrote in his diary a week later: 'The Americans behaved – as always – in a contemptible fashion. They threw our wounded from the bridge into the Waal and shot the few home guard they took prisoner.' The throwing of wounded into the river was almost certainly not true, yet it reflected the fear and hatred which German troops felt for the American airborne, having been told by Nazi propaganda that they were all recruited from the toughest jails.

The Irish Guards passed back a radio message to announce that the 3rd Battalion had reached the railway bridge, but the Guards Armoured Division understood that they had reached the great road bridge, a kilometre further on. Major Trotter gave the word to Sergeant Robinson to prepare. The Grenadiers, however, were still fighting against Euling's battalion of SS panzergrenadiers in and around the Valkhof, and the rest of Trotter's

Shermans were firing rapidly in support. Euling's command post was in the sixteenth-century brick tower, the Belvedere, between the Valkhof and the bridge. A German artillery observation officer, after his radio set had been destroyed, had managed to continue obtaining fire support from across the river by shooting flares at the intended target.

'The King's Company of the Grenadiers, with the tallest men in the regiment,' wrote Major Stanley, 'stormed the fort after breaking in through an unguarded alley.' Their commander was killed, with a bullet through the head. Euling's panzergrenadiers claimed to have shot eighteen Grenadiers in the head. Captain Bestebreurtje later saw the slogans Euling's men had painted on walls in the Valkhof. 'We black ones trust the Führer'; 'Our faith is loyalty' (which was the SS motto); 'Rather death than tyranny'; 'The coward is a scoundrel'; 'Death to the Murderers of the Homeland'; and 'We believe in Adolf Hitler and our victory'.

Robinson commanded his troop from a Firefly Sherman with the powerful 17-pounder gun. He was given absolute radio priority so that he could keep in constant touch with divisional headquarters. 'It seemed the whole town was burning,' Robinson remembered, as the four tanks charged towards the ramp. His tank was hit just as they got to the bridge and his radio was knocked out, so he took over the next Sherman, much to the anger of the sergeant who commanded it.

Captain Lord Carrington, the second-in-command of No. 1 Squadron (and much later Margaret Thatcher's foreign secretary), stood in the turret of his tank knowing that he was next to go. Close by, Lieutenant Tony Jones, of the 14th Field Squadron Royal Engineers, was also ready. His task was to deal with any wires and explosive charges as soon as the tanks crossed over. 'The sight of tracer flashing down the centre of the huge road bridge really made me feel we had a chance of capturing it intact,' he recorded. 'I can still see Peter Carrington's face as he looked down from the turret of his tank before going over. He looked thoughtful, to say the least of it.'

Colonel Vandervoort later recalled that 'It was pretty spectacular. When the lead tank reached the crest of the bridge, it came under fire from an 88mm gun sandbagged into the side of the highway about 100 or so yards from the north end of the bridge. The tank and the 88 exchanged about six rounds apiece with the tank spitting .30 tracers all the while. Quite a show in the gathering dusk. The tank was not hit and the 88 ceased fire.' Sergeant Robinson thought that his tank had knocked it out with a direct hit from their main armament.

During the dash across the bridge, Robinson had not realized that a German rifleman high in the superstructure of the bridge had been shooting at him. He was too busy directing his own tank's fire and operating the turret-mounted Browning to gun down fleeing German infantrymen. Robinson and his crew could feel their tank bumping over the bodies of those they had killed, and later found their tank tracks covered in blood. The scene was also observed from the village of Lent by Brigadeführer Harmel, who said, 'I always had a cigar in my mouth, and in critical moments I would light it . . . when I first saw the British tanks I lit the cigar.'

Robinson and his tanks carried on for a little way through Lent to where the road goes under the railway line. Paratroopers from the 82nd Airborne opened fire at them and they fired back, but fortunately both sides realized their mistake before anyone was hurt. In their relief, the paratroopers jumped on the tank, kissing it and, it seems, the tank commander. But from then on accounts diverge wildly: the Guards refusing to advance without orders and the paratroopers accusing them of cowardice and abandoning their airborne comrades. Carrington arrived some time afterwards and a defensive perimeter was formed with the four tanks facing outwards. Robinson, Carrington and their crews stayed awake either by walking around or by sitting against one of the tanks. They shared a bottle of whisky which Carrington had brought with him, while they waited for a company of the Irish Guards to join them.

Some highly coloured American accounts describe officers from the 82nd Airborne berating Carrington for his refusal to advance because he had been ordered to await infantry support. One even claimed that he had put his Thompson sub-machine gun to Carrington's head. It is rather more likely that the righteous indignation of the Americans was so intense that they convinced themselves in hindsight that they really had told the British what they thought of them.*

Just behind Robinson's tanks, Lieutenant Jones of the 14th Field Squadron had begun cutting wires as soon as they were on the road bridge. A troop of his Royal Engineers arrived immediately afterwards and began removing the explosive charges. It proved anxious work, as officers from Cook's battalion also found. 'Countless Krauts who had been trapped in the middle of the bridge when both ends had been secured had sought temporary refuge high up in the steel girders. From these vantage points they continued to fire at us and also at the vehicles as they passed beneath them.

---

* Eisenhower's chief of staff, General Walter Bedell Smith, said after the war, 'I doubted that the British armor could get up there [to Arnhem]. Ours might have.' Brigadeführer Harmel, on the other hand, insisted that 'they would have stood no chance once they got there, because by this time . . . Arnhem was in German hands.'

In spite of the darkness we constantly sprayed them with automatic fire. As dawn broke a gruesome sight greeted the eyes. Intertwined grotesquely throughout the massive steel girders were the bodies of dead Krauts, looking for all the world like a group of gargoyles leering hideously at the passers-by hundreds of feet below.'

Both Grenadiers and Cook's paratroopers were convinced that they had taken the Nijmegen road bridge first. Perhaps inevitably in the circumstances few accounts tally, even on the same side. Several American versions indicate that the tanks were across first, and a few British ones that American paratroopers were there already. Such a debate, however, is futile. It is far more important to understand the reasons for the British failure to advance on to Arnhem that night. Tucker and his paratroopers were understandably furious. Cook's battalion and the engineers manning the boats had suffered 89 dead and 151 wounded. They naturally believed that the only reason for their semi-suicidal crossing of the Waal in full daylight was because every hour counted if XXX Corps was to save the 1st Airborne at Arnhem. Otherwise, the attack could have waited until after dark.

Horrocks must shoulder most of the blame for the resulting damage to Anglo-American relations. He had supported Gavin's plan for the assault crossing of the Waal. To underline the urgency, he had emphasized to Tucker's officers the desperate situation which the 1st Airborne Division faced, and the American paratroopers were better able than most to imagine what it would be like for their British counterparts. Then as soon as they had achieved their objective with heavy losses and almost unbelievable courage, nothing happened. Horrocks even wrote in his memoirs: 'Another hurdle had been overcome and I went to bed a happy man.'

There were many good reasons why the Guards Armoured Division, and especially the Grenadiers, could not push on that night. For a start, the Grenadier group had suffered heavy casualties in Nijmegen, and they were still fighting Euling's panzergrenadiers until after 22.00, so they could not disengage. And apart from Robinson's troop, all their tanks were low on ammunition and fuel. This was why Brigadier Gwatkin and Major General Adair decided to switch back to having the Irish Guards in the lead, but due to the chaos in the burning city of Nijmegen the Irish Guards tanks had not yet been resupplied with ammunition after their massive expenditure in support of the crossing.

Horrocks, on the other hand, should have foreseen these problems and ensured that some well-prepared battle group was waiting and ready to advance rapidly north towards Arnhem through the night. He was not one of those fixated by the doctrine that armour should operate only in daylight.

'I was a great believer in using tanks at night,' he wrote. 'I tried it on three occasions and was successful each time. It has a shattering effect on the morale of the enemy.' Horrocks may have been exhausted once again from his injuries, but this was not the moment to go 'to bed a happy man'.

Whether or not the road to Arnhem was wide open that night has been another area of debate, but even the strongest and freshest battle group with General George Patton lashing them on would have been lucky to get through. That afternoon the Germans had retaken the Arnhem road bridge and were sending panzergrenadiers and Tiger tanks south to Nijmegen. The simple truth is that XXX Corps was too late, and so was the capture of the Nijmegen bridge as a result of defending the Groesbeek heights.

On the German side there was fury, frustration and bewilderment. As soon as Robinson's tanks had crossed, Brigadeführer Harmel – who was watching from the village of Lent – went straight to Reinhold's command tank. He radioed Bittrich to warn him that the Allies were over the Waal. Teleprinters began chattering and telephones ringing in various headquarters, with a good deal of shouting. Model's chief of staff Generalleutnant Hans Krebs was having to field a lot of difficult calls, sometimes by pretending that nothing had changed. At 18.35, 'On being asked by the chief of staff of the Wehrmacht Befehlshaber Niederland about the blowing up of the bridges over the Waal, the chief of staff of the Army Group explained that the Nijmegen bridges should not be blown up for the time being.' In another communication at the same time, he insisted that with the forces rapidly despatched from Arnhem, including two panzergrenadier battalions, several Tigers and assault guns, 'the breakthrough on to the north bank of the Waal should be sealed off.' Less than an hour later, the operations officer at II SS Panzer Corps rang Model's headquarters to report that the enemy was now definitely established across the Waal. 'The situation is extraordinarily tense.'

Some German officers, including Brigadeführer Harmel of the SS *Frundsberg*, tried to claim that despite Model's order not to blow the bridge the plunger had been pushed but nothing happened. Harmel even said that he gave the order as the Grenadier tanks were crossing, but this version of events was presumably the reaction of an officer hoping to protect himself from Hitler's fury. Others maintain even less convincingly that its demolition was delayed so that the remnants of Euling's battalion could escape.

Model was angry and embarrassed. That morning he had again refused Bittrich's request to blow the two bridges and withdraw to the north bank. He had insisted that 'the bridgehead be maintained'. He had been convinced that Reinhold's and Euling's SS panzergrenadiers would be able to hold on, so when he heard about the Allied crossing he made noises about putting both men in front of a court martial. (In fact both Reinhold and Euling instead received the Knight's Cross for their leadership and bravery.) Model could hardly deny the existence of his own order. SS-Obergruppenführer Rauter stated, 'The commander-in-chief of the Army Group, Generalfeldmarschall Model, informed me personally that he reserved for himself [the decision] to blow the Nijmegen bridge. He wanted the bridge to be left intact in all circumstances.' Model may have been a brutal commander-in-chief, but he was not one to try to pass the blame on to a subordinate. When the frantic telephone calls came from the Wolfsschanze in East Prussia, Bittrich's headquarters described the outcome simply. 'The question from the Wehrmacht command staff about the responsibility for the failure to blow the bridges was answered by Army Group.' At that stage of the war, only Model could have faced Hitler's fury and got away with it.

Brigadier General Gavin had not been able to see his men's feat of arms crossing the Waal. At about 13.30 when still at the power station, he had received an urgent call over the radio from his chief of staff, who had been calling him without success for nearly an hour and a half. 'General, you'd better get the hell back here, or you won't have any division left.' Major attacks had developed in the north against Wyler and Beek, against Groesbeek in the centre, and in the south against Mook. They consisted of Kampfgruppe Becker in the north, Kampfgruppe Greschick in the centre from the 406th Division and Kampfgruppe Hermann in the south, with the first six battalions from Meindl's II Fallschirmjäger Corps supported by some Mark V Panther tanks.

Gavin drove off rapidly in his Jeep back to the divisional command post. He felt bitter that bad weather in England and a shortage of aircraft had yet again delayed the arrival of the 325th Glider Infantry Regiment. His forces were far too stretched to defend a sector some fifty kilometres long. The greatest danger was in the south, where the attack on Mook threatened the Heumen bridge and the XXX Corps supply line. Gavin's insistence on bringing in airborne artillery early paid off when the 456th Parachute Field Artillery managed to slow the German advance, with help from a squadron of tanks from the Coldstream Guards. There was fighting in the streets of Mook and in the houses.

Gavin, on reaching his command post, was surprised to see Major General Matthew Ridgway, the commander of XVIII Airborne Corps, talking to members of his staff. Gavin concentrated on studying the situation map, rather than on the courtesies of briefing his superior officer. Things looked so dire that he felt he had to leave for Mook straight away, and did so, without acknowledging Ridgway's presence. Ridgway did not forgive Gavin's behaviour for some time. He was already in a foul mood after the bombing in Eindhoven where he had become separated from General Brereton, but above all because Browning was commanding the corps in action and not him. The bad British planning and their lack of drive exasperated him and seemed to confirm his worst prejudices.

When Gavin reached the edge of Mook, he found a paratrooper with a bazooka 'shaking visibly', and a Coldstream Guards tank on fire which had run over an American mine. He told the sergeant and lieutenant who were with him to go up on to the embankment with their rifles and start firing as fast as they could to give the impression of a strong defence. A paratrooper from the 505th then appeared with a prisoner, 'a real apple-cheeked kid about eighteen, a fine, tough-looking kid'. He was in Fallschirmjäger uniform. Gavin went forward, squirming on his belly across a road and then on to the line of foxholes ahead to reassure his men that reinforcements were coming. This was doubly impressive considering that the young commander was in such pain from his back that he found his hands were becoming numb. During a lull a few days later, he visited the doctor who, unaware of the cracked spine, said it was just part of the nervous system reacting to the stress of battle. Gavin carried on. 'Physical damage to you doesn't mean much in battle if you're really into the battle,' he observed later. 'If you are so excited and carried away you don't know things like that. You can get shot without knowing what's happening to you.' Gavin made a habit of deliberate understatement. Horrocks was tickled by his casual remark, 'We're just having a bit of a patrol,' when his men were launching a major raid or attack.

Mook was retaken in a counter-attack, but by then Gavin had moved north. Kampfgruppe Becker had advanced through Wyler to take Beek, and was pushing towards Berg en Dal. Brigadier Gwatkin, having heard of the threat, sent a troop of Q Battery, 21st Anti-Tank Regiment in their M-10 Achilles tank destroyers to Beek, which certainly helped. Gavin arrived to encourage the men in the front line, and was relieved to find that their battalion commander, Lieutenant Colonel Louis Mendez, appeared well in control.

The Kampfgruppe Greschick attacking Groesbeek proved to be the least of Gavin's worries. German riflemen had infiltrated the small town the previous night through a culvert underneath the railway track and in this way they managed to reach the centre. They stood little chance against the better-trained and better-armed American paratroopers. Father Hoek recounted that they dug a large grave for seven German soldiers that day, but left it open in case there were any more, and there certainly were. Groesbeekers greatly admired the relaxed way American paratroopers set off to fight, a gun in one hand and an apple in the other.

Further south, the 101st was also under pressure as the Germans tried to cut Hell's Highway in two places. At dawn the 107th Panzer-Brigade, with a motorized battalion of Fallschirmjäger, attacked Son again. 'They drove their tanks up to the canal bank,' Lieutenant Colonel Hannah reported, 'and pinned down most of the personnel in one of our battalions.' Major General Taylor found his command post in a school under direct fire. A XXX Corps convoy rolling north was under threat, but fortunately the 15th/19th Hussars were still in the area, and counter-attacked with the 1st Battalion of the 506th. They were then supported by part of the 44th Royal Tank Regiment which had been heading towards Helmond, with the 2nd Battalion. There were anxious moments for the 101st Airborne Military Police Platoon guarding nearly 2,000 prisoners in a cage, little more than 400 metres away from the Panthers. 'Our own command post and supporting troops pulled out and left us sitting practically on the front lines,' wrote a sergeant. 'We had our interpreters tell the prisoners to lie down and be quiet.' There was also a Luftwaffe attack, but fortunately no prisoners were hit.

The 107th Panzer-Brigade withdrew, somewhat battered by the British armoured squadrons. That evening, it reported the loss of seven tanks and twelve half-tracks. Even so, Colonel Hannah was struck by how badly Allied intelligence had 'underestimated the enemy strength and degree of organization from the beginning of the operation. In every case, the Germans far exceeded the expected rate of reorganization, and were able to launch a coordinated attack with infantry and armor by D plus 2 [19 September] which was entirely unexpected.'

With none of the 101st Airborne's supply trucks getting through the congestion on Hell's Highway, the paratroopers were on short rations. Having used up their initial three days' supply, they had to live off turnips, as well as food captured from the Germans or donated by ever-generous Dutch civilians. Fortunately for the Allies, B Squadron of the Household Cavalry Regiment discovered that day a vast German food store at Oss. (It also engaged a steamer flying the Nazi flag and three barges sailing along the Waal, which prompted regimental headquarters to reply to its report: 'Congratulations on brilliant naval action. Splice Mainbrace.')

General Taylor reinforced the Son crossing with a battalion and decided to move his headquarters to Kasteel Henkenshage, on the western edge of

St Oedenrode. An advance detail then returned to say that German tanks were attacking the new command post. Taylor called Lieutenant Colonel Cassidy at St Oedenrode and said to him: 'Can you clear them out? I don't like tanks round me.' Cassidy, who had six tanks from the 44th Royal Tank Regiment attached to his battalion, took them up the road to sort out the situation.

That day one of Cassidy's platoons captured a prisoner from Heydte's 6th Fallschirmjäger-Regiment after an engagement. He told them that his patrol had been sent out specially to destroy Sergeant McCrory's tank. The Irish Guards sergeant, meanwhile, had been asked by Cassidy to see if he could help evacuate any survivors from two British tanks knocked out by Panzerfausts on the road to Koevering. 'If all they have up there is a bazooka,' McCrory replied, 'we shall knock it out.' The American who wrote the report for Brereton's headquarters was clearly mesmerized by the larger than life Sergeant McCrory.

When they reached the two damaged Shermans, McCrory climbed down from his tank and went to the first one. The commander was very badly wounded. 'He saw that he was still breathing but that his skull was laid back and his brains hanging out and that another shard had ripped his abdomen open and bared his intestines. He was beyond help. An American soldier then witnessed McCrory 'suddenly spring from the tank and run forward rapidly about 20 yards towards the right hand ditch, pulling out his revolver as he ran. As he came to it, he fired down and a little forward four or five times.' McCrory returned to the tank with a dead suckling piglet in his hand. He threw it to the American, saying: 'Tonight, we'll eat.'

McCrory continued the advance, taking the place of the two knocked-out tanks. He carried on in his slowly grinding vehicle even when they came under fire from a German 88mm gun concealed in a house. He fired three rounds of 75mm into the house, 'then skip-fired three more rounds into the garden, getting the 88'. Six dead Germans were found inside. By now the Sherman tank was almost level with a monastery. 'McCrory figured the steeple was being used for an [observation post] and said to his gunner: "Aim right for the cross." The gunner hesitated. McCrory told him again: "I said aim for the cross." So he fired and ruined whatever usefulness the steeple might have had.' A German armoured reconnaissance vehicle appeared and the gunner hit that with his first round.

The Bailey bridge at Son had been an obvious choke point on the XXX Corps supply route, but in Generaloberst Student's view 'The most sensitive spot was Veghel, the "wasp-waist" of the enemy corridor.'

Veghel, in the words of Captain Laurence Critchell, was 'a neat, cheerful and homey little town . . . with plane-trees and a village square'. Although disappointed not to find any tulips or windmills, the captain relished the fact that 'Colonel Johnson found himself in the sort of setting he liked best. It was bristling with comic-opera war.' So many people wanted to provide information on the Germans that Johnson's staff had to post reliable members of the underground outside their headquarters to filter all those demanding an audience. 'The collaborators were routed out of their homes for a long-delayed retribution. The girls were mostly rather young and sensual-featured, and they went undemonstrably to have their hair shorn; they seemed to accept it as an expected fate . . . and the Dutch crowds who watched the tonsorial administration of justice displayed none of the sickening and almost animal glee that French crowds showed on similar occasions. They were amused, that was all.'

The gaiety of the young in the streets was infectious, when they sang and danced in clothes of symbolic orange and scarves made from parachute silk. And their parents never complained when soldiers dug foxholes and slit trenches in their lawns and rosebeds. But the idyll of liberation came to an abrupt end during the afternoon of Tuesday 19 September when German artillery began to bombard the town. Paratroopers in their foxholes dropped out of sight 'like prairie dogs'.

The 59th Infanterie-Division attacked Veghel from Schijndel. Student himself went to observe. 'I watched a flak-platoon from the Reichsarbeitsdienst, which with its two large 88mm guns was shooting at American snipers who sat in the tall trees and hindered our attack from the flank. Meanwhile east of the canal around Dinther, in the marshy and difficult forest and scrub terrain, the Fallschirm-Marsch-Bataillon under Major Jungwirth was fighting its own small war . . . But with their light weapons they could not prevent the reinforced 1st Battalion of the 501st from taking Dinther and Heeswijk on 20 September.'

The battalion was hardly reinforced. It was just superbly led, and executed a brilliant encircling manoeuvre. Colonel Johnson had finally given in to the pleading of Lieutenant Colonel Harry Kinnard that he mount a sweep along the canal to the north-west towards Heeswijk, where all their jump casualties had been captured by the Germans in the castle there. Kinnard had argued that because the corridor was so narrow, their only hope of holding off the Germans was by offensive action. Kinnard's operation that day was hugely successful, netting 480 prisoners for the cost of two men wounded. Some of the prisoners were so young that they had not even started shaving. If Kinnard's battalion had been reinforced, as Student tried to claim, then its auxiliaries had consisted of Dutch volunteers on bicycles acting as unarmed scouts, pedalling ahead and off to the flanks. Johnson, impressed by Kinnard's results, decided to repeat the exercise next day, with two battalions this time. They would mount a night attack due west to Schijndel. The battle for Hell's Highway was about to escalate rapidly.

Although finally free of German occupation, the citizens of Nijmegen were in no mood to celebrate. The carnage from the battle for the bridge shocked all those who saw it. 'It was there that I saw precisely what war really signifies,' wrote Father Wilhelmus Peterse, whom the Americans named 'the priest on the bridge', after his ministrations in the wake of the fighting. 'Mutilated bodies. Severely wounded and dying soldiers. The road was littered with hand grenades.' The casualties were all German, but that did not of course stop Father Peterse from kneeling to comfort the dying and help the wounded, while captured German medics worked on their fellow countrymen under the eye of an American officer.

German soldiers concealed in cavities below the bridges emerged to surrender. Lieutenant Jones, the Royal Engineer, was assisted by a prisoner with excellent English but without any boots, who showed him where the explosives were concealed. The prisoners, who included some marines and a few Russian Hiwis in Wehrmacht uniform, were marched to the southern end. Suddenly a shot rang out and an American airborne officer fell dead. The SS officer responsible who had concealed himself in the girders was riddled with bullets.

When German prisoners from the bridge were escorted into the town, 'Their reception by the civilian population was none too friendly,' observed Father Peterse, 'but wars aren't won that way.' Albertus Uijen also witnessed their reception. 'There is whistling and jeering at German prisoners-of-war . . . They walk with their arms raised. One of them cannot keep this up. One hand is practically gone, just a lump of raw flesh. Blood is pouring down. Their appearance is awful. Black as soot or sallow, sweaty, torn uniforms, no more helmets or belts, no more badges, no more buttons even. It is a dreadful sight. Suddenly I am struck again by the beastliness, the absurdity of war.' The American paratroopers escorting them tell the Dutch, who are hooting and hissing, to stay calm.

'The inner town was one great heap of ruins,' Father Peterse recorded. 'On Burchtstraat an enormous tank was buried under the rubble of houses that had collapsed. Occasional shots were heard among the ruins. No doubt some foolish Germans who wanted to vent their rage.' Volunteers, in overalls and gloves, were already collecting the dead from the streets on horse-drawn wagons and recording unexploded shells for disposal later. In the less damaged southern part of Nijmegen, an American paratrooper 'noted that there were lots of mounds of earth and wooden crosses stuck in the narrow grassy area between street and sidewalk. The local people had gathered up the German corpses and buried them.' But the fighting and the terrible fires had been too much for many people, not just the homeless. They trekked out to neighbouring villages where they were touched by the generosity of strangers welcoming them into their homes. The flames and smoke from the city could be seen from a great distance.

That night Field Marshal Montgomery sent a characteristically confident signal to General Eisenhower: 'My appreciation of the situation in the MARKET area is that things are going to work out all right . . . The British airborne division at Arnhem has been having a bad time but their situation should be eased now that we can advance northwards from Nijmegen to their support. There is a sporting chance that we should capture the bridge at Arnhem which is at present held by the Germans and is intact.'

18

Arnhem Bridge and Oosterbeek
Wednesday 20 September

Wednesday dawned with light rain, which did little to dampen the flames around the north end of Arnhem bridge and the town centre. One of the few civilians left in the area gazed in horror at the church of St Walburgis and noted that 'the towers looked like great columns of fire'.

Frost's force suspected that they did not have what Monty considered a 'sporting chance' of holding the bridge, yet they also guessed that their presence had more than inconvenienced the Germans. Brigadeführer Harmel, while directing operations in Nijmegen from the north bank of the Waal, longed to hear that the British 1st Airborne had been crushed. 'Damn them, but they're stubborn!' he cursed. He desperately needed the road bridge opened because the improvised ferry system at Pannerden simply could not cope with reinforcements and supply. Bittrich's headquarters felt obliged to explain to higher command that the delay in eliminating Frost's battalion was due to their 'fanatical doggedness'. Frost and his men would never have accepted the word 'fanatical', but they would have acknowledged a thoroughly British bloody-mindedness.

Ammunition was almost totally exhausted. Not a single PIAT round remained to deal with armoured vehicles. Although Frost was no longer optimistic about their chances, a belief had taken hold that 'this is our bridge and you'll not set one foot on it.' A signaller told him that they had made contact with divisional headquarters. Frost had his first chance to talk to Urquhart, who told him that things were very difficult for them too. Frost assured him that they would hold on as long as possible but ammunition was the problem, along with medical supplies and water. He then asked about XXX Corps. Urquhart knew little more than he did, and Frost sensed that he and his men would not be relieved. Jokes about the Guards Armoured Division stopping to blanco their belts and polish their boots were no longer

funny. The day before he had discussed with Freddie Gough of the reconnaissance squadron what they should do if they had to break out. The
obvious direction was due west to Oosterbeek, but Frost thought it might be
better to slip out in groups towards the north through the back gardens.

The desire to know the whereabouts of XXX Corps continued to pre-
occupy everyone. Captain Bill Marquand in brigade headquarters sent a
signalman up into the attic with a 38 Set. Desperate to make contact, he was
broadcasting in clear, over and over again: 'This is the 1st Para Brigade calling Second Army.' There was still no response.

More and more buildings had been destroyed by fire or shelling. Often
the two were linked as the Germans used phosphorus shells to accelerate the
process. After capturing the second last house on the eastern side, the Germans sent in pioneers to fix charges to the underside of the bridge so that
it could be blown if British tanks did break through from Nijmegen. A
counter-attack led by Lieutenant Jack Grayburn forced them back, and
sappers removed the charges. The Germans attacked again and Grayburn,
wounded twice already, was killed with a burst of machine-gun fire from a
tank. He was awarded a posthumous Victoria Cross.

Accompanied by panzergrenadiers in their camouflage smocks, a battalion of Royal Tiger tanks reached Arnhem that morning, making a terrible
noise as it crossed the Willemsplein from the direction of Velp. 'However,
a sixty-ton panzer colossus', Generaloberst Student acknowledged, 'could
not be very effective in the narrow streets and the house-to-house fighting.'
They at least did not run the risk of crushing gun crews. Artillery pieces
fired on a smooth asphalt surface meant that the gun could run back up to
ten metres each shot, and it was not easy to jump clear in time. Kampfgruppe Brinkmann, meanwhile, 'passed from a period of exceptionally
savage night fighting', Brigadeführer Harmel wrote, 'to a technique of
smoking out individual pockets of resistance with Panzerfausts and flamethrowers'. With the British blinded by smoke, Brinkmann's force advanced.
'A great many prisoners, mostly wounded, were taken.'

In the school, Captain Eric Mackay issued two pills of Benzedrine to
each of his sappers but took none himself. 'The men were exhausted and
filthy,' Mackay recorded. 'I was sick to my stomach every time I looked at
them. Haggard and filthy with bloodshot red-rimmed eyes. Almost everyone had had some sort of dirty field dressing and blood was everywhere.'
Their faces, with three days' growth of beard, were blackened from fighting
fires. Parachute smocks and battledress trousers had been cut away by medics to tend their wounds. Everyone suffered from a terrible thirst. They had
been drinking the rusty water from those radiators which had not been hit.

The Van Limburg Stirum School now looked like a sieve. 'Wherever you looked you could see daylight.' It was the last British redoubt holding out on the east side of the bridge, which is why the Germans again concentrated such firepower upon it. Mackay was concerned that it might collapse on top of them, as Harmel had hoped, with his tactic of blasting the building systematically from the top. Shells from one of the newly arrived Mark VI Tigers set fire to it once more early in the afternoon.

Mackay recognized that they urgently needed to do something for the thirty-five wounded men in the cellars. Major Lewis had himself just been hit in an explosion. There were only fourteen able-bodied men left, so if the fires in the building intensified, or if the floors began to collapse, they would not have time to get them out. They decided to break out so that the school could be surrendered and the remaining wounded in the cellars left to be cared for by the Germans. With six men acting as vanguard with their remaining Bren guns, and eight acting as stretcher-bearers for four of the wounded, they made their move. But the break for freedom was short-lived. Almost all were captured.

Ringsdorf from the Kampfgruppe Brinkmann recorded seeing someone look out from a cellar aperture. 'My immediate reaction was to toss a hand grenade through the cellar window. Then I heard a voice shouting "No! No!", and the sound of moans. I had already pulled the pin on my grenade so I tossed it in the direction of another building. Then, I went down into this cellar alert for any trap, and entered saying "Hands up!" The cellar was full of wounded English soldiers. They were very frightened, so I said "It's OK, it's good." I took them prisoner and had them taken back to be tended . . . These wounded men were quite helpless and many had to be carried away. They looked terrible.' Ringsdorf showed impressive restraint, because his company commander Obersturmführer Vogel, whom he had greatly liked, had just been cut almost in half by British machine-gun fire.

Frost was discussing the situation with Major Douglas Crawley, one of his company commanders, when they were both badly wounded by a mortar bomb. Captain Jimmy Logan, the medical officer, suggested morphine, but Frost refused, as he needed to keep his wits about him. He fought the pain and nausea for as long as possible, and could not even face drinking whisky. He told Major Freddie Gough to take over command but to check all important decisions with him first. Eventually he accepted morphine and was carried down to the cellar of brigade headquarters on a stretcher.

Although Frost still wanted to hold on to their positions, they had lost the houses closest to the bridge. The Germans were soon on the ramp. Using tanks, they shunted the burned-out carcasses of Gräbner's reconnaissance vehicles to one side. So just before Tucker's paratroopers and the Gren-adiers secured the road bridge at Nijmegen, the *Frundsberg* was already sending through those first reinforcements of panzergrenadiers and Tiger tanks.

When Frost awoke that evening it was dark. He heard 'some shell shock cases gibbering'. Many more started shaking uncontrollably every time there was an explosion. Apparently there was one soldier whose black hair went white in the course of less than a week from stress. The doctor, Cap-tain Logan, warned that the building was on fire, so Frost sent for Gough and told him to take over command in full. First they would move those fit to fight and the walking wounded – only around a hundred remained – then Gough was to arrange a truce to hand the wounded over to the Germans. One paratrooper wrote, 'It was undoubtedly the right decision, but some men who were in a bad state felt aggrieved at being abandoned, even though the battalion doctor and medical orderlies were staying with them.'

As soon as the truce began the Germans tightened the ring. They then insisted that they must take the British Jeeps to evacuate the wounded. By that stage Gough was in no position to refuse such a condition. When the truce to remove the wounded began in earnest, Lieutenant Colonel Frost removed his badges of rank. Captain Logan went out with a Red Cross flag. There was a shot, and he yelled back 'Cease fire!' 'Only wounded in here,' he added. The shooting died away. Outside, he explained to a German offi-cer that they needed to get everyone out before the building burned down or collapsed. The officer agreed and gave his orders. As German soldiers came down the stairs, 'a badly wounded paratrooper brought out a Sten gun from under his equipment, complete with full magazine, with every intention of giving the Germans a fitting reception, but luckily he was over-powered and the gun taken from him.'

A German officer entered the cellar in greatcoat and steel helmet, carry-ing an MP-40 sub-machine gun. He looked around at the dreadful sight, and told the men following to help the wounded out. Both Germans and British carried them out before they could be burned to death. Frost was taken out on a stretcher and laid on the embankment next to the bridge. He found himself next to Crawley, with whom he had been wounded. 'Well,' he remarked, 'it looks as though we haven't got away with it this time.'

'No,' Crawley replied, 'but we've given them a damn good run for their money.' But Frost felt anguished at leaving his battalion in such a state. 'I had been with the 2nd Battalion for three years. I had commanded it in every battle it had fought and I felt a grievous loss at leaving it now.'

Lance Bombardier John Crook, when told to surrender, found it harshly ironic to be surrounded by the German prisoners he had been guarding. He smashed his rifle, 'a forlorn action in the circumstances'. A 'big SS panzer-grenadier' pointed a sub-machine gun at him, shouting '*Hände hoch!*' Then some of their German prisoners tried to console him and his comrades by patting them on the back, saying '*Kamerad.*' There were altogether some 150 German prisoners, many of them wounded.

In the courtyard wounded British paratroopers were greeted by the sight of a 6-pounder anti-tank gun on its side, with the rubber tyres still burning and the crew dead around it. Some of their guards, from the army and not the Waffen-SS, allowed them some food and something to drink, before moving them on. The paratroopers were both shaken and secretly gratified to see the numbers of German dead lying around. But the sight hardened the mood of some SS panzergrenadiers.

After a thorough search for hidden weapons, half a dozen paratroopers and sappers were forced to stand against a wall. The SS panzergrenadiers formed a semi-circle facing them and they were joined by a very young soldier with a flamethrower in the middle. One of them gave the order to prepare to fire. 'Say your prayers boys,' a paratrooper said out loud, and another began to recite 'The Lord is my shepherd, I shall not want.' Suddenly an SS officer ran up shouting, '*Das ist verboten. Nein! Nein! Nein!*' The panzergrenadiers lowered their weapons with obvious reluctance.

A member of the underground who had been fighting with the para-troopers was identified by the Germans, because both his hands were bandaged from terrible burns. He had tried to pick up a phosphorus bomb to throw it away. 'He was forced to his knees and shot through the back of the head by a German officer.'

As the truce came to an end, Major Digby Tatham-Warter took charge of some of the survivors, who had left the buildings where wounded were being evacuated. They took up new positions in a garden area behind bri-gade headquarters and the ruins of a few houses, but their perimeter was now tiny and almost every building was on fire. Others tried to escape dur-ing the night through the German cordon, hoping to get through to the 1st Division at Oosterbeek. Very few made it.

Most of the wounded were taken off in the captured Jeeps to a church where a British doctor treated their wounds. The more serious cases were taken directly to the St Elisabeth Hospital. The surgeon Dr Pieter de Graaf, who had ordered the wounded to be moved back from the windows because of all the shooting in the area, was struck by how little shouting there was in the British army. When a group of SS came in to round up malingerers among the German patients, the SS doctor started shouting orders in all direc-tions. 'Nobody really cared,' de Graaf noted. 'The man yelled because there was nothing he could do but make a noise. The British and Dutch doctors just went about their business, pretending he wasn't there.' There had been only one civilian casualty in the last two days. An elderly patient had stuck his head out of an upstairs window to see what was going on, and was shot by a sniper. He was buried in the hospital grounds along with the bodies of British soldiers.

Although the fighting around the hospital was over, the Germans were still nervous. A tank rumbled down the road towards the St Elisabeth Hos-pital, its tracks making a metallic screeching sound. The turret traversed round to the right, with the gun pointing at the main entrance of the hospital. The hatch opened and a German officer in black panzer uniform appeared. He shouted that he wanted to see the director, claiming that he had been shot at from the hospital building, and unless he appeared imme-diately he would open fire with his tank. The German surgeon came out instead. Originally captured by the British, he had in theory assumed con-trol when the Germans retook the hospital, but he continued to work with Dutch and British doctors as before. He told the panzer officer that he had been very well treated and he was sure nobody had fired from the hospital. The tank commander calmed down and carried on along the road towards Oosterbeek, where the next battle was about to take place.

On the previous afternoon, stragglers from those other battalions which had tried to reach the bridge had started to appear in Oosterbeek. They had presented a sorry sight. A heavy officer and NCO casualty rate over the last two days meant that most men were leaderless. The disaster they had expe-rienced attempting to fight into Arnhem had risked undermining good order and military discipline. A company sergeant major in the 11th Battalion recounted that during the retreat a staff sergeant, whom he had charged with an offence in the past, drew his revolver to scare him, saying, 'Now we are all equal. Nobody will know.' And yet reassuringly the sergeant major had also overheard a private say to his companion, clearly another Londoner and fellow fancier, 'I'll be glad to get back to my pigeons.'

The commanding officer of the Light Regiment, Lieutenant Colonel 'Sheriff' Thompson, was alarmed to find that there was no covering force in front of his pack howitzers just below Oosterbeek church. 'Some troops of 11 Para Battalion [were] very shaky,' he noted. Thompson began to organ-ize the remnants of the four battalions into a defence line facing east to protect his guns. Having lost at least three-quarters of their strength, the

1st, 3rd and 11th Parachute Battalions as well as the South Staffords were now reduced to less than 450 men combined. They became known for the time being as Thompson Force. Under the command of the redoubtable Major Robert Cain, the South Staffords based themselves near Oosterbeek church in the laundry. The old rectory of the ter Horst family, already the aid station for the Light Regiment, would also become an improvised hospital for the south-eastern sector of the perimeter.

Private William O'Brien in the 11th Parachute Battalion limped into the church, and lay down on one of the pews for a sleep. The church had been badly battered and he could see the sky overhead through the shell-damage to the roof. 'I began to think of my own skin now,' O'Brien admitted. 'It seemed to me they had got us into something they had no business getting us in.' But according to his account an unnamed Dutch lady (who was probably Kate ter Horst) came to encourage the wounded, saying, 'Have courage, God is with you.' A number were not convinced that He was, but they were impressed by her bravery during bombardments, and the occasional malingerer was shamed into returning to his post.

The 4th Parachute Brigade under Hackett had still not yet managed to reach any form of safety after their bruising battle the day before against the *Hohenstaufen* blocking line along the Dreijenseweg. The survivors of the 10th and 156th Parachute Battalions were at less than half their strength. With brigade headquarters, they prepared defensive positions south of the railway line. Hackett wanted to push on east to Oosterbeek during the hours of darkness, leaving before midnight, but General Urquhart told him to stay where he was and make his move after dawn.

Hackett was right to be concerned. Urquhart evidently had not known that the Border Regiment had pulled back its company from the key crossroads to the south which Hackett's force would need to use. During the night, the Germans moved in and took up positions in that area both on the Wolfheze road and around where the Breedelaan reached the Utrechtseweg. So when the 156th Battalion led off next morning, it had a fearful fight against infantry and assault guns to clear a way through. From 270 men, the battalion was reduced to just 120 men still capable of fighting.

With pressure building up from the Kampfgruppe Krafft to the north and from Kampfgruppe Lippert's SS Unteroffizier Schule Arnheim to the west, Hackett's force was almost surrounded. He ordered the 10th Battalion to strike off to the north-east, which seemed the only way out. But in the woods contact was lost, and Hackett found himself moving with just the remnants of the 156th Battalion, his headquarters and a sapper squadron.

Sheltering in a ditch, Major Geoffrey Powell saw Hackett run through enemy fire to where three Jeeps stood. One was ablaze, another next to it was packed with ammunition and the third had a trailer with the badly wounded Lieutenant Colonel Derick Heathcoat-Amory strapped to a stretcher. Hackett leaped into the driver's seat, shielding his face from the flames, started the Jeep and drove it out of range, thus saving the wounded man's life. Powell thought Hackett deserved a VC. Heathcoat-Amory, the head of the Phantom detachment with a direct radio link to the War Office, was later Harold Macmillan's chancellor of the exchequer.

Further on the enemy fire was so strong that when Powell and the remnants of the 156th Battalion found a large crater in the woods they slipped into it and took up all-round defence. With the other brigade personnel, they were about 150 strong. It was less than a thousand metres from the Hartenstein and safety, but German strength was increasing. Staff Sergeant Dudley Pearson, who was Hackett's chief clerk, found himself next to a terrified young soldier who just fired his rifle vertically in the air. Exposed to mortar fire, their losses were heavy, especially among officers. Pearson also saw one collapse beside him, shot with a bullet through the throat. The commanding officer of the 156th, Lieutenant Colonel Sir Richard Des Voeux, was killed, so was his second-in-command Major Ernest Ritson, and Hackett's brigade major.

After the defenders had held off German attacks for most of the afternoon, Hackett announced that they were going to break out by charging straight through the German line towards British positions some 400 metres away. Powell agreed that, however suicidal it might appear, it was certainly better than staying there to be picked off as their ammunition ran out. 'So we lined up on the rim of the hollow and waited for Hackett to order us forward.'

Hackett first went to say goodbye to the wounded whom they had to leave behind. A corporal refused to come. He insisted on remaining so that he could give them covering fire. When their cavalry brigadier shouted 'Charge!' the paratroopers burst out screaming and shouting, and firing their Sten guns. Pearson saw Hackett, also armed with rifle and bayonet, pause above one cowering young German soldier, change his mind and push on. The astonished Germans in front of them scattered and, with the loss of half a dozen men, the remaining ninety broke through to positions held by the Border battalion from the airlanding brigade. The 10th Battalion, bringing their wounded commanding officer, Lieutenant Colonel Smyth, also reached the Hartenstein perimeter. But they too were down to about seventy men, close to a tenth of their original strength.

*

The 21st Independent Parachute Company, reinforced by sixty glider pilots and a troop of airborne sappers, fought back against the Luftwaffe Kampfgruppe from Deelen backed by assault guns. They were a kilometre due north of the Hartenstein, and based themselves on a large house called Ommershof. The Germans had crossed the railway line during the night and were hoping to slip through to cut them off. The inexperienced Luftwaffe conscripts were facing some formidable fighters, including the German-speaking Jewish pathfinders, who had no intention of giving ground. A German officer approached shouting, '*Hände hoch!*', demanding their surrender. The commander of the sapper detachment told his men to hold their fire, but then hurled back abuse when the German continued to demand their submission. A burst of Bren-gun fire made the irritating man dive for cover, and the battle continued.

Late in the afternoon, during a slight lull after another attack, the defenders were surprised to hear music through the trees. A German loudspeaker van was playing Glenn Miller's 'In the Mood'. The paratroopers were even more amused when it was replaced by a voice calling to them in English. 'Gentlemen of the 1st Airborne Division, remember your wives and sweethearts at home.' It then tried to claim that many of their senior officers, including General Urquhart, had been captured, so it was perfectly honourable for them to surrender. This provoked catcalls and insults and whistling, then firing. 'Stayed in position all day,' wrote a paratrooper called Mollett. 'Plenty of mortaring and sniper fire, so made myself a humdinger of a little trench . . . Got another cert when a bunch of Jerries came right out into the open in front of us, also several possibles. Heard a mobile speaker in the distance – funny shooting Jerries to dance music.'

A little further down the railway track towards Arnhem were the King's Own Scottish Borderers, minus two companies cut off during the retreat from the landing zone. They were dug in around the 'White House', the small Hotel Dreijeroord. Colonel Payton-Reid, who had felt so embarrassed on being welcomed there as a liberator, could only prepare for one of the most devastating battles in the regiment's history. They were facing a reinforced Kampfgruppe Krafft, backed by tanks and assault guns. On Wednesday 20 September, the Borderers held off the probing attacks without too much difficulty, but the real fight would come on the morrow.

On the western side the Border Regiment, which up until now had not seen heavy fighting, became involved in several different battles as the SS Kampfgruppe Eberwein advanced. The withdrawal in front of Division von Tettau had meant abandoning the Wolfheze Institute, where an

SS-Hauptsturmführer was convinced that a British general was being secretly treated. When Dr van de Beek denied this, a gun was thrust into his back. 'If you are lying, it will cost you your neck.' Still at gunpoint, Dr van de Beek had to give the SS a guided tour of every room in the Institute. No general was found, so the Germans took away a British military chaplain who had been helping tend the wounded.

The companies of the Border Regiment were clearly too spread out as the retreat gathered speed on the Tuesday. Three of them were pulled back and brought closer together over a front not much more than a kilometre and a half wide, running south from the Utrechtseweg. But as the woods were quite dense, there was little communication. The Borders had to dig in well because the mortar stonks came in suddenly to catch men out in the open. And because there were gaps between the three companies, small groups of SS and even a tank managed to filter through. One of the few remaining 17-pounder anti-tank guns, directed in person by Colonel Loder-Symonds, destroyed it conclusively. D Company had been reinforced with some RAF radar operators who had never fired a rifle before. So 'our RSM walked up and down the parapet of their trench', wrote the company commander, 'giving them weapon training instruction during the battle.'

A Company was on its own, between the railway line and the Utrechtseweg. With a platoon of glider pilots on its right, it faced Lippert's SS Unteroffizier Schule Arnheim, probably the best unit in the Division von Tettau. A glider pilot lieutenant called Michael Long bumped into a German soldier at close quarters in dense undergrowth. They both shot at each other at point-blank range, the German with a sub-machine gun, and Long with his Smith and Wesson revolver. Long, shot through the thigh, was the more badly wounded. He had only managed to hit the German's ear, so the immobilized lieutenant became the prisoner. The German bandaged his leg, and Long bandaged his head. Then the German's platoon commander, Oberleutnant Engelstadt, arrived. He and Long chatted pleasantly about where they had fought in the war. Engelstadt had been in Italy, Russia and the western front. Long asked which he had preferred. Engelstadt glanced round at his men, then bent down with a grin on his face. 'The west,' he replied. 'Anything's better than Russia.'

While the perimeter was starting to close during the latter part of Wednesday, many inhabitants of Oosterbeek tried to escape. They took what they could carry and fashioned crude white flags, often just a handkerchief or napkin tied to a stick.

A Polish war correspondent in the woods south of the Amsterdamseweg was approached by women in tears, asking where they could possibly go to escape the fighting. 'We heard a great scream above the thunder of the artillery,' he wrote. 'A large group of children came running through the trees and tried to make their way across the uneven terrain, falling and getting up again. There were more than ten of them led by a girl of about sixteen: the eldest of the children no more than ten years old and all running after her.' Those civilians who decided to stay either moved mattresses down into their cellar if they thought it strong enough, or sought shelter with neighbours. Many found that 'the Tommies' wanted to come in for a wash and a cup of tea and a little rest. But even those who had filled their baths to the brim feared that water might soon be a major problem.

In the middle of the northern part of the perimeter, the Hotel Hartenstein was losing its elegance by the hour. Paratroopers ripped the shutters off to provide covering for their trenches. German shells had already started to break open the roof, and smoke from burning Jeeps blackened the white walls. The large and solid figure of General Urquhart brought reassurance to many, but there was not very much he could do now that they were trapped. The sad remnants of his division would hold on in the hope that if they maintained their bridgehead north of the Rhine, then the Second Army could use it as soon as they had cleared their way from Nijmegen through the polderland of the Betuwe, or the 'Island'.

The American forward air controller with the 1st Airborne, Lieutenant Paul Johnson, reported how they came under heavy mortar fire. An RAF sergeant helping the team was killed. He and his men were well dug in, but their vehicles and equipment remained exposed. 'As the shelling grew heavier the rest of them practically lived in their slit trenches.' He thought the radio operators behaved bravely under fire, considering it was the first time they had been in combat.

Since there was little he could do outside the Hartenstein, the other American lieutenant, Bruce Davis, went out on patrol at night. 'Three of us went after a machine-gun nest and found it about four hundred yards from divisional headquarters. There were six men sitting by it doing nothing. We threw two grenades and then went back. On the way back I shot a sniper, who fell about twenty feet out of a tree, hit in the head. I think that was one of the most satisfying sights I have ever seen. He was either careless or over-confident, for he had chosen a tree higher than the others and not very thick with foliage, and making a beautiful target. He did not even see me.'

Encirclement at Oosterbeek by SS forces represented an even greater danger to the many Dutch volunteers assisting the British. One of the most remarkable was Charles Douw van der Krap, a naval officer, who had fought in the defence of Rotterdam against the German invasion in 1940. He had been imprisoned by the Germans in a camp in Poland, from which he had recently escaped to take part in the early phase of the Warsaw Uprising. Reaching Arnhem just before the airborne landings, van der Krap was ready to offer his services at the Hartenstein. Lieutenant Commander Arnoldus Wolters, a Dutch liaison officer who knew of him by reputation, asked him to turn some forty Dutch volunteers into a company. But, because of the shortage of weapons and ammunition, their main task was to retrieve supplies parachuted behind German lines.

Douw van der Krap longed to hit back at the Germans but he did not believe that the British could win, and that would mean the sacrifice of these brave young men for little advantage. 'The British would be taken prisoner, the Dutch boys would be shot on the spot,' he explained to Urquhart's intelligence officer, Major Hugh Maguire. Maguire listened carefully and had to agree with his pessimistic assessment. The young volunteers were told to disband and go home. The majority left with great reluctance, yet a number insisted on fighting to the end, while several more went to work in one of the improvised hospitals.

While the British were surrounded they also held a considerable number of German prisoners, who were placed in the hotel tennis courts under guard. The regimental sergeant major in charge of them was astonished to see how few of them were wounded, 'which annoyed me at the time as we were getting it outside the courts'. It was perhaps confirmation of the renowned accuracy of German mortar teams. The prisoners' rations handed to a German officer were exactly the same as those the British were receiving. 'The portion worked out to half a biscuit and about a sixth of a sardine per man. This was done with great care and each German filed by to collect some. They were very sullen about it.'

When the Hartenstein came under heavy mortar fire that day, one of Bruce Davis's American radio operators was hit. Colonel Warrack drove him in a Jeep straight to the dressing station at the Hotel Schoonoord, but while he was still there the Germans overran the hospital. To avoid becoming a prisoner Warrack hurriedly 'removed his tabs and badges of rank, and worked as a private'. Warrack, a large cheerful man, was not easy to conceal, but he got away with it.

The southern road to Oosterbeek church was not the only route left open following the retreat from the battle round the St Elisabeth Hospital. A kilometre or so to the north, a group of South Staffords arrived out of breath at the crossroads in Oosterbeek by the Schoonoord. Many stragglers claimed

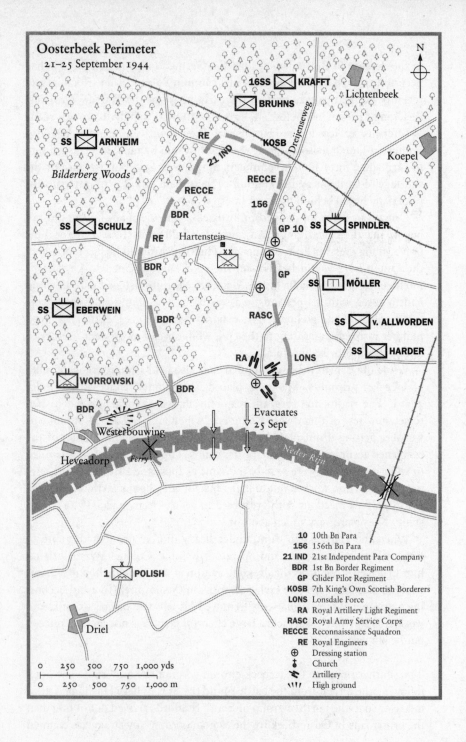

Oosterbeek Perimeter
21–25 September 1944

N

16SS KRAFFT

BRUHNS

Lichtenbeek

SS ARNHEIM

Bilderberg Woods

RE
21 IND

KOSB
Dreijenseweg

Koepel

RECCE

RECCE
156

BDR
GP 10

SS SPINDLER

RE
Hartenstein

XX

SS SCHULZ

GP

BDR

SS MÖLLER

SS EBERWEIN

RASC

BDR

SS v. ALLWORDEN

RA
LONS

SS HARDER

WORROWSKI

BDR

BDR

Westerbouwing

Evacuates
25 Sept

Heveadorp
Ferry

Neder Rijn

1 POLISH

Driel

| 0 | 250 | 500 | 750 | 1,000 yds |

| 0 | 250 | 500 | 750 | 1,000 m |

10   10th Bn Para
156   156th Bn Para
21 IND 21st Independent Para Company
BDR   1st Bn Border Regiment
GP   Glider Pilot Regiment
KOSB 7th King's Own Scottish Borderers
LONS Lonsdale Force
RA   Royal Artillery Light Regiment
RASC Royal Army Service Corps
RECCE Reconnaissance Squadron
RE   Royal Engineers
⊕   Dressing station
✝   Church
𝄃𝄂   Artillery
\|// High ground

to have panzers right behind them to justify their panic, but the appearance of three German tanks proved they were not exaggerating. A troop from the 2nd (Airlanding) Anti-Tank Battery was fortunately present and managed to fight them off.

The attackers came from Kampfgruppe Möller. According to Hans Möller, the British 6-pounder anti-tank gun they came up against also killed Obersturmbannführer Engel at the head of his company. There was little left of him from the direct hit. Möller's pioneers from the *Hohenstaufen* now had some 20mm light flak guns, two tanks and an assault gun supporting them. These vehicles quickened their advance around the Utrechtseweg by flattening garden fences. The Kampfgruppe had also been reinforced with RAD, Kriegsmarine and Luftwaffe personnel. They had no training in street fighting, 'but those that survived, soon learned'.

Demands to surrender were ignored, Möller wrote later, 'or answered with caustic remarks, such as "focken Germans"'. He claimed that the British also gave more 'humorous answers over loudspeakers' by playing 'Lili Marlene' or 'We'll Hang Out our Washing on the Siegfried Line'. But there was no doubt about the intensity of the fighting. 'Anyone who was rash enough to venture to look out of a window, would be found with a hole in his head.'

Despite the heavy gunfire outside the Schoonoord, the volunteers carried on washing patients using a bucket and soap. Kneeling by their patient, they threw themselves flat at each explosion. The wounded who were not completely incapacitated put on their netted parachute helmets, which looked incongruous in bed. According to Hendrika van der Vlist, one of the British doctors announced that patients must take care of the medical cards attached to their battledress, because all their medical details were recorded there. 'You mustn't lose it,' he joked, 'otherwise the wrong arm or leg might be amputated.' This apparently raised a big laugh.

Suddenly, shouts came from the hotel kitchens. Some of the Jews who had been released from the prison in Arnhem had been in the hotel kitchens chatting with a few of the walking wounded and orderlies. Being unaware of the Nazi racial persecution, the British soldiers could not understand why they had been locked up just for being Jewish. They knew astonishingly little of the Nazis' racial policies. In the middle of this conversation, a Waffen-SS officer appeared. He pointed his gun at one of the British medical orderlies and shouted: 'Weapons. Do you have weapons?' He then pushed open the swing doors through to what had been the dining room and was now another ward.

This huge officer appeared in the doorway in full combat kit. He had black stubble, an unwashed face and a Waffen-SS camouflage jacket. According to Hendrika van der Vlist, he looked around with glittering eyes. Other Germans followed. All the British medical orderlies raised their hands in the air. None of them were armed. While this was happening, the Jews escaped from the house through a back door. Sister Suus entered the dining room, and took the threatening German by the arm. She said very calmly. 'This hospital has just been shot at.'

'No, Sister, no!' he replied. 'We're not like the Americans. We don't shoot at a hospital.' She pointed to the bullet holes in the wall. He quickly insisted on seeing his wounded compatriots. A British doctor came over, and Hendrika van der Vlist accompanied them to translate. The British doctor pointed out the German wounded. The German officer shook the hand of the first one and congratulated him on being free again. He asked how he had been treated. There was a note of challenge in his voice. Hendrika did not think that the wounded German looked delighted at the announcement of his liberty. He just replied that he had been very well looked after. According to Colonel Warrack, who was watching incognito, there could have been one exception, through no fault of the medical staff. An ardent young Nazi had refused morphia and any help for four hours. He had a shattered knee joint and must have been suffering considerably. 'Eventually he gave in shouting "*Kamerad!*" and allowed himself to be treated.'

The officer also insisted on seeing the operating theatre, where a German soldier was undergoing minor surgery. On looking at his compatriot, he suddenly said, '*Muss das sein?*' – 'Does this have to be?' – as if the war was simply an unfortunate misunderstanding with tragic consequences. German officers often tried to claim that they had never wanted the war. '*Wir haben es nicht gewünscht.*' It had been forced on them. The commanding officer of the field ambulance, the imperturbable Lieutenant Colonel Arthur Marrable, still puffing gently on his pipe, said to his staff, 'Good show, chaps. Don't take any notice of the Jerries. Carry on as if nothing has happened.'

The sudden German advance in eastern Oosterbeek posed another serious problem. It made it much more dangerous to transport the wounded from the Schoonoord to the surgical department in the Hotel Tafelberg, though such transfers were still possible when the firing was less intense. As a result one of Marrable's doctors had to take off a soldier's shattered foot with an escape file for sawing through prison bars as all the amputation saws were in the Tafelberg on the other side of the front line.

The Hotel Vreewijk, just across the road from the Schoonoord, had been turned into a post-operative centre, but soon it was much more. A courageous young woman called Jannie van Leuven arrived with a horse and cart loaded with wounded men, whom she had collected and then driven through firefights. Her clothes were so soaked with the blood of the wounded she had cared for that she was given battledress, which she wore until they were all captured later. Although the Schoonoord was clearly marked with many Red Cross symbols, the machine-gun fire continued and an assault gun fired four rounds into the building. The wide windows at the front of the hotel were 'gaping holes bordered by wicked glass stilettos'. The utterly vulnerable wounded could do little but pull their blankets over their faces as a defence against flying glass, which made them look a little like children trying to hide under the bedclothes. Mortaring was constant and several men were re-wounded by shrapnel. Plaster dust covered the faces and heads of the staff as if they had been in a fight with flour bombs. Both Dutch volunteers and Royal Army Medical Corps personnel were astonished at how uncomplaining their patients were, showing little more than 'the mirthless grin of pain'.

The fighting in both Arnhem and Oosterbeek caused deep mental wounds as well. Psychological breakdown from combat fatigue could produce many strange forms of behaviour. One man, although hardly wounded physically, would take off all his clothes and walk round the room, pumping his arms and making noises like a locomotive. From time to time, he would utter a string of curses and say, 'Blast this fireman, he was never any good.' Another casualty would wake people at night, bend over them and stare into their eyes to ask, 'Have you got faith?' At the St Elisabeth Hospital, Sister Stransky had a strange encounter with a case of German combat fatigue. A Wehrmacht soldier appeared armed with a pistol. Sister Stransky, a Viennese, refused to allow him to come in. He kept repeating to her, 'I have come all the way from Siberia with a new weapon to rescue the Führer.' When still refused entry, he sat down on the steps of the hospital entrance and began sobbing. Some died with great calm. A sergeant who knew he was dying said to a medic, 'I know I'm not going to live. Would you please just hold my hand.'

The main German attack that day was aimed against the south-east corner, on the lower road towards Oosterbeek church. Colonel Thompson had asked for some more officers to help get the sector organized for defence, and he was sent Major Richard Lonsdale, the second-in-command of the 11th Parachute Battalion. Lonsdale, an Irishman who had won the Distinguished Service Order in Sicily, was the officer who had been wounded in the hand by flak shrapnel just before jumping. He went forward to sort out the defence line, about a kilometre in front of Colonel Thompson's howitzers.

Suddenly a soldier shouted, 'Look out, they're coming!' Lonsdale saw three German tanks coming out of the woods on to the road some 300 metres away. Infantry were also advancing behind a self-propelled assault gun. Lance Sergeant John Baskeyfield of the South Staffords was in command of a 6-pounder anti-tank gun. He and his crew destroyed two tanks, in each case by waiting until they were within a hundred yards. Baskeyfield, although wounded badly in the leg, and alone after the other crew members had been killed or wounded, carried on loading and firing. In a renewed German attack, his 6-pounder was knocked out, so he crawled across to another, the crew of which had all been killed. Baskeyfield manned it single-handed and, firing two shots, knocked out another self-propelled assault gun. 'Whilst preparing to fire a third shot, however, he was killed by a shell from a supporting enemy tank.' Baskeyfield was awarded a posthumous Victoria Cross.

A little later flamethrowers set off a panic, and one group of South Staffords who broke and ran had to be rounded up by an officer and ordered back into the line. The Germans renewed their attacks several times that afternoon. At one point a German self-propelled assault gun was tucked in on the far side of one house, so Major Robert Cain spent a considerable time playing a form of deadly pétanque, firing PIAT bombs over the top of the roof on high elevation as if it were a mortar. A gunner officer, Lieutenant Ian Meikle, bravely clung on behind the chimney above, trying to guide him on to his target. It cost Meikle his life when a German shell hit the chimney, while the constant firing of the PIAT perforated Cain's eardrums.

Two tanks appeared and Cain engaged them too with his PIAT. Wanting to make sure that the one he had hit was properly knocked out he fired again, but this time the PIAT bomb exploded in the launcher. 'There was a flash and the major threw the PIAT in the air and fell backwards,' a glider pilot sergeant reported. 'Everyone thought he had been hit by a shell from the tank exploding. He was lying with his hands over his eyes. His face was blackened and swollen. "I think I'm blinded," he said.' His face was riddled with tiny metal fragments. They lifted him on to a stretcher and he was carried away. At the aid station, his sight returned, so after a short rest he discharged himself and went back. He soon heard a cry of 'Tigers!', so he ran to the 6-pounder anti-tank gun. Cain called to another soldier to help him and they achieved a first-round hit, which brought the tank to a halt. 'Reload!' Cain shouted. 'Can't, sir,' came the reply. 'Recoil mechanism's gone. She'll have to go into the workshops.' Cain clearly appreciated the calm and professional answer.*

---

* Cain, the only winner of a Victoria Cross at Arnhem to survive the battle, was the father-in-law of Jeremy Clarkson.

Towards evening, Lonsdale was given permission to pull back to the church with the remnants of the three battalions. As most of them recovered in the battered church, Lonsdale, head bandaged and arm in a sling, went up into the pulpit and addressed them in stirring style. Thompson Force was officially redesignated Lonsdale Force the next day. The 1st and 3rd Battalion men were positioned south of the church on the polderland stretching down to the river, with the South Staffords around the church and the 11th north of the road. Company Sergeant Major Dave Morris of the 11th moved into the Vredehof, or Peace House. The door was barricaded with two pianos, so they climbed in through a window. In the cellar they found fifteen civilians, including three children and a month-old baby. Rather surprisingly, the owner of the Peace House, Frans de Soet, begged a rifle off the paratroopers, and he joined CSM Morris in the attic next day, sniping from a skylight.

Back in England, Major General Sosabowski's Polish Independent Parachute Brigade suffered agonies of impatience and frustration. They had watched the first wave take off on the Sunday. Lieutenant Stefan Kaczmarek thought it looked so powerful that he felt 'a joy that almost hurt' at the idea that the war would soon be over. But then, after two days of cancellations, Sosabowski and his officers became understandably angry at the lack of information. They had already been to the airfield once and been sent back.

At 08.45 hours on Wednesday morning, Lieutenant Colonel George Stevens, the 1 Airborne Corps liaison officer with the Poles, brought a new order. They were not to land near the Arnhem road bridge, but to the west near the village of Driel. If the Arnhem bridge was still in airborne hands, they wondered, then why were they being dropped well to the west? They began to suspect that things had gone badly wrong. All Colonel Stevens would say was that the brigade was to be dropped south of the Neder Rijn and was 'to cross by means of the ferry'.

Sosabowski briefed the battalion and company commanders on the new plan, and the brigade emplaned for a 12.30 take-off. This was delayed another hour. But 'after having started engines, take-off [was] again postponed for 24 hours because of bad weather.' A report from the First Allied Airborne Army implied, however, that the real reason for this cancellation was to give priority to supply drops, but in the event 'most of the supplies dropped to the 1st Airborne Division fell into enemy hands.' 'The soldiers, exhausted by a whole day of tense anticipation, return to the camp, embittered,' a Polish paratrooper wrote. 'In the evening they gather around radio receivers to hear news from Warsaw – now dying – which had awaited their help.'

That evening at 22.00, Colonel Stevens returned to say that the 'position was desperate'. The 1st Airborne Division urgently needed reinforcements as it was surrounded. Communications with the continent had clearly not improved, as Stevens thought that the northern part of Nijmegen and the bridges there were still in German hands. He admitted that the present state of affairs was 'entirely different from the one anticipated'. He did not need to add that the role of the Polish brigade was now simply to help pull British chestnuts out of the fire. That was all too plain.

Sosabowski, who had never had any confidence in the whole plan for Market Garden, now lost his temper. He had consistently objected to the fact that his anti-tank guns would be landed by glider with the British on the north side. Now that the Germans held the Arnhem bridge, it meant that his brigade would be dropped on the south bank, without any anti-tank defence. Sosabowski told Stevens to inform First Allied Airborne Army headquarters that if he did not receive a proper briefing on what was happening at Arnhem, he would not go. He said that General Brereton should be 'asked to make a decision. He [Sosabowski] maintained that the former task being cancelled, the introduction of the Brigade Group into battle should be preceded by adequate information regarding own troops and enemy position.' An hour later, Colonel Stevens discovered that General Brereton was somewhere on the continent, but even his own headquarters did not know where, and General Browning had not been in touch for more than twenty-four hours. It was hardly surprising that Sosabowski despaired of his superior officers.

19

Nijmegen and Hell's Highway
Thursday 21 September

On the German side, confusion continued all through the night over whether German troops were still fighting in Nijmegen, south of the Waal road bridge. Bittrich reported to Model's headquarters, 'no further report has been received from the bridgehead for the last two hours, garrison appears to be destroyed.'

Hauptsturmführer Karl-Heinz Euling had commanded the defence of the Valkhof and Hunner Park partly from the Belvedere tower, and partly from a house near by. The fighting had carried on well after Sergeant Robinson's troop had charged across. And yet around midnight Euling had somehow managed to escape with almost sixty of his men as well as with a small group of Fallschirmjäger under Major Ahlborn.

Euling claimed that the collapse of buildings in the raging fires gave the impression that he and his men had perished. In fact they had climbed down the steep hill of the Valkhof and gone under the bridge while more British tanks thundered across above them. They were in darkness down below because the Valkhof bluff shielded them from the fires in the town above. Euling had then led his men in single file down the street 'in a casual manner, as if they were Americans'. Euling asserts that he and his men pushed along the riverbank to the east of Nijmegen, where they found boats and crossed over to the north bank of the Waal. Since both the Americans and the underground had searched and found none, this seems unusually fortunate.

While Euling and his SS panzergrenadiers were greatly admired for their bravery, a reserve unit under Major Hartung on the north bank had apparently 'dispersed without orders' on the appearance of the British tanks. They had run back to Bemmel and even as far as Elst, where they were rounded up by part of the 10th SS Panzer-Regiment and brought back into line, no doubt at gunpoint. By dawn on 21 September, II Panzer Corps reported that a defence line had been established running from Oosterhout to Ressen and on to Bemmel, blocking the Allied advance less than four kilometres north of the road bridge. This line was stiffened with some Mark IV tanks which had been ferried across at Pannerden. These forces were supported by the *Frundsberg* artillery regiment also at Pannerden. Harmel transferred his command post to the ferry point, because supplies were not getting across in sufficient quantities.

Despite Generalfeldmarschall Model accepting responsibility for the failure to blow the bridge, Generaloberst Jodl noted that Hitler was still raging about 'the idiocy of allowing undemolished bridges to fall into enemy hands'. Generalmajor Horst Freiherr von Buttlar-Brandenfels of the Wehrmacht high command continued to demand more details to account for 'why the Nijmegen bridge was not destroyed in time'. Model's chief of staff had to explain that the order had been given immediately after the first Allied landings. The situation at Arnhem had shown that this order was entirely justifiable. If the bridge at Arnhem had been blown, it would have been impossible to reinforce Nijmegen. And as for the bridge at Nijmegen, that could always be recaptured with an attack from the east by the II Fallschirmjäger Corps.

Both British and American commanders were conscious of the danger. On Brigadier Gwatkin's orders, M-10 tank destroyers from the 21st Anti-Tank Regiment followed on in the early hours, just behind the first company of the 3rd Battalion Irish Guards. Captain Roland Langton with a squadron of their tank battalion was also on the way, but in the dark they had trouble finding the infantry from their 3rd Battalion. Despite their casualties from the day before, Major Julian Cook's battalion pushed forward at dawn with the tank destroyers in support for another kilometre. 'Every inch of this advance was hotly contested,' Cook wrote. 'The Krauts had all the advantages. They controlled the orchard, the ditches, the farmhouses etc.' Cook and his men had hit Harmel's defence line. They could do little more until the Irish Guards group was ready to deploy.

With the fighting across the Waal and the counter-attacks from the Reichswald, the 82nd Airborne's casualty rate over the last twenty-four hours rose to more than 600 men in need of hospital treatment. The 307th Airborne Medical Company had just created a casualty clearing station out of a former monastery in a southern suburb of Nijmegen. The paratroopers called it 'the Baby Factory' because SS soldiers were thought to have mated there with racially selected young women.* Locals joked that this Strength through Joy centre should be called the 'Lustwaffe'.

The American doctors and medics were greatly assisted by large numbers of women volunteers. They had to cope with one aid man drinking the surgical spirit used for sterilizing medical instruments, and American paratroopers desperate for souvenirs to send home. One GI kept offering a Dutch nurse more and more money for her Red Cross brooch. She was, however, shocked by the racial tensions in the US Army. Whenever she looked after black soldiers from a quartermaster battalion, a white soldier would make a snide comment: 'Is that your new boyfriend?'

That day the 307th was able to send some casualties back by road to the 24th Evacuation Hospital at Leopoldsburg over the Belgian frontier. This solution did not last once the Germans started attacking Hell's Highway in earnest. The company, which had been reinforced with an extra group of surgeons, was certainly hard-worked. It carried out 284 major operations and 523 ordinary operations. As one might expect, 78 per cent were 'extremity cases, hands, arms, feet and legs'.

The 307th's mortality rate in the circumstances was impressively low at just 2.5 per cent. Military medicine had made huge advances since the First World War, with penicillin, glucose drips, oxygen, anti-tetanus, sulfa powder and improved anaesthetics. Rapid evacuation by Jeep also made a difference. The company's doctors encountered only a single case of gas gangrene, a casualty who did not arrive until thirty hours after his injury. The old triage system from the previous war, which left those with major head and stomach wounds to die, was largely replaced. The 'usual procedure followed was to admit seriously wounded to the shock room directly from the admitting room'. The use of a total of 10,000 gallons of oxygen and 45 million units of penicillin sodium made an enormous difference. So did blood transfusions. 'Blood was a major factor in saving the shock cases and most of the ones with massive hemorrhages,' the 307th report stated. As well as using 1,500 units of plasma, the team supplemented their blood bank by calling on lightly wounded patients to act as blood donors.

Sergeant Otis L. Sampson, who had been badly hit by 88mm shrapnel,

* In 1942, on Himmler's orders, the SS took over this monastery called the Berchmanianum for his *Lebensborn* project. An SS Vorkommando from Munich adapted the monks' cells and living space so that sixty 'Aryan' women and a hundred 'race pure' children could be housed there in 'Lebensborn Gelderland'. No children were born there in the end because the place had not been finished until late 1943.

was taken to the Baby Factory by Jeep. 'I was carried into the hospital on a low legged stretcher', he recorded, 'and deposited on the floor in the hall-way. Here I was given two quarts of blood: I could feel life flow back into my body. A major looked me over and told an attendant to take my clothes off and turn me on my back. I informed him, "Major I'm hit in the back." "I know," he said, "but your stomach is where the shrapnel is. If this was World War I, with the wound you have, you wouldn't survive. You can have a drink of water if you care to, it won't do you any harm." '

The attendant tried to walk off with his paratrooper jump boots, saying, 'Where you're going, you won't need them.' An outraged Sampson tried to crawl off the stretcher to stop him so the major ordered the attendant to bring them back. In the ward, Sampson watched the doctors draw the sheet over the faces of those who had died. But not all patients were badly hit. A German pilot had parachuted from his plane and he came down in sight of their window. 'His chute had been caught on some object and he was left dangling.' Two paratroopers, both walking wounded, immediately went out to relieve the pilot of his watch and pistol.

The German pilot was from one of the fighters which had attacked Nijmegen in the early afternoon, causing a sudden panic. The remaining population thought that the city was about to be bombed like Eindhoven, and crammed into the closest air-raid shelter. The fighters also machine-gunned the Baby Factory. When Captain Bestebreurtje went there to have his wounds dressed, the doctor said to him, 'Do you know what those German bastards did? They flew over and strafed the hospital in spite of the fact that we have a big red cross on it. And do you know what I was doing when they came over? I was saving the life of a German – and I happen to be a Jew.'

After the battle of the Nijmegen bridges, there was a great deal of clearing up to do. Many were struck by one image. On the road bridge on the Nijmegen side a dead German in rigor mortis had an arm outstretched which appeared to be pointing across the river. Altogether eighty dead Germans were found on the bridge, and 'during the morning', wrote Lieutenant Tony Jones of the Royal Engineers, 'a great many more prisoners were winkled out – an extra-ordinary assortment, old and young, SS, police, Wehrmacht, Marines, some temporarily arrogant (but only for a short time), but most completely dazed and bewildered. The equipment captured and lying about was even more varied – 88mm guns, 50mm, 37mm, a baby French tank, Spandaus, Hotch-kiss machine-guns, new rifles and old 1916 long barrel and long bayonet rifles, mines and bazookas, grenades of every sort, size and description. It was almost a foundation for a War Museum.'

In Nijmegen itself, the conditions were far worse with much of the northern part of the town burned out. 'The city looks awful and is heavily damaged,' the director of the concert hall wrote. 'Many burned blocks of houses, craters in the roads, mountains of glass and rubble, uprooted trees, a terribly sad sight.' The great De Vereeniging concert hall itself had more than a thousand windowpanes broken.

All around the Valkhof the destruction was of course even more terrible, 'a chaos of shelled trenches, bits of uniform, dried pools of blood, shot-up vehicles and weapons'. German bodies were still lying in the street, some covered with coats. According to one eyewitness, Americans were wandering laconically amid the scene. 'One American paratrooper was eating his lunch out of a tin next to the body of a German soldier.' Wounded civilians were taken to the St Canisius hospital 'where they were being operated on eight or ten at a time'. People in villages, having heard of the destruction inflicted on Nijmegen, immediately donated what they could, especially food, to help those who had lost everything.

Out of 540 Jews in Nijmegen in 1940, only sixty or so were left four years later. Simon van Praag had been hidden by a Catholic priest and had to spend much of the time in the dark to evade discovery or denunciation. To remain concealed while the battle raged and houses were set on fire must have been terrifying. There was little relief when the ordeal ended, and he emerged into daylight to see the city half-destroyed from the fighting.

Although artillery shells were still landing in Nijmegen, the final departure of the Germans meant that the Dutch red, white and blue flag came out again and the purges recommenced. 'Prostitutes who served members of the German occupation forces', wrote Cornelis Rooijens, 'have their hair cut off with big shears and are wrapped in pictures of prominent Nazis at the hands of the city rabble and professional idlers.' And Martijn Louis Deinum also saw captured members of the NSB paraded, including 'a woman with a portrait of Hitler hanging round her neck and with a completely shaven head'. Many disliked these forms of revenge, while others rather resented the way that British soldiers tried to interfere. 'Generally speaking they don't have the same hatred of the Germans as we have,' a woman wrote. 'I told them that they could not imagine what these years had been like for us. They think that the shearing of the heads of those who have had relations with the Germans is so awful, that whenever they have a chance, they will try and stop it.'

By 11.00 that morning, Model's headquarters heard that 'so far 45 enemy tanks have crossed over the bridge towards the north.' These presumably were a mixture of Q Battery tank destroyers and Irish Guards Shermans. Brigadier Gwatkin had told the Vandeleur cousins that they were to advance at the normal speed of an approach march, fifteen miles in two hours. But they could see immediately that the dyke embankment, with a road along the top and flanked by boggy polderland, 'was a ridiculous place to operate tanks'. An advance on a one-tank front, with no chance of man-oeuvring off the road, would be suicidal. But of course they had no option but to follow orders. Montgomery's refusal to listen to Prince Bernhard's advice and the failure of planners to consult army officers from the Netherlands army had been a major mistake.

At 10.40, Captain Langton was ordered to advance twenty minutes later, although the Irish Guards war diary indicates that finally they did not advance until 13.30. Langton thought at first that Lieutenant Colonel Giles Vandeleur was joking. All they had was a road map. The order came, 'don't stop for anything.' Langton was furious when the Typhoons he had been promised failed to appear. In fact they had come, but communications had broken down.

'The Typhoons had begun arriving, a squadron at a time,' the forward air controller, Flight Lieutenant Donald Love, recounted. '[Squadron Leader] Sutherland tried to contact them but the VHF set in the contact car had gone dead. It was absolutely horrible . . . The Typhoons were milling around overhead and on the ground, shelling and mortaring was going on. I felt frustrated and exasperated. There was nothing to be done. The Typhoons had strict instructions not to attack anything on speculation.' Love's mood was not improved when their RAF radio operator suffered a nervous collapse.

The four leading Shermans were knocked out one after another. The first three 'within a minute'. As another Guards officer put it, they were lined up 'like metal ducks in a fairground booth waiting to be shot down'. The defence line contained 88mm guns, self-propelled assault guns and at least two Royal Tigers hidden in woods. Giles Vandeleur shouted across to his cousin that if they sent any more tanks up the road 'it would be bloody murder'.

Langton, left with just four Shermans in the squadron, was joined a few minutes later by Colonel Joe Vandeleur, who arrived with his cousin Giles. Langton asked whether they could get air support. Vandeleur shook his head and told him quite inaccurately that all aircraft were being tasked to support the drop of the Polish Parachute Brigade. 'But we could get there if we had the support,' Langton persisted. Vandeleur again shook his head and said that he was sorry. He ordered Langton to stay where he was until further orders. According to Flight Lieutenant Love, Colonel Joe Vandeleur then went off on foot into the woods with a drawn service revolver, looking 'like [something out of] a Wild West film', to carry out his own reconnaissance on foot. Langton was furious and he became even more bitter that afternoon when he watched over to their left German fighters attacking the Polish drop near Driel without any Allied aircraft coming to their aid.

'When I saw that "Island" my heart sank,' said the Guards Armoured Division commander. 'The Island' was the name given to the flat, wet polderland of the Betuwe between the Waal and the Neder Rijn. 'You can't imagine anything more unsuitable for tanks.' Adair was short of infantry when the task ahead was clearly 'a job for infantry', so he persuaded Horrocks to push the 43rd Infantry Division through instead. It faced a hard fight. With the Arnhem bridge now open, Harmel's defence line was strengthened by the first part of Kampfgruppe Brinkmann, with Bataillon Knaust and a company of Mark V Panther tanks reaching Elst.

At first light that morning, the Household Cavalry Regiment sent two troops of D Squadron over the Waal to reconnoitre to the west. They came under heavy shelling and three White scout cars were damaged, but they managed to slip through Harmel's defence line in the mist. They headed for Driel, where the Polish Parachute Brigade was due to drop.

Stranded in England by one delay after another, Major General Sosabowski and his men were living in a state of unbearable tension. They longed to get into battle in the Netherlands, and yet their thoughts were in Warsaw with the Home Army's desperate defence. At 03.00 on 21 September, Lieutenant Colonel Stevens received a signal from First Allied Airborne Army confirming the new drop zone near Driel, and stating that the ferry was still in British hands. It also said that the bridge at Nijmegen had been taken, and British artillery would soon be within range to support the airborne division at Oosterbeek. Later in the morning, Brigadier General Floyd L. Parks, the chief of staff, First Allied Airborne Army, again assured Sosabowski that the ferry was in the hands of 1st Airborne Division. This was true at the time, but a German attack later that morning would push back the company of the Border Regiment guarding it and enable the Wehrmacht to destroy it.

At 07.00, the men of the Polish Parachute Brigade reached their three airfields. The fog lingered so thickly that the outlines of hangars, aircraft and buildings could scarcely be made out, but as it was warmer than on previous days, the Poles were determined to believe that this time they would take off. A young Polish officer described the scene: 'A bustle of paratroopers can be seen around, before and behind the Dakotas, their equipment and personal kits carelessly scattered about on the cement runway. Some, in groups, are engaged in discussions, some take their time to rest, others visit their friends from neighbouring Dakotas. No one goes off too far, though, to be ready to load up at a moment's notice. The men look for signs that might tell them that this time lift-off will not be cancelled. But it is delayed again, hour after hour.'

Soon after 14.00 hours, the mist had cleared just enough so the signal was given. Seventy-two aircraft took off from Saltby and Cottesmore, and another forty-six from Spanhoe. The larger group managed to find a window in the weather over the North Sea, but the troop carriers from Spanhoe were ordered to return, to the furious disbelief of their passengers. After they had landed and heard that the other group had carried on, their feelings of uselessness, 'though it is not of our doing, throws us into despair, awakens feelings of helpless rage and a sort of envy towards our comrades on the ground'.

At 16.05 hours, a German signaller in the Dunkirk pocket reported a large number of Allied aircraft. Standartenführer Harzer ordered Oberstleutnant von Swoboda's flak brigade to stand by in its new position south-west of the Arnhem road bridge. Sixty fighters on nearby airfields were ordered to take off. German accounts at this point became carried away with excitement. 'The concentrated fire of the flak hit them like a burning fist,' was just one exultant phrase. The Germans claimed that they had shot down forty-three Allied planes. One German eyewitness estimated a 60 per cent casualty rate among the paratroopers, but Polish accounts show such ideas to be wildly optimistic.

German flak was certainly heavy. Polish paratroopers, ardent Catholics for the most part, described the tracer arcing up towards them as 'a rosary of sparks'. Five C-47 troop carriers were shot down and another sixteen damaged. German troops in about company strength were on or near the drop zone. 'There was intense shooting aimed at the aircraft and also at the descending force of paratroopers,' the brigade war diary stated.

Only a handful of men were shot as they came down. 'Those who've been found by a bullet also land,' ran one Pole's romantic view of death in battle. 'Their bodies float down under the white canopy slowly, majestically, as if they, too, were about to go into battle.' Yet out of Sosabowski's reduced force of 957 men, no more than four were killed and twenty-five wounded or injured. 'Some close-quarter combat with knives and hand grenades followed. Enemy resistance was soon overcome and eleven prisoners taken.' Their greatest anxiety was the inexplicable absence of the 1st Battalion and half the 3rd Battalion. They had no idea that they had been ordered back and feared that they had been shot down.

Their chaplain, Father Alfred Bednorz, saw the steeple of Driel church and went immediately to pay a visit on the local priest, presumably conversing in Latin. 'I introduce myself as a Polish Army chaplain. The vicar is surprised, "How did a Polish priest get here?" I smile and point to the sky. He understands that the paratroopers who have just dropped here are Poles. We embrace each other like brothers. The vicar runs to his desk and hands me a lovely antique cross. "May this cross be a remembrance of our liberation from the Hitlerites."'

Soon after landing, Sosabowski was greeted by Cora Baltussen, a member of the underground, who arrived on a bicycle. She warned him that the ferry had been destroyed and the Germans now held that stretch of the north bank. While setting up his command post in a farmhouse on the edge of Driel, Sosabowski sent off a reconnaissance patrol to the bank of the Neder Rijn to check on the ferry. But the patrol returned to confirm what Cora Baltussen had told him. The 1st Airborne across the river was under machine-gun and mortar fire, and the remains of the railway bridge were also in German hands. There was no sign of any boats.

At 22.30 that evening, Captain Ludwik Zwolański, the Polish liaison officer from Urquhart's headquarters, appeared, still wet and muddy in his shirt and undershorts from having swum the river. He was known as the 'black bandit' because of his swarthy features. Not knowing the password, he cursed loud enough for a fellow officer to recognize his voice and clear him with the sentries. He pointed out Sosabowski's command post and Zwolański entered and announced himself, saluting smartly. 'Captain Zwolański reporting, sir.'

Sosabowski, who had been bent over a table studying the map, turned and stared at him in amazement. 'What the hell are you doing here, Zwolański?' he demanded. Zwolański explained that Urquhart had sent him to say that rafts would be provided to bring his men across the river that night. The fact that Zwolański himself had had to swim was hardly encouraging. Sosabowski nevertheless moved both battalions down towards the river. No rafts had appeared by 03.00 hours so Sosabowski brought the bulk of his men back to Driel to dig in. The riverbank would be far too exposed in daylight.

Zwolański had also brought an order from Urquhart that Sosabowski himself should cross the river at the first opportunity to report to 1st Airborne headquarters. Sosabowski had no intention of doing anything of the sort. He considered it madness for a commander to leave his troops in such a way, and when he later heard what had happened to the British, with the divisional commander, one brigadier and the commander of the recce squadron all separated from their men, he considered his decision even more justified.

While Browning wanted the Polish brigade to cross the river to reinforce the 1st Airborne Division and stave off disaster, Obergruppenführer Bittrich and Model's headquarters believed that the new landings in the Betuwe south of the Neder Rijn were intended 'to establish the link with advancing enemy forces coming north from Nijmegen'.

Bittrich's defence line around Ressen was managing to block the road running north towards Elst and Arnhem. The 4th/7th Dragoon Guards had more luck to the west round Oosterhout. 'British tanks moving in column', the 1st Battalion of the 504th reported, 'came to the area in front of the company about 17.30. They cleaned out German strongpoints, scared off a Mark IV tank coming out of Oosterhout, knocked out two tanks and a half-track on the road leading to Oosterhout, and wiped out a German mortar position. Bren gun carriers killed, wounded or drove out about 50 Germans in the orchard.' This was the correctly chosen route if you were to pass the exam for the Netherlands Staff College. As it happened, that was the day the Dutch troops of the Princess Irene Brigade passed through Eindhoven and Nijmegen to an emotional welcome from their fellow citizens. They were lucky to get through, because the XXX Corps route was about to earn its nickname of Hell's Highway.

On 21 September, Colonel Johnson of the 501st Parachute Infantry Regiment, building on Kinnard's offensive strategy to defend Veghel, launched a regimental night attack towards Schijndel. Generaloberst Student went to see Generalleutnant Poppe in the school which he had made his command post at the southern edge of the town. Student asked how things were. Poppe replied drily: 'The situation is somewhat spreckled.' By that he meant that they were under attack in Schijndel and would have to get out, but the Americans were about to get a nasty shock when attacked from the east by the 107th Panzer-Brigade reinforced with paratroopers and an SS battalion under Oberst Walther.

Kinnard's 1st Battalion was advancing when a 20mm gun mounted on a truck opened up on them. Kinnard saw his men throwing themselves into the ditches on either side of the road. The Germans were deliberately firing high with the 20mm using tracer, while at the same time another machine gun using ordinary ball ammunition was scything away at knee height. Not realizing that the Germans were up to their old tricks, Kinnard ran up the road, ordering his men to get up and push on. 'Keep moving!' he shouted. 'That fire's going way high.' 'Maybe it is, Colonel,' a private answered him

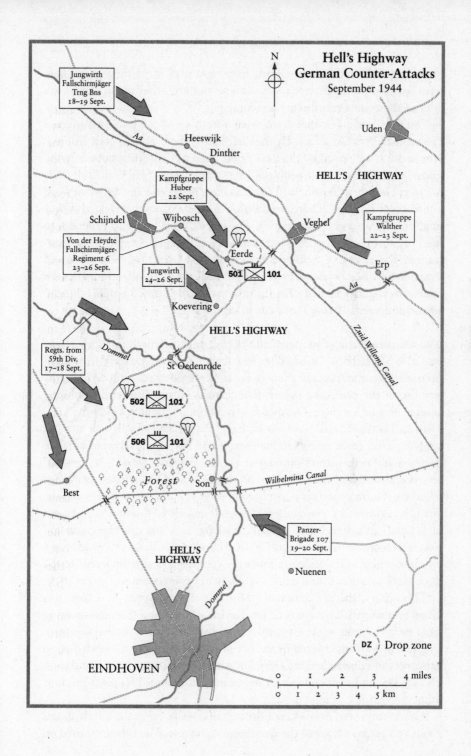

N

**Hell's Highway
German Counter-Attacks**
September 1944

Jungwirth
Fallschirmjäger
Trng Bns
18–19 Sept.

Aa

Heeswijk

Dinther

Uden

HELL'S HIGHWAY

Kampfgruppe
Huber
22 Sept.

Schijndel

Wijbosch

Veghel

Kampfgruppe
Walther
22–23 Sept.

Von der Heydte
Fallschirmjäger-
Regiment 6
23–26 Sept.

Eerde

Erp

501 ☒ **101**

Aa

Jungwirth
24–26 Sept.

Koevering

HELL'S HIGHWAY

Dommel

St Oedenrode

Zuid Willems Canal

502 ☒ **101**

506 ☒ **101**

Forest   Son

Wilhelmina Canal

Regts. from
59th Div.
17–18 Sept.

Best

Panzer-
Brigade 107
19–20 Sept.

**HELL'S
HIGHWAY**

Nuenen

Dommel

EINDHOVEN

DZ Drop zone

0   1   2   3   4 miles

0   1   2   3   4   5 km

out of the darkness, 'but we already have eight men hit in the legs.' Others went forward in the ditches at a crouching run until they could engage the crew of the 20mm gun and force them to flee.

Entering Schijndel, they found that a number of the houses contained German soldiers fast asleep. By the early hours, the town had been secured. Kinnard was contacted by the local priest, who was also an organizer in the underground. 'Keep your people off the streets,' he begged him. 'Tell them not to get out their bunting and to act as if we're unwelcome. Get that word out to them tonight.' There would probably be a counter-attack, and they might not be able to hold the town. The priest agreed and also promised to send off scouts on bicycles to see where German forces might be concentrating. The people of Schijndel fortunately did what they were asked and stayed inside their houses even after dawn had come. One paratrooper in the street was slightly startled when a shutter suddenly opened beside him, and a hand appeared offering him a cup of ersatz coffee.

The German tactic of perpetual attacks against the length of Hell's Highway also affected St Oedenrode. Lieutenant Colonel Cassidy's battalion prepared to counter-attack at 06.30 on 21 September, but supporting artillery fire in the preceding moments fell short, killing three and wounding another five of his men. The attack against the monastery which the Germans had occupied still went ahead. Each platoon had two British tanks in support. They faced heavy German fire, but it was very inaccurate, as if the enemy was firing without aiming at all. By the time Cassidy's men had seized and searched the buildings, all the Germans had slipped away. But a sudden German artillery bombardment at around 10.00 hours hit the 502nd's regimental command post, wounding Colonel Michaelis and most of his staff in a tree burst. Cassidy, walking back towards the command post, was blown into a ditch and lightly wounded. He had to take command of the regiment and decided to move the command post temporarily to the monastery, where it would enjoy slightly better protection.

The bitter fighting continued. 'Mortar Sergeant James A. Colon was killed by a sniper. Pfc Robert L. Deckard was killed by a German shooting from near-by cover while Deckard was trying to help a wounded German. Lieutenant Larson, covered by the fire of several of his men, crawled up to the covert and dispatched the Germans with two grenades and a round from his .45. The 2nd Platoon leader, Lieutenant Wall, a squad sergeant and four others were badly wounded.'

Things improved only when a British tank, well over to the left flank and about 150 yards in front of the paratroopers, traversed its turret. 'It fired on an 88 directly confronting the infantry and knocked it out. Then it scored a direct hit on a self-propelled gun near the 88.' This 'seemed to pop the cork out of the bottle'. Germans 'began to spring up like mushrooms' from the field in front, ready to surrender. 'The officers were neatly groomed as if they had been planning a capitulation.' One German soldier insisted that he had to retrieve his soap and toilet articles from his kitbag. 'Someone booted his pants and he moved along.' At 16.00 hours 'a tank crossed the company front about 600 yards out. A six-pounder [anti-tank gun] which was attached gave it a round which hit just behind the tank and caused it to spin round with its tail toward C Company. A Sherman tank then poured three rounds into the Tiger and it exploded and went up in flames.'

Cassidy received orders to fall back on St Oedenrode, but that night the Germans reoccupied the monastery. Two days later it cost a British armoured regiment and an infantry battalion heavy losses to retake it. Horrocks's Club Route was far too narrow to defend effectively, because of the delays to the two British formations flanking his XXX Corps. American parachute battalions and British armoured squadrons were having to dash up and down and back and forth like firefighters. General Taylor compared their role to that of US Cavalry troops defending railroad lines, outposts and settler trails from attacks by Native American tribes.

Constant interruptions, caused by German artillery shooting up convoys, meant that most American units were receiving only about a third of the K-rations they were due. The great German ration store at Oss discovered by the Household Cavalry Regiment was used to supplement diets. But because neither side could spare sufficient troops to secure the town, a strange situation developed. Each side sent armed parties to take supplies. 'At this time what was apt to happen', the Household Cavalry Regiment stated in its war diary, 'was that the British drew rations in the morning – Germans in the afternoon. What a wonderful nation we are for standing in queues.' A British officer observed that the German supplies from Oss were forcing his Guardsmen to admit that perhaps their ration packs of 'compo' were not the worst in the world after all. 'German rations are *not delectable*,' an American officer emphasized. With dry sausage made out of horsemeat and the rock-hard bread called *Dauerbrot*, American paratroopers found them even worse than the British compo variety, which they received from time to time. In compo packs, they liked only the treacle pudding. As for Player's cigarettes, 'they tasted like warm wind and were hard to draw.' Another paratrooper said that smoking British cigarettes was 'like sucking cotton through a straw'.

*

For Gavin's 82nd Airborne, the attacks were coming not from both sides of the highway, but from the Reichswald still. Meindl's II Fallschirmjäger Corps had taken Feldt's Kampfgruppen under command because 'his forces were not equal to meeting a serious, systematic attack and still less so to carrying out an attack themselves.'

Some of the most intense fighting was for a commanding feature, Den Heuvel, which predictably became known as Devil's Hill. Kampfgruppe Becker from the 3rd Fallschirmjäger-Division attacked relentlessly. At one point Company A of the 508th ran out of machine-gun ammunition, with most riflemen down to five rounds each. An NCO who had been back to battalion headquarters appeared with four bandoliers just in time. They were also short of food. Constant attacks, especially at night, left the company exhausted. They tied empty canvas bandoliers together to run from foxhole to foxhole so that they could jerk each other awake whenever there was an enemy incursion. Company A managed to hold on until they were finally relieved on the night of 23 September.

The 3rd Battalion in Beek was hit by a sudden onslaught before dawn on 21 September. One company was virtually surrounded, but the others launched a fierce counter-attack and the young Fallschirmjäger were forced out of the town for good shortly before dusk.

Once darkness fell, the paratroopers of the 508th could see searchlights over to the left, probing the night sky from Nijmegen. Anti-aircraft batteries were firing away at German night bombers attempting to destroy the Waal bridge, which Generalfeldmarschall Model had so obstinately refused to demolish.

20

Oosterbeek
Thursday 21 September

Although resistance at the road bridge in Arnhem had come to an end the evening before, some groups had still not given in. Lieutenant Barnett's defence platoon was determined to fight on. Trapped in a burning building, they knew that their only chance was to break out through the back, where Germans were waiting for them. 'I took a dozen or so [men],' Barnett recounted, 'and told them to fix their bayonets and we charged them. They were in a back garden and they got up and ran before we reached them. We were shouting "Whoa Mahomet!" and I think we scared more of them to death than we actually killed with bullets.' They made their way down towards the river to pass under the bridge, but suddenly they saw the unmistakable silhouette of a Tiger tank. They froze at the sight, and it took them a little time before they worked out that it had been knocked out and abandoned. It was the one from Panzer-Kompanie Hummel. They spent the rest of the night concealed under the bridge, as German patrols searched for survivors.

On hearing Major Gough's order to break out towards Oosterbeek, the American OSS officer Lieutenant Todd had made a run for it with a small group. In the confusion and smoke, he managed to get out of the battle area. On finding himself alone he climbed a tree which had somehow escaped the conflagration, and strapped himself to a branch. A very uncomfortable night did little more than preserve his freedom until the next morning, when he was spotted.

Panzergrenadiers combed the battlefield. 'It was terrible,' wrote Horst Weber. 'The trenches were full of bodies. There were bodies everywhere.' Weber then discovered two British paratroopers playing dead. 'Going past two bodies I turned around to glance at them casually – and I met their eyes. I covered them with my pistol, and smiling I said to them "Good morning, gentlemen. Shall I bring you your breakfast now?" ' He escorted them up to the church. Outside, weapons had been dropped in a pile. He watched his prisoners carefully because after the ferocious defence he could not rule out the possibility that they might grab one.

Lance Corporal John Smith, a brigade signaller, had been in another group trying to break out but they ran into a detachment of SS and were marched off. They were held in something like a church hall, which had a piano on the stage. One of the paratroopers could not resist going up and started playing jazz on it. The German guards, in a good mood after their victory, roared with laughter.

One paratrooper, who had remained in the slit trenches behind brigade headquarters during the night, recorded how they were mortared and had to fight off several counter-attacks. 'We had by late morning been reduced to small groups and had been given orders by one of our officers that it was now every man for himself.' He and three others decided to head for the St Elisabeth Hospital, dodging from house to house. They had two Sten guns and a handful of bullets left between them. They hid in an office, but were soon discovered by one of the many German patrols searching for survivors. 'Within half an hour we were rejoining a considerable number of our compatriots, having our hands shaken by SS troops, and sharing their cigarettes. Many of these SS men we found, we had fought in North Africa, Sicily and Italy. I myself was most surprised to find that they were still under the impression that they would win the war – how can one argue with a fanatic?' A number of SS also adopted what one paratrooper called their 'usual "We-should-be-on-the-same-side" gambit', arguing that the British should join them in the fight against the Soviet hordes.

A paratrooper from Lewis's company of the 3rd Battalion was surprised to find that the young German soldier searching him was trembling. Many more panzergrenadiers, however, were in an expansive mood. Some handed out the chocolate taken from British parachute containers which they had collected. 'Occasionally, one would stop and pat a British soldier on the shoulder and offer his congratulations. "Nice fight, Tommy." ' A German officer asked a sapper where he had been fighting before. Following regulations, he refused to answer. In a perfect English accent, the officer replied, 'Never mind, you are a very brave man, but also very foolish.'

Another German officer hit one of his soldiers for sneering at the British prisoners. Victory at Arnhem gave the Waffen-SS the opportunity to show how *ritterlich* – how chivalrous – they could be. At the collecting point, after they had dropped their weapons, Major Gough passed the word that all prisoners were to put on a good show when they set off. So they fell in smartly, dressed by the right and marched with their heads high. One group let rip with a final 'Whoa Mahomet!'

The panzergrenadier Rottenführer Alfred Ringsdorf reflected on what they had just been through. 'No one who has lived through such a terrible experience, whose life has hung by a thread, can tell me that he was not afraid. I don't care if he has the Knight's Cross with diamonds, I am sure he was afraid.' After the battle at the bridge, those in the company who had survived were assembled in a park on the edge of Arnhem. 'It was when we were gathered all together that I consciously heard a bird singing. It was like coming back to life, as if during the battle I had been living in suspension. I was suddenly alive again and realized that I had come through it alive.'

Horst Weber from the same 21st SS Panzergrenadier-Regiment wrote, 'When the English came out after having surrendered they came out holding their heads high. They looked proud and not at all defeated. But I felt sorry for them because they looked so worn, haggard and exhausted. When it was clear that we had defeated the English, the first thing we thought about was getting hold of their food supplies and cigarettes. I was so intent on getting a share of the loot that I refused to help an English soldier whose legs had been shot away. He was propped against a wall and helpless to do anything.' Weber described how as seventeen- and eighteen-year-olds who 'were always hungry' he and his comrades could not believe the rations, the first-aid kits, the instant coffee and all the luxuries which they found in parachute containers. 'And there was soap,' Weber recorded, 'something we had not seen for years. We had been washing with sand. We all wanted to grab these things and take some home with us. We were war children, only interested in what we could get.' They were particularly impressed by sulfa powder. 'In our army many soldiers died of gangrene because we had no penicillin.'

Some of Weber's comrades were not above taking items of enemy uniform from the dead. Even in the usually well-equipped Waffen-SS, there could be a mixture of uniforms. Some wore the tiger camouflage smocks, some field grey, and many wore British or American trousers because they were far more resilient than the German issue, which fell to pieces. American paratrooper boots were the most highly prized, but any German captured wearing a pair was likely to be shot on the spot. Allied matériel had become such a preoccupation, even at the highest levels, that Model's chief of staff soon issued an order forbidding troops in a strong position to shoot down gliders. 'They carry valuable booty, especially heavy weapons, motor vehicles and motorcycles.'

*

As soon as the resistance from Frost's men had ceased, the Kampfgruppe Knaust and the panzergrenadiers from the 10th SS *Frundsberg* were ordered south to strengthen the line around Elst. According to Knaust, some of Gräbner's men from the *Hohenstaufen* reconnaissance battalion were found badly wounded, but still just alive, in the half-tracks which had been shot up on the bridge three days before. Several suffered from terrible burns. Ringsdorf also described going to Elst that morning in half-tracks. 'We went over the bridge on which lay burned-out vehicles. The drivers were still inside. They were burned and charred black.'

Knaust's reaction on seeing the terrain of the Betuwe, or the Island, was the same as General Adair's. It was impossible country for tanks, with water-logged polder on either side of the raised road. His Kampfgruppe's panzer company was soon greatly strengthened with Royal Tigers and some Pan-thers – Knaust estimated some forty-five altogether. His battalion was also reinforced by a naval battalion of sailors from cruisers and U-boats – 'they were terrific men, most of them NCOs, but unfortunately had absolutely no idea how to fight on land. As for the so-called Luftwaffe Field Battalion, it reported to me in Elst at twilight. It was my first and only glimpse of this battalion. By dawn it had disappeared.' Knaust stayed awake on Pervitin, the German army's methamphetamine pills.

Bittrich visited Knaust that day. 'Another 24 hours,' Bittrich said to him, 'we need another 24 hours.' He emphasized that they must not let the Brit-ish through as he had yet to eliminate the 1st Airborne at Oosterbeek. Only then could they switch the bulk of II Panzer Corps south. Knaust, the experienced panzer commander, sited each tank himself. Instead of stomp-ing around on his crutches, the one-legged commander travelled around in a motorcycle sidecar, which was far more manoeuvrable and presented a smaller target in the event of air attack.

Bittrich had placed the newly arrived SS *Nederland* battalion between the bridge and Arnhem railway station, as a backstop behind the Knaust Kampfgruppe. Führer headquarters in East Prussia still feared that Mont-gomery might break through, with sheer weight of tank numbers. Bittrich was under pressure from the Oberkommando der Wehrmacht (OKW) to eliminate the remains of the 1st Airborne at Oosterbeek as rapidly as possible. Hitler demanded a swift conclusion to that battle so that a major counter-attack could be launched towards Nijmegen. They believed that the British at Oosterbeek must be almost out of ammunition, and since 'there is no doubt that the German Luftwaffe controls the air space over Arnhem,' supplies were not getting through. Resistance, they deduced, would therefore be very short-lived.

Bittrich had reported the night before that they had already taken 2,800 prisoners north of the Neder Rijn, and that General von Tettau's left flank on the railway line east of Wolfheze had made contact with the right flank of Harzer's *Hohenstaufen*, so the British were entirely surrounded. But all was not well within the so-called Division von Tettau, because of the furious rows its commander was having with SS-Obersturmbannführer Lippert. Bittrich therefore decided to give the *Hohenstaufen* command over all forces surrounding the 1st Airborne Division.

An hour before first light, British officers in the Oosterbeek perimeter blew whistles to wake men in their slit trenches ready for dawn stand-to. Some wag shouted out, 'Off-side!': a weak joke which still produced some much needed laughter. A couple of glider pilots who had slept through the whistle, awoke later with a shock to find a German lying by their trench. He had waited for them to wake so that he could give himself up. He was in his forties, and simply did not want to fight any more. Considering the perilous situation of those to whom he was surrendering, he must have been either uninformed or desperate. A private from the 1st Para Battalion was so exhausted that he fell asleep later during the battle. When he woke up he astonished one of his comrades who had assumed he was dead.

The attack did not develop until 08.00, with half an hour of heavy shelling and a mortar stonk before the infantry came in, supported with direct fire from flak batteries. The noise was overwhelming. 'The only way Taffy and I could converse', a private in the South Staffords recorded, 'was to shout in each other's ear.' The machine-gun fire was so intense that Major Lonsdale had to visit his sector's positions north of Oosterbeek church in a Bren-gun carrier. Lonsdale, according to Hackett's chief clerk, was 'a figure to inspire terror', with one arm in a blood-soaked sling, another blood-stained bandage wrapped around his head and another large bandage around his leg.

'Usual morning "hate" shortly after first light,' Major Blackwood of the 11th Parachute Battalion wrote in his diary that day. 'John Douglas and a mortar bomb reached the same spot simultaneously. Bunny Speake received the larger portion of a shell in his stomach and chest. This left Guy Black-lidge and myself as the only officers. An interesting day, mortared and shelled continually and the tanks gave us no respite. Our gun crews were magnificent and brewed up at least two Tigers. It was my misfortune to inhabit a trench some twenty yards to the flank of our 17 pounder which almost concussed my head off at every shot.'

Major Robert Cain of the South Staffords also distinguished himself again, having recovered overnight from the PIAT round which blew up in his face. 'The next morning', the citation for his Victoria Cross continued, 'this officer drove off three more tanks by the fearless use of his PIAT, on each occasion leaving cover and taking up positions in open ground with complete disregard for his personal safety.' Afterwards, Cain had to pull back to Oosterbeek church, with most of his men in the nearby laundry which its owner refused to leave.

The defenders were soon going to need every round of anti-tank ammunition. In the middle of the day, the 503rd Heavy Panzer Battalion reached Arnhem with forty-five Royal Tigers, along with another panzergrenadier battalion, the 171st Artillery Regiment from Zutphen and the SS-Landstorm *Nederland* of Dutch Nazi volunteers, which Bittrich placed behind the Arnhem bridge.

The south-western part of the perimeter manned by the Border Regiment was the principal objective for General von Tettau's forces. Three platoons had been sent forward to defend the steep hill at Westerbouwing which overlooked the Neder Rijn and the ferry across to Driel. It had a café on its summit to enjoy the scenic view over the river and the Betuwe beyond. The hill was of great importance, but the Border battalion could spare no more men to defend it.

At 08.00 that morning, the Worrowski battalion of the *Hermann Göring* Division's Unteroffizier Schule attacked, supported by a few antiquated Renault tanks captured in 1940. The battle was fierce. The platoons were pushed off. B Company then counter-attacked, but suffered such losses that it had to pull back to the gasworks along the riverbank. One private with a PIAT managed to knock out three of the four tanks.

B Company had clearly put up a courageous fight against a greatly superior force. 'There seemed to be hundreds of them,' a lance corporal recorded, 'like a football crowd. We opened up with everything.' Oberstleutnant Fullriede recorded in his diary that 'the Worrowski battalion during the attack on Oosterbeek lost all its officers except for a lieutenant, and half of its men.' Fullriede, who belonged to the *Hermann Göring* Division, was appalled by the casualties caused when sending barely trained scratch units into action. 'Despite the OKH's ban', he wrote of the army high command, 'some 1,600 recruits were sent back to Germany, as their deployment would simply turn into child murder.'

The remnants of B Company retreated to the large white house of Dennennoord, which belonged to Jonkheer Bonifacius de Jonge, a former governor-general of the Dutch East Indies who had retired to Oosterbeek for its famed peace and quiet. He tried to be philosophical when his tennis court was ruined by shellfire and the whole house shook. And the water shortage meant that they had to fill buckets at a well in the neighbouring farm, which was extremely dangerous. He recorded in his diary that day how twelve wounded men appeared and were given something to eat in the kitchen. 'They wanted to give themselves up as they had hardly any ammunition left. I then told them that this was impossible for as long as they had even one round left. An officer came to see what was happening, and thank God, took them with him. But an hour later they were back again. There is no leadership and cohesion. The situation is more than precarious. Parachutists are being dropped with the idea that they can look after themselves for three days, but then the Army has to come to relieve them, and that Army has not come. The house is still standing, but that is all one can say.' The lawns around the house were then ruined with slit trenches and weapons pits, and the wounded were moved into Jonkheer de Jonge's wine cellar.

D Company of the Border Regiment, halfway between the river and the Utrechtseweg, was also hard hit during that first major attack on the perimeter. It was heavily mortared throughout the day, causing many casualties from tree bursts. And in the fairly dense woods around, troops from SS Kampfgruppe Eberwein managed to infiltrate this extended line without too much difficulty. It was one thing to fight off troops attacking head-on, but constant harassing fire from behind as well was not good for morale. Since the company was close to a small hamlet and unable to send back wounded for treatment, the medical orderly and some courageous local inhabitants cared for them in their houses.

The 7th King's Own Scottish Borderers, another battalion from Hicks's airlanding brigade, also prepared to defend their White House on the northern tip of the perimeter, the Hotel Dreijeroord. The commanding officer, Lieutenant Colonel Payton-Reid, described 'the eerie atmosphere of a haunted house. The moon shone through shot-holes in the walls, casting weird shadows, prowling footsteps could be heard on every enemy side and one felt that faces were peering through every window.' Trees all around had been shredded by shrapnel. A huge chestnut tree had been brought down, and the hotel was surrounded by shattered roof tiles from the firing. Shredded curtains flapped in the wind 'like ghosts'.

The 'Battle of the White House' began at dawn with German snipers who had tied themselves to trunks of trees high in the branches. All positions came under heavy Nebelwerfer fire, the six-barrelled mortar sometimes known by the British as the 'moaning minnie' because the noise it made was like a braying scream. Loudspeaker vans broadcast messages claiming that Montgomery had forgotten them and that, as they were surrounded, they should surrender.

The main attack began that afternoon. The Kampfgruppe Krafft advanced behind an intense mortar barrage, but when the moment came for them to charge, 'Everything opened up,' Colonel Payton-Reid recorded. 'Riflemen and Bren gunners vied with each other in production of rapid fire; mortars, their barrels practically vertical, lobbed bombs over our heads at the minimum possible range, anti-tank guns defended our flanks and Vickers machine-guns belched forth streams of bullets as only Vickers can. The consequent din was reinforced by a stream of vindictive utterances in a predominantly Scottish accent.' German survivors went to ground, but they were cleared when 'we went for them with the bayonet in the good old-fashioned style, with more blood-curdling yells.'

The Borderers, although reduced to just 270 men, managed to inflict massive casualties on their attackers. Their regimental history records how Headquarters Company and D Company were hotly engaged. 'Major Cochrane and Drum Major Tait with Bren guns, and Provost Sergeant Graham with a Vickers machine-gun killed dozens of Germans.' Little quarter was given or expected. Apparently, 'Major Gordon Sherriff, when accompanying the commanding officer on a tour of the 7th KOSB positions, met a German and killed him with his hands.' A Company was overrun, and the rest of the battalion was forced back, but the ground was retaken in a wild bayonet charge. By then no company commanders were left, and only a single wounded sergeant major remained on his feet.

That night Major General Urquhart ordered the Borderers back to a block of houses just a few hundred metres north of the Hartenstein. The new positions turned into a suburban battlefield in which self-propelled assault guns would dominate the street, and house-to-house fighting became savagely intimate. British soldiers claimed that they could tell if Germans were present purely from the smell of stale tobacco.

Part of the reconnaissance squadron attached to the remnants of the 156th Para Battalion came under pressure around midday. 'We got our first sight of Jerry infantry on the move,' Lieutenant John Stevenson wrote in his diary. 'They were going in and out of the houses on the other side of the crossroads towards a bakery which was the largest house in our defensive area. As fast as they came, we knocked them down. We had three men and a machine-gun in the bakery. [The Germans] set it on fire with incendiary bullets and our chaps had to get out. We were uncertain whether [the Germans] had got into the bakery themselves, and as the building dominated our other positions, we thought it best to knock it down completely. We turned the PIAT on it from fifty yards range which knocked a great hole in the wall and must have made things most uncomfortable for anyone inside. We made sure by patrolling to the house and lobbing grenades into what was left of it until we were quite sure there was no one there. They more or less left us alone for the rest of that day, leaving behind their dead and wounded. By then we had killed a lot of Jerries.'

The perimeter's defenders were not just drooping on their feet from exhaustion, they were short of ammunition and desperately hungry. The American air support officer Lieutenant Paul Johnson reported that 'the rations were running low so we decided to cut down and make what was left last as long as possible.' But his group was better off than most as they still had their Jeeps, which had been well stocked.

The key problem came from the supply containers dropping outside the perimeter, because the lack of radio contact meant that the RAF did not have a clear idea of the defended area. Smoke from the fighting obscured the coloured panels, and it was no good firing Very lights or setting off smoke grenades because the Germans were doing the same, having captured the plans which revealed all the signals. And when containers were retrieved, they often lacked food. 'Resupply has come in,' wrote Corporal George Cosadinos, 'but the majority dropped in the wrong place. All we received were 6 pounder [anti-tank] shells. You can't eat them!' Even greater fury was provoked by containers, filled not with food or ammunition, but with maroon berets, battledress, belts and even blanco.

Other units were longing for 6-pounder shells, but they would probably receive 17-pounder shells after their 17-pounder had been knocked out. The Germans, on the other hand, seemed to suffer no shortage of ammunition. Thanks to Model's organization, it came all the way to each unit in the same trucks which brought it to the Netherlands. Lieutenant Johnson observed that when the defenders opened fire, 'almost immediately the Germans came back with their mortars working over the area thoroughly.'

Everyone's attention was on the sky when the RAF supply planes approached, and many admitted to having their heart in their mouth, imagining the bravery required to keep the plane on course through the fire from the surrounding flak batteries. 'My eye caught one of the burning Dakotas,' wrote Lance Bombardier Jones. 'For the briefest second two figures appeared at the doorway. One had a chute and the other didn't and they were jumping on the one chute. As they came out of the doorway, they parted. The one floated down in his chute; the other fell to earth like a stone. I can still picture him falling, his arms akimbo, diving head first towards the ground.' Despite the loss in aircraft, the supply drop on 21 September proved to be more successful than most, and certainly a lot more than on subsequent days. The Light Regiment Royal Artillery had been down to less than thirty rounds per gun, and its effectiveness was saved by that day's delivery of nearly 700 rounds of 75mm shells for the howitzers.

With impressive self-control on the part of finders, a large proportion of the parachuted rations was handed over for the wounded. While German soldiers exulted in their booty from above, and often tormented their adversaries with the fact, a few British soldiers were so hungry that sometimes they unwisely cooked chickens or rabbits without gutting them. They had no compunction about searching the pockets and pouches of the dead, whether German or British, to see if they contained any rations. Breakfast for the lucky ones consisted of half an oatmeal block, crumbled into water to make porridge. Most of their food came from vegetable gardens and orchards, and many paratroopers suffered from diarrhoea from eating unripe pears and apples. Those away from the Hartenstein had to rely on the store cupboards of generous households. British soldiers were often too shaken to take in how little the average Dutch family had survived on during the occupation. And this was to become far more serious after the battle. The only item which still seemed to exist in reasonable quantities was tea leaves. The soldiers handed them over to the family of the house they were defending, and the owners would make pots of tea for everyone. But there was almost no milk available, and the water shortage was becoming acute.

The desperation for tea was so great that some soldiers would do almost anything to obtain more. Lieutenant Jeffrey Noble's batman, Private McCarthy, went out under German fire, searching one container after another. He finally managed to find a box, and ran back to be cursed by Noble for taking such risks, but no doubt he was a hero to his comrades.

As well as tea, the British gave their Dutch hosts cigarettes, sweets and chocolate in addition to bully beef and sardines from parachute containers. Having been rather too generous with cigarettes at the beginning, they then had to ask for the odd one back. They were also surprised to find that in Oosterbeek many people grew their own tobacco. But the British had much to be grateful for, especially the way civilians cared for their wounded, and even just the exhausted. One husband noted that when some tired and dirty paratroopers arrived in their cellar and there was no water, 'my wife cleans their faces with eau de cologne.'

Some Dutch boys would slip through German positions to deliver apples and vegetables. Others, excited by the danger, took crazy risks to obtain supplies, from British containers and even from German sources. Lucianus Vroemen and a friend came across an unoccupied half-track. They discovered cans of sardines, some bottles of French wine and packs of pale Hungarian tobacco. They wondered whether to take a pistol as well, but decided against it. They were intrigued rather than shocked by the dead German soldiers whose pockets they searched. When they handed their booty over, British paratroopers begged them not to be so reckless.

Feeding the hundreds of wounded became an increasingly difficult task. Near the Tafelberg, four sheep were spotted wandering around. Jan Donderwinkel, a local volunteer helper, noted that they were promptly shot, skinned, butchered and turned into stew. Also caring for the patients was becoming increasingly difficult in the midst of a battlefield. No more surgery could be performed for the moment at the Tafelberg as the ceilings had been brought down by shellfire, in both the offices used as operating theatres.

Part of Hackett's 4th Parachute Brigade managed to push the Germans out of the Hotel Schoonoord. The shortage of water had made life almost impossible for the nurses, who could not now wash the bodies of the wounded, and the medical staff could not wash their hands. They were so short of field dressings and bandages or gauze that volunteers went from house to house with baskets begging for sheets which could be cut up as bandages. In some cases the medical staff even resorted to taking them off the dead for reuse, yet more and more wounded were arriving every hour.

'The noise of battle became distinctly unpleasant', the padre of the Glider Pilot Regiment reported from the improvised hospital. He came across 'a lad who physically was unharmed, but mentally badly shocked'.

'Padre, I'm cold,' the boy said. 'Can you get me another blanket?' He explained that there were none spare because many of the wounded did not have one. The boy asked to be tucked in, and begged him to say a prayer. 'I get frightened with all the noise.' The sound of battle continued in the surrounding streets. Having apparently succeeded in calming him, the padre continued on his rounds. Next morning, not finding the boy, Padre Pare asked where he was. 'He died two hours after you left him,' came the reply. 'It was the noise outside.'

Padre Pare continued in his attempts to comfort the disturbed or take down messages to mothers or loved ones. He had to try to sound optimistic, however bleak the outlook. Colonel Warrack reported that the wounded were 'pathetically anxious for news of XXX Corps'.

On the Marienbergweg on the eastern side of Oosterbeek, SS soldiers shot a young Dutch woman trying to help a wounded English paratrooper, but fortunately they failed to kill her. She was brought to the Schoonoord with a badly smashed arm. Yet firing stopped when orderlies carrying stretcher cases appeared to cross the road from the Schoonoord to the Vreewijk. At one point during the fighting, a medical orderly saw an old Dutchman walk along the road from Oosterbeek station. 'When he reached the crossroads, he looked to the right and left, put up his umbrella, and calmly walked across the street and disappeared in the direction of the Tafelberg Hotel.'

While the Schoonoord, the Tafelberg, the Vreewijk and the ter Horst house down by the church became ever more battered and squalid, medical services in the field often reeked of earlier wars. Arie Italiaander, a Dutch commando attached to the reconnaissance squadron, found himself having to act as surgeon after a mortar round exploded by the Hotel Hartenstein. 'The wounded man's foot had almost been torn off,' and Italiaander, who had a good knife, was asked to cut it off completely, which he did. 'The wounded man, who'd been given a morphine injection and was smoking a cigarette, smiled bravely.' The Germans, who could see what was going on, held their fire. Later, Italiaander buried the boot, with the foot inside, somewhere near his trench.

In theory, every man given morphine was supposed to have the dose marked in indelible blue ink on his forehead. When they ran out of morphine, they did not tell the wounded. Instead the medical orderly would say: 'What would you be wanting morphia for? Morphia's for people who are really hurt. You're not.' The 1st Airborne did receive one fresh consignment towards the end of the battle. A Mosquito fighter-bomber came in very low and dropped morphine supplies wrapped in blankets.

With German and British wounded lying side by side in the improvised hospitals, the hostility of the battlefield often gave way to the shared humanity of suffering. Sapper Tim Hicks had been shot in the neck. His body felt numb and he feared that he had been paralysed, but to his relief the pain came and he sensed he would walk again. His comrades took him to an aid station for the wounded. 'There was a soldier lying next to me,' he wrote. 'I couldn't see him, but I could hear him. He was moaning and crying. We got shelled and he reached over and took my hand and squeezed it. He seemed to get quieter then and it gave me a sense of comfort too. In the morning I looked over and saw he was German. He was young, about my age, 21 or 22. He had a terrible wound in his right side. He was conscious and when he saw me looking at him, he smiled and mumbled something. I shared what water I had in my water bottle with him.'*

Even the St Elisabeth Hospital, under German control, had no water. So to clean up the place, which was spattered with blood, Sister van Dijk organized a column of nursing staff and volunteers to proceed under Red Cross flags to the riverbank to fill buckets and other containers with water. They were never fired at, but they had to pick their way through the dead. 'There were men lying everywhere – British and German. On the ground were arms and legs without men and we had to be very careful not to step on grenades.'

The regimental aid post of the Light Regiment in the ter Horst rectory down by Oosterbeek church was in a far worse state. The house was smashed by shellfire, and they had nearly a hundred cases with just a single doctor, Captain Martin. That day a German tank opened fire on the house. 'A shell blew in one of the walls of the room with stretcher cases,' an orderly wrote. 'Bricks and wood covered the men. Captain Martin and I began uncovering them. There was another explosion and everything went black. Five stretcher cases were killed by the second blast. Captain Martin was wounded in both legs.' Martin, having patched himself up, carried on.

General Urquhart, on a morning tour of the sector with Colonel Loder-Symonds, was shaken by the number of corpses piled in the garden. He told Colonel Thompson of the Light Regiment to see that they were buried, because it was 'bad for morale'.

Urquhart, Loder-Symonds and Thompson then entered the cramped battery command post in the back of the laundry. At 09.35 hours, the forward observation officer there had broken into the radio net of an unidentified British unit, saying 'we are the people you have been trying to meet'. He was ordered off, but he persisted. 'We are being heavily shelled and mortared. Can you help us?' Using veiled speech, the two officers cautiously began an identification process, well aware of German attempts to cause mischief.

The forward observation officer handed the microphone and headset to Loder-Symonds. He identified himself, with 'This is Sunray,' the standard

---

* It is worth remembering that the mortally wounded Elizabethan hero and poet warrior Sir Philip Sidney died in Arnhem from wounds received on the battlefield of Zutphen on 22 September 1586. Although hard hit, he had offered the last of his water to another casualty with the immortal words 'Thy necessity is greater than mine.' He had been fighting alongside the Dutch against the *furia española* of the Castilian infantry.

code for a commander. To move the process forward, he said that his first name was Robert. He was then asked to identify a mutual friend. This he did, and with great satisfaction, he turned to Urquhart to announce that they had now made contact with 64th Medium Regiment, with the 43rd Division. Not only were they now at last in touch with XXX Corps, they could call up fire support from Nijmegen. 'The tense atmosphere in the command post relaxed in a sense of elation,' Thompson noted.

The 64th Medium Regiment had driven through the night from the Belgian frontier to Nijmegen. Within an hour of their first contact with the forward observation officer in Oosterbeek, one of their troops was ready to fire its 4.5-inch guns on one of the three targets they had been given. Fire mission followed fire mission throughout the day, and by 16.00 the regiment was augmented with a battery of 155mm 'Long Tom' howitzers. Even though the range was fifteen kilometres, 1st Airborne recorded that they were firing with 'uncanny accuracy', even at German breakthroughs into the perimeter. The American Paul Johnson of the air support party, who admitted their failure to help the airborne division, described how the Light Regiment's forward observation officers 'were able to adjust the fire of some of the XXX Corps 155mm. guns. They managed to knock out two assault guns and damage a third thus saving the southeast flank from a dangerous attack.'

The other advantage for the Light Regiment came later in the afternoon. While the Polish Independent Parachute Brigade was dropping near Driel, every German gun was firing in its direction. This finally gave the gunners at Oosterbeek the chance to bring up ammunition, improve their gun pits and fling out all their empty shell cases.

Any lull in the firing that day was a relief for the civilians still trapped in their cellars in Oosterbeek. During the bombardments, parents sometimes made their children wear saucepans on their heads like helmets. Such lulls would also provide relief from children crying and even the opportunity to go upstairs and stretch cramped legs, with up to twenty-five people sheltering in a single house. Some would slip out to find out which houses were still standing and who was still alive. A few more families would seize the opportunity to flee, taking the old and infirm with them, often sitting them on cushions in a wheelbarrow. A few old people simply refused to move. Lieutenant Michael Dauncey of the Glider Pilot Regiment was checking out a house that day, to see whether they should turn it into a strongpoint. He went upstairs to examine the rooms, and opened a door. There, sitting up in a large bed, was an old lady wearing a bed jacket. They bowed and smiled to each other, and Dauncey withdrew, closing the door. He never knew what happened to her as the battle intensified.

The real danger to civilians during the battles came from SS panzer-grenadiers, clearing houses by throwing grenades down into the cellar. An unexpected danger was children playing with unexploded ordnance. A sergeant witnessed one soldier approaching a child who was holding a grenade with the pin out. He managed to take it off him, but lost his own hand as a result.

Wounds were totally unpredictable, especially during one of the frequent mortar stonks that day. One person recorded eighteen mortar bursts in a single minute at one point. The American Lieutenant Bruce Davis was hit in the feet by shards from an explosion, just as he was diving head first into a foxhole near the Hartenstein. Having little to do once the pieces of metal had been removed, he limped around during lulls trying to raise morale with rumours of XXX Corps arriving. 'I think I must have promised them an armored division for breakfast four days in a row,' he reported later.

Davis was above all interested in the enemy. He observed that the SS were prepared to attack, but ordinary German infantrymen were scared of the red berets 'and would not attack without the help of armor or self-propelled guns'. As an indication of German nervousness, he noted a thirty-second burst of fire from an MG-42 machine gun. The fact that German machine-gunners were firing such long bursts, from five seconds all the way up thirty, indicated how frightened they were, he wrote in his report. 'There was constant evidence that the British infantry had given Jerry the scare of his life. And the amazing thing about the British infantry was that they carried on with the light-hearted abandon of a Sunday school class on the first spring picnic.'

While many had been in tears when the supply planes came over and the pilots demonstrated such incredible courage, death was so commonplace that almost everyone became callous. On the eastern flank just north of the Utrechtseweg, a group of glider pilots playing cribbage would stop from time to time between hands so that one of their number could pick off a German soldier.

The loudspeaker van returned to the northern part of the perimeter, again playing Glenn Miller's 'In the Mood', before switching to appeals to lay down their arms. This was rapidly followed by 'the shouting of the German Jews in the 21st [Independent Parachute Company] urging them "to go fuck yourselves" in German'. But their hatred at times became irrational and uncontrollable. A pathfinder sergeant recorded how a large group of Germans emerged from the woods waving white handkerchiefs. A German Jew in Sergeant Sullivan's platoon shouted out in German, 'Who are you?'

'Signalmen,' they answered.

'Come here.'

Halfway to the British lines, the paratroopers opened fire, slaughtering the entire section.*

Another pathfinder noted that evening in his diary, 'Can hear our own artillery on the other side of the river very plainly now. Hope they hurry up and join up with us, for we can't hold out much longer.' And Major Black-wood with 11 Para wrote, 'XXX Corps of Second Army should have reached us by yesterday, but at least we have contacted them by wireless. Their mediums are giving us noble support, this afternoon breaking up a strong enemy counter attack before it was properly launched. By dusk our sole remaining anti-tank gun was knocked out and a bloody Tiger was still whining around just over the crest. We waited for it with 82 grenades, but it did not come in, and glad we were when a Polish anti-tank gun and crew appeared and dug in among us. The remnants of 1st Airborne Division, as far as we can make out, are now holding a box some one and a half miles square, with Jerry on three sides and the Rhine on the fourth.'

---

* A platoon commander in the 21st Independent Parachute Company called Gerald Lamarque wrote a successful novel about the pathfinders at Arnhem called *The Cauldron* under the nom de plume 'Zeno'. He wrote it in prison when serving a sentence for murder and received the Arthur Koestler prize.

21

Black Friday 22 September

American paratroopers of the 101st Airborne and British armoured regiments defending Hell's Highway would remember 22 September as Black Friday. This was the start of three days of relentless German attacks on the route. 'At one point,' wrote a captain in the 506th Parachute Infantry Regiment, 'the men were so weary that [on] the order to rest, [they] fell almost as one to the ground without even attempting to remove their packs, falling immediately into deep slumber.'

The principal German objective was still Veghel, which Generaloberst Student had identified as the best choke point on the XXX Corps route. Colonel Johnson in Veghel soon realized that his regimental attack on Schijndel had been ill timed. During the morning of 22 September, there was some desultory shooting in Schijndel by a few Germans stranded in the town and 'a vigorous house-to-house rat-hunting campaign' by Kinnard's battalion killed fifteen of them. The real threat was heading for Veghel.

At 09.30 that morning, Generalfeldmarschall Model had sent an order demanding that 'Today's attack must definitely cut off the enemy's route of advance.' He also called for the 245th and the 712th Infanterie divisions to be brought up as soon as possible. 'Make my left flank strong!' From the west, three battalions of Kampfgruppe Huber from the 59th Division, supported by five Panther tanks and artillery, was advancing 'to take the canal bridge west of Veghel and blow it up'. Meanwhile from the east, General von Obstfelder had sent Kampfgruppe Heinke and the 107th Panzer-Brigade from north of Helmond.

As soon as the danger became evident Johnson contacted Major General Taylor, who had moved the 101st Airborne's divisional command post to the Kasteel Henkenshage on the edge of St Oedenrode. Unlike at Son, this command post was now well defended with the 502nd Parachute Infantry Regiment and the 377th Parachute Field Artillery. Taylor had already sent Johnson a squadron of the 44th Royal Tank Regiment, and now promised to send some British self-propelled artillery.

While Kampfgruppe Walther and the 107th Panzer-Brigade advanced from the east, the German encircling attack from the west cut Hell's Highway between Veghel and Uden. This forced General Adair in Nijmegen to send back the 32nd Guards Brigade to reopen it. The 2nd Battalion of the 506th, including Major Winters's Easy Company, reached Uden just in time with a couple of British tanks. A furious attack on the first German patrol to approach Uden gave the impression that the town was strongly held. The German counter-attack caused panic in Veghel. Inhabitants tried to crowd into the hospital for safety. 'At one moment many hundreds of people, scared and hysterical, were crowding outside the main door, waiting to be let in,' Dr Schrijvers recorded. He had to address them and advise them to go back to their own cellars. The hospital's basement was being used to shelter the wounded.

The British tanks supporting Kinnard's battalion at Schijndel had been recalled in haste to Veghel, where Brigadier General Anthony McAuliffe (who later led the defence of Bastogne in the Ardennes) took command. Lieutenant Colonel Julian Ewell's 3rd Battalion was brought back to Eerde ready to support the tanks. He was able to hand his 150 prisoners over to the Dutch underground, whose members guarded them with captured German weapons. Kinnard left wounded prisoners in the care of their German doctors, well aware that they would be reincorporated into the Wehrmacht, but he had little choice in the circumstances. He gave the underground the German vehicles they had captured, all except a well-stocked mobile field kitchen. This black cooker on wheels with a chimney was popularly known as a 'Gulaschkanone'. Kinnard also armed members of the underground with German rifles and machine pistols and asked them to escort his 250 prisoners back to Veghel, while his battalion established a defence line along some sand dunes south-west of Eerde.

Johnson had only a single battalion and the 377th Parachute Field Artillery in Veghel as the attack began at 10.30. He was fortunate that part of Colonel Sink's 506th Parachute Infantry Regiment was within striking distance, and the 321st Glider Field Artillery took up position by the canal to engage the Panther tanks over open sights. Another squadron of British tanks and the self-propelled artillery sent by General Taylor also arrived just in time to make a difference.

Even in the midst of the furious fighting, a Dutch family asked Pfc John Cipolla to join them for dinner. He could not resist the invitation to a table laid with a tablecloth. Just after they had sat down, his Top Sergeant glanced in as he passed the window, carried on a couple of paces, did a double-take and then dashed back to yell at him that he should get his butt outside where he belonged. Cipolla grabbed a chicken leg and his rifle, thanked the family and ran for the door.

By mid-afternoon, it was clear that the Germans would not be able to destroy the bridge at Veghel. At 16.30, Student informed Model's head-quarters that the 59th Division had been within a thousand metres of it. The Germans did manage to blow the bridge over the Zuid Willems Canal, but Kampfgruppe Huber was encircled and almost destroyed in the battle. When Colonel Sink told McAuliffe that they had wiped out a German attack, killing 140 of them, McAuliffe retorted: 'You're exaggerating.' Sink insisted that he come and count the bodies.

One paratrooper lieutenant who had been wounded during the attack on Veghel admitted later, 'I was afraid that if the Germans captured our aid station, they would shoot me, as some of my men had done to the Germans in Normandy.' A sergeant later acknowledged that only their padre, Father Sampson, had managed to stop him from committing murder in Veghel, when he came across a badly wounded German soldier. 'I had hoped many times if I was ever like this, some German soldier would put a bullet in my brains and end it for me. I was about to do this for the poor devil when I felt a hand on my shoulder. It was Father Sampson. He prevented me from doing this for which I have been thankful.'

As the Germans started to withdraw, General Taylor called the 2nd Tactical Air Force. They sent in a large force of RAF rocket-firing Typhoons to engage the tanks. This prompted wild cheering from the paratroopers on the ground as they watched each aircraft peel off, roll and dive followed by the whoosh of the rockets. That day the deployment of the 107th Panzer-Brigade away from Helmond enabled VIII Corps, on the right of XXX Corps, to seize a bridgehead there with little loss. Confusion and bad com-munications had undermined the German attack. The chaos was such that, early in the morning, some officers in a staff car drove into Veghel thinking it was still in German hands and were shot or captured. Even a paymaster drove into the town before the battle started, an American officer reported, 'with the idea of paying off the German garrison in the town, to find out to his sorrow that the garrison was in a PW cage down the street, so we just threw him in there. He was truly mad.' Once the battle died down, the local restaurant did a brisk trade with famished soldiers, offering ham and eggs for 3 guilders, which was $1.10, or $15.30 in today's money.

Major General Taylor may have been satisfied with the outcome at Veghel, but he was not pleased that 'it required seven days to bring in all the elements of the 101st Airborne Division. During this time the Division was obliged to protect the landing field with considerable forces while carrying out ground missions. This reduced the strength available for the essential tasks of the Division.' The 101st, he emphasized, only just held on to its twenty-four-kilometre sector. They were 'weak at every critical point' which required 'the most energetic shifting of troops to meet the numerous threats as they developed along this long corridor'.

Death was doubly shocking when it came unexpectedly during peaceful moments. In Eerde, looking out of the window of a windmill after the battle for Veghel was over, Corporal Richard Klein observed to Jacob Wingard, the paratrooper beside him, that it seemed as if the Germans had conceded this particular area. A few moments later a shot hit Wingard. He knew it was fatal. He said 'I'm dead' three times, then died.

While the 101st was overstretched along its sector of Hell's Highway, Gavin's 82nd Airborne was still fighting off attacks from Meindl's II Fall- schirmjäger Corps. Gavin was also deeply dissatisfied with the length of time troop carrier command was taking to deliver his division. His 325th Glider Infantry Regiment had still not arrived. He too realized the need to keep a numerically superior enemy off balance by constant attacks. The Sherwood Rangers Yeomanry began its association with the 82nd that day, supporting the 3rd Battalion of the 508th in a reconnaissance in force towards Wercheren, north-east of Beek.

Gavin's intelligence staff were suffering from a lack of information on enemy strength, mainly because they had no prisoners to interrogate. Div- isional headquarters had been sending out firm instructions that German prisoners must be captured for interrogation and not just shot. Battalion commanders became desperate for prisoners because demands for them from divisional headquarters increased. They even started offering expenses-paid trips to Paris to anybody who brought one in. A paratrooper in the Beek sector decided to have a go after consuming rather too much captured German Schnapps. 'To the surprise of the troopers round him', reported Captain Ferguson, 'and before anyone could stop him, this trooper picks up his rifle, cocks his helmet on his head, and starts walking across the level Waal River flood plain towards the German lines some two to three hundred yards away. Everyone watched in amazement, including General

Gavin, as this trooper walked across this open space in full view of the enemy up to a culvert and called for the "Krauts" to come out with their hands up. The surprised Germans, three or four, meekly came out, and with a little urging from the trooper, made their way to our lines. General Gavin met the trooper, still rather tipsy, and pinned the Silver Star on him.'*

Capturing prisoners for interrogation was often a far more dangerous activity. 'On one patrol into Germany,' a paratrooper recorded, 'Lieutenant Megellas captured several Germans. The following night, our over-eager regimental staff ordered another patrol (different company) into the same area. As expected, the patrol was ambushed by a strong German force and suffered many killed and wounded. The lieutenant leading that patrol received multiple gunshot wounds and was crippled for life.'

In spite of their attacks from the Reichswald and against Hell's Highway, the Germans were dismayed to find how rapidly British forces were building up in the Betuwe between the Waal and the Neder Rijn. At 10.30 Obergruppenführer Bittrich telephoned Model's chief of staff Krebs to warn him that they were pushing in much greater strength up the Nijmegen–Arnhem railway line. He was having to send his last reserves into the battle south of Elst. Fifteen minutes later Krebs rang back with Model's reply that 'a link-up between the forces advancing from Nijmegen to Arnhem with the enemy west of Arnhem is to be prevented by every means.' It was not entirely clear whether this meant the 1st Airborne north of the Rhine or the Polish brigade on the south side. Krebs was under great pressure that morning, for Generalfeldmarschall von Rundstedt was demanding to know when they were going to destroy the Nijmegen bridge. They could only answer that they intended to blow it up that night.

Major General Ivor Thomas's 43rd Wessex Division was now taking over the main advance from the Guards Armoured Division on the Nijmegen–Arnhem axis, and also advancing north-west towards Driel. The night before, Brigadier Hubert Essame's 214th Brigade had crossed the Waal by both the railway bridge and the road bridge. It would attack Oosterhout with the 7th Somerset Light Infantry and protect the left flank of the 129th Brigade, which was to attack the German defence line that ran from the main road to Ressen. It was manned by the Kampfgruppe Knaust with two

---

* The 82nd subsequently captured a panzergrenadier called Heinrich Ullman. He was sent back to the United States as a prisoner of war and, on being released, applied for US citizenship, joined the army and went into the 82nd Airborne at Fort Bragg.

infantry battalions, a machine-gun battalion, twenty 20mm light flak guns and, most decisive of all, two batteries of 88mm guns. But that night, after the loss of Oosterhout, Knaust would pull them back to Elst.

'At first light under cover of the morning mist', two troops of the Household Cavalry Regiment had slipped through the German forces around Oosterhout at half an hour's interval. They headed on to Valburg to scout out the best route to Driel to make contact with Sosabowski's Polish Parachute Brigade. They were followed later by the 5th Duke of Cornwall's Light Infantry and B Squadron of the 4th/7th Dragoon Guards.

Early that morning in Oosterbeek, Major General Urquhart sent for his chief of staff, Lieutenant Colonel Charles Mackenzie. He told him to take Lieutenant Colonel Eddie Myers, their chief engineer officer, and cross the Neder Rijn. He was to go on to Nijmegen to see Browning and Horrocks in person, because Urquhart did not believe that they appreciated the gravity of the situation. 'It is absolutely vital that they should know that the division, as such, no longer exists, and that we are merely a collection of individuals hanging on.' Mackenzie was to make it clear that if supplies did not reach them in the course of the night to come, it might be too late. Myers was to accompany him, as he should advise on the crossing. This was the same Myers who had played such a central part in Special Operations Executive's great coup, the blowing up of the Gorgopotamos railway viaduct in Greece in 1942.

Mackenzie and Myers set off in a Jeep carrying the rubber dinghy, but then had to seek shelter in the church at Oosterbeek because of heavy shelling. This delay meant that the river mist was breaking up by the time they reached the bank of the Neder Rijn. They could hear sounds of battle when they reached the far side, but there was no sign of the Polish reception party they had been told to expect.

Sosabowski, unable to do anything else, was making his men dig their slit trenches deeper in the orchards surrounding Driel. He wobbled around them on a woman's bicycle, shouting 'Deeper! Deeper!' Some of his men called back asking if he had a driver's licence.

It was about this time that 2nd Lieutenant Richard Tice was killed. Tice was an American volunteer of Polish extraction, who had joined the brigade despite hardly speaking the language. He was much liked by his men who referred to him as 'the Cowboy' because he looked so American. Tice had experienced a premonition of his death 'before we even jumped', one of his NCOs said. At about 15.00, a group of soldiers appeared a few hundred metres away. Some of the men saw they were Germans, but Tice was convinced they must be friendly. As they approached to within about 300 metres, a voice called, 'Don't shoot, don't shoot!'

'Those are our boys, Americans!' Tice rejoiced, but his men were not convinced. He allowed the line of soldiers to come closer. Suddenly they dropped to the ground and opened fire. Tice's platoon fired back. He gave the order to his men 'Retreat one by one towards the farm.' He stayed behind with Corporal Gredecki and a light machine gun to cover them, but the gun was hit and put out of action. The two men, now vulnerable, ran back shooting behind them with their personal weapons. Tice threw himself down next to an apple tree to fire at the Germans with his Sten gun, but he was hit several times and died.

Some time later, when Sosabowski was visiting another of his companies, armoured vehicles were sighted. The Poles assumed they were German, but they turned out to be British Daimler armoured cars and White scout cars from the two troops of Household Cavalry commanded by Captain Wrottesley and Lieutenant Young. Mackenzie and Myers had arrived, so Young's troop acted as a relay station to allow Mackenzie to speak to Horrocks's chief of staff at XXX Corps. He passed on the message from Urquhart to Horrocks: 'We are short of ammunition, men, food and medical supplies. DUKWs are essential, 2 or 3 would be sufficient.* If supplies do not arrive tonight it may be too late.' Mackenzie insisted on a meeting with Browning in Nijmegen. Myers meanwhile warned Sosabowski that they had only rubber dinghies to ferry his men across the Neder Rijn.

The Household Cavalry as a reconnaissance force was supposed to avoid combat if possible, but when some German tanks were sighted Wrottesley and Young 'had great difficulty in preventing the Poles somewhat naturally from taking over as tanks their armoured cars and scout cars' as they were the only vehicles available. Sosabowski's men had only PIATs, because their anti-tank guns were all north of the river. Once the tanks had moved away, Sosabowski then wanted to send patrols in all directions. A reply from General Horrocks was transmitted in answer to Urquhart's message. 'Everything possible will be done to get the essential through.'

Urquhart's feelings of impatience can be easily imagined, with XXX Corps so near and yet so far. The curse of bad communications made everything worse. All he could hope to do was to try to maintain morale while waiting for Mackenzie to return with definite news. The Hotel Hartenstein was in a sorry state, with its roof shot to pieces and its walls riddled in all

---

* DUKWs were six-wheeled amphibious trucks.

directions. Outside, every man needed to be within a jump of a slit trench. Fortunately, the trenches had a reasonably soft bottom as soldiers had padded them with parachutes. But 'the great snag about mortars', Major Blackwood observed, 'is that the bomb arrives with no warning whistle.'

The other danger came from German snipers strapped in the tall beech trees. They waited for a soldier to make a dash to collect water and would take their shot. As soon as a sniper's position was identified Bren gunners would blast him out of his tree. PIAT rounds were now too precious to be used. They had to be reserved for tanks and the self-propelled assault guns. One well-concealed German sniper had a macabre sense of humour. He was hidden high in some trees which overlooked the only well close to the Hartenstein. 'He would allow us to approach the well,' a glider pilot recorded, 'usually through a hail of mortar bombs, and then solemnly shoot holes in the bucket as it appeared over the edge of the well. A true sadist!'

German mortar teams were impressively accurate because they always managed to avoid the hotel tennis courts, where their compatriots were held. The Germans caged there complained constantly about the lack of food, when in fact they were receiving no less than their captors. According to the American air controller Lieutenant Bruce Davis, a German major, a veteran of the First World War, addressed them in the following terms: 'These men have stood up under the most terrible artillery bombardment I have ever seen. They have fought on without food and without sleep for several days. Even though they are our enemies, they are the bravest men I have ever seen. When you complain, you make me feel ashamed of being German. I suggest that you be quiet and follow their example.'

A corporal in the 1st Airborne Provost Company, who was guarding them, was amused when a lightly wounded German sergeant complained that he thought it unfair that the Americans should use .45 bullets, which were so much larger than the German 9mm. His lieutenant remarked that they had so many prisoners packed in, 'it's getting like bloody Wimbledon.'

Hunger and exhaustion after five days of fighting had its effect on the defenders. Members of the 21st Independent Company just to the north were so tired that they had not dug in the night before. 'Found we'd been sleeping amongst a lot of Jerry graves, so it was a good job we didn't dig in,' a pathfinder observed. 'Thank goodness Jerry likes his sleep and doesn't worry us much during the night.'

That morning of Friday 22 September, Major Blackwood in the 11th Para Battalion started with the usual morning 'hate' of mortar bombardment. The only difference was that it was raining quite heavily. 'The company was withdrawn to the reinforced concrete church for a much needed rest and an opportunity to eat and clean weapons. The mud plays hell with Sten working parts and our .45 automatics have proved useless, being far too susceptible to dirt and grit in the working parts. Managed some hot stew and tea and cleaned all magazines etc. About 1100 hrs we moved to the "comparatively quiet sector" of the western flank where, with some Borders, we dug in along the edge of a large park facing enemy held buildings some 400 yards away. As our [machine guns] were in position on our left we had little peace. Mortaring was incessant and extremely heavy and a Spandau had a periodic crack at us. We sat tight all day, beating off several infantry attacks, the casualties from which were in each instance collected by German stretcher parties under the charge of a very agitated and uneasy Hun who vigorously waved a large Red Cross [flag] and shouted repeatedly: "You no fire! Red Cross flag!" But Jerry himself is observing the rules of war rather well.'

Blackwood was summoned to an orders group by Brigadier Hicks. He was told to prepare an attack 'across four hundred yards of perfectly flat and open ground, surmounting en route four 15 foot wire fences, entering and clearing three enemy held buildings, clearing an orchard some hundreds of yards long, attacking and clearing part of a village, and consolidating against inevitable counter-attack. This was rather a tall order as my force consisted of ten paratroopers, six glider men and two cooks.' Fortunately for Blackwood and his men, the attack was then cancelled. He kept going on benzedrine tablets and a large bottle of Dutch brandy.

The large park was almost certainly Dennenoord, belonging to the former governor-general, Jonkheer Bonifacius de Jonge. De Jonge noted that morning that it had been quite peaceful until about 10.00 when a sudden bombardment hit the house and gardens, and smashed their conservatory. 'We took our mattresses down to the servants' hall.' With the wounded lying everywhere, they now had almost sixty people in the house, and only a few candles for light. Goats and cows had been killed in the meadows outside, but he observed that you were risking your life trying to butcher them for meat.

The German attack on the western flank of the perimeter had begun with Kampfgruppe Lippert attacking on either side of the Utrechtseweg, supported by the 171st Artillery Regiment. To its south, Kampfgruppe Eberwein advanced, supported on its right by the Worrowski battalion, which had lost so many men when taking the heights of Westerbouwing the day before. But it was the sailors of the Schiffs-Stamm-Abteilung, armed with French rifles from 1940, who suffered the most. They were 'heavily battered'. Armament improved only when captured British weapons began to be distributed, with ammunition obtained from parachute containers.

Standartenführer Harzer, who was now in command of the Division von Tettau as well, noted that the scratch units lacked field kitchens, and Luftwaffe units would abandon the tanks they were supposed to be protecting. Harzer moved in some SS NCOs to improve battle discipline. 'It was the task of Division *Hohenstaufen* to imbue the motley units of all branches of the service with their fighting spirit.' A no doubt exasperated General von Tettau sent round an order pointing out that 'in the fighting over the last few days, no fewer than six tanks have been lost through locally unsuitable deployment by junior commanders, and infantry failing to accompany them. We cannot afford such losses any more.' Panzer Company 224 was now reduced to three tanks and its commander had clear instructions to pull them out the moment infantry support disappeared.

Harzer was heartened by the arrival at midday of the first Royal Tiger tanks of the 503rd Heavy Panzer Battalion, but he soon recognized that these seventy-two-ton monsters could be deployed only one at a time, otherwise the brick streets of Oosterbeek would break up under their weight. 'Whenever a "Königstiger" makes a turn,' Harzer wrote, 'the pavement is hurled aside.'

Model's headquarters suddenly had an unsettling thought. They felt they could not rule out more landings. 'The enemy can still deploy another three or four airborne divisions,' the situation report stated that day.

Lieutenant Johnson, the other American officer at Oosterbeek, noticed that the Germans were now avoiding infantry attacks. 'Instead they would run up a tank or self-propelled gun and knock us out of the houses, then move the tank back before we could bring up an anti-tank gun or PIATs to combat it. They also had some flame-throwers which they used to good advantage. At any time they wished they could bring down heavy mortar and arty fire on our little strong points making them quite uncomfortable. It was a slow process for them but they seemed to know that they had plenty of time . . . The men made many successful counter-attacks to regain these lost positions but the Germans would just repeat the process of using armor, artillery and automatic weapons and eventually we didn't have enough men left to do any counter-attacking.'

Lieutenant Stevenson of the reconnaissance squadron also noticed the change in tactics. 'We saw very little sign of German infantry at all on Friday. Jerry settled himself down to swamp the area with mortar fire and knocked down the houses systematically with [self-propelled] guns. These guns hit every house in our area at least once at very short range. We always heard the creaking of their tracks as they came along and it wasn't pleasant.'

They decided to ambush the next assault gun, so an NCO and a trooper went into a slit trench at the crossroads. 'About half an hour had gone by when one came creaking up again. The trooper let fly and hit with his first shot at about seventy yards. Unfortunately the shot immobilised the vehicle but not its guns. The crew must have recovered very quickly and they brought machine-gun fire to bear on the slit trenches killing and wounding two glider pilots who were in the next trench to our chaps. Luckily the trooper and the NCO were able to get out quick.'

The wounded were evacuated, but it was far too dangerous to collect the dead. Some of the corpses had been there for days and had begun to swell, stretching their battledress as if it had been pumped up. It was a very unpleasant sight and young, inexperienced soldiers could be badly affected. Outside the perimeter, the two Dutch boys who went foraging for their paratrooper friends decided to bury one of the crew members of a crashed transport aircraft. As they were digging, they were stopped by two Wehrmacht soldiers who demanded to know what they were doing. When they explained, one of them asked angrily: 'Why are you burying a murderer? They have bombed our cities and killed our women and children. They don't deserve to be buried, but to lie in a field and rot.'

With water available now only from lavatory cisterns and radiators in the houses, men in slit trenches were reduced to drinking from the puddles left by that morning's downpour. Benzedrine euphoria still prompted some soldiers to believe that the whole of the Second Army was about to arrive to save them. A paratrooper, hearing tank tracks, shouted to his companion, 'I knew they wouldn't let us down!' And round the corner came a Royal Tiger.

By the sixth day, the stress was beginning to tell when Harzer's SS Pioneers launched an attack using flamethrowers, supported by 20mm flak guns. Paratroopers began to run back towards the Hartenstein headquarters in a sudden panic. Two glider pilot sergeants in their slit trench were astonished to see a Jeep come round the corner of the hotel, with General Urquhart standing in it bolt upright. His face was red and angry as he began roaring at the panic-stricken paratroopers: 'Get back there, you bastards! You're no bloody good to me!' Some of the soldiers began to move back, shame-faced. Sergeant Hatch remarked disapprovingly to his companion in the trench: 'A bloody general doing the job of a sergeant!' Combat fatigue even drove some to suicide, usually a muzzle in the mouth or under the chin.

With so many attacks on the perimeter that day, the gunners of 64 Medium Regiment had to provide no fewer than thirty-one different fire missions. A battery of 5.5-inch guns was also brought up to increase the support. Once again the accuracy of their fire left observers filled with admiration. As an officer in the Somerset Light Infantry in the Betuwe wrote, 'I doubt if any experienced infantry officer would deny that the Royal Artillery, during the Second World War, were the most professionally competent people in the British Army.' He was right, but he should also have mentioned the Royal Engineers.

House cellars in Oosterbeek within the diminishing perimeter were by now desperately overcrowded. The noise of explosions and firing, the inability to move and the unhygienic conditions due to the lack of water led to high levels of stress, made worse by fear. A Catholic, sheltering under the bombardment with a small group of friends, described their 'voices raised in a heart-wrenching and rhythmic "Hail Mary" to the accompanying shelling. Louder and louder this prayer sounded like a cry for help as outside the walls tremble. It is unbearable!'

For those in the cellars, the news that they were now in the front line was brought by apologetic British soldiers, announcing that their house was now a fire position. And yet the Dutch were still amused by what they saw as the almost excessive politeness of the British soldier. 'Thank goodness there are also funny moments,' an anonymous woman diarist wrote. 'Yesterday evening, just when we were all going down into the cellar to sleep, and the children were already asleep, a Tommy comes very quietly down the stairs and says: "Would you mind keeping as quiet as possible and not to use any lights?" A Boche would simply have said "Shut your mouth!"'

Because of the 1st Airborne's hopeless radio communications it was only on this, the sixth day of Operation Market Garden, that the First Allied Airborne Army had any idea of its losses. Colonel Warrack reported that the division had suffered more than 2,000 casualties, while 'the strength of the medical personnel was reduced to 18 officers and 120 other ranks.' This was down from a total strength of 31 officers and 371 other ranks. Some medics had been taken as prisoners by the Germans from the St Elisabeth Hospital, but the loss of stretcher-bearers had been disastrous. Many German soldiers and even SS respected the Red Cross symbol, but others targeted medical personnel because they knew the effect it had on morale. A corporal with the 16th (Parachute) Field Ambulance refused to wear an armband. 'I learned in North Africa, the only purpose Red Cross markings served was to make you a better target.'

All the improvised hospitals within the perimeter were under fire. A young volunteer who entered the aid centre in the Hotel Tafelberg was amazed that the building had not yet burned down. 'It is a complete hell for the patients,' he wrote. 'Try and imagine how ghastly it must be to lie in a bed with a leg amputated and to find that the wall next to you has been hit and with it your neighbour for the second time – only this time he doesn't make it. This is what happens here. The curtains have been closed to catch the flying glass. A small flickering candle the only light in the hall. Some patients groan at every sound, some bite their lips in silence. In the operating theatre English and Dutch doctors work together by candlelight. I don't think they get much sleep. I walk through a hall where at least a hundred English are still lying on stretchers and mattresses on the floor. I suppose they must be the lightly wounded. At least I hope so.'

Conditions in the old rectory, Kate ter Horst's house next to Oosterbeek church, were just as pitiful. The walls were pockmarked all over by rifle fire and they had fifty-seven fatal casualties piled in their garden, giving off the sickly-sweet smell of decaying corpses. This 'tall slim Dutchwoman with the blonde hair and the calm ice-blue eyes' became known as the 'Angel of Arnhem'. She helped care for the 250 men brought to the regimental aid post set up in her house, even though she had five children to look after. She comforted the wounded and dying by reading aloud from a Bible in the King James version. Her voice and the fine, familiar prose calmed the fears of all who listened to her.

Kate ter Horst was also a keen observer of the young men in their care. She described Rod, a sandy-haired Scot 'who looks like a man of forty . . . It always strikes me how these young men, most of them not older than 20 or 25 in their voice and gesture, have a control and a sense of responsibility, a self-discipline, which makes them look more like family fathers than young men just coming from college or university.' In five years of war, Rod found the fighting in Oosterbeek the worst he had experienced. 'This is no fight,' he told her. 'This is murder.'

While parts of the perimeter had to be withdrawn, the Hotel Schoonoord had been recaptured. The hospital area, which by now included nine buildings, was under intense mortar fire. 'A number of wounded were killed or re-wounded in their beds,' Colonel Warrack reported. 'It was one of the most tragic experiences to see these men who had been wounded in the battle coming to the medical services for help and protection and finding themselves still in the front line and even more exposed than in slit trenches. There was never a murmur even when mortar bombs burst in the wards.' The fighting around the hospital continued, but this time a British soldier, who began firing from a shellhole in the garden, compromised the hospital's neutrality.

The wounded were always thirsty, and as it had rained hard in the early hours, the staff and volunteers had rigged every waterproof cape and pipe available to catch the water off the roof and gutters in buckets and every receptacle available. 'Water! We want it now so badly,' wrote Hendrika van der.Vlist. 'The lavatories have become dunghills.' She was still interested in the striking differences between their German patients. An officer, although a prisoner, loudly demanded a tetanus injection, which he insisted was standard practice in German hospitals. He also demanded to be exchanged for a British officer in German captivity. She asked an ordinary soldier, with whom she chatted easily, if he had voted for Hitler. He replied that he had been a schoolboy then. 'Well, how old are you?' she asked, having thought he was in his thirties. 'Twenty-three,' he replied. Seeing her surprise, he added: 'The war has made me old.' In an attempt to lighten the atmosphere, Hendrika said, 'Fortunately the war is nearly over, so you can become young again.' He replied, 'When the spirit is old, you can't become young again.'

She was struck by the pessimism of the young Germans in comparison to the optimism of most of the British soldiers, even when badly wounded. But then she reflected, 'What kind of future lies ahead of them? If they do come out of this war alive, only misery awaits them.' She remembered that the mother of one of her pupils had remarked that soon you would want to be 'anything rather than German'. Only a Ukrainian in the SS, another patient, was likely to be worse off after the war. He was no volunteer, but that would not save him if he was returned to the Soviet Union.

There were also Polish wounded from their anti-tank squadron. They were put together to help each other and keep up their spirits. The German patients were clearly frightened of the Poles, but not of the British. Yet a shared fate often seemed to bring the wounded of both sides together. When a new stretcher case was brought in, Hendrika bent over to ask in English where he was wounded. '*Verstehe nicht*,' he replied. 'Don't understand.' With the blanket over him, she had not spotted the German uniform. The British paratrooper next to him raised his head in interest and asked if he were German. She nodded. He offered the German his own plate of food. Later, the German stopped a helper from giving another newly arrived soldier a glass of water. 'The comrade should not drink, sister, he has a stomach wound.'

The number of dead was mounting at the Schoonoord too. The Royal Army Medical Corps sergeant major directed the stretcher-bearers to stack the bodies out in the garden now that there was no more room left in the hotel garage. Nights were the most difficult time, with no electricity. The staff had to step over bodies and limbs with only a match for light. A company sergeant major from the 11th Parachute Battalion observed that the wounded around him longed for anything which reminded them of home and family life. 'A woman came in and brought a young, week-old baby with her. All the men asked to see the baby.'

The Schoonoord was soon retaken by the Germans. They brought in armed sentries pretending to guard it, but as the building lay on the front line it provided them with a way of forcing back other British positions, since they could not shoot in the direction of the hospital.

That night, Sosabowski ordered Lieutenant Albert Smaczny's company to cross the river, but its men had no boats of their own. The 9th Field Company Royal Engineers, who had tried to improvise rafts out of Jeep trailers the night before, admitted failure. The sappers in the perimeter would instead have to ferry the Poles in six tiny reconnaissance boats and an RAF dinghy. They had hoped to create a ferry, hauled back and forth across the river, which could bring two Poles over at a time, but the current was strong and the signal cable kept breaking, so the sappers were reduced to paddling back and forth with only one Pole.

The dark brought further chaos. 'Without any means to cross the river,' Smaczny wrote, 'we were forced to wait a long time before two rubber dinghies arrived, navigated by engineers. Some of the boats could seat no more than two people. After a while, two more rubber boats arrived, manned by British engineers. We began crossing by twos, sometimes one by one. Every now and then the enemy flashed a rocket over the crossing and volleys from German Spandaus searched for targets on the river. I made it to the other side.'

Glider pilots were supposed to lead them to the church in Oosterbeek, but the one taking Smaczny's group lost his bearings, and they stumbled into a German anti-tank gun crew eating their meal. 'Suddenly, I heard a terrified voice from a few steps away, "*Herr Feldwebel, sie sind Tommies!*" I realized that we had walked into a concentration of German troops.' A messy little battle followed, with the Poles extricating themselves with a synchronized hurling of grenades. But as they approached the British lines they came under fire again, and Smaczny yelled at them not to shoot. Altogether only fifty-two Polish paratroopers were ferried across the river that night.

Other mishaps included two Sherman tanks from the 4th/7th Dragoon Guards, which were escorting a battalion of the Duke of Cornwall's Light Infantry to Driel. They ran on to Polish mines laid across the road and then fired at the Household Cavalry armoured cars. This advance force from the 130th Infantry Brigade had managed to skirt round the German positions near Valburg. And to make matters worse, the two DUKW amphibious trucks bringing desperately needed medical supplies for the 1st Airborne became stuck in the deep mud of the riverbank.

In the course of the day, Generalfeldmarschall Model reorganized the command structure in the Netherlands, with the Fifteenth Army taking responsibility from the North Sea to Rhenen, and Student's First Fallschirm Army the eastern part from Rhenen to Roermond.

Meanwhile in Versailles, General Eisenhower had called a major conference at his headquarters in the Trianon Palace Hotel to discuss strategy. 'Everyone there but Monty,' Admiral Ramsay noted in his diary. Montgomery had sent a signal the previous morning: 'For operational reasons consider I cannot leave this front to attend your conference Versailles tomorrow. Will send my chief of staff who has my full views on all matters.' Montgomery claimed to be too busy directing the battle for Arnhem, but since there was little he could usefully do, many took his absence to be a deliberate snub to Eisenhower.

Montgomery's decision to send his chief of staff Major General de Guingand was seen by American officers as a devious tactic. 'A chief of staff is not authorized to make commitments for him,' noted Bradley's aide. 'Monty can repudiate them at will.' Apparently prior to the conference there had been a good deal of betting at SHAEF that the field marshal would not appear. And General Omar Bradley himself later said, 'We checked up afterward and found Monty hadn't done a damn thing that day except sit around his [command post]. There was no reason in the world why he couldn't have come down to attend that conference except his own vanity and feeling of importance. He was too good to go to Ike's headquarters.'

There was perhaps another reason. Despite Montgomery's message to Eisenhower that he thought there was still 'a sporting chance' of taking the bridge at Arnhem, he must have sensed by then that a terrible disaster was taking place, which would considerably damage his reputation. After all his demands for priority in the north to get across the Rhine, he cannot have wanted to face Bradley, Patton and Eisenhower across the table in Versailles. And he cannot have been keen to encounter General Bedell Smith, or Strong, whose fears about German strength in the southern Netherlands he had ridiculed. The very next day Montgomery wrote in his diary 'I am very doubtful myself now if they [1st Airborne] will be able to hold out, and we may have to withdraw them.' And the fact that he never once visited Horrocks during the entire battle confirms the impression that he was keeping his distance, a rare event for 'Master'.

The other architect of the fatal plan, Lieutenant General Boy Browning, was far more loath to admit the reality of the situation. General Brereton, the commander of the First Allied Airborne Army, wrote in his diary on 23 September: 'An encouraging message came from General Browning in reply to an offer by General Hakewill-Smith, commander of 52nd Lowland Division [the airlanding formation in the First Allied Airborne Army], to send a complete force in gliders to aid the Red Devils. General Browning's message follows: "Thanks for your message but offer not, repeat not, required as situation better than you think. We want lifts as already planned including Poles. Second Army definitely require your party and intend fly you in to Deelen airfield as soon as situation allows." ' It is hard to imagine how Browning can have convinced himself that things were 'better than you think'.

Browning had moved his headquarters into Nijmegen, with his caravan in a garden on Sophiaweg. His aide Eddie Newbury noted how the atmosphere became increasingly strained, with Browning unable to stop twisting the end of his moustache. The general, who could not stand inactivity, had no useful command function except over the British 1st Airborne, with which he was not even in contact. He had no reason to interfere with Gavin's impressive handling of his sector, so the only formation effectively under him was the Princess Irene Brigade of the Royal Netherlands Army defending the bridge at Grave.

Operation Market Garden had been devastating for the 1st Airborne Division, but it was about to produce a far greater humanitarian disaster. At General Eisenhower's request, the Dutch government-in-exile had called for an all-out railway strike to assist the airborne invasion. The Germans were outraged and intended to exact revenge. At 18.45 on Friday evening, 22 September, Generalleutnant von Wühlisch, the chief of staff of the Wehrmacht commander-in-chief, rang Model's headquarters and spoke to Generalleutnant Krebs about German retaliatory measures for Dutch support to the Allies. 'The destruction of Rotterdam with the blowing up of the electricity works etc. would cause disturbances among the civil population,' he said. 'An outbreak of panic is possible.' Krebs suggested that they could postpone demolitions, which included water supplies as well as the electricity stations, for twenty-four hours.

Wühlisch then went on to say that 'as a counter-measure against the Dutch railway workers' strike, it is intended to seal off Amsterdam and The Hague from supplies etc. to enforce the restoration of rail traffic.' This marked the first step in German revenge for Dutch 'treason'. It would lead to the deliberate famine of the Hunger Winter.

22

Saturday 23 September

The fate of the 1st Airborne Division at Oosterbeek was also affected by the German attacks on Hell's Highway. They prevented Horrocks from bringing any more troops forward to reinforce the two divisions north of Nijmegen in the Betuwe. Only a single infantry brigade from the 43rd Wessex Division could be spared to join the Poles at Driel and cross the Neder Rijn to reinforce Urquhart's exhausted force. XXX Corps was virtually immobilized as German artillery engaged convoys coming up its supply route.

Once again Veghel was the principal German objective, with the 107th Panzer-Brigade and Kampfgruppe Walther attacking from the east and Kampfgruppe Huber coming from the west. The latter force was supported by Oberstleutnant von der Heydte's 6th Fallschirmjäger-Regiment advancing from Boxtel on Veghel. Heydte was scathing about the replacements and reserves scraped together to hold the line in the Netherlands. He knew that the bulk of his soldiers simply lacked the training to launch a proper attack. To make things worse, he had been ordered to send one of his battalions to sort out a crisis in the sector of the 245th Infanterie-Division. In exchange Heydte had received from the 2nd Fallschirmjäger-Regiment 'a battalion of even lower fighting qualities, with poor officers, far from satisfactory in respect of discipline and addicted to arbitrary action, pilfering and outrages against the civilian population'.

Colonel Johnson had Kinnard's 1st Battalion of the 501st holding the sand dunes at Eerde which lay across Heydte's line of advance. Assault guns and a Jagdpanther tank destroyer pounded away at the windmill in the little village and at the church steeple. A German mortar round hit an ammunition truck in the street causing a number of casualties, both killed and wounded. Another shell, exploding outside the command post, wounded the British liaison officer and sliced off part of Colonel Johnson's ear. Kinnard, standing there with them, suffered no more than a bad headache.

Johnson called for help from the 44th Royal Tank Regiment. Nine tanks arrived soon afterwards, but several of them were 'brewed up' by the Jagdpanther. American paratroopers tried to brave the flames to rescue crewmen, but in vain. They were reduced to charred corpses. American accounts claim that the other British tank commanders were so reluctant to advance after this disaster that they had to clear the dunes themselves. Kinnard's plan was a pincer movement, but as an eyewitness noted, 'what had begun as a tactical move became a soldier's fight.'

Heydte complained that his whole attack had started half an hour late. 'The battalion on the right had to attack across flat ground that offered practically no cover, while the battalion on the left attacked through thick brushwood. Towards midday, the right battalion was halted in a wooded fringe south-east of Schijndel, and the left battalion lost its way and strayed into the right battalion's sector.' Heydte, however, had clearly had 'little confidence in the outcome' from the start, as Generalleutnant Poppe observed. Having seen the American paratroopers in action, Heydte knew that the majority of his inexperienced men did not stand a chance against their far-better-trained opponents in a straight fight.

Johnson was able to call on artillery support from St Oedenrode, but Kinnard's paratroopers, charging from position to position, often in close-quarter combat, made it impossible for the forward observers to call down fire which would not hit their own men. The battalion mortars in weapon pits by Eerde were in direct sight and could be much more precise. By 13.00, Heydte decided to call off the attack because of his casualties. The paratroopers of the 501st, showing an astonishing stamina on their short rations, had outfought their attackers magnificently, as Heydte himself acknowledged.

An American platoon commander recounted, 'I saw them, in twos and threes, jump into machine-gun nests. I saw some of our men go individually at foxholes containing two or three Germans. What we did in those moments we could hardly remember afterwards, because we had not time to think. It was courage such as I'd never imagined possible – almost foolish courage – and I doubt if any group of men could have held their ground against it.'

East of Veghel, Kampfgruppe Walther and the 107th Panzer-Brigade were badly mauled by air strikes from the RAF.'s Second Tactical Air Force and counter-attacks from the 32nd Guards Brigade sent back by Horrocks. At 20.50 Generalleutnant Krebs issued an order from Army Group B's new position just south of Krefeld, that Panzer-Brigade 107 should renew its attack north-westwards. Student's chief of staff replied that 'Brigade 107 has suffered very high losses. The commanders of the panzer brigade, the panzer battalion and the panzergrenadier battalion have fallen.' Major Berndt-Joachim Freiherr von Maltzahn's evacuation due to his serious wounds was keenly felt by his men. The brigade was left with just three tanks and two assault guns still serviceable, an estimate later corrected to twelve tanks which were battleworthy. In any case the Kampfgruppe Walther and the remnants of the panzer brigade had to withdraw rapidly, because the British VIII Corps advancing through Helmond threatened their rear.

The German attacks on Hell's Highway made the removal of casualties to the 24th Evacuation Hospital in Leopoldsburg impossible for the next four days. The 101st Airborne suffered 163 cases of combat exhaustion during its time in the Netherlands, and 30 per cent of them returned to duty after treatment within the divisional area. Far more serious was the shortage of plasma for battle wounds. The 82nd Airborne medics in the Baby Factory were also running short of essential supplies. 'No more traffic from the south', Martijn Louis Deinum wrote in his diary. Temporarily cut off from the rest of the Allied army, Nijmegen took stock of the situation. As a result of the fighting and the deliberate fire-raising, more than 16,000 were homeless.

Another reason for the rapid withdrawal of the 107th Panzer-Brigade that day was the sight overhead of C-47 Dakotas, towing Waco gliders, heading for the drop zone just over the Maas–Waal Canal. General Gavin's 325th Glider Infantry Regiment and the 80th Airborne Anti-Aircraft Battalion were arriving, five days late. He sent the Glider Infantry, supported by Sherman tanks of the Sherwood Rangers Yeomanry, to widen the bridge-head round Mook for VIII Corps to occupy. East of Nijmegen the 2nd Battalion of the 504th Parachute Infantry Regiment, also supported by a squadron of the Sherwood Rangers, managed to push back the northern wing of General Meindl's II Fallschirmjäger Corps as far as Erlekom. 'A short but bitter battle ensued,' the battalion reported. 'Three enemy tanks and one half-track were knocked out and the enemy was completely routed leaving many dead. We had two British tanks supporting us which accounted for the enemy tanks.'

Meindl complained that he was still short of ammunition, but he at least received the 190th Infanterie-Division under the Austrian Generalleutnant Ernst Hammer. It was given the whole of the Reichswald sector between Kranenburg and Gennep. And while the 325th Glider Infantry became responsible for the southern part, Tucker's 504th Parachute Infantry

26. 101st Airborne welcomed between Son and St Oedenrode.

27. German tanks for the Knaust Kampfgruppe arriving on a *Blitztransport*. The Allies never imagined how quickly the Germans could bring in panzers from right across Germany.

28. Waffen-SS prisoners taken by the British 1st Airborne west of Arnhem.

29. German artillery forcing a convoy to halt on Hell's Highway.

30. An RAF shot of the bridge showing the wreckage of Gräbner's reconnaissance battalion.

31. Kate ter Horst, the 'Angel of Arnhem', who calmed the wounded by reading from the Bible.

32. Major General Roy Urquhart outside the Hotel Hartenstein.

33. A Light Regiment 75mm pack howitzer east of the Bilderberg Hotel, 19 September.

34. One of the Luftwaffe ground crew in action north of Oosterbeek, 19 September.

35. A Stug III of the 280th Assault Gun Brigade near the Rhine Pavilion after the destruction of the 1st and 3rd Parachute Battalions.

36. SS panzergrenadiers in Arnhem amid abandoned British equipment, 19 September.

37. Civilians evacuated from the St Elisabeth Hospital.

38. Polish paratroopers facing yet another cancellation due to bad weather.

39. Sappers and 3rd Battalion Paras from the school north of the Arnhem bridge forced to surrender.

40. Paratroopers from the 1st Battalion using a shell hole for defence.

41. C Company 1st Battalion of the Border Regiment on 21 September preparing to repel a German assault on the western flank of the Oosterbeek encirclement.

42. Luftwaffe anti-aircraft gunners of the Flak Brigade von Swoboda on the Amsterdamseweg engaging RAF supply flights.

43. Desperate paratroopers trying to signal to the RAF pilots to drop their loads within the perimeter.

44. A Waffen-SS half-track of the *Hohenstaufen* on the Dreijenseweg with supply parachutes caught on trees behind.

45. American paratroopers under artillery fire close to Hell's Highway.

46. Walking wounded from Hotel Schoonord taken prisoner on 20 September.

47. After the defeat of Frost's battalion on Arnhem bridge, Kampfgruppe Brinkmann prepares to cross to the south into the Betuwe to face the British troops pressing up from Nijmegen.

48. A mixture (*l* to *r*) of Waffen-SS, German army soldiers and Luftwaffe in the Betuwe, or 'the Island', between Arnhem and Nijmegen.

49. On 24 September the Germans begin the forced evacuation of Arnhem and the surrounding areas. This act of reprisal for Dutch support to the Allies would also allow them to loot the city unhindered.

50. On 14 April 1945, Canadian troops finally liberate a deserted and ruined Arnhem.

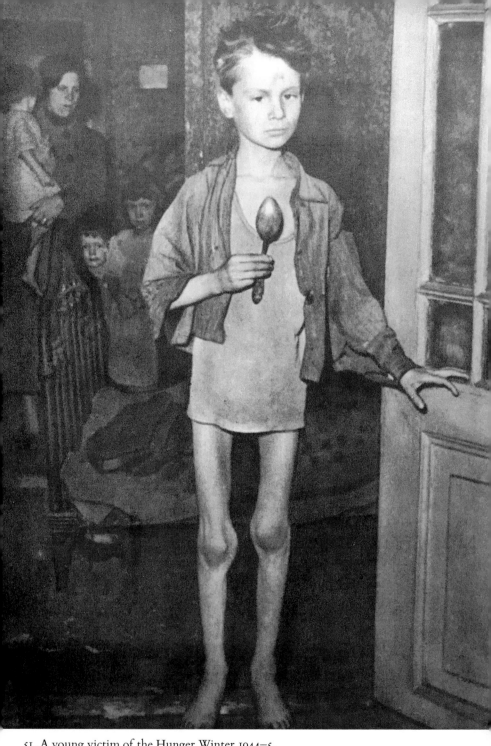

51. A young victim of the Hunger Winter 1944–5.

Regiment took over the northern sector from the Waal down to Groesbeek. The Den Heuvel woods lay to its front, as well as some of the original landing zones. 'Skeletons of gliders lay silhouetted like ghosts all along no-man's land,' wrote Captain Adam A. Komosa. 'They were stripped of their canvas fabric by the Germans who in all probability used it for shelter.'

Gavin's headquarters was still demanding prisoners for interrogation, so F Company was ordered to mount a night attack into the woods, following an artillery barrage. It was hardly a silent operation to snatch a lone sentry. 'Angry exchanges of machine-gun and small arms fire now took place. Much shouting, some screaming, and a hell of a lot of swearing was heard.' They returned with a prisoner, still arguing. 'Let me throw my bayonet through that son of a bitch.' 'Look you stupid ass!' Sergeant Bishop shot back. 'If we don't bring this dried up little bastard back to the CP alive, we'll have to come out here tomorrow night and do this all over again.'

Not long afterwards, another patrol was sent out to seize a prisoner. While they were away, a German patrol came through 3rd Battalion's lines and killed the brother of one of the men out on patrol. When they returned with their prisoner, they wanted to shoot him as soon as they found out what had happened. Their platoon commander stopped them from killing the German and took him to the battalion command post after he had been roughed up. 'The prisoner would not talk,' Major Cook recorded. 'I interviewed him and knowing that he understood English, told him I would give him two minutes to start talking or else I would kill him as he was of no further use to me. When the two minutes were up, I dramatically pulled out my .45 and the S-3 Captain Keep, and the S-2 Captain Carmichael, who were on either side of the prisoner, stepped away. For once I saw real fear in a man's eyes and he started answering questions.'

The Sherwood Rangers, one of the most effective British armoured regiments, had taken over from the Coldstream. They worked closely with the 82nd Airborne on its Reichswald flank. The American paratroopers had no idea what Yeomanry meant, but they recognized the word 'Rangers' and assumed that they were an armoured equivalent of the elite American force. The cavalrymen certainly admired the fighting qualities of the 82nd. In a battle near Beek, Lieutenant Stuart Hills saw one paratrooper 'continuing to fire his weapon with a leg and an arm blown off'. The commanding officer of the Sherwood Rangers, Lieutenant Colonel Stanley Christopherson, liked General Jim Gavin and considered his paratroopers to be the best infantry they had worked with – 'tough, brave and cheerful'. But 'maybe on some occasions', Christopherson wrote in his diary, 'they were too tough, especially in the treatment of their prisoners, whom they seldom took.

I shall never forget seeing a Jeep full of American paratroopers driving along with the head of a German pierced with an iron stake and tied to the front. This spectacle haunts me still.'

British paratroopers at Oosterbeek could be tough too. On 23 September, a wounded officer from the 1st Para Battalion was lying in an aid station near the Tafelberg. 'Next to me was one of our chaps with his fingers blown off coolly smoking a fag held between the bloody stumps of his fingers. Somehow summed up the airborne soldier I thought.' Tobacco was not the main preoccupation by then. 'Food becoming very short,' a pathfinder wrote that day. 'Only got a couple of biscuits and a dab of jam all today. Had to break into my emergency ration.'

Despite heavy rain at dawn, the battle continued relentlessly. '07.00 terrific mortar barrage,' Lieutenant Stevenson of the reconnaissance squadron noted. 'S[elf] P[ropelled] guns came up again and began systematically destroying every house which might give shelter. All this time, in the cellars of almost every house, were Dutch civilians, women and children, who had been caught up in the battle. By now we were losing count of time. More SP guns and more shellfire.' Brigadier Hicks, who was not a man to exaggerate, described the shelling at Oosterbeek as 'the worst and the most hellish that I had ever experienced, including the shelling of World War I in the trenches'.

Inevitably cases of psychological breakdown increased, even among the bravest. A glider pilot recorded how one man locked himself in a shed near Oosterbeek church and began firing his Sten gun all around the walls, shouting 'Come on you bastards!' He killed himself in the end. Physical exhaustion, a captain wrote later, almost reached 'a point that being killed would be worth it'.

'My lads mostly OK,' Major Blackwood wrote in his diary, 'though two cases of shell-shock: one a stout warrior who had wakened in his trench to find his pal's severed head in his lap.' In Oosterbeek church they ate some compo which had been reinforced with two Angora rabbits brought in by a sergeant. 'We did raise a grin by looking at our filthy beards in a small mirror. The gunners were using the church as an O[bservation] P[ost] and the astute Hun brought his 88s to bear on us. One of the shells upset the rabbit stew. Had to abandon the church. Roof came down. In foxholes outside near British 75[mm] gun positions. The whole area around our trenches was pitted with holes, and between us and the river lay the inevitable dead cows and a neatly disembowelled horse.'

The pitiless determination of the Waffen-SS was once again evident. A Dutch engineer called de Soet saw a dozen German soldiers, with their hands in the air, guarded by four British paratroopers. There was an explosion and it appeared that a German had thrown a grenade among them for having surrendered.

Major Powell of the 156th reflected on the fact that he had caught fleas because their battalion headquarters was in a chicken house. He expected the perimeter to be overrun at any moment, but the Germans were relying on their tanks and self-propelled assault guns to smash the houses around their heads. There was less support from the 64th Medium Regiment that day. They could manage only twenty-five fire missions. Ammunition reserves had become a concern now that the Germans had cut the XXX Corps supply route, and their own division was also calling for support. Some soldiers tried to keep up their spirits in the old way by singing 'Lili Marlene' or playing records. An Austrian soldier claimed that when their record came to an end, the British would yell 'Play another one, Fritz!', and the Germans would shout 'Play another one, Tommy!' when one of theirs finished.

On the western side at Dennenoord, Jonkheer Bonifacius de Jonge wrote, 'Every day is worse than the day before.' The house had been hit with three shells that Saturday. Only the central staircase was intact. The gasworks just to their south had been hit and were blazing. The house was stifling with everybody packed into the basement, where soldiers were sitting on the floor back to back. Their expressions were dead after so many days without food or sleep. The former governor-general's wife offered a soldier some cognac to pep him up. 'But I'm not wounded,' he said. 'You should not give me that.'

Bonifacius de Jonge tried to distract their little granddaughter Neelsje from the firing by taking candles out of packets and putting them back in again. 'But when all the wounded are lying down, you can see Neelsje skipping between the blood-soaked mattresses, and hopping over the blood-drenched bandages and torn battledress, and with a soft smile, those poor wretches reach out to her. Occasionally this is heart-wrenching.'

The Hotel Schoonoord found itself under German control again that day. An Unteroffizier, who looked very pleased with himself, brought a considerable number of men to guard the place. After making sure that the German wounded were still receiving good treatment, he announced, 'I see the British are not the Russians.' He announced that all German patients who could be moved would be evacuated. But he also insisted on posting guards at all the windows, which only encouraged the Polish paratroopers in the area to shoot at them. They could not look at a German with a weapon and not want to kill him. At one stage a German machine-gunner took up position at a top-floor window, which prompted outraged protests from the British doctors.

The hotel had suffered badly in the fighting. A number of the ceilings were starting to collapse, which was hardly comforting to the wounded underneath. A detachment of SS selected those British wounded who could still walk and marched them off to Arnhem. The padre of the Glider Pilot Regiment found himself in a conversation with one of the young panzer-grenadiers. 'It is the Jews we hate,' the young SS soldier said. 'The Jews and the Russians.'

'Why do you hate the Jews?'

'Because they started the war.'

'Why do you hate the Russians?'

'Why we hate the Russians?' The young Nazi gave the padre a pitying smile. 'Because . . . well, you would know if you saw them.'

Colonel Warrack had to send out an order to the regimental aid posts telling them not to evacuate any more wounded as nothing could be done for them in the dressing stations and hospitals. The wounded lying on the floor had to share a blanket. Soldiers still fighting passed the bulk of the food supplies retrieved from containers back to the wounded, yet undernourishment remained a major problem. Even more critical was the lack of medicines. 'Supplies of morphia and bandages were getting low,' Warrack noted in his report. 'It was bad enough to run short of food and water,' a Dutch volunteer wrote, 'but the worst was to run short of morphia and see men staring at the ceiling, crying silently in pain.' With no source of fresh water, apart from catching rain from the odd downpour, they could not clean patients or operate. 'Surgery was impossible and rest, warmth and fluids were difficult.' Although water was so precious, Lieutenant Colonel Marrable, the commanding officer of 181 (Airlanding) Field Ambulance, still insisted that all officers should shave, which they did in the same single mess tin of cold, murky water. Every shop in Oosterbeek and most empty houses had been stripped. So 'a couple of sheep were acquired and despatched with the aid of a Sten gun by Captain Griffin, the air landing dentist, and turned into stew.'

The greatest lack at the dressing station in the ter Horst house was anti-gangrene serum. 'At first many of the wounds were not serious,' a medical orderly said, 'but they began developing gangrene. It only takes a few hours . . . We were taking out four or five dead every day.' NCOs in the Royal Army Medical Corps could display an astonishing courage and determination, as one wounded paratrooper testified. A German tank began to shell the ter Horst house. An RAMC corporal seized a Red Cross flag, and went right up to the tank. When the commander appeared out of the turret, he asked angrily why they were shelling a house clearly marked with a Red Cross. The tank commander apologized, turned his tank around and trundled back towards Arnhem.

At 13.05, Model's Army Group B headquarters heard that Hitler was outraged to find that the 1st Airborne had not yet been eliminated. He had just ordered that 'the 15 Tiger tanks were to be deployed by II SS Panzer Corps'. Soon afterwards, another message came through to say that Heavy Panzer Battalion 506 with Royal Tigers and Panzerjäger Battalion 741 were on their way to strengthen Bittrich's SS Panzer Corps and Meindl's II Fallschirmjäger Corps.

Bittrich's troops in the Betuwe had been forced back from the line at Ressen to Elst by the 129th Brigade. Well aware of the build-up of British forces to reinforce the Poles at Driel, Bittrich wanted to attack west towards Valburg to cut their route, but the Kampfgruppe Knaust's panzer company had lost three tanks from the attack by the Somerset Light Infantry and the 4th/7th Dragoon Guards on Oosterhout. And he could not use his Tiger tanks because the cross-country routes would collapse under their weight. Bittrich also ordered the 30th Machine-Gun Battalion to take positions down by the Neder Rijn to cover the crossing places.

General der Flieger Christiansen, the Wehrmacht commander-in-chief Netherlands, issued a bombastic order of the day congratulating the Division von Tettau 'under the unerring and energetic leadership of General von Tettau'. Oberst Fullriede of the *Hermann Göring* Division must have felt sick on reading it. Christiansen was claiming that the enemy was being pushed back towards the east, and yet Tettau was complaining that they could not advance because of the fire from 64th Medium Regiment, which he believed was Polish heavy artillery.

A company from the reconnaissance battalion of the *Frundsberg*, under Obersturmführer Karl Ziebrecht, was ordered to push along the north bank of the Neder Rijn to watch the other shore at Driel. The rest of the reconnaissance battalion was on the other side of the river with the Swoboda flak brigade, along the railway line between Elden and Elst facing the Poles. During the day, the rest of the 130th Brigade pushed on via Valburg to Driel, partly concealed by the driving rain. At the same time the 214th Brigade attacked Elst with the 7th Somerset Light Infantry, the 1st Battalion of the Worcestershire Regiment and a squadron of the 4th/7th Dragoon Guards.

Rottenführer Alfred Ringsdorf of the 21st Panzergrenadier Regiment was sitting in a house in Elst playing the piano. He did not hear the

Shermans approaching until a shell went right through the room, fortunately missing the piano. But Major Knaust's powerful reserve of Tiger tanks began firing, and the Shermans pulled back, having destroyed one Mark V Panther.

'We had four Tiger tanks and three Panther tanks,' Horst Weber recounted. 'We were convinced that we would gain another victory here, that we would smash the enemy forces. But then Typhoons dropped these rockets on our tanks and shot all seven to bits. And we cried. We cried from sheer rage, that there could be such injustice, that the soldiers on one side should have everything and the soldiers on the other side should have nothing. We would see two black dots in the sky and that always meant rockets. Then the rockets would hit the tanks which would burn. The soldiers would come out all burnt and screaming with pain.'

Weber admitted that when Typhoon fighter-bombers knocked out these tanks, he and his fellow panzergrenadiers had been 'running for our lives as fast as we could', but then Knaust had appeared in his half-track brandishing one of his crutches, yelling 'Go back! Go back!' And because it was Major Knaust, they felt ashamed and did as they were told. The young panzergrenadiers clearly worshipped him, even though he was not a member of the Waffen-SS. 'He saved our front line down at Elst. I would have done anything for him.'

Knaust re-formed the line. He gave the *Frundsberg* panzergrenadiers two Tiger tanks next to their position. 'It was like a partnership. We gave each other mutual protection. We saw to it that no infantry could attack the tanks from the side and the Tigers protected us from the Shermans. But most important the Tigers helped us to fight our fear.'

Colonel Mackenzie arrived at Browning's headquarters after various adventures he could have done without. According to the Household Cavalry war diary, he 'had quite an exciting experience when the Daimler armoured car in which he was travelling became involved in a fire fight with an enemy half-track and he as loader fired off eight rounds'. The armoured car had then overturned. Mackenzie had very nearly been captured when German infantry advanced in extended line, 'like they were out on a partridge shoot', searching for the crew, and shouting 'Come out, Tommy!'

Browning's aide Eddie Newbury noted that they had been shaken by Mackenzie's appearance. He had 'quite a stubble of beard and his clothes were dirty and dishevelled and he looked very tired'. Browning said later that Mackenzie and Myers were 'putty coloured like men who had come through a Somme winter'.

Whatever illusions Browning still had should have been shattered by

Mackenzie's report on conditions within the perimeter. Mackenzie did not spare his feelings, yet he felt afterwards that Browning had still not grasped the gravity of their predicament. Providing their armoured taxi service once more, the Household Cavalry ran Mackenzie and Myers back to Driel so that they could cross over the Neder Rijn that night, with more Polish paratroopers, to report to General Urquhart.

The chief concern for General Horrocks was not the battle for Elst. It was of course the fate of the 1st Airborne at Oosterbeek. He sent his chief of staff Brigadier Pyman down to see General Dempsey, the commander of the Second Army, who had come up as far as St Oedenrode. It was decided that a last effort should be made to reinforce the airborne division's bridgehead. If that failed, and there were reports that the Germans were preparing an all-out attempt to crush the perimeter, then the surviving paratroopers would be evacuated back across to the Betuwe side. Dempsey authorized Horrocks and Browning to take that decision without reference to higher authority. They could make up their minds the next day at a conference to be held at 43rd Division headquarters at Valburg.

Urquhart showed his two brigadiers, Hicks and Hackett, and Colonel Loder-Symonds the message he intended to send to Browning describing their situation. It ended: 'Morale still adequate, but continued heavy mortaring and shelling is having obvious effects. We shall hold but at the same time hope for a brighter 24 hours ahead.'

The morning's rain gave way to clearer skies. On their own initiative, Lieutenant Johnson of the American air support party and a Canadian officer Lieutenant Leo Heaps had crossed the Neder Rijn before dawn in a dinghy. They went to Sosabowski's command post in Driel and briefed his staff on the situation in the perimeter. The two lieutenants had a hot meal and a proper drink for the first time in over a week.

With the clear skies, they could look back across the Neder Rijn to the north bank from where they had come to watch Allied aircraft in action. 'We saw the first real air support of the operation. For more than half an hour Typhoons and Thunderbolts strafed and bombed the German anti-aircraft gun positions. Then the Stirlings and Dakotas came in with their resupply loads. From Driel I saw flares go up from our perimeter across the river to mark the DZ and almost immediately the Germans on three sides of the Division area also shot up flares. It was damn heartbreaking to see those so badly needed supplies drop up to 5,000 yards away from the Division. No more than ten percent were recovered by the Division. I would have given my right arm for a radio set that could have contacted those planes to guide them to the right area. Two Dakotas were set ablaze by the anti-aircraft fire but both kept right on going till they could drop their load. Just one man got out of the two planes before they hit.' Altogether 123 British Stirlings and C-47 Dakotas transported the supplies that day. Six were lost and sixty-three damaged. German anti-aircraft fire was reducing the RAF transport fleet at such a rate that resupply could not continue much longer.

That afternoon, Major General Sosabowski received a signal message that assault boats were on their way. 'I was not very pleased,' he said. 'I could not understand why they wanted to sacrifice specially trained airborne troops in an assault crossing when the 43rd Division had the boats and was trained in making assaults. But I had my orders.'

The sky had cleared entirely by dusk, leaving a starlit night. Colonel Myers on the southern bank was supervising the distribution of the 130th Brigade's assault boats to the Polish brigade. He had every sympathy for the Poles. The boats were of a different type and size to what they had been told. They did not arrive until 02.00 and only ten proved capable of floating. Two others had been holed in transit by German fire. No engineers were provided with the boats, so the Poles, who had never been trained in river crossings, had great difficulty paddling them. Instead of a whole battalion crossing, only 153 Polish officers and men reached the north bank in the few hours of darkness left. Many others were killed or wounded by the German 30th Machine-Gun Battalion, firing over the water on fixed lines. The casualties were brought back to the southern bank. Sosabowski, who was watching from the dyke, halted the operation shortly before dawn. He had probably heard the American joke that 'The British would fight to the very last ally.' It might well have crossed his mind that night.

23

Sunday 24 September

Having spent most of the night on the dyke watching the 8th Company crossing, Major General Sosabowski had not gone to sleep until after dawn. He was woken at 10.00 to be told that General Horrocks had arrived in an armoured car, accompanied by Lieutenant Colonel Stevens, the liaison officer. Sosabowski was surprised and pleased to see Horrocks, especially since the route from Nijmegen via Valburg was still open to German attack. He wondered why Browning, his direct superior, had not come too. The two men climbed the church tower at Driel, and from the steeple Sosabowski was able to point out the key features, including the Westerbouwing heights which the Germans had taken from the Border Regiment. Urquhart's 1st Airborne Division now had less than a kilometre of river frontage and the Germans were trying to cut it off entirely.

Horrocks listened, but provided very little information himself. He did not reveal that his chief of staff Brigadier Pyman and Major General Ivor Thomas, the commander of the 43rd Division, had already planned the river crossing to take place that night. Instead, he simply instructed Sosabowski to come to Thomas's headquarters at Valburg for a conference at 11.30 that morning.

Sosabowski sent a runner to fetch his interpreter Lieutenant Jerzy Dyrda, who was observing the north bank of the Neder Rijn from the dyke. Horrocks had already departed by the time Dyrda reached the farmhouse. Sosabowski told him to bring a machine gun and grenades. He, Dyrda and Stevens would leave in a Jeep driven by Sergeant Juhas. Dyrda was slightly mystified why Sosabowski should have been summoned back from the front for a conference.

There had been one good piece of news for Sosabowski, although it was astonishing that he had not been informed of it before. The 1st Battalion and part of the 3rd Battalion had not perished as he had feared. They had finally been flown over the day before, to be dropped in the comparative safety of the 82nd Airborne Division's sector near Groesbeek. There had been a strong wind so a number of men had suffered broken legs when dragged, but the important thing was that the rest of the brigade was on its way to Driel.

Shortly before reaching the small town of Valburg, Sosabowski's Jeep was halted by British military police who signalled for them to leave the road. They were directed to an orchard where a large tent had been erected in a clearing. Horrocks and Browning stood outside waiting for them. 'The greeting of the two generals was clearly very cool,' Dyrda noticed. 'I did not see the smallest display of friendliness on the part of the British generals and brigadiers towards Gen Sosabowski.'

Sosabowski had not met Major General Thomas, the commander of the 43rd Division. Thomas, both humourless and self-satisfied, was probably the most thoroughly disliked general in the whole British army. His officers referred to this obsessive martinet as 'General von Thoma' because of his Prussian obsession with outward form. Thomas would tear a strip off commanding officers if latrines had not been dug according to regulation size the moment their troops seized an objective. He was also known as 'the Butcher' due to his pitiless attitude to losses in achieving an objective.

Sosabowski asked Horrocks whether he could bring Lieutenant Dyrda with him into the meeting as his interpreter so that there would be no misunderstandings. Horrocks refused, insisting that it was not necessary. But Dyrda appealed to Browning, who knew him from previous discussions, and Browning agreed. Horrocks could not then refuse, which did not improve his mood. Once inside, he would not let Lieutenant Dyrda sit beside Sosabowski. He insisted that he stand behind him, which was surprisingly petty. Dyrda began to suspect that Horrocks did not want another Polish officer present as a witness. Even more striking was the way that Sosabowski and Dyrda were left on one side of the table, while all the senior British officers sat opposite them. It looked like a court martial, not a conference between allies. Even Colonel Stevens, the liaison officer, did not sit on the Polish side. Horrocks, flanked by Browning and Thomas, sat facing Sosabowski.

Dyrda's account, the only detailed one of the Valburg conference which exists, was written in a strong tone of moral outrage at the British generals' treatment of Sosabowski. He failed to remember that Sosabowski had always been the most outspoken critic of the whole Market Garden project, and now that his warnings had proved entirely justified Browning and Horrocks must have expected another outburst against disastrous British planning. They were clearly determined to keep Sosabowski in his place right from the start.

Horrocks chaired the conference. He announced that the intention was still to establish a strong bridgehead north of the Rhine. Two crossings were to be made that night under the command of Major General Thomas, to whom the Polish Parachute Brigade would report. He then handed over to Thomas, who announced that the 4th Battalion of the Dorset Regiment and the 1st Battalion of the Polish brigade would cross the river opposite the Heveadorp ferry. They would take extra ammunition to distribute to the 1st Airborne Division. At the same time, the remaining troops of the Polish Parachute Brigade would cross in approximately the same place as the night before. 'Both crossings were to be commanded by Brigadier B. Walton, commander of his 130th Infantry Brigade,' Dyrda noted down. 'Boats would be supplied by 43rd Infantry. All the instructions were delivered in a very peremptory tone, with a shade of superiority.' Thomas gave no details about what sort of boats, nor how many, would be provided, nor whether they would be crewed by engineers, and he provided no information about smokescreens or artillery support. In fact so little information was offered that Horrocks could have briefed Sosabowski at Driel and avoided his trip to Valburg.

The two Polish officers were taken aback. To command the operation Thomas had not only chosen a man junior in rank to Sosabowski, but one who had never been near the river. It looked like a deliberate provocation. When Sosabowski was told that his 1st Battalion would be transferred to Brigadier Walton, he pointed out with considerable self-control that he commanded the Polish Independent Parachute Brigade, and he would decide which battalion was selected for a particular task.

British sources, based on the official history of the 43rd Wessex Division, claim that Sosabowski lost his temper at this point and said to Horrocks, 'I am General Sosabowski, I command the Polish Para Brigade. I do as I like.' Horrocks, according to this story, retorted: 'You are under my command. You will do as I bloody well tell you.' 'All right,' Sosabowski is supposed to have conceded. 'I command the Polish Para Brigade and I do as you bloody well say.' This is almost certainly apocryphal, just the sort of anecdote exchanged in an officers' mess after dinner. Sosabowski was a passionate patriot who did not suffer fools gladly, whatever their rank, and it is hard to believe that he would have said 'I do as you bloody well say.' Nothing even resembling this exchange is included in Dyrda's account.

Dyrda had good reasons for suspecting that Horrocks and Browning wanted to evade responsibility for the disaster, and would try to 'argue that

Sosabowski's objections, stubbornness and intractability hindered them from providing effective help to the 1st Airborne Division'. But he does not acknowledge Sosabowski's misunderstanding of the situation. Sosabowski argued that, instead of the plan presented by Thomas, a major crossing of the Neder Rijn in divisional strength should be made further to the west, and the German forces surrounding the 1st Airborne should be enveloped from the rear. This was impracticable since the British lacked the boats and the bridging equipment to get a sufficiently large force across in time, and in any case Thomas could spare no more than a brigade. But Sosabowski was entirely correct to point out that Thomas's plan to land the Dorsets and his 1st Battalion at the Heveadorp ferry, right under the dominating Wester-bouwing heights held by the Germans, was reckless at the very least. German machine-gun positions covering the river meant that the operation just described was not a crossing, but an opposed assault.*

As soon as Dyrda had finished translating, General Thomas rose and, ignoring everything Sosabowski had said, announced that the crossings would be carried out at 22.00 and in the places he had stated. Sosabowski had exercised great self-control up until that point, but the deliberately rude refusal of an officer of equal rank to respond to his suggestion drove him to fury. He had far more experience than anyone else present and had a much better idea of the terrain. And he could sense that Horrocks and Browning, who never opened his mouth during the meeting, had no real intention of continuing the battle for Arnhem. The operation described by Thomas was clearly just a face-saving gesture.

Sosabowski's lack of sleep compounded the exasperation he felt at the futile suffering which the whole ill-planned enterprise had caused. He stood up and in his own rather fractured English warned that the sacrifice of the

---

* Horrocks never mentioned the Valburg conference in his memoirs. He claimed that he went straight from Driel to see General Dempsey at St Oedenrode. Even more astonishingly, he wrote: 'It is always easy to be wise after the event but, knowing what I do now, I think it would have been better to have committed the 43rd Division on a different axis. Instead of passing them through the Guards on the 22nd, I should have ordered General Thomas to carry out a left hook across the lower Rhine much farther to the west and so attack the Germans, who were engaged with the 1st Airborne Division, from behind.' He seems to have forgotten that this was precisely what Sosabowski had recommended, and what he had rejected out of hand. It is also worth repeating that Sosabowski's plan of encirclement from the west was the only one accepted by the Dutch army's staff college, when they failed any officer who proposed advancing straight up the Nijmegen–Arnhem road.

Dorsets and his 1st Battalion would be utterly wasted. He again emphasized that the Dorsets were being sent to their deaths against Westerbouwing. If the British did not have the means to launch a major attack, then they must withdraw Urquhart's division. Thomas tried to interrupt, but Sosabowski shot back: 'Don't forget that for the past eight days, not only Polish paratroopers, but also the best sons of Britain, volunteer soldiers of your airborne division, have been dying for nothing on the Rhine.'

'The briefing is over,' Horrocks announced angrily. 'Orders issued by General Thomas are to be carried out.' He turned to Sosabowski. 'And if you, General Sosabowski, are unwilling to carry out the orders you've been given, we shall find another commander for the Polish parachute brigade, one who will carry out our orders.'

No further word was addressed to Sosabowski by officers from XXX Corps as they trooped out, but General Browning stayed behind and invited him to lunch in Nijmegen. This lifted some of his gloom, and he accepted in the hope that he might persuade Browning to change Horrocks's mind. But when he heard from Browning that there were hardly any boats for the crossing that night, his views on the sluggishness and incompetence of XXX Corps exploded. Dyrda warned him afterwards that this had not been wise. Browning and Horrocks were old friends and would stick together if they felt the British army was being criticized. Sosabowski was furious with Lieutenant Dyrda, whom he thought had overstepped the mark with his frankness. He refused to speak to him again, but after the war he realized that Dyrda had been right. He had played straight into the hands of his opponents.

Horrocks, as already mentioned, was in a bad physical and mental state from his serious wounds and was in constant pain. Montgomery should never have given him such stressful responsibilities. Browning too was unwell with a persistent cold which he could not shake off. Sosabowski was indeed a difficult character, but that was no justification for the way he was treated. As Urquhart recognized, it was a completely unnecessary insult to have placed him under a young and inexperienced brigadier. Both Horrocks and Browning must have played a part in convincing Montgomery that the Polish Parachute Brigade had been reluctant to fight.

On his return from the meeting the day before in Nijmegen with General Browning, Colonel Charles Mackenzie sat on the south bank of the Neder Rijn. 'I thought about what I would report to the general,' he wrote later. 'I could either tell him what I thought, that after seeing the situation on both sides of the river, I was convinced that a crossing from the south side would not be successful. Or I could tell him, as I was told, that [XXX Corps] were doing their best, that there would be a crossing and that we should hold on.' After some time, 'I decided to tell him what [Horrocks and Browning] told me; that they were doing everything possible and that there would be a crossing. I felt it would be easier for him to keep people going if I put it that way.' Back at divisional headquarters, Mackenzie reported to Urquhart, who took care to show no feelings one way or the other.

Their surroundings in the Hartenstein were desperate. The formerly immaculate hotel grounds were now like 'a stretch of open-cast mining, all slit trenches and bomb holes', while the building itself looked 'as if it would fall down if you pushed it'. There were more than thirty wounded in the divisional aid post. Among the many victims of the German mortar fire at the Hartenstein were Brigadier Hackett and his chief clerk, Staff Sergeant Pearson. Pearson had been offended by the sight of his brigadier having to eat with his fingers, so he went off in search of a knife and fork for him. That was when he was hit by mortar shrapnel. He managed to drag himself to the aid post in the Hartenstein only to find Hackett joining him, clutching his stomach from a severe abdominal wound. The two of them were later evacuated on the same Jeep to the St Elisabeth Hospital as prisoners of the Germans. Hackett had no fewer than fourteen holes in his intestine. Brigadier Lathbury, who was already a patient there, heard that Hackett had only a 50 per cent chance of surviving.

At 09.00 on 24 September, Colonel Warrack went to see General Urquhart. He persuaded him that he should be allowed to contact the senior German medical officer to 'arrange for the evacuation of the wounded to a safer area in German held territory', since evacuation over the river was clearly quite impossible. 'The Divisional Commander made it quite clear that under no circumstances whatever must the enemy be allowed to think that this was the beginning of a crack, and it must be clearly understood that this measure was being adopted purely on humane grounds.' Fire was to be lifted for a period that afternoon 'to allow the battlefield to be cleared of wounded so that both sides could get on with the fight'.

Colonel Warrack, who could move without difficulty between the Hartenstein and the Schoonoord under the Red Cross flag, approached a German doctor there. This turned out to be SS-Stabsarzt Egon Skalka, the senior medical officer in the SS *Hohenstaufen*. Skalka, an Austrian from Carinthia, was only twenty-nine years old. He wore a well-tailored uniform, had wavy hair and reeked of eau de cologne. His immaculately manicured hands, with a gold SS signet ring, indicated that he did not stoop to surgery himself. Warrack asked for a meeting with the divisional commander. Skalka agreed, and the two men then drove in a Jeep under a Red Cross flag to the *Hohen-staufen* command post at the Villa Heselbergh on the Apeldoorn road out of Arnhem.*

Warrack had to wait while Skalka went in to see his divisional commander. Skalka claimed that Harzer was angry because he had not blindfolded Warrack and had not sought approval first. 'What do you mean dragging him here without permission?' Harzer then went next door to Bittrich's office to ask him about the truce and the evacuation of British wounded. Bittrich immediately agreed to the idea. Skalka meanwhile rang the regional senior medical officer to request every available ambulance and vehicle.

Bittrich and Harzer went to speak to Warrack and expressed the standard German regret that 'there should be this fight between our two countries', with the subtext that they should both be fighting the Soviets together. The ceasefire and the evacuation were quickly agreed, but Urquhart had been right to fear that this démarche would only encourage the Germans to think they were about to win. Harzer plied Warrack with sandwiches and gave him a bottle of brandy to take to Urquhart. He and his officers also offered stocks of morphine, taken from British containers dropped outside the perimeter.†

Skalka then took Warrack to the St Elisabeth Hospital to see the British wounded there. They were in beds with sheets and were very well cared for by Dutch doctors and nurses as well as the German nuns. Warrack was of course struck by the contrast with his wounded back in Oosterbeek, where the lack of water meant that surgery was impossible. By the time they returned to the Schoonoord, the ceasefire had started. German military trucks were lined up, but because British army stretchers were too long to fit in sideways, only three could be fitted in lengthways. This meant that three times as many vehicles would be needed. Colonel Marrable had

---

* Skalka later claimed that he had made the approach, not Warrack. He said he had heard of the plight of the wounded from Harzer through German signals intercepts. According to his version, Skalka drove into the perimeter with a captured Tommy on the front of a Jeep waving a large white flag.

† Harzer wrote from his prison camp after the war to Urquhart, hoping for a testimonial to the *Hohenstaufen*'s chivalrous behaviour. 'As a result of the Nuremberg trial the entire Waffen-SS has been pronounced a criminal organization. I appeal to the British combat soldiers, in recognition of the fair battle at Arnhem, to remember that time and to acknowledge the fairness of conduct at least of those German soldiers who were involved in that operation.' He asked without success for a letter back from Urquhart 'confirming my statements'.

quietly told his staff that they must get the badly wounded away as quickly as possible, but they should then go slow on all the others just in case XXX Corps arrived to save them from prison camp.

As Urquhart had expected, one of the German doctors tried to persuade Colonel Warrack that the British should surely surrender because there were so many British wounded. He should do all he could to persuade his divisional commander. According to Hendrika van der Vlist, who was interpreting, Warrack listened in silence, then shook his head slowly and said calmly, 'No. We have not come to surrender. We have come to fight.'

'Yes, I too can understand that,' the SS doctor had to answer. 'It was just a suggestion.'

During the evacuation of the wounded, the Germans managed to take over some of the Red Cross Jeeps. (The next time they were seen by the Allies was in the Ardennes, when they were used by Otto Skorzeny's commandos masquerading in American uniforms.) They also seized the Hotel Tafelberg packed with wounded.

A diminutive German soldier, his helmet almost over his eyes, began screaming at one of the Dutch nurses for helping British soldiers. A British medical orderly walked over to him and shouted down into his face, 'If you don't shut up, I'm going to knock your block off.' This unexpected reaction silenced him completely. The partial ceasefire at least gave a number of civilians trapped within the perimeter the chance to escape. As they passed German positions, panzergrenadiers taunted the refugees with comments about what their friendship with the British had done for them.

At 16.00 hours the Germans brought troops forward to the Schoonoord, so as to use its buildings as cover for an attack. Lieutenant Colonel Marrable firmly ordered them out of the hospital buildings, but he could not persuade them to pull back. The presence of the German guards who remained provoked the newly arrived Poles, who immediately started shooting at them. 'At considerable risk from both sides, Lieutenant Colonel Marrable went across to parley with the Poles and managed to restore peace for the moment.' Another doctor, Captain Mawson, had a far more difficult task trying to persuade Major Wilson of the 21st Independent Parachute Company to give up his well-prepared positions now that the German advance placed the Schoonoord right in the cross-fire.

The Waffen-SS kept up the pressure, threatening to destroy the Schoonoord if the British did not abandon certain buildings. They brought up two self-propelled assault guns, but Wilson's pathfinders managed to destroy one of them and persuade the other to withdraw. It was a constant struggle to keep the panzergrenadiers out of hospital buildings, yet as

Warrack observed, 'It was rather surprising how quickly a tough-looking SS corporal with a Spandau and a garland of bullets round his neck "jumped to it" when told (in English) to "get the hell out of here, and be quick about it", all this accompanied by an angry look and a gesture to the Red Cross armband.'

Only once the four-hour ceasefire had finished did Bittrich dare tell Army Group B headquarters about it. Model was furious. 'What in God's name were you thinking of?' he demanded. 'The enemy benefited from this truce.' But Model was still prepared to protect Bittrich, and made sure that Führer headquarters never heard of the incident. Hitler would have been apoplectic. He was still issuing orders that bore little relation to what was happening on the ground, and Generalfeldmarschall von Rundstedt passed on his latest that morning. 'The Führer has ordered that the enemy in the area Arnhem–Nijmegen–Mook, as well as to the east, must be destroyed as quickly as possible, and the gap in the front north of Eindhoven will be closed through concentric attacks.' Model simply replied that the elimination of the Oosterbeek perimeter was expected the next day.

German generals continued to expect further airborne landings, and Bittrich was relieved to hear that the Heavy Panzer Battalion 506 with more Tiger tanks would arrive later that day. After the river crossing of the night before, the *Hohenstaufen* pioneer battalion now found itself up against Polish paratroopers. Möller claimed that respect for the wounded and dead 'changed suddenly'. The Poles just wanted to kill Germans.

Their reinforcement of the British defenders produced a great boost to morale. 'Midday the owner of the house comes up from the cellar', one of the pathfinders wrote in his diary, 'and cooks us a meal from his scanty rations. It mainly consisted of potatoes and spinach, anyway it was very acceptable. Just as it was ready, we see movements in the next house. Some strange-looking blokes give me the thumbs-up and victory sign, and we realise that they are the advance guard of the Poles who apparently [parachuted] on the other side of the river. Everyone's spirits rise.'

The Poles themselves had found little to encourage them in the Oosterbeek perimeter. 'It seemed that everywhere you looked there was either an Englishman, a Pole, a German, a Dutchman or a dead cow,' wrote Corporal Władysław Korob. Officer Cadet Adam Niebieszczański found the body of a British major lying in front of a slit trench in the sun. Afraid that the corpse might decompose, he and a companion decided to throw it into another slit trench and bury it there, but as they each grabbed either arms or legs, the major opened his eyes in astonishment. He had just been enjoying a sleep in the open air during the ceasefire. After making their apologies, Niebieszczański and his comrades had the good fortune to find a parachute container with tins of Christmas pudding. These provided such solid nourishment that they felt full for the rest of the day. Lieutenant Smaczny, who had been one of the first to cross, recounted that their tactic for retrieving a container was for one group to mount a fake attack off to the side, with grenades and much shouting, while another group sneaked round to grab it.

During the lull, a gunner who could speak German joined up with some Poles and began to converse. But 'to his utter disbelief and despair, one of the Poles remarked that once they had finished with the Germans, they had to get ready for the next war – with the Russians.' Like almost all British soldiers at the time, he had heard only heroic accounts of Red Army prowess from newspapers and newsreels. He had no knowledge of the Soviet treatment of Poland.

The newly arrived Polish paratroopers were taken aback at the state of their British allies. 'Everyone had red eyes from lack of sleep, and white lips from lack of water,' Corporal Korob observed. Most men had lost a stone or more in that week, from sheer exhaustion and malnourishment. Some of the wounded still being looked after in cellars became delirious, shouting, 'Kill them! Kill them!' At the same time, there was no more betting among those still on their feet about who could shoot the most Germans. Men could be so mindlessly tired that they found themselves wishing for any wound which would allow them to go and lie down somewhere. Near Oosterbeek church, some skivers slipped away from their trenches to a brick barn behind an undertaker's premises to sleep secretly in a dusty old hearse, the sort drawn by black horses with ostrich plumes.

With nerves so frayed, men lost their temper more easily over little things. They were also much slower in their reactions and understanding. Officers and NCOs had to repeat themselves several times for something to sink in. After Captain Springett Demetriadi of the Phantom detachment with divisional headquarters had transmitted Urquhart's signal to Browning, which described their dire state, he said that 'it was like sending our own epitaph'. Their sense of humour had also changed. It now became deeply cynical. Demetriadi's Phantom colleague Lieutenant Neville Hay said, 'Do you know why they called this Operation Market?' 'No.' 'Because we've bought it.'

At the north-eastern tip of the perimeter, the battalion of the King's Own Scottish Borderers was down to seven officers and less than a hundred men. Those who had the strength went on sniper hunts. The rest waited in their battered houses for another attack. Men of the reconnaissance squadron next to them were heartened to see rocket-firing Typhoons come to their aid for the first time, attacking German positions with impressive accuracy. 'Jerry obviously didn't like this and we had a respite from shelling,' Lieutenant Stevenson wrote in his diary. Once that show was over, they found themselves back to mortar stonks and sniping from houses less than fifty metres away. 'An SS tough had been wounded in the street and was kicking up a hell of a row about it. Our chaps could not get to him because of sniper fire so they gave him a lullaby of Lili Marlene through the window – the sort of mad thing people were doing.' They had received no rations for four days and lived mainly on fruit, and yet 'the greatest privation was lack of cigarettes.'

Major Blackwood and his survivors from the 11th Para Battalion were also suffering from a chronic shortage of food and cigarettes because the containers dropped out of reach. 'Heavily blitzed and sniped at all day,' Blackwood wrote that day in his diary. 'Our rocket-firing Typhoons came over and strafed along both flanks. A lovely sight. As usual Dakotas arrived and dropped containers most of which dropped in Hun territory. I raise my hat to these airmen. They fly in through the heaviest flak to give us our stores. I saw two of them set ablaze by the terrific barrage, yet the pilots held them steady and the crews continued to pitch out the door loads . . . It is difficult even to secure the few containers which do drop in our lines. If we rush to them immediately, Jerry gets cracking on them with his mortars. If we wait till dark some sneaking rats from another sector get there first. Today we got nothing.'

It was doubly infuriating for the defenders to imagine how much the enemy enjoyed their rations. 'We ate well, even luxuriously, thanks to the British supplies,' Standartenführer Harzer remembered. 'There were things in the supply containers which we had not seen for years, such as chocolate and real coffee.'

On 24 September, the 129th Brigade from Thomas's 43rd Division continued to attack the Kampfgruppe Knaust round Elst. The British had already found that the polderland and small orchards of the Betuwe were even more difficult for the attacker than the *bocage* in Normandy.

Hell's Highway between St Oedenrode and Veghel remained a key target for the Germans. Heydte's 6th Fallschirmjäger-Regiment launched another attack, even after their losses in the 'battle of the dunes' by Eerde and the virtual destruction of Kampfgruppe Huber. The unexpected success of the Battalion Jungwirth, raiding the main XXX Corps route near the village of Koevering, encouraged Heydte to join them in shooting up a long British supply convoy. Columns of smoke could be seen from quite a distance and the stench of burning rubber spread too. The Americans later claimed that the British had stopped for tea when they were shot up, but in fact they had been halted by reports of German assault guns ahead. Supported by some light flak guns, Major Hans Jungwirth's men and Heydte's force had plenty of time to loot the trucks they had not destroyed. They even captured some officers in staff cars oblivious to the danger, and two Sherman tanks.

Two battalions of the 506th Parachute Infantry Regiment were sent down the route from Veghel supported by several tanks. A battalion of the 502nd came from the other direction and a British unit arrived from the 50th Division. Jungwirth's force, supported by Heydte, was nearly surrounded the next day, but the damage inflicted on British convoys and the blockage of Hell's Highway for another two days represented an extraordinary achievement for such a small and inexperienced battalion. 'Our pleasure at this success was short-lived', Heydte wrote, yet this rupture to XXX Corps's supplies helped convince Dempsey and Horrocks that any hope of reinforcing the 1st Airborne north of the Rhine was over-optimistic. Unfortunately, Major General Thomas's crossings planned for that night were still going ahead.

The first priority was to provide urgent medical supplies, which the DUKWs had failed to deliver when they became bogged down in the mud. Lieutenant Colonel Martin Herford, Captain Percy Louis and four soldiers from 163 Field Ambulance crossed in daylight to the north bank 'in a boat loaded with medical stores and flying Red Cross flags. They were not fired on.' But as soon as they landed, German troops surrounded them. They were told that they could not take the medical stores through to the 1st Airborne Division, but they would be used to treat British prisoners of war. Louis and the four orderlies were allowed then to cross back to British lines. That evening Captain Louis tried again after dark with fresh supplies. Heavy firing was heard after they landed, and Louis was never seen again.

Lieutenant Colonel Gerald Tilly, the commanding officer of the 4th Battalion the Dorsetshire Regiment, received a briefing that afternoon. He met Brigadier Ben Walton at Driel and they went up the church tower, just like Horrocks and Sosabowski that morning. Walton told him that they had to broaden the base of Oosterbeek perimeter, so Tilly's battalion would cross in the amphibious DUKWs which were on their way. This was hardly encouraging, after the fate of the DUKWs the night before. Walton implied that the Dorsets would be followed rapidly by the rest of the Second Army. Considering the lack of craft and bridging equipment available, this seemed unconvincing.

Tilly went to brief his company commanders, but at 18.00 hours a runner arrived to ask Tilly to report once again to Brigadier Walton at a house just south of Driel. Walton told him that the large-scale operation was off. Instead Tilly was to take his battalion across the Neder Rijn to help hold the perimeter until they could evacuate the airborne division. He was to take as few men as possible. 'The idea was to create a diversion until the airborne was withdrawn.'

On returning to the orchards where his battalion was dispersed, Tilly, with understandable reluctance, selected about 300 men and 20 officers to go with him. He felt that his battalion was being 'sent to its certain death' for no good reason, so he left his second-in-command and adjutant behind. Tilly took Major James Grafton, one of his company commanders, aside afterwards. 'Jimmy, I must tell you something because someone other than me has to know the real purpose of this crossing. We're not going over to reinforce the bridgehead. We're going over to try and hold it while the airborne is withdrawn. I'm afraid we're being chucked away to get the airborne out.' Grafton was stunned by this announcement and for a moment just stared at Tilly.

'May I ask, sir, if the men have been informed of the decision?' Tilly replied that they had not, and that he must not say anything to anyone else, even an officer. Walton had given Tilly two identical copies of the evacuation plan to be handed to General Urquhart. Tilly kept one himself and gave the other to Grafton.

After nightfall, the Dorsets and the Polish Parachute Brigade prepared for the crossing. As the night wore on Tilly's anger grew. The rations they had been promised failed to arrive, and there was still no sign of the boats at 22.00 when General Thomas had insisted the operation would begin. Like most of Operation Market Garden, almost everything went wrong, usually due to incompetence compounded by bad luck. Part of the convoy which was supposed to head for Driel with rubber dinghies failed to take a turning to the left and drove straight up the Nijmegen–Arnhem road and through the front line. The Germans let the convoy carry on into the town of Elst where the trucks were surrounded by Knaust's panzergrenadiers, to the astonishment of the Royal Army Service Corps drivers. Their captors were rather disappointed to find only dinghies when they had hoped for rations and of course cigarettes. Two other trucks from the remainder of the convoy had become bogged down, and in the end only nine boats arrived.

The Dorsets did not receive their boats until 01.00 on the Monday morning. As for the rest of the Polish Parachute Brigade, they had three rubber dinghies which could carry two soldiers each and three six-passenger rubber boats. 'Frequent flares light up the crossing area,' ran the entry in the brigade war diary. A lumber-yard was also burning on the north bank, perhaps set alight deliberately by the Germans to provide illumination for their machine guns which were otherwise firing on fixed lines. The flames were reflected on the water as the Dorsets paddled hard, using rifle butts and entrenching tools in their fight against the strong current. The Poles even used their hands – as they too lacked paddles. Three artillery regiments from XXX Corps fired over their heads, but despite their accuracy by day, they were unable to suppress the positions of the 30th Machine-Gun Battalion which were so close to the front line of the perimeter.

In his impatience, Colonel Tilly had insisted on taking the first boat. It landed on a sandy strip on the north bank, and he ran out white tape to guide other boat parties in. But Tilly and his group were on their own. The others had not followed them, because he had miscalculated their route and had landed behind German lines. Tilly and his boatload had started to climb part of the Westerbouwing heights when they bumped into some German reservists, who might have been happy to surrender. In the chaotic encounter, Colonel Tilly was hit on the head by a stick grenade, which fortunately did not explode, but as more German troops arrived he had to destroy his copy of the evacuation plan before surrendering.

B Company under Major White was hard hit, both during the crossing and on arrival. The Dorsets had set out with 18 officers and 298 men. Only five officers and fewer than a hundred men would return. Sosabowski's warning to General Thomas about the dangers of the Heveadorp–Westerbouwing route had been sadly vindicated. At 02.15, after only seventy-five minutes, Brigadier Walton called a halt because enemy fire was so intense. According to the Polish Parachute Brigade's war diary, the Dorsets tried further crossings at 04.00. But Walton's decision was a great relief to the Poles of the 1st Battalion, waiting to cross behind the Dorsets. They had arrived only just before midnight, having marched through the night from Valburg. The other two Polish battalions further to the east managed to land no more than 153 men unwounded on the north bank. Browning and Horrocks would try to use this as evidence against Sosabowski and his brigade, despite the fact that machine-gun fire had sunk half their boats. Browning implied that Sosabowski had held back his men to preserve them.

Unlike the rest of the Dorsets, Major Grafton and most of A Company landed safely and crossed the polderland to Oosterbeek church. There Grafton found Major Lonsdale, still bandaged up from his wounds but completely at his ease, and apparently 'as welcoming as a host at a country house weekend'. A padre took the package with the evacuation plan straight to General Urquhart at the Hartenstein.

Lieutenant Colonel Eddie Myers, the 1st Airborne's chief engineer, managed to cross unharmed in a DUKW. He brought with him a letter to Urquhart from Browning. Browning assured him that 'the Army is pouring to your assistance', and ended with the assertion that he, Browning, was busy directing the defence of the corridor, a statement which would have surprised Major General Taylor and Brigadier General Gavin. 'It may amuse you to know that my front faces in all directions, but I am only in close contact with the enemy for about 8,000 yards to the south-east, which is quite enough in present circumstances.' This claim to be directing the battle of Hell's Highway is even more unconvincing in the light of Browning's later admission in private that his headquarters staff had proved to be thoroughly unsatisfactory.

Myers also brought a rather more important letter from Major General Thomas. Preparations for the evacuation of the remnants of the 1st Airborne Division were in hand, and the withdrawal was to be called Operation Berlin. Urquhart should send a signal as soon as he decided that they could hold on no longer.

That night members of the Arnhem underground gathered secretly in the cellar of the Penseels' townhouse on the Velperplein. They met to discuss what they should do next, now that the 1st Airborne was on the point of defeat. They had done everything they could to help, from providing vital intelligence on German movements to guarding prisoners. Right under the Germans' noses, they had even brought in medical supplies which had dropped outside the perimeter. But all this in the end had not been enough.

The mood was grim, with the feeling that the British could have made a lot more use of them. A British officer had admitted to one of their number, Albert Horstman, that as a result of the many inaccurate reports they had received from the Resistance in France they had wrongly assumed it would be the same in the Netherlands. A number of those present argued that they should join the fight, whether or not the Germans had won. Others considered this a futile sacrifice, especially since the war was clearly going to continue for some time.

Their leader, Piet Kruijff, persuaded them that they should not take up arms and throw their lives away. There was still work for them as the occupation went on north of the Neder Rijn, as well as providing intelligence for the Allies in the Betuwe. And there were already large numbers of British soldiers in hiding who needed help to rejoin their own side. Kruijff himself would later slip into the St Elisabeth Hospital and extract first Brigadier Lathbury and then Brigadier Shan Hackett from right under the Germans' noses. Hackett described Kruijff as 'about forty years old, spare of figure, with an intelligent bird-like face and a watchful eye'. Both senior officers would be concealed by Dutch families and then smuggled back to British lines. But in the mind of the Wehrmacht commander-in-chief Netherlands, the underground were simply 'terrorists'. He said that even the population in areas liberated by the Allies was 'armed and organized in terrorist groups'.

24

Operation Berlin
Monday 25 September

One of the many ironies of Operation Market Garden was that the German retreat to Elden in the early hours of 25 September coincided with the British decision to withdraw the 1st Airborne Division. Kampfgruppe Knaust had suffered such heavy losses in the battle against the 129th Brigade and the 4th/7th Dragoon Guards that Bittrich ordered it to pull all the way back from Elst to either side of Elden. This was less than two kilometres from the southern end of the Arnhem road bridge which the 1st Airborne had failed to secure. By coincidence the 129th Brigade was about to be replaced by another from the 50th Northumbrian Division, so the Germans were not pursued during their withdrawal. Bittrich reported that 'the enemy followed only cautiously'.

General Urquhart, having received Thomas's letter with details of Operation Berlin shortly before dawn, came to a decision within two hours. The division could not survive in its present state of exhaustion, lack of ammunition and supplies. The Germans were trying to cut them off from the riverbank and then they would be trapped. He ordered his radio operator to call up the 43rd Division headquarters. The decision went back up the chain of command for final confirmation. 'Spoke to Horrocks on the blower using arranged code,' General Dempsey wrote in his diary. 'Two alternatives were "Little One" for withdrawal; "Big One" for further crossing.'

'I think it must be the Little One,' said Horrocks.

'I was going to tell you it would have to be the Little One anyway,' he replied. Dempsey then informed Field Marshal Montgomery that the withdrawal would be carried out that night, and he assented. He had little choice.

Montgomery's official biographer remarked of this moment that 'Monty's bid for the Ruhr via Arnhem had proved nothing less than foolhardy.' Staff officers at his tactical headquarters had never seen 'the Master' look so

quiet and withdrawn. The sacrifice of the 1st Airborne Division was grave
enough. Market Garden had also used up the striking power of the Second
Army and led it into the blind alley of the Betuwe, where it could do nothing. Even Montgomery's great supporter Field Marshal Brooke concluded
that his strategy had been at fault. 'Instead of carrying out the advance on
Arnhem he ought to have made certain of Antwerp in the first place,' he
wrote in his diary. The failure to secure the Scheldt estuary leading to that
vital port now stood out as a glaring lapse of judgement.

After Model's prediction to Führer headquarters that they would crush
the *Kessel*, or cauldron, as they called the besieged area of Oosterbeek, the
Germans had to make a big push that day. The volume of fire reached
unprecedented levels, with mortars, artillery, assault-gun and tank fire.
Kampfgruppe Spindler now had its company of fifteen Royal Tigers from
Heavy Panzer Abteilung 506. The American fighter control officer Lieutenant Bruce Davis 'counted 133 shells around the hotel [Hartenstein] between
07.20 and 08.05'. A Nebelwerfer firing its 'screaming meenie' rockets was
having the greatest effect on the defenders' nerves. But to their surprise and
joy RAF fighter-bombers appeared for the second day running and a
Typhoon obliterated the Nebelwerfer with rockets.

At 07.50, Bittrich's headquarters reported to Army Group B, 'Enemy in
besieged area of Oosterbeek still maintaining a bitter defence. Each house
has been turned into a fortress.' At 09.00, Urquhart informed Colonel
Warrack of the decision to pull back across the Neder Rijn. It would be
impossible to take the wounded, so the medical services would stay behind
to help them in captivity. Warrack accepted this without a murmur: it was
the role required of the medical corps. He went to the command post of the
Light Regiment to make sure that the XXX Corps artillery to the south
knew the exact positions of all the dressing stations and aid posts. Only one
shell from the 64th Medium Regiment was thought to have hit a medical
centre.

Across the river, the Polish headquarters and aid station at Driel were
also under heavy fire. 'On the first day of the battle,' Lieutenant Władysław
Stasiak wrote, 'the doctors had looked no different from any other doctors working in regular hospitals. Now they had replaced their white caps
with paratrooper helmets. Under their white gowns they wore protective
armoured vests.' At least their casualty clearing station did not have too many
examples of combat fatigue to deal with. Only two Polish paratroopers had
suffered 'complete nervous breakdown', and another committed suicide in
his slit trench.

At 10.30 the Germans attacked south of the Hartenstein from round the

Tafelberg, which they had captured the day before. 'Found a hundred Germans in woods between Hartenstein and river,' Bruce Davis reported. 'Afraid Germans had wind of plan, so radioed 43rd Division artillery to hit them in the surrounding woods, especially on the southern side between Hartenstein and the riverbank.' It was Colonel Loder-Symonds who was in radio contact with 64th Medium Regiment. 'We fired mediums within 100 yards of our own troops, which was very tricky,' he said later. In fact they were firing more or less into the centre of the perimeter itself. Major Blackwood and his remnants of the 11th Parachute Battalion were rather too close for comfort. 'Our gunners called down a barrage of Second Army mediums to crush a threatened counter-attack. Some of the guns were firing short and we got the full benefit. The whole earth quaked with the explosions, so did we.' The rain was pouring down as well as the shells that morning. 'We snitched an umbrella from a ruined house and set it up,' Blackwood noted. 'Unmilitary but useful.'

At midday, Colonel Warrack was back at the Hotel Schoonoord. The wounded were evacuated by thirty German ambulances, Jeeps and even handcarts while the firing continued. The Schoonoord was then refilled with wounded from other sites, which were overcrowded. Skalka had insisted on starting with the Schoonoord alone, even though there were many badly wounded in the Tafelberg. Warrack, to conceal the gravely weakened state of the division, had told him at their first meeting that there were only 600 patients, but the true figure was more than three times larger.

The Germans were taking the British wounded to a barracks in Apeldoorn, the Willem III-Kazerne, which was being converted into a makeshift hospital by captured British doctors and orderlies. Hendrika van der Vlist decided that she should go with them to help. She found herself having to deal with some Dutch SS. 'I felt ashamed for my compatriots in front of the English, but I have to try to get on with them.' She could do little when the Dutch SS discovered that the British wounded had Dutch currency, with Queen Wilhelmina's portrait, which was banned in German-occupied territory. The SS started to frisk each man and take the money. The British began to object strongly. 'Explain to them, Sister. We are not taking real money from them,' the SS men said. 'This is just junk.'

The arrival of Polish reinforcements meant that they could take over some positions where only a handful of British remained unwounded. Mevrouw Kremer-Kingma found the Poles very different when they assumed the defence of her house. After their officer had been killed, the Pole who took command pointed to the entrance. 'When the Germans enter this house,' he declared, 'we will defend ourselves to the end in the cellar.'

'What about us?' the Dutch civilians asked in horror. The Poles thought it over and agreed not to fight in the cellar. They would leave that to the family. In another house defended by Poles, the parents were crying over their little boy who had lost most of one buttock ripped off by shrapnel. Officer Cadet Adam Niebieszczański gave him his last square of chocolate, and the brave little boy managed to smile his thanks as he put it in his mouth.

Captain Zwolański, the liaison officer at the Hartenstein who had swum the Neder Rijn in both directions, was now suffering from dehydration. 'We haven't had water to drink for two days,' he wrote. 'The small quantities we still have, are for the wounded only.' He decided to make a run for the nearest well as soon as the artillery barrage died down. Two British soldiers agreed to go with him, but knowing that a sniper covered the door, they were well aware that they all had to charge out together. Any pause between them would give him time to aim. 'We bound from tree to tree, drop into ditches, and finally get to a cluster of bushes by the well. The two Englishmen, hidden behind a small mound of earth, crawl up closer to the well. As soon as they've pulled up the bucket and put it down, one of them takes a look and is lightly wounded in the hand. We still fill up our canteens with water. We retrace our steps quickly to get to the ruins of the headquarters before another artillery barrage begins.'

Smoking saved one man's life. During one of the more intense bombardments, a British lieutenant from a slit trench next to Lieutenant Smaczny ran over to ask for a cigarette. As the barrage intensified, the lieutenant could not go back and decided to smoke the cigarette in Smaczny's company. Several seconds later a mortar shell hit the very centre of the British lieutenant's slit trench a couple of metres away, blowing it to pieces.

Early in the afternoon, the main German attack came in on the eastern flank round Oosterbeek church in an attempt to cut the British off from the river. Lonsdale Force and a glider pilot group found themselves in the thick of it. SS panzergrenadiers supported by pioneers with flamethrowers, assault guns and several Royal Tigers threatened the Light Regiment's howitzers. Some of the gunners were firing over open sights at ranges of less than fifty metres, and one battery was overrun. The last remaining anti-tank guns were brought into position. 'There are few more terrifying noises than the whine and rattle of an approaching tank,' wrote Major Blackwood with Lonsdale Force that afternoon. But they held their ground. 'Something grimly humorous', he added, 'in seeing a frantically scurrying Hun legging it in vain with bullets kicking up the mud at his heels.'

Major Cain of the South Staffords, who felt comparatively spruce after seizing an unexpected opportunity for a shave, once again demonstrated extraordinary courage. Now out of PIAT ammunition, he grabbed a 2-inch mortar and went into action. 'By skilful use of this weapon and his daring leadership of the few men still under his command,' the citation for his Victoria Cross continued, 'he completely demoralised the enemy who, after an engagement lasting more than three hours, withdrew in disorder.'

Urquhart had told his officers not to announce the withdrawal until early evening, just in case anyone was taken prisoner. At Dennenoord on the western flank the previous night, the former governor-general Jonkheer Bonifacius de Jonge had thought that they were about to be saved. He had been convinced that the Allied artillery firing from the south was supporting a major crossing of the river. The anti-climax was considerable. 'So many wounded came in during the afternoon that we could not cope any more. The men were lying on top of each other it was so full, and cooking wasn't possible. The major said that during the coming night they would pull back across the river to Driel with all who were still able to move. So the whole plan is a total failure. All these victims, all this suffering, all this for nothing!'

Major Powell was also dismayed when he heard at the Hartenstein that they were to withdraw that night. He had thought that the arrival of the Dorsets meant that the Second Army would be across the river at any moment. He felt sickened when thinking of all that wasted effort and so many lives lost. Major Blackwood, on the other hand, had no illusions when he heard of the evacuation that night. 'It was a bitter moment, but with food and ammo exhausted, anti-tank guns all knocked out and men dazed with nine days of shelling and mortars, there is no alternative.'

Once the decision to leave had been taken, Major General Urquhart had called in Charles Mackenzie, Eddie Myers and other members of his staff. He explained that, having studied the evacuation of Allied forces at Gallipoli as a young officer, he planned to follow a similar plan. In the course of the night the bulk of the division would be pulled back to the riverbank, following white tapes in the dark provided by the engineers. A rearguard would stay in place on the flanks until almost the very end to prevent the Germans from realizing what was afoot. While Urquhart based his plans on Gallipoli, Brigadier Hicks muttered about 'another Dunkirk'. He was not alone.

At 17.30 details of the evacuation plan were distributed to all officers.

The old British army rule of 'last in, last out' unfortunately meant that the Poles would form the main rearguard. A British major relayed the order to the commander of the 8th Company, Lieutenant Smaczny: 'The 8th Company is to stay in its positions and cover the evacuation. The company will be relieved at the right time. The order to leave positions will be delivered by a runner.' Smaczny suspected that the order would become a death sentence for him and his company.

For Polish paratroopers this was a particularly bitter moment. They had not been in Warsaw fighting alongside their compatriots. And with the Red Army at the gates of their capital, they had no idea whether they would ever be allowed home. Their dead in Oosterbeek were buried where they had fallen – usually in shell craters, trenches or foxholes. On their graves, their companions placed a helmet and erected a simple cross made of tree branches, marked with a dog-tag or sign bearing the rank, name, nationality and date of death. Having completed the burial, soldiers said a short prayer. 'Their eyes welled up with tears – tears of grief for the loss of the fallen, tears of grief for a failed hope.'

Even though the prospect of leaving the hell of Oosterbeek was a relief, the idea of crossing the river again under fire did not appeal to them. They felt they had been lucky to have got through the first time. 'To expect such a miracle to happen again is clearly an abuse of divine patience.' Orders came that they were to leave everything except their weapons. 'Haversacks are lined up neatly so the Germans cannot say that the Poles have fled in panic.'

The three journalists with the 1st Airborne, Stanley Maxted and Guy Byam of the BBC and Allan Wood of the *Daily Express*, were told that they could take a haversack each. Byam in his report recorded that 'Many were so tired that when they smiled, they smiled as if it hurt them to move their mouths.' Steel-studded army boots had to be wrapped in strips of blanket for silence. As the rain poured down, all welcomed it as it would help screen them from the enemy. 'We were never happier to see rain,' wrote Brigadier Hicks. Many took the opportunity to use their capes to catch the water to drink.

The Phantom signals detachment with divisional headquarters smashed their radio set and destroyed their one-time code-pads in a stove in the Hartenstein kitchen. Lieutenant Bruce Davis helped burn documents and used the ash to blacken his face. He then went out and sat in a slit trench to accustom his eyes to the dark. He took a last look at the surroundings. 'I have never seen such a scene of destruction.' The great beech trees around the Hartenstein had been smashed and shredded by mortar fire. 'The smell of gunpowder was still everywhere. The big four story house was a shambles. Part of the roof was blown in. There was no window left in the place – there hadn't been for days – the walls were blown in in several places and the dead were everywhere. We had not been able to bury the dead from the first.'

A gunner could not help noticing, as they left their wrecked house near the church at Oosterbeek, that the wooden-framed sampler saying 'Home Sweet Home' in English was still in place on the wall, after virtually everything else had been destroyed. 'When the order to pull out came,' a pathfinder sergeant recounted, 'I had a terrible fear for the Dutch in the cellars, especially the youngsters. We had weapons. They had nothing. We were leaving. They were staying.'

Headquarters personnel were divided into groups of ten and told that nobody was to open fire unless ordered by their leader. Just as they were about to set off, General Urquhart filled a cup with whisky and passed it round, as if in a farewell communion, and then the glider pilot chaplain led them in the Lord's Prayer.

Troops from the 43rd Division mounted a feint attack from the village of Heteren, four kilometres west of Driel, firing machine guns and mortars across the river to give the impression of an assault crossing there. Then, at 21.00, XXX Corps artillery opened a covering barrage, hitting targets all around the edge of the perimeter. 'The Second Army guns started in real earnest,' a pathfinder wrote. 'I've never heard such a noise, it beat anything Jerry has put over.' The Germans were convinced, as was the intention, that the weight of artillery must be supporting a crossing in strength: that the British were reinforcing the airborne division, not withdrawing it.

For civilians still in Oosterbeek, the bombardment was terrifying. People in cellars lay curled up underneath their mattresses. 'At the back of our house,' an anonymous diarist wrote, 'a great round hole appeared after a shell exploded. Windows and doors were splintered. Huge holes appeared in the ceiling. Cupboard doors were like a colander from the shrapnel; lamp shades, chair covers, everything was destroyed. Over the fireplace a portrait of [Queen] Juliana and [Prince] Bernhard with their children, looked at me as if this was a daily occurrence.'

Heavy rain and darkness made visibility so bad that some groups of para-troopers took three hours to reach the riverbank. Even the white tapes set up by the sappers were hard to see. Men were told to hold on to the bayonet scabbard or shirt-tail of the man in front to avoid becoming lost. When someone halted, everyone behind would bump into the back of the man in front. With their muffled boots and the urge for silence, they could hear the patter of rain on the leaves and, at odd moments close to the perimeter, German soldiers chatting in low voices. At every change of direction along the route stood a glider pilot sergeant to make sure everyone followed the right way. 'Every now and then a flare would go up on the flanks,' wrote Major Blackwood, 'and then long files of freezing exhausted men would be struck into immobility till the brilliant light died.'

Other units, including Poles, passed the Smaczny company's position and expressed surprise that they had not left. They had to explain the 8th Company's orders to form the rearguard. The Germans began to fire mortars, which they normally never did at night. Many feared that this signified that they had discovered what was afoot. Since almost everyone was in the open by then and not in slit trenches, casualties were inevitable. A private in the Border Regiment never forgot one of the victims. 'We passed along the road and there was a wounded fellow, and he was crying for his mother and everyone felt really sorry, but no one was in a position to help him.'

As Colonel Payton-Reid led the remnants of the King's Own Scottish Borderers down to the Neder Rijn, they passed the Hartenstein 'which now loomed ghostly and lifeless through the darkness'. Departing through such scenes of death put everyone in a sombre mood. More died on the way to the riverbank. Lieutenant Bruce Davis wrote in his report, 'We walked along a road and behind hedges until we reached an open field commanded by a German machine-gun. As we crawled, a very bright light went up, but they apparently did not see us. We moved on into woods again. We stopped to rest and as we squatted down, the man behind me pitched forward on his face. I thought he had seen something and hit the dirt. Then I rolled him over and saw that he was dead. He was the fourteenth man to be killed within a few feet of me, the others by mortar fire.'

On approaching the dyke in front of the riverbank, Myers's Royal Engineers made each group lie down to wait until beckoned forward. 'We settled down on the grass to wait our turn on the boats,' the pathfinder continued. 'By now it was raining fairly heavily, and the clouds were low, which I think was the only thing which kept us from being seen. Jerry was sending up lots of flares and occasional bursts of mortar fire on the banks of the river.' Others lay down flat in the mud. As Byam described it, 'Long lines of men hugged the ground so as to stand the best chance of not being hit by enemy mortar shells.'

Operation Berlin, although rapidly put together, was a greatly improved example of organization and execution. Lieutenant Colonel Mark Henniker, the Commander Royal Engineers of the 43rd Division, had the 20th and

23rd Canadian Field Companies in addition to his own men. The Canadians had twenty-one flat-bottomed wooden storm boats with Evinrude outboard motors while the British sappers had canvas assault boats. When the Canadian officers were summoned to a briefing that morning, Henniker had still been given no idea of the number of men to be brought off and it was not even certain where the embarkation point was to be. The 'orders were that we should continue until the beach was cleared'. They then found that they needed bridging equipment for crossing dykes and ditches.

Having surmounted all these problems, the first boat was launched at 21.20 but it had a major leak from a rip. The next boat set off, but was sunk by a direct hit from a mortar shell. Its crew was never seen again. The third boat was far more successful. Its crew would complete fifteen trips before they were relieved. The first boats reached the north bank at 21.40, and groups ran crouching down the bank and into the water to climb aboard. The rippling surface of the river was still lit by the flames from the blazing timber-yard. To their left and right, Bofors guns fired tracer at regular intervals marking the outside edges of the perimeter and the bank towards which the boats should steer. It was not easy with the strong current, and the heavy rain caused endless trouble to the outboard motors. They stalled frequently, which meant that boats were swept down river, and then had to fight their way back.

German machine guns firing attempted to sweep the river, but since they were sited on higher ground they did not have nearly the same effect as they would have done if firing on a horizontal plane. The voices of the Canadian sappers were found to be cheerful and encouraging, and they did much to soothe the fears of their passengers. Because of the rain one Canadian could not start the outboard motor. He told the last two soldiers to arrive to start paddling with their rifle butts. Seeing a soldier in front of him who was apparently uninjured, one of them asked why he was not helping. The man turned and said quite calmly, 'I've lost an arm.'

Many boats were hit by either mortar or machine-gun fire, so Corporal Korob and a fellow Polish paratrooper decided to swim. The two men found a large log and then, holding on for dear life, kicked away. Many others also set out to cross the Neder Rijn on their own. Most of those attempting to keep their personal weapon with them drowned as a result. Lewis Golden, a signals lieutenant, asked if any of his group wanted to join him swimming the river. Only Company Sergeant Major Clift and Golden's batman, Driver Hibbitt, responded. 'We stripped off our smocks, blouses, trousers and boots,' Golden wrote, 'but I for one kept my beret tightly on my head because it held in position my silver cigarette case which I was intent on saving. We threw our firearms into the river and swam off.' Hibbitt was not a strong swimmer. The other two tried to save him when he floundered, but lost him as he slipped from their grasp.

Three glider pilots, impatient with the long queues, found a small boat further down the riverbank. In it were the bodies of two young civilians who had been shot. They climbed in without removing the bodies and began to paddle with their rifle butts, but the boat began to sink. The two bodies floated to the surface beside them, and the three men abandoned ship rapidly. They swam back to the shore, where they joined a queue for the Canadian boats. Another group was more fortunate. They found an abandoned assault boat, which had been badly holed by machine-gun fire. After rounding up a couple of other officers and several men they set out. One group paddled hard, using their rifle butts, while the rest bailed as fast as they could, using their helmets. Every few minutes they swapped roles, until they reached the far shore completely exhausted.

Some men acted as helpers, standing in the water to load the walking wounded into the boats. When the boat left, they floated in the water holding on to its side and allowing themselves to be dragged across. But if the boat came under fire, they could let go and swim the rest of the way.

As the night drew on, hundreds of men still waiting to be evacuated became increasingly nervous. 'As dawn broke grey,' the 23rd Canadian Field Company reported, 'the trouble began. Each trip became more hazardous. Little fountains marked where the mortar bombs had struck the water, debris of boats and struggling men marked the hits.' The sapper boat crews did not falter, and kept going. But 'it was impossible to regulate the number of passengers carried in boats at times. Men panicked and stormed onto the boats, in some cases capsizing them. In many cases they had to be beaten off or threatened with shooting to avoid having the boats swamped . . . They were so afraid that daylight would force us to cease our ferrying before they were rescued.'

Sosabowski heard from his men how an officer shouted furiously at a mass of British troops fighting to get on a boat, 'Get back! Behave like Englishmen!' But Lance Corporal Harris from the 1st Parachute Battalion also witnessed a group of Poles rush a boat. 'They did not fancy being taken prisoner by the Germans, no doubt because of what happened in their own country to prisoners-of-war.' Harris himself threw his rifle in the river and stripped off his boots and battledress. Having placed his pay-book and lighter in his beret and jammed it on his head, he set off in just his underwear. Weak after so little food and rest, he feared that the strong current would carry him away, but he just managed to reach the other side.

Colonel Henniker ordered operations to cease at 05.45, 'when it became evident that any further attempts to bring off men would be suicidal for the boat crews'. But Lieutenant Russell Kennedy of the 23rd Canadian Field Company, carried on even after dawn. The artillery tried firing smoke shells, but in the damp conditions they achieved little. On his penultimate crossing, Kennedy took captured German lifebelts in case any straggler wanted to swim. 'He made two trips with these, leaving about a hundred for those who cared to use them. Each trip he brought back a boatload of men. In the first trip he had about five casualties. In the second hardly a man got out unhit, many were dead. It was a gallant effort, but he could not be allowed to try again.'

The rearguard, Smaczny's 8th Company and another group under Lieutenant Pudełko, had both waited all night for a runner to bring them the order to abandon positions as they had been promised. They waited in vain, not knowing whether the messenger had been killed or had lost his way in the dark, or perhaps the officer responsible had simply forgotten. Just before dawn, when there could be no doubt that his company had fulfilled its duty, Smaczny ordered his men to pull back. Pudełko did the same, but when both groups reached the river they found they were too late. There were hardly any boats to be seen, just many wounded lying on the mud flats. Pudełko was killed in the water. Most of the others were captured when the Germans moved in. Father Hubert Misiuda, the chaplain of the 3rd Battalion, had been carrying wounded to the boats, and he refused to abandon those left behind. 'Over the past three days, the chaplain had moved about the battle field, blessing, hearing confessions, dressing wounds, recording deaths, collecting dog-tags. Throughout those days and nights, when he himself was on the verge of a mental breakdown, he encouraged those who were losing spirit.' Misiuda was shot in the water as he helped others on to one of the last boats.

At 06.00, one of the Poles recorded, 'the last boat left keeps coming back. German rockets shine so brightly that they clearly illuminate not only us standing on the river bank, but also those on the other side, as they crawl to get over the dyke which now offers the only cover.' The regimental sergeant major of the Light Regiment, having seen his men away, decided it was time for him to depart. He stripped completely as he had seen three other men drown. When he reached Driel, he found Major J. E. F. Linton there 'in a lady's blouse and flannel trousers'. Local villagers and farmers, as soon as they had realized what was happening, had turned out with any spare clothes they had for the swimmers who arrived, shivering uncontrollably. Soldiers who had swum the river naked were embarrassed by their nakedness, but not the women who passed them items of clothing and clogs.

When Major Geoffrey Powell reached the southern shore he turned back to look at where they had come from. 'I stared at it for a few seconds and then, all at once, I realised I was across. It was a feeling of complete disbelief. I simply could not believe I had got out alive.' From the river, men followed a white guide tape over a muddy dyke. Although exhausted and shivering, one paratrooper with a fine voice began to sing the song 'When the Lights Go On Again'. More and more voices joined in until it seemed as if a couple of hundred were singing together.

The Germans, having finally woken up to the fact that the 1st Airborne was escaping, opened fire with some shells aimed at Driel. On the way to the village, Lieutenant Hay stopped to speak to a captain from the 43rd Division. 'My God!' he replied. 'Don't stand here. It's dangerous.' Hay could not help laughing, for it was the safest spot he had been in for more than a week. On reaching Driel, Major Cain was greeted by Brigadier Hicks, who walked over and looked closely at him. 'Well,' he said, 'here's one officer at least who's shaved.' Cain smiled. 'I was well brought up, sir.'

In the barn at Driel, the survivors were given a mug of hot tea laced with rum and a blanket to put round their shoulders. Some forty stretcher-equipped Jeeps were waiting for the wounded. The rest still had another long walk in front of them to get to the dressing station, from where trucks would collect them. Many were so tired that they fell asleep as they walked.

According to the First Allied Airborne Army, 1,741 men of 1st Airborne Division, 160 Polish paratroopers, 75 Dorsets and 422 glider pilots were evacuated that night. A few more escaped the following night. 'We came back 4 officers and 72 men,' wrote Colonel Payton-Reid, the commanding officer of the King's Own Scottish Borderers. This was almost exactly one-tenth of the battalion strength on the roll call after their landing nine days before.

In one of the groups left on the north bank a British officer, seeing that the situation was hopeless, told the men around him that they had no alternative but to surrender. He waved a white handkerchief, but the Germans opened fire in response, killing him on the spot.

As the Germans moved in on the survivors huddled on the muddy shore, a Polish soldier was appalled when he saw four British paratroopers stand up in a tight circle and link their arms together, then one of them pulled the pin from a grenade which he did not drop. 'There was an explosion and the four men fell.' Lieutenant Smaczny had no more than twenty men left in his company as they approached the riverbank. They suddenly heard shouts and bursts of firing in the air. Smaczny and his men found themselves rounded up along with a large group of British paratroopers. He ordered his men to throw down their weapons immediately. Fortunately, the Poles had their grey berets in their pockets, and not on their heads, so they were not immediately identifiable.

The German guards marched this large group of prisoners off together, but after a time they halted. A German SS officer shouted out that all Poles should step forward. Knowing the hatred the Germans, and especially the SS, felt for the Poles, a British officer passed Smaczny his red beret and shouted out in bad German: 'There are no Poles here.' Smaczny and his men feared that they would be ordered to take off their parachute smocks, which would reveal the Polish white-eagle patches on their uniforms underneath, but at that moment XXX Corps artillery fired another bombardment from south of the river, and their guards hurried them on.

A number of the prisoners rounded up on the north bank wondered afterwards whether they should have risked swimming across alone. It is hard to tell how many drowned that night. According to an account from Rhenen, twenty-five kilometres downstream, 'Dead English soldiers drifted down the Neder Rijn. The boys hauled them out of the water with boat-hooks, and pulled them on to the bank, where they were collected by the Red Cross to be buried in civilian cemeteries. It became a routine.'

25

Oosterbeek, Arnhem, Nijmegen
Tuesday 26 September

The guns had fallen silent. Windows which still had panes in them no longer rattled with the boom of artillery. 'There was something different,' the glider pilot padre remembered of that morning in the Hotel Schoonoord. 'I could not grasp it for a moment and then I realized. Everywhere was unnaturally quiet.' He joined the medical corps sergeant major who was staring out. That was when the Rev. Pare heard the news. The Second Army had not crossed to the north bank in the night, as they had believed from the heavy volume of XXX Corps artillery fire. Instead, the remains of the 1st Airborne Division had pulled back across the Neder Rijn. It was a bitter pill, as he acknowledged, but 'spirits began to rise – the battle was over and we were still alive. Dutch lads and girls were very unhappy. I believe their dismay was far greater than ours.'

This was a very dangerous time for all the Dutch who had helped the British. The Germans were determined to identify them. 'When we woke up the next morning, all was quiet,' wrote C. B. Labouchere. 'A quietness we had not experienced for nine days. Not a shot was heard.' The German authorities ordered the population of Oosterbeek to leave immediately. Along the road, the SS lined up the 150 German prisoners released from the tennis courts to look for any civilians they could identify from the Hartenstein. Knowing how recognizable he was from his height and clothes, Labouchere wondered how he would get past them without being spotted. 'I saw two old ladies, pushing a small cart loaded with luggage and blankets. I offered my help. With an old lady on each side of me, the blankets thrown over my shoulders, I bent over the cart I was pushing and did everything I could think of to look at least twice my age.' In this way Labouchere managed to return to his wife and daughter in Velp on the far side of Arnhem – no civilians were allowed through the town – and found their house already crowded with sixteen refugees from the fighting.

The few surviving crews in the Sturmgeschütz-Brigade were warming the engines of their self-propelled assault guns, ready to move out for the morning attack, when they caught sight of a column of British prisoners. They gazed in astonishment, hardly daring to believe that the battle was finally over. Ordered out of her home like everyone else, Kate ter Horst had to put her children and bags on a handcart and set off with a friend, not really knowing where to go. Some Dutch SS took great satisfaction in yelling at a group of women, 'You see. You celebrated too soon!' One of the women wrote philosophically, 'Just for a moment I look behind me, flames and smoke billow from the house. We feel separated from it. We still have our lives.'

Squads of SS had begun searching for concealed stragglers in the ruined houses. 'Every now and again,' wrote Colonel Warrack, 'there was an exchange of small arms fire in the distance as if someone resisted giving himself up.' A number of paratroopers had been so exhausted that they had slept right through the evacuation and now, suddenly wakened, they fought back. The majority, however, consisted of men who had not been removed to one of the dressing stations and were too badly wounded to be taken across the river.

Jan Eijkelhoff was with three wounded British soldiers in the cellar of a house when a German voice shouted from above. 'Is anyone here?'

'Yes,' the soldiers yelled back. Two German soldiers charged down the stairs. One of them began screaming, 'You are our prisoners! Hands up!' He had clearly worked himself up into a frenzy, because he started to insult them, saying they were mercenaries and anything else that came into his head. Eijkelhoff described how one of the wounded soldiers, listening to him impassively, pulled out a packet of cigarettes and offered him one. The German was so astonished, he stopped shouting and just stood there with his mouth half-open.

By mid-morning, the Germans had found 300 British soldiers in Oosterbeek, a number which had doubled by the afternoon. The wounded were carried out and dumped on the pavement for collection later. The beautiful village of Oosterbeek had been transformed by the fighting into a wilderness of broken trees and lampposts, smashed bricks from shellholes in the roads and overhead wires brought down. A whiff of cordite and burning lingered in the air. The only pleasant smell was the scent of resin, from fir trees blasted by shells. Oberstleutnant Fullriede of the *Hermann Göring* Division visited Oosterbeek that morning. 'German and English dead are lying around everywhere,' he wrote in his diary. 'The trees are festooned with coloured parachutes with which the English were trying to supply their troops. Two of our Panther tanks stand there with their burned crews inside.'

Those prisoners able to walk were rounded up. According to a sergeant in the 10th Parachute Battalion, German officers really did say to British prisoners 'For you the war is over.' One officer, with an amused air, studied a small, dishevelled man with a badly scratched face and wearing an unfamiliar dark-blue uniform. 'I don't want Frenchmen, only British,' he said in English.

'I ain't no bleeding froggie,' the man retorted. 'I'm in the Navy.'

'You will be telling me in a minute that you sailed up the Rhine in a submarine,' the officer replied. It turned out that this prisoner was a Fleet Air Arm fitter who had worked at the same aerodrome as one of the transport squadrons. He had been offered a ride to Arnhem on one of the aircraft, and had decided to go along and help push out the bundles. But the plane was hit and he had no option but to parachute along with the crew. His face was lacerated from landing in bushes.

The prisoners were marched to Arnhem under guard, unshaven, eyes red from lack of sleep, with dirty bandages round their injuries and filthy uniforms. They sang while marching, and grinned or made V for Victory signs whenever they saw German propaganda cameras or photographers. A middle-aged Dutch lady bicycled past one group on an old-fashioned upright machine singing 'God Save the King' at the top of her voice in English. This produced a rousing cheer. Some prisoners also sang the 'Internationale' or the 'Red Flag' to provoke their captors. The Germans were utterly bemused by the British compulsion to joke in adversity. A captured glider pilot, facing a panzergrenadier who was pointing a Mauser rifle at his chest, took a small mirror from his pocket to examine his growth of beard. With a straight face, he asked his captor whether there was a dance in town that night.

A number of prisoners were picked out for interrogation. German intelligence officers would pretend to fill in Red Cross forms to obtain their home address and next-of-kin details, but would also slip in a question of military importance for the unwary. Exhausted men were not on their guard and keen to let their families know they were alive, so they often let slip much more information than just their name, rank and number.

Colonel Warrack warned his remaining doctors that the Germans intended to move all the wounded to the barracks in Apeldoorn. In what was left of the Schoonoord, 'Major Frazer started a plaster clinic to immobilise as many fractures as he could for the journey – he worked at this all day and undoubtedly saved many bones and limbs.' Warrack was surprised and relieved by the help of Stabsarzt Skalka and the other German doctors. 'The attitude of the Germans all through was one of respect,' he wrote in his report, 'and they were invariably correct in the way they treated us.'

*

Model had no idea of the night's events when he visited Bittrich's command post on the northern edge of Arnhem early that morning. 'Bittrich, when will things finally be over here?' he demanded. Bittrich had also not yet heard the news. He claimed later that he had hardly washed or shaved during the battle, and had slept in a chair or sitting in his staff car. 'Herr Generalfeldmarschall,' he replied, 'yesterday and the day before we fought as we have never fought before. We threw everything we had in against them.' At that moment a despatch rider arrived on a motorcycle and sidecar with the news that the British had ceased fighting.

'Well, thank God!' Model exclaimed. Bittrich was finally able to send off the signal, 'North bank of the Neder Rijn west of Arnhem clear of enemy.' He could now concentrate his forces south of the Rhine in the Betuwe, but first he obtained Model's permission to decorate Knaust and Harzer with the Knight's Cross. He also made a tally of their losses. Out of 3,300 casualties, 1,100 were dead. British losses, they estimated, came to 1,500 dead and 6,458 prisoners including 1,700 wounded, a figure which was increased to 1,880 three days later.

German satisfaction at their victory was great. 'The SS has once again proved itself in an outstanding way and had the decisive share in the destruction of the English 1st Parachute Division,' a Luftwaffe officer wrote in a letter. One of Krafft's men, Sturmmann Bangard, declared, 'The victory at Arnhem again proved to our enemies that Germany too is still in a position to strike a decisive blow.' A member of the *Hohenstaufen* in Velp boasted to a Dutch audience, 'We'll be back in Paris by Christmas!' And the officer in charge of the Oberkommando der Wehrmacht's war diary claimed that the Allies had intended to achieve the equivalent of Germany's decisive defeat of the Netherlands in May 1940, but 'the greater fighting spirit was, and remained, on the German side.'

Model and Bittrich did not allow themselves the luxury of celebration or complacency. Army Group B allocated the 363rd Volksgrenadier-Division for deployment on the north bank of the Neder Rijn, while more scratch units were assembled to prepare 'for renewed airborne landings'. Model also ordered the 9th Panzer-Division and part of the 116th Panzer-Division to be ready to move immediately. They would be used for the counter-attack demanded by Führer headquarters to sweep the Allies from the Betuwe.

General Boy Browning's failure to go to Driel during Operation Berlin did not endear him to the officers of the 1st Airborne Division. His only gesture was to send his Jeep to bring Major General Urquhart back to his headquarters in Nijmegen. Urquhart arrived in the early hours, still drenched, unshaven and filthy, and then had to wait for Browning. 'When he did appear,' Urquhart wrote, 'he was as usual immaculately turned out. He looked as if he had just come off parade instead of from his bed in the middle of a battle. I tried to display some briskness as I reported: "The division is nearly out now. I'm sorry we haven't been able to do what we set out to do." ' Browning offered him a drink. 'You did all you could,' he said. 'Now you had better get some rest.' Urquhart described it as a 'totally inadequate meeting'.

Later in the day, Charles Mackenzie with a fellow officer trudged wearily along the road from Driel towards the Jeeps and trucks which would take them to Nijmegen. 'We hardly spoke,' he recounted. 'There wasn't much we could say.'

No transport had been provided for the Polish paratroopers. They had to march all the way back to Nijmegen. With 1,283 officers and soldiers left out of total of 1,625, Sosabowski had asked Browning if they could be allowed trucks too, but Browning gave an angry refusal and later accused Sosabowski of distracting him with trivial details at an important moment. Browning also appears to have started a story that Sosabowski had held back his battalions on the night of 24–25 September and let the Dorsets cross instead. In fact Major General Thomas had ordered Sosabowski at 21.45 hours to hand his boats over to the Dorsets.

Captain Robert Franco, the surgeon in the 82nd Airborne, happened to see survivors of the 1st Airborne as they reached Nijmegen. 'One look at them told the story,' he said. The American lieutenant Paul Johnson had been there when the first survivors began to arrive in the early hours. 'First they were given a shot of rum then some hot food and tea and after eating they went to a long table of clerks, gave their name, rank and organization and were assigned a bed for the night and as much of the morrow as they wanted. What a crew they were: dirty, wet, unshaven and haggard yes, but not cowed nor defeated. Their spirit was wonderful, as was their discipline. Even those who had lost all their clothes in the river did not try to hurry past the others and get quickly into a warm bed.'

Johnson, whose American team of ten had been attached to the 1st Airborne to ensure air–ground communications with fighters and fighter-bombers, had a meeting in Nijmegen the next day with the Second Army staff officer responsible for air support. 'He was very surprised when we told him about our VHF difficulties . . . It looks as though the planes never were on our frequencies at all.'

That evening, General Browning insisted on giving a party to celebrate their return and Brigadier Hicks's forty-ninth birthday the day before.

Neither Urquhart nor Hicks had 'much taste' for champagne in the circumstances. 'It was an ordeal even to have to face such food, let alone consume it,' Urquhart wrote. Browning had also invited Horrocks. Urquhart longed to ask him what had taken XXX Corps so long, but he found that Horrocks had his own hypnotic technique. 'It was his habit to work on anyone with his hands, his eyes and his voice, and in the process he tended to get closer and closer to his victim.' On that particular evening, Urquhart 'found his hypnosis far from soothing', and he never managed to ask why the advance up the Club Route had been so slow.

The survivors from the division were billeted in three red-brick school buildings in Nijmegen. Many tried to make the best of the food, hot tea and beds on offer. Some slept for forty-eight hours. Other were in a form of shock from their losses. 'Someone walked around asking "Where's the 1st Battalion?" and a corporal, with tears in his eyes, answering "This is it." Near him stood a handful of bedraggled men.' So few men appeared from the Light Regiment that Gunner Christie also 'felt like crying'. Hackett's 4th Parachute Brigade was reduced to 9 officers and 260 soldiers from more than 2,000.

A corporal of horse in the Household Cavalry saw the paratroopers when they arrived. 'They looked like hell. Dirty and cut up and all of them needing a bath and shave and some sleep.' Some of them shouted angrily at members of the Guards Armoured Division, 'What, you've only just arrived?', 'Did you have a nice drive up?' or 'Where the hell have you been mate?'

One paratrooper shouted to an Irish guardsman, 'Having a good rest chum?' 'Glory be to God,' replied the Irishman, 'and haven't we been fighting since D-Day, not Friday!' The priority awarded to special forces and airborne was not popular in regular regiments. According to one Guards officer, their tank crews jeered the paratroopers, shouting, 'Some people have all the fucking luck – one battle and home to England.'

The antagonism did not entirely fade with the passage of time. In 1984, at the fortieth-anniversary commemoration of the battle in Arnhem, Colonel (by then Major General) John Frost shook his fist in the direction of Nijmegen from where the Guards Armoured Division was supposed to have come, and roared, 'Do you call that fighting?'

Operation Market had finished badly, and now Operation Garden was dragging on. German attacks on Hell's Highway round Veghel and Koevering were at their last gasp, mainly because of the advance of VIII Corps and XII Corps on either side. By the next day, men of the 327th Glider Infantry were able to take their first bath in Veghel. 'Give a soldier a letter, a plate of hot chow, a clean pair of socks and a dry blanket, and he thinks he's in heaven,' wrote the poet Louis Simpson with the 327th. 'Today I had a shower and lost my nice warm crust, also the barnyard smell which Elisabeth [sic] Arden will never capture in a bottle.'

The main active battlegrounds left in the last week of September were the Betuwe to the north of Nijmegen and the Groesbeek heights and Mook to the east and south-east. Mook by then was 'a town of broken glass, bricks and smouldering ruins'. The medical station of the 1st Battalion of the 325th Glider Infantry was in the ruins of a house. German dawn attacks came through 'low, dense fog' which could lift suddenly, but Gavin knew that he had to keep jabbing at the enemy too. He now had the division in full strength as well as British armour and artillery in support. Round Mook they also benefited from good intelligence provided by the local underground group, Den Bark. 'Beards were heavy and faces dirty,' a sergeant in 325th recounted, as they smoked a last cigarette before an advance. 'Several British tanks stood along the road with engines idling. A column of men silently moved along the hedgerow to the road and climbed on the backs.' Someone spotted the tall figure of Gavin with his rifle, and the murmur was passed on, 'General Jim's here.'

Further north, the 82nd faced a German build-up of forces in the Reichswald, but having finally cleared the area between Beek and Groesbeek, and secured Den Heuvel or Devil's Hill, they were in a much stronger position. It had been a bitter fight, with no opportunity to move the wounded. A sergeant claimed that 'on taking Devil's Hill, I had five men with stomach wounds that sat up propped against trees. They took twelve to fifteen hours to die and I didn't hear a whimper or sound out of any of them.'

Following Gavin's insistence on offensive night patrols, a sergeant of the 504th took his squad to check out a farmhouse in the Den Heuvel woods. 'A German officer came out of the door spouting a lot of furious German words at us. We took him prisoner. Upon interrogation at headquarters we found that he was a company commander and he had assumed us to be replacements sent to his company who were making too much noise.' A paratrooper in the 505th received a different sort of surprise. Fast asleep in his foxhole, he awoke with a terrified start to find a huge German towering over him. He wondered if he could grab his rifle before the man killed him, but in fact the German was trying to push a piece of paper into his hands. Printed on both sides in German and English, it promised safe conduct to any German who surrendered.

Few of the German reinforcements possessed maps or had any idea where they were. A paratrooper in the 505th described how he watched three of them walk down the road straight into his platoon's position. 'They were challenged and made the mistake of attempting to fire their weapons. They were shot down – two wounded and one dead. The wounded were taken care of by our medics.' Soon afterwards a Dutchman and his wife from a nearby farm appeared with a wheelbarrow, recovered the dead German and buried him in a field behind their barn.

Meindl's II Fallschirmjäger Corps had also been reinforced with artillery. As British Lancasters flew over to bomb Cleve on a rare daylight raid, German gunners fired coloured smoke shells on to American positions hoping that the formation overhead would drop its bombs there. In such wooded terrain, spotting for gun and mortar batteries was a problem. On one sector a lieutenant recorded that the Germans 'were using a large high smoke stack as [an observation post] for days. It was dumb of us not realising where all the screaming meemies [Nebelwerfer rockets] were coming from and direct hits too. We finally got a tank to blow it down. What a sight to see those Krauts fly a hundred feet with no chute!' The Sherwood Rangers proved their worth again two days later, when the Germans launched a strong counter-attack with tanks towards Berg en Dal. C Squadron managed to destroy four tanks. One was a Panther which tried to escape by reversing into a house, but the gunner in the Sherman 'kept pumping shells into it and the house collapsed in flames around the tank'.

Gavin's men had to endure some heavy barrages, which triggered the odd case of nervous collapse. During one particularly intense bout of shelling a young paratrooper kept saying over and over again: 'What are they trying to do to us? Kill us?' Unable to stand it, he shot himself in the foot to ensure he was invalided out. In a striking contrast, another boy in the 505th, who had received a 'Dear John' letter, 'proceeded to commit suicide by volunteering for every hazardous detail until a sniper got him'.

Wounded American paratroopers were still being taken back to the Baby Factory in Nijmegen for treatment, and their longing for souvenirs had not abated. One day an SS trooper taken in the Betuwe was brought in on a stretcher. 'He was calm,' a patient from the 508th observed, 'until a lanky, unshaven paratrooper came over and started to pace around the stretcher.' The SS man was uneasy to begin with, but when the paratrooper reached down to his boot and pulled out his knife, the German really started to shake with fear. 'The paratrooper reached over with his knife and neatly cut off the Jerry's Waffen-SS [cuff]band as a souvenir.' Paratroopers and glider infantry alike seized on items to send home, both German and typically Dutch. Wooden clogs were particularly popular, but how the army post office coped is not recorded.

For the citizens of Nijmegen who had remained, little seemed to have changed. 'We are still being shelled by the Germans on a daily basis,' wrote Martijn Louis Deinum. 'Great English activity in the skies and then the moment they go, German planes come to shoot at the city. We are getting less frightened as we are getting used to all the noise, but we are looking awful and have lost a lot of weight.' Deinum spoke too soon. 'In the evening we had a very heavy German bombardment. It was terrible . . . One feels so vulnerable. Then the noise of low-flying aircraft. The tension rises, no one says a word, an explosion and the blast. We hear glass smashing and rubble falling.' On the order of Führer headquarters, the Luftwaffe was targeting the Nijmegen bridge with every available bomber. Hitler was so preoccupied with the matter that Generalfeldmarschall von Rundstedt's headquarters had to ring immediately after the attack to see whether it had been successful. Next evening, Rundstedt's chief of staff rang Model's headquarters to ask 'whether the Nijmegen bridge could be blown up by army pioneers', but the chief operations officer replied that so much explosive was needed that it could not be achieved with small boats. The Luftwaffe also attempted a 'piggyback' attack, when one aircraft carried another aircraft packed with explosives and then released it at the last moment at the target, but they never hit it.

Soon after nightfall, the last of the British wounded from Oosterbeek had been transferred to the barracks in Apeldoorn, a town which XXX Corps should have captured two days before according to the Market Garden timetable. They were accompanied by the remaining medical personnel and six Dutch nurses, including Hendrika van der Vlist. A number of wounded remained in the St Elisabeth Hospital, including Brigadiers Lathbury and Hackett and Major Digby Tatham-Warter, all of whom were later smuggled out by Piet Kruijff and his colleagues in the underground before the Germans had worked out who they were.

Colonel Warrack had already met the senior German medical officer in Apeldoorn, Oberstleutnant Zingerlin, whom he considered 'a very reasonable, efficient man'. Zingerlin was responsible for some 2,000 German casualties, many of whom were in Queen Wilhelmina's palace of Het Loo, which the Wehrmacht had taken over as a military hospital. Together they had chosen the barracks for the British wounded, and Royal Army Medical Corps personnel cleaned it out and laid straw in time for the first arrivals. Soon after it had filled with patients from Oosterbeek, the SS turned up, suspicious of this British hospital in their midst, and carried out a thorough search.

Still hoping that the Second Army would break across the Rhine, Warrack tried every trick he could think of to keep the wounded in Holland. He insisted that they could be evacuated to Germany only by proper hospital train, even when the Germans were sending back their own wounded in cattle trucks. He also asked that Generalfeldmarschall Model should give permission for drops of Allied medical supplies, as his teams had virtually nothing left and the Germans could supply only paper bandages. Three surgical teams from Amsterdam promised to help with blankets and stores. They even arranged the transfer of some complicated cases to Dutch hospitals, one of which was St Joseph's in Apeldoorn.

The mortally wounded sometimes took a long time to die. In St Joseph's, a boy from Carlisle in Cumberland screamed so loudly when orderlies tried to lift him to take him for an X-ray that they had to leave him. His deterioration was sudden and rapid. A German nurse later told Private Andrew Milbourne that the boy was dying. That night, while some were chatting in the ward, they heard him, 'in a hoarse, croaking voice try to sing the first few bars of "God Save the King". A deathly hush fell over the ward.' Listening to the boy, cold shivers ran up and down Milbourne's spine as he instinctively tried to lie to attention in his bed. Everyone remained silent. Nurses moved the dying boy into a side-ward. Milbourne got up and followed him there. He was still trying to sing the national anthem. Half an hour later he was dead.

26

The Evacuation and Looting of Arnhem
23 September to November 1944

Generalfeldmarschall Model had not waited until the end of the battle in Oosterbeek to deal with the population of Arnhem, just three kilometres to the east. On Saturday 23 September, Anna van Leeuwen wrote in her diary, 'Panic rumours – the whole of Arnhem has to be evacuated.'

Stories spread about the summary executions carried out on those inhabitants who had sheltered or cared for British wounded during the battle. One anonymous diarist wrote that 'three families including their children were shot'. Another wrote, 'Our houses were full of English soldiers. When the German soldiers found them, ten people including Dr van Zwol and Mr Engelsman from the furniture shop, were put against the wall and shot.' They also heard of German soldiers clearing the areas of the town which had been fought over. 'Grenades were thrown into the cellars and no attention was paid to the cries of inhabitants in those cellars. There were many civilian victims as a result.' Recent research has shown that 188 civilians were killed just in the city of Arnhem during the battle, of whom some forty are thought to have been summarily executed by the Germans. The stresses of the evacuation, Allied shelling and air activity and other factors raised the civilian death toll by another 2,000.

The Germans gave the impression that the evacuation of the city had been ordered by the municipal authorities headed by members of the NSB. In fact the order had been given to the burgemeester by Obersturmführer Helmut Peter, the commander of the SS *Hohenstaufen* Feldgendarmerie company. He even made a barely veiled threat that if the evacuation was not carried out, then 'carpet bombings must be taken into account.'

The divisional commander Standartenführer Harzer later insisted that he had received the order from Generalfeldmarschall Model in person. He claimed that the intention had been to evacuate Arnhem and the surrounding area 'in order to avoid further heavy losses among the civil population through carpet bombing, artillery fire and street fighting'. This meant that approximately 150,000 people were to be ejected from their homes. He recounted that the 'Oberbürgermeister' came to his command post soon afterwards, and 'We agreed how the evacuation of the population of Arnhem could and must proceed in the most humane possible way.' Such humanitarian concerns were hardly credible. The decision was made two days after the end of fighting in the city, and the real reasons became cruelly apparent in a very short space of time. Harzer, in a letter of 23 September addressed to Seyss-Inquart's Kommissariat in den Niederlanden, claimed that he had ordered the evacuation to be carried out over three days 'on military grounds'. In a bid to escape further responsibility for what followed, Harzer asserted after the war that he was no longer in charge of Arnhem after 28 September.

It was terrifying news, and not just for the old and infirm. A number of German deserters hiding in the town knew that the Waffen-SS preferred to beat deserters to death rather than shoot them, because they did not deserve a bullet. Jews who had been divers concealed by friendly townsfolk were equally horrified, as were scores of British soldiers, cut off during the battle and hidden by civilians. They could not be left behind without food or knowledge of the language, so families took them along disguised in civilian clothes, although their army boots often betrayed them, because nobody had shoes to spare. Some civilians were tricked by SS men dressed in British uniforms asking for help so that under interrogation they could be forced to reveal where other paratroopers might be hidden. When groups of British prisoners captured at Oosterbeek were marched through the town to the railway station for shipment to camps in Germany, Dutch civilians cheered or made gestures of solidarity, despite being warned that they would be shot if they even looked at them.

It soon became clear that the evacuation was part of '*Vergeltungsmassnahmen gegen die Zivilbevölkerung*' – 'Retaliatory measures against the civil population'. The burgemeester's deputy announced that 'Everyone will have to try to make their getaway themselves. There are no means of transportation. Hospital patients are to be carried on flat, horse-drawn wagons to Otterloo.' The claim that there were 'no means of transportation' was rather undermined by the number of Germans driving wildly all over the place in captured Jeeps with black crosses painted over the Pegasus symbol. Some of them appear to have been drunk. Albert Horstman with the LKP underground saw a Jeep with two German soldiers in it, one dressed as a bride and the other as a bridegroom, having looted shop windows.

The process of evacuation would start with Arnhem town centre. Anyone who tried to stay behind risked execution. It seemed ironic that on the morning of the order to evacuate, the water supply was finally restored in Arnhem. Much of the centre was still burning or smouldering. The SS blamed the fires on the 'vandalism of the British', yet they would not allow the Dutch to put them out. (The volunteer firemen who at great risk tried to limit the damage were most unfairly and illogically accused of collaboration at the end of the war.) Those from the town centre, who had slept fully clothed every night during the fighting to be ready to flee in case their house caught fire, felt bitterly aggrieved at having to leave just as the worst dangers were over.

A woman on the eastern edge of Arnhem wrote that day, 'Those from the centre are coming to seek shelter in the suburbs. In the afternoon the rumour goes that before the night is over the whole city has to be evacuated and that the inhabitants will have to walk to Zutphen or Apeldoorn. At 17.00 posters go up saying that the whole centre of the city must be cleared by eight o'clock. There was a stream of thousands of people with all types of transport. It was a sad sight. They all came to Velp. How they all found a place to stay is a mystery. They cannot fit any more in Molenbeke. Twenty in a house is normal. A woman came who had only just had a baby the night before, pushing it in a handcart.' The road to Velp was littered with burned-out military vehicles from the fighting.

The next day, Sunday 24 September, the same woman wrote: 'At four in the morning more people were herded out of the city . . . At eleven an order came that the whole city has to be evacuated and the road to Apeldoorn is still open.' The orders were posted on trees and buildings. Some compared it to 'a Biblical Exodus', with thick, dark smoke over the city and charred paper and soot gently raining down 'like black snow'. The Germans had been torching more houses 'as a reprisal for so-called collaboration'.

A telephone engineer called Nicholas de Bode described the scene: 'An old lady walking through the town with a birdcage and a bird in it in one hand and carrying a family photo album covered in red velvet, and a cushion under her other arm.' He asked her why she took those things and not food or clothing for the winter. She replied that the bird was the only living thing she had. If she lost her album then she lost her family, and she would not be able to sleep unless she had her favourite cushion. Another old woman was being pushed along in a household chair with wheels attached to its legs. 'There were not dozens of them or hundreds, there were thousands and thousands and they did not know where to go.' He believed that they were not weeping, but 'stunned, sick in their hearts'.

Anna van Leeuwen saw in the long columns of refugees patients from the mental institution at Wolfheze. 'Many have to walk, which is very sad, the sick ones are transported on flat carts. The heavily disturbed were tied together with ropes in case they ran off.' Albert Horstman spotted 'a woman, dressed in a fine fur coat and wearing high heels, walking on the road to Ede, crying her heart out'. He also witnessed 'an old man with a grey beard suddenly dropping dead beside the road, and the panic and the sorrow this caused among his children and grandchildren who were with him'.

To identify themselves as non-combatants, adults wore a white armband or carried a white flag, often just a pillowcase attached to a broomstick. Children trudged along in the rain beside their parents. Copying their parents, they tied a handkerchief to a stick. The Voskuil family were forced to leave Oosterbeek on 26 September, with mevrouw Voskuil on a handcart because she had been badly hurt by a grenade. As the British wounded were taken out of their house, an SS man gestured to the destruction all around, with tram-wires down, branches and felled trees everywhere, 'Well, you see the result of being friends with the British.' At one moment a mother saw her little son staring at a corpse which had been blown in two. She was terrified that he would be traumatized by the sight, but he turned to her, pointed down and said, 'Look, Mummy, half a man.' He then stepped over the corpse and walked on with his stick and handkerchief over his shoulder.

Many carried their possessions bundled up in a knotted white sheet slung over their backs. Babies were carried because their perambulators were needed for supplies such as a sack of potatoes. Dogs often sat in a box on the back of bicycles, which were wheeled along, not ridden. The more fortunate with handcarts brought rabbits and chickens in wicker cages, sometimes even a goat tied on behind. In northern Arnhem they passed the cemetery which was in a terrible state, with headstones overturned and bones scattered around by shellfire ripping up the graves.

'A big problem for the fleeing people of Arnhem was their domestic animals,' the zoo-keeper Anton van Hooff pointed out. 'They mostly took them along until they were outside the city and then turned them loose. If the animals were able to follow them, they were allowed to do so. In all other cases they just had to remain behind. At about eleven this morning some people came along with a small dog which was almost exhausted. Just in front of the zoo they asked a German soldier whether he would shoot the little animal. The soldier tied the dog to a tree and then started shooting at it, but only managed to wound it in the leg.' Finally, Anton van Hooff's father insisted on taking it and bandaged up the wounded leg.

Not everyone behaved according to stereotype. One mother had taken her small son as far as she could go before dropping exhausted by the side of the road. 'All of a sudden,' her son recounted years later, 'a luxurious car stopped and a German officer, saluting, asked if we wanted a ride. I piped up: "Yes, please." ' He drove them on to the next town. Most Germans, however, showed little sympathy. 'Two soldiers from the *Hermann Göring* Division started to laugh when they saw our poor little caravan and called out: "Ha ha! And you were so happy when the English came." '

Nobody knew how such multitudes would be able to feed themselves on their seemingly endless march to find accommodation. Ration coupons were worthless when all the villages around had run out of food. Nobody could move west or south because of the fighting in Oosterbeek and in the Betuwe, so more than 35,000 people flocked to Velp just to the east. 'The rest have trudged on to other places. The Germans are taking all men between twenty and sixty to bury the dead . . . A few brave people want to go back to Arnhem to see if their house is all right, but they are seized by Germans and forced to bury bodies.' German pickets also halted the refugee columns, to seize any able-bodied men for forced labour on defences on the line of the River IJssel. Supervised by the Organisation Todt, they had to work until they collapsed from exhaustion or disease. They were then discharged, without food or means of transport.

By Thursday more than 50,000 people had crammed into Velp. Orders then came that the whole of the north bank of the Neder Rijn was to be evacuated, which raised the estimated total to 200,000 refugees. Yet villages and towns inland were already overcrowded because the Germans had forcibly evacuated the population along the North Sea coast.

Some stayed behind in Arnhem, ignoring the order to leave. Gerhardus Gysbers, an antiquarian bookseller, remained even though his shop was ruined, with the windows smashed and his books scattered in the street outside. On the other hand, his father's house by the school opposite the Willemskazerne was almost untouched. 'Everything was as they had left it on the afternoon of 17 September,' he wrote. 'Meat was still on their plates and their knives and forks still lay across their plates. Only one thing had been added. A large, very dead, black cat was stretched out full length across the table.' Whether or not the death or departure of cats had made a difference, an old force swelled to fill the vacuum. 'Everywhere you looked you saw rats,' he added. A fellow citizen who returned secretly to Arnhem came across a macabre German joke. Eleven shop-window mannequins had been hanged from trees. It rapidly became clear that as well as punishing the population for aiding the Allies, the true purpose of forcing the

Dutch from their homes north of the Neder Rijn was to loot the whole area unobserved.

Even in the first week after the airborne invasion, the Dutch in the region had also suffered from American and British looting. 'Some of them are great people,' Martijn Louis Deinum wrote of the American paratroopers in Nijmegen, 'but it's a great shame there is so much rabble amongst them, as they steal everything.' Even officers joined in, believing they deserved it after risking their lives for the Dutch. One group from the 508th in Nijmegen decided that they wanted a drink. But they had trouble getting the stopper out of the barrel, 'so Lieutenant Lamb told everyone to stand back and fired two shots from his Colt .45 and everyone crowded round with their canteen cups as the beer spewed from the holes.'

Others were interested in more durable and valuable items. 'Some of the soldiers had heard that Holland is the land of diamonds,' wrote one of Brigadier General McAuliffe's staff officers. 'They had visions of going back to the States with pockets full of sparklers. With the use of bazookas, many large iron safes in Holland got the treatment.' A corporal in the 101st also recounted how 'some of our troopers used a bazooka to open a bank vault and "liberated" a substantial amount of Dutch money. General Taylor did visit our battalion to inform us that this was not proper behaviour with regard to our allies.' At the end of the war the Allies had to make a joint settlement of £220,000 (£9 million in today's money) to the Dutch authorities for looting just in the area of Nijmegen.

The British military authorities put up placards in English ordering troops to stop looting empty houses as the population had suffered enough, yet all too many soldiers could not resist the easy pickings of war. A private of the 3rd Parachute Battalion at the Arnhem road bridge was quite frank on the subject. 'It was against all regulations, but everybody did it,' he said later. 'The lads had piled up some nice treasures. I got four drawers full of beautiful cutlery that must have been worth a £100 or more. My sister was getting married and I thought it would make a wonderful wedding present.' Even without the prospect of prison camp, he had no idea how he would take it home. All too often soldiers plundered, then dumped their swag later.

During the battle there had even been some looting by Dutch civilians with the argument that if they did not take it, then the Germans would. In Arnhem, Dutch housewives seized all the linen from the Hotel De Zon.

But these comparatively isolated acts were dwarfed when the Germans started to vent their rage on the local population for having supported the British.

Reichskommissar Seyss-Inquart had made a declaration that all of Arnhem was forfeit, based on Reichsmarschall Göring's decree of 14 August 1943. 'In consequence of the enemy's terror attacks on the civil population in Reich territory, the Führer has made the following decision: In future enemy public and private property in the occupied territories is to be ruthlessly drawn upon for the replacement of property such as house furnishings, furniture, domestic utensils, linen, clothing etc. destroyed by enemy terror attacks.' Another document from Göring addressed to the occupation authorities in the Netherlands claimed to justify German harshness: 'The attitude of the Dutch population in connection with this [the Allied bombing of Germany] is especially striking in a way unknown in any other occupied territory, in that it shows its malicious joy at the results of the terror attacks on Reich territory in a spiteful and unconcealed fashion.'

Even hospitals and nursing homes were looted. At Diaconessenhuis the NSB deputy burgemeester Arjen Schermer found four officers, headed by an Oberstleutnant, representing the Wirtschaftskommando for economic warfare, 'whose task it is to send part of everything that has been left behind in Arnhem in the way of serviceable goods to Germany, and place [the other] part at the disposal of Reichskommissar Seyss-Inquart'. Schermer tried to mitigate this order by seeking permission to take items useful for the refugees, such as blankets and food, and hand them over to the Red Cross. On one of the last days before the St Elisabeth Hospital was evacuated, German soldiers came to steal all the bandages, Sister Christina van Dijk recounted. 'We had to laugh as they had taken boxes and boxes of sanitary towels.'

Looting was in theory methodical. The Germans used long metal rods to probe gardens for any silver and other valuables buried there. Recent brick and paintwork was knocked out or ripped apart to search for paintings concealed in false walls. Safe deposit boxes were no protection, and Arnhem was a very rich area. So-called Räumungskommandos – or 'eviction task forces' – led by local Nazi Party officials or members of Organisation Todt were brought in, then German bureaucracy had to list everything that was taken once factories, shops and houses had been cleared (and before they were set on fire to conceal what had been done).

Yet Nazi methods seldom worked as they were supposed to. State plunder became personal opportunity, as revealed in a letter from a member of a Räumungskommando from Westphalia, supposedly collecting furniture for bombed-out families in Essen and Düsseldorf: 'My dear Emmy, I send you all best greetings from Arnhem. The fur coat you will get via the fastest means possible. I have now been able to fulfil your dearest wish. But there are many more things to come. You will be amazed. I have found one large wireless, six small radios, underwear for you and Ingrid. For you a hair-dressing cape and a dressing gown. The most wonderful bed and damask table cloth, an electric iron, and an electric kettle. Also, to put it briefly, here everything is for the taking, what one can only dream about. Tinned meats and butter. So dear Emmy, you can see that we are living in para-dise. We have such wonderful beds here, such as simply do not exist in Germany.' With Christmas coming in the near future, Wehrmacht officers, NCOs and Organisation Todt men all found presents for their families to send home.

Some freebooters from the Nazi Party clearly had even greater ambi-tions, as a letter from Reichsführer-SS Heinrich Himmler to Reichsleiter Martin Bormann indicated. Nazi Party Gauleiters had been told that their 'salvage commandos' were not allowed to take valuable paintings. 'Temmler, the leader of the Gaukommando from Düsseldorf, had already in the course of several weeks in Arnhem been attempting to open the safes in the branches of the major banks. He was forbidden to do this by the Reichs-kommissar [Seyss-Inquart]. He then approached Generalleutnant [Walter] Lackner, the commander of the [2nd] Fallschirmjäger-Division and asked him to put some welders at his disposal. The General refused on the grounds that his paratroopers were not safe-breakers.' The security police estab-lished that Temmler's Gaukommando, with six leaders and 300 men, had blown open the safes of the Amsterdamsche Bank, the Nederlandsche Bank and the Rotterdamsche Bank and had attempted to open the safe at a fourth bank. They got away with valuable paintings, precious metals and currency estimated to be worth many millions of Reichsmarks. 'One incomplete list runs to 34 artworks.'*

Temmler had set himself up in a house with some Dutch girls, who worked there, to whom he gave silver, textiles and food as presents. 'The walls of his bedroom were decorated with tasteless nude photographs and swastika emblems.' He lived a life of luxury, giving banquets, and acquired three grand pianos. Himmler was concerned that the prestige of the Nazi Party would suffer in the Netherlands with such shameless behaviour.

* In November 2017, one of these paintings stolen in Arnhem, a Dutch old master, *The Oyster Meal* by Jacob Ochtervelt, was finally returned to the daughter of its owner by the City of London Corporation after its provenance was confirmed.

'While the troops are fighting the bravest and toughest of battles, these young men were robbing in Arnhem with similar zeal.'

Attempts to preserve property were futile. Three days after the battle was over, Jonkheer Bonifacius de Jonge went to see the town commandant to try to obtain a signed protection order for his house, to preserve his wine cellar. He had no satisfaction, so he and his family packed everything they could fit in one car and departed. Dennennoord was looted the next day. The zoo in north Arnhem suffered in a different way. German soldiers came in and openly stole the animals' food, which they would then sell at inflated prices. Johannes van Hooff, the director of the zoo, put his passionate complaints to SS-Hauptsturmführer Dornstein. They were brushed aside with a bored '*Es ist Krieg*' – 'It's war.'

The Dutch were shocked not so much by the blatant robbery as by the senseless destruction and defilement. It suggested an incoherent rage against the world, *Germania contra mundum*. 'Around us,' wrote an eyewitness, 'there are endless groups of Moffen who enter deserted houses and take anything they want. Whatever they don't want – chairs, tables, wardrobes – they smash up with axes.' When German soldiers invaded the Hotel De Zon, they drank what they could from the wine cellar, then smashed the remaining bottles so that nobody else could enjoy them. 'Tubs of butter were smeared across the street. In the shops vats of syrup and flour were thrown over the floor. The "Herren" walked through the mess and then smeared it all over the furniture of the rooms. Shop windows were also systematically destroyed and the contents displayed taken. A tank drove into the V & D store and destroyed the interior.' The Nazis liked to imagine that they were far more civilized that the Soviets, yet their sack of Arnhem, in its viciousness and waste, was remarkably similar to the Red Army's looting of Germany in 1945.

27

The Island of Men
September to November 1944

The region of the Betuwe between the Waal and the Neder Rijn had become known as 'the Island of Men', because most of the women had been evacuated. The reclaimed polderland of orchards and marshy grazing existed above water only thanks to the surrounding dykes. In the words of an American paratrooper, 'the land was as flat as a pool table.' And however much they liked the local people, paratroopers did not like fighting there as the weather deteriorated. As soon as they dug a foxhole, water seeped in from the bottom and began rising.

Having done the job they came to do, American troopers felt they should not be kept there as ordinary infantry. So did their commanders, who were furious at the way Montgomery clung on to them. American generals suspected that Montgomery, who had always wanted command over US Army formations as well as British and Canadian, was exploiting the situation. 'One of the strange things about Market Garden', wrote Brigadier General Jim Gavin, 'is that for the first time in our history we had American divisions placed under the command of a foreign army.' An outraged General Brereton warned Eisenhower's headquarters that the two divisions had suffered a 35 per cent casualty rate. 'This totals 7,382 highly trained airborne troops which are irreplaceable . . . their continued use as ground troops will preclude their being used in airborne operations until late spring.'

The commander of XVIII Airborne Corps, Major General Ridgway, was probably the angriest of all. He found it 'hard to accept Monty's promise that he will have them out by November 1st'. Events proved him right. The 82nd Airborne did not leave until almost halfway through November and the 101st was not released until almost the end. Anti-Monty jibes grew in popularity. When King George VI visited American headquarters in Belgium and Luxembourg, he wore the uniform of a field marshal. 'This caused

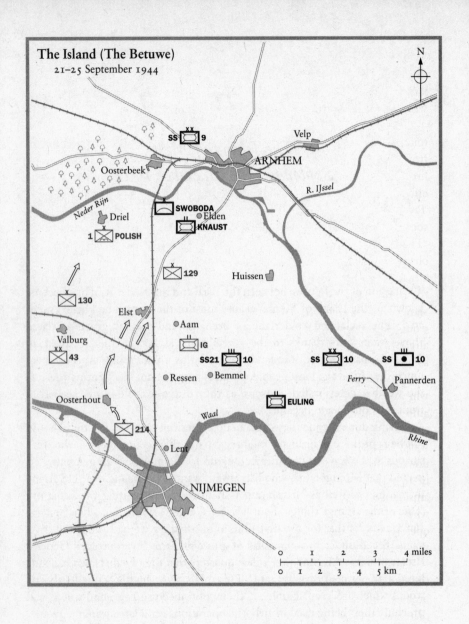

The Island (The Betuwe)
21–25 September 1944

N

SS 9

Velp

ARNHEM

Oosterbeek

R. IJssel

Neder Rijn   Driel

SWOBODA   Elden

1 POLISH   KNAUST

129   Huissen

130

Elst   Aam

Valburg   IG

43   SS21 10   SS 10   SS 10

Ressen   Bemmel   Ferry   Pannerden

Oosterhout   EULING

Waal   Rhine

214

Lent

NIJMEGEN

0   1   2   3   4 miles
0   1   2   3   4   5 km

the jokesters to ask if he outranked Monty.' American suspicions were largely justified, but the British Second Army, like the Canadian First Army, was also suffering from an acute manpower shortage.

General Maxwell Taylor had his own reason for disliking their extended tour of duty in the Betuwe. On a visit to the 3rd Battalion of the 501st in the front line near Heteren on the Neder Rijn, he ordered the mortar platoon to fire at a tree stump in the distance to demonstrate their accuracy and the effect. The paratroopers warned him that the Germans would retaliate. Taylor insisted, the Germans did react and everyone had to take cover. As soon as there was a lull, Taylor decided to leave, once more against advice. 'That is when he got his Purple Heart – shell fragment in his posterior,' observed an officer who had been present. 'We were caught in a mortar attack,' Taylor's bodyguard recorded. 'I turned and, seeing Taylor on the ground, ran back and picked him up. As I stumbled with him over my shoulder, with shells bursting all around us, I heard him mutter, "Dammit – wounded right in the ass!"' The general could no doubt imagine the jokes already. Taylor was not greatly liked by his men, and certainly not admired as much as Ridgway and Gavin.

When the 501st moved to Heteren, one company took over a brick factory which had housed a German field hospital. There were still body parts from amputations which had to be cleaned up. A hungry hog wandered in. One trooper who had worked in an abattoir volunteered to fell it, as they did not want to shoot with the Germans so close. He thwacked the hog which went down, but as the trooper took his bow, the hog jumped up again and ran out of the factory, with the trooper chasing him. The Germans watched in amazement at the sight, but did not fire. The hog returned to the factory, where somebody shot it with their .45 pistol. German artillery then did open fire. A number of paratroopers were not keen to eat the pork, when they thought about what it might have consumed.

The 508th Parachute Infantry Regiment from the 82nd Airborne also did time in the Betuwe with the British 50th Division. They were in an apple orchard, where at least the fruit was finally ripe which reduced the risk of diarrhoea. 'It was here in the ditch that I celebrated my twentieth birthday,' Dwayne Burns wrote. Their foxholes were 'just big mud puddles'. He received a handsome pen and pencil set as a present from home.

'Burns, if you get killed, can I have it?' First Sergeant Scanlon asked. 'Sure,' Burns replied, 'as long as you aren't the one pulling the trigger.'

The only form of entertainment on offer was watching dogfights in the sky, for there was considerable air activity along the Neder Rijn. On 28 September, the fighter pilot Leutnant Hans-Dietrich Student, son of

Generaloberst Student, had been shot down and killed over Arnhem. Burns was watching two P-51 Mustangs. 'Boy, that is the life,' Burns remarked. 'Go out for a little flying. Shoot up a few Germans, then go home, have a nice dinner with your girlfriend and have a good warm bed to sleep in at night. Boy, what a hell of a way to fight a war! Bet he does not even know that we are sitting down here in the mud in the same clothes that we jumped in over a month ago.' But one of the planes was then hit by flak and exploded into the ground. The paratroopers were suddenly convinced that it was better to be 'down on the ground where it's safe'.

Both the 82nd and the 101st carried out night patrols along the Neder Rijn bank at night, because the Germans often sent raiding parties over in rubber dinghies. One night a patrol from Easy Company in the 506th bumped into a group of Germans. Both sides threw grenades at each other to little effect. The lieutenant commanding the Americans shouted, 'Fix bayonets!', but he was the only person to have brought one with him. 'No one in their right mind would carry one of those rattling things on a night patrol,' observed one of his paratroopers, Earl McClung. He and his buddies used them only for digging foxholes. The lieutenant fixed his on his carbine, jumped up and ran a few paces before enemy fire forced him to throw himself flat. He was furious to find nobody had followed him. McClung answered anonymously in the dark: 'Lieutenant, you are the only one with a bayonet, so you go ahead and we'll give you all the fire cover we can.' This provoked 'a few giggles up and down the line'.

Further west at Opheusden a German company advanced on positions held by the 506th Parachute Infantry Regiment. 'One of our American mortar rounds exploded where a cluster of enemy lay couched,' wrote Captain Sweeney of the Headquarters Company. 'A German soldier leaped up, running frantically towards our lines. His hand was blown off above the wrist. The blood was gushing like water from a garden hose. He was obviously bleeding to death. Captain Madden, our battalion surgeon, rushed out to meet the stricken enemy warrior. The firing stopped as all watched the American medical officer promptly apply a tourniquet to the mutilated arm and gently lead the grateful enemy soldier to the American lines for shelter and care.' This, according to the American company commander, 'undoubtedly influenced the enemy's decision to surrender'.

Mortars almost certainly inflicted more fatal wounds on both sides than bullets. When inspecting positions along a dyke, Colonel 'Jump' Johnson of the 501st demonstrated his usual disregard for danger when mortar shells came over, while the officers and soldiers with him threw themselves flat. Johnson laughed, but the 'next one to come had his name on it', their padre

Father Sampson recorded. His last words to his replacement, Lieutenant Colonel Julian Ewell, were: 'Julian, take care of my boys.'

American paratroopers were not impressed by British infantry tactics on the Island. Private Donald Burgett described an attack by the 5th Duke of Cornwall's Light Infantry. They advanced 'shoulder to shoulder across the open fields' firing their rifles from the hip, 'working the bolts and firing again'. With sad admiration he thought, 'This sort of attack went out with the bloody assaults of our Civil War.' Like the Americans, the British stuck the dead man's rifle, with a fixed bayonet, upright into the ground to mark each corpse to be collected later.

One of the other disadvantages of being on the Island for American paratroopers was that British military authorities provided the rations, which included a good deal of tough mutton from Australia. They wanted fresh meat instead. 'We ate off the poor Dutch people,' a soldier in the 508th admitted later. 'Most houses had rabbit hutches alongside, so we ate a lot of rabbit.' The only exception to their dislike of British provisions was the rum ration. Even though it had the colour and viscosity of heavy engine oil, much trade was done by those with a taste for strong alcohol. 'One of our boys got drunk', wrote a staff sergeant in the 505th, 'and went hunting with a tommy gun. He came back singing with two tame rabbits and was placed under arrest in his foxhole until he was sober.'

Above all American troopers dreamed of steak, so a considerable number of cows were killed with .30 machine guns and butchered on the spot. 'Too many cows were ending up as steaks because they did not know the password,' Padre Sampson wrote. As the volume of complaints from Dutch farmers rose, General Taylor ordered a crackdown. A $500 fine was introduced for the killing of cattle. Shortly after taking command of the 501st, following Johnson's death, Colonel Ewell went to visit his three battalions to underline the message. Lieutenant Colonel Ballard tried to explain away the cornucopia of fresh meat acquired by his battalion. 'The cattle had been hit by 88 shells, the pigs had stepped on mines and the chickens had just died, presumably from battle fatigue.' Just then a squealing pig came running past, chased by four paratroopers firing at it. 'I suppose you're going to tell me now', Ewell said to Ballard, 'that damn pig is attacking your men.'

American military authorities in Europe were rather more concerned about serious crime, as the First Allied Airborne Army revealed in a Daily Bulletin: 'Reports that military personnel are securing funds from unlawful sources, such as captured enemy currency, barter with prisoners of war, black market operations and similar methods, have been brought to the attention of this headquarters.' American soldiers had acquired large numbers of old Belgian 100-franc notes, and 'numerous forgeries of Allied Military French Francs' were in circulation. In their spare time some paratroopers were playing the currency markets and even 'dealing in gold bullion'. Paratroopers would not, however, forgive anyone who profited at the expense of his comrades. Inspections revealed that one man had been stealing morphine, Lieutenant La Riviere noted. He was almost certainly selling it on the black market. 'Rivers' revealed that the man was thoroughly beaten up by his own platoon before being handed over to the military police. 'The man turned out to be a hardened criminal.'

It is difficult to believe, but some locals seemed to think that British troops on the Island were angelic in comparison. 'All the houses are occupied by English soldiers,' one of them wrote later. 'They have taken over and the [Dutch] men that stayed behind are guests. They don't mind because even though they don't understand each other, there is a lot of goodwill. We are not frightened like we were of the Germans. They are very polite, and won't make our life needlessly difficult. They give us cigarettes and also food including rice, which none of us have eaten for many years. We give them milk and eggs, which they receive politely and offer to pay for.' He then added, 'We thought the whole thing would go on for a few days but it lasted for seven months.' The biggest blow to their livelihoods came on 2 December 1944 when the Germans blew the dyke, just east of the destroyed Oosterbeek railway bridge. This caused extensive flooding in the Betuwe.

For British troops, the failure of Market Garden led to a sense of anticlimax made worse by the relentless rains of early autumn. When the 11th Armoured Division took over a sector on the east flank of XXX Corps, a limerick, probably written by a British officer, was distributed anonymously in a leaflet:

> As I sit on the banks of the MAAS
> I reflect that it's really a FAAS
> At my time of life
> And miles from my wife
> To be stuck in the mud on my AAS

The Germans were unimpressed by what they saw as British nine-to-five soldiering as they prepared to sit out the winter. '*Bei Nacht will der Tommy schlafen,*' they said – 'At night Tommy likes to sleep.' Montgomery had picked the worst terrain imaginable, with the endless saturated polders and the Rhine in its various forms hedging them in. There was only one way to go, come the spring, and that was east across the Maas and into the Reichswald, which also allowed little room for manoeuvre with tanks.

The people still in Nijmegen had the impression that they were almost in the front line. 'We still feel ourselves to be in the middle of the war,' Martijn Louis Deinum wrote in his diary. 'German shells are falling ceaselessly and we therefore can't feel safe yet.' He clearly could not quite fathom what he called 'the optimistic indifference of the English'.

The focus of German attacks remained the two bridges over the Waal. The British had surrounded the road bridge with searchlights and anti-aircraft guns to fight off the night bombers and the piggyback aircraft. The most dramatic attempt, however, came from frogmen. The British became aware of this threat after a clumsy German reconnaissance and so installed 17-pounder anti-tank guns to cover the approaches. The twelve frogmen from Marine Einsatzkommando 65, who had trained in Venice, were briefed at Brigadeführer Harmel's command post at Pannerden. Harmel warned them that 'the enemy guard on the bridge was exceptionally alert'. On the night of 28 September three groups of four frogmen each launched their half-ton torpedo mines ten kilometres upriver. The speed of the current made the task exceptionally difficult and only one of the mines was correctly positioned. This destroyed part of the rail bridge. The road bridge was undamaged. Of the twelve frogmen, only two escaped downstream without being captured. Of the ten who were taken, three died from their wounds.

The 82nd Airborne had its own unofficial secret weapon in the form of Private Theodore H. Bachenheimer in the 504th Parachute Infantry Regiment. Bachenheimer, a twenty-one-year-old German-born Jew, was a self-appointed spy. Both his parents had been in the theatre, and when they emigrated to the United States they went to live in Hollywood. Bachenheimer still spoke English with a German accent, and had only gained American citizenship while training at Fort Bragg. When the 504th had been at Anzio, Bachenheimer would slip through enemy lines and queue up with German soldiers at a field kitchen to gather intelligence, an exploit for which he received the Silver Star.

On 18 September when the Allies had no troops in Nijmegen, Bachenheimer had slipped into the railway station, where many German soldiers were enjoying a meal in the restaurant. Aided by a Dutch railway engineer, he took over the public address system. After issuing an order to all the

Germans in the station to surrender, he fired his sub-machine gun in front of the microphone. This caused the forty Germans in the station to run out in panic. After the capture of Nijmegen, his speciality was seizing German soldiers for interrogation. Bachenheimer worked closely with Jan Postulart, a local leader of the underground, known as 'Zwarte Jan', or 'Black John'.

Colonel Tucker's regimental adjutant remembered Gavin saying he did not know whether Bachenheimer should be court-martialled for his irregular activities or be given a field promotion to officer. During a visit to her lover, Jim Gavin, the writer and war correspondent Martha Gellhorn described Bachenheimer's headquarters in a *Collier's* article as 'a small overstuffed room in an old Nijmegen school'. There he debriefed his network of agents, listened to German informers, interviewed prisoners, worked with the Dutch underground and received British and American officers who needed information. Gellhorn sat in on one interrogation. 'No detail was too large or too small for Bachenheimer, who was a very capable and serious human being. Neither could anyone shake his modesty,' she wrote. 'Bachenheimer had an extraordinary talent for war, but in reality he was a man of peace.'

The self-appointed spy went off across the German frontier to Cleve and to the Betuwe. The local underground headquarters near Tiel was on the fruit farm owned by the Ebbens family, who were all captured by the SS and executed. Bachenheimer was also taken by the Germans and shot, supposedly attempting to escape, on the night of 22 October. Few believed that. He had been shot in the back of the head and through the neck. The most inexplicable part is that Bachenheimer's body was found wearing the uniform of an American lieutenant pilot.

Gellhorn left some memorable descriptions of Nijmegen under shellfire during her visit. 'The Dutch sweep up broken glass every morning in a despairingly tidy way, but there is no transport to cart glass away, so, under the dripping autumn trees and along the shell-marked street, there are neat mounds of rubble and glass.' She was also intrigued by the way a society dealt with traitors of different degrees. 'The police and the underground have been busy rounding up the collaborators and tracking down German agents in the town. They put the collaborators in a big schoolhouse, which is pock-marked with shell holes, and they feed them as they feed themselves, and they await the return of the Dutch government so that proper trials may be held. The schoolhouse has the awful, familiar smell of dirty bodies . . . The Dutch are not brutal to these people, and the prisoners are lightly guarded. One is always surprised to see what kind of people are arrested; one is most surprised by their apparent poverty. There are rooms with dreary-looking young women, ill, lying in bed with very small babies. These are the women who lived with German soldiers and are now the mothers of Germans. There are rooms of old people, who either trafficked with Germans, or worked for the Dutch Nazi government, or denounced, or in some way harmed, the true Dutch and the country. There is a nun in one room, looking very frozen and unforgiving. And alongside her are two stupid, homely girls who worked in the Germans' kitchens, and were soldiers' delights as a side line.'

After the last paratroopers in Oosterbeek had surrendered, the 9th SS Panzer-Division *Hohenstaufen* departed for Siegen in Germany. On 28 September Model briefed the commanders of the 9th and 116th Panzer divisions, both from the German army, on his operation for the II SS Panzer Corps to win back the Betuwe. Bittrich was not happy with the plan, and his scepticism about attacking in such terrain was soon shown to have been justified. Both divisions had trouble reaching Arnhem. The 116th Panzer had been involved in the fighting round Aachen and was then slowed by Allied fighter-bomber attacks. Model refused to delay the attack any longer, even though not all their units had arrived.

On 1 October at 06.00 the two divisions advanced towards Elst under cover of fog, but 'in the face of strenuous enemy resistance only insignificant gains were made,' Harmel reported. The Royal Tigers of the 506th Heavy Panzer Battalion appear to have played a very reluctant role in the whole operation. The Irish Guards halted the 9th Panzer attack on Aam. British artillery took a heavy toll of German attacks across open ground, just as Bittrich had feared. By 4 October the 10th SS *Frundsberg* had suffered so many casualties that it was renamed Kampfgruppe Harmel. The following day Bittrich requested an end to the offensive. Model insisted that it should continue, but on 8 October the American advance on Aachen forced Rundstedt to withdraw the 116th Panzer-Division. To impede the resupply of German troops on the Island, Allied bombers destroyed the Arnhem road bridge, which Frost's force had battled so fiercely to preserve. For some this truly underlined the final failure of Market Garden.

Following the end of Model's offensive, the Germans prepared defensive positions up the River IJssel east of Arnhem. Large numbers of half-starved Soviet prisoners of war were put to work and locals took pity on them, as a young Dutchman remembered: 'When these Russians were secretly given bottles of beer from the restaurant by granny they did not know what to do with the crown caps. To drink the beer they broke off the bottlenecks and drank from the damaged bottles. They also appeared to be rather hungry. In addition to the eggs we gave them, they were mad about bars of soap, which they literally devoured without any further ado. They also cut up and tore apart a dead horse while it was still warm, and ate the meat on the spot.'

Almost 500 members of the 1st Airborne were still in hiding after the battle north of the Neder Rijn. Major Digby Tatham-Warter wanted arms drops so that, with the underground, the British stragglers could act as a guerrilla force assisting any fresh attempt to cross the river. But after the failure of Market Garden, the Allies had given up any further idea of crossing the Rhine in the Netherlands.

The forced evacuation of Arnhem by the Germans meant that British soldiers hidden in the area needed to be moved to the west, to avoid capture and to prevent German reprisals against the families who had helped them. The Arnhem underground, led by Piet Kruijff, brought out a large number from Arnhem and Oosterbeek, including Brigadiers Lathbury and Hackett. Kruijff was already in touch with a team of Belgian SAS commanded by Captain Gilbert Sadi-Kirschen, operating to the west since 15 September. Together they worked with the underground round Ede, led by Bill Wilde-boer, to conceal British soldiers in surrounding villages. Eventually so many British were congregating in the area that it became far too dangerous to keep them. The SAS team contacted Special Forces headquarters at Moor Park for advice, while the underground, using the PGEM electricity company telephone network, contacted British intelligence in Nijmegen. A plan called Operation Pegasus evolved to smuggle as many as possible across the Neder Rijn on the night of 22 October. With American paratroopers from the 101st Airborne guarding the crossing point, and American combat engineers manning the boats, 138 airborne and shot-down Allied air crew were brought back to safety.

Airey Neave of MI9, the organization responsible for escaping military personnel, decided to mount Pegasus II a month later with a similar number of people.* Unfortunately they ran into a German position in the woods north of the river, and the whole effort ended in disaster. From then on mass crossings were avoided. Small groups continued during the very hard winter which followed the battle of Arnhem, including one in February with

---

* Airey Neave, the first officer to escape from Colditz Castle, became the moving spirit behind MI9 and after the war worked with the International Military Tribunal at Nuremberg. He became a Member of Parliament and Margaret Thatcher's favourite adviser until he was assassinated in 1979 by Irish republicans in a car-bomb attack at the House of Commons.

Brigadier Hackett, now sufficiently recovered from his wounds to make the attempt.

Hackett and Colonel Graeme Warrack were taken separately in stages by underground groups across the Neder Rijn closer to the sea and into the western end of the Betuwe, which was still occupied by the Germans. Hackett was content to do what he was told by their capable escorts. 'It was like being a child again,' he wrote later, 'led by the hand in a crowd. I had neither power to influence events nor curiosity to enquire into their nature.'

Local boatmen who knew the marshes and the channels of the Waal estuary ran a courier service with electric-powered canoes provided by the Canadian army between liberated and occupied Holland. On a windy night, Hackett was taken across by one of them, and shortly before dawn after a long journey through the reed-banked waterways they reached the southern side. By chance, the sector was held by the 11th Hussars, and friends from the war in the Western Desert were there waiting to greet him. 'It was wonderfully comforting to know I was among them. There was perhaps no other regiment in the army which was better known and liked in mine.' And in the house by the small quay was 'the great bulk of Graeme Warrack, the big man, full of warmth and cheer'. Warrack, who was almost twice the size of Hackett, boomed, 'Here he is! The little man at last.'

28

The Hunger Winter
November 1944 to May 1945

On 28 September, Harold Nicolson went to the House of Commons to hear Winston Churchill's statement on the end of the battle. 'On my way there,' he wrote in his diary, 'I consider how, were I in his place, I would treat the Arnhem surrender. On the one hand it was necessary to represent it as an episode of relative unimportance in proportion to the wide sweep of the war. On the other hand it was necessary not to suggest to anxious parents that it had all been no more than an incident. Winston solved this difficulty with mastery. He spoke of the men of the 1st Parachute [sic] Division with great emotion. "'Not in vain' is the boast of those who returned to us. 'Not in vain' is the epitaph of those who fell.'"'

Even allowing for the usual compulsion to put on the best face after a debacle, the self-congratulation and buck-passing among senior Allied commanders was bewildering. General Brereton claimed in October that 'Despite the failure of Second Army to get through to Arnhem and establish a permanent bridgehead over the Neder Rijn, Operation Market was a brilliant success.' The implication was that any blame must lie with Horrocks and XXX Corps, not with the First Allied Airborne Army.

Horrocks in turn blamed Urquhart and his men. 'The 1st Airborne Division plan was fundamentally unsound and it fought a bad battle,' he said after the war. 'They did not know how to fight as a division.' Dempsey also blamed Urquhart's plan, still unaware that Brereton and Major General Williams had left him little alternative. The 1st Airborne 'had little chance of success because their own plan was so bad', he said. It 'was not a good division, as a division. The men were gallant enough but they were not skilled tactically and they didn't know how to fight a regular battle once they were on the ground.' Urquhart, as one would have expected, did not blame anyone and did not rock the boat. He ended his report thus: 'Operation

Market was not 100% a success and did not end quite as was intended. The losses were heavy but all ranks appreciate that the risks involved were reasonable. There is no doubt that all would willingly undertake another operation under similar conditions in the future. We have no regrets.'

Nobody, it seemed, knew, or dared to question, how the whole operation had evolved. Eisenhower wrote to Brereton, 'The perfection of your staff work is demonstrated by the complete coordination between air, ground and airborne forces, and this coordination has resulted in maximum tactical effect.' Seldom has a compliment been so far from the reality.

Montgomery had been determined to bring the Allied air forces to heel by imposing his plan, apparently unaware that they, not he, had the final say. Then Browning, who had at last been given the field command he longed for, did nothing when faced with Major General Williams's refusal to allow his aircraft near the Arnhem and Nijmegen bridges. This eliminated any hope of surprise, the only advantage enjoyed by lightly armed airborne forces. Even Brereton's headquarters later admitted that 'The time between landing and getting into position was relatively long – between two and three hours. [In fact it was closer to six hours.] Thereby the advantage of surprise at Arnhem was lost.' And Williams, with some justification, rejected the idea of two lifts in a day, which offered the only chance of delivering sufficient forces to their objectives. So Browning must bear a large proportion of the blame because he failed to go straight back to Montgomery and insist that, with these limitations, the whole operation should be reconsidered.

In fact the fundamental concept of Operation Market Garden defied military logic because it made no allowance for anything to go wrong, nor for the enemy's likely reactions. The most obvious response would have been for the Germans to blow up the bridges at Nijmegen, and it was only Model's own defiance of military logic which allowed Market Garden its sole hope of success. All the other deficiencies which emerged, such as bad communications and lack of ground–air liaison, simply compounded the central problem. In short, the whole operation ignored the old rule that no plan survives contact with the enemy. Such hubris always seems to provoke Murphy's law. As Shan Hackett indeed said much later, 'Everything that could go wrong did go wrong.'

Montgomery blamed the weather, not the plan. He even asserted at one point that the operation had been a 90 per cent success, since they had got nine-tenths of the way to Arnhem. This prompted the scorn of Air Chief Marshal Arthur Tedder, Eisenhower's deputy, who observed, 'one jumps off a cliff with an even higher success rate, until the last few inches.' Prince Bernhard, on hearing of Montgomery's optimistic assessment of the battle, is said to have remarked, 'My country cannot afford another Montgomery victory.' But at least the field marshal issued a well-deserved tribute to the 1st Airborne Division. In an open letter which he gave to Urquhart as he was about to fly back to England, he finished: 'In years to come it will be a great thing for a man to be able to say: "I fought at Arnhem." '

The Germans analysed the British failure with acute professional interest, especially the way they lost '*Überraschungserfolg*' – 'the effect of surprise'. The great flaw in the plan at Arnhem, as Oberstleutnant von der Heydte pointed out later, was that the British paratroop brigade that landed on the first day was not strong enough and that forces were not dropped on both sides of the river. 'They made an astounding mess of things at Arnhem,' he concluded. Both German and Dutch officers disagreed with Williams's claim that the south bank of the Neder Rijn near the bridge was unsuitable for gliders and paratroops. And the strength of the flak batteries was grossly exaggerated, as Generaloberst Student pointed out. As a result, he added, the British lost 'surprise, the strongest weapon of airborne troops. At Arnhem the enemy didn't play this trump card and it cost him the victory.' Bittrich, who had had great respect for Montgomery's generalship up until then, changed his opinion after Arnhem.

To expect Horrocks's XXX Corps to advance from the Meuse–Escaut Canal, just inside Belgium, for 103 kilometres along a single road to Arnhem simply asked for trouble. Even with air superiority, it was exactly the sort of action which the German general staff would have dismissed as a *Husarenstück* – an ill-thought-out cavalry raid. The rate of advance required did not allow for any hold-ups. And despite mounting evidence to the contrary, Montgomery still believed that the Germans would be incapable of reacting rapidly to form an effective defence. General David Fraser, who as a Grenadier subaltern took part in the battle for Nijmegen, wrote later, 'Operation Market Garden was, in an exact sense, futile. It was a thoroughly bad idea, badly planned and only – tragically – redeemed by the outstanding courage of those who executed it.'

For Sosabowski's troops it represented a double tragedy. In the first week of October they 'received the painful message that Warsaw had fallen. News ran through the ranks like lightning. That is when true exhaustion and gloom came over the troops.' Nobody else, it seemed, cared about the fate of Poland.

Two Polish paratroopers, Stanley Nosecki and Gasior, his comrade in the anti-tank battery, returned to their base in England together. They found that they were the only two from their Nissen hut to have survived.

Suddenly Gasior (almost certainly a *nom de guerre*), who was a veteran of the Spanish Civil War and the French Foreign Legion, burst out in sadness and anger. 'We are being killed, no one is helping us. Our brothers in Warsaw are being killed and no one is helping them. We'd better not sit in this empty barracks, as there is too much sentiment and too much bitterness. Let's get out of here.'

Outside the camp a US Army truck driven by a black soldier stopped for them. He recognized them as Polish paratroopers and offered them a lift to Northampton. 'You fellows deserve a good time,' he said. In Northampton, the two Poles walked into a hotel. 'We met a sergeant of the RAF, his beautiful wife and his mother-in-law, a distinguished lady.' They talked about Arnhem and Oosterbeek, of which the sergeant must have heard a great deal within the RAF. They all had dinner together, and then went to the bar afterwards. By then it was too late for Nosecki and Gasior to return to camp, so they decided to stay at the hotel. One of them, almost certainly Gasior, ended up sleeping with 'the distinguished lady'. The brief break from the tragic gloom of the Polish camp and the kindness of those they met were enough to restore their sanity.

Major General Sosabowski had even more reason than his soldiers to feel abandoned and ill-used. Neither Horrocks nor Browning could forgive him for his criticism of British planning and command. When Sosabowski informed Browning that the Polish government intended to award him the star of the Order Polonia Restituta, he replied, 'I am going to be absolutely candid, and I say to you that the award of a Polish decoration at the present time, to me is unfortunate. As you must be most fully aware, my relationship with yourself and your brigade has not been of the happiest during the last few weeks; it has been very different, in fact.' Sosabowski immediately wrote back to apologize 'if at any time my opinion was not expressed in such a way or words you would have liked'.

Browning was not mollified. He saw Sosabowski's outspoken criticism as insubordination. He continued to convince himself that during the crossing on 24 September Sosabowski had held his men back to spare them, when in fact the Poles had been ordered to hand over their boats to the Dorsets. Browning's views clearly reached Montgomery, who had strongly resented the Polish government-in-exile's reluctance to hand over the Polish Parachute Brigade until the invasion of Normandy. He proceeded on 17 October to write to Field Marshal Brooke, saying, 'Polish Para Brigade fought very badly and the men showed no keenness to fight if it meant risking their own lives. I do not want this brigade here and possibly you might like to send them to join other Poles in Italy.' This was an outrageous slander. But as

Browning's biographer wrote, it was Boy 'who was to wield the knife' in a letter to Lieutenant General Sir Ronald Weeks, the deputy chief of the general staff, who was responsible for Allied formations.

'Ever since the 1st Polish Parachute Brigade Group was mobilised in July,' Browning wrote on 24 November, 'Major General Sosabowski proved himself to be extremely difficult to work with. The "difficulty" was apparent not only to commanders under whom he was planning but also to staff officers of the other airborne formations concerned. During this period he gave me the very distinct impression that he was raising objections and causing difficulties as he did not feel that his brigade was fully ready for battle.' This was untrue. Sosabowski was perfectly confident that his brigade was ready, even though it had been allowed little in the way of parachute training facilities.

'This officer', Browning continued, 'proved himself to be quite incapable of appreciating the urgent nature of the operation, and continually showed himself to be both argumentative and loath to play his full part in the operation unless everything was done for him and his brigade.' Nothing was said about the insulting way Horrocks and Thomas had treated Sosabowski at Valburg from the moment he arrived, nor was it mentioned that Sosabowski had again been correct to point out the dangers of sending the Dorsets across to Westerbouwing. All Browning could then complain about was Sosabowski's request for some trucks to bring his paratroopers back to Nijmegen. 'This officer worried both me and my staff (who were at that time fighting a very difficult battle to keep the corridor open from inclusive Nijmegen to Eindhoven) about such things as two or three lorries to supplement his transport. I was forced finally to be extremely curt to this officer, and ordered him to carry out his orders from then on without query or obstruction. Both commander XXX Corps and commander 43 Division will bear out my criticism of the attitude of this officer throughout the operation.'

Sosabowski, aware of Browning's campaign to have him dismissed, demanded to know the charges against him, but even the Polish commander-in-chief, General Kazimierz Sosnkowski, could do little to defend him. In the second week of November, Sosabowski was transferred to a largely fictitious job of inspector of replacement units. Outraged, the Polish Parachute Brigade was close to mutiny, and it was Sosabowski who had to calm his men down. On 7 December, after a fruitless correspondence and meetings, General Stanisław Kopański, the chief of staff, wrote from the Polish forces' headquarters in the Rubens Hotel on Buckingham Palace Road, 'Whether you are at fault or not, your collaboration with the British encountered difficulties which were practically speaking impossible to resolve. Leaving you in charge of the parachute brigade would be detrimental to the brigade as it would be removed from the 21st Army Group's order of battle. As you know full well, the issues of equipment, supplies, training conditions and even to a degree replacements, are in the hands of the British.' It was a sad end to a shameful episode.

To say that Browning and Horrocks tried to make the abrasive Sosabowski a scapegoat for the failure of Market Garden is going too far, but their behaviour towards him was disgraceful. After the Arnhem debacle, Browning could not remain as commander of the airborne corps, so he went off as chief of staff to Admiral Lord Louis Mountbatten at South East Asia Command. The remnants of the 1st Airborne Division took no further part in the war until, at the time of the German surrender in May 1945, they were flown to Norway to disarm the 350,000 German troops still there. The division was officially disbanded in August.

Field Marshal Montgomery's period of reflection on Arnhem did not last long. His claim that Market Garden had failed because he had received insufficient support was not well received at Eisenhower's headquarters. His attempt to hold on to the two American airborne divisions then made things worse. Montgomery was his own worst enemy. He still did not give absolute priority to capturing the north side of the Scheldt estuary, so the port of Antwerp remained unusable. And the fact that more than 60,000 German troops of the Fifteenth Army had escaped across the Scheldt to take part in the September attacks on Hell's Highway did not improve his popularity with American officers.

'Monty tried to wave Antwerp aside,' Air Chief Marshal Tedder recounted later. 'He kept brushing it aside, until Ike had to get very determined with him.' On 5 October Eisenhower held another conference in Versailles. Montgomery could not avoid it this time as Field Marshal Brooke was to be present. With the tacit support of Eisenhower and Brooke, Admiral Ramsay returned to the charge over Antwerp, and castigated Montgomery in front of all the American generals. Montgomery was furious. Afterwards he signalled Eisenhower, 'Request you will ask Ramsay from me by what authority he makes wild statements to you concerning my operations about which he can know nothing. True facts are that Canadian Army attack began two days ago and tonight is reported to be going much better than at first . . . The operations are receiving my personal attention . . . You can rely on me to do every single thing possible to get Antwerp opened for shipping as early as possible.' In fact it took another month, until 8 November, to clear German troops from the north side and almost another three weeks to clear the mines in the estuary. Not until 28 November, twelve weeks after the capture of Antwerp, did the first ships enter its port.

Thinking that he had silenced his critics, Montgomery revived his argument that he should have single command over the campaign to capture the Ruhr, and thus command over all American forces north of the Ardennes. This challenge to Eisenhower's authority was destroyed on 16 October when Montgomery received the supreme commander's letter suggesting that if he disagreed with his orders, then the matter should be referred to higher authority. Montgomery had no choice but to submit immediately. The joint chiefs of staff would not hesitate to back Eisenhower against him. Unfortunately for Anglo-American relations, the field marshal had still not learned his lesson.

German generals thought Montgomery was wrong to demand the main concentration of forces under his command in the north. Like Patton, they reasoned that the series of canals and great rivers – the Maas, the Waal and the Neder Rijn – made it the easiest region for them to defend. 'With obstacles in the form of water courses traversing it from east to west,' wrote General von Zangen, 'the terrain offers good possibilities to hold on to positions.' General der Panzertruppe Eberbach, whom the British had captured in Amiens, was recorded telling fellow generals in captivity: 'The whole point of their main effort is wrong. The traditional gateway is through the Saar.' The Saar was where Montgomery demanded that Patton's Third Army be halted.

The failure of Operation Market Garden was bad for British morale. But for the Dutch the consequences affected the whole population, not just the 180,000 people forced from their homes on the north bank of the Neder Rijn. The scenes of battle were bad enough. Arnhem was 'a dead town'.* 'I have been in the city!' wrote Andries Pompe-Postuma, who slipped back secretly. 'Burned districts, shelled houses, bare trees, general destruction everywhere. Unrecognizable streets, and all of it empty, empty. Only military vehicles are thundering by. Bleak. After the bloody Moffen took everything, the Organisation Todt took whatever was left.' In Nijmegen, which had suffered so much from German shelling and fire-raising, 2,200 civilians are estimated to have died, 5,500 were disabled and 10,000 wounded. Some

---

* The Netherlands official history records an estimated total of more than 3,600 civilian deaths in Operation Market Garden, including 200 in Arnhem, 100 in Wolfheze and 200 in Oosterbeek.

The Hunger Winter

——— Front line, December 1944

NORTH SEA

N

Delfzijl

NETHERLANDS

IJsselmeer

IJssel

Haarlem

Amsterdam

Deventer

Leiden

Amersfoort

Apeldoorn

The Hague

Grebbe Line

Rotterdam

Arnhem

Waal

Maas

Nijmegen

Rhine

G E R M A N Y

Walcheren
Island

Eindhoven

Scheldt Estuary

Antwerp

Meuse

Scheldt

Cologne

Brussels

Aachen

B E L G I U M

Namur

Liège

Sambre

0   10   20   30   40   50 miles

0   10 20 30 40 50 km

22,000 houses were either wholly or more than three-quarters destroyed, and only 4,000 remained unscathed.

The Nazis wanted revenge on the Dutch population as a whole for having helped the Allies and they intended to use the twin weapons of oppression and starvation. In a secret report dated 25 September, the Dutch government-in-exile also heard that 'women and children are being taken as hostages as reprisals against railway strikers and that alternatively the houses and belongings of strikers are being destroyed.' Reichskommissar Seyss-Inquart's order that no food should be distributed in any areas of the Netherlands under German control was not just a temporary measure to break the railway strike, it remained in place.

Another 40,000 men between the ages of seventeen and forty were sent to Germany on forced labour from Rotterdam alone, making a total of around 400,000 Dutch civilians over the course of the war. Many members of the underground, who had helped and fought so bravely beside the Allies, were executed by the Germans. Some 3,000 people were shot during the occupation, and the largest proportion of that total was linked to Operation Market Garden. In Apeldoorn on 2 October, Hendrika van der Vlist saw bodies in the street showing signs of torture, with little placards attached to their clothes saying 'Terrorist'. No men were to be seen. They were either in hiding, along with a quarter of a million others in the Netherlands, or they had been rounded up for forced labour under the Organisation Todt. German operations seizing men for work were known as '*Razzias*'. It was almost as if they wanted to make sure that all men of military age were under their control.

On 28 September, at the urging of Queen Wilhelmina in London, Prime Minister Pieter Gerbrandy wrote to Winston Churchill. After paying tribute to the bravery of the attempt to break through at Arnhem, he wrote of the consequences to the people of the Netherlands. 'Many railway strikers and members of the resistance movement have been and are being executed, and the strongest reprisals are being taken against members of their families. Starvation in the big cities – the term is not too strong – is imminent. Destruction of port installations, wharves, factories, power plants, bridges etc., is being carried out by the Germans on a very extensive scale.'

The Foreign Office resisted the government-in-exile's request that the British issue a public warning to the Germans about atrocities in the Netherlands. 'We have always been opposed to limited warnings of this kind, both because they probably have not the slightest effect on the Germans and because, if made too frequently, they debase the currency of international declarations.' What they could not say was that, after the failure at Arnhem,

Allied military strategy had little interest in liberating more of the Netherlands. All attention was now focused on the east. Generals were bound to
argue that the only way to stop the suffering everywhere was to defeat Germany as rapidly as possible, without being deflected from that objective.
Even if the Canadian and British armies had received priority in supplies
during the hard winter to come, it is difficult to see how they could have
crossed the swollen Neder Rijn and breached the German defence line
without massive casualties.

The cities of The Hague, Amsterdam and Rotterdam were the most vulnerable to starvation because of the size of their populations, and also the
greater distances people needed to walk in order to find food. As a result
the three cities accounted for more than 80 per cent of the total death toll
during the winter of 1944–5, with Rotterdam suffering the most. After the
Germans had seized almost all the available grain, eggs, dairy products and
livestock, the only foods available were sugar beets made into a disgusting
mash and potatoes, which soon became very hard to obtain. Even tulip bulbs
could be found only on the black market. City-dwellers had to forage in the
countryside with a bicycle or perambulator, taking articles of value to barter
with farmers. Once the country was locked in deep snow and ice, they had
to ask for a place to sleep before they attempted to return.

At first barter often offered the only means of survival. 'Cigar-shops and
hundreds of other shops around had been transformed into bartershops,
but now there was nothing left to barter and hunger was all there was. People
just collapsed where they stood out of sheer exhaustion.' London was
informed of a typhoid epidemic in Amsterdam and diphtheria in Rotterdam. The mortality rate from tuberculosis more than doubled. The onset of
starvation and vitamin-deficiency, combined with the cold, reduced everyone's resistance. 'We have holes in our hands and feet because of the lack of
Vitamin A, which is very horrible and difficult.'

The government-in-exile in London tried to discuss the possibility of
allowing Swedish ships to bring in food supplies, but Churchill replied that
the Germans would simply take them for themselves. The chiefs of staff, on
the other hand, did not object. A plan was agreed with Eisenhower, yet the
first two ships did not arrive until late January 1945. Even then SHAEF
was concerned that the Germans would use the neutral ships as a front for
their own operations.

As the winter progressed, the daily ration was reduced from 800 calories
a day to 400, and then to 230. Short-term desperation became so intense
that there were reports of the rich buying the ration books off the poor,
'with obvious results'. Only inhabitants who had lost more than a third of

their body weight, certified by a doctor, were entitled to extra food collected by the Church. The diet of sugar beets often provoked diarrhoea and vomiting, weakening people further. According to one report, 'five times as many males were suffering from starvation as females,' while another stated that 75 per cent of the victims were male. This seems very similar to the pattern during the Siege of Leningrad where studies confirmed that men had far smaller reserves of fat.

The cold forced people to smash up furniture, floorboards, doors and doorframes to make firewood. Abandoned houses were stripped. Anyone caught looting was made to write '*Ik ben een plunderaar*' on a board. They were then shot and the board propped against their body as a warning. Wooden coffins were replaced by cardboard substitutes.

'The need was such', wrote someone in The Hague, 'that the dead bodies were unburied and left above ground for 14 to 18 days. There was no transport and there were no coffins available. For the survivors it was frequently impossible to live inside their houses because of the stench of death and so they had to go outside. When small children died the parents were told "take your child's body to the cemetery yourself."'

In Amsterdam things were not quite so bad. 'The bodies are collected by bicycle and cart and then taken as luggage to the cemetery,' wrote Jan Peters, a law student. 'There they are put on top of one another. The family is not allowed to come. It is like being in a market-hall. Efficiency! The whole lot in a big hole. There are people who are left for weeks above ground. The funeral directors are rushed off their feet. You have to pay them in advance, and if you have a little butter or sugar to give them then there is a chance you can still acquire a coffin made of wood.'

'It is no surprise', Peters continued, 'that under the circumstances and the black-market prices, people are dying of hunger in droves, especially old people and very small children. The Germans have stolen most vehicles of transport in order to take practically everything that moves or not. Which is one of the reasons for the lack of food. Life has become very raw! I have often seen people just slowly crumbling and falling on the street, also in the queues standing outside the Central Kitchens. There are lots of beggars in the streets, mostly in the shape of singers with awful voices. People are going to houses and begging for a slice of bread or a potato. The other side of all this is the thriving black market in the Jordaan [district]. Some streets are packed with people shuffling along with boxes in order to buy things at outrageous prices. In the cafés Big Business goes on. You can literally buy anything. On the street corners there are look-outs. The Police do nothing. They are busier stealing a bag of potatoes from people who have just returned from a long trek to the Wieringermeer with their prams.' German officials and officers sometimes made a killing from the black market. According to Oberstleutnant von der Heydte, the SS ran their black market in coffee from the Netherlands.

Every form of physical and moral resistance disintegrated as starvation gripped. Members of the Wehrmacht in Rotterdam apparently bragged that they did not need to go to a brothel and pay. According to a Kriegsmarine midshipman called Hoffmann, they boasted that 'for half a loaf of bread they could get anything they wanted from Dutch girls.'

As more and more reliable evidence reached London of the developing humanitarian crisis, the political pressure to do something increased, if only to avoid social unrest later. When Montgomery heard that the Netherlands government-in-exile was complaining that he was not doing enough to relieve the situation, he wrote to Eisenhower. 'The issue is quite clear. I have no troops available for attacking the Germans in West Holland. If the Germans withdraw from West Holland, I must go east and fight them. I cannot go east and fight the Germans and also go into West Holland with my present resources. I can do one of these two alternatives, not both . . . So it is not clear to me why I am being made the scapegoat. Except that it is quite normal for me to collect any mud that is being slung about!!'

There were also acute shortages in the liberated parts of the Netherlands, as well as Belgium. Montgomery to his credit kicked up such a fuss in February that he forced SHAEF to start distributing food reserves, because civilians were receiving only about a third of the calories which Allied soldiers enjoyed. Famished children hung around Allied camps to dip into the swill barrel into which the uneaten food from mess kits had been emptied. A number offered themselves in exchange for food. Young women, who had fraternized with the Germans and had their hair shorn, wandered around rejected by everyone. Many were forced to turn to prostitution.

'The Germans became nastier and nastier as their military position became less secure,' wrote a member of the underground as reprisals mounted. On the night of 7 March 1945 members of the Dutch underground, wearing German uniforms, set out to hijack a vehicle on the road from Apeldoorn to Arnhem. There was little traffic so they stopped a BMW motorcar which happened to contain SS-Obergruppenführer Hanns Albin Rauter. In the shoot-out which followed, Rauter was wounded and feigned death while his companions were killed. A German patrol arrived and took him to hospital. His attackers escaped. Himmler, ignoring the random nature of the ambush, saw the event as a repeat of the assassination of Reinhard Heydrich in Prague. He ordered that 500 hostages should be executed in the Netherlands in revenge. In the end only half that number were shot, including 117 who were brought to the site of the attack in buses. They were then executed in a long line by green-uniformed Ordnungspolizei, who had served in the Kampfgruppe Rauter during the battle.*

A fear of growing Communist influence played a part in galvanizing attitudes in London during March, but until Seyss-Inquart had been placed under real pressure no agreement on the distribution of relief supplies could be made. Following Montgomery's crossing of the Rhine at Wesel on 24 March 1945, the First Canadian Army swung left on 5 April, trapping the Germans and Seyss-Inquart in western Holland behind the Grebbe Line. What remained of Arnhem was liberated ten days later, but 3.6 million civilians still starved in the principal cities. As the Red Army prepared to attack Berlin, Seyss-Inquart made overtures through the Dutch underground. To save his neck, he thought he might be able to arrange a separate deal which would somehow make the Netherlands neutral again. He offered to halt executions and to allow food supplies to enter the occupied areas, and he would cease fighting providing the Allies did the same. But if they attacked, the Germans would destroy the dykes and flood the country. As this démarche offered the only chance of providing food to the starving cities, the Allies were prepared to talk.

On 28 April Montgomery's chief of staff, Major General Freddie de Guingand, and senior Canadian officers met German representatives near Amersfoort. Eisenhower's headquarters had informed General Alexei Antonov, the chief of staff of the Red Army's supreme command, the Stavka. Stalin was concerned that German troops in Holland might be transferred to the east. The western Allies assured him that they were prepared to include a prohibition of any such movement in their conditions, even though 'no routes are now available to the Germans for transfer of troops from this area.' Since Stalin suspected that the Americans and British might want to make a separate peace, General Ivan Susloparov, the Red Army representative at Eisenhower's headquarters, was to attend every meeting.

Montgomery's intelligence chief, Brigadier Bill Williams, accompanied de Guingand. He described how the leading German entered and gave a Nazi salute. 'Freddie decided not to return the salute and then decided to

---

* Rauter remained in hospital until he was arrested by British military police in May after the German surrender. The British handed him over to the Dutch authorities; he was tried in The Hague and finally executed in the prison of Scheveningen on 24 March 1949.

avoid shaking hands . . . To make the Russians happy, we had asked for a representative. They sent the perfect man for the job – he was nine foot high, very impressive, and completely dumb. I shan't forget the look on the German's face when he suddenly discovered he was standing under this giant's chin.' The Germans were sent back to discuss details with Seyss-Inquart and inform him that he must attend two days later. A provisional agreement was reached that the Germans were not to fire at aircraft dropping supplies, while the Allies would halt in their present positions in the Netherlands and would cease all bombing operations. The next day, squadrons of American B-17 and British Lancaster bombers appeared over designated drop zones by the worst-hit cities and 500 tons of food supplies were bundled out to reception committees. Altogether 10.4 million rations had been prepared for delivery by sea and by air, once bomber squadrons had been released by the Allied air forces.

Just before 13.00 on 30 April, Eisenhower's chief of staff General Walter Bedell Smith reached Achterveld, eight kilometres east of Amersfoort. He and Seyss-Inquart were to meet in the village school which had two entrances, one for each delegation. The 1st Canadian Corps had arranged everything and provided guards. The main street was packed with staff cars and crowds of local onlookers, fascinated by the spectacle. Freddie de Guingand, Bill Williams and General Susloparov were there first. 'The Russians with their uniforms,' the Canadians reported, 'which appeared to have come quite recently from the tailor's shop, with sparkling epaulettes, caused great interest and when a trim, pleasant-looking female interpreter appeared, also handsomely attired in the uniform of a lieutenant, the crowd literally goggled.'

The Germans arrived from Amersfoort, and climbed out of their cars. 'The whole party, headed by Seyss-Inquart, moved into the village school. The eyes of every officer, other rank and villager were on the central figures in this drama. Leading the procession, limping along slightly in advance, moved the hated Seyss-Inquart, Reichskommissar of the Netherlands. He was escorted by two SS officers in their black uniforms with silver badges. In cold, matter-of-fact language the points connected with this food distribution were discussed. At the same time, the nature of the whole proceedings became more and more obvious. Here were the Allies, forced by a set of circumstances beyond their control to negotiate with this man, one of the worst of the war criminals.'

'Bedell was tough at first,' Williams recounted later, 'then to our disgust, he wheedled. Spoke of his German blood. When Seyss-Inquart was not impressed he got tough again . . . Incidentally [Prince Bernhard] had come in a car which had been stolen by the Resistance from Seyss-Inquart. However, Seyss-Inquart came in another just like it, and with him there was a woman who screamed out when she saw Bernhard's car and demanded where the three parcels were that she had left in it when it was stolen.'

'The arrangements about the introduction of food into west Holland were agreed,' the official report continued. 'Further arrangements are being made tomorrow between the local commanders for necessary daily truces to let food convoys in and these may well lead to a general truce on that front in order to simplify the problem. No definite agreement about surrender was made by Seyss-Inquart, but the general opinion was that he was prepared to nibble if the cheese looks attractive.'

Even though German officers were already escaping on Red Cross trains to Germany, Generaloberst Johannes Blaskowitz, the military commander in the Netherlands who replaced Student, felt that they could not give in while resistance continued elsewhere. Bedell Smith insisted on a private talk with Seyss-Inquart to persuade him to surrender now rather than later. At one point during the discussion, General Bedell Smith said to Seyss-Inquart, 'I wonder if you realize that I am giving you your last chance.'

'Yes, I realize that,' the Reichskommissar replied.

'The consequences to you yourself will be serious. You know what your acts have been here. You know the feeling of the Dutch people toward you. You know you will probably be shot.'

'That leaves me cold,' Seyss-Inquart said.

'It usually does,' Bedell Smith replied.*

On 5 May, five days after Hitler's suicide, General Blaskowitz signed the surrender of Wehrmacht forces in the Netherlands in a hotel in Wageningen just west of Oosterbeek.†

Food supplies had poured into the country in the course of the previous week by ship, air and truck. Civilians flocked to greet the Canadian troops. One report asserted that 'the food situation is not as serious as had been anticipated. Starvation conditions are not, repeat not, apparent. Malnutrition exists in urban centers, but no indications have been found in country

---

* Seyss-Inquart was not shot, but hanged, on 16 October 1946 after being condemned as a war criminal at the International Military Tribunal at Nuremberg.
† Blaskowitz, whom Hitler distrusted because he had strongly criticized SS crimes in Poland, is said to have committed suicide in the prison at Nuremberg even though he knew he was going to be acquitted. Mystery surrounds his death. One theory holds that he was thrown from the window by members of the SS.

districts. Undernourishment is especially noticeable in Rotterdam.' Some officers seemed to think that the government-in-exile had been exaggerating the famine. Their view was based entirely on those they saw who welcomed them in the streets, but as the head of the SHAEF mission in the Netherlands pointed out: 'On the advent of Allied troops, the soldiers were greeted with cheers and bunting, and made their progress through a smiling countryside. But it was deceptive because men and women who are slowly dying in their beds of starvation unfortunately cannot walk gaily about the streets waving flags.'

Estimates of those who died from starvation usually range from 16,000 to 20,000 people, but it is impossible to assess how many more died from disease brought on and accelerated by severe malnutrition. All one can say for certain is that the death rate would have climbed exponentially if the SHAEF supplies had not arrived when they did. The emaciated figures who greeted the troops reaching Rotterdam and Amsterdam, especially in the poorer areas, were compared to the victims of concentration camps.*

Liberation did not automatically bring feelings of undiluted joy or relief. Many Dutch could not understand why the Allies had taken so long to come to their aid. They were also suspicious of SOE's disastrous handling of agents in 1942, permitting the German Abwehr to capture, torture and kill them in Operation North Pole. And those from the Betuwe and the north bank of the Neder Rijn found it hard to forgive the pointless artillery duels during the autumn and winter of 1944, which destroyed towns and villages without any attempt to advance and secure them.

When the forcibly evacuated citizens of Arnhem and Oosterbeek returned to their devastated homes in the summer of 1945, many were shaken to find that the battle was being refought for the film *Theirs is the Glory*. Some of the real participants took part, including Kate ter Horst who read Psalm 91, as she had to the wounded in her house. Others, especially young Dutchmen acting in German uniform, seem to have enjoyed the work and the advantages it brought in the way of food.

Despite the communal efforts to clear rubble and restore essential

---

* Nobody knew about the long-term effects, but one piece of recent research has indicated that 'Girls born to Dutch women who were pregnant during a famine at the end of the Second World War had an above-average risk of developing schizophrenia.' Another, earlier study indicated that those who had survived by eating tulip bulbs did better than those who had included wheat in their diet, but when they consumed American bread parachuted in at the liberation, they rapidly succumbed to coeliac disease.

services, it was not enough to revive the devastated towns. In the summer of 1945 an appeal was launched to the rest of the country to help Arnhem. Amsterdam virtually adopted Arnhem, and craftsmen arrived to help rebuild the city. The story spread, thanks to the public relations skills of Burgemeester Matser, and assistance came from all directions. The reconstruction of Arnhem was finally completed in 1969.

Although the Dutch had much to forgive in the wake of Operation Market Garden, their instinctive generosity to Allied troops at the time and ever since towards the veterans has been one of the most moving legacies of the Second World War. One story is particularly poignant, especially amid the astonishing courage shown by civilians and soldiers alike.

A lieutenant of the Parachute Regiment, who was very happily married, suffered a psychological breakdown under heavy shelling. Along with two medical orderlies in a similar state, he hid in the smaller cellar of a large country house on the western edge of Oosterbeek. The place was owned by the Heijbroek family who were sheltering in the larger cellar. But the three men, evidently still frozen by fear, stayed put throughout the battle and made no attempt to rejoin their unit.

They were still there on 26 September, after the evacuation of Urquhart's men across the Neder Rijn. The Heijbroek family ran a great risk. If British soldiers were found in their house, they would be executed. They had to beg the Englishmen to escape when the Germans ordered the population of Oosterbeek to abandon their homes. One of the Heijbroek sons, Daan, a member of the local resistance, finally persuaded the three soldiers to follow him after dark down to the Neder Rijn, where they could swim across to Allied lines on the southern bank. The three roped themselves together because one of the medical orderlies was a weak swimmer, but they struggled in the strong current. The lieutenant and the poor swimmer drowned. The other medical orderly survived by cutting himself free and floating downstream.

Two years after the war, the young widow of the lieutenant visited Oosterbeek and met the Heijbroek family. She returned once more and married Henri Heijbroek, the elder brother of Daan who had led her husband to the riverbank.

Notes

ABBREVIATIONS

AAMH	Archief Airborne Museum Hartenstein, Oosterbeek
AHB	Air Historical Branch, RAF, Ministry of Defence, Northwood
ALDS	'Arnheim, der letzte deutsche Sieg', Generaloberst Kurt Student, *Der Frontsoldat erzählt*, no. 5, 1952
BArch-MA	Bundesarchiv-Militärarchiv, Freiburg-im-Breisgau
CBHC	Chester B. Hansen Collection, USAMHI
CBW	Centralna Biblioteka Wojskowa, Warsaw
CRCP	Cornelius Ryan Collection of World War II Papers, Mahn Center for Archives and Special Collections, Ohio University, Athens, OH
CSDIC	Combined Services Detailed Interrogation Centre, documents in the National Archives, Kew
DDEP	Dwight David Eisenhower Papers, DDE Presidential Library, Abilene, KS
EC-UNO	Eisenhower Center, World War II Archives and Oral History Collection, University of New Orleans, courtesy of the National WW II Museum, New Orleans, LA
FCPP	Forrest C. Pogue Papers, OCMH, USAMHI
FLPP	Floyd Lavinius Parks Papers (Diary chief of staff First Allied Airborne Army), USAMHI
FMS	Foreign Military Studies, USAMHI
GAA	Gelders Archief Arnhem
GA-CB	Gelders Archief-Collectie Boeree, Collection of Papers of Colonel Theodor A. Boeree

HKNTW	L. de Jong, *Het Koninkrijk der Nederlanden in de tweede Wereldoorlog*, vol. 10a: *Het laatste jaar*, Amsterdam, 1980 (The Netherlands Official History)
HvdV	Hendrika van der Vlist, *Die dag in september*, Bussum, 1975
IWM	Imperial War Museum, London
JMGP	James M. Gavin Papers, USAMHI
KTB	Kriegstagebuch, or war diary
LHCMA	Liddell Hart Centre of Military Archives, King's College London
MPRAF	Museum of the Parachute Regiment and Airborne Forces, Duxford, Cambridgeshire
NARA	National Archives II, College Park, MD
NBMG	Nationaal Bevrijdingsmuseum Groesbeek
NIOD	Nederlands Instituut voor Oorlogsdocumentatie, Amsterdam
OCMH	Office of the Chief of Military History
PISM	Polish Institute and Sikorski Museum, London
PP	*The Patton Papers*, ed. Martin Blumenson, New York, 1974
PUMST	Polish Underground Movement Study Trust, London (Studium Polski Podziemnej Londyn)
RAN	Regionaal Archief Nijmegen
RHCE	Regionaal Historisch Centrum Eindhoven
RvOD	Rijksinstituut voor Oorlogsdocumentatie, *Het proces Rauter*, Ministerie van Onderwijs, *Kunsten en Wetenschappen*, 's-Gravenhage, 1952
TNA	The National Archives (formerly the Public Record Office), Kew
USAMHI	US Army Military History Institute, Carlisle, PA
WLB-SS	Württembergische Landesbibliothek, Sammlung Sterz, Stuttgart

1 THE CHASE IS ON!

p. 1 'Never let it be said . . .', Stuart Hills, *By Tank into Normandy*, London, 2003, p. 148

'Along the main supply routes . . .', CBHC, Box 4, Folder 13

'This was the type . . .', Brian Horrocks, *A Full Life*, London, 1960, p. 195

p. 2 'open and rolling . . .', Hills, *By Tank into Normandy*, p. 148

'To travel at top speed . . .', ibid.

'their odd assortment . . .', TNA WO 171/837

'de-lousing', ibid.

'I have a surprise . . .', Horrocks, *A Full Life*, p. 198

p. 3 'was exactly like . . .', ibid.

'Goddamit, I'm tired . . .', CBHC, Box 4, Folder 13

Montgomery on 1.9.44, Nigel Hamilton, *Monty: The Field Marshal 1944–1976*, London, 1986, pp. 8–14

'The Field Marshal thing . . .', PP, p. 535

'Monty made a Field Marshal . . .', Robert W. Love and John Major (eds.), *The Year of D-Day: The 1944 Diary of Admiral Sir Bertram Ramsay*, Hull, 1994, p. 129

p. 4 'neat and trim . . .', 'Give me 400,000 . . .', CBHC, Box 4, Folder 13

'to go through . . .', PP, p. 539

'According to German conceptions . . .', OKW KTB, FMS B-034

'It is amazing . . .', Forrest C. Pogue interview with Bedell Smith 13.5.47, OCMH WWII Interviews, USAMHI

p. 5 'the spirit of competition . . .', 'Les jeux sont faits . . .', TNA WO 171/837

'It was our longest . . .', TNA WO 171/1256

'The chief trouble . . .', TNA WO 171/837

p. 6 'fired five rounds . . .', 'proved of enormous value . . .', ibid.

'The people dressed better . . .', Major Edward Eliot, 2nd Bn Glasgow Highlanders, IWM 99/61/1

'An event that surpasses . . .', Diary Uffz. Heinrich Voigtel, 3.9.44, Stab/Beob.Abt. 71, 59 160 A, WLB-SS

'the conversation of officers . . .', 2.9.44, Fullriede Tagebuch, BArch-MA MSG2 1948; also RAN 80/328

'The Italians are . . .', Oskar Siegl, 6.9.44, Feldpostprüfstellen 1944, BArch-MA RH13/49, 62

'We Germans . . .', A. Schindler, Reichenberg, 10.9.44, Feldpostprüfstellen 1944, BArch-MA RH13/49, 65

'for operations in Germany', 1.9.44, Raymond G. Moses Collection, USAMHI

'everyone was getting as excited . . .', CBHC, Box 41

'everything we talk about . . .', CBHC, Box 4, Folder 13

p. 7 'future operations . . .', CBHC, Box 42, S-2

'We both consider . . .', M148 Montgomery Papers, quoted Hamilton, *Monty: The Field Marshal*, p. 18

'between Wesel and Arnhem', ibid., p. 22

2 'MAD TUESDAY'

p. 9 'Compatriots . . .', C. A. Dekkers and L. P. J. Vroemen, *De zwarte Herfst. Arnhem 1944*, Arnhem, 1984, p. 18

Prins Bernhard, TNA HS 7/275

'Never have we enjoyed . . .', Diary mej. Crielaers, RHCE D-0001/1383/2042

For *Dolle Dinsdag* ('Mad Tuesday'), see among others Karel Margry, *De Bevrijding van Eindhoven*, Eindhoven, 1982; H. Lensink, NIOD 244/313; HKNTW, pp. 265ff.; Jack Didden and Maarten Swarts, *Einddoel Maas. De strijd in zuidelijk Nederland tussen September en December 1944*, Weesp, 1984; Diary Albertus Uijen, RAN 579/23-33; Antonius Schouten, CRCP 123/35; Sister M. Dosithée Symons, St Canisius Hospital, CRCP 123/39

p. 10 'Many vehicles . . .', H. Lensink, NIOD 244/313

'women on their laps . . .', Louis van Erp, CRCP 120/18

'Cognac Tuesday', P. Nuis, CRCP 93/5 the 'wrong' Netherlanders, Didden and Swarts, *Einddoel Maas*, p. 22

'The attitude of . . .', Feldkommandantur Utrecht, 28.12.43, BArch-MA, RW 37/v21, quoted Gerhard Hirschfeld, *Nazi Rule and Dutch Collaboration: The Netherlands under German Occupation 1940–1945*, Oxford, 1988, p. 307

p. 11 'Yesterday evening . . .', 'The "Gentlemen" . . .', letter to Gefreiter Laubscher, 7.9.44, Feldpostprüfstellen 1944, BArch-MA RH13/49, 24

'The feeling of the civilian . . .', Frau Chr. Jansen, Niederbieber-Neuwied, 17.9.44, Feldpostprüfstellen 1944, BArch-MA RH13/49, 42

'I cannot convey . . .', Kanonier Felix Schäfer, OKH-Funkstelle, 10.9.1944, WLB-SS

p. 12 'an economic advantage', HKNTW, p. 266

Eindhoven destruction, RHCE D-0001 Nr. 2042

'the fact that railway . . .', Oberleutnant Helmut Hänsel, 15.9.1944, Heeres-Bezugs-Abnahmestelle für die Niederlande, 36 610, WLB-SS

Netherlands government-in-exile and attacks on locomotives, TNA FO 371/39330

'It was a wonderful sight . . .', Paul van Wely, CRCP 122/5

'Organised fascism . . .', Hirschfeld, *Nazi Rule and Dutch Collaboration*, p. 310

'Resistance against the occupying forces . . .', *Deutsche Zeitung in den Niederlanden*, TNA FO 371/39330

p. 13 'The Dutch are not just . . .', Oberleutnant Helmut Hänsel, 4.9.44, Heeres-Bezugs-Abnahmestelle für die Niederlande, 36.610, WLB-SS

'My longing for . . .', 'Some details about the Battle of Arnhem', GA-CB 2171/1

'They wear civilian . . .', Dagboeken Burgers, AAMH

'A very wet and stormy . . .', 4.9.44, Robert W. Love and John Major (eds.), *The Year of D-Day: The 1944 Diary of Admiral Sir Bertram Ramsay*, Hull, 1994, p. 131

'was extremely difficult . . .', NARA RG407, 270/65/7/2

pp. 13–14 'a stout, dapper little man . . .', 'Then each man raised . . .', Stuart Hills, *By Tank into Normandy*, London, 2003, pp. 153–4

p. 14 'a most remarkable sight . . .', TNA WO 171/837

Château d'Everberg, 'just like a hotel', Alistair Horne and David Montgomery, *The Lonely Leader: Montgomery 1944–1945*, London, 1994, p. 328

'were forced to go borrowing ...', CBHC, Box 4, Folder 13

p. 16 'slight opposition ...', War Diary, 2nd (Armoured) Bn, Irish Guards, TNA WO 171/1256

'we would have to stop ...', TNA WO 171/837

'the retreat of the Germans ...', Diary mej. Crielaers, RHCE D-0001/1383/2042

p. 17 'to build a new ...', ALDS

'the Führer "the Greatest Commander ...', Heydte, TNA WO 208/4140 SRM 1180

'Those new paratroop ...', CSDIC, TNA WO 208/4140 SRM 1156

'The fighting strength ...', BArch-MA RL33/115

7th Fallschirmjäger-Division, Generaloberst Kurt Student, FMS B-717

'a calm and experienced ...', 'small and barely mobile ...', ibid.

p. 18 'And then ...', ibid.

For Chill's 85th Division at this time, see Jack Didden, 'A Week Too Late?', in John Buckley and Peter Preston-Hough (eds.), *Operation Market Garden: The Campaign for the Low Countries, Autumn 1944*, Solihull, 2016, pp. 74–98

'He is an officer who ...', Major Zapp, Sich. Rgt 16, TNA WO 208/4140 SRM 1126

p. 19 'Model is the grave-digger ...', Obersturmbannführer Lönholdt, 17 SS Pz Gr Division, TNA WO 208/4140 SRM 1254

'He is a first-rate artist ...', SS Standartenführer Lingner, TNA WO 208/4140 SRM 1206

Model not allowing officers to speak, Oberst Wilck, commander of Aachen, TNA WO 208/4364 GRGG 216

'a little Hitler', TNA WO 171/4184

p. 20 'He was guilty', GA-CB 2171/1

For the fate of Arnhem Jews, see Margo Klijn, *De stille slag. Joodse Arnhemmers 1933–1945*, Westervoort, 2014

Jews in Eindhoven, Margry, *De Bevrijding van Eindhoven*

p. 21 'The Jewish problem ...', RvOD, p. 615

The camp at Vught, Didden and Swarts, *Einddoel Maas*, p. 26

Sachsenhausen and Ravensbrück, HKNTW, vol. viii, p. 61

'an almost total lack ...', J. Presser, *Ashes in the Wind: The Destruction of Dutch Jewry*, London, 1968, p. 495

p. 22 'In the Netherlands he made ...', CSDIC, TNA WO 208/4178 GRGG 341

Englandspiel, for the most detailed account see M. R. D. Foot, *SOE in the Low Countries*, London, 2001

Destruction of Nijmegen, 22.2.44, HKNTW, vol. viii, p. 96

3 THE FIRST ALLIED AIRBORNE ARMY

p. 23 'Saturday, 2 September', Maj J. E. Blackwood, 11 Para, 4th Parachute Brigade, NIOD 244/1237

'gutless bugger', Montgomery to F. de Guingand, TNA WO 205/5D

'I must emphasize . . .', Brereton to Eisenhower, 20.8.44, FAAA, NARA RG331/Entry 254/Box19

p. 24 Operations cancelled, HQ FAAA, 12.9.44, NARA RG498 290/56/2/3, Box 1466

Kansas City Kitty etc., FAAA, NARA RG331/Entry 254/Box18

'one of the General's . . .', Miss Claire Miller MBE, CRCP 107/26

p. 25 'the suave and polished . . .', CBHC, Box 4, Folder 13

'Sir, I have the honour . . .', HQ FAAA, NARA RG331/Entry 254/Box19

'Require airborne operation . . .', M148 quoted Montgomery Papers, Nigel Hamilton, *Monty: The Field Marshal 1944–1976*, London, 1986, p. 22

'You will immediately . . .', FAAA, NARA RG331/Entry 253/Box5

p. 26 'to seize control of Allied strategy', Professor Gary Sheffield, RUSI presentation, 20.11.2013

'peace could be maintained . . .', CBHC, Box 4, Folder 13

'We discussed plans . . .', Dempsey Diary, 4.9.44, TNA WO 285/9

'the British and the Poles . . .', Lt Stefan Kaczmarek, Polish Parachute Brigade, CRCP 132/38

p. 27 'But the Germans, General . . .', Maj Gen R. E. Urquhart (with Wilfred Greatorex), *Arnhem*, Barnsley, 2008, p. 17

'planning geniuses', Maj Gen Sosabowski, CRCP 132/45

'Believe me . . .', Lt Robin Vlasto, A Company, 2nd Para Bn, CRCP 111/7

'Large forces of airborne troops . . .', FAAA, NARA RG498 290/56/2/3, Box 1466

'a plan to lift . . .', FLPP, Box 2

'believed that the Air Forces . . .', FAAA, NARA RG498 290/56/2/3, Box 1466

'small size of [the] island . . .', Brereton to Montgomery, 9.9.44, TNA WO 205/197

'we didn't work in the serious way . . .', Brig E. T. Williams, FCPP, Box 24

p. 28 Brereton failure to invite AOCs 38 and 46 Groups, letter Leigh-Mallory to Brereton, 6.9.44, NARA RG331/Entry 253/Box5

'Sir, I am very sorry . . .', etc., Sosabowski, CRCP 132/45, and PISM A.v.20 31/19

'being strongly opposed . . .', Dempsey Diary, 8.9.44, TNA WO 285/9

p. 29 'in view of increasing . . .', etc., ibid.

'Eisenhower himself . . .', M524 Montgomery Papers, quoted Hamilton, *Monty: The Field Marshal*, p. 44

p. 30 'Did you send me these?' etc., LHCMA 15/15/48 and LHCMA Gale 11/22

'absolute priority', etc., Tedder to Portal, 10.9.44, Tedder Papers, Duplicates 1944, July–September, p. 347, AHB

p. 31 'alarmed at the administrative . . .', LHCMA Gale 11/22

'fantastic to talk of marching . . .', Tedder to Portal, 10.9.44, Tedder Papers, Duplicates 1944, July–September, p. 347, AHB

'fixed with [Browning] . . .', etc., Dempsey Diary, 10.9.44, TNA WO 285/9

p. 32 Codeword 'New', TNA WO 205/692

'The commander-in-chief Northern . . .', Eisenhower to Brereton, FAAA, NARA RG331/Entry 254/Box19

'Airborne Army HQ . . .', M196 Montgomery Papers, quoted Hamilton, *Monty: The Field Marshal*, p. 58

List of attendees, 10.9.44, FAAA, Brig Gen Floyd L. Parks Diary, FLPP

Browning and control over planning, see Sebastian Ritchie, *Arnhem: Myth and Reality. Airborne Warfare, Air Power and the Failure of Market Garden*, London, 2011, pp. 180–81

'a tentative skeleton ...', FAAA, NARA RG331/Entry 254/Box20

'would be more ...', 'in the belief ...', FAAA, NARA RG331/Entry 254/Box20

p. 33 'estimate of flak differed ...', Lt Col John Norton, G-2, 82nd Airborne, CRCP 100/3

'General Williams stated ...', Parks Diary, FLPP

'Arnhem bridge – and hold it', Urquhart, *Arnhem*, p. 1

p. 35 'No we did not dictate ...', Pogue interview with Bedell Smith, 13.5.47, OCMH WWII Interviews, USAMHI

'normal sized coup de main ...', TNA CAB 106/1133

Hollinghurst memo, 11.9.44, kindly provided by John Howes

Taylor and Gavin upset about their DZs, FCPP, Box 24

'in seven separate areas ...', Brereton memo, 11.9.44, TNA WO 219/4997

101st Airborne responsibility reduced to twenty-five kilometres, Ritchie, *Arnhem: Myth and Reality*, p. 119

p. 36 'One of the greatest ...', Norton, CRCP 100/3

'The airmen had the final ...', Urquhart, *Arnhem*, p. 7

'Arnhem depended ...', FCPP, Box 24

Prince Bernhard, HKNTW, p. 385

'enemy appreciation ...', Brig E. T. Williams, FCPP, Box 24

p. 37 'Went on to see Ike ...', Robert W. Love and John Major (eds.), *The Year of D-Day: The 1944 Diary of Admiral Sir Bertram Ramsay*, Hull, 1994, p. 137

'Your decision ... Revised Operation Comet ...', DDEP, Box 83, and TNA WO 205/693

p. 38 'a great victory', 'produced electric results ...', M196 Montgomery Papers, quoted Hamilton, *Monty: The Field Marshal*, pp. 57–8

'Thank you for sending ...', DDEP, Box 83

'objected strenuously', Omar N. Bradley, *A Soldier's Story*, New York, 1964, p. 410

'Monty does what he pleases ...', PP, p. 548

4 DOUBTS DISMISSED

p. 39 'the whole brigade ...', Lt Robin Vlasto, A Company, 2nd Para Bn, CRCP 111/7

'Come on ...', Lt Col Charles Mackenzie, GSO1, 1st Airborne, CRCP 108/3

'barracks bag ...', 'We also took every ...', Joseph F. Brumbaugh, I/508/82, EC-UNO

p. 40 60 per cent losses, Edward C. Boccafogli, B/I/508/82, EC-UNO

'Combat is a place ...', Brumbaugh, EC-UNO

'Let Patton win ...', Capt Patrick J. Sweeney, H, 506/101, CRCP 98/40

'eager beaver', 'that he would not rest ...', Capt A. Ebner Blatt, Medical Detachment, 502/101, CRCP 97/31 'that a military police . . .', Gordon Carson, 506/101, EC-UNO

'Screaming Eagles – Help! . . .', Maj Richard Winters, E/506/101, EC-UNO

'The English are a very . . .', Louis Simpson, *Selected Prose*, New York, 1989, p. 92

'killers under the silk', unnamed American officer observing Polish paratroopers in training, PISM A.v.20 31/16 35

p. 41 'As Poles we knew we . . .', Cpl Bolesław Wojewódka, CRCP/47

'My Scottish girlfriend . . .', Stanley Nosecki memoir, PISM A.v.20 31/38 26

'*Stary*', 2nd Lt Jerzy Lesniak, 1st Bn, 1st PPB, CRCP 132/41

'Order Regarding Preparations . . .', PUMST A 048–055

'unless you become . . .', PISM A.v.20 31/60 28

'refused to accept . . .', ibid.

'the defeat of Germany . . .', 'Support for the Rising. Air Support documentation', PUMST (2.3.2.1.3.1/4) file A.053

p. 42 'I made every effort . . .', Gen Sosnkowski, 16.8.44, PISM A.v.20 31/16 16

'to walking into Germany . . .', Lt Stefan Kaczmarek, Polish Parachute Brigade, CRCP 132/38

Meeting at Moor Park, 12.9.44, War Diary, 1st Polish Parachute Brigade Group, PISM A.v.20 31/27

p. 43 'Sosabowski permitted himself . . .', 14.9.45, PISM A.v.20 31/19

'the bridgehead to be held . . .', War Diary, 1PIPB, PISM A.v.20 31/27 3

'in order to enable . . .', ibid.

'Some of them were . . .', Brig P. H. W. Hicks, 1st Airlanding Brigade, CRCP 112/3

For the fate of 1st Airborne if not deployed, see John Peaty, 'Operation MARKET GARDEN: The Manpower Factor', in John Buckley and Peter Preston-Hough (eds.), *Operation Market Garden: The Campaign for the Low Countries, Autumn 1944*, Solihull, 2016, pp. 58–73

p. 44 'persist in presenting . . .', memo to General H. H. Arnold from Brereton, JMGP, Box 15

'The general consensus . . .', Generaloberst Kurt Student, FMS B-717

For the battle for Geel, see Jack Didden, 'A Week Too Late?', in Buckley and Preston-Hough (eds.), Operation Market Garden, pp. 85–7; Stuart Hills, *By Tank into Normandy*, London, 2003, pp. 157–72; and Heydte, BArch-MA RL33 115

'I ought to have known . . .', Hills, *By Tank into Normandy*, p. 157

5 THE DAY OF THE HATCHET

p. 46 'When news arrived . . .', O'Zahlm.d.R. Heinrich Klüglein, Heeres Kraftfahrzeugpark 550, Utrecht, 8.9.44, WLB-SS

p. 47 'a big child with . . .', GA-CB 2171/24d

'*Bekämpfung von Terroristen und . . .*', ibid.

'Model is in your . . .', ibid.

'That the English . . .', ibid.

'England only has two . . .', ibid.

Rauter, Model and Krebs, see also RvOD

Wehrmachtbefehlhaber der Niederlande, Hauptmann Ritter von Schramm, BArch-MA MSG2 2403

'parachute landing . . .', 10.9.44, 3. Jagddivision KTB, BArch-MA RL8 171, 3

p. 48 Trevor-Roper report, TNA CAB 154/105. I am most grateful to Max Hastings for passing me this detail

'XIX Corps on the 14th . . .', CBHC, Box 4, Folder 13

p. 49 'Although he had a wife . . .', GA-CB 2171/29b

'feeling of combat superiority', II SS Panzer Corps, FMS P-155

p. 50 Three Mark V Panthers, BArch-MA RS3-9, pp. 3–4

Kampfgruppe Walther, FMS P-188

Ultra decrypts on II Panzer Corps, 5 & 6.9.44, TNA DEFE 3/221

'The operation was conceived . . .', Pogue interview with Bedell Smith, 13.5.47, OCMH WWII Interviews, USAMHI

'the only reinforcements . . .', NARA RG498 290/56/2/3, Box 1466

p. 51 'I have my own . . .', FCPP, Box 24

'waved [Bedell Smith's] objections . . .', Charles B. MacDonald, *The Siegfried Line Campaign*, OCMH, Washington, DC, 1963, p. 122; see also Kenneth Strong, *Intelligence at the Top*, London, 1968, p. 49

'He worried about . . .', Brig E. T. Williams, FCPP, Box 24

'In point of fact . . .', Harmel, GA-CB 2171/24

For photo-reconnaissance mission, see Sebastian Ritchie, *Arnhem: The Air Reconnaissance Story*, AHB, 2015

p. 52 'with their uncanny . . .', TNA WO 171/837

'We reached the area of the bridge . . .', 3rd Bn Irish Guards, TNA WO 171/1257

'Our success . . .', War Diary, 2nd (Armoured) Bn, Irish Guards, TNA WO 171/1256

Lt Rupert Buchanan-Jardine, HCR, TNA WO 171/837 and CRCP 114/46

p. 53 Reaction in Eindhoven, Diary mej. Crielaers, RHCE D-0001/1383/2042

'We hear artillery fire . . .', ibid.

'guarded by totally . . .', 13.9.44, Fullriede Tagebuch, BArch-MA MSG2 1948

'several days' respite', 'Top up . . .', TNA WO 171/837

'XXX Corps' advance . . .', FAAA, NARA RG331/Entry 253/Box6

Air support conference, FAAA, NARA RG331/Entry 254/Box20

p. 54 Lieutenant Colonel C. D. Renfro, CRCP 96/1

'I had no idea at all . . .', Maj Gen R. E. Urquhart (with Wilfred Greatorex), *Arnhem*, Barnsley, 2008, p. 10

'You had better . . .', etc., ibid., p. 15

'an airborne division was . . .', ibid.

p. 55 Browning and Gale, Richard Mead, *General 'Boy': The Life of Lieutenant General Sir Frederick Browning*, Barnsley, 2010, p. 120

'cheerful, red-faced . . .', Urquhart, *Arnhem*, p. 10

p. 56 For the 1st Airborne's signals problems, see the analysis in Lewis Golden, *Echoes from Arnhem*, London, 1984, pp. 139–69

6 FINAL TOUCHES

p. 57 'The houses of teachers ...', 11.9.44, Diary Johanna Marie Fokkinga, RAN 579/662

Teachers into hiding, Diary Albertus Uijen, RAN 579/23-33

Furniture to be sent to Germany, P. C. Boeren, city archivist Nijmegen, CRCP 124/1

Nijmegen threat of executions for sabotage, Diary Albertus Uijen, RAN 579/23-33

'nine terrorists shot', 07.45h, 16.9.44, BArch-MA RH 19 IX/22, 187

'a camouflaged terrorist', 21.50h, 15.9.44, H.Gr.B., Feindlagebeurteilungen, BArch-MA RH 19 IX/19, 3

Munitions dump near Arnhem, anonymous diary, NIOD 244/1040

p. 58 'We did not know what danger was', Lucianus Vroemen, CRCP 121/26

Dr van der Beek, NIOD 244/5

'The lunatic asylum ...', 'Slag bij Arnhem', GA-CB 2171/1

Urquhart's request to bomb Wolfheze, CRCP 93/3

Kruijff's group, Albert Horstman, LKP, CRCP 120/28

p. 59 Reprisals threatened in Arnhem, NIOD 244/1040

Nicholas de Bode, PTT engineer, CRCP 120/11

PGEM, GA-CB 2171/17

'patriotic little fairytales', HKNTW, p. 384

'did not think the resistance ...', Prince Bernhard, CRCP 120/2

p. 60 '*Deutsche Wehrmacht* ...', Oosterbeek, *Niet tevergeefs. Oosterbeek September 1944*, Arnhem, 1946, p. 17

Wouter van de Kraats, CRCP 125/8

pp. 60-61 'He came up only ...', 'Any other questions ...', Wilhelm Bittrich, Boeree interview, GA-CB 2171/33a

p. 61 'campaign books', ibid.

'a little dancer', Walter Harzer, Boeree correspondence, GA-CB 2171/25

'*Keiner über Achtzehn*', Harmel, GA-CB 2171/25

'I haven't heard a thing', Walter Harzer, Boeree interview, GA-CB 2171/25

p. 62 'like a paradise ...', Diary Leutnant Gustav Jedelhauser, CRCP 130/3

'Each day we await ...', 15.9.44, Fullriede Tagebuch, BArch-MA MSG2 1948

'The situation facing ...', 15.9.44, H.Gr.B., KTB, BArch-MA RH 19 IX/5, 238

'as bad as can be ...', BArch-MA RL33 109/5

Heydte and church towers, TNA WO 208/4140 SRM 1195

'With an elegant leap ...', Heinz Volz, 'Fallschirmjäger Regiment von Hoffman', *Der Deutsche Fallschirmjäger* 2/55, quoted Robert Kershaw, *It Never Snows in September*, London, 1976, p. 27

p. 63 'considerable', BArch-MA RL33 109/5

'Some of the barely trained ...', 15.9.44, Fullriede Tagebuch, BArch-MA MSG2 1948

Allied airpower in the west, L. Brümmer, BArch-MA RH 13 v.54

'The fireworks at the front . . .', Adolf Kutsch, Stab/Sich.Btl.772, 9.9.44, 10 731A, WLB-SS

Market air plan, FAAA, NARA RG331/Entry 254/Box20

p. 64 'The Groesbeek high ground . . .', TNA CAB 106/1133

505th Parachute Infantry Regiment in Sicily, JMGP, Box 1

'Sir, you've ordered . . .', Capt Eddie Newbury, Browning's ADC, CRCP 108/5

7 EVE OF BATTLE – SATURDAY 16 SEPTEMBER

p. 65 'This next operation . . .', TNA WO 171/837

'Club Route', HKNTW, p. 366

p. 66 Briefing, Brian Horrocks, *Corps Commander*, London, 1977, pp. 96–100

'impressed with his enthusiasm . . .', Lt Col C. D. Renfro, CRCP 96/1

'First we'll take . . .', Lt Col Charles Pahud de Mortanges, CRCP 122/32

Napoleonic maxim, Major Jhr Jan Beelaerts van Blokland, Princess Irene Brigade, CRCP 127/39

p. 67 Horrocks sickness, Brian Horrocks, *A Full Life*, London, 1960, pp. 191–2

'for the breakout . . .', Horrocks interview, 15.5.46, LHCMA 15/15/130

For an analysis of the Guards Armoured Division and manpower, see John Peaty, 'Operation MARKET GARDEN: The Manpower Factor', in John Buckley and Peter Preston-Hough (eds.), *Operation Market Garden: The Campaign*

for the Low Countries, Autumn 1944, Solihull, 2016, pp. 58–73

p. 68 'a big mistake', Sir Michael Howard, conversation with the author, 16.12.15

'Oh, Christ!', Lt Col J. O. E. Vandeleur, CRCP 102/17

'Orders were issued . . .', War Diary 3rd Bn Irish Guards, TNA WO 171/1257

'a half-moan', Maj Edward Tyler, 2nd (Armoured) Bn, Irish Guards, CRCP 115/33

'We have 48 hours . . .', Capt Roland Langton, 2nd (Armoured) Bn, Irish Guards, CRCP 115/4

'Gentlemen, my officers . . .', Lt Neal W. Beaver, H/3/508/82, CRCP 105/27

p. 69 'which made it sound . . .', Dwayne T. Burns, F/II/508/82, EC-UNO

'the usual old-men . . .', Capt Carl W. Kappel, H/504/82, CRCP 103/1

'We were damned sure . . .', ibid.

'I'm supposed to tell you . . .', ibid.

'Everyone is serious . . .', PISM A.v.20 31/32 43

'the Poniatowski bridge . . .', PISM A.v.20 31/38 26

p. 70 'and volunteered *en masse* . . .', E. J. Vere-Davies, D Company 1 Para, AAMH, DOOS NO: 038

'Bring it back . . .', Capt R. Temple, 4th Parachute Brigade HQ, CRCP 117/36

'Something was . . .', 16.9.44, Diary Martijn Louis Deinum, NBMG 5.3.20548

'You just wait until . . .', HvdV, p. 22.

'halt on or near . . .', 16.9.44, H.Gr.B., KTB, BArch-MA RH 19 IX/5, 232

p. 71 Hitler's announcement of Ardennes offensive, Diary of General der Flieger Kreipe, FMS P-096

'The battle in the west . . .', 16.9.44, H.Gr.B., KTB, BArch-MA RH 19 IX/5, 241

'in Ostend harbour . . .', 16.9.44, 11.20h, H.Gr.B., KTB, BArch-MA RH 19 IX/90

Harmel journey to Berlin, SS-Brigadeführer Harmel, FMS P-163, and CRCP 130/13

p. 72 'regarded me as a . . .', GA-CB 2171/24a

'I simply cannot remember . . .', GA-CB 2171/24c

'The English cannot afford . . .', Krafft Diary, TNA WO 205/1124

'Life there was . . .', SS-Sturmmann K. H. Bangard, SS-Panzergrenadier-Ausbildungs- und Ersatz-Bataillon 16, GA-CB 2171/24a.

'Some troopers were dancing . . .', Dwayne T. Burns, F/II/508/82, EC-UNO

p. 73 'We were disenchanted . . .', S/Sgt Neal Boyle, E/II/506/101, EC-UNO

'Lieutenant, I've got . . .', Lt Edmund L. Wierzbowski, H/III/502/101, CRCP 98/5

8　AIRBORNE INVASION – SUNDAY MORNING 17 SEPTEMBER

p. 74 'Luftwaffe reaction was hesitant', Allied Air Operations Holland, TNA AIR 37/1214

Smoked haddock, Sgt Robert Jones, 2nd Para Bn, CRCP 110/50

Frost's preparations, John Frost, *A Drop Too Many*, Barnsley, 2008, p. 124

p. 75 'There's old Johnny . . .', Pvt James Sims, 2 Para, CRCP 111/1

Browning's teddy bears, Richard Mead, *General 'Boy': The Life of Lieutenant General Sir Frederick Browning*, Barnsley, 2010, p. 125

'Look, Charles . . .', Col Charles Mackenzie, GSO1, 1st Airborne Division, CRCP 108/3

'to pass away . . .', Harry Butcher, *Three Years with Eisenhower*, London, 1946, p. 573

Bottle of sherry, Capt B. W. Briggs, HQ 1st Para Brigade, CRCP 109/30

'Up with the Frauleins' . . .', Urquhart, CRCP 93/3

'The chaps are just the same . . .', S/Sgt Leslie Gibbons, D Squadron, quoted George Chatterton, *The Wings of Pegasus*, London, 1982, p. 187

p. 76 'what all those blonde girls . . .', Lt Sam H. Bailey, 505/82, CRCP 104/4

'The gold and white vestments . . .', Laurence Critchell, *Four Stars of Hell*, New York, 1947, p. 113

Self-inflicted injuries, Brig Gen Anthony C. McAuliffe, CRCP 96/9, and Richard L. Klein, III/501/101, CRCP 97/11

p. 77 'Just step out . . .', JMGP, Box 15

'Hook your safety . . .', 2nd Lt William 'Buck' Dawson, JMGP, Box 15

p. 78 'How many days' . . .', Lt Col C. D. Renfro, NARA RG407, Entry 427B, ML 2124

Artillery regiments, TNA WO 171/1256

Binoculars and telescopes, C. A. Dekkers and L. P. J. Vroemen, *De zwarte herfst. Arnhem 1944*, Arnhem, 1984, p. 22

'Germans stumbling . . .', Gerhardus Gysbers, antiquarian bookseller, CRCP 120/20

St Catharina Gasthuis, Willem Tiemens, CRCP 121/22

Sister Christine van Dijk, CRCP 120/15

Dutch joke on RAF inaccuracy, Jan Voskuil, CRCP 125/22

p. 79 'Fire engines [are] unable . . .', anonymous diary, NIOD 244/1040

'air raids on flak positions . . .', H.Gr.B., KTB, 17.9.44, BArch-MA, RH 19 IX/5, 249

'a badly burnt rabbit . . .', Ton Gieling, GAA 1557/1511

Dr Marius van de Beek, neurologist, NIOD 244/5

The men had 'dived', Heimrich Bisterbosch, CRCP 120/10

p. 80 'Annoying red tape . . .', ALDS

p. 81 'not ready for use', GA-CB 2171/4

'it felt like the start . . .', Lt Col J. O. E. Vandeleur, CRCP 102/17

Nuns in convent, Lt James J. Coyle, E/II/505/82, CRCP 92/9

'tiny checker box fields', Dawson, JMGP, Box 15

'jumped up and released . . .', Lt Col Harold W. Hannah, CRCP 96/7

p. 82 KOSB brewing tea, Sergeant William Oakes, Glider Pilot Regiment, CRCP 116/41

White silk scarf, Philip H. Nadler, F/II/504/82, CRCP 103/12

'Blitz Creek', Dawson, JMGP, Box 15

'They're leaving the cancellation . . .', L/Bdr Percy Parkes, Light Regiment RA, CRCP 113/55

'stayed afloat for . . .', FAAA, NARA RG331/Entry 254/Box20

'Wow!', JMGP, Box 15

'some [were] cocky . . .', Pvt James Sims, 2nd Para Bn, CRCP 111/1

'We tried to fake . . .', CRCP 97/3

'Gory, Gory . . .', Sgt Paddy Campbell, 2nd Para Bn, CRCP 110/34

'slept most of the distance . . .', Lt Col Patrick Cassidy, I/502/101, FAAA, NARA RG331/Entry 254/Box20

p. 83 'He was shot . . .', Pfc Patrick J. O'Hagan, E/II/505/82, CRCP 104/73

'a fugitive from the . . .', S/Sgt Paul D. Nunan, D/I/505/82, CRCP 104/72

'We could see the tracers . . .', Chaplain Kuehl, quoted T. Moffatt Burriss, *Strike and Hold*, Washington, DC, 2000, p. 105

'golf balls of red tracer', CRCP 104/74

'It was a feeling . . .', CRCP 92/9

p. 84 'Look, they're giving you . . .', CRCP 92/9

'The sky was black . . .', British Broadcasting Corporation, *War Report: A Record of Dispatches Broadcast by the BBC's War Correspondents with the Allied Expeditionary Force, 6 June 1944–5 May 1945*, London, 1946, p. 233

'What's that stuff?', Col Frank J. McNees, 435 TCG, CRCP 107/16

'there is no way to fight back', Dwayne T. Burns, F/II/508/82, EC-UNO

'instructions for flying . . .', Melton E. Stevens, 326th Airborne Engineer Bn, Veterans Survey, 101st Airborne Division, USAMHI, Box 2

Jeep filled with explosive, Capt Eric Mackay, 1st Para Sqn RE, CRCP 110/55

'sweating out the flak', FAAA, NARA RG331/Entry 254/Box20

p. 85 'Well, there goes the wing', CRCP 96/1

'Cassidy, the green light is on', CRCP 97/1

'Long live Stalin!', Stevan Dedijer in *Princeton Alumni Weekly*, 21.12.94, EC-UNO

'suddenly chickened out . . .', Diary Lt Col Harold W. Hannah, CRCP 96/7

Lieutenant Colonel Warren R. Williams, HQ/504/82, CRCP 103/26

p. 86 'By now [we're] getting . . .', Edward R. Murrow, CBS, in British Broadcasting Corporation, *War Report*, pp. 233–4

'then a falling plane . . .', William True, EC-UNO

'the plane throttling . . .', Capt Arthur W. Ferguson, III/504/82, CRCP 102/23

'Get ready . . .', JMGP, Box 15

'The medics had . . .', Capt Patrick J. Sweeney, H, 506/101, CRCP 98/40

p. 87 'a Jeep came flying . . .', Gordon Carson, E/II/506/101, EC-UNO

'Among the hundreds of gliders . . .', Capt Adam A. Komosa, 504/82, CRCP 103/5

'The transparent insincerity . . .', Lt Col John Frost, CO 2 Para, CRCP 110/42

Captain Eric Mackay, 1st Para Sqn RE, CRCP 110/55

Glider disintegrated, Warrant Officer Allan Schofield, 38 Group RAF, CRCP 117/32

'We were almost at the . . .', Chatterton, *The Wings of Pegasus*, p. 183

Cows on landing zone, Sgt Roy Hatch, Glider Pilot Regiment, CRCP 116/2

p. 88 'Driver advance!', Brian Horrocks, *A Full Life*, London, 1960, p. 212

'It was the first time I had . . .', J. O. E. Vandeleur, CRCP 102/17

'mush', Lt John Quinan, 2nd (Armoured) Bn, Irish Guards, CRCP 115/21

'one of those little striped . . .', Flt Lt Donald Love, CRCP 115/17

p. 89 'As he fell . . .', Quinan, CRCP 115/21

'And this extraordinary combination . . .', Maj Edward Tyler, 2nd (Armoured) Bn, Irish Guards, CRCP 115/33; and TNA WO 171/1256

'Frankly, he was dead . . .', Quinan, CRCP 115/21

'I caught a movement . . .', J. O. E. Vandeleur, CRCP 102/17

9 THE GERMAN REACTION – SUNDAY 17 SEPTEMBER

p. 91 'In the distance . . .', SS-Sturmmann K. H. Bangard, 16 SS Training and Replacement Battalion, CRCP 131/9

'What a wonderful sound . . .', SS Sturmbannführer Sepp Krafft, GA-CB 2171/24a

'I was suddenly startled . . .', ALDS

p. 92 'This will be the decisive . . .', Diary Leutnant Gustav Jedelhauser, CRCP 130/3

'[Model] ran to his bedroom . . .', GA-CB 2171/24c

p. 93 Schoonoord Hotel, CRCP 125/3

'A panic flight . . .', Dr Erwin Gerhardt, CRCP 131/21

'Command post attacked . . .', BArch-MA RL8 171, 4

Krafft Battalion account based on KTB, SS Panzergrenadier- Ausbildungs- und Ersatz-Bataillon 16, TNA WO 205/1124, and GA-CB 2171/24a

'It was Sunday . . .', Bangard, CRCP 131/9

'the spine-chilling . . .', etc., Krafft, GA-CB 2171/24c

'pulled up his pants', ibid.

'Battalion, prepare to march!', Bangard, CRCP 131/9

'In a feverish hurry . . .', SS-Sturmmann K. H. Bangard, CRCP 128/2

p. 94 'It was up to me . . .', etc., GA-CB 2171/24c

Battalion strength, KTB, SS-Panzergrenadier- Ausbildungs- und Ersatz-Bataillon 16, TNA WO 205/1124

'Attack immediately . . .', KTB, TNA WO 205/1124

'In this present fight . . .', ibid.

p. 95 'Paratroopers have landed . . .', GA-CB 2171/25

'Cirrocumulus?' Pionier-Bataillon 9, SS Kampfgruppe Brinkmann, BArch-MA N756 158A

p. 96 'We learn that . . .', Diary Gefr. Schulte-Fabricius, 19.9.44, WLB-SS

'The RAD commander . . .', Stelzenmüller, CRCP 132/18

Harmel at Bad Saarow, 'could rely only . . .', SS-Brigadeführer Harmel, FMS P-16

p. 97 The telephone rang, GA-CB 2171/1

'Our commanders are simply . . .', Fullriede Tagebuch, BArch-MA MSG2 1948

'Yes, but can you . . .', etc., GA-CB 2171/24d; see also RvOD, p. 614

10 THE BRITISH LANDINGS – SUNDAY 17 SEPTEMBER

p. 98 Death of Corporal Jones, Pvt Alfred Jones, CRCP 114/12

'Blue Bonnets . . .', Lt Col Robert Payton-Reid, KOSB, CRCP 111/36, MPRAF

'made a bad landing . . .', etc., Diary Col Graeme Warrack, GAA 1557/322; FAAA, NARA RG331/Entry 256/Box35

p. 99 'Is this journey absolutely . . .', Diary Leutnant Martin, Mohren-Bataillon, Rautenfeld-Regiment, published in *Veghelse Courant*, 19.3.49

'Are you a postman?', Jan Donderwinkel, CRCP 125/1

'Our glider had a rough . . .', Lt John Stevenson, 'Arnhem Diary', *Reconnaissance Journal*, vol. 4, no. 1, Autumn 1947

Gough's insistence on parachuting, Maj C. F. H. Gough, 1st Airborne Reconnaissance Squadron, CRCP 114/17

p. 100 Barnett and batman, Lt Patrick Barnett, Defence Platoon, 1st Parachute Brigade, CRCP 109/26

Locals cutting rigging lines, AAMH 50EO 0782

'Brace, there is no point . . .', Cpl Terry Brace, 16th (Para) Field Ambulance, CRCP 109/29

Military police detachment, CRCP 109/29

p. 101 Lieutenant Paul B. Johnson air support party, FAAA, NARA RG331/Entry 253/Box1

'Tiger Rag', Maj E. M. Mackay RE, 'The Battle of Arnhem Bridge', *Royal Engineers Journal*, Dec. 1954, p. 306

Left side of the road, L/Bdr James Jones, 1st Light Regiment RA, CRCP 113/52

'Casualties had been lighter . . .', DDMS 1st Airborne Division, Diary Col

Graeme Warrack, GAA 1557/322; FAAA, NARA RG331/Entry 256/Box35

p. 102 Lieutenant Bucknell's troop, Gough, CRCP 114/17

Hicks's main concern, Brig P. H. W. Hicks, 1st Airlanding Brigade, CRCP 112/3

p. 103 'The General drove up . . .', Hibbert quoted John Waddy, *A Tour of the Arnhem Battlefields*, Barnsley, 2011, p. 59

'The people were shouting and pointing . . .', Jan Voskuil, CRCP 125/22

'Not bloody likely . . .', Jan Eijkelhoff, CRCP 125/3

'Everywhere the Churchill . . .', Stuart Mawson, *Arnhem Doctor*, Staplehurst, 2000, p. 40

'The British soldiers arrive', Oosterbeek, *Niet tevergeefs. Oosterbeek September 1944*, Arnhem, 1946, p. 17

p. 104 'They're together some place . . .', Gough, CRCP 114/17

'Hold a mess-tin out . . .', Pvt James Sims, 2nd Para Bn, CRCP 111/1

'He got to the middle . . .', Lt Peter Barry, 2 Para, CRCP 100/32

p. 105 'They might have surrendered . . .', Lt H. A. Todd, CRCP 102/5

'like a triumphal procession', Lt Robin Vlasto, A Company, 2nd Para Bn, CRCP 111/7

'Am I going to be . . .', Cpl Terry Brace, 16th (Para) Field Ambulance, CRCP 109/29

'*Chocolade!*', Pvt William Lankstead, 2 Para, CRCP 110/52

'casualties were almost . . .', Diary Col Warrack, DDMS 1st Airborne Division, GAA 1557/322; FAAA, NARA RG331/ Entry 256/Box35

p. 106 'dozens of nurses . . .', Sister Christine van Dijk, CRCP 120/15

'While they were singing . . .', Ton Gieling, GAA 1557/1511

'Now we are free', etc., Sister Christine van Dijk, CRCP 120/15

'Well, we'll have two . . .', Louis van Erp Taalman Kip, neurologist, CRCP 120/18

'I'm looking for a . . .', Bittrich, GACB 2171/24c

p. 107 'The Division will reconnoitre . . .', ibid.

'taking every man . . .', Meindl, FMS B-093

'fastest possible provision . . .', Cassidy, CRCP 128/4

'The almost complete lack . . .', Generaloberst Dessloch, CRCP 129/12

p. 108 'landings and parachute jumps . . .', 17.9.44, Kreipe Diary, FMS P-069

American airborne division Warsaw, CRCP 128/4

'landed in Warsaw', 19.05, H.Gr.B., KTB, BArch-MA RH 19 IX/90, 32

'quite an excitement', etc., 17.9.44, Kreipe Diary, FMS P-069

'Here I sit with . . .', Cassidy, CRCP 128/4

11 THE AMERICAN LANDINGS – SUNDAY 17 SEPTEMBER

p. 109 'In order not to offer . . .', General der Infanterie Reinhard, LXXXVIII Corps, FMS B-156 and B-343

'The Tommies are coming!', 'like a Mexican . . .', P. Nuis, CRCP 93/5

p. 110 'Go away . . .', 'the Fallschirmjäger pushed . . .', report of 13.3.1949, Municipality of Nijmegen, CRCP 99/25

p. 111 'came very close to being shot . . .', Cpl Ray Lappegaard, CRCP 97/12

Dutch widow, Sgt Richard R. Clarke, G3/101, CRCP 96/5

'The Dutch even gathered . . .', Cpl Richard L. Klein, III/501/101, CRCP 97/11

'When a man landed . . .', After Action Report, 506th Parachute Infantry Regiment, CRCP 96/1

Hollowed-out haystacks, FAAA, NARA RG331/Entry 254/Box20

p. 112 'a beautiful Dutch girl . . .', ibid.

'double A bridge', Dr Leo Schrijvers, CRCP 126/22

'Better than anyone . . .', ALDS

Five tanks, Lt William C. Dwyer, E/I/502/101, NARA RG407, Entry 427B, Box 19182, ML2235

'the fighter-bombers attacked . . .', FAAA, NARA RG331/Entry 254/Box20

'in good shape', FAAA, NARA RG331/Entry 254/Box20

p. 114 'Within sight of the first . . .', Lt Bates R. Stinson, NARA RG407, Entry 427B, Box 19182, ML2235

'You're supposed to . . .', Stevan Dedijer in *Princeton Alumni Weekly*, 21.12.94. Stevan Dedijer, Headquarters/101, EC-UNO

Action in Son, FAAA, NARA RG331/Entry 254/Box20

'stunned by the surprise . . .', ibid.

'God damn . . .', Maj Richard Winters, 506/101, EC-UNO

The Bridge at Son, Lt Col Hannah, G-3/101, NARA RG407, Entry 427B, Box 19182, ML2235

p. 115 'a float of barrels and timbers . . .', Melton E. Stevens, 326th Airborne Engineer Bn, Veterans Survey, 101st Airborne Division, USAMHI, Box 2

'We received ovations . . .', Diary Lt Col Harold W. Hannah, G.3 CRCP 96/7

Dr Leo Schrijvers, CRCP 126/22

'The march was terribly . . .', FAAA, NARA RG331/Entry 254/Box20

p. 116 'stepped out from the cover . . .', Lt Edmund L. Wierzbowski, H, III/502/101, CRCP 98/5

'Coming down the road . . .', ibid.

Three half-tracks, FAAA, NARA RG331/Entry 254/Box20

Wierzbowski's command, Wierzbowski, CRCP 98/5

p. 117 NSB mayor lynched, George Hurtack, C/I/506/101, CRCP 98/21

'You're mayor', Maria de Visser, CRCP 126/24

'looking extremely martial . . .', Cornelis de Visser, CRCP 126/24

p. 119 'torture racks . . .', Francis L. Sampson, *Look Out Below!*, Washington, DC, 1958, p. 85

'quite a bit of flak', Guy R. Anderson, HQ/I/505/82, NARA RG407, Entry 427B, Box 19182, ML2235

'All of the 18 paratroopers . . .', 2nd Lt Raymond L. Blowers, 436TCG, NARA RG407, Entry 427B, Box 19182, ML2235

'had a helluva landing . . .', JMGP, Box 15

Shooting machine-gunner, Capt Arie Bestebreurtje, CRCP 101/7; Gavin lecture at US Army War College, JMGP, Box 1

p. 120 'All guns ready to fire . . .', JMGP, Box 1

'We got out of . . .', Joseph F. Brumbaugh, I/508/82, EC-UNO

Browning's command post, Col George Chatterton, Glider Pilot Regiment, CRCP 108/2

Browning's tent and sleeping trench, Capt Eddie Newbury, Browning's aide, CRCP 108/5

'We joke and laugh . . .', Dwayne T. Burns, F/II/508/82, EC-UNO

'with the aid of . . .', First Allied Airborne Army, NARA RG331/Entry 254/Box20

p. 121 'The field was covered . . .', Hauptfeldwebel Jakob Moll, Ersatz-Bataillon 39, CRCP 132/12

'frightened out of his wits', Fr H. Hoek, Groesbeek, CRCP 122/44

'They hardly noticed . . .', Diary Petronella Dozy, NBMG 9.7.8082379105

'smiling kids', Brumbaugh, EC-UNO

'solidly built . . .', Diary Petronella Dozy, NBMG 9.7.8082379105

'One of the Americans . . .', J. H. M. Verspyck, NIOD 244/204

p. 122 'Cowboy Joe', Pfc Leonard J. Webster, CRCP 105/16

'You dirty Krauts . . .', T. Moffatt Burriss, *Strike and Hold*, Washington, DC, 2000, p. 105

Colonel Reuben H. Tucker, 504/82, CRCP 100/7

Tiled roof, Capt Louis A. Hauptfleisch, Rgtl Adjutant, 504/82, CRCP 102/29

'in very brief . . .', Lt James H. Nelson, E/II/504/82, NARA RG407, Entry 427B, Box 19182, ML2235

'Just about this time . . .', ibid.

p. 123 'People were nervous . . .', 'goose-stepping . . .', Diary Martijn Louis Deinum, NBMG 5.3.20548

'the most unpleasant . . .', Diary Albertus Uijen, RAN 579/23-33

'Men, women and children . . .', ibid.

'We are not interested . . .', Bestebreurtje, CRCP 101/7

'a helluva [German] reaction . . .', 'killer instinct', Gavin interview, 20.1.67, CRCP 101/10

p. 124 Nazi eagle at the infantry barracks, Diary Albertus Uijen, RAN 579/23-33

'We heard the first . . .', Diary Martijn Louis Deinum, NBMG 5.3.20548

Nijmegen bridge defences, Georg Jensen, CRCP 132/4

'Just east of Groesbeek . . .', Lt Winston O. Carter, HQ/III/505/82, CRCP 104/16

'tree row', Arthur Schultz, C/I/505/82, EC-UNO

p. 125 RAF Bomber Command, FAAA, NARA RG331/Entry 254/Box20

'the quick "ride into . . .', Lt Col C. D. Renfro, CRCP 96/1

'to take [his] time . . .', Lt Col J. O. E. Vandeleur, DSCN 6212, CRCP 102/17

'In my opinion . . .', Brian Horrocks, *Corps Commander*, London, 1977, p. 103

12   NIGHT AND DAY ARNHEM – 17–18 SEPTEMBER

p. 126 'I am all alone!', anonymous diary, GAA 1557/163

'somewhat of an unholy . . .', Rev Fr Bernard Egan, CRCP 110/40

p. 127 Lieutenant John Grayburn VC, 2nd Para Bn, Citation, CRCP 110/45

Determined to display conspicuous gallantry, Pvt Ronald Holt, A Company, 1st Para Bn, CRCP 110/49

p. 129 C Company, 2 Para, TNA CAB 106/1133

'Their morale was not . . .', Emil Petersen, RAD, CRCP 132/18

p. 130 'We fought hand to hand . . .', 1st Parachute Squadron RE, Maj E. M. Mackay, 'The Battle of Arnhem Bridge', *Royal Engineers Journal*, Dec. 1954, pp. 305ff.

p. 131 'When you hear a boom . . .', Oosterbeek, *Niet Tevergeefs. Oosterbeek September 1944*, Arnhem, 1946, p. 39

'With the coming . . .', Hauptsturmführer Möller, BArch-MA, N 756-158/A

'just like shooting . . .', Jan Voskuil, CRCP 125/22

'Good morning!', HvdV, p. 37

p. 132 'Arnhem–Nijmegen road . . .', 20.00h, 17.9.44, BArch-MA RH 19 IX/22, 175

'order that the bridge . . .', interview with Bittrich, GAA 2171 33a

'Arnhem road bridge . . .', WBNdl, 18.9.44, BArch-MA RH 19 IX/12, 219

p. 133 'Destruction of Rotterdam . . .', 11.00h, H.Gr.B., KTB, BArch-MA RH 19 IX/5, 258

Reinforcements, 'temporarily motorized', H.Gr.B., KTB, BArch-MA RH 19 IX/90, 26, 27

Police battalion from Apeldoorn, GA-CB 2171/24c

SS-Werferabteilung 102, II.SS-Pz. Korps, H.Gr.B., KTB, BArch-MA RH 19 IX/5, 250

p. 134 'someone from the army', Hans-Peter Knaust, CRCP 130/13

'air-landed enemy from the west . . .', 22.15h, 17.9.44, H.Gr.B., KTB, BArch-MA RH 19 IX/5, 253

Desertion of SS guard battalion *Nordwest*, Collection P. A. Berends, GAA 1557/1438

Kampfgruppe Lippert, 'limited to rolling . . .', GA-CB 2171/1

'with a counter-attack . . .', H.Gr.B., KTB, BArch-MA RH 19 IX/90, 32

'Around us frightened . . .', Pionier-Bataillon 9, SS Kampfgruppe Brinkmann, BArch-MA N756/158A

p. 135 'We all acted . . .', Horst Weber, I/21 SS Pzgr-Rgt, CRCP 131/1

'saw some Dutch civilians . . .', Alfred Ringsdorf, I/21 SS Pzgr-Rgt/10 SS Pz-Div, CRCP 130/14

'A cold mist rising . . .', Pvt James Sims, 2nd Para Bn, CRCP 111/1

p. 136 'I had a good . . .', report by Lt H. A. Todd on Claude Mission, JMGP, Box 15, and CRCP 102/5

'One badly wounded . . .', Sims, CRCP 111/1

'Armoured cars coming . . .', Lt Col John Frost, CO 2 Para, CRCP 110/42

p. 137 'Several German infantrymen . . .', Todd on Claude Mission, JMGP, Box 15, and CRCP 102/5

'Cease fire, you . . .', Mackay, 'The Battle of Arnhem Bridge', p. 307

p. 138 'a ghostly feeling', Maj Richard Lewis, C Company, 3rd Para Bn, CRCP 111/20

'Whoa Mahomet!', Mackay, 'The Battle of Arnhem Bridge', p. 307

'Will we be getting . . .', Sims, CRCP 111/1

'I thought you were . . .', Frost, CRCP 110/42

Kampfgruppe Knaust, Bob Gerritsen and Scott Revell, *Retake Arnhem Bridge: Kampfgruppe Knaust, September–October 1944*, Renkum, 2014, p. 53

p. 139 Assumption of fighting in the Betuwe, Gerhardus Gysbers, CRCP 120/20

'looking as white . . .', anonymous diary, NIOD 244/1040

'turned out to be . . .', 'the hands of the large clock . . .', Coenraad Hulleman, LO, CRCP 120/30

'The noise it made . . .', Horst Weber, CRCP 131/1

'Advancing on high ground . . .', E. J. Vere-Davies, AAMH DOOS NO: 038

p. 140 'Under fire from across the river . . .', AAMH 50EO 0782

'Smoke and fire . . .', 'the smouldering body . . .', 'A dead civilian . . .', Pvt Walter Boldock, HQ 1 Para, CRCP 109/28

'everywhere, many of them . . .', Albert Horstman, CRCP 120/28

'It felt exactly . . .', RSM John C. Lord, 3rd Para Bn, CRCP 111/21

'she sat there staring . . .', Ton Gieling, GAA 1557/1511

Sister Christine van Dijk, CRCP 120/15

p. 141 'around 120 strong', 3.15h, 18.9.44, BArch-MA RH 19 IX/22, 165

13 ARNHEM – THE SECOND LIFT – MONDAY 18 SEPTEMBER

p. 142 'volatile', Col Charles Mackenzie, GSO1, 1st Airborne Division, CRCP 108/3

'fallen to pieces . . .', Brig P. H. W. Hicks, 1st Airlanding Brigade, CRCP 112/3

'somewhat confusing', etc., ibid.

p. 143 March routine, Pvt Robert Edwards, D Company, 2nd South Staffords, CRCP 111/47

'About 10.30 . . .', Lt Bruce E. Davis, 306th Fighter Control Squadron, FAAA, NARA RG331/Entry 253/Box1

'I flew into . . .', BArch-MA N756 390/B

p. 144 'was ashamed to . . .', Adriaan Beekmeijer, No. 10 Commando, attached 1st KOSB intelligence section, CRCP 127/30

Jagdgeschwader 11, BArch-MA RL8 171

'The Führer becomes . . .', 18.9.44, Kreipe Diary, FMS P-069

'weather in the United Kingdom . . .', Brereton to Eisenhower, 1.9.44, TNA WO 219/2121

'The hours literally . . .', Hicks, CRCP 112/3

p. 145 16th (Para) Field Ambulance, Diary of Events, DDMS, 1st Airborne Division, CRCP 109/3

'Can you turn . . .', HvdV, p. 37

181st (Airlanding) Field Ambulance, Major Guy Rigby-Jones, CRCP 109/20

pp. 145–6 Volunteers in the Schoonoord, Jan Eijkelhoff, CRCP 125/3

p. 146 Nebelwerfer strike on aid station, Cpl Geoffrey Stanners, 16th (Para) Field Ambulance, CRCP 110/24

'Thank God . . .', 'I'm ordered . . .', SS-Brigadeführer Heinz Harmel, 9th SS Panzer-Division, GA-CB 2171/1

'Me?', interview Walter Harzer, 9th SS Panzer-Division, GA-CB 2171/25

p. 147 'totally shot to pieces', 'utterly inexplicable', Harmel, BArch-MA N756 162

'I could see . . .', SS-Brigadeführer Harmel, FMS P-163

'It was the best . . .', Horst Weber, 1st Bn, 21st SS Panzergrenadier-Regiment, CRCP 131/1

'They're here!', Rev. G. A. Pare, Glider Pilot Regiment, CRCP 117/1

Aircraft deployed 18.9.44, FAAA, NARA RG331/Entry 254/Box20

p. 148 'a much warmer . . .', Davis, FAAA, NARA RG331/Entry 253/Box1

'slumped back with . . .', Capt Frank King, CRCP 113/4

'At 13.55 . . .', etc., Maj J. E. Blackwood, 11 Para, 4th Parachute Brigade, NIOD 244/1237

p. 149 'Five of the gliders . . .', Pare, CRCP 117/1

On the heath with its sandy tracks, S/Sgt Les Frater, Glider Pilot Regiment, CRCP 116/21

'Someone shot one . . .', CRCP 114/30

'so we handed . . .', Pvt Reginald Bryant, B Company, 156th Para Bn, CRCP 112/34

Death of Lieutenant John Davidson, Maj John Waddy, 156th Para Bn, CRCP 113/33

p. 150 'They are young . . .', PISM A.v.20 31/38 26

'the hatred of . . .', Pvt Alan Dawson, 21st Independent Parachute Company, CRCP 114/7

'found three young boys . . .', Sgt Stanley Sullivan, 21st Independent Parachute Company, CRCP 114/12

'traitors all', Garrit Memelink, CRCP 121/6

'They shouted back . . .', Maj B. A. Wilson, MPRAF

'We were interrogating . . .', Waddy, CRCP 113/33

'Look here, Charles . . .', Mackenzie, CRCP 108/3

p. 151 'the two brigadiers . . .', Hicks, CRCP 112/3, Mackenzie, CRCP 108/3

'Stop flapping around . . .', Stuart Mawson, *Arnhem Doctor*, Staplehurst, 2000, p. 34

'picking up *en route* . . .', Blackwood, NIOD 244/1237

'seemed more surprised . . .', Mawson, *Arnhem Doctor*, p. 35

p. 152 'Most of the German . . .', Anonymous, Arnhem, NIOD/244/1400

'We were raring to fight . . .', Weber, CRCP 131/1

'more leopardy-looking', Sgt Ralph Sunley, 10 Para, CRCP 113/29

p. 153 'The fighting in this part . . .', Harmel, FMS P-163

'our most enjoyable . . .', Lt Col John Frost, CO 2 Para, CRCP 110/42

14 THE AMERICAN DIVISIONS AND XXX CORPS – MONDAY 18 SEPTEMBER

p. 154 'leisurely pace', Lt Col J. O. E. Vandeleur, CRCP 102/17

Student's claim, ALDS

59th Division, Generalleutnant Walter Poppe, FMS B-149

'They've been annihilated . . .', Lt Edmund L. Wierzbowski, H, III/502/101, CRCP 98/5

p. 156 'cussing colonel . . .', CRCP 97/35

'The Germans at this point . . .', Capt LeGrand K. Johnson, F/II/502/101, NARA RG407, Entry 427B, Box 19182, ML2235

'the fields ahead . . .', FAAA, NARA RG331/Entry 254/Box20

'In a day and a half . . .', Capt Ernest D. Shacklett (medical corps), II/502/101, NARA RG407, Entry 427B, Box 19182, ML2235

'a shell had just hit . . .', FAAA, NARA RG331/Entry 254/Box20

p. 157 'We were in a . . .', Pfc Albert F. Jones, B/II/502/101, CRCP 97/53

'When we had a . . .', Shacklett, NARA RG407, Entry 427B, Box 19182, ML2235

'like bats out of hell', etc., FAAA, NARA RG331/Entry 254/Box20

p. 158 'A bazooka rocket . . .', ibid.

'These men are not Germans . . .', RHCE D-0001/1383

'Stable boys . . .', TNA WO 171/837

p. 159 'the crowd goes . . .' RHCE D-0001/1383

'running fire-fights', FAAA, NARA RG331/Entry 254/Box20

'Everywhere you look . . .', J. F. Fast, Eindhoven, NIOD 244/191

'After four years . . .', Diary Frans Kortie, CRCP 122/24

'Where did you say . . .', FAAA, NARA RG331/Entry 254/Box20

'The flags are out . . .' RHCE D-0001/1383

p. 160 'Don't shoot! . . .', Dr J. P. Boyans, CRCP 122/17

'And the people grabbed . . .', Richard Winters, E/II/506/101, EC-UNO

'He and his wife . . .', RCHE SISO 935.4

'At 3 o'clock, with screaming . . .', J. F. Fast, Eindhoven, NIOD 244/191

'When we are over . . .', Louis Simpson, *Selected Prose*, New York, 1989, p. 128

'The land is flat . . .', ibid., pp. 128–9

p. 161 'I skirted a pit . . .', ibid., p. 129

X-ray machine, Capt Robert B. Shepard, HQ/II/327/101, CRCP 98/55

'in some places . . .', FAAA, NARA RG331/Entry 254/Box20

'Our helmets came flying . . .', Walter Cronkite letter, 13.9.67, CRCP 96/6

'Seventy-five percent . . .', Signalman Kenneth Pearce, CRCP 96/1

p. 162 'Germany's worst soldiers', GA-CB 2171/1

'railway security guards . . .', BArch-MA N756 162

'10th SS Panzer-Division . . .', BArch-MA RS2-2 32, p. 4

'We still need the . . .', GA-CB 2171/24c

p. 163 'a fantastic fellow . . .', 'with great vigour', SS-Brigadeführer Harmel, FMS P-163

RAD to Valkhof, P. C. Boeren, city archivist Nijmegen, CRCP 124/1

'makeshift formation', General der Kavallerie Kurt Feldt, FMS C-085

'I had no confidence . . .', ibid.

'It was with the . . .', ibid.

p. 164 'We don't care . . .', Gavin lecture at US Army War College, JMGP, Box 1

'Three grim-looking . . .', Diary Martijn Louis Deinum, NBMG 5.3.20548

'Some brush their teeth . . .', Diary of mevrouw C. W. Wisman, RAN 579/665

p. 165 'that this would be . . .', Gavin interview 20.1.67, CRCP 101/10

'Father, cover!', Fr H. Hoek, Groesbeek, CRCP 122/44

'as everyone would be enemy', 'were not very careful . . .', Lt Wayne H. Smith, F/II/508/82, NARA RG407, Entry 427B, Box 19182, ML2235

'The people came out of their homes . . .', Dwayne T. Burns, F/II/508/82, EC-UNO

'I pulled my .45 and . . .', Pfc Joe Tallett, C/I/505/82, EC-UNO

p. 166 'a legend in the regiment', ibid.

'The C Company troopers . . .', Lt Jack Tallerday, C/505/82, CRCP 105/9

Other accounts, Arthur Schultz, C/I/505/82, EC-UNO, and CRCP 105/2; Gerald Johnson, C/I/505/82, EC-UNO

'A few of the most enterprising . . .', B. Warriner, 434th Troop Carrier Group, USAAF, EC-UNO

p. 167 'At 15.30, 18 September . . .', Memorandum for Charles B. MacDonald, Office of the Chief of Military History from Major Thomas P. Furey, 8.3.54, JMGP, Box 15

'He drove at a . . .', Capt Eddie Newbury, Browning's ADC, CRCP 108/5

'a quiet night', TNA WO 171/1257

'delayed until 10.00 hours . . .', TNA WO 171/1256

Aalst, War Diary, 2nd (Armoured) Bn, Irish Guards, TNA WO 171/1256

p. 168 Vandeleurs' swim, J. O. E. Vandeleur, CRCP 102/17

'What's the matter . . .', Flt Lt Donald Love, CRCP 115/17

Assault guns, Maj Edward Tyler, 2nd (Armoured) Bn, Irish Guards, CRCP 115/33

German guns north of Aalst, War Diary, 2nd (Armoured) Bn, Irish Guards, TNA WO 171/1256

'The English are coming . . .', Diary Jeanette Roosenschoon Gartion, RHCE 13154:1/10794

'whatever the Dutch and Belgians . . .', RHCE D-0001/1383

p. 169 'all those orange flags . . .', Lt John Quinan, 2nd (Armoured) Bn, Irish Guards, CRCP 115/21

'They were drinking . . .', J. O. E. Vandeleur, CRCP 102/17

107 Panzer-Brigade and the Soeterbeek Bridge, RHCE D-0001/1383; also *Eindhovens Dagblad*, 31.1.66

'A train approached . . .', Tallett, C/I/505/82, EC-UNO

'there were quite a few . . .', 2nd Lt Jack P. Carroll, 505/82, NARA RG 407, Entry 427B, Box 19182, ML2235

'a group of people in fine . . .', Tallett, C/I/505/82, EC-UNO

p. 170 SS trooper and grenade, P. Nuis, CRCP 93/5

'Anybody still here?', Elias H. Broekkamp, Nijmegen, CRCP 123/14

'While the Prior . . .', Fr Wilhelmus Peterse, CRCP 123/30

'In the St Annastraat . . .', P. Nuis, CRCP 93/5

'The fires are taking on . . .', Diary Albertus Uijen, RAN 579/23-33

p. 171 'It looks as if . . .', ibid.

15 ARNHEM – TUESDAY
19 SEPTEMBER

p. 174 'I was obsessed by . . .', AAMH 50EO 078

'The pioneers fired . . .', Hans Möller, SS Pionier-Bataillon 9, BArch-MA N756 158A, 59

'Germans', Maj Robert Cain VC, 2nd South Staffords, CRCP 113/44

p. 175 'Wires and cables down . . .', Maj J. E. Blackwood, 11 Para, 4th Parachute Brigade, NIOD 244/1237

'but at about 11.00 . . .', Pvt Maurice Faulkner, CRCP 111/49

p. 176 Warrack report, FAAA, NARA RG331/Entry 256/Box35

SS panzergrenadier crying, Signalman Stanley Heyes, 3rd Para Bn, CRCP 111/19

'13.00 hrs, message . . .', Blackwood, NIOD 244/1237

p. 177 Cain at St Elisabeth Hospital and Den Brink, Cain, CRCP 113/44

'like animals escaping from . . .', Stuart Mawson, *Arnhem Doctor*, Staplehurst, 2000, p. 57

'As I came down . . .', Rev. G. A. Pare, Glider Pilot Regiment, CRCP 117/1

p. 178 'The Germans are coming! . . .', GSO1, 1st Airborne Division, CRCP 108/3

LKP underground, Albert Horstman, CRCP 120/28

'a BBC set, brought . . .', FAAA, NARA RG331/Entry 253/Box1

p. 179 'Come on, Sir . . .', Maj John Waddy, 156th Para Bn, CRCP 113/33

'It was ludicrous . . .', Maj G. Powell, 156th Para Bn, CRCP 113/18

p. 181 'a country parson . . .', Sgt Francis Fitzpatrick, 10th Para Bn, CRCP 112/48

'Finally, as the German . . .', Victoria Cross citation, *London Gazette*, 1.2.45

'All through the operation . . .', Lt Bruce E. Davis, 306th Fighter Control Squadron, USAMHI and FAAA, NARA RG331/Entry 253/Box1

'See my first live Jerry . . .', Diary H. E. L. Mollet, GAA 1557/27

'Third lift here!', Pare, CRCP 117/1

p. 182 'The landing took place . . .', Stasiak in Jerzy Kisielewski (ed.), *Polscy spadochroniarze. Pamiętnik żołnierzy*, Newtown, 1949, p. 291, CBW

'The British could not help . . .', PISM A,v.20 31/38

'Absolute hell . . .', Maj Francis Lindley, 10 Para, CRCP 113/5

'tears in his eyes', Pvt James Jones, 10 Para, CRCP 113/2

'Later in the afternoon . . .', FAAA, NARA RG331/Entry 253/Box1

'Three minutes' flying . . .', etc., Flying Officer Henry King, CRCP 117/30

p. 183 'Now we too smoked . . .', Hans Möller, SS Pionier-Bataillon 9, BArch-MA N756 158A, 5

'and a few hours later . . .', Interview Walter Harzer, 9th SS Panzer-Division, GA-CB 2171/25

p. 184 'Knaust, can we hold . . .', Bob Gerritsen and Scott Revell, *Retake Arnhem Bridge: Kampfgruppe Knaust, September–October 1944*, Renkum, 2014, p. 60

'It would seem a miracle . . .' Interview Walter Harzer, 9th SS Panzer-Division, GA-CB 2171/25

Upright piano riddled with bullets, Coenraad Hulleman, CRCP 120/30

'On Tuesday morning . . .', Lt D. R. Hindley, 1st Para Squadron RE, CRCP 117/36

p. 185 'Bretherton, for a split . . .', Sgt Norman Swift, A Troop, 1st Para Squadron RE, CRCP 111/5

'We're all going to die', Sapper Gordon Christie, B Troop, 1st Para Squadron RE, CRCP 110/36

Alfred Ringsdorf, I/21 Pzgr-Rg/10 SS Pz-Div, CRCP 130/14

'We bound up our . . .', Maj E. M. Mackay RE, 'The Battle of Arnhem Bridge', *Royal Engineers Journal*, Dec. 1954, pp. 305ff.

'We were now getting . . .', Diary unknown paratrooper, 2 Para, CRCP 94/3

p. 186 German counter-attack, report by Lt H. A. Todd on Claude Mission, JMGP, Box 15

'Great joy . . .', Mackay, 'The Battle of Arnhem Bridge', pp. 305ff.

'We now had over . . .', Todd on Claude Mission, JMGP, Box 15

Logan and Egan, Rev Fr. Bernard Egan, CRCP 110/40

'And to think . . .', Cpl Eric Gibbins, 2nd Para Bn, CRCP 110/43

'The bullet went in . . .', Todd on Claude Mission, JMGP, Box 15

p. 187 'It was all over . . .', Mackay, 'The Battle of Arnhem Bridge', pp. 305ff.

'Oh yes, Digby's quite a leader', Maj C. F. H. Gough, 1st Airborne Reconnaissance Squadron, CRCP 114/17

'I thought I'd go and see . . .', Lt Patrick Barnett, Defence Platoon, 1st Parachute Brigade, CRCP 109/26

'He told me to get . . .', Pvt Arthur Watson, C Company, 3rd Para Bn, CRCP 111/32

'tall, languid', etc., Gough, CRCP 114/17

p. 188 'After a pause . . .', Horst Weber, 1st Battalion, 21st SS Panzergrenadier-Regiment, CRCP 131/1

'Stand still you sods . . .', Signalman James Haysom, 1st Para Brigade, CRCP 110/47

'At every house . . .', Blackwood, NIOD 244/1237

'A sergeant whose boots . . .', Pvt Robert Edwards, D Company, 2nd South Staffords, CRCP 111/47

'You white-livered . . .', S/Sgt Dudley Pearson, chief clerk, 4th Para Brigade, CRCP 113/17

'hundreds of airborne running . . .', Sgt Stanley Sullivan, 21st Independent Parachute Company, CRCP 114/12

p. 189 'which at four o'clock . . .', etc., Col R. Payton-Reid, CRCP 112/15

'casualties were coming in fast', Diary of Events, DDMS, 1st Airborne Division, FAAA, NARA RG331/Entry 256/Box35

'Nurse, cold towel! . . .', HvdV, p. 44

p. 190 'A week ago . . .', ibid., p. 46

Sturmgeschütz Brigade, Wilhelm Rohrbach, CRCP 132/18

p. 191 'They looked incredibly . . .', Lt Col John Frost, CO 2 Para, CRCP 110/42

Tiger tank at the school, Maj Richard Lewis, C Company, 3rd Para Bn, CRCP 111/20

'Thus ended the first . . .', H.-G. Köhler, Schwere Panzer Abteilung 506, B.Arch-MA MsG2 5173/3

Model and Nijmegen, Chef Gen. St.H.Gr. 15.20h, 19.9.44, H.Gr.B., KTB, BArch-MA RH 19 IX/90, 45

'for the complete . . .', ibid.

'It seemed impossible . . .', Pvt James Sims, 2nd Para Bn, CRCP 111/1

p. 192 'They had been shot down . . .', Lt Patrick Barnett, Defence Platoon, 1st Parachute Brigade, CRCP 109/26

'As night came . . .', GA-CB 2171/1

'Then if they tried . . .', Weber, CRCP 131/1

'The houses were burning . . .', Alfred Ringsdorf, I/21 Pzgr-Rg/10 SS Pz-Div, CRCP 130/14

'it was one man . . .', ibid.

p. 193 'You can read the newspaper . . .', anonymous diary, NIOD 244/1040

16 NIJMEGEN AND EINDHOVEN – TUESDAY 19 SEPTEMBER

p. 194 'No sign of enemy . . .', War Diary, 2nd (Armoured) Bn, Irish Guards, TNA WO 171/1256

Wierzbowski's little force, Lt Edmund L. Wierzbowski, H, III/502/101, CRCP 98/5

p. 195 'propped against . . .', ibid.

Fired their last rounds, ibid.

'It was an express drive . . .', Frank Gillard, in British Broadcasting Corporation, *War Report: A Record of Dispatches Broadcast by the BBC's War Correspondents with the Allied Expeditionary Force, 6 June 1944– 5 May 1945*, London, 1946, pp. 236–7

Browning on 19.9.44, Col George Chatterton, Glider Pilot Regiment, CRCP 108/2

'asking if it were true . . .', Daphne du Maurier, letter, 29.3.67, CRCP 108/1

'General "Boy" Browning . . .', Capt A. G. Heywood, 2 Grenadier Guards, CRCP 115/7

pp. 195–6 'I was really living', interview Gavin, 20.1.67, CRCP 101/10

p. 196 'sweep through', Maj Gen Sir Allan Adair, Guards Armoured Division, CRCP 114/38

'suggested that the town . . .' Heywood, CRCP 115/7

'It was a lovely . . .', Maj H. F. Stanley, 1st Motorized Battalion, Grenadier Guards, CRCP 102/17

p. 197 Jan van Hoof, Fr Anton Timmers SJ, Official Waalbridge report of 13.3.49, for the Municipality of Nijmegen, CRCP 102/17, and RAN; Capt Arie Bestebreurtje, CRCP 93/1 and 101/7

Meeting with Horrocks, Gavin letter to General Smith, OCMH, 17.6.54, JMGP, Box 15

'Captain Franco . . .', Capt Robert Franco, 2/505/82, CRCP 104/33

p. 198 'the British custom . . .', Maj R. Winters, E/II/506/101, Veterans Survey 101st Airborne Division, USAMHI, Box 2

'where it was rumoured . . .', Stanley, CRCP 102/17

'nice souvenir', Gerardus Nicolaas Groothuijsse, CRCP 101/7

p. 199 Bridge approach blocked, TNA WO 205/1125

'The town was on fire . . .', 2nd Lt Jack P. Carroll, 505/82, NARA RG407, Entry 427B, Box 19182, ML2235

2nd Battalion paratroopers on rooftops, Gavin lecture at US Army War College, JMGP, Box 1

'The town is surrounded . . .', Diary Albertus Uijen, RAN 579/23-33

p. 200 'It is only when . . .', Cornelis Rooijens, CRCP 123/34

'Some Germans throw . . .', P. Nuis, CRCP 93/5

'they shot left and right . . .', Diary Johanna Marie Fokkinga, RAN 579/662

'We hear that a . . .', R. W. Van den Broek, Nijmegen, NIOD 244/850

'a fierce hand-to-hand . . .', Lt William J. Meddaugh, E/II/505/82, CRCP 104/3

'The racket of guns, mortars . . .', Diary Martijn Louis Deinum, NBMG 5.3.20548

'As evening falls . . .', Nuis, CRCP 93/5

p. 202 'The centre of the town . . .', Rooijens, CRCP 123/34

'After the violent street fighting . . .', SS-Brigadeführer Harmel, FMS P-163

'Commanding general . . .', 21.30h, 19.9.44, H.Gr.B., KTB, BArch-MA RH 19 IX/90

'OK, we will do the best . . .', Capt Louis A. Hauptfleisch, Regimental Adjutant 504/82, CRCP 102/29

'and occasionally . . .', Chatterton, CRCP 108/2

p. 203 Gittman and accidental shot, T. Moffatt Burriss, *Strike and Hold*, Washington, DC, 2000, pp. 108-9

'Hell, yes!', FAAA, NARA RG331/Entry 254/Box20

p. 204 '16.00, counter-attack . . .', H.Gr.B., KTB, BArch-MA RH 19 IX/90, 45

'The tanks turned . . .', D/I/502/101, NARA RG407, Entry 427B, Box 19182, ML2235

'Our men wanted . . .', ibid.

'the tanks were . . .', FAAA, NARA RG331/Entry 254/Box20

'one of the worst massacres . . .', Capt LeGrand K. Johnson, F/II/502/101, NARA RG407, Entry 427B, Box 19182, ML2235

p. 205 'The operation was hardly more . . .', CRCP 93/5

Hauptmann Wedemeyer, RHCE D-0001/1383/2042

107th Panzer-Brigade, Lt Col Hannah, G-3 101, NARA RG407, Entry 427B, Box 19182, ML2235

'with big orange bows in their hair', Diary Jeanette Roosenschoon Gartion, RHCE 13154:1/10794

'A dummy in the uniform of a Dutch Nazi . . .', RHCE 10166.94

'We are free . . .', Door J. Slagboom, RHCE 14475

p. 206 'Stop that nonsense!', etc., Dr J. P. Boyans, CRCP 122/17

Brereton to Dempsey headquarters, TNA WO 219/4998

'every time he goes . . .', CBHC, Box 4, Folder 13

'We will never forget . . .', Diary mej. Crielaers, RHCE D-0001/1383/2042

'huge explosions', RHCE D-0001/1383

p. 207 'A dreadful night . . .', J. F. Fast, Eindhoven, NIOD 244/191

'We all knew what . . .', Diary mej. Crielaers, RHCE D-0001/1383/2042

227 killed and 800 wounded, HKNTW, p. 511

17 NIJMEGEN – CROSSING THE WAAL – WEDNESDAY 20 SEPTEMBER

p. 208 'It was a pretty tense . . .', Maj H. P. Stanley, 1st Motorized Battalion, Grenadier Guards, CRCP 102/17

Homeless fed at hospital, Sister M. Dosithée Symons, St Canisius Hospital, CRCP 123/39

Q Battery 21st, Anti-Tank Regiment, TNA WO 205/1125

'From the first five minutes . . .', Stanley, CRCP 102/17

p. 209 'Charlie Rutland . . .', ibid.

p. 210 'a wonderful shoot . . .', ibid.

'I sat there gritting . . .', Maj Gen Sir Allan Adair, Guards Armoured Division, CRCP 114/38

'left out of battle', Sgt Peter Robinson, No. 1 Squadron, 2nd (Armoured) Bn, Grenadier Guards, CRCP 115/22

'We saw green, grassy . . .', Lt Henry B. Keep, letter to his mother, 20.11.44, JMGP, Box 15

'a veritable wall . . .', Capt Carl W. Kappel, H/504/82, CRCP 103/1

p. 211 'Fortunately, none of them . . .', Keep, letter to mother

'the current was too swift . . .', Gavin Correspondence, letter to General Smith, OCMH, 17.6.54, JMGP

'put the fear of God . . .', Maj Edward Tyler, 2nd (Armoured) Bn, Irish Guards, CRCP 115/33

'As the hour of three o'clock . . .', Lt Virgil F. Carmichael, III/504/82, CRCP 102/16

p. 212 'shouldered the boats like . . .', Sgt T4 Albert A. Tarbell, HQ/II/504/82, CRCP 103/21

Preparations for the crossing, Capt W. A. Burkholder, HQ/III/504/82; 2nd Lt H. H. Price, I/III/504/82, NARA RG407, Entry 427B, Box 19182, ML2235

'ran away', Lt Col Giles Vandeleur, CRCP 115/36

'saying his Rosary . . .', Carmichael, CRCP 102/16

'one-two-three-four', Maj Julian Cook, III/504/82, CRCP 102/17

'a rather incongruous vision . . .', Keep, letter to mother

'There was smoke . . .', Lt John Gorman, 2 Irish Guards, CRCP 115/2

p. 213 'It was a horrible, horrible . . .', Giles Vandeleur, CRCP 115/36

'In everyone's ears . . .' Keep, letter to mother

'Doctors were little more . . .', Lt Hyman D. Shapiro, III/504/82, CRCP 106/52

'I felt as naked . . .', Keep, letter to mother

p. 214 'I was horrified . . .', Gorman, CRCP 115/2

'My God! . . .', Lt Col Giles Vandeleur, CRCP 102/17

'as unconcerned as if . . .', Tyler, CRCP 115/33

'All along the shore line . . .', Keep, letter to mother

'When we finally . . .', S/Sgt Clark Fuller, H/504/82, CRCP 102/25

p. 215 'I think these paratroopers . . .', TNA WO 205/1125

'The soldiers were very young . . .', quoted Bob Gerritsen and Scott Revell,

Retake Arnhem Bridge: Kampfgruppe Knaust, September–October 1944, Renkum, 2014, p. 87

'through some vigorous . . .', Carmichael, CRCP 102/16

Seventy-five German bodies, British Broadcasting Corporation, *War Report: A Record of Dispatches Broadcast by the BBC's War Correspondents with the Allied Expeditionary Force, 6 June 1944–5 May 1945*, London, 1946, p. 243

'ordinary run of the mill . . .', Lt Richard G. La Riviere, H/III/504/82, CRCP 103/7

Scattered banknotes, Shapiro, CRCP 106/52

p. 216 Railway bridge massacre, Lt Edward J. Sims, H/III/504/82, Veteran Survey 82nd Airborne, Box 1, USAMHI; Kappel, CRCP 103/1; La Riviere, CRCP 103/7

'There was confusion . . .', Burkholder, NARA RG407, Entry 427B, Box 19182, ML2235

'I did see old German men . . .', Cpl Jack Louis Bommer, HQ Company/504/82, CRCP 102/11

'You captured yours . . .', Kappel, CRCP 103/1

175 prisoners at railway bridge, Burkholder, NARA RG407, Entry 427B, Box 19182, ML2235

Cutting off fingers for wedding rings, La Riviere, CRCP 103/7

'The Americans behaved . . .', 27.9.44, Fullriede Tagebuch, BArch-MA MSG2 1948

Message confusion over which bridge, War Diary, 2nd (Armoured) Bn, Irish Guards, TNA WO 171/1256

p. 217 'The King's Company . . .', Stanley, CRCP 102/17

'We black ones . . .', Capt Arie Bestebreurtje, CRCP 101/7

'It seemed the whole town . . .', Robinson, CRCP 115/22

'The sight of tracer . . .', Lt A. G. C. Jones, troop commander, 14 Field Squadron RE, CRCP 102/17

'It was pretty spectacular . . .', Lt Col B. H. Vandervoort, CRCP 105/14

p. 218 'I always had a cigar . . .', SS-Brigadeführer Heinz Harmel, 10th SS Panzer-Division, GA-CB 2171/17

American officer threatening Carrington, T. Moffatt Burriss, *Strike and Hold*, Washington, DC, 2000, p. 124

'I doubted that the British . . .', Pogue interview with Bedell Smith, 13.5.47, OCMH WWII Interviews, USAMHI

'they would have stood no chance . . .', Harmel, GA-CB 2171/17

'Countless Krauts . . .', Keep, letter to mother

p. 219 'Another hurdle had been . . .', Brian Horrocks, *A Full Life*, London, 1960, p. 221

p. 220 'I was a great believer . . .', ibid., p. 197

'On being asked by . . .', 18.35h, 20.9.44, H.Gr.B., KTB, BArch-MA RH 19 IX/90, 62

'the breakthrough on to the . . .', ibid., 52

'The situation is extraordinarily . . .', 19.30h, H.Gr.B., KTB, BArch-MA RH 19 IX/90, 62–3

Harmel's claim about Nijmegen Bridge, *Der Freiwillige*, Nr. 7/8 1981, p. 49, BArch-MA N756 163/A 'the bridgehead be maintained', H.Gr.B., KTB, BArch-MA RH 19 IX/90

p. 221 'The commander-in-chief . . .', letter Rauter, Scheveningen, 10.10.48, GA-CB 2171/24d; and RvOD, p. 617

'The question from the Wehrmacht . . .', II SS Panzerarmeekorps, BArch-MA RS2-2 32, p. 6

German attack on 20.9.44, BArch-MA RH24-203/4, pp. 55–6

p. 222 'shaking visibly', Gavin lecture at US Army War College, JMGP, Box 1

'We're just having . . .', Horrocks, *A Full Life*, p. 229

p. 223 Grave for seven German soldiers, Fr H. Hoek, Groesbeek, CRCP 122/44

Americans setting off on patrol, Jhr van Grotenhuis van Onstein, Groesbeek, CRCP 123/1

'They drove their tanks . . .', Lt Col Hannah, G-3/101, NARA RG407, Entry 427B, Box 19182, ML2235

'Our own command . . .', T/Sgt D. Keimer, 101st Airborne Military Police Platoon, EC-UNO

'underestimated the enemy . . .', Hannah, NARA RG407, Entry 427B, Box 19182, ML2235

Rations problem, XVIII Airborne Corps, NARA RG498 290/56/2/3, Box 1466

'Congratulations on brilliant . . .', 2HCR War Diary, TNA WO 171/837

p. 224 'Can you clear them . . .', FAAA, NARA RG331/Entry 254/Box20

'If all they have . . .', ibid.

'He saw that he was . . .', ibid.

'then skip-fired three . . .', ibid.

'The most sensitive spot . . .', ALDS

p. 225 'a neat, cheerful . . .', Laurence Critchell, *Four Stars of Hell*, New York, 1974, pp. 120–1

'like prairie dogs', ibid.

'I watched a flak-platoon . . .', ALDS

p. 226 'It was there that I saw . . .', etc., Fr Wilhelmus Peterse, CRCP 123/30

'There is whistling . . .', Diary Albertus Uijen, RAN 579/23-33

'The inner town was . . .', Peterse, CRCP 123/30

p. 227 'noted that there were . . .', Joseph F. Brumbaugh, I/508/82, EC-UNO

'My appreciation of the situation . . .', DDEP, Box 83

18 ARNHEM BRIDGE AND OOSTERBEEK – WEDNESDAY 20 SEPTEMBER

p. 228 'the towers looked . . .', Piet Hoefsloot, CRCP 120/25

'Damn them, but they're . . .', SS-Brigadeführer Harmel, FMS P-163

'fanatical doggedness', II SS Panzerarmeekorps, BArch-MA RS2-2 32, p. 5

'this is our bridge . . .', Lt Col John Frost, CO 2 Para, CRCP 110/42

p. 229 'This is the 1st Para . . .', Signalman Stanley Copley, 1st Para Brigade, CRCP 110/1

'However, a sixty-ton . . .', ALDS

'passed from a period . . .', Harmel, FMS P-163

'The men were exhausted', Capt Eric Mackay, 1st Para Squadron RE, 'The Battle of Arnhem Bridge', *Royal Engineers Journal*, Dec. 1954, pp. 305ff.

p. 230 'Wherever you looked . . .', ibid.

'My immediate reaction . . .', Alfred Ringsdorf, I/21 Pzgr-Rg/10 SS Pz-Div, CRCP 130/14

p. 231 'some shell shock cases . . .', Frost, CRCP 110/42

'It was undoubtedly the right decision . . .', Pvt James Sims, 2nd Para Bn, CRCP 111/1

'a badly wounded paratrooper . . .', ibid.

'Well, it looks as though . . .', etc., Frost, CRCP 110/42

p. 232 'a forlorn action . . .', L/Bdr John Crook, Light Regiment RA, CRCP 113/48

'Say your prayers boys . . .', Sapper Gordon Christie, B Troop, 1st Para Squadron RE, CRCP 110/36

'He was forced . . .', Sims, CRCP 111/1

p. 233 'Nobody really cared . . .', Dr Pieter de Graaf, CRCP 120/19

Tank at hospital, Ton Gieling, GAA 1557/1511

'Now we are all equal . . .', CSM Dave Morris, 11 Para, CRCP 113/8

'Some troops of . . .', Lt Col William Thompson, 1st Light Regiment RA, CRCP 114/1

p. 234 'I began to think . . .', Pvt William O'Brien, 11 Para, CRCP 113/13

p. 235 Heathcoat-Amory and Phantom, David Bennett, 'Airborne Communications in Operation Market Garden', *Canadian Military History*, vol. 16, issue 1, Winter 2007, p. 40

Terrified young soldier, S/Sgt Dudley Pearson, chief clerk, 4th Para Brigade, CRCP 113/17

'So we lined up . . .', Maj G. Powell, 156th Para Bn, CRCP 113/18

p. 236 'In the Mood', 'Gentlemen of the . . .', Capt Harry Faulkner-Brown, 4th Para Squadron RE, quoted John Waddy, *A Tour of the Arnhem Battlefields*, Barnsley, 2011, pp. 146–7

'Stayed in position . . .', Diary H. E. L. Mollett, GAA 1557/27

p. 237 'If you are lying . . .', Dr Marius van de Beek, CRCP 126/24

'our RSM walked up . . .', Maj Charles Breese, D Company, 1 Border, CRCP 111/42

'The west', Lt Michael Long, Glider Pilot Regiment, CRCP 116/32

p. 238 'We heard a great . . .', HKNTW, p. 380

'As the shelling . . .', Lt Paul B. Johnson, FAAA, NARA RG331/Entry 253/Box1

'Three of us went . . .', Lt Bruce Davis, FAAA, NARA RG331/Entry 253/Box1

p. 239 'The British would be . . .', Charles Douw van der Krap, CRCP 125/2, and Jan Eijkelhoff, CRCP 125/3

'which annoyed me . . .', RSM William Kibble, CRCP 109/13

'removed his tabs and badges of rank . . .', Diary of Events, DDMS, 1st Airborne Division, FAAA, NARA RG331/Entry 256/Box35

p. 241 'but those that survived . . .', Hans Möller, SS Pionier-Bataillon 9, BArch-MA N756 158A, 61

'or answered . . .', ibid.

'You mustn't lose . . .', HvdV, pp. 56–7

'Weapons? Do you have . . .', ibid., p. 57

p. 242 'This hospital has just been . . .', ibid., p. 58

'Eventually he gave in . . .', Diary of Events, DDMS, 1st Airborne Division, FAAA, NARA RG331/Entry 256/Box35

'Does this have to be . . .', HvdV, pp. 59–60

'Good show, chaps . . .', Stuart Mawson, *Arnhem Doctor*, Staplehurst, 2000, p. 89

p. 243 'gaping holes bordered . . .', ibid., p. 83

'the mirthless grin of pain', ibid., p. 81

'Blast this fireman . . .', 'Have you got . . .', Cpl T. Brace CRCP 109/29

'I have come all the way . . .', Sister Stransky, St Elisabeth Hospital, CRCP 121/20

'I know I'm not . . .', Cpl Terry Brace, RAMC, CRCP 109/29

'Look out . . .', Maj Richard T. H. Lonsdale, 2ic 11 Para, CRCP 113/6

p. 244 'Whilst preparing to fire . . .', Lance Sgt John Baskeyfield VC, South Staffordshire Regiment, *London Gazette*, 23.11.44

Major Robert Cain VC, *London Gazette*, 2.11.44

'There was a flash . . .', S/Sgt Richard Long, Glider Pilot Regiment, CRCP 116/33

'Tigers!', Maj Robert Cain VC, 2nd South Staffords, CRCP 113/44

p. 245 The Peace House, CSM Dave Morris, 11 Para, CRCP 113/8

'a joy that almost hurt', Lt Stefan Kaczmarek, Polish Parachute Brigade, CRCP 132/18

'to cross by means . . .', War Diary, 1st Polish Parachute Brigade Group, PISM A.v.20 31/27

'most of the supplies . . .', FAAA, NARA RG331/Entry 254/Box20

'The soldiers, exhausted . . .', Jerzy Kisielewski (ed.), *Polscy spadochroniarze. Pamiętnik żołnierzy*, Newtown, 1949, p. 292, CBW

p. 246 'position was desperate', 'entirely different from the one anticipated', PISM A.v.20 31/27 3

'asked to make a decision . . .', ibid.

19 NIJMEGEN AND HELL'S HIGHWAY – THURSDAY 21 SEPTEMBER

p. 247 'no further report . . .', H.Gr.B., KTB, BArch-MA RH 19 IX/90, 64

Fallschirmjäger under Major Ahlborn, SS-Brigadeführer Harmel, FMS P-163

'in a casual manner . . .', Erich Kern, *Buch der Tapferkeit*, Starnberger See, 1953, p. 111

'dispersed without orders', Harmel, FMS P-163

p. 248 Defence line, BArch-MA RS2-2 32, p. 7

Artillery at Pannerden, SS-Brigadeführer Heinz Harmel, 9th SS Panzer-Division, GA-CB 2171/1

'the idiocy of allowing . . .', CRCP 128/4

Generalmajor Buttlar, H.Gr.B., KTB, BArch-MA RH 19 IX/90, 72

'Every inch of . . .', Maj Julian Cook, III/504/82, CRCP 102/17

'Lebensborn Gelderland', *Trouw*, 25.5.96

p. 249 'Lustwaffe', Johanna Bremen, Nijmegen, CRCP 123/13

'Is that your new . . .', Bremen, CRCP 123/13

'extremity cases . . .', 307th Airborne Medical Company, FAAA, NARA RG331/Entry 256/Box35

'Blood was a major . . .', ibid.

p. 250 'I was carried into . . .', Otis Sampson, JMGP, Box 15

'Do you know . . .', Capt Arie Bestebreurtje, CRCP 101/7

'during the morning . . .', Lt A. G. C. Jones, troop commander 14 Field Squadron RE, CRCP 102/17

p. 251 'The city looks awful . . .', etc., Diary Martijn Louis Deinum, NBMG 5.3.20548

'a chaos of shelled . . .', 'One American paratrooper . . .', Diary Johanna Marie Fokkinga, RAN 579/662

'where they were being . . .', Cornelis Rooijens, CRCP 123/34

Simon van Praag, CRCP 123/33

'Prostitutes who served . . .', Rooijens, CRCP 123/34

'a woman with a portrait', Diary Martijn Louis Deinum, NBMG 5.3.20548

'Generally speaking . . .', Diary mevrouw C. W. Wisman, RAN 579/665

'so far about 45 enemy . . .', 11.00h, 21.9.44, BArch-MA RH 19 IX/22, 119

p. 252 'was a ridiculous . . .', Lt Col Giles Vandeleur, CRCP 102/17

'don't stop for anything', Capt Roland Langton, 2nd (Armoured) Bn, Irish Guards, CRCP 115/14

Timings of attack, War Diary, 2nd (Armoured) Bn, Irish Guards, TNA WO 171/1256

'The Typhoons had begun . . .', Flt Lt Donald Love, CRCP 115/17

'within a minute', War Diary, 2nd (Armoured) Bn, Irish Guards, TNA WO 171/1256

'like metal ducks in a . . .', Capt Michael Willoughby, Coldstream Guards, CRCP 115/44

'it would be bloody . . .', Lt Col J. O. E. Vandeleur, CRCP 102/17

'But we could get there . . .', Langton, CRCP 115/4

p. 253 'like [something out of] a Wild West film', Love, CRCP 115/17

'When I saw . . .', Maj Gen Sir Allan Adair, Guards Armoured Division, CRCP 114/38

Brigadier General Parks's assurance, Maj Jerzy Dyrda, 'Przemilczana odprawa w historiografii bitwy o Arnhem', *Wojskowy Przegląd Historyczny*, issue 1 (127), 1989, pp. 125–37; and FAAA, NARA RG331/Entry 254/Box20

'A bustle of paratroopers . . .', 2Lt Sz. Relidziński, in Jerzy Kisielewski (ed.), *Polscy spadochroniarze. Pamiętnik żolnierzy*, Newtown, 1949, p. 299, CBW

p. 254 'though it is not of our . . .', PISM A.v.20 31/32 41

'The concentrated fire . . .', Kern, *Buch der Tapferkeit*, p. 107

'a rosary of sparks', Kisielewski (ed.), *Polscy spadochroniarze*, p. 301, CBW

'There was intense . . .', War Diary, 1st Polish Parachute Brigade Group, PISM A.v.20 31/27

'Those who've been . . .', Kisielewski (ed.), *Polscy spadochroniarze*, p. 303, CBW

'Some close-quarter combat . . .', 957 men, War Diary, 1st Polish Parachute Brigade Group, PISM A.v.20 31/27

p. 255 'I introduce myself . . .', Fr Alfred Bednorz, in Kisielewski (ed.), *Polscy spadochroniarze*, p. 305, CBW

Reconnaissance patrol, S/Sgt Woll Juhas, CRCP 132/37

'Captain Zwolański reporting . . .', Maj Gen Sosabowski, CRCP 132/45

Urquhart's order to Sosabowski, PISM A.v.20 31/60

p. 256 'to establish the link . . .', 21.35h, 21.9.44, H.Gr.B., KTB, BArch-MA RH 19 IX/90, 76

'British tanks moving . . .', C/I/504/82, CRCP101/1

'The situation is somewhat . . .', ALDS

'Keep moving! . . .', FAAA, NARA RG331/Entry 254/Box20

p. 258 'Keep your people . . .', ibid.

Cup of coffee, Schijndel, Laurence Critchell, *Four Stars of Hell*, New York, 1974, pp. 128–30

'Mortar Sergeant James . . .', FAAA, NARA RG331/Entry 254/Box20

'It fired on an . . .', ibid.

p. 259 'At this time . . .', TNA WO 171/837

'German rations are *not* . . .', FAAA, NARA RG331/Entry 254/Box20

'they tasted like . . .', Critchell, *Four Stars of Hell*, p. 145

'like sucking cotton through . . .', Carl Cartledge, 501/101, EC-UNO

p. 260 'his forces were not equal . . .', General der Fallschirmtruppen Eugen Meindl, FMS B-093

20 OOSTERBEEK – THURSDAY 21 SEPTEMBER

p. 261 'I took a dozen or so . . .', Lt Patrick Barnett, Defence Platoon, 1st Parachute Brigade, CRCP 109/26

Lieutenant Todd, Report by Lt H. A. Todd on Claude Mission, JMGP, Box 15

'It was terrible . . .', Horst Weber, 1st Battalion, 21st SS Panzergrenadier-Regiment, CRCP 131/1

p. 262 Piano on the stage, L/Cpl John Smith, Royal Signals, 1st Parachute Brigade, CRCP 109/22

'We had by late morning . . .', Diary unknown paratrooper, 2 Para, CRCP 94/3

'usual "We-should-be . . .', Signalman James Haysom, 1st Para Brigade, CRCP 110/47

Trembling soldier, Pte Arthur Watson, C Company, 3rd Para Bn, CRCP 111/32

'Never mind, you are . . .', Sapper Gordon Christie, B Troop, 1st Para Squadron RE, CRCP 110/36

pp. 262–3 Marching off from collecting point, Capt B. W. Briggs, HQ 1st Para Brigade, CRCP 109/30

p. 263 Final 'Whoa Mahomet!', Diary unknown paratrooper, 2 Para, CRCP 94/3, and CRCP 92/9

'No one who has lived . . .', Alfred Ringsdorf, I/21 Pzgr-Rg/10 SS Pz-Div, CRCP 130/14

'When the English came out . . .', Weber, CRCP 131/1

'They carry valuable . . .', Generalleutnant Krebs, 1.10.44, H.Gr.B., Feindlagebeurteilungen, BArch-MA RH 19 IX/19, 52

p. 264 Gräbner's men still alive, Hans-Peter Knaust, CRCP 130/13

'We went over the bridge . . .', Ringsdorf, CRCP 130/14

'they were terrific men . . .', Knaust, CRCP 130/13

'Another 24 hours . . .', ibid.

'there is no doubt . . .', Walter Harzer, 9th SS Panzer-Division, GA-CB 2171/25

p. 265 Bittrich's report 20.9.44, II SS Panzerarmeekorps, BArch-MA RS2-2 32, p. 7

Lippert and Tettau, Wilhelm Bittrich, Boeree interview, GA-CB 2171/24c

'Off-side!', Sgt Edward Basnett, Glider Pilot Regiment, CRCP 116/12

German soldier surrendering, S/Sgt Holt, Glider Pilot Regiment, CRCP 116/28

Falling asleep during the battle, Pvt Walter Boldock, HQ Company, 1st Para Bn, CRCP 109/28

'The only way . . .', Pvt Robert Edwards, D Company, 2nd South Staffords, CRCP 111/47

Lonsdale in Bren-gun carrier, Cpl Mills, Interview MPRAF

'a figure to inspire terror', S/Sgt Dudley Pearson, chief clerk, 4th Para Brigade, CRCP 113/17

'Usual morning "hate" . . .', Maj J. E. Blackwood, 11 Para, 4th Parachute Brigade, NIOD 244/1237

p. 266 'The next morning . . .', Maj Robert Cain VC, 2nd South Staffords, *London Gazette*, 2.11.44

'There seemed to be . . .', L/Cpl Wilson, 12 Platoon, quoted John Waddy, *A Tour of the Arnhem Battlefields*, Barnsley, 2011, p. 131

'the Worrowski battalion . . .', 21.9.44, Fullriede Tagebuch, BArch-MA MSG2 1948

p. 267 'They wanted to give themselves . . .', Jhr B. C. de Jonge, AAMH 50N00635

'the eerie atmosphere . . .', 'like ghosts', Col R. Payton-Reid, CRCP 112/15

p. 268 'Everything opened up . . .', ibid.

'Major Cochrane and . . .', etc., Hugh Gunning, *Borderers in Battle*, Berwick-on-Tweed, 1948, p. 198

'We got our first sight . . .', Lt John Stevenson, 'Arnhem Diary', *Reconnaissance Journal*, vol. 4, no. 1, Autumn 1947

p. 269 'the rations were running . . .', Lt Paul Johnson, FAAA, NARA RG331/Entry 253/Box1

'Resupply has come in . . .', Cpl George Cosadinos, 1st Para Squadron RE, diary, CRCP 109/5

'almost immediately . . .', Johnson, FAAA, NARA RG331/Entry 253/Box1

'My eye caught . . .', L/Bdr James Jones, 1st Light Regiment RA, CRCP 113/52

p. 270 Ammunition resupply Light Regiment RA, Lt Col R. G. Loder-Symonds, CRA, MPRAF

Private McCarthy's search for tea, Lt Jeffrey Noble, 156th Para Bn, CRCP 113/13

'my wife cleans their faces . . .', Oosterbeek, *Niet Tevergeefs. Oosterbeek September 1944*, Arnhem, 1946, p. 44

p. 271 Lucianus Vroemen, CRCP 121/26

Sheep at Tafelberg, Jan Donderwinkel, CRCP 125/1

Tafelberg operating theatres, Diary of Events, DDMS, 1st Airborne Division, FAAA, NARA RG331/Entry 253/Box1

'The noise of battle . . .', Rev. G. A. Pare, Glider Pilot Regiment, CRCP 117/1

'pathetically anxious . . .', DDMS, 1st Airborne, FAAA, NARA RG331/Entry 256/Box35

p. 272 Dutch young woman shot, Jan Lammerts, *Oosterbeek, September 1944*, Vereniging Vrieden van het Airborne Museum, Oosterbeek, 1988, p. 76

'When he reached the . . .', Cpl Geoffrey Stanners, 16th (Para) Field Ambulance, CRCP 110/24

'The wounded man's foot . . .', Arie Italiaander, No. 2 (Netherlands) Troop, 10 Commando, attached Reconnaissance Squadron 1st Airborne, CRCP 127/3

'What would you be wanting . . .', Cpl Terry Brace, 16th (Para) Field Ambulance, CRCP 109/29

Mosquito fighter-bomber with morphine, Maj Guy Rigby-Jones, 181st (Airlanding) Field Ambulance, CRCP 109/20

'There was a soldier lying . . .', Sapper Tim Hicks, C Troop, 1st Para Squadron RE, CRCP 110/8

p. 273 'There were men lying . . .', Sister Christine van Dijk, CRCP 120/15

'A shell blew in one of the . . .', Cpl Roberts, RAMC, MPRAF

'bad for morale', Lt Col William Thompson, 1st Light Regiment RA, CRCP 114/1

'we are the people . . .', War Diary, 64th Medium Regt RA, TNA WO 171/1059

'We are being heavily . . .', Lt Col I. P. Tooley, RA, 'Artillery Support at Arnhem', *Field Artillery Journal*, April 1945

'This is Sunray', 'Some details about the Battle of Arnhem', GA-CB 2171/1

p. 274 'uncanny accuracy', FAAA, NARA RG331/Entry 254/Box20

'were able to adjust . . .', Johnson, FAAA, NARA RG331/Entry 253/Box1

Saucepans on their heads like helmets, Jan Voskuil, CRCP 125/22

Up to twenty-five people, anonymous diary, NIOD 244/1040

Old lady in bed, Lt Michael Dauncey, Glider Pilot Regiment, CRCP 116/18

p. 275 Child with grenade, L/Sgt Harold York, CRCP 115/49

'I think I must have promised . . .', Lt Bruce E. Davis, 306th Fighter Control Squadron, USAMHI and FAAA, NARA RG331/Entry 253/Box1

Glider pilots playing cribbage, S/Sgt George Baylis, CRCP 116/13

'In the Mood', S/Sgt Holt, Glider Pilot Regiment, CRCP 116/28

'the shouting of the German Jews . . .', Signalman Kenneth Pearce, CRCP 114/30

'Who are you?', Sgt Stanley Sullivan, 21st Independent Parachute Company, CRCP 114/12

p. 276 'Can hear our own . . .', Diary H. E. L. Mollett, GAA 1557/27

'XXX Corps of Second . . .', Blackwood, NIOD 244/1237

21 BLACK FRIDAY 22 SEPTEMBER

p. 277 'At one point . . .', Capt Patrick J. Sweeney, H, 506/101, CRCP 98/40

German attack on Veghel, Kreipe Diary, FMS P-069

'a vigorous house-to-house ...', FAAA, NARA RG331/Entry 254/Box20

'Today's attack ...', 09.30h, 22.9.44, H.Gr.B., KTB, BArch-MA RH 19 IX/90, 81

'to take the canal ...', Generalleutnant Walter Poppe, 59th Infanterie-Division, FMS B-149

Kampfgruppe Heinke and the 107th Panzer-Brigade, 10.15h, 22.9.44, H.Gr.B., KTB, BArch-MA RH 19 IX/90, 82

p. 278 Kampfgruppe Walther, Poppe, FMS B-149

'At one moment ...', Dr Leo Schrijvers, CRCP 126/23

p. 279 Pfc John J. Cipolla, CRCP 97/4

Student claims 59th Division within a thousand metres, 22.9.44, H.Gr.B., KTB, BArch-MA RH 19 IX/90, 83

'You're exaggerating', interview with Brig Gen Anthony C. McAuliffe, CRCP 96/9

'I was afraid that if ...', Lt Eugene D. Brierre, CRCP 96/19

'I had hoped many times ...', Sgt Desmond D. Jones, III/501/101, CRCP 97/7

'with the idea of ...', Lt Bates R. Stinson, NARA RG407, Entry 427B, Box 19182, ML2235

p. 280 'it required seven days ...', FAAA, NARA RG331/Entry 254/Box20

'I'm dead', Cpl Richard L. Klein, CRCP 97/11

'To the surprise of ...', Capt Arthur W. Ferguson, 3/504/82, CRCP 102/23

Heinrich Ullman, Capt Arthur W. Ferguson, 3/504/82, CRCP 102/23

p. 281 'On one patrol into Germany ...', Edward J. Sims, WWII Veterans Survey, 82nd Airborne, Box 1, USAMHI

'a link-up between ...', 10.45h, 22.9.44, H.Gr.B., KTB, BArch-MA RH 19 IX/90, 82

Ressen line, War Diary, 2nd (Armoured) Bn, Irish Guards, TNA WO 171/1256

p. 282 'At first light ...', 2HCR War Diary, TNA WO 171/837

'It is absolutely vital ...', Col Charles Mackenzie, GSO1, 1st Airborne Division, CRCP 108/3

'Deeper! Deeper!', Albert Smaczny, OC 8 Company, 3rd Bn, 1st Polish Parachute Brigade, CRCP 132/44

'before we even ...', etc., Cpl K. Gredecki, cited Jerzy Kisielewski (ed.), *Polscy spadochroniarze. Pamiętnik żołnierzy*, Newtown, 1949, p. 313, CBW

p. 283 Myers warning on dinghies, Maj Gen Sosabowski, CRCP 132/45

'had great difficulty ...', 2HCR War Diary, TNA WO 171/837

p. 284 'the great snag about ...', Maj J. E. Blackwood, 11 Para, 4th Parachute Brigade, NIOD 244/1237

'He would allow us to ...', S/Sgt Dennis Ware, Glider Pilot Regiment, CRCP 117/14

'These men have stood ...', Lt Bruce E. Davis, 306th Fighter Control Squadron, USAMHI and FAAA, NARA RG331/Entry 253/Box1

German sergeant and calibre of bullets, Cpl Leonard Formoy, 1st Airborne Provost Company, CRCP 110/4

'Found we'd been sleeping ...', Diary H. E. L. Mollett, GAA 1557/27

pp. 284–5 'The company was withdrawn ...', Blackwood, NIOD 244/1237

p. 285 'We took our mattresses down . . .', Jhr B. C. de Jonge, AAMH 50N00635

'heavily battered', 'H.G' Schiffs-Stamm-Abt., 18.45h, 22.9.44, H.Gr.B., KTB, BArch-MA RH 19 IX/90, 87

p. 286 'It was the task . . .', interview Walter Harzer, 9th SS Panzer-Division, GA-CB 2171/25

'in the fighting . . .', Tettau, BArch-MA RH26-604 1, 8; Divisions-Befehl Nr. 15, BArch-MA MSG2 13622

'Whenever a "Königstiger" . . .' Harzer, GA-CB 2171/25

'The enemy can still . . .', 22.9.44, H.Gr.B., Feindlagebeurteilungen, BArch-MA RH 19 IX/19

'Instead they would run . . .', Lt Paul Johnson, FAAA, NARA RG331/Entry 253/Box1

'We saw very little . . .', Lt John Stevenson, 'Arnhem Diary', Reconnaissance Journal, vol. 4, no. 1, Autumn 1947

p. 287 'Why are you burying . . .', Hendrik Valk, CRCP 121/24

'I knew they wouldn't . . .', Sgt William Fenge, CRCP 116/20

'Get back there . . .', Sgt Roy Hatch, Glider Pilot Regiment, CRCP 116/26

'I doubt if any . . .', Sydney Jary, 18 Platoon, Bristol, 1998, p. 60

p. 288 'voices raised in a . . .', HKNTW, p. 379

'Thank goodness there are also . . .', Anonymous, NIOD 244/1349

'the strength of . . .', ADMS, 1st Airborne, FAAA, NARA RG331/Entry 256/Box35

'I learned in North Africa . . .', Cpl Geoffrey Stanners, 16th (Para) Field Ambulance, CRCP 110/24

'It is a complete hell for the . . .', HKNTW, p. 391

p. 289 'tall slim Dutchwoman . . .', Maj Gen R. E. Urquhart (with Wilfred Greatorex), Arnhem, Barnsley, 2008, p. 126

'who looks like a man . . .', Kate A. ter Horst, CRCP 93/7

'A number of wounded . . .', Diary of Events, DDMS, 1st Airborne Division, FAAA, NARA RG331/Entry 256/Box35

p. 290 'Water! We want it now . . .', etc., HvdV, pp. 75–9

p. 291 'A woman came in and brought . . .', CSM George Gatland, 11th Para Bn, CRCP 112/50

'Without any means . . .', Kisielewski (ed.), Polscy spadochroniarze, p. 316, CBW

Fifty-two Polish paratroopers, War Diary, 1st Polish Parachute Brigade Group, PISM A.v.20 31/27

p. 292 'Everyone there but Monty', Robert W. Love and John Major (eds.), The Year of D-Day: The 1944 Diary of Admiral Sir Bertram Ramsay, Hull, 1994, p. 129

'For operational reasons . . .', Montgomery to Eisenhower, 09.30, 21.9.44, DDEP, Box 83

'A chief of staff is not . . .', CBHC, Box 4, Folder 13

'We checked up afterward . . .', CBHC, Box 42 S-19

'I am very doubtful myself . . .', Montgomery diary, quoted Richard Mead, General 'Boy': The Life of Lieutenant General Sir Frederick Browning, Barnsley, 2010, p. 140

p. 293 'An encouraging message came . . .', Brereton Diaries, p. 354

'The destruction of Rotterdam ...', etc., H.Gr.B., KTB, BArch-MA RH 19 IX/90, 86

22 SATURDAY 23 SEPTEMBER

p. 294 'a battalion of even ...', Heydte, 6th Fallschirmjäger-Regiment, FMS C-001

p. 295 'what had begun ...', Laurence Critchell, *Four Stars of Hell*, New York, 1947, p. 141

'The battalion on the right ...', Heydte, FMS C-001; and BArch-MA RL33 109

'little confidence in ...', Poppe, FMS B-149

'I saw them, in twos ...', Lt James Murphy, A/I/501/101; Critchell, *Four Stars of Hell*, p. 141

p. 296 'Brigade 107 has suffered ...', 23.9.44, H.Gr.B., KTB, BArch-MA RH 19 IX/90, 97

Casualty evacuation, FAAA, NARA RG331/Entry 256/Box35

'No more traffic from ...', Diary Martijn Louis Deinum, NBMG 5.3.20548

'A short but bitter battle ...', FAAA, NARA RG331/Entry 254/Box20

p. 297 'Skeletons of gliders ...', Capt Adam A. Komosa, 504/82, CRCP 103/5

'Angry exchanges ...', ibid.

'The prisoner would not talk ...', Maj Julian Cook, 3/504/82, CRCP 102/17

'continuing to fire his weapon ...', Stuart Hills, *By Tank into Normandy*, London, 2003, p. 187

'tough, brave and cheerful', etc., Stanley Christopherson, *An Englishman at War*, London, 2014, p. 451

p. 298 'Next to me was one ...', E. J. Vere-Davies, 1 Para, AAMH DOOS NO: 038

'Food becoming very short ...', Diary H. E. L. Mollett, GAA 1557/27

'07.00 terrific mortar ...', Lt John Stevenson, 'Arnhem Diary', *Reconnaissance Journal*, vol. 4, no. 1, Autumn 1947

'the worst and the most ...', Brig P. H. W. Hicks, 1st Airlanding Brigade, CRCP 112/3

'Come on you bastards!', Sgt Edward Mitchell, Glider Pilot Regiment, CRCP 116/37

'a point that being killed ...', Capt Benjamin Clegg, CRCP 112/36

'My lads mostly OK ...', Maj J. E. Blackwood, 11 Para, 4th Parachute Brigade, NIOD 244/1237

pp. 298–9 Grenade thrown among prisoners, Oosterbeek, *Niet tevergeefs. Oosterbeek September 1944*, Arnhem, 1946, pp. 54–5

p. 299 156th Battalion, Maj G. Powell, 156th Para Bn, CRCP 113/18

'Play another one ...', Joseph Sick, CRCP 132/18

'Every day is worse than the day ...', etc., Jhr B. C. de Jonge, AAMH 50N00635

'I see the British ...', HvdV, p. 90

p. 300 'It is the Jews we hate ...', Rev. G. A. Pare, Glider Pilot Regiment, CRCP 117/1

'Supplies of morphia ...', Diary of Events, DDMS, 1st Airborne Division, FAAA, NARA RG331/Entry 256/Box35

'It was bad enough ...', Jan Eijkelhoff, CRCP 125/3

'Surgery was impossible ...', 'a couple of sheep were ...', Diary of Events,

DDMS, 1st Airborne Division, FAAA, NARA RG331/Entry 256/Box35

'At first many of the wounds . . .', Cpl Roberts, RAMC, MPRAF

pp. 300–301 RAMC co–rporal at ter Horst house, Cpl Daniel Morgans, 1st Para Bn, CRCP 110/14

p. 301 'the 15 Tiger . . .', 13.05h, 23.9.44, H.Gr.B., KTB, BArch-MA RH 19 IX/90, 97

Troop movements Betuwe and Neder Rijn, BArch-MA RH26-604 1

'under the unerring . . .', BArch-MA RH26-604 1, 17

pp. 301–302 Piano in Elst, Alfred Ringsdorf, I/21 Pzgr-Rg/10 SS Pz-Div, CRCP 130/14

p. 302 'We had four Tiger . . .', etc., Horst Weber, 1st Battalion, 21st SS Panzergrenadier-Regiment, CRCP 131/1

'running for our lives . . .', ibid.

'had quite an exciting . . .', 2HCR War Diary, TNA WO 171/837

'like they were out on a . . .', Col Charles Mackenzie, GSO1, 1st Airborne Division, CRCP 108/3

'quite a stubble of beard . . .', Capt Eddie Newbury, CRCP 108/5

'putty coloured . . .', Maj Gen R. E. Urquhart (with Wilfred Greatorex), *Arnhem*, Barnsley, 2008, p. 145

p. 303 'Morale still adequate . . .', ibid., p. 150

Lieutenant Paul Johnson, FAAA, NARA RG331/Entry 253/Box1

'We saw the first real air . . .', ibid.

p. 304 Stirlings and C-47 casualty rate, FAAA, NARA RG331/Entry 254/Box20

'I was not very pleased . . .', Maj Gen Sosabowski, CRCP 132/45

Assault boats, Lt Wiesław Szczygieł, CRCP 132/44; and War Diary, 1st Independent Polish Parachute Brigade Group, PISM A.v.20 31/27

'The British would fight to . . .', Komosa, CRCP 103/5

23 SUNDAY 24 SEPTEMBER

p. 305 11.30 that morning, War Diary, 1st Polish Parachute Brigade Group, PISM A.v.20 31/27

Dyrda's account, Maj Jerzy Dyrda, 'Przemilczana odprawa w historiografii bitwy o Arnhem', *Wojskowy Przegląd Historyczny*, issue 1 (127), 1989, pp. 125–37

pp. 305–6 1st Battalion, 1st Polish Independent Parachute Brigade, PISM A.v.20 31/32

p. 306 'The greeting of the . . .', Dyrda, 'Przemilczana odprawa w historiografii bitwy o Arnhem', pp. 125–37

'the Butcher', Richard Mead, *General 'Boy': The Life of Lieutenant General Sir Frederick Browning*, Barnsley, 2010, p. 140 n. 9

p. 307 'Both crossings were to be . . .', ibid.

'I am Major General Sosabowski . . .', Hubert Essame, *The 43rd Wessex Division at War 1944–1945*, London, 1952, pp. 132–3

pp. 307–8 'argue that Sosabowski's objections . . .', Dyrda, 'Przemilczana odprawa w historiografii bitwy o Arnhem', pp. 125–37

p. 308 'It is always easy . . .', Brian Horrocks, *A Full Life*, London, 1960, p. 231

p. 309 'Don't forget that . . .', Dyrda, 'Przemilczana odprawa w historiografii bitwy o Arnhem', pp. 125–37

'I thought about what . . .', Col Charles Mackenzie, GSO1, 1st Airborne Division, CRCP 108/3

p. 310 'a stretch of open-cast . . .', Sgt Dwyer, quoted Stuart Mawson, *Arnhem Doctor*, Staplehurst, 2000, p. 122

Hackett and Pearson, S/Sgt Dudley Pearson, chief clerk, 4th Para Brigade, CRCP 113/17

Hackett's chances at St Elisabeth Hospital, Brig G. Lathbury, CRCP 110/12

'arrange for the evacuation . . .', Diary of Events, DDMS, 1st Airborne Division, FAAA, NARA RG331/Entry 256/Box35

p. 311 Skalka and German intercepts, Karl Schneider, 'Ein Sieg der Menschlichkeit', *Der Landser*, Nr. 847, March 1993, pp. 67–8, GAA 1557/1478

Skalka driving into perimeter under white flag, SS-Stabsarzt Dr Egon Skalka, CRCP 131/6

'What do you mean dragging . . .', Diary of Events, DDMS, 1st Airborne Division, FAAA, NARA RG331/Entry 256/Box35

'there should be this fight . . .', Warrack, ibid.

'As a result . . .', Harzer letter, 15.11.46, GA-CB 2171/25

p. 312 'No. We have not come . . .', HvdV, p. 106

'If you don't shut up . . .', Maj John Waddy, 156th Para Bn, CRCP 113/33

'At considerable risk . . .', Diary of Events, DDMS, 1st Airborne Division, FAAA, NARA RG331/Entry 253/Box1

p. 313 'It was rather surprising . . .', ibid.

'What in God's name . . .', GA-CB 2171/24c

'The Führer has ordered . . .', H.Gr.B., KTB, BArch-MA RH 19 IX/5, 436

Elimination of the Oosterbeek perimeter, 20.30h, 24.9.44, H.Gr.B., KTB, BArch-MA RH 19 IX/90, 111

'changed suddenly', Hans Möller, SS Pionier-Bataillon 9, BArch-MA N756 158A, 61

'Midday the owner of the house . . .', Diary H. E. L. Mollett, GAA 1557/27

'It seemed that everywhere . . .', Cpl Władysław Korob, CRCP 132/40

pp. 313–14 The apparently dead major, Cadet Adam Niebieszczański, CRCP 132/42

p. 314 Seizing containers, Albert Smaczny, OC 8 Company, 3rd Battalion, 1st Polish Parachute Brigade, CRCP 132/44

'to his utter disbelief . . .', Gunner Robert Christie, 1st (Airlanding) Light Regiment RA, CRCP 113/45

'Everyone had red eyes . . .', Korob, CRCP 132/40

'Kill them! Kill them!', Jan Voskuil, CRCP 125/22

'it was like sending our own epitaph', Capt Springett Demetriadi, Phantom, CRCP 116/7

'Do you know why . . .', ibid.

p. 315 'Jerry obviously . . .', Lt John Stevenson, 'Arnhem Diary', *Reconnaissance Journal*, vol. 4, no. 1, Autumn 1947

'Heavily blitzed and sniped . . .', Maj J. E. Blackwood, 11 Para, 4th Parachute Brigade, NIOD 244/1237

'We ate well . . .', Harzer, GA-CB 2171/25

p. 316 'pleasure at this success . . .', 6th Fallschirmjäger-Regiment, FMS C-001 'in a boat loaded . . .', Capt Percy Louis, FAAA, NARA RG331/Entry 256/Box35

p. 317 'The idea was to create . . .', Lt Col Gerald Tilly, 4th Dorsets, CRCP 116/4 'sent to its certain death', ibid.

'Jimmy, I must tell . . .', Maj James Grafton, 4th Dorsets, CRCP 116/5

'Frequent flares . . .', War Diary, 1st Polish Parachute Brigade Group, PISM A.v.20 31/27

p. 318 Dorsets try further crossings, ibid. 'as welcoming . . .', Grafton, CRCP 116/5

p. 319 'the Army is pouring to . . .', letter Browning to Urquhart, 23.9.44, CRCP 108/7, and Urquhart, *Arnhem*, pp. 163–5

Meeting of Arnhem underground, Albert Deuss, CRCP 120/14

Bringing in medical supplies, FAAA, NARA RG331/Entry 256/Box35

British officers admit underestimation of Dutch underground, Albert Horstman, LKP, CRCP 120/28

'about forty years old . . .', Gen Sir John Hackett, *I was a Stranger*, London, 1977, p. 34

p. 320 'armed and organized in terrorist groups', 19.25h, 25.9.44, H.Gr.B., Eingegangene Einzelmeldungen, BArch-MA RH 19 IX/22, 63

24 OPERATION BERLIN – MONDAY 25 SEPTEMBER

p. 321 'the enemy followed . . .', II SS Panzerarmeekorps, BArch-MA RS2-2 32, p. 8

'Spoke to Horrocks . . .', LHCMA, Dempsey papers, 15/15/30

'Monty's bid for the Ruhr . . .', Nigel Hamilton, *Monty: The Field Marshal 1944–1976*, London, 1986, p. 89

p. 322 'Instead of carrying out . . .', Field Marshal Lord Alanbrooke, *War Diaries 1939–1945*, London, 2001, p. 600

Kampfgruppe Spindler and Royal Tigers, Hans Möller, SS Pionier-Bataillon 9, BArch-MA N756 158A, 61

'Enemy in besieged . . .', 07.50h, 25.9.44, H.Gr.B., Eingegangene Einzelmeldungen, BArch-MA RH 19 IX/22, 68

Warrack visiting Light Regiment, Diary of Events, DDMS, 1st Airborne Division, FAAA, NARA RG331/Entry 256/Box35

'On the first day . . .', Władysław Klemens Stasiak, *W locie szumią spadochrony. Wspomnienia żołnierza spod Arnhem*, Warsaw, 1991, p. 172

'complete nervous breakdown', Col Jan Golba, Polish Army Medical Corps, PISM A.v.20 31/43 17

p. 323 'Found a hundred Germans . . .', Lt Bruce E. Davis, 306th Fighter Control Squadron, USAMHI and FAAA, NARA RG331/Entry 253/Box1

'We fired mediums . . .', Lt Col R. G. Loder-Symonds, CRA, MPRAF

'Our gunners called down a . . .', Maj J. E. Blackwood, 11 Para, 4th Parachute Brigade, NIOD 244/1237

'I felt ashamed . . .', HvdV, p. 116

p. 324 'When the Germans enter . . .', A. L. A. Kremer-Kingma, Oosterbeek, *Niet tevergeefs. Oosterbeek September 1944*, Arnhem, 1946, p. 117

Wounded boy, Cadet Adam Niebieszczański, CRCP 132/42

'We haven't had water . . .', Zwolański in Jerzy Kisielewski (ed.), *Polscy spadochroniarze. Pamiętnik żołnierzy*, Newtown, 1949, pp. 334–5, CBW

British lieutenant and cigarette, Smaczny in ibid., p. 326, CBW

'There are few more terrifying . . .', Blackwood, NIOD 244/1237

p. 325 'By skilful use . . .', *London Gazette*, 2.11.44

'So many wounded . . .', Jhr B. C. de Jonge, AAMH 50N00635

Powell at the Hartenstein, Maj G. Powell, 156th Para Bn, CRCP 113/18

'It was a bitter . . .', Blackwood, NIOD 244/1237

'another Dunkirk', Brig P. H. W. Hicks, 1st Airlanding Brigade, CRCP 112/3

p. 326 'The 8th Company is to . . .', Stasiak, *W locie szumią spadochrony*, p. 172

'Their eyes welled up . . .', ibid.

'To expect such a miracle . . .', 'Haversacks are lined up . . .', Wieczorek in Kisielewski (ed.), *Polscy spadochroniarze*, p. 338, CBW

'Many were so tired . . .', Guy Byam, British Broadcasting Corporation, *War Report: A Record of Dispatches Broadcast by the BBC's War Correspondents with the Allied Expeditionary Force, 6 June 1944–5 May 1945*, London, 1946, p. 252

'We were never happier . . .', Hicks, CRCP 112/3

Phantom signals detachment, Lt Neville Hay, Phantom with 1st Airborne, CRCP 116/8

'I have never seen such . . .', Lt Bruce E. Davis, 306th Fighter Control Squadron, USAMHI and FAAA, NARA RG331/Entry 253/Box1

p. 327 'Home Sweet Home', Gunner Ralph Cook, Light Regiment RA, CRCP 113/47

'When the order to pull out . . .', Sgt Stanley Sullivan, 21st Independent Parachute Company, CRCP 114/12

Urquhart and glider pilot chaplain, S/Sgt Les Frater, Glider Pilot Regiment, CRCP 116/21

'The Second Army guns . . .', Diary H. E. L. Mollett, GAA 1557/27

Germans convinced the British were reinforcing, Hauptmann Ritter von Schramm, BArch-MA MSG2 2403, p. 4

'At the back of our house . . .', Anonymous, NIOD/244/1400

p. 328 'Every now and then . . .', Blackwood, NIOD 244/1237

'We passed along the road . . .', Pvt Henry Blyton, Border Regiment, CRCP 109/27

'which now loomed ghostly . . .', Col R. Payton-Reid, CRCP 112/15

'We walked along a road . . .', Davis, USAMHI and FAAA, NARA RG331/Entry 253/Box1

'We settled down on the grass . . .', Mollett, GAA 1557/27

'Long lines of men . . .', Guy Byam, British Broadcasting Corporation, *War Report*, p. 252

p. 329 'orders were that we . . .', Maj M. L. Tucker, 23 Canadian Field Company RCE, CRCP 117/39

'I've lost an arm', Pvt Arthur Shearwood, 11 Para, CRCP 113/24

Swimming with a log, Cpl Władysław Korob, CRCP 132/40

'We stripped off . . .', Lewis Golden, *Echoes from Arnhem*, London, 1984

p. 330 Three glider pilots, Sgt Roy Hatch, Glider Pilot Regiment, CRCP 116/26

The helpers, Cpl George Potter, 1st Para Battalion, CRCP 110/18

'As dawn broke grey . . .', report on evacuation, 23 Canadian Field Company RCE, CRCP 117/39

'Get back! . . .', Maj Gen Stanislaw Sosabowski, *Freely I Served*, Barnsley, 2013, p. 188, and HKNTW, p. 394

'They did not fancy . . .', L/Cpl Thomas Harris, 1st Para Bn, CRCP 110/7
p. 331 'when it became evident . . .', 'He made two trips . . .', Maj Gen R. P. Pakenham-Walsh, *History of the Corps of Royal Engineers*, vol. ix, Chatham, 1958, p. 320

Smaczny in Kisielewski (ed.), *Polscy spadochroniarze*, p. 326, CBW

Lieutenant Pudełko's company, Mieczysław Chwastek, 3rd Bn, Polish Parachute Brigade, CRCP 132/36

'Over the past three days . . .', Kisielewski (ed.), *Polscy spadochroniarze*, p. 342, CBW

'the last boat left keeps . . .', PISM A.v.20 31/36 14

'in a lady's blouse . . .', RSM Siely, 1st Light Regiment RA, MPRAF

Naked men embarrassed, Payton-Reid, CRCP 112/15
p. 332 'I stared at it for a few . . .', Maj G. Powell, 156th Para Bn, CRCP 113/18

'When the Lights Go On Again', Frater, CRCP 116/21

'My God! Don't stand . . .', Lt Neville Hay, Phantom with 1st Airborne, CRCP 116/8

'Well, here's one . . .', Maj Robert Cain VC, 2nd South Staffords, CRCP 113/44

Numbers evacuated night of 25/26 September, FAAA, NARA RG331/Entry 254/Box20

'We came back . . .', Lt Col Robert Payton-Reid, KOSB, MPRAF

He waved a white handkerchief, Kisielewski (ed.), *Polscy spadochroniarze*, p. 342, CBW

'There was an explosion . . .', Chwastek, CRCP 132/36
pp. 332–3 Smaczny's 8th Company at the riverbank, Lt Albert Smaczny, OC 8 Company, 3rd Bn, 1st Polish Parachute Brigade, CRCP 132/44
p. 333 'Dead English soldiers . . .', Jan Blokker, *Achter de laatste brug*, Amsterdam, 2012, p. 99

25 OOSTERBEEK, ARNHEM, NIJMEGEN – TUESDAY 26 SEPTEMBER

p. 334 'There was something different . . .', Rev. G. A. Pare, Glider Pilot Regiment, CRCP 117/1

'When we woke up . . .', C. B. Labouchere, 'Herinneringen aan de slag om Arnhem', GAA 2869/15.

'You see. You celebrated . . .', etc., Oosterbeek, *Niet tevergeefs. Oosterbeek September 1944*, Arnhem, 1946, p. 60
p. 335 Sturmgeschütz-Brigade, Wilhelm Rohrbach, CRCP 132/18

'Every now and again . . .', Diary of Events, DDMS, 1st Airborne Division, FAAA, NARA RG331/Entry 256/Box 35

'Is anyone here?', etc., Jan Eijkelhoff, CRCP 125/3

Numbers of British soldiers found in Oosterbeek, 11.45h, 26.9.44, H.Gr.B., KTB, BArch-MA RH 19 IX/90, 129

'German and English dead . . .', 26.9.44, Fullriede Tagebuch, BArch-MA MSG2 1948

p. 336 'For you the war . . .', Sgt Ralph Sunley, 10 Para, CRCP 113/29

'I don't want . . .', Signalman Victor Reed, 1st Para Brigade, CRCP 110/20

Dutchwoman singing 'God Save the King', L/Bdr James Jones, 1st Light Regiment RA, CRCP 113/52

Glider pilot and mirror, S/Sgt George Baylis, CRCP 116/13

'Major Frazer . . .', Diary of Events, DDMS, 1st Airborne Division, FAAA, NARA RG331/Entry 256/Box35

p. 337 'Bittrich, when will things . . .', interview Bittrich, GA-CB 2171/24c

'North bank of . . .', BArch-MA RH 19 IX/12, 271

German estimates of losses, H.Gr.B., KTB, BArch-MA RH 19 IX/90, 125

1,880 wounded, 29.9.44, H.Gr.B., KTB, BArch-MA RH 19 IX/90, 167

'The SS has once again . . .', Erwin, 28.9.1944, WLB-SS

'The victory at Arnhem . . .', SS-Sturmmann K. H. Bangard, 16 SS Training and Replacement Battalion, CRCP 131/9

'We'll be back in Paris by Christmas!', Lucianus Vroemen, CRCP 121/26

'the greater fighting spirit . . .', Hauptmann Wilhelm Ritter von Schramm, OKW, BArch-MA MSG2 2403, p. 4

'for renewed airborne . . .', 26.9.44, 9th SS Panzer-Division *Hohenstaufen*, BArch-MA RS3-9, pp. 3–4

p. 338 'When he did appear . . .', Maj Gen R. E. Urquhart (with Wilfred Greatorex), *Arnhem*, Barnsley, 2008, pp. 179–80

'We hardly spoke . . .', Col Charles Mackenzie, GSO1, 1st Airborne Division, CRCP 108/3

Trucks for the Poles refused, PISM A.v.20 31/60

'One look at them . . .', Capt Robert Franco, 2/505/82, CRCP 104/33

'First they were given . . .', Lt Paul B. Johnson, FAAA, NARA RG331/ Entry 253/Box1

'He was very surprised . . .', ibid.

p. 339 'much taste', Brig P. H. W. Hicks, 1st Airlanding Brigade, CRCP 112/3

'It was an ordeal . . .', 'It was his habit . . .', Urquhart, *Arnhem*, pp. 184–5

'Someone walked around . . .', Sgt Stanley Sullivan, 21st Independent Parachute Company, CRCP 114/12

'felt like crying', Gunner Robert Christie, 1st (Airlanding) Light Regiment RA, CRCP 113/45

Hackett's 4th Parachute Brigade, Capt R. Temple, 4th Pct Bde Hq, CRCP 117/36

'They looked like . . .', 'What, you've only just . . .', Corporal of Horse William Chennell, 2HCR, CRCP 114/47

'Where the hell have you been mate?', Capt Roland Langton, 2nd (Armoured) Bn, Irish Guards, CRCP 115/4

'Having a good rest . . .', Maj Edward Tyler, 2nd (Armoured) Bn, Irish Guards, CRCP 115/33

'Some people have all . . .', Charles Farrell, *Reflections 1939–1945*, Edinburgh, 2000, p. 106

'Do you call that fighting?', Stuart Hills, *By Tank into Normandy*, London, 2003, p. 175

p. 340 'Give a soldier a letter . . .', Louis Simpson, *Selected Prose*, New York, 1989, pp. 95–6

'a town of broken glass . . .', etc., S/Sgt J. C. Reynolds, 325th Glider Infantry, JMGP, Box 15

'on taking Devil's Hill . . .', Sgt Frank C. Taylor, A/1/508/82, CRCP 105/37

'A German officer came out . . .', Sgt Theodore Finkbeiner, H/504/82, CRCP 102/24

German surrendering with safe-conduct pass, ibid.

p. 341 'They were challenged . . .', Pfc Joe Tallett, C/I/505/82, EC-UNO

'were using a large . . .', Lt Sam H. Bailey, 505/82, CRCP 104/4

'kept pumping shells . . .', Hills, *By Tank into Normandy*, p. 187

'What are they trying . . .', Pfc Robert S. Cartwright, HQ/1/505/82, CRCP 104/17

'Dear John' letter, Sgt James T. Steed, F/505/82, CRCP 105/5

'He was calm . . .', Pfc James R. Allardyce, 1/508/82, CRCP 105/25

p. 342 'We are still being . . .', Diary Martijn Louis Deinum, NBMG 5.3.20548

Rundstedt's headquarters, 01.05h, 27.9.44, H.Gr.B., KTB, BArch-MA RH 19 IX/90, 140

'whether the Nijmegen bridge . . .', 23.30h, 27.9.44, H.Gr.B., KTB, BArch-MA RH 19 IX/90, 146

'piggyback', 26.9.44, JMGP, Box 1

'a very reasonable, efficient man', FAAA, NARA RG331/Entry 256/Box35

p. 343 'in a hoarse, croaking voice . . .', Pvt Andrew Milbourne, 1st Para Bn, CRCP 110/13

26 THE EVACUATION AND LOOTING OF ARNHEM – 23 SEPTEMBER TO NOVEMBER 1944

p. 344 'Panic rumours – the whole . . .', Anna van Leeuwen, GAA 1557/1053

'three families including . . .', anonymous diary, NIOD 244/1040

'Our houses were full of . . .', anonymous diary, GAA 1557/163; other versions include 'a local doctor and four others', H. Lensink, NIOD 244/313

'Grenades were thrown . . .', Lensink, NIOD 244/313

Civilian casualties, Reinier Salverda, 'Beyond a Bridge Too Far: The Aftermath of the Battle of Arnhem (1944) and its Impact on Civilian Life', in Jane Fenoulhet, Gerdi Quist and Ulrich Tiedau (eds.), *Discord and Consensus in the Low Countries 1700–2000*, London, 2016, p. 110

Obersturmführer Peter, 9th SS Panzer-Division *Hohenstaufen*, BArch-MA RS3-9/28

'carpet bombings must be . . .', P. R. A. van Iddekinge, *Arnhem 44/45. Evacuatie, verwoesting, plundering, bevrijding, terugkeer*, Arnhem, 1981, p. 52

p. 345 'in order to avoid further heavy . . .', Harzer letter, 13.10.75, 9th SS Panzer-Division *Hohenstaufen*, BArch-MA RS3-9/5, p. 3

'on military grounds', 9th SS Panzer-Division *Hohenstaufen*, BArch-MA RS3-9/29, p. 1

SS dressed in British uniforms, Pieter van Aken, Wolfheze, CRCP 126/24

British prisoners marched through Arnhem, Lensink, NIOD 244/313

'Retaliatory measures against the civil population', WBfh.Nd., 24.9.44, BArch-MA RS3-9 5

'Everyone will have to try . . .', Arjen Schermer, NSB deputy mayor, CRCP 121/17

German soldiers in Jeep, Albert Horstman, LKP, CRCP 120/28

p. 346 Evacuation starting with town centre, Lensink, NIOD 244/313

'vandalism of the British', Sturmmann K. H. Bangard, 16 SS Training and Replacement Battalion, CRCP 131/9

Dutch not allowed to put the fires out, anonymous diary, NIOD 244/1040

'Those from the centre . . .', ibid.

'At four in the morning . . .', ibid.

'a Biblical Exodus', Johannes van Hooff, CRCP 120/25

'An old lady walking . . .', Nicholas de Bode, PTT engineer, CRCP 120/11

p. 347 'Many have to walk . . .', Anna van Leeuwen, GAA 1557/1053

'a woman, dressed in a . . .', Horstman, CRCP 120/28

'Well, you see . . .', 'Look, Mummy . . .', Jan Voskuil, CRCP 125/22

'A big problem for . . .', Anton van Hooff, CRCP 120/26

p. 348 'All of a sudden . . .', anonymous diary, GAA 1557/163

'Two soldiers from the . . .', anonymous, NIOD 244/1400

'The rest have trudged on . . .', anonymous diary, NIOD 244/1040

Gerhardus Gysbers, antiquarian bookseller, CRCP 120/20

Shop-window mannequins, NIOD 244/1400

p. 349 'Some of them are . . .', Diary Martijn Louis Deinum, NBMG 5.3.20548

'so Lieutenant Lamb . . .', Woodrow W. Millsaps, H, III/508/82, EC-UNO

'Some of the soldiers had heard . . .', Capt Harrell, CRCP 96/7

'some of our troopers . . .', Cpl Ray Lappegaard, CRCP 97/12

Allied settlement for looting, Sean Longden, *To the Victors the Spoils: D-Day and VE Day: The Reality Behind the Heroism*, London, 2007, p. 238

Placards against looting, Collection Herman Jeansen, RAN 764/7

'It was against all regulations . . .', Private Arthur Watson, C Company, 3rd Para Bn, CRCP 111/32

pp. 349–50 Dutch looting, anonymous diary, NIOD 244/1040

p. 350 'In consequence of the . . .', RvOD, pp. 622–3

'whose task it is to . . .', Schermer, CRCP 121/17

'We had to laugh . . .', C. A. Dekkers and L. P. J. Vroemen, *De zwarte herfst. Arnhem 1944*, Arnhem, 1984, p. 107

German bureaucracy, Tj. de Boorder and W. Kruiderink, *Rovers plunderen Arnhem. Een verhaal van Oorlog, Ballingschap, Vernieling en Massale Roof*, Arnhem, 1945

p. 351 'My dear Emmy', Räumungskommando, 'eviction task force', GAA 1557/244

'salvage commandos', etc., letter by teleprinter Himmler to Bormann about looting of Arnhem, 23.2.45, BArch-MA N756 390/B

Dutch old master, 'Lord Mayor of London returns Nazi-looted Old Master', *Art Newspaper*, 6.11.2017

p. 352 Attempt to obtain protection order, Jhr B. C. de Jonge, AAMH 50N00635

'*Es ist Krieg*' – 'It's war', Johannes van Hooff, CRCP 120/25

'Around us, there are . . .', Lensink, NIOD 244/313

27 THE ISLAND OF MEN – SEPTEMBER TO NOVEMBER 1944

p. 353 'the land was as flat . . .', Joseph F. Brumbaugh, I/508/82, EC-UNO

'One of the strange things . . .', JMGP, Box 15

'This totals 7,382 highly trained . . .', FAAA, NARA RG331/Entry 254/Box19

'hard to accept Monty's promise . . .', CBHC, Box 4, Folder 14

'This caused the jokesters . . .', 14.10.44, ibid.

p. 355 'That is when he got his . . .', Cpl Richard L. Klein, CRCP 97/11

'We were caught . . .', Stevan Dedijer in *Princeton Alumni Weekly*, 21.12.94, EC-UNO

Heteren and the hog in the brick factory, Carl Cartledge, 501/101, EC-UNO

'It was here in the ditch . . .', Dwayne T. Burns, F/II/508/82, EC-UNO

p. 356 'Fix bayonets!', Pfc Earl McClung, 3/E/II/506/101, EC-UNO

'One of our American mortar . . .', Capt Patrick J. Sweeney, H, 506/101, CRCP 98/40

'next one to come . . .', Francis L. Sampson, *Look Out Below!*, Washington, DC, 1958, p. 93

p. 357 'shoulder to shoulder . . .', Burgett, quoted David Bennett, *A Magnificent Disaster: The Failure of Market Garden: The Arnhem Operation, September 1944*, Philadelphia, PA, 2008, p. viii

'We ate off . . .', Brumbaugh, EC-UNO

'One of our boys . . .', S/Sgt William L. Blank, 505/82, CRCP 104/8

'Too many cows were ending . . .', Sampson, *Look Out Below!*, p. 94

$500 fine, S/Sgt William L. Blank, Veterans Survey, 82nd Airborne, Box 2, USAMHI

'The cattle had been hit . . .', Sampson, *Look Out Below!*, p. 94

'Reports that military personnel . . .', FAAA, NARA RG331/Entry 254/Box18

p. 358 'The man turned out to be . . .', Lt Richard G. La Riviere, H/3/504/82, CRCP 103/7

'All the houses . . .', J. W. Lammert, NIOD/244/629

'As I sit on the banks . . .', 11th Armoured Division, TNA WO 171/4184

'*Bei Nacht will der* . . .', TNA WO 171/4184

p. 359 'We still feel ourselves . . .', Diary Martijn Louis Deinum, NBMG 5.3.20548

'the enemy guard . . .', GA-CB 2171/1

British version of events, TNA WO 171/4184

Details on Pfc Theodore H. Bachenheimer, 504/82, CRCP 101/6

p. 360 Tucker's regimental adjutant, Captain Louis A. Hauptfleisch, 504/82, CRCP 102/29 'a small overstuffed room ...', *Collier's*, 23.12.44

'The Dutch sweep up ...', ibid.

p. 361 'in the face of strenuous ...', SS-Brigadeführer Harmel, FMS P-163

'When these Russians ...', Johannes van Hooff, CRCP 120/25

p. 362 Operation Pegasus, FAAA, NARA RG331/Entry 253/Box2

p. 363 'It was like being ...', Gen Sir John Hackett, *I was a Stranger*, London, 1977, p. 188

'It was wonderfully comforting ...', ibid., p. 197

28 THE HUNGER WINTER – NOVEMBER 1944 TO MAY 1945

p. 364 'On my way there ...', Nigel Nicolson (ed.), *Harold Nicolson Diaries 1907–1963*, London, 2004, pp. 301–2

'Despite the failure ...', FAAA, NARA RG331/Entry 256/Box34; and Narrative of Operation Market, Headquarters FAAA, 9.10.44, NARA RG498 290/56/2/3, Box 1466

'The 1st Airborne Division plan was ...', Horrocks interview, 15.5.46, LHCMA 15/15/130

'had little chance of success ...', Dempsey interview, 4.6.46, LHCMA 15/15/30

pp. 364–5 'Operation Market was not ...', 1st Airborne Division Report on Operation Market, FLPP

p. 365 'The perfection of your ...', FAAA, NARA RG331/Entry 253/Box1

'The time between landing and getting ...', FAAA, NARA RG331/Entry 256/Box34

'Everything that could go ...', Hackett to Michael Howard, conversation with the author, 16.12.15

'one jumps off a cliff ...', Vincent Orange, *Tedder: Quietly in Command*, p. 289, quoted Rick Atkinson, *The Guns at Last Light*, New York, 2013, p. 286

p. 366 'My country cannot afford ...', Prince Bernhard, CRCP 92/9

'In years to come ...', quoted Maj Gen R. E. Urquhart (with Wilfred Greatorex), *Arnhem*, Barnsley, 2008, p. 189

German analysis, BArch-MA RS3-9/5, p. 80; FMS P-163; FMS C-001

'*Überraschungserfolg*' – 'the effect of surprise', 9th SS Panzer-Division *Hohenstaufen*, BArch-MA RS3-9/5, p. 82

'They made an astounding mess ...', TNA WO 208/4140 SRM 1195

'surprise, the strongest ...', ALDS

Bittrich on Montgomery, interview Bittrich, GA-CB 2171/24c

'Operation Market Garden ...', David Fraser, *Wars and Shadows: Memoirs of General Sir David Fraser*, London, 2002, pp. 241–2

'received the painful message ...', PISM A.v.20 31/34

p. 367 'We are being killed ...', Stanley Nosecki, PISM A.v.20 31/38 26

'I am going to be absolutely ...', 2.10.44, Lt Gen F. A. M. Browning to Sosabowski, PISM A.v.20 31/60

'if at any time ...', ibid.

'Polish Para Brigade fought ...', 17.10.44, quoted Richard Mead, *General 'Boy': The Life of Lieutenant General Sir Frederick Browning*, Barnsley, 2010, p. 164

p. 368 'who was to wield the knife', ibid., p. 165

'Ever since the 1st Polish . . .', PISM A.v.20 31/60

'This officer . . .', ibid.

'Whether you are at fault or not . . .', PISM A.v.20 31/60

p. 369 'Monty tried to wave . . .', FCPP, Box 24

'Request you will ask Ramsay . . .', Montgomery to Eisenhower, 9.10.44, DDEP, Box 83

p. 370 'With obstacles in the form . . .', General der Infanterie Gustav von Zangen, FMS B-475

'The whole point . . .', CSDIC, TNA WO 208/4177

'a dead town', Cornelis Doelman, *Arnhem. Stad der bezitloozen*, Arnhem, 1945, p. 21

3,600 civilian deaths, HKNTW, p. 511

'I have been in the city!', Andries Pompe-Postuma, GAA 1557/1022

Nijmegen casualties, RAN B248

p. 372 'women and children . . .', TNA FO 371/39330

40,000 men from Rotterdam, TNA WO 208/4156

3,000 shot during occupation, 250,000 'divers', HKNTW, p. 513

'Terrorist', HvdV, p. 134

'Many railway strikers . . .', TNA WO 208/4156

'We have always . . .', ibid.

p. 373 Asking for places to sleep, J. S. H. Weinberg collection, Folder 10, RHCE 10166:94

'Cigar-shops and hundreds . . .', ibid.

'We have holes in . . .', ibid.

For negotiations on the Swedish ships and delivery of supplies, see William I. Hitchcock, *Liberation: The Bitter Road to Freedom 1944–1945*, London, 2009, pp. 103–7

'with obvious results', TNA WO 202/838

pp. 373–4 Church meals, Elsa Caspers, *To Save a Life*, London, 1995, p. 12; and J. S. H. Weinberg collection, Folder 10, RHCE 10166:94

p. 374 'five times as many males . . .', SHAEF Mission to Netherlands, 15.5.45, TNA WO 202/838

75 per cent of the victims male, Collection S. H. A. M. Zoetmulder, RHCE 10086:6

'*Ik ben een plunderaar*', Ian Gardner, *Deliver Us from Darkness*, New York, 2013, p. 61

'The need was such . . .', letter The Hague, 9.5.45, J. S. H. Weinberg collection, Folder 10, RHCE 10166:94

'The bodies are collected . . .', letter, 1.3.45, Jan Peters, Collection S. H. A. M. Zoetmulder, RHCE 10086:3

'It is no surprise . . .', ibid.

p. 375 SS black market in coffee, Heydte, CSDIC, TNA WO 208/4140 SRM 1189

'for half a loaf of bread . . .', Fähnrich zur See Hoffmann, TNA WO 208/4156

'The issue is quite clear . . .', Montgomery to Eisenhower, 20.2.45, TNA WO 32/16168

'The Germans became nastier . . .', Caspers, *To Save a Life*, p. 121

p. 376 'no routes are now . . .', TNA WO 106/4420

'Freddie decided not . . .', Brig E. T. Williams, FCPP, Box 24

p. 377 10.4 million rations, TNA WO 208/4420

'The Russians with their . . .', TNA WO 106/ 4420

'The whole party . . .', ibid.

'Bedell was tough at first . . .', FCPP, Box 24

p. 378 'The arrangements about the . . .', TNA WO 106/4420. For agreement, see also 1 Cdn Corps, 6.5.45, TNA WO 205/1073

'I wonder if you . . .', Walter Bedell Smith, *Eisenhower's Six Great Decisions: Europe 1944–45*, New York, 1956, p. 199; D. K. R. Crosswell, *Beetle: The Life of General Walter Bedell Smith*, Lexington, KY, 2010, p. 913

'the food situation is not . . .', TNA WO 208/4420

p. 379 'On the advent of Allied . . .', Maj Gen J. G. W. Clark, SHAEF Fortnightly Report No. 16, 15.5.45, TNA WO 202/838

16,000 dead, Hitchcock, *Liberation*, p. 122; 18,000, Ian Buruma, *Year Zero: A History of 1945*, London, 2013

'Girls born to Dutch women . . .', 'Holocaust trauma led to gene changes in offspring', Helen Thomson, *Guardian*, 22.8.2015

pp. 379–80 For the revival and rebuilding, see Doelman, *Arnhem*, p. 2; and Reinier Salverda, 'Beyond a Bridge Too Far: The Aftermath of the Battle of Arnhem (1944) and its Impact on Civilian Life', in Jane Fenoulhet, Gerdi Quist and Ulrich Tiedau (eds.), *Discord and Consensus in the Low Countries 1700–2000*, London, 2016

p. 380 Heijbroek story, Lt Col Th. A. Boeree papers, GA-CB 2171/47

Bibliography

Alanbrooke, Field Marshal Lord, *War Diaries 1939–1945*, London, 2001

Allport, Alan, *Browned Off and Bloody-Minded: The British Soldier Goes to War 1939–1945*, New Haven, 2015

Ambrose, Stephen E., *Band of Brothers*, New York, 1992

—— *Citizen Soldiers*, New York, 1998

Amsterdam, *Amsterdam tijdens den Hongerwinter 1944–1945*, Amsterdam, 1946

Atkinson, Rick, *The Guns at Last Light*, New York, 2013

Barr, Niall, *Yanks and Limeys: Alliance Warfare in the Second World War*, London, 2015

Bauer, Cornelis, *The Battle of Arnhem*, New York, 1968

Bedell Smith, Walter, *Eisenhower's Six Great Decisions: Europe 1944–45*, New York, 1956

Bekker, C. D., *K-Men: The Story of the German Frogmen and Midget Submarines*, London, 1955

Belchem, David, *All in the Day's March*, London, 1978

Bennett, David, 'Airborne Communications in Operation Market Garden', *Canadian Military History*, vol. 16, issue 1, Winter 2007

—— *A Magnificent Disaster: The Failure of Market Garden: The Arnhem Operation, September 1944*, Philadelphia, PA, 2008

Bennett, Ralph, *Ultra in the West*, New York, 1980

Bentley, Jr, Stewart W., *Orange Blood, Silver Wings: The Untold Story of the Dutch Resistance during Market Garden*, Milton Keynes, 2007

Bestebreurtje, A. D., 'The Airborne Operations in the Netherlands in Autumn 1944', *Allgemeine schweizerische Militärzeitschrift*, vol. 92, no. 6, 1946

Blair, Clay, *Ridgway's Paratroopers: The American Airborne in World War II*, New York, 1985

Blokker, Jan, *Achter de laatste brug*, Amsterdam, 2012

Blumenson, Martin (ed.), *The Patton Papers 1940–1945*, New York, 1996

Blunt, Roscoe C., *Foot Soldier: A Combat Infantryman's War in Europe*, Cambridge, MA, 2002

Boeree, Th. A., *De slag bij Arnhem en 'het verraad van Lindemans'*, Oosterbeek, undated

Bollen, Door Hen and Jansen, Herman, *Het manneneiland. Kroniek van de gebeurtenissen in de Over-Betuwe van september 1944 tot juni 1945*, Zutphen, 1982

Boorder, Tj. de and Kruiderink, W., *Rovers plunderen Arnhem. Een verhaal van oorlog, ballingschap, vernieling en massale roof*, Arnhem, 1945

Booth, T. Michael and Spencer, Duncan, *Paratrooper: The Life of James M. Gavin*, New York, 1994

Boscawen, Robert, *Armoured Guardsman: A War Diary, 6 June–April 1945*, Barnsley, 2001

Bradley, Omar N., *A Soldier's Story*, New York, 1964

Brereton, Lewis H., *The Brereton Diaries*, New York, 1946

British Broadcasting Corporation, *War Report: A Record of Dispatches Broadcast by the BBC's War Correspondents with the Allied Expeditionary Force, 6 June 1944–5 May 1945*, London, 1946

Buckley, John, *Monty's Men: The British Army and the Liberation of Europe*, London, 2013

Buckley, John and Preston-Hough, Peter (eds.), *Operation Market Garden: The Campaign for the Low Countries, Autumn 1944*, Solihull, 2016

Burgett, Donald R., *The Road to Arnhem*, New York, 2001

Burriss, T. Moffatt, *Strike and Hold*, Washington, DC, 2000

Buruma, Ian, *Year Zero: A History of 1945*, London, 2013

Butcher, Harry, *Three Years with Eisenhower*, London, 1946

Caspers, Elsa, *To Save a Life*, London, 1995

Chatterton, George, *The Wings of Pegasus*, London, 1982

Christopherson, Stanley, *An Englishman at War*, London, 2014

Clark, Lloyd, *Arnhem*, London, 2009

Critchell, Laurence, *Four Stars of Hell*, New York, 1947

Crosswell, D. K. R., *Beetle: The Life of General Walter Bedell Smith*, Lexington, KY, 2010

Dagboeken, *Niet tevergeefs, Oosterbeek September 1944*, Arnhem, 1946

Deenen, Tienus, Kamp, Aloys and Stalpers, Frank, *De Beerzen in oorlogstijd 1940–1945*, Middelbeers, 1994

Dekkers, C. A. and Vroemen, L. P. J., *De zwarte herfst. Arnhem 1944*, Arnhem, 1984

D'Este, Carlo, *Eisenhower: Allied Supreme Commander*, New York, 2002

Devlin, Gerard M., *Paratrooper*, New York, 1979

Didden, Jack, 'A Week Too Late?', in John Buckley and Peter Preston-Hough (eds.), *Operation Market Garden: The Campaign for the Low Countries, Autumn 1944*, Solihull, 2016, pp. 74–98

Didden, Jack and Swarts, Maarten, *Einddoel Maas. De strijd in zuidelijk Nederland tussen September en December 1944*, Weesp, 1984

Doelman, Cornelis, *Arnhem. Stad der bezitloozen*, Arnhem, 1945

Dover, Victor, *The Sky Generals*, London, 1981

Dyrda, Major Jerzy, 'Przemilczana odprawa w historiografii bitwy o Arnhem', *Wojskowy Przegląd Historyczny*, issue 1 (127), 1989, pp. 125–37

Eisenhower, Dwight D., *Crusade in Europe*, London, 1948

Essame, Hubert, *The 43rd Wessex Division at War 1944–1945*, London, 1952

Farrell, Charles, *Reflections 1939–1945: A Scots Guards Officer in Training and War*, Edinburgh, 2000

Fenoulhet, Jane, Quist, Gerdi and Tiedau, Ulrich (eds.), *Discord and Consensus in the Low Countries 1700–2000*, London, 2016

Foot, M. R. D. (ed.), *Holland at War against Hitler: Anglo-Dutch Relations 1940–1945*, London, 1990

—— *SOE in the Low Countries*, London, 2001

Fraser, David, *Wars and Shadows: Memoirs of General Sir David Fraser*, London, 2002

Frost, John, *A Drop Too Many*, Barnsley, 2008

Gardner, Ian, *Deliver Us from Darkness*, New York, 2013

Gavin, James M., *On to Berlin*, New York, 1985

Gerritsen, Bob and Revell, Scott, *Retake Arnhem Bridge: Kampfgruppe Knaust, September–October 1944*, Renkum, 2014

Giskes, H. J., *London Calling North Pole*, London, 1953

Golden, Lewis, *Echoes from Arnhem*, London, 1984

—— *There is War*, privately printed, 2012

Govers, Frans, *Corridor naar het verleden, Veghel. Een snijpunt in Oost-Brabant 1940–1945*, Hapert, 1983

Greelen, Lothar van, *Verkauft und verraten. Das Buch der Westfront 1944*, Welsermühl, 1963

Gregg, Victor, *Rifleman*, London, 2011

Guingand, Major General Sir Francis de, *From Brass Hat to Bowler Hat*, London, 1979

Gunning, Hugh, *Borderers in Battle*, Berwick-on-Tweed, 1948

Hackett, General Sir John, *I was a Stranger*, London, 1977

Hagen, Louis, *Arnhem Lift*, London, 1993

Hamilton, Nigel, *Monty: The Field Marshal 1944–1976*, London, 1986

Hastings, Max, *Armageddon*, London, 2004

Heaps, Leo, *The Grey Goose of Arnhem*, London, 1976

Heide-Kort, Ans van der, *Zij komen . . . Dolle Dinsdag 5 september–Bevrijding mei 1945*, Driebergen-Rijsenburg, 1989

Heintges, Jos (ed.), *Son en Breugel 1944–1994*, Eindhoven, 1994

Hills, Stuart, *By Tank into Normandy*, London, 2003

Hinsley, F. H., *British Intelligence in the Second World War*, vol. 3, part 2, London, 1988

Hirschfeld, Gerhard, *Nazi Rule and Dutch Collaboration: The Netherlands under German Occupation 1940–1945*, Oxford, 1988

Hitchcock, William I., *Liberation: The Bitter Road to Freedom 1944–1945*, London, 2009

Horne, Alistair and Montgomery, David, *The Lonely Leader: Montgomery 1944–1945*, London, 1994

Horrocks, Brian, *A Full Life*, London, 1960

—— *Corps Commander*, London, 1977

Iddekinge, P. R. A. van, *Arnhem 44/45. Evacuatie, verwoesting, plundering, bevrijding, terugkeer*, Arnhem, 1981

—— *Door de lens van De Booys. Een Arnhemse reportage 1944–1954*, Utrecht, 1999

Ingersoll, Ralph, *Top Secret*, London, 1946

Jary, Sydney, *18 Platoon*, Bristol, 1998

Jong, Dr L. de, *Het Koninkrijk der Nederlanden in de tweede wereldoorlog*, vol. 10a: *Het laatste jaar*, Amsterdam, 1980

Keizer, Madelon de and Plomp, Marijke (eds.), *Een open zenuw*, Amsterdam, 2010

Kerkhoffs, Bert, *Arnhem 1944. Slag van de tegenslag*, The Hague, 1994

Kern, Erich, *Buch der Tapferkeit*, Starnberger See, 1953

Kerry, A. J. and McDill, W. A., *The History of the Corps of Royal Canadian Engineers*, vol. ii, Ottawa, 1964

Kershaw, Robert, *It Never Snows in September*, London, 1976

—— *A Street in Arnhem*, London, 2014

Kisielewski, Jerzy (ed.), *Polscy spadochroniarze. Pamiętnik żołnierzy*, Newtown, 1949

Klaauw, Bart van der and Rijnhout, Bart, *Luchtbrug Market Garden*, Amsterdam, 1984

Klijn, Margo, *De stille slag. Joodse Arnhemmers 1933–1945*, Westervoort, 2014

Koskimaki, George E., *Hell's Highway: A Chronicle of the 101st Airborne in the Holland Campaign*, Philadelphia, PA, 2003

Lamb, Richard, *Montgomery in Europe 1943–45*, London, 1983
Lammerts, Jan, *Oosterbeek, September 1944*, Vereniging Vrienden van het Airborne Museum, Oosterbeek, 1988
Longden, Sean, *To the Victors the Spoils: D-Day and VE Day: The Reality behind the Heroism*, London, 2007
Love, Robert W. and Major, John (eds.), *The Year of D-Day: The 1944 Diary of Admiral Sir Bertram Ramsay*, Hull, 1994
Lunteren, Frank van, *The Battle of the Bridges*, Oxford, 2014

MacDonald, Charles B., *The Siegfried Line Campaign*, OCMH, Washington, DC, 1963
Mackay, Major E. M., 'The Battle of Arnhem Bridge', *Royal Engineers Journal*, December 1954, IWM Docs 22796
McManus, John C., *September Hope*, New York, 2012
Margry, Karel, *De bevrijding van Eindhoven*, Eindhoven, 1982
Martens, Allard and Dunlop, Daphne, *The Silent War: Glimpses of the Dutch Underground and Views on the Battle for Arnhem*, London, 1961
Mawson, Stuart, *Arnhem Doctor*, Staplehurst, 2000
Mead, Richard, *General 'Boy': The Life of Lieutenant General Sir Frederick Browning*, Barnsley, 2010
Middlebrook, Martin, *Arnhem 1944: The Airborne Battle*, Barnsley, 1994

Neillands, Robin, *The Battle for the Rhine 1944*, London, 2005
Nichol, John and Rennell, Tony, *Arnhem: The Battle for Survival*, London, 2011
Nicolson, Nigel, *The Grenadier Guards 1939–1945*, vol. i, Aldershot, 1945
—— (ed.), *The Harold Nicolson Diaries 1907–1963*, London, 2004
North, John, *North-West Europe 1944–5*, London, 1953

Oosterbeek, *Niet tevergeefs. Oosterbeek September 1944*, Arnhem, 1946
Orde, Roden, *The Household Cavalry at War*, Aldershot, 1953
Overmans, Rüdiger, *Deutsche militärische Verluste im Zweiten Weltkrieg*, Munich, 2000

Pakenham-Walsh, Major General R. P., *History of the Corps of Royal Engineers*, vol. ix, Chatham, 1958
Paul, Daniel and St John, John, *Surgeon at Arms*, London, 1958
Peatling, Robert, *No Surrender at Arnhem*, Wimborne Minster, 2004

Peaty, John, 'Operation MARKET GARDEN: The Manpower Factor', in John Buckley and Peter Preston-Hough (eds.), *Operation Market Garden: The Campaign for the Low Countries, Autumn 1944*, Solihull, 2016, pp. 58–73

Pereira, J., *A Distant Drum*, Aldershot, 1948

Pogue, Forrest C., *Pogue's War: Diaries of a WWII Combat Historian*, Lexington, KY, 2001

Powell, Geoffrey, *The Devil's Birthday*, London, 1984

—— *Men at Arnhem*, Barnsley, 1998

Presser, J., *Ashes in the Wind: The Destruction of Dutch Jewry*, London, 1968

Reddish, Arthur, *A Tank Soldier's Story*, privately published, undated

Revell, Scott, Cherry, Niall and Gerritsen, Bob, *Arnhem: A Few Vital Hours*, Renkum, 2013

Rijksinstituut voor Oorlogsdocumentatie, *Het proces Rauter*, Ministerie van Onderwijs, Kunsten en Wetenschappen, 's-Gravenhage, 1952

Ritchie, Sebastian, 'Learning the Hard Way: A Comparative Perspective on Airborne Operations in the Second World War', *Royal Air Force Air Power Review*, vol. 14, no. 3, Autumn/Winter 2011, pp. 11–33

—— *Arnhem: Myth and Reality: Airborne Warfare, Air Power and the Failure of Market Garden*, London, 2011

—— *Arnhem: The Air Reconnaissance Story*, Air Historical Branch RAF, 2015

—— 'Airborne Operations from Normandy to Varsity', *Journal of the Royal Air Force Historical Society*, vol. 59, 2015, pp. 76–106

—— 'Learning to Lose? Airborne Lessons and the Failure of Operation Market Garden', in John Buckley and Peter Preston-Hough (eds.), *Operation Market Garden: The Campaign for the Low Countries, Autumn 1944*, Solihull, 2016, pp. 19–36

Rosse, Earl of and Hill, E. B., *The Story of the Guards Armoured Division*, Barnsley, 2017

Rossiter, Mike, *We Fought at Arnhem*, London, 2012

Ryan, Cornelius, *A Bridge Too Far*, New York, 1974

Salverda, Reinier, 'Beyond a Bridge Too Far: The Aftermath of the Battle of Arnhem (1944) and its Impact on Civilian Life', in Jane Fenoulhet, Gerdi Quist and Ulrich Tiedau (eds.), *Discord and Consensus in the Low Countries 1700-2000*, London, 2016

Sampson, Francis L., *Look Out Below!*, Washington, DC, 1958

Schneider, Karl, 'Ein Sieg der Menschlichkeit', *Der Landser*, Nr. 847, March 1993, pp. 67–8

Schretlen, Trees, *Nijmegen '44-'45. Oorlogsdagboek van Trees Schretlen*, Groesbeek, 2014

Schrijvers, Peter, *The Crash of Ruin: American Combat Soldiers in Europe in World War II*, New York, 1998

Seth, Ronald, *Lion with Blue Wings: The Story of the Glider Pilot Regiment 1942–1945*, London, 1955

Shulman, Milton, *Defeat in the West*, London, 1988

Simpson, Louis, *Selected Prose*, New York, 1989

Sims, James, *Arnhem Spearhead*, London, 1978

Sosabowski, Major General Stanislaw, *Freely I Served*, Barnsley, 2013

Stainforth, Peter, *Wings of the Wind*, London, 1988

Stasiak, Władysław Klemens, *Go! Album wspomnień spadochroniarza*, Wap., West Germany, 1947

—— *W locie szumią spadochrony. Wspomnienia żołnierza spod Arnhem*, Warsaw, 1991

Stevenson, Lieutenant John, 'Arnhem Diary', *Reconnaissance Journal*, vol. 4, no. 1, Autumn 1947

Strong, Kenneth, *Intelligence at the Top*, London, 1968

Tedder, Lord, *With Prejudice: The War Memoirs of Marshal of the RAF Lord Tedder GCB*, London, 1966

ter Horst, Kate A., *Cloud over Arnhem, September 17th–26th 1944*, London, 1959

Tieke, Wilhelm, *Im Feuersturm letzter Kriegsjahre. II. SS-Panzerkorps mit 9. u. 10. SS-Division 'Hohenstaufen' u. 'Frundsberg'*, Osnabrück, 1976

Tooley, RA, Lieutenant Colonel I. P., 'Artillery Support at Arnhem', *Field Artillery Journal*, April 1945

Urquhart, Major General R. E. (with Wilfred Greatorex), *Arnhem*, Barnsley, 2008

Vandeleur, J. O. E., *A Soldier's Story*, London, 1967

Vlist, Hendrika van der, *Die dag in September*, Bussum, 1975

Waddy, John, *A Tour of the Arnhem Battlefields*, Barnsley, 2011

Warrack, Graeme, *Travel by Dark*, London, 1963

Weigley, Russell F., *Eisenhower's Lieutenants: The Campaign of France and Germany 1944–1945*, Bloomington, 1990

Woollacott, Robert, *Winged Gunners*, Harare, Zimbabwe, 1994

Zee, Henri A. van der, *The Hunger Winter: Occupied Holland 1944–45*, Lincoln, NB, 1982

Acknowledgements

There would have been little point in writing yet another book on Operation Market Garden without adding a good deal of new material and human detail to the story. As it turned out there was far more than I ever expected, and for that I am deeply grateful to all the people who helped me at every turn.

I owe a huge debt to Rick Atkinson, who so generously passed on all his notes from both American and British archives. It was also Rick who sent me to the Mahn Center for Archives and Special Collections in the Alden Library at Ohio University, which holds the Cornelius Ryan papers. Ryan had a superb team of researchers and interviewers who provided him with a staggering quantity of material, most of which he never used. I am deeply grateful to Douglas McCabe, the then Curator of Manuscripts, whose advice and generous help made all the difference to my work there.

In the United States, the knowledge and assistance of other archivists also proved invaluable. I once again owe a great deal to Dr Tim Nenninger of the National Archives at College Park, Maryland; to Dr Conrad Crane and his colleagues at the United States Army Military History Institute in Carlisle, Pennsylvania; and to Lindsey Barnes and Taylor Benson at the Eisenhower Center, World War II Archives and Oral History Collection, University of New Orleans, courtesy of the National WW II Museum in New Orleans.

In the Netherlands I am especially grateful to Robert Voskuil who, with his unrivalled knowledge, guided us around the battlefields and corrected many misapprehensions, always explaining what had changed since 1944 and what had remained the same. Archivists who greatly helped the research included Hubert Berkhout at the Nederlands Instituut vor Oorlogs Dokumentatie, Amsterdam; Geert Maassen, the head of collections at the Gelders

Archief Arnhem; Derek Prins and Freek Huitink of the Regionaal Archief Nijmegen; Jan Suijkerbuijk, service co-ordinator Regionaal Historisch Centrum Eindhoven; Conservator Rense Havinga of the Nationaal Bevrydings Museum Groesbeek; and Marieke Martens and Tim Streefkerk of the Airborne Museum Hartenstein at Oosterbeek. H. C. Moolenburgh kindly offered his research into the King Kong saga, and the de Bourgraaf family in Oosterbeek generously loaned the manuscript diary of Piet van Hooydonk.

For Polish sources, I would very much like to thank Dr Andrzej Suchcitz of the Polish Institute and Sikorski Museum; Ms Jadwiga Kowalska of the Polish Underground Movement Study Trust, London (Studium Polski Podziemnej w Londynie); Sławomir Kowalski from the Polish Army Museum; and the staff of POSK, the Polish Cultural Association in London, for all their help.

In Germany Frau Elfriede Frischmuth at the Bundesarchiv-Militärarchiv, Freiburg-im-Breisgau, Gunnar Goehle at the Feldpost Archiv in Berlin, and once again Frau Irina Renz, the archivist of the Sammlung Sterz at the Württembergische Landesbibliothek in Stuttgart, were all a great help. Dr Jens Westemeier at the Rheinisch-Westfälische Technische Hochschule Aachen generously shared his own research into the Waffen-SS; and Professor Dr Clemens Schwender, the great expert on Feldpost sources, also kindly provided material.

It has been a very great pleasure as well as a huge benefit to work with Angelique Hook on Dutch sources, Angelica von Hase on German and Anastazja Pindor on Polish archive material. Their diligence and professionalism in research and translation have literally made all the difference. They, and Robert Voskuil, also checked the final version of the text and pointed out some necessary corrections, but naturally any mistakes which remain are entirely my responsibility.

Once again I owe a great deal to Sebastian Cox, the head of the Ministry of Defence's air historical branch, and above all to his colleague Dr Sebastian Ritchie, the author of *Arnhem: Myth and Reality* and *Arnhem: The Air Reconnaissance Story*. They have provided much valuable advice and detail on the air side of Operation Market Garden and helped me clarify my thoughts, even if we did not end up in entire agreement over the thorny issue of planning responsibilities.

I am also most grateful for the observations, suggestions and advice of many people, including Professor Sir Michael Howard, the late Professor M. R. D. Foot who taught me a lot over the years about airborne and special operations, Professor Allan Millett, Field Marshal Lord Bramall, John

Howes, Michael Bottenheim, Harry de Quetteville, Maurice Kanareck, Lieutenant General Mark Carleton-Smith, Lieutenant General Sir John Lorimer, Menzies Campbell (Baron Campbell of Pittenweem) and Judith Urquhart, the daughter of Major General Roy Urquhart. Louise Baring generously lent me books, as did my old friend Sir Max Hastings who once again also provided intriguing tips and quotes.

At Penguin Venetia Butterfield has provided wonderful encouragement, Daniel Crewe has proved a masterly editor, and John Hamilton who designed the jacket for *Stalingrad* twenty years ago has again shown himself to be a peerless art director. It has also been hugely reassuring to work with Peter James as the copyeditor once again. At Penguin in the United States Kathryn Court and Victoria Savanh have been ideal editors. I am also blessed once more with Alex Hippisley-Cox's inspired planning and handling of publicity. And Andrew Nurnberg, who has been my literary agent and great friend for the last thirty-five years, has again advised me superbly. His outstanding team has continued to maintain excellent relations with all my foreign publishers, and Robin Straus has handled everything in the United States to perfection.

Finally my eternal gratitude and love go to my editor of first resort Artemis Cooper for having agreed to marry me in the first place and then to have put up with me for so long. This book is dedicated to her.

Index

 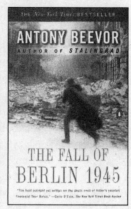 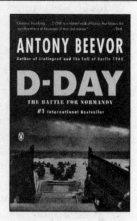